The Evolution of Rights in Liberal Theory

The Evolution of Rights in Liberal Theory

IAN SHAPIRO

Yale University

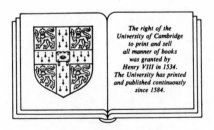

The right of the
University of Cambridge
to print and sell
all manner of books
was granted by
Henry VIII in 1534.
The University has printed
and published continuously
since 1584.

Cambridge University Press

Cambridge
New York   New Rochelle
Melbourne   Sydney

Published by the Press Syndicate of the University of Cambridge
The Pitt Building, Trumpington Street, Cambridge CB2 1RP
32 East 57th Street, New York, NY 10022, USA
10 Stamford Road, Oakleigh, Melbourne 3166, Australia

First published 1986
Reprinted 1988

Printed in the United States of America

Library of Congress Cataloging-in-Publication Data
Shapiro, Ian.
The evolution of rights in liberal theory.
Bibliography: p.
1. Civil rights – History. 2. Liberalism – History.
I. Title.
JC571.S45   1986   323.4'09   86–2657

British Library Cataloguing in Publication Data
Shapiro, Ian
The evolution of rights in liberal theory
1. Rights (Philosophy)
I. Title
323.4'01   B105.R5

ISBN 0 521 32043 7 hard covers
ISBN 0 521 33853 0 paperback

To the memories of
H.A.S. and S.M.

Contents

Acknowledgments

To discuss seriously ideas that one knows to be half-baked, and to criticize them constructively in the early stages of their formulation, is never easy, and without Douglas Rae's enthusiastic execution of these tasks this book would not have been written. Debts to others have also accumulated at various stages. In this regard I should like especially to thank Michael Walzer for diligently reading the long and often painfully roving drafts of an author who, as he once observed, has a tendency to chew more than he has bitten off. I hope I have done enough swallowing for him, and certainly I have benefited greatly from his advice. I also owe substantial debts to Quentin Skinner and Richard Ashcraft, both of whom went well beyond the call of duty in reading the entire manuscript and commenting extensively and constructively on it. Both will find arguments in the final version with which to disagree, but both have helped me develop my thesis while saving me from myself in more ways than I care to think about; for this I remain indebted.

Others who have read and commented helpfully on large parts of various drafts, or offered important advice in other ways, include Carol Fessler-Mendoza, William Galston, Jennifer Hochschild, Jeffrey Isaac, David Johnston, John Kane, Adolph Reed, Jr., Rogers M. Smith, and Steven B. Smith. Research assistance was provided by Frederick Bartol and Chihoe Hahn. I would like to thank, without in any way implicating, all of the above.

Financial assistance was provided by fellowships from Yale University between 1978 and 1982 and a Newcombe Fellowship from the Woodrow Wilson National Fellowship Foundation in Princeton for 1982–83. I am grateful to both these institutions.

ix

Finally I must thank Judy for helping in innumerable ways with the manuscript itself and for tolerating long periods of absence when writing was in progress – and worse periods of presence when it was not.

Part I
Introduction

1

Anatomy of an ideology

This is a book about the evolution of an ideology. Its goal is to show, in a more detailed and systematic way than has hitherto been attempted, why particular ways of talking about economic, social, and political rights became central to the Western liberal tradition around the time of the English Civil War, how these ways of talking have since evolved in that tradition, and in what respects they condition, shape, and constrain arguments about politics and public morality in contemporary Anglo-American political discourse.

The Western liberal tradition that will concern us is the one espoused by the principal architects of its political theory. This is not to say that the study of influential traditions of political theory is the only, even the best, way of trying to penetrate the many complexities that constitute a political ideology, but it is my claim that a detailed analysis of the writings held in great esteem in the established institutions of a culture can reveal much of importance about its underlying values and predispositions that might otherwise go unnoticed. My outlook is thus explicitly anthropological. My goal is to grasp, explain, and think critically about the values and beliefs that constitute our contemporary political culture. This I hold to be integral to discerning how, and in which directions, those values and beliefs might evolve in the future, and how, if at all, they might be influenced to evolve.

I. THE HISTORICAL STUDY OF CONTEMPORARY IDEAS

The basic goal is critically to evaluate contemporary arguments about right and justice, but my approach is necessarily historical for four related reasons. It is, first, a striking feature of the recent contractarian revolution in American po-

3

litical theory that its most influential proponents make explicit appeal to the intellectual authority of a contractarian tradition believed to have emerged in England in the seventeenth century and to have established itself in France and Germany in the eighteenth. John Rawls regards Locke's *Second Treatise,* Rousseau's *Social Contract,* and Kant's ethical works beginning with the *Foundations of the Metaphysics of Morals* as "definitive of the contract tradition." His aim is to "present a conception of justice which generalizes and carries to a higher level of abstraction" their arguments (1971:11; cf. also 32 ff, 112, 132). Although more equivocal about Hobbes, he is nonetheless impressed by his greatness and employs some of the main arguments of *Leviathan* in the course of developing his own views (ibid.: 11n, 240, 269). Robert Nozick, too, develops his account in *Anarchy State and Utopia* by building on what he takes to be Locke's state of nature (1974:10–25). In addition to such appeals, these writers (like many more minor figures they have influenced) rely heavily, as we will see, on conceptual tools, modes of reasoning, and assumptions about human nature and rationality that they take to be characteristic of this older contractarian tradition, particularly in its early English variants.

One should not, however, overlook the fact that the modern contract theorists have been deeply influenced by other powerful intellectual currents as well, most notably utilitarianism and legal positivism (against which they reacted but which left indelible marks on their arguments), post-Kantian deontological moral philosophy, and developments in modern economic and psychological theory. I will try to show how these various movements have been adapted to fit within the evolving contractarian tradition, which latter in important and usefully identifiable ways continues to define the basic outlook of the modern writers: they articulate and reproduce it.

Second, the liberal rights tradition, viewed more broadly, has itself evolved over time and these modern writers are to some extent products of that evolution. They are products in that they invoke the tradition's authority, but also because they are influenced by it in ways of which they are frequently unaware. In contrast to those commentators who identify "mod-

4

ernity" with a single unit-idea, be it the decline of objective moral standards, the supremacy of "possessive individualism," or "the emotivist self,"[1] I argue that the liberal view of rights is an ensemble of related doctrines, beliefs, and assumptions about the nature of persons, value, legitimacy, and ends. The relations among these are complex and have changed over time, more as an internally complex organism with many (and often conflicting) needs adapting to a changing environment, than as a radical disjunction with the past or a single characteristic simplifying assumption that constitutes the motif of modernity. The tradition as I describe it has been through four distinct incarnations or "moments," which I designate as transitional, classical, neo-classical, and Keynesian. These are not presented as historically or conceptually exhaustive categories and their heuristic utility is intended primarily to be thematic and comparative. I do hold, however, that some sense of the changing socioeconomic conditions that gave rise to them is essential to grasping why the modern arguments are presented in the forms that they are, why they confront the particular difficulties that they do, and why, these difficulties notwithstanding, they retain such powerful intellectual and ideological appeal.

A third reason for an historical approach derives from this fact of evolution. From an intellectual point of view (though not, as we will see, necessarily from an an ideological one) the modern arguments can usefully be thought of as lethal mutations of the earlier ones. The seventeenth-century arguments confronted important intellectual difficulties within their own terms of reference, but they exhibited an underlying intellectual coherence which the modern arguments lack, mainly because they relied on a view of scientific knowledge that was not to survive the eighteenth century. The modern writers try to combine a substantive appeal to the arguments of the early English contract theorists with a methodological appeal to Kant's ethics; in this conjunction reside some of their most intractable difficulties. My argument on this point is comparable in form, though not in content, to the claim in the opening

1 See Strauss (1953), Macpherson (1962), and MacIntyre (1981).

pages of *After Virtue*. Like MacIntyre I argue that contemporary writers have fragmented an older tradition by appropriating parts of it while leaving behind crucial premises that gave those parts their underlying coherence. Like him I argue that an understanding of the processes by which this occurred is essential to a full critical evaluation of the modern arguments. I do not, as MacIntyre (1981:35) does, locate the reasons for these changes in the mere follies of philosophers, or in what Richard Rorty (1979:136ff) has, with unintended irony, referred to as our "optional" commitment to the enlightenment epistemology of Descartes and his successors–which can be jettisoned once we come to understand its muddled genesis.[2] The history of dominant ideas is far more intertwined with the evolution of social structures and practices than this therapeutic metaphor suggests. Philosophical predispositions are deeply embedded in peoples' consciousnesses, at levels of which they are typically unaware. These beliefs hold together less abstract views which serve important material ends. In contrast to these voluntarist accounts of the historical evolution of ideas, I argue that a much greater role has been played by extraintellectual factors and I am skeptical of the extent to which we might return to the arguably more coherent contentions of earlier writers. Many of our most fundamental philosophical beliefs are integral to social practices in which we engage unreflectively every day. Those beliefs are required, in nontrivial ways, by those social practices, thus generating important limitations on how we might reasonably expect beliefs to change. Understanding the intricate relationships between theory and practice and how these relationships have evolved historically will reveal the dimensions of the task facing those who advocate altering the beliefs that constitute the dominant intellectual culture. We need to take much better account of our actual circumstances, how they have come to be what they are, and how they influence our own values and actions, if we are seriously to argue for the pursuit of significantly different values in the contemporary political world.

2 For discussion of Rorty's historical thesis and its implications for the history of ideologies, see Shapiro (1982:550–3ff).

A final, and related, reason for an historical approach is that it helps to get at the tenacity of this ideology over time; to grasp the historical power of its core ideas, which have persisted through the various mutations and been reproduced as dominant institutions and practices have replicated themselves. To speak of the tenacity and continuing dominance of a liberal ideology of individual rights in this way is to some extent to take issue with recent work by historians of political thought. In particular, no one who comes to this field of inquiry can fail to admire and come to terms with J.G.A. Pocock's brilliantly argued thesis in *The Machiavellian Moment* and elsewhere, seriously questioning the claim that liberal ideas have been as influential historically as is often supposed. I do not doubt that a powerful strand of republican ideology, emphasizing civic virtue and idealizing the values of civic humanism and republican citizenship (in contrast to the characteristically liberal focus on jurisprudence and the centrality of individual rights), can be traced from the Florentine Renaissance through the writings of some seventeenth-century followers of Harrington. Nor do I doubt that these ideas, which might usefully be characterized as an Atlantic republican tradition, played a significant role in shaping American revolutionary ideology, or that they have since continued to play important (if changing) roles in the evolution of American political ideas. I do question, however, the extent to which these two ideologies have evolved exclusively of one another historically, either in their geneses or in all the historical periods in which Pocock holds them to have been distinct, but it would take a different book to show this definitively.[3] In concentrating here on the evolution of liberal ideas and in trying to document and explain their continuing historical influence, I am not supposing that these are the only ideas of significance in shaping the values dominant in Anglo-American culture, or that they have evolved uninfluenced by the evolution of republican political thought. My interest is in understanding why liberal ideas have retained their powerful appeal over

3 For a recent summary of Pocock's views on this incommensurability before the Scottish jurisprudence of the eighteenth century and after 1789, see Pocock (1981:353–68).

7

time, these and other competing influences notwithstanding. We might say that I am concerned to explain the ideological appeal of the view that Pocock is concerned to debunk.

II. THE STUDY OF IDEOLOGY AND THE ANTHROPOLOGY OF POLITICAL THEORY

If my concern is with a major intellectual tradition and the canonical figures who comprise it, my venture differs at root from conventional studies of The Greats, whose principal focus tends to be on interpreting what are taken to be their Fundamental Insights into the human condition. The questions I am asking concern why they are thought to have these Fundamental Insights; my interest in them is from the point of view of an evolutionary anthropology of establishment values. Such an enterprise requires interpretation of canonical texts, but it is interpretation undertaken from a different point of view, with different goals in mind, than most modes of textual exegesis.

My enterprise differs, also, from the attempts by Quentin Skinner and his followers to reread the history of ideas as what they take to be the history of ideologies. My disagreements with these writers, and my realist alternatives to their hermeneutic procedures, have been set out and defended elsewhere, and need not detain us now.[4] Skinner and his followers focus exclusively on an internal reading of texts, geared toward the detailed recovery of authorial intention. My view is that, insofar as we are concerned with the history of *ideologies,* such analysis, while necessary, will never be sufficient. It must be supplemented by an external analysis that goes beyond the realm of authorial intent and locates the texts, as well as the traditions they constitute, in the broader processes of socioeconomic change that give rise to them *qua* ideological entities, and which they are instrumental in reproducing.[5] This is not to relegate the text to the realm of the

---

4 See Shapiro (1982:335–78).
5 There are some affinities between my use of the terms "internal" and "external" and H.L.A. Hart's use of them in his discussion of the relation between moral and legal rules in *The Concept of Law* (1961:168–80). For more extensive discussion of my uses of them see Shapiro (1982:554–63).

epiphenomenal (the relationship between ideologies and the causal reproduction of the social world is vastly more intricate than this notion suggests), nor is it to hold the quite fashionable view that authorial intent is intrinsically irrecoverable, and, anyhow, irrelevant, to textual exegesis – which latter depends exclusively on the meaning imputed by the reader. The intentions of the authors of canonical texts are indeed manipulated by subsequent generations (it is doubtful that the process of canonization could otherwise occur). Attention to the ways in which this process occurs can be highly instructive in tracing the evolution of an ideology and in thinking critically about it. Although texts become relatively autonomous of their authors once written or, as Pocock (1984:31) has noted, there is a certain "refraction and recalcitrance" to uttered speech or written language, which means it can be manipulated by others, such processes of manipulation are never without limits. These limits derive partly from the meanings of the words themselves, not because they do not change over time, but because they exist in weblike, mutually interdependent, relationships with other parts of our conceptual vocabularies. As Hanna Pitkin (1972:175–6ff) has pointed out in relation to the concept of justice, the very fact that we use this term and its cognates in a whole mesh of interrelated and overlapping ways places limits on its manipulability in a given usage. We do (or fail to do) justice to meals as well as criminals, to an author's intentions as well as to a corrupt politician, to our convictions as well as to our students, and this whole network of overlapping meanings cannot simply be detached from a single substantive use for a particular ulterior purpose. The web of connected meanings ensures a certain amount of continuity over time and space, although the degree of this will vary and is unlikely to invite much that is useful in the way of theoretical generalization.

The debate on whether or not we impute meanings to texts tends to be conducted at so high a level of abstraction that it entirely misses these issues, which are frequently crucial to grasping in concrete historical terms how ideologies evolve. It may be that the arguments of canonized writers are systematically misapplied in ways that they would never have endorsed

9

or perhaps in some cases even have understood, but this is typically the result of bending, stretching, and pulling at parts of arguments, of subtly manipulating the contexts in which they are held to apply, of being half-true to an author's intentions, not of distorting them wholesale. Just as powerful ideologies invariably have some significant connection with reality, make straightforward sense of some realm of experience, and depend on these facts for their justificatory appeal when misapplied in other contexts for other purposes,[6] so it would be a mistake to think that there are not elements of Locke's argument, as the argument he made, which, while doubtless manipulable into the service of various competing political goals, nonetheless retain a powerful straightforward appeal in their own right and contribute to his continuing influence in the liberal tradition as a result. For this reason close attention to the internal aspects of the argument and their connection with evolving external aspects of it can be essential to getting at its ideological force over time. Nozick's "misreadings" of Locke, Rawls's of Kant, we will see, reveal a great deal about the modern evolution of liberal ideology.[7]

In short, though I follow Skinner in conceiving of ideologies in functional terms and in analyzing them by reference to the practices they are instrumental in legitimating or attacking, we differ both in our accounts of what such analysis requires and in that we are not, ultimately, interested in the same social practices. Skinner focuses on an internal hermeneutic analysis to get at the ideological force of the argument for its author. I supplement this with an external analysis in which I try to get at the more complex relationship between the meaning of the text for the author and its role in the evolving tradition, and to locate these in the broader processes of socioeconomic reproduction and change of which they are

6 I am here following Walzer's discussion of the concept of ideology (Walzer, 1983:12ff).
7 This does not go to the question of whether I, as reader, can be certain I understand the text in the sense of being sure I know what Locke's intentions in writing it really were, or that I can be certain of having grasped Nozick's reading of Locke's intentions. Obviously to say that Nozick misreads Locke is to presume a correct reading of Locke (and of Nozick). For reasons given elsewhere (Shapiro, 1982: 575–8), I see no a priori reason to suppose that such correct readings are intrinsically unavailable.

a part. Finally, where Skinner's focus is exclusively historical, my emphasis is on comprehending contemporary ideas historically: my interest in the evolution of the liberal rights tradition is geared toward a better critical understanding of its dominant contemporary manifestations.

III. THE LIBERAL IDEOLOGY OF INDIVIDUAL RIGHTS

If the liberal rights tradition is to be thought of as an internally complex set of doctrines, beliefs, and assumptions that have evolved over time while retaining a relatively enduring underlying structure, more needs to be said about how these processes of change and persistence occur, and about the underlying structure itself. We need a better sense of our animal's basic anatomy and of how this directs and limits its activities in an environment that is itself evolving over time.

i. Ideologies as conservative adaptive mechanisms

A useful start to thinking about this problem can be made by considering W. V. Quine's seminal discussion of knowledge and belief in "Two Dogmas of Empiricism." The two "dogmas" that Quine was concerned to overturn were Kant's analytic/synthetic distinction and the related correspondence theory of truth, which in his view rested on a misleading reduction of the relationship between language and experience. In contrast to the empiricist view of beliefs deriving from sense-data, which in turn correspond to particulars in the world, he averred:

The totality of our so-called knowledge or beliefs, from the most casual matters of geography and history to the profoundest laws of atomic physics or even of pure mathematics and logic, is a man-made fabric which impinges on experience only along the edges . . . [it] is like a field of force whose boundary conditions are experience. A conflict with experience at the periphery occasions readjustments in the interior of the field. Truth values have to be redistributed over some of our statements. Reevaluation of some statements entails reevaluation of others, because of their logical interconnections – the logical laws being in turn simply certain further statements of the system, certain further elements of the field. Having reevaluated one statement we must reevaluate some others, which may be statements

11

logically connected with the first or may be the statements of logical connections themselves. But the total field is so underdetermined by its boundary conditions, experience, that there is much latitude of choice as to what statements to reevaluate in the light of any single contrary experience. No particular experiences are linked with any particular statements in the interior of the field, except indirectly through considerations of equilibrium affecting the field as a whole. (Quine, 1953:42–3)

For Quine there is no simple correspondence between language and experience (although there is a more complex adaptive relationship), and there is no analytic/synthetic distinction. Beliefs that are commonly thought to be analytic are those toward the center of the "field" on which a great many others depend, and our "natural tendency to disturb the total system as little as possible" leads us always to focus revisions on specific statements (often but not necessarily empirical) as close to the edge of the system as possible (ibid.:44).

Leaving aside the issue of whether this constitutes an adequate ontological account of the nature of knowledge,[8] as a descriptive account of how beliefs generally, and political ideologies in particular, operate and evolve, Quine's account seems to me deeply plausible and, for reasons that will emerge shortly, very useful. For one thing, Quine's analogy captures the intrinsically messy nature of peoples' beliefs, and of the relations among those beliefs. In contrast to one predominant Whiggish tendency, to expect beliefs to exist in neat, tidy structures of ascending levels of generality, this view captures their fluid nature and the much looser notion of consistency with which people actually operate. Second, Quine's account captures the complexly interlocked nature of more and less general beliefs which requires us always to go to the more general to understand the less general, without making large and implausible claims about the transcendental validity of some list of "key" terms or categories. Third, the field analogy makes it clear that from this point of view there is no sharp distinction between theoretical principles and empirical beliefs, which intuitively conforms to the way ideologies preserve

---

8 Aspects of this issue are taken up in the final chapter.

themselves. Consider how monetarists can find a construction of "the facts" to support the view that Reagan's policies have worked while Keynesians can find a different one to show they have failed; how Marxists can produce constructions of "the facts" to show that there is a long-term declining tendency in the rate of profit, though neo-classical economists can hold that "the facts" disconfirm this. Quine's analogy captures the verity that empirical beliefs need not necessarily be less "basic" than theoretical beliefs; some empirical beliefs will be closer to the center of a "field" and less amenable to revision than some theoretical beliefs, and the desire to hold onto particular empirical beliefs may generate complex theoretical modifications. Fourth, Quine's account is sensitive to the truth that many parts of a system of beliefs can be implicit or unconscious, at least until they meet with recalcitrant experiences, or need to be adapted to accommodate other adaptive changes. Even in these cases agents may be more or less conscious of the ways in which they modify their beliefs. People can quite consistently hold mutually inconsistent beliefs, so long as these inconsistencies are not seen to be mutually threatening. Finally, an advantage of this view of ideologies over, for instance, a Wittgensteinian one, is that though it requires no correspondence theory of truth, it does rest on a view of language as situated in and adapting to a world that is at least partly external to itself, and it therefore directs our attention to those features of the world to which particular elements of language adapt, in addition to the internal imperatives generated by the requirements of language itself.[9] This account of the structure of belief systems is thus broadly consistent with the realist account of ideologies which I have defended elsewhere.[10]

ii. Anatomy of an ideology

If Quine's analogy supplies a general account of how ideologies operate, how does this help us to probe the underlying structure of the modern liberal tradition? At the heart of this tradition is a particular view of rights that powerfully con-

9 For a good critical account of the Wittgensteinian view see Bloor (1983).
10 Shapiro (1982:563f).

strains arguments about politics and public morality in the contemporary Anglo-American world. Its influence is sometimes latent, sometimes manifest, and the forms it has taken have varied historically, but its continuing power cannot be overestimated. Indeed, as I will suggest, its influence is so great that we should reject as misleading the widespread belief that liberalism faces a fundamental choice between contractarianism and utilitarianism: this view of rights is integral to them both.

The underlying structure of rights. People who talk or make assumptions about rights are talking or making assumptions about one of a family of moral and political concepts that are essentially formal and relational. These concepts express complex substantive relationships among different terms or variables. A claim about rights generally involves a fourfold assertion about the *subject* of entitlement, the *substance* of entitlement, the *basis* for entitlement, and the *purpose* of entitlement.[11] It generally makes sense, therefore, to ask: *who* is entitled, to *what*, on what *basis*, for what *purpose*? All users of the term do not typically address themselves to all aspects of its fourfold relational nature, nor are they necessarily aware that all these aspects exist. We will see that some of the greatest difficulties modern writers confront derive ultimately from a systematic blindness to some of them. The relational schema should be conceived of as part of the underlying grammar of the term "right," and just as in other areas speakers can be more and less aware of the grammatical rules which structure their discourse, so here these rules of intelligibility will often function invisibly. They are part of the core meaning of the term; they constitute that component of its meaning which is essentially reapplicable over its various intelligible uses.

A full philosophical defense of this claim would take us far afield and is not necessary for my purposes here.[12] Some gen-

---

11 This relational account is similar to, and based on, MacCallum's (1972:174–93) discussion of the concept of freedom as a triadic relation among accounts of persons, restraining conditions, and actions.

12 For a summary discussion of "core" theories of meaning see Shapiro (1982:540–46). For a fuller account see Graham (1977:94–102).

eral remarks will, however, be helpful in fleshing out this analytical schema and in explaining its usefulness and limitations.

Consider for a moment what things would be like if the term "right" were used without conforming to these relational requirements. Imagine someone who said that there were rights that attached to no one, they were just *there*, as if they fell off trees in the fall and grew again in the spring. Or imagine how you would react to someone who said: "Oh yes, people have rights, but they are not rights to anything at all: they are just rights." We should make no sense of this kind of usage and would doubt that the speaker understood what it meant. So also with a claim that people have rights, but not by virtue of any natural, rational, moral, or positive authority – they just have them in the same way as they have teeth. The meaning of the idea of right is inseparably bound up with that of legitimacy. If someone said he had a right and responded to our question "By virtue of what authority?" with "None" (not "None of your business," "My own," "Because I am a human being," or "Because I say so," but simply "None") we would doubt that he understood what the word meant. We would encounter comparable difficulties with a claim that rights existed and attached to people but served no purpose (not that they had become redundant like an appendix, or were seldom or never invoked, or that we did not know what their purpose was, but simply that they served no purpose whatsoever). The claim, then, is that it is a condition for the intelligibility of talk about rights that it be expressible in terms of the quadratic schema, that intelligible claims about rights must be able to supply answers to the fourfold question: who is entitled, to what, on what basis, and for what purpose?

It might reasonably be asked what the "historical status" of this schema is. My use of the Austinian tactic here of what "we" would find intelligible glosses over the historical or cultural ranges within which these claims are held to be true. Let us leave aside the question of whether there could be a culture in which no rights existed at all. Could there be a culture in which people used the term in such a way that it had some affinities with our understanding of it but did not conform to this schema, at least in some respects, or perhaps in a way that bears no resemblance to our usage at all? The response that in that case we should not be able to understand it is never very satisfactory, partly because the issue in arguments about the indeterminacy of translation is often not this type of case, but the one where we think we have a correct translation but someone questions our grounds for thinking this. There are tremendously complex philosophical problems raised here, but it is legitimate to sidestep them for two reasons.

First, no special epistemological status is claimed for this schema. It is offered as an analysis of the core meaning of the term "right," which should be taken only to mean that if the term is used in such a way as to violate the injunctions entailed by this analysis, it is difficult to see how it could be intelligible. To this extent we could say that these conditions for the use of the term are quite close to the centers of our metaphorical Quinean fields. In addition, we are talking here about conditions for the intelligibility of utterances about rights, not conditions that make them plausible or convincing.[13] This is not to say that first and second order questions are unrelated. Part of my historical thesis will be that the negative libertarian view of rights that has had so much influence in the liberal tradition rests on a misconception of the second order nature of the term "right." The claim is simply that assertions about rights will be translatable into the schema if they are coherent, because the schema embodies what is essentially reapplicable in what the term means. It is part of the internal grammar of the term which functions independently of whether people who use the term coherently realize this, and this is partly why it can be a useful heuristic device in bringing hidden assumptions to the fore and in comparing different arguments. For instance, we will see that one influential substantive account of rights holds that it is possible to specify the right independently of the good, indeed that the idea of right, if taken seriously, requires that we do this. My schema, if accurate, reveals such claims to be fallacious, because reference to the

13 My claim thus differs, for instance, from the much stronger (and in my view implausible) claim of Rawls (1971:48ff) that our "considered judgments" on substantive questions of right and justice can be expected to command unanimity. Rawls's claim is discussed in Chapter 5.

substance of rights and their purposes clearly requires a conception of the good. And indeed when we examine the substantive arguments of defenders of this "independence" thesis,
we find that they obviously do embody conceptions of the
good in what they say, or imply, concerning the second and
fourth terms in the relation. It is in this sense that intelligibility requires conformity to the schema whether protagonists
typically realize it or not.

Second, this study is quite historically and culturally specific.
It is concerned with developments in the Anglo-American liberal tradition since the English Civil War. From points of view
such as that of the narrative historian this range might be
thought to be very broad, but it means that many of the formally possible problems relating to indeterminacy of translation do not arise. Whether the term "soul" means something
different than it does to us in a culture where people believe
that they carry their souls in boxes, whether two people could
systematically believe they both have the same understanding
of the same term when they do not, whether I could invent a
private language, these questions are not presented in this
context. There can be, however, substantial difficulties in recovering enough of the contexts in which people wrote to see
why they made the assumptions they did, or in being sure that
we have grasped the argument in its own terms of reference.
But these are questions of a much lower order, and do not
entail anything about the intrinsic inaccessibility of old books.

Underlying structure and substantive argument. Assuming, then,
that the schema is taken on trust, what does it tell us about the
concept of a right? On its own, very little: conformity to the
schema is a necessary condition for an assertion being about
rights, but it is by no means sufficient.[14] The formal, empty

14 Parent (1974:154) makes this point in relation to MacCallum's triadic account of
   freedom. This is something of a misplaced criticism, however, since the object of
   MacCallum's analysis was to demonstrate that arguments that often purport to be
   about alternative definitions of freedom are often in fact arguments about the
   different (substantive) characterizations of the variables in his triad. His point was
   not that conformity to his triad is a sufficient condition for talking about freedom
   but rather that it is necessary. MacCallum would be the first to acknowledge that
   talking about freedom involves talking about many other things as well. It is
   precisely to those things that he wished to direct our attention.

17

character of the schema points to the fact that assertions about rights rest on and entail a great many substantive propositions about other things, some abstract, some normative, and some empirical. This is a point of far-reaching implications, for it militates against the tendency of the whole deontological ethical tradition to treat substantive moral and political questions as questions of "ideal theory" which are then applied to the "second best" situations of the actual world. We will see that moral arguments about rights are deeply embedded in assumptions and beliefs about how the world actually operates causally, and claims which purport to be purely hypothetical and theoretical invariably require such assumptions. This should not surprise us once we think about the problem in terms of the schema. If a claim about rights, for instance, is partly a claim about what there are rights to, about the substance of rights, or the things that have value, this will obviously rest on assumptions about how those things are in fact created and distributed. Thus an apparently purely normative question concerning whether we ought to have a right to what we make is intrinsically empirically loaded with assumptions about how things are made, what constitutes "making," and why different persons have different capacities to make different things. For a moral claim to our right to what we make to have substantive content, it engages these questions willy nilly. It is a virtue of the schema that it brings such engagements to the surface and makes them explicit.

If the schema places some basic limitations on intelligible uses of the term "right," this is not all that constitutes the skeleton to its main uses in the liberal tradition since the English Civil War. The Anglo-American liberal tradition has evolved, since the seventeenth century, in such a way as to view certain substantive characterizations of the terms in the relation, certain ways of talking about rights, as central and basic to moral and political philosophy. These ways of talking have evolved with, and been functional to, changing circumstances, although I will argue that it is misleading to think, as Macpherson and others appear to, that they merely reflect those changing circumstances, or that these ways of conceiving of rights have not themselves undergone significant changes.

In Part II, I trace the emergence and consolidation of individual rights theories in their early modern forms. Employing my quadratic schema to delineate the domain of investigation, I examine the accounts of rights in the writings of Hobbes and Locke, who are held to typify the emergence and classical consolidation of the liberal ideology of individual rights. In Part III, I undertake a parallel analysis of the modern rights theories of Nozick and Rawls who are argued to typify the neo-classical and Keynesian moments in this ideology.

Each chapter is divided into an "internal" discussion of the argument and an "external" analysis which focuses more explicitly on its ideological consequences. In the first of these I try to recover the meaning of the argument within its own terms of reference. Such critical judgments as are offered do not seek to question those terms of reference. In the second half of each chapter I move beyond those terms of reference, examine their consequences for the evolving liberal tradition, and offer more general critical judgments. Part IV begins with a comparative discussion of the earlier and later theories. It is argued that, although all these arguments have had (different) powerful ideological components, the seventeenth-century arguments were generally more coherent and made better intellectual sense, within their own terms of reference, than the modern arguments. For various historical and conceptual reasons, however, I contend that it is unrealistic to suppose that the seventeenth-century arguments can fruitfully be applied to our contemporary reality and its characteristic political dilemmas. I conclude with a more general discussion of the limits to a coherent general theory of rights or justice in our contemporary world, and with a critique of the deontological turn in modern liberal theory.

Part II
The early arguments

2

The transitional moment

I. INTRODUCTION

My aim at the outset is to exhibit the subject of our investigation in its earliest recognizably modern form, through an analysis of the account of rights at the heart of Hobbes's political theory. My interpretation of Hobbes's argument shares some affinities with C. B. Macpherson's, but it differs in three main respects. First I will argue that, although the major socioeconomic forces that influenced Hobbes's argument were intimately bound up with the emergence of capitalism in England, Macpherson's "possessive market" model misses the transitional character of English society during this period, and that partly for this reason it provides an inadequate and misleading basis for understanding the historical role of Hobbes's argument in the evolution of liberal ideology. Second, if Hobbes's argument contained many elements of what was to become the classical variant of the liberal ideology of individual rights, several ideas central to that later ideology were absent, the most important being the concept of equilibrium. This made a vast difference to the ideology's practical imperatives, particularly with respect to the social, economic, and political functions of the state in an emerging market economy—for it entailed very different assumptions about how markets functioned in practice. Macpherson's excessively general "possessive market" model leads him to miss these and other important implications of Hobbes's arguments. Finally, although Hobbes played a central role in articulating much of the vocabulary and underlying grammar of the modern liberal rights tradition, and in transforming the language of natural rights he inherited into a recognizably modern form, his argument was embedded in a view of the nature of moral knowledge which (while essential to his own argument's underlying coherence) is anathema to the modern liberal consciousness. In this regard Hobbes's argument is undeniably premodern, but it remains useful for understanding some of the greatest difficulties the modern arguments confront.

II. HOBBES'S THEORY OF RIGHTS

Hobbes is renowned for the view that man in a state of nature has a right to life, that this right is perpetually threatened by the chaos that prevails in the state of nature, and that he consequently agrees, in a simultaneous act with all others, to submit to an absolute sovereign. The precise nature and basis of the rights and obligations thus generated have been the subject of intensive dispute,[1] but it is clear that although some residual right to life remains (the moral status of which is somewhat ambiguous), to all intents and purposes man's positive political rights are those granted by the sovereign at his pleasure. An individualsit theory of contract thus generates a command theory of law. Hobbes's account of rights, however, contains a good deal more of interest which can be gleaned by looking at it more closely.

i. The subject of rights

Hobbes was a member of a ruling class and, whatever the complex redistributions of power and wealth occurring within that class during this period,[2] he exhibited the ruling-class fear of the masses, quite widespread in Tudor and early Stuart England, so convincingly documented by Christopher Hill. Hill points out that a recurrent theme in early Stuart literature was a strong upper-class mixture of fear of and contempt for the "many headed monster" (Sidney's phrase in *Arcadia*), the marauding rabble of dispossessed poor. It can be discerned in the writings of Spenser, Barnable Googe, Sir Thomas Browne, Thomas Fuller, and many others. The same sentiment is re-

---

1 Warrender (1957:278–98ff, 1965:89–100), Plamenatz (1965:73–87), Pennock (1965:101–16), Wernham (1965:117–39), Tuck (1979:119–39).
2 Stone (1965:1–134). For a useful summary of Stone's views as they relate to Hobbes see Wood (1980:437–52).

flected in many political tracts of the propertied class. Richard
Morison, for whom "all men almost [are] at war with them
that be rich," Francis Thynne, Sir Thomas Ashton, the Duke
of Albermarle, Sir John Oglander, and Sir Thomas Went-
worth all expressed views similar to that of Deloney, who asserted in 1597 that "[t]he poor hate the rich because they will
not set them on work; and the rich hate the poor because they
seem burdensome."[3] Such rulling-class sentiments intensified
during the extensive lower-class unrest in the decades immediately preceding the Civil War.[4] The fear was a natural response to visible social consequences of economic and demographic changes in progress: urbanization (particularly in the
south) and the growth of a wage laboring class (by the time of
the Civil War comprising close to one half the population of
England) at a time of prolonged economic crisis marked by
extensive unemployment and underemployment.

Although demographic statistics for the period are uncertain, it appears that the trend of increasing population growth
characteristic of the sixteenth century continued throughout
the seventeenth (Hill, 1961:23). Nominal wages rose in the century before 1640, but this rise was more than offset by the
continuous rise in prices, which began in the 1520s (Outhwaite,
1969:7–15) and took on sudden spurts in the 1540s, 1590s,
and 1630s, producing a decline in the real purchasing power of
wages (Bowden, 1967:594–616). In 1641 the opinion was expressed that "the fourth part of the inhabitants of most of the
parishes of England are miserable poor people, and (harvest
time excepted) without any subsistence," and in the 1680s King
estimated that laborers, cottagers, and paupers constituted as
much as 47 percent of the population (ibid.:598). Real wages
fell by about two thirds over the sixteenth century, and although they began to rise slowly at the end of the century, a
worker born in 1580 would never earn half of his grandfather's
wage (Hill, 1961:24; Everitt, 1967:435). This marginalization
produced a large and growing population living at or near the
poverty line and concentrated in the towns, especially London,
whose population may have increased eight-fold between 1500

3 Quoted in Hill (1968:302. Cf. also 300–1).
4 For further discussion and evidence, see Hill (1961:23–8, 1968:306–14, 1972:39–56).

and 1650. These "masterless men" were not tied to the feudal system and were thus threatening to it. In 1569 a government inquiry concluded that there were 1300 of them, mainly in the north; by the turn of the seventeenth century it was estimated that there were 30,000 in London alone (Hill, 1972:39–41).

Hobbes's attitude to the new urban masses was ambiguous. At one level he obviously felt the ruling-class fear; he thought uncontrolled mobs had provided one of the forces necessary to make the rebellion against the king successful. Since they were not in fear of the law they would fight for money and the merchants who had more of it than the crown were hence able to buy their allegiance. In *Behemoth* Hobbes wrote:

Truly, I think, if the King had had money, he might have had soldiers enough in England. For there were very few of the common people that cared much for either of the causes, but would have taken any side for pay or plunder. But the King's treasury was very low, and his enemies, that pretended the people's ease from taxes, and other specious things, had the command of the purses of the City of London, and of most cities and corporate towns in England, and of many particular persons besides. (Hobbes, 1966, VI:166)

In Hobbes's view, the masses were a powerful and potentially dangerous force, willing "to serve under them that had the greatest plenty of money," and it is in this context that his discussion of the state of nature should be comprehended.[5] *Pace* Macpherson (1962:20), for Hobbes the state of nature was no theoretical construct; he thought it actually prevailed in much of the world and had prevailed in England with the breakdown of legal order during the Civil War:

It may peradventure be thought, there was never such a time, nor condition of warre as this; and I believe it was never generally so, over all the world: but there are many places, where they live so now. For the savage people in many places of *America*, except the government of small Families, the concord whereof dependeth on naturall lust, have no government at all; and live at this day in that brutish manner, as I said before. Howsoever, it may be perceived what manner of life there would be, where there were no common

5 For a useful discussion of Hobbes's views of the role of the masses in the Civil War, see Ashcraft (1978:27–62).

Power to feare; by the manner of life, which men that have formerly lived under a peacefull government, use to degenerate into, in a civill Warre. (Hobbes, 1968:187)

Yet, despite his fear that society must inevitably degenerate into civil war once the masses cease to be controlled by an absolute power, Hobbes recognized with a kind of Tocquevillean foresight that these masses were to be the stuff of the politics of the future. Dangerous and threatening as they were, a political system, to survive, must appeal to their interests – not as a member of this or that class and not for some higher good: these "overmighty subjects" had to be appealed to in terms of their individual interests.

Leviathan was not directly aimed at the masses. For Hobbes the war of all against all and the relentless drive for power infected the entire social landscape, and was present not least within the ruling classes themselves. He was a first-hand witness to the decline of the aristocracy that Lawrence Stone has so masterfully chronicled, to the corruption and squabbling for advancement that accompanied and exacerbated the inflation of honors, and to the growing sale of titles and offices to meet the urgent financial needs of the crown.[6] It seems certain that Hobbes regretted the breakdown of aristocratic values that these events appeared to accelerate, and that he disliked the growing influence of merchants and money in politics (Thomas 1965:189–215).[7] He saw these as events to be reckoned with – again perhaps the comparison with Tocqueville's attitude toward equality is instructive – in the attempt to generate the social consensus necessary for political stability. For Hobbes thought it essential for people, in their own interests, to assent to the arrangements he advocated if political stability was to be assured. This is reflected in his opening remarks in *Leviathan* where he says:

[Y]et, when I shall have set down my own reading orderly, and perspicuously, the pains left another, will be onely to consider, if he also

---

6 See Stone (1965:37–61, 71–88, 191–232), Wood (1980:441–7).
7 In section II(ii) of this chapter it is argued that Thomas's account, while a useful corrective to Macpherson's, nonetheless understates the significance of Hobbes's views for the liberal ideology of individual rights.

find not the same in himself. *For this kind of Doctrine, admitteth no other Demonstration.* (Hobbes, 1968:83, emphasis added)

The ways in which his principles are to be communicated to the common people are bound up with a complex theory of political education which need not concern us in detail now.[8] Suffice it to note here that Hobbes did not believe that the masses must be terrorized into submission, as Thomas (1965:203ff) and others have suggested. He had a powerfully egalitarian conception of rationality, and believed that the major barriers to the universal acceptance of the laws of nature as he articulated them derived neither from any constitutional inadequacy of the common people, nor from any difficulties with the ideas themselves. (These latter, we will see, he held to be unambiguously and conclusively demonstrable.) The political confusion of the common people derived instead, for Hobbes, from ideological distortions generated by religious, economic, and intellectual groups for partisan political reasons.[9] He thus responded to critics who maintained that "though the Principles be right, yet Common people are not of capacity enough to be made to understand them" in the following terms:

I should be glad, that the Rich, and Potent Subjects of a Kingdome, or those that are accounted the most Learned, were no lesse incapable than they [the common people]. But all men know, that the obstructions to this kind of doctrine, proceed not so much from the difficulty of the matter, as from the interest of them that are to learn. Potent men, digest hardly any thing that setteth up a Power to bridle their affections; and Learned men, any thing that discovereth their errours, and thereby lesseneth their Authority: whereas the Common-peoples minds, unless they be tainted with dependance on the Potent, or scribbled over with the opinions of their Doctors, are like clean paper, fit to receive whatsoever by Publique Authority shall be imprinted. (Hobbes, 1968:378–9)

The implications of this for modern doctrines of individual consent will concern us in detail later. Notice here that in

---

8 Aspects of this issue are taken up in section II(iii) of this chapter. For a comprehensive discussion of Hobbes's theory of political education see Johnston (1981: 189–91).
9 For a useful discussion of Hobbes's views on ideological distortion of political beliefs see Ashcraft (1978:27–62).

ascribing rights indiscriminately to all in the state of nature, and holding that all must be convinced individually that the Leviathan functions in their interests, Hobbes is doing more than just rejecting the feudal order. He is acknowledging that the breakdown of that order has radically changed the whole basis of politics.

It would thus be misleading to suggest that Hobbes was entirely against all the developments that had produced mass politics as he understood them. The many attacks on knowledge from authority throughout his writings and his belief that scientific principles are rationally demonstrable to and understandable by all bespeak considerable enthusiasm for the possibilities generated by this "new subjectivity." It was the fact that peoples' rational capacities had been sullied and exploited in the service of various religious, economic, and political causes that was the problem, which he saw it as his task to address.[10]

ii. The substance of rights

For Hobbes there are no restrictions in the state of nature on what people have rights *to* (in the absence of some system of authority all have a right to everything against all), but following the contract people are entitled only to what the law permits. Even property rights are regarded as postcontractual, distributed by the state, an anticommon-law view that clearly identified Hobbes with the royalist position that all property is subject to the crown (Thomas, 1965:223ff). There is a powerful authoritarian component to this view, as is often pointed out, but to pay too much attention to it obscures other elements of his account that are important here. It is true that Hobbes allows the state unlimited power, but it is also clear that the "absolute and arbitrary" power of the sovereign should be exercised through published rules, that its functions are seen as fundamentally regulative of private interaction, and that a very wide area is envisaged where private rights of exclusive dominion (over objects and actions) prevail. It is important not to conflate a regulative state with a minimal one.

10 For further analysis of Hobbes's views on these issues see Johnston (1981).

For Hobbes, writing in a situation of political and social chaos, where national markets in important commodities such as land, labor, and food were still in the process of establishing themselves, regulation could and often did mean very considerable intervention.

Hobbes's view of the relation between state and society can perhaps best be gleaned by considering his account of the economic functions of the state. In chapter 24 of *Leviathan*, entitled "Of the Nutrition and Procreation of the Common-Wealth," he outlines the following six such functions: first, the sovereign arbitrarily distributes land among the subjects and thereby creates property rights. This constitutes *"Mine,* and *Thine,* and *His* that is to say in one word Propriety" (Hobbes, 1968:296). The existence of a civil law, Hobbes argues, is a necessary condition for the creation and maintenance of property rights, and should it be *"abandoned, or but negligently guarded . . . there is nothing that any man can be sure to receive from his Ancestor, or leave to his children"* (ibid). This account may sound remarkably unbourgeois but two points should be noted. First, Hobbes is at this stage dealing with the original endowment of property rights. In his account of commutative justice subsequent changes among individuals are effected through voluntary contract. It is only initial distribution that Hobbes deals with in this way, and it is worth pointing out that it was to become characteristic of liberal accounts of property that they would fail to offer a satisfactory treatment of the initial endowments of property rights – focusing exclusively on the mechanisms of subsequent distributional change, and assuming that questions of initial endowment were of now more than historical concern.[11] It is thus to Hobbes's account of commutative justice that modern liberal theories of property ownership and exchange most closely conform. Commutative justice "is the Justice of a Contractor." It concerns "Performance of a Covenant, in Buying and Selling; Hiring and Letting to Hire; Lending and Borrowing; Exchanging, Bartering, and other acts of Contract." In all such transactions the value of things contracted for "is measured by the Appetite of the

---

11 This issue is taken up in Chapter 4.

Contractors: and therefore the just value, is that which they be contented to give." It is on this basis that Hobbes rejects the traditional distinction between commutative and distributive justice, arguing that the notions of merit to which the latter was tied are not relevant to the justice of market transactions (Hobbes, 1968:208).

Hobbes's refusal to grant property rights against the state, and his medieval views on the rights of the starving poor to relief through theft if this was the only alternative to starvation, separate his view from a developed bourgeois account of property as Thomas (1965:223, 225–7) has argued. This should not, however, lead us to overlook the significance of Hobbes's account for the evolution of liberal views. Hobbes grounds all property rights in positive law and thereby links the state to the preservation of private property. The subject has no property right against the sovereign (and can therefore legitimately be taxed) but his property right against other subjects is inviolable: "The Propriety which a subject hath in his lands, consisteth in a right to exclude all other subjects . . . and not to exclude their Soveraign" (1968:297). It is simply not true, then, that Hobbes "provided no effective guarantees for private property" as Thomas claims. For Thomas, "in the one issue where property rights . . . were seriously disputed, Hobbes abandoned the interests of possessing classes altogether" (Thomas, 1965:224, 223). Even if this were accurate historically (which is hard to imagine when we think of the social and political implications of enclosure or the more general perceived threats to property before and during the Civil War),[12] it misses the fact that Thomas elsewhere acknowledges: for Hobbes "the commonwealth exists to provide a framework of security in which wealth may be pursued, but [that it is] not to interfere with its distribution," and that "he favoured what we should regard to-day as an extreme state of internal *laisser-faire*" so that in general his economic position was, "in the context of his age, extremely advanced and it constitutes the most obviously *bourgeois* aspect of his thought" (ibid.:228–9).

12 See section II(i) of this chapter.

Second, Hobbes was writing in a volatile political and legal context. The state had for over a century been taking a powerfully active role in the destruction of feudal property relationships and the creation of modern transmissibility in land. Both through its own confiscation and sale of church lands after the Reformation and through its central role in dismantling feudal land law, the state in late Tudor and early Stuart England *was* distributing "initial" property rights in their modern form of exclusive transmissible dominion. This is, in significant part, how "bourgeois" property relations were created in England.[13] In simultaneously adhering to a view of ownership in terms of exclusive dominion, and charging the state with responsibility of distributing property in accordance with it, Hobbes was, however unconsciously, sanctioning changes in English land law that had been in motion for some time and which were to become central to the modern system of private law on which developed capitalism would rest.

The second function of the state concerns taxation. The sovereign may tax the subject when the public need arises:

In the Distribution of land, the Common-wealth it selfe, may be conceived to have a portion, and possesse, and improve the same by their Representative; and that such portion may be made sufficient, to sustein the whole expence to the common Peace, and defence necessarily required. (Hobbes, 1968:298)

The amount of taxation that will be required is to be determined by circumstances, but what is interesting from our point of view is that Hobbes was clear that it must be limited to whatever is necessary for the maintenance of internal peace and national security. He thus opposed the creation of a stock of public property on the grounds that it would invariably generate waste and corruption:

[T]he nature of men being as it is, the setting forth of Publique Land, or of any certaine Revenue for the Common-wealth, is in vaine; and tendeth to the dissolution of Government, and to the condition of meere Nature, and War, as soon as ever the Soveraign Power falleth into the hands of a Monarch, or of an Assembly, that

13 For discussion of evidence see sections II(iii) and III of this chapter.

are either too negligent of mony, or too hazardous in engaging the publique stock, into a long, or costly war. (Ibid.)

Thus Hobbes advocated limited taxation to finance a regulative state whose economic functions were seen as confined to those necessary for the maintenance of civil peace and national security. This interpretation is reinforced by his account of public goods: although the twelfth law of nature dictates, on the basis of equity, that those things held in common should be equally available to all, things should only be held in common to begin with if they "*cannot be divided*" (1968:212). Since all were held to have an equal interest in the limited public functions ascribed to the state, Hobbes was later able to argue that people should all be taxed equally: "Seeing then the benefit that every one receiveth thereby . . . is equally dear to poor, and rich; the debt which a poor man oweth them that defend his life, is the same which a rich man oweth for the defence of his" (ibid.:386).

Third, the state regulates foreign trade to ensure that no individual can furnish a foreign power with "means to hurt the Common-wealth" (ibid.:299) or import things inimical to its safety. Fourth, the sovereign regulates the mode but, significantly from our standpoint, not the substance of contract.

[I]t belongeth to the Common-wealth (that is to say, the Soveraign,) to appoint in what manner, all kinds of contract between Subjects (as buying, selling, exchanging, borrowing, lending, letting, and taking to hire,) are to be made; and by what words and signes they shall be understood for valid. (Ibid.:299)

Fifth, the sovereign establishes and regulates the value of money, which is the "Bloud of a Common-wealth" (ibid.:300); and sixth, it ensures the "procreation" of the commonwealth by licensing the founding of colonies abroad. A seventh function is dealt with in the course of Hobbes's discussion of the province of the sovereign: the state should provide maintenance for the unemployable, for "as it is Uncharitablenesse in any man, to neglect the impotent; so it is in the Soveraign of a Common-wealth, to expose them to the hazard of such uncertain Charity" (ibid.:387). But the able-bodied idle should be

33

forced to work. To ensure that employment be available, laws should be passed to encourage "all member of Manifacture that requires labour." The state should not intervene directly in the production process to create employment, but it should create conditions conducive to the expansion of private generated employment. If this does not solve the problem, the unemployed should be "transplanted into Countries not sufficiently inhabited" (ibid.).

These constitute a complete list of the economic functions of Hobbes's state. Within the limits imposed by them individuals are free to enjoy liberty by "praetermission":

The Liberty of a Subject, lyeth therefore only in those things, which in regulating their actions, the Soveraign hath praetermitted: *such as is the Liberty to buy, and sell, and otherwise contract with one another, to choose their own aboad, their own diet, their own trade of life, and institute their children as they themselves think fit, & the like.* (Hobbes, 1968:264, emphasis added)

The state, then, remains silent as to the substance of individual trades and contracts (which it nonetheless regulates and enforces), as well as most other activities that contemporary liberals typically regard as comprising the private sphere.

We seem to be confronted by the paradox that Hobbes the political absolutist advocates a highly restricted state in matters economic, as Letwin (1972:163–4) has noted. Despite the state's absolute power, its actions are conceived of as indirect and regulative, as revealed in the discussions of unemployment and taxation; it is supportive of the institution of the market, revealed in the account of contract and individual freedom; and it is limited, revealed in the discussion of the limits to public property as well as by the fact that Hobbes does not ascribe any further economic roles to the state.

How are we to reconcile this economic minimalism with Hobbes's political absolutism? This has not been squarely confronted in the Hobbes literature. Commentators have tended to ignore his chapter on the economic functions of the state and Letwin's explanation, that Hobbes was a complicated thinker (1972:162–4), is less than fully satisfactory. To address this issue three factors should be borne in mind. First, it seems clear that Hobbes perceived no necessary connections between economics and politics. Ashcraft (1978:27–62) points out that, in his history of the Civil War, Hobbes acknowledged the social usefulness of merchants and the social cohesion that could result from an order based on "market-friendship," but that he inveighed against the prevalent view that only republicanism was compatible with the development of commercial wealth. He thought it misleadingly false, for instance, to suggest a connection between Dutch republicanism and prosperity. In Hobbes's view as expressed in *Behemoth,* the true interests of merchants were quite compatible with those of the monarchy; it was their ignorance of this and their being "passionately carried away" that led them to oppose the king. Since for Hobbes all ideas originate from "the motions of the mind," the place to deal with deceptive ideologies was in the universities (ibid.:49–50). He believed there was no necessary relationship between a country's economic prosperity, or lack of it, and its type of government.[14]

Second, Hobbes could hardly on the one hand subscribe to the increasingly widespread view that production for exchange is the source of society's wealth, and on the other condemn the activities of the merchants who appeared to be the driving force behind this production. The view that the capacity to produce for exchange is the source of wealth had become common currency among English economic and political writers by the mid-seventeenth century. During the middle third of the century dozens of writers, simultaneously concerned with the problem of the poor and the sources of national wealth, began to reject the mercantilist identification of wealth with precious metals, as well as medieval conceptions of wealth as "the bounty of a dread God or in the gifts of a reluctant Nature" (Johnson, 1937:239). Instead they began to define national prosperity as inhering in the capacity to produce for exchange. Appleby has shown that the belief that the capacity to labor is a source of wealth was affirmed in much of the pamphlet literature on

14 On this subject see also Thomas (1965:214–15).

trade and the poor throughout the century, a view which reflected the "dawning realization that art could produce more than nature" (Appleby, 1978:135–57).

Perhaps the most systematic formulation of this view came from Hobbes's contemporary William Petty (whom Marx regarded as the founder of political economy).[15] Petty formulated a labor theory of value in which he distinguished the "natural," "real," or "true price current" (which depends on "the few or more hands requisite to necessities of nature") from the "political" price (which depends "upon the paucity of Supernumerary Interlopers into any trade over and above all that are necessary"). He thereby set out the terms of the central problem that would preoccupy the classical economists of the eighteenth and nineteenth centuries, how labor and demand interact in the determination of value or price. Petty himself tried to compute relative prices in terms of comparative labor times: If a man can bring an ounce of silver to London from Peru in the same time as he can produce a bushel of corn, "then one is the natural price of the other." If, in virtue of technological innovation, he can bring two ounces in the same time as he formerly did one, "then Corn will be as cheap at ten shillings the bushel, as it was before at five shillings, *caeteris paribus*" (Petty, 1899 [1662], I:89–91, 50–1). Petty recognized that such computations implied some basic unit of value in terms of which commodities are commensurable with one another. This brought him, in *The Political Anatomy of Ireland,* to what he regarded as "the most important Consideration in Political Oeconomies" which is "how to make a *Par* and *Equation* between Lands and Labour, so as to express the Value of any thing by either alone" (ibid. [1691], I:181). To tackle this Petty developed the notion of simple labor, to which all labor can be reduced.[16]

Hobbes and Petty had worked together in the 1640s, and although Petty's discipleship of Hobbes was primarily for his

---

15 See the discussion in *Theories of Surplus Value* (1963, I:178–82, 354–63).

16 Appleby uncovering in the seventeenth-century English literature on trade and the poor, long before the demise of physiocratic ideas in France, so much of the language of what was to become classical political economy, is an important corrective to the assertions of Tribe (1978) and others that the language of classical economics did not emerge before the eighteenth century.

politics, it is possible that Hobbes influenced Petty in his formulation of the labor theory of value.[17] That Hobbes embraced a version of this view is indicated by his comments on
the poor already mentioned, by his celebrated assertion in
chapter 10 of *Leviathan* that the "*Value*, or WORTH of a man,
is as of all other things, his Price; that is to say, so much as
would be given for the use of his Power. . . ." (1968:151–2), by
a discussion of labor as a commodity and source of wealth in
Behemoth where Hobbes claims that merchants produce wealth
". . . by making poor people sell their labor to them [mer-
chants] at their own prices" (1966, VI:321), and by his discussion of labor-value and trade in chapter 24 of *Leviathan*. In
this instance Hobbes is arguing that few countries are large
enough to be self-sufficient and few do not produce surpluses
in some commodities. Thus:

the superfluous commodities to be had within, become no more superfluous, but supply these wants at home, by importation of that
which may be had abroad, either by Exchange, or by just Warre, or by
Labour: for a mans Labour also, is a commodity exchangeable for
benefit, as well as any other thing: And there have been Commonwealths that having no more Territory, than hath served them for
habitation, have nonethelesse, not onely maintained, but also en-
creased their Power, partly by the labour of trading from one place to
another, and partly by selling the Manifactures, whereof the Materials
were brought in from other places. (Hobbes, 1968:295)

Clearly this passage reveals no mercantilist predisposition for
particular types of imports over exports, or balance of trade –
anything, including labor, which can be exchanged for benefit
brings advantage. It is true that Hobbes treats just war as an
alternative mechanism of accumulation to production for exchange. War was a principal mode of accumulation under late
feudalism and the fact that Hobbes acknowledges both these
mechanisms signals the transitional juncture in English economic history at which he stood. This should not, however, be
overstated. Hobbes was for the most part in the mainstream of

17 This is suggested by Charles Hull, editor of Petty's economic writings; see Petty
(1899 [1691]:lxi, lxiii, lxxiii). See also Reik (1977:79, 210). On the influence of
early versions of the labor theory of value in seventeenth-century writing on
wages, employment, depopulation, and the poor see Coleman (1956:280–95).

the advanced economic thinking of his day in regarding the capacity to labor as the source of wealth, and production for trade as indispensable to the health of a commonwealth. It is therefore not surprising that he did not criticize the economic activities of merchants. He was compelled to endorse their economic behavior and claim that it was compatible with the political arrangements he advocated.[18]

A third point concerns the absence of the concept of equilibrium from economic and political writing during this period. It was not until the turn of the eighteenth century that writers began seriously to contend that the economic system could regulate itself without any interference from the state; it was much later still that the notion of equilibrium would be directly applied to politics generally. This meant, in Hobbes's England, that one could quite consistently advocate market-based social and economic organization without holding anything like the view that the system could be self-regulating. Indeed for Hobbes absolutist political institutions would be essential to sustain this organization. The driving force behind his politics was that without decisive control by the sovereign, society would collapse into disorder. In the early eighteenth century Mandeville would become notorious for his metaphorical understanding of the social mechanism in terms of the harmonious activities of bees. Hobbes, by contrast, employs this analogy in reverse: where bees (and ants) were correctly labeled political by Aristotle because they "live sociably one with another," this is because among them the "Common good differeth not from the Private" so that although "by nature enclined to their private [goods], they procure thereby the common benefit." But man differs in that he is continually in competition for honor and dignity, his "Joy consisteth in comparing himselfe with other men," he "can relish nothing but what is eminent," and his rational capacities enable him to question the "administration of their

18 As Ashcraft puts it, Hobbes could "leave the bourgeois economic arrangements of society–in so far as they existed–as they were, provided the political *ideas* of merchants and educated gentlemen were reformed in accordance with Hobbesian principles" (Ashcraft, 1978:49).

common businesse" (1968:225–6). In these circumstances the common good must be preserved by the state. It will otherwise be undermined by the private activities of individual men.

Hobbes's account of the state as essentially regulative of economic activity, the substance of which latter is inherently private, rests on a broader negative libertarian view of society summed up in his epithet that "The Greatest Liberty of Subjects, dependeth on the silence of the Law" (1968:271). Hobbes conceives of social relationships as essentially private, their form, but never their content, regulated by the state. This view was significant not only for economic life, it was central to the demands for religious toleration that dominated so much of English politics at this time, and is required by the Protestant view of man's religious life as essentially private. Although Hobbes took great pains to argue that his laws of nature were compatible with the laws of God, he made a sharp distinction between civil and ecclesiastical law and acknowledged the privacy of man's relationship with God. Indeed, he used this to deny the legitimacy of Catholicism against the English crown on the grounds that a "private opinion" (of the Pope) could never be set up against the "Publique Person" of the civil authority. He even defended freedom of the individual rational conscience (which Locke was accused of plagiarizing in *The Reasonableness of Christianity*). Although this did not generate any political guarantees of toleration for nonconformists, it did recognize the sanctity of religious beliefs. Hobbes held that "true" religious beliefs by definition could not conflict with civil power, since they require acknowledgment of the legitimate authority and domain of that power; in this way he largely avoids the *political* question of religious toleration. He does acknowledge, however, that it would be madness for someone knowingly to condemn himself to eternal damnation at the command of the sovereign, and in the case where the sovereign is an infidel, defiance will in some circumstances be understandable, but "if they do [defy], they ought to expect their reward in Heaven" (ibid., 625ff). Hobbes believed that if religion does not overstep its legitimate (private) boundaries and interfere with civil matters, conflict between church and state will not arise.[19]

So although Hobbes's sovereign is allowed unlimited power, we have seen that the sphere in which private rights are to function is expected to be quite extensive in economic, social and religious life. People will make voluntary agreements with one another that will be enforced by the state; they will be free within the limits of the law, to make, do, exchange, and believe as they please.

iii. The basis for rights

Hobbes is perhaps best known for introducing into English political theory a view of law as resting on a generalized agreement among equal individuals, which both constitutes civil society and confers legitimacy on the actions of the state. All positive rights are embedded in a command theory of law whose legitimacy derives from this contract. The aim of the contract is the preservation of man's natural right to life that would otherwise be perpetually threatened. This view is rightly regarded as innovative not only because of its fundamental egalitarianism, the centrality it attached to the notion of individual consent, its secularism and its rationalism, but also because it marks a decisive break with feudal conceptions of law. With the Royalists, Hobbes rejected outright the common-law case that the law derived its legitimacy from an Ancient Constitution which was older than, and placed limits on, the authority of the crown. But unlike conventional defenders of absolutism such as Filmer, who linked their patriarchal defenses of prerogative to theories of divine right, Hobbes defined legitimate authority as the power to command obedience, the de facto presence of which was regarded as decisive evidence for the existence of the contract. Hobbes's view of

---

19 I do not claim to do justice to the highly contentious and voluminous literature currently emerging on Hobbes's religious views, and on the relevance of his religious arguments to his political theory. I would only claim, *pace* Warrender, that had Hobbes not offered a secular formulation of his argument, the logic of which was in principle separable from his religious arguments, he would never have been canonized in the liberal tradition. For this reason I sidestep the debates on his religious views. For a reinterpretation of their significance in light of Hobbes's changing views on the political importance of rhetoric, see Johnston (1986).

the contract was thus innovative in its accounts of the parties to the contract, the nature of their agreement with the sovereign, and the consequences of that agreement.

For Hobbes, man's rights in the state of nature seem at first sight to have a purely descriptive status. He defines natural right as:

THE RIGHT OF NATURE, which Writers commonly call *Jus Naturale* [which] is the Liberty each man hath, to use his own power, as he will himselfe, for the preservation of his own Nature; that is to say, of his own Life. (Hobbes, 1968:189)

This is sharply contrasted with, and separated from, natural law:

For though they that speak of this subject, use to confound *Jus*, and *Lex*, *Right* and *Law;* yet they ought to be distinguished; because RIGHT, consisteth in liberty to do, or to forbeare; Whereas LAW, determineth, and bindeth to one of them: so that Law, and Right, differ as much, as Obligation, and Liberty; which in one and the same matter are inconsistent. (Ibid.:189)

Natural rights thus indicate the human capacity for free action. This conceptual division marks an important shift in the Western tradition away from emphasis on natural law to the centrality of individual natural rights, as can perhaps be gleaned from the fact that in European languages other than English there is not the same linguistic distinction. The German word *Recht*, the Italian *diritto* and the French *droit* are all used to signify law in the abstract as well as right, so closely bound up are the etymologies of these ideas historically. They all exhibit the conflation Hobbes identifies in the Latin *ius* when he detaches the idea of right from that of law by insisting that natural rights are mere capacities, quite independent of any conception of law. Hobbes's natural rights do not even have the status of what Hohfeld referred to as "privileges" (and which his followers have come to refer to as "liberties"), rights that correlate only with the "no-right" of others to interfere with one's right—while imposing no additional affirmative obligations on those others.[20] For Hobbes man's natural

---

20 Hohfeld (1923:7, 38f). For a useful account of Hohfeld's views see Flathman (1976:38–47).

state is literally a state in which the right of all *against all* prevails and people's rights are limited by nothing more (or less) than their capacities for enforcement.

Morality inheres in the laws of nature which Hobbes regards as postulates for rational action and derivable from a correct understanding of the human condition. They are not, strictly speaking, laws at all, for a law, "to speak properly and accurately, is the speech of him who by right commands somewhat to others to be done or omitted" and natural laws, even though they are "delivered by God in the holy Scriptures," are not "in propriety of speech" laws at all; they are "nothing else but certain conclusions, understood by reason, of things to be done and omitted . . . as they proceed from nature" (Hobbes, 1966, II:49–50). The exact moral status of these natural laws is complex and elusive, but in one important respect Hobbes stands traditional natural law arguments on their heads: the various Ockhamist, Gersonist, and neo-Thomist traditions, while significantly different from one another, had all recognized the existence of *some* relationship between natural right and law, such that natural rights were either derived from natural law or at least limited by it. Even if the relationship was not one of symmetrical correlativity – as in the writings of the "subjective" theorists influenced by the revival of the Roman law conception of a right as a *facultas*, a liberty or power – natural law placed some limitations on man's natural rights, as will be seen in the next chapter.[21] To Hobbes, however, natural laws are derived from his account of man's natural capacities, which are taken to be, or at least in isomorphic correspondence with, man's natural rights.

Man's *civil* rights, those rights granted (or indirectly secured) by the actions of the sovereign, have an important moral force which inheres in the legitimacy of the contract. Once we try to pin down the nature of this moral force, however, we seem to find two distinct arguments. First is the claim that *in making* the agreement man authorizes the actions of the sovereign, that the act of agreeing is itself morally decisive. Second is the claim that the contract confers legitimacy be-

21 Chapter 3, Section II(iii). For useful discussions of the evolution of these various traditions see Skinner (1978, vol. I), Tuck (1979), and Finnis (1980:205–10).

cause it is *rational* for men to make it; it is a rational imperative dictated by the laws of nature which are in turn derived from a scientific analysis of the human condition.[22] On the face of it these appear to be very different arguments, perhaps even mutually contradictory. The first, supported by Hobbes's accounts of free action, promising and mutual renunciation of rights, corresponds most neatly with modern rights-based theories of contract. The second, which allows Hobbes to defend the imposition of commonwealths by force, the denial of any individual rights against the state, and the granting to the state of unlimited power, reads far more like a theory of interests. It is these features of his account that are generally singled out by liberals for criticism.

In fact, there was no contradiction here for the historical Hobbes because he had a different view of the ontological status of moral knowledge from that which the preceding dichotomy implies. Though Hobbes believed subjective assent played an important role in validating moral judgments, he was not a subjectivist in anything like our sense of the word. He thought that moral predicates could only meaningfully attach to individuals, that terms like "good" had no intrinsic meaning, that Aristotle was wrong in defining "good" simply as "that which all men desire . . . since different men desire and shun different things, there must need be many things that are *good* to some and *evil* to others . . . one cannot speak of something as being *simply good* since whatsoever is good, is good for someone or other" (1972:47). He thought moral knowledge to be radically mind-dependent in that it depended ultimately on introspection. None of this, however, was thought to entail that it could not be known with absolute certainty. On the contrary, one of his central aims in writing *Leviathan* was to supply such a conclusive demonstration. This apparent paradox can be explained only by reference to his theory of scientific knowledge.

It should be remembered that although *Leviathan* is a study of the "matter, form, and power of a commonwealth ecclesiasti-

---

22 Hence the so-called Taylor thesis which postulates a kind of schizophrenia between moral and psychological theory in Hobbes's argument. See Taylor (1965:35–55). For a useful critical discussion of this view see Minogue (1972:70–84).

cal and civil" Hobbes begins it with an account of the nature of sense-experience and scientific knowledge. He outlines a sense-data theory of perception, remarkable in its anticipation of Hume, according to which all knowledge is reducible to sense-impressions. Knowledge is divided into two classes, history, which is knowledge of fact, and science, which is knowledge of consequence. These classes are further subdivided into knowledge that in some way depends on man's will, such as civil history or civil philosophy, and that which does not, such as natural history or physics.[23] It is important to recognize that in classifying a mode of activity as scientific, there is no distincton between different types of consequences. Similarly, although all factual knowledge is reducible to sense-data, there is no ontological difference between objects of sense experience that exist inside the mind and those which exist outside it.[24] A desire is as much an object of sense-experience as a tree and a triangle. This is not to say that Hobbes makes no distinciton between a priori and a posteriori knowledge – we will see in a moment that he does – but simply that he regards all knowledge, even mind-dependent knowledge, as grounded in sense-experience. Scientific knowledge consists in the rational deduction of true consequences from true premises, which latter are either unambiguous "definitions" or accurate reflections of sense-experience.

Reason is defined in terms of, and held to be wholly reducible to, addition and subtraction. Its purpose is the discovery of "consequences," but these are conceived of far more broadly than entailment relationships. They include logical consequences, causal consequences, and moral consequences. Thus

23 Hobbes's classifications of the different sciences are not altogether consistent through the different writings. In *Leviathan* (1968:147–9) ethics is regarded as part of natural philosophy and politics part of civil philosophy, suggesting that only the latter depends on the human will, but in the (later) *de Homine* (1972:41) they are classified together as both being will-dependent and hence open to a priori demonstration.

24 There are, however, methodological differences in how these different phenomena can be known. Since the hallmark of genuine knowledge is subjective certainty, the kind of certainty we can have of a mathematical proof we understand, it follows that phenomena in the mind can only be known, ultimately, by introspection. In this regard there seems to be an essentialist component to Hobbes's view of science despite the epistemological nominalism (and ultimately, one must suspect, in tension with it) that has been well analyzed by Dorothea Krook (1956:3–22). This will be evident in my discussion of his view of truth in the next paragraph but one.

44

arithmeticians teach us to add and subtract in numbers, logi-
cians to compute with the "consequences of words," political
writers "add together *Pactions,* to find mens *duties;* and Lawyers, *Lawes,* and *facts,* to find what is *right* and *wrong* in the
actions of private men." Reason, then, is applicable to "what
matter soever there is place for *addition* and *subtraction*"
(1968:110–111). All men reason alike in the sense that coherence requires conformity to the basic laws of addition and
subtraction, but reason is not a natural capacity such as sense
or memory. It is learned by "industry," through language,
commonly misused, and its correct and unambiguous use is
the source of all scientific knowledge (ibid.: 110–16).

Truth is a slippery concept in Hobbes's writing. It is held
to be an attribute of language, not of the world, and is defined as "the right ordering of names in our affirmations"
(1968:105). This is actually a definition of coherence or consistency and in many places Hobbes uses the term in precisely this sense. But it is clear from his discussion of the uses
and abuses of speech, of absurdity, and from his sense-data
theory of perception that he thinks true statements reflect or
correspond to, or are reducible to, statements that reflect or
correspond to, particulars in the world. Thus truth consists
in the right ordering of names, but the names correspond to
particulars in the world, "there being nothing in the world
Universall but Names; for the things named, are every one
of them Individuall and Singular" (1968:102). An important
class of these are "Names positive" which are "put to mark
somewhat which is in Nature" (ibid.:107). Although absurdity
can result from unclear definitions and confusion of predicates with the subjects of which they are predicated, it can
also result from misidentifying particulars in the world as
universals or confusing our descriptions of bodies with the
bodies themselves (ibid.:114). In his discussion of historical
knowledge, Hobbes asserts that "[w]hatsoever . . . we conceive, has been perceived first by sense, either all at once, or
by parts; a man can have no thought, representing any thing,
not subject to sense" (ibid.:99). His various attacks on Carte-
sianism and scholasticism turn on his claims that such notions
as "immaterial substance" and "incorporeal substance" are

meaningless because they have no real referents. Despite his nominalism Hobbes clearly operates, at times, with a conception of truth as unambiguous correspondence.

When Hobbes comes to distinguish a priori from a posteriori knowledge his prototypical empiricism begins to wane. For Hobbes this distinction is not between knowledge which is true by definition and knowledge which depends on experience; the essential distinction is between truths which are functions of the human will and those which are not. A priori knowledge can be known with certainty because we *make* it. This is a so-called "workmanship" or "creationist" theory of knowledge which conferred on the moral sciences an epistemological status in pre-Humean empiricist thought vastly superior to any they have enjoyed in the Anglo-American tradition of philosophy ever since. For Hobbes the pure or "mathematical" sciences can be known a priori, but the "mixed mathematics" such as physics depend on "the causes of natural things [which are] not in our power" and the "greatest part of them . . . is invisible" (1972: 42). He put it more fully in the Epistle Dedicatory to his *Six Lessons to the Professors of Mathematics:*

Of arts, some are demonstrable, others indemonstrable; and demonstrable are those the construction of the subject whereof is in the power of the artist himself, who, in his demonstration, does no more but deduce the consequences of his own operation. The reason whereof is this, that the science of every subject is derived from a precognition of the causes, generation, and construction of the same; and consequently where the causes are known, there is place for demonstration, but not where the causes are to seek for. Geometry therefore is demonstrable, for the lines and figures from which we reason are drawn and described by ourselves; and civil philosophy is demonstrable, because we make the commonwealth ourselves. But because natural bodies we know not the construction, but seek it from the effects, there lies no demonstration of what the causes be we seek for, but only what they may be. (Hobbes, 1966, VII:183–4)

It is this geometrical, or pure "mathematical" model which is taken by Hobbes to be paradigmatic of the moral sciences,[25] so that:

---

25 For further discussion see Child (1953:271–83).

politics and ethics (that is, the sciences of *just* and *unjust,* of *equity* and *inequity*) can be demonstrated *a priori;* because we ourselves make the principles – that is, the causes of justice (namely laws and covenants) – whereby it is known what *justice* and *equity,* and their opposites *injustice* and *inequity,* are. For before covenants and laws were drawn up, neither justice nor injustice, neither public good nor public evil, was natural among men any more than it was among beasts. (1972:42)

This argument implies that the central task for a science of ethics must be an account of the human will, and in offering his account of this Hobbes bridges the gap between the argument from rights and that from interests for the legitimacy of the contract. His aim is to give an account of the will that enables him to deduce the indubitable rationality of the contract, to show that given the nature of the human will it must be in man's interest to contract – at the same time arguing that the state derives its legitimacy from man's decision to make it.

For Hobbes the will is an appetite, one of the "voluntary motions" that has "interior beginnings" in the mind; it is the result of man's deliberative capacity to do or forbear, the "last Appetite, or Aversion, immediately adhaering to the action, or to the omission thereof" (1968:127), but that it resides in the mind does not mean that its consequences cannot be scientifically studied. This view of moral knowledge being characterized by subjective certainty grounded in the purposive acts of individual wills has had a lasting impact on liberal moral and political thought. With geometry it lost its preeminent status as the archetypical science, not because of changes in conceptions of moral knowledge but because of changes in what came to be regarded as criteria for genuine science: specifically the replacement of apodictic certainty with intersubjective demonstrability, prediction, and experiment that came to characterize empiricist thought in the nineteenth century. *These* developments turned the subjective certainty that the early empiricists considered the hallmark of moral knowledge into "mere" subjectivism, opening the way for the emotivist revolution in ethics. Hobbes perceived no tension between his identification of moral knowledge with subjective certainty and his scientific pretensions; for him the mind-dependence or otherwise of

47

facts had no bearing on their epistemological status, and the will-dependence of moral actions made them understandable with the certainty of geometry.

If Hobbes was not himself a subjectivist in anything like the modern sense of the term, it is nonetheless true that in the political and moral isolation of the individual he made several decisive moves that would be crucial for the incorporation of a subjectivist ethos into liberal rights theories. His account of the contract was innovative politically because of its treatment of the relationship between man and the state. The state, as we saw, derives its legitimacy from a universal reciprocal agreement among all men to renounce the right of nature. Although the idea of legitimate government resulting from some sort of contract was by no means new in the seventeenth century, medieval conceptions of contract had assumed powerful corporatist views of society and were interlaced with ascending and descending feudal rights and obligations. Hobbes's account differed not only in its treatment of the makers of the contract as equal, but, as Gierke (1934, I:61ff) long ago pointed out, because his account rules out the possibility of any legitimate social or political institution – such as the church, local or regional associations, or the common law – other than the state and thus leaves the state and the individual as the only significant political actors in society.

One of the main reasons that Hobbes's account proved to be of such lasting influence lies in its compatibility with the monumental changes in English public and private law that occurred in the seventeenth century, providing the basis for the modern, secular, national states of the post-Enlightenment period. Central among these changes was the destruction of an independent basis for public law, and the growing tendency to perceive it as secondary to, and derivative of, the system of private law. This was implied, for instance, in the act abolishing the office of king in 1649. After declaring void "all fealty homage and allegiance which is or shall be pretended to be due unto any of the issue and posterity of the late king, or any claiming under him," the act decisively separates the public interest from any autonomous rights the ruler might be thought to have had, by declaring the ruler unnecessary to the public interest, where previously he had been regarded as the embodiment of it; and by convicting the king of treason, where treason previously had been defined in terms of thoughts or deeds against the crown.[26] Never again would an English monarch be granted rights that were not ultimately a function of the rights of the people. This denial of any other source of legitimate authority is also embodied in the act of the same year abolishing the House of Lords.[27] The Lords had derived their rights through the feudal hierarchy from the crown. Once the crown ceased to have any legitimate independent authority so too must the Lords. This dismantling of the medieval system of public law was not reversed at the Restoration. Although vestiges of medieval public law have remained, in characteristic English fashion, down through the present, when Royal institutions were reinstated they were firmly grounded in and limited by the private law rights of the common law. The abolition in 1641 and 1642 of the Star Chamber, High Commission, and other prerogative courts also sharply underscores these developments.[28] These courts, which had functioned independently of the common law and had expanded their jurisdictions throughout the later fifteenth and sixteenth centuries, had been principal mechanisms of Royal control over the legal system. Their abolition more than any other single development signaled the triumph of the doctrine of the rule of law. Thus, though Hobbes opposed the innovative anti-Royalist claims of the common lawyers, by grounding the authority of his absolutist state exclusively in the contract among individuals he was sanctioning a view of public law that had elective affinities with the larger historical changes in English law that were in motion. His claim that power is absolute and indivisible is not to be confused with the traditional defenses of absolutism, such as Filmer's, which invariably argued for a legitimating lineage of Royal power that

26 Act of March 17, 1649, reprinted in Gardiner (1889:294–6).
27 Act of March 19, 1649, reprinted in Gardiner (1889:296–7).
28 Thus the act abolishing the Star Chamber laid it down that "neither His Majesty nor his Privy Council have or ought to have any jurisdiction, power or authority ... to examine or draw into question, determine or dispose of the lands, tenements, hereditaments, goods or chattels of any the subjects of this kingdom, but that the same ought to be tried and determined in the ordinary Courts of Justice and by the ordinary course of the law." Reprinted in Gardiner (1889:183).

49

functioned independently of, or was a source of, the rights of the subject.[29]

Hobbes isolated the individual morally by making him the only meaningful subject of moral predicates, and by considering his wants, needs, and aspirations in isolation from those of all others, except insofar as these latter can assist or retard the pursuit of his own goals. We have already seen that he rejected what today we should refer to as intuitionist and extrinsic conceptions of the good in favor of a relational view tied to the wants and needs of individuals. If, for Hobbes, moral predicates can attach only to individuals, they are individuals of a very special sort, for they are conceived of in this (moral) context in their prepolitical state. In his taxonomy of the sciences in *Leviathan* (1968:149), ethics and the sciences of justice and injustice are regarded as subdivisions of natural philosophy, derivable from the nature of the human passions and speech. Ethics is thus quite separate from civil philosophy which results from "the accidents of *Politique* bodies" which generate the institution of commonwealth and the political rights and duties of sovereign and subject. For Hobbes, moral questions are in no sense a function of political relationships; on the contrary, morality is prior to and gives rise to political relationships via the contract. This view was reinforced by the radical antiholism implied by Hobbes's resolutive-compositive method: the way to understand a complex social mechanism such as a commonwealth is to take it to pieces and examine the component parts – in this case the agents who have contracted to create it – ruling out the possibility that the whole might in any epistemologically loaded sense be more than the sum of its parts, or that the nature of those parts can be grasped only in relation to the mechanism as a whole. When Hobbes makes the further move of considering man *qua* moral agent only after he has completed this disassembly, he is able to supply a philosophical basis for treating all moral questions in terms of

29 This independent lineage rested on patriarchial conceptions of authority – taken over from Bodin in Filmer's case – in terms of which governmental authority was held to be identical to both familial and monarchical authority. The ultimate basis of all three kinds of authority was held to be divine. See Tully (1980:55f). This issue is taken up further in Chapter 3 section II(ii).

private individuals, and for deriving all moral and political relationships from relationships among individuals.

Hobbes's conception of morality is derived directly from his account of natural man's passions. It is this that enables him to make the prepolitical individual's wants, needs, and aspirations the foundation of his system of ethics, and hence his naturalist account of political legitimacy. The only sense in which Hobbes considers social relationships in his ethics is where individual desires are overdetermining and thus generative of conflict. He never considers moral questions as arising from man's political interrelationships. They result directly from man's natural capacities and passions, which are taken as axiological.[30] His refusal to regard man's passions as in any sense even conditioned by civil relationships led to the objection of Rousseau and countless others that he attributes obviously civil characteristics of the society of his day to "natural" man. There is truth to such claims but more to the point is this whole view of morality as predicated of isolated individual wills in the first place. This generates the notion that it is possible to have a science of morality that is entirely ahistorical and ignores all social facts, and which makes morality essentially a private affair, since man *qua* moral agent is logically prior to and a condition for the creation of a public sphere. This provides a new legitimating basis for the system of public law.

The historical tenacity of Hobbes's account must be understood in terms of its elective affinity with historical changes that were in process. While the system of public law was coming to be exclusively based on and legitimated by the common law, this latter was itself in a period of innovative change. The notion that the common law had existed since time immemorial, that it was rooted in an Ancient Constitution lost in the mists of time, was being displaced due to the discovery by Spelman and others that English law was largely feudal in character and German in origin, and had been imported at

---

30 Although Hobbes pays serious attention to the distinction between "vital" motions that include basic animal needs and "voluntary" motions (1968:118–30) this is not to be confused with a nature/nurture distinction of any kind. For Hobbes, as we have seen, all issues about morality fall into the latter (voluntary) category. This has no bearing on their presocial or, better, asocial character.

the time of the Norman Conquest (Pocock, 1957:70–123).[31] The doctrine of the rule of law could thus not be based on an historical claim; it must rest on a direct moral claim about the nature of the relationship between ruler and people. It is in this period that the common law begins, in the two critical areas of land law and contract, to take on the appearance of modern private law.

Although in many respects feudalism never became fully established in England,[32] the system of land law was the exception. Following the Conquest, all land became part of the system of tenures that derived ultimately from the crown.[33] If English land law was more perfectly feudalized than any in Europe, it was also the first to go into decline. England's relatively powerful medieval monarchy was able to destroy local suzerainties which the French, for example, were unable to do successfully. Henry VIII's seizure of church land (about one-sixth of all the land in England was seized during the 1530s) and subsequent sale of much of the land to pay for his wars in Scotland and France, did much to create the beginnings of modern transmissibility in land (Tigar and Levy, 1977:203–6). Although it is mistaken to imply, as Tigar and Levy do in many places, that there was a single homogeneous bourgeoisie which until the Civil War allied itself to the crown against the church and feudal landowners, and then against the crown in alliance with the common lawyers,[34] and although it is true

31 More recent scholarship has shown that this development was not as revolutionary as Pocock, in *The Ancient Constitution and the Feudal Law*, thought. Some of Hobbes's contemporaries believed that an historical view of the common law was compatible with a Hobbesian view of sovereignty. See Tuck (1979:83, 132ff). I sidestep these debates noting only that Hobbes's detaching the theory of sovereignty from all considerations of history and tradition was to be decisive for its incorporation into the ideological grammar of the modern liberal tradition. This is taken up in section III of this chapter.
32 See Maitland (1920:161–3).
33 For discussion of the impact of the Conquest on English land law see Nasmith (1875:561–88).
34 Thus the constant references to "the legal ideology of the bourgeoisie," to "the alliance of the bourgeoisie and the common lawyers," and to the partial responsibility of "the bourgeoisie" for the creation of the absolutist powers of the Henrican monarchy. They refer to the "alliance of the bourgeoisie and the common lawyers" during the Civil War, and to Coke as a "major architect of the alliance's ideology" (Tigar and Levy, 1977:216–18, 226–7). This is gross oversimplification, since it presumes a homogeneous bourgeois class that simply did not exist. See Brenner (1973:53–107).

that the redistribution of land took several centuries,[35] there is no doubt that Henry's actions spelled the beginning of the end of feudal land law. By the end of his reign not only had he established the fact of a considerable market in land, but he had also enacted statutes enabling the buying and selling of land and its effective transmissibility through wills (Tigar and Levy, 1977:196–210).

The legal consolidation of these developments began in the mid-seventeenth century. A statute of 1660 abolished a great many feudal tenures[36] and although tenures continued, nominally, to be granted by the crown, this meant the de facto end of the large majority of feudal rights and obligations. It was at this time that the common law shed much of its medieval machinery, either by statute or simply by being allowed to obsolesce, and was replaced by modern conveyancing in land (Holdsworth, 1937, VI:624–9). Property assumed its modern form of exclusive dominion and became a predicate of its owner, conferring rights and powers of exchange on him, no longer entailing social or political obligations. The individual property owner became the central figure in the land law.

These developments were critically helped by the incorporation of the commercial side of the law merchant into the common law. First in relation to internal trade and, by the end of the century, in relation to all trade, the special law and courts of the law merchant were replaced by common law courts, and the principles of the mercantile side of the law merchant were absorbed into the common law. Although the complete incorporation of the law merchant was not achieved until the time of Lord Mansfield, by the late seventeenth century it had ceased to be a separate body of laws administered by separate courts (Holdsworth, 1956, I:568–73). This is the principal mechanism by which modern principles of contract entered the common law and transformed its entire basis, replacing the feudal system of rights and obligations with the individual contractor as the linchpin of the system of private law. And this is why, although Bacon and Hobbes lost the battle with the common lawyers, they ultimately won the war. It was the Hobbesian

35 See Hexter (1979:71–116).
36 The statute is reprinted in Nasmith (1875:588).

conception of contract as individual voluntary agreement that was to triumph, even if gradually, and from within. The survival of the common law was only achieved via its immense modification, the decisive beginning of which was Coke's declaration, in 1601, that the law merchant was part of the common law (Tigar and Levy, 1977:217–27). Many vestiges of the medieval system of conveyancing survived well into the eighteenth century, but the movement of the contracting agent to the center of the common law implied by this incorporation ensured that in triumphing the common law would spawn a new system of private law.

iv. The purposes of rights

For Hobbes, the purpose of natural rights, or the right of nature, is self-preservation. He breaks, as we saw,[37] with much of the natural law tradition in not deriving his right to self-preservation from natural law, but by turning it instead into an axiom, taking to a logical extreme a position that had first been developed in its seventeenth-century form by Hugo Grotius.[38] All civil rights and obligations, although the immediate result of the command theory of law, derive ultimately – via the contract – from this right to self-preservation. As we saw,[39] however, Hobbes envisaged an organization of society which sustains many other broadly defined civil rights, a wide area of negative freedom, created and regulated by the state, in which people have rights of exclusive dominion over their actions and property against one another. Hobbes regards the institutional relationships guaranteeing these civil rights as essential to man's survival, but he also sees them as central to the realization by man of his natural capacities. It will thus be necessary to look more closely at his account of those capacities to get at the purpose of these institutional relationships, and of the rights and obligations he believed that they entailed.

Hobbes believed that man's capacity to desire is such that

---

37 See section II(iii) of this chapter.
38 See Finnis (1980:207ff).
39 See section II(ii) of this chapter.

there are no limits to the number of things that will be desired or to the quantities in which they will be desired. The renowned axiom that man has a "perpetuall and restlesse desire of Power after power, that ceaseth onely in Death" (1968:161) is paradigmatic of a view of man as driven by an imperative to accumulate power, wealth and prestige. This is partly the result of man's insecurity in the state of nature, but it is important to realize that Hobbes regards it as a permanent part of the human condition, and as such it infects his account of the purpose for which civil rights, indeed all the institutions of civil society, exist. Hobbes's view of man's capacity to desire as intrinsically insatiable rests on a pluralist conception of human goods which in turn generates an essentially utilitarian rationale for the civil rights and institutions he envisages. There are four different but mutually reinforcing roots to this pluralism.

To begin with the definition of goods, Hobbes makes two moves which combine to locate the value of an object in the state of mind that it evokes rather than any property intrinsic to the object itself. The first is his argument, already discussed,[40] that goods must always be understood relationally in terms of individuals; that the only sense in which assertions about goods are meaningful is when they take the logical form "good for x" where x is an individual. The second move is to reduce all conceptions of good and evil to the desires of individuals. "*Good* and *Evill*," he says with an almost Stevensonian ring, "are names that signifie our Appetites, and Aversions" (1968:216). In this way it is the individual appetite which is the ultimate measure of value.

The second source of pluralism concerns the variability of goods. Goods can differ not only for different individuals, but for the same individual over time. The appetites and aversions that determine good and evil

in different tempers, customes, and doctrines of men, are different: And divers men, differ not onely in their Judgment, on the sense of what is pleasant, and unpleasant to the tast, smell, hearing, touch, and sight; but also of what is comformable, or disagreeable to Reason, in the actions of common life. Nay, the same man, in divers

40 See section II(iii) of this chapter.

times, differs from himselfe; and one time praiseth, that is, calleth Good, what another time he dispraiseth, and calleth Evil. (Ibid.: 216)

It is partly this plurality of individual conceptions of the good which, in Hobbes's view, generates inevitable conflict and ultimately war in the state of nature, and which dictates the necessity for a state to prevent that conflict by implementing rational imperatives that function in the interests of all. Although all men are in principle capable of rational behavior, their private appetites and mutual distrust mean that, although they know that peace, and hence the laws of nature which are conducive to peace, is desirable, they cannot (individually) implement the laws. The laws of nature thus in part derive their force from an appeal to the plurality of private conceptions of the good, which Hobbes regards as endemic to the human condition.

A third, related, source of pluralism is that Hobbes sees the value of goods as dependent in practice on something very like effective demand. Hence the controversial assertion in chapter 10 of *Leviathan* that value "is not absolute; but a thing dependent on the need and judgment of another." The following passage gives an even clearer illustration of this view of effective demand as the determinant of a good's value:

An able conductor of Souldiers, is of great Price in time of War present, or imminent; but in Peace not so. A learned and uncorrupt Judge, is much Worth in time of Peace; but not so much in War. And as in other things so in men, not the seller, but the buyer determines the Price. For let a man (as most men do,) rate themselves as the highest Value they can; yet their true Value is no more than it is esteemed by others. (1968:152)

The "true value" of a good is thus its market value. This operationalist view is connected to Hobbes's identification of goods with individual states of mind, because in the absence of any alternative basis for the value of an object, the object becomes synonymous with what is taken to be its value; once this move is made, the only way in which we can know the value to society of an object is to observe what social agents, by their actions, implicitly agree to be its value. In other words Hobbes commits himself to something very like a doctrine of revealed preference. It is thus an important consequence of his view of effective demand as the determinant of "true value" that it imports the idea of individual agreement, or consent as revealed through the market, into the heart of his theory of value.

The final source of pluralism in Hobbes's conception of the good derives from his subsumption of wants and needs under the general category of desires. Here the claim is not that Hobbes makes no distinction between wants and needs (we will see in a moment that he does) but rather that his identification of both needs-based and wants-based desires with individual states of mind makes them behaviorally equivalent psychological imperatives. For Hobbes, desires are a species of the "Voluntary Motions" (1968:118). In addition to the purely "vital motions," the things necessary for the physical continuation of life, man's imagination generates desires and capacities of a quite different order. Hobbes sees all desires as needs in the sense that they result in irresistible psychological drives, and the intrinsic insatiability of the human capacity to desire means that there is no simple threshold between essential and inessential desires. All desires are wants, on the other hand, in that their satisfaction or nonsatisfaction involves deliberative acts of the will.

Although there is thus no basic distinction between needs and wants, there are two importantly different classes of things desired: those things which are universal goods in the sense that all men must rationally desire them, and particular goods which lack this quality. The primary universal goods are self-preservation, peace, and security, but it is Hobbes's argument that all the laws of nature embody goods of this type; given his account of human nature they must be desirable to all. It would be a mistake, however, to attribute to Hobbes some kind of threshold notion, a view of primary or basic goods; the laws of nature are conceived of rather as structural conditions which enable individuals to pursue their private goals without generating chaos, war, and death. The laws of nature are general injunctions—to seek peace wherever possible, to preserve oneself, to observe basic norms of reciprocity, to keep promises—without which social life would, in Hobbes's view, be impossible.

57

A law of nature is a "Precept, or generall Rule, found out by Reason, by which a man is forbidden to do, that, which is destructive of his life, or taketh away the means of preserving the same . . ." (1968:189). Although these laws are discoverable by reason and in principle knowable to all, the fact that in practice reason is subordinated to the passions means that people will not abide by these rules without being forced to. But the rules themselves, defined as rational imperatives for the most effective realization of individual desires, have more in common with modern doctrines of rule-utilitarianism than traditional conceptions of natural law. Hobbes's account of the good is not fully utilitarian because his individuals are power-maximizers not pleasure-maximizers, and because he was more concerned with the avoidance of civil war than with the promotion of happiness. The blueprints for social engineering that consumed the attention of the classical utilitarians could only emerge in a vastly more stable, expansionary, and optimistic age. Yet the fact that he takes individuals as maximizing their subjectively identified goods as the basis for his account of the social good, together with his transformation of natural law from a set of divine injunctions which give rise to natural rights into a set of rules for the most effective realization of individual goals, means that the seeds of a utilitarian conception of the good are deeply embedded in his own. The quasi-rule-utilitarian status of Hobbes's natural laws is of cardinal importance because these are the injunctions he expects the sovereign to enforce in civil society. They shape the basic institutional structure of the Leviathan and reinforce the role of the state as regulator of the interactions of private individuals in pursuit of their separate goals.

A final point that should be noticed concerning Hobbes's account of human desires is that, though the capacity to desire is intrinsically insatiable, there is no sense in which this generates a dialectical or developmental view of human nature. It is natural man who is conceived of as having these capacities and drives and they are regulated, but in no way altered, by the institutions of civil society (as they are altered, for example, in different ways, according to Rousseau, Hegel, and Marx). There is no developmental theory of needs or capacities, which would require that they be seen, at least in part, as functions of social institutions and relationships. Human desires, drives, and capacities are seen as presocial, or, better, nonsocial, and, when man *is* in society, essentially private except insofar as their effective realization requires regulation. Each individual strives continuously after his goals, but this has no intrinsic effect on either his own needs or capacities or those of anyone else. It is worth stressing again that in offering this interpretation I am not attributing to Hobbes the doctrines of individualism or subjectivism in their modern forms. His view of the ontological status of moral knowledge, discussed in section II(iii) of this chapter, as well as his belief that he could deduce a predictive account of man's voluntary behavior from a materialist theory of the passions, decisively separates him from these traditions. My claim is that he made moves that constituted important necessary conditions for the emergence of individualism and subjectivism in their modern forms.

III. IDEOLOGICAL CONSEQUENCES OF HOBBES'S ARGUMENT

What were the consequences for the liberal ideology of individual rights of Hobbes's account? What is so special about his argument that gives Hobbes his immense status in the liberal tradition and shapes so powerfully both the vocabulary and the grammar of that tradition? In the foregoing analysis of Hobbes's discussion of rights I have begun to sketch answers to these questions. Here my aim is to spell out in greater detail the implications of that analysis via a discussion of five consequences for the liberal tradition of the Hobbesian account.

A central and basic consequence of the Hobbesian view is that the private individual becomes the subject of all legitimate rights. At the most general level, Hobbes regards all moral assertions as meaningfully predicable only of individuals, and his science of morality is deduced from his theory of man in his natural state. The moral imperatives embedded in the laws of nature are rational imperatives for the survival of naturally private individuals. These imperatives do not become unneces-

sary, as they do for Rousseau, after the institution of civil society. The rational imperatives of the laws of nature are embedded in and enforced by the laws of the Leviathan and the actions of the sovereign; they regulate the interaction between
private individuals *in* society, and indeed they make such interaction possible. In this way Hobbes is able to identify natural
man with private man, and so present a view of society as based
on and reducible to relationships between private individuals as
part of the natural order of things. Hobbes is able to reduce
society to a collection of private relationships and render the
notion of a public sphere unintelligible except as a complex
description of these private relationships. Whereas defenders
of absolutism had hitherto derived the rights of the ruler either
directly from his supposed relationship with God or from a
complex structure of patriarchal authority inherited from
Adam; whereas medieval theories of natural law had attributed
rights and jurisdictions to the church quite independently of
the secular rights in society; whereas the feudal land law had
reinforced a complex asymmetrical structure of ascending and
descending rights and obligations; and whereas medieval public law had acknowledged independent local and regional jurisdictions, Hobbes denied the existence of any legitimate rights
other than those of the individual and the sovereign, and those
of the latter he derived directly from those of the former. All
social interaction was made by definition private. The existence
of a public sphere was merely to facilitate private interaction.
This is a move of immense ideological significance because it
provides for the germination of the liberal notion that the state,
as representative of the public sphere, is fundamentally unde-
sirable, an illegitimate intruder except where its actions facilitate private interaction. What was to be decisive in the creation
of a liberal conception of law was not that the private sphere
should be considerable in size (in many ways this sphere was
greater in the preabsolutist feudal period than at any time
since) but rather that the public sphere was seen as derived
from, reducible to, and legitimated by the private sphere. This
was central to Hobbes's account of legitimacy.

A second consequence of Hobbes's account concerns his
separation of rights from obligations. Instead of conceiving of

rights and obligations in terms of reciprocal correlative relationships, both being grounded in natural law, or some other theory of the good, rights are conceived of as indicative of the basic human capacity for autonomous action. In the state of nature man's rights are conceived of as whatever he can in fact do, and in civil society this is limited only by the law; it is not changed in any essentials, except that the law imposes limitations on others to respect a person's right through the machinery of voluntary agreement. Property rights are regarded as individual rights to exclusive dominion and are taken as the basic model of rights generally; they are seen as spheres of private action. Rights become religious, economic, legal, social, and moral spheres surrounding individuals that can only be entered by other individuals via mutual consent. The only sense in which this view of rights entails a theory of obligation is that all are obliged not to violate the private spheres of others. The definition of these spheres is quite general. For this reason Hobbes's *civil* rights might be thought of as Hohfeldian "liberties" as they relate to all other individuals (but not as they relate to the state), since they impose "no-rights" on others which are enforced by the state. There are endemic problems for general accounts of this kind in that they are overdetermined. The condition of one individual's satisfaction of his right becomes the violation of another's; the spheres, as it were, overlap. Whatever the drawbacks attending this view of rights (and we will see in subsequent chapters that they are considerable), it has been immensely influential in shaping the liberal tradition, in which it has become axiomatic to regard private property rights and moral rights thus conceived as analytically identical indicators of human freedom.

A third consequence of the Hobbesian account is that the substance of rights is defined in terms of negative freedom. Apart from those natural rights that are never given up, man's civil rights are defined as those areas where he is not prohibited by law from acting as he chooses – what Hobbes refers to as liberty the sovereign has "praetermitted": the liberty to buy and sell, make contracts, choose where to live, what to eat, what work to do, and how to raise children. "The Greatest Liberty of Subjects, dependeth on the silence of the Law"

(1968:271). Hobbes's plural theory of the good reinforces this negative libertarianism. Since individual conceptions of the good differ, except in cases where it leads him into conflict with the law, the individual should define and pursue his own individual goals. Hobbes did not go as far as Mandeville, for whom the pursuit of private good was synonymous with promotion of the public good, but he thought it inevitable that people would in fact pursue what they took to be their private goods and that a political system, if it is to survive, must acknowledge – even build on – this fact. One of Hobbes's principal explanations in *Behemoth* of the outcome of the Civil War was that the king and his followers lacked the resources to appeal to the self-interest of the masses.

Although Hobbes gives no clear definition of the size of and limits to the private sphere (he thinks this will vary with circumstances in the same way as will the level of taxation), we have seen that he expects it to comprise the vast majority of day-to-day social and economic interaction. It is unquestionably intended to include activities relating to the production, exchange, and consumption of wealth, all of which are conceived of as intrinsically private activities, grounded in the individual capacities to work and desire. Little as Hobbes liked the merchants whom he blamed, in large part, for causing the Civil War, and strong as was his personal distaste for excessive preoccupation with material gain, Hobbes recognized the importance of merchants from the point of view of generating wealth. His criticisms of the merchants were political and ideological, not economic. He thought the merchants had been misled concerning ways to attain their self-interested goals, but he accepted the inevitability, even desirability, of those goals (Ashcraft, 1978:46–51). Hobbes's assumption that there is a radical distinction between the public sphere of politics and the private sphere encompassing most of social, economic, familial, and religious life – which latter is preserved and regulated but not as a rule directly entered into by the state – would harden into one of the basic organizing categories of the liberal moral outlook. If Hobbes's views on the compatibility of the interests of merchants with those of the monarchy were a little naive,[41] the more general assumption on which they rested, while no less naive, was radically innovative and of lasting historical importance.[42]

This negative libertarian view of social life in general, and of the production, exchange, and consumption of wealth in particular, was also of great importance in the subsequent history of the liberal ideology of individual rights. Indispensable as it obviously is to the functioning of a capitalist market, it became deeply embedded in the emerging social system. Hobbes did not intend to justify such a system nor had he any very clear idea of what it was. His negative libertarianism survived and achieved the preeminent status it did in the dominant ideology because of its affinity with these emerging economic and social relations. It provided the conceptual tools for the construction of an ideology that could legitimate these relations. An important consequence of this negative libertarianism was that it provided for the notion of toleration as the basic yardstick for political freedom. This to an extent reflects the historical fact that one of the principal ideological battles of the seventeenth century was for religious toleration, a notion Hobbes openly endorsed. It is most interesting from our point of view, however, because it marks a separation of liberal rights theories from the communalist rights theories of the seventeenth century (such as those of the Levellers) and the radical rights theories of the eighteenth century and beyond, all of which emphasized participation, not toleration, as the central measure of a free society.[43]

A fourth consequence of Hobbes's account is that the class of objects and actions to which there are private individual rights is potentially infinite. There is a basic equation of doing, knowing, and making at the root of Hobbes's creationist or workmanship view of the world which generates the notion that I can own my actions, or be proprietor of them, in the same way as I can own or be proprietor of an object I have

---

41 On this subject see Thomas (1965:215ff).
42 Its contemporary manifestations will concern us in some detail in Chapters 4 and 5.
43 These issues are taken up in greater detail in Chapter 3.

made. In this way the individual private property right is the conceptual model for rights in general. Hobbes implicitly accepted the growing orthodoxy that the value of objects to which there are rights, of property, is some function of the work required to produce those objects and of the effective demand for them on the market. Since the capacity to demand includes both needs and wants, and since the latter are regarded as intrinsically insatiable, it follows that there are no necessary limits to what there may be private rights *to,* or at least no limits other than those imposed by technological barriers to what can be produced. This was a period in which wealth was seen increasingly as dynamic and continuously expanding, inhering in the capacity to work, not in land or in precious metals. Hobbes never articulated a *theory* of production, but his "making" model of ownership implied such a view. His dynamic account of demand was sufficient to entail that the value of objects to which there might be private rights was intrinsically unlimited and in practice determined on the market, that is, by what people will in fact pay for them. Whatever we believe to be the value of our property, its true value "is no more than it is esteemed by others" (1968:152).

The expansion of this workmanship model of proprietorship to a general model of action entailed that just as there were no intrinsic limits to objects that could be owned, exchanged, and consumed in the private sphere of the market, there were likewise no intrinsic limits to the actions that could be performed. Individuals' freedom of action varies with their capacities. The only sense in which individuals may influence others' actions is via their voluntary interactions in the market. Aside from this constraint, provided they remain within the law, there are no limits to what people may do, and no one to whom they are accountable for their actions. This view had three significant implications.

First, the notion that entitlement is conferred by some combination of making and voluntary exchange forms the basis of market-based conceptions of distributive justice that can, and would, be used to legitimate monumental inequalities, so long as these are worked through the market. Second, the view that individuals own what they make in virtue of their ownership of their actions takes the capacity for individual action as given, as prior to and independent of man's social relationships. It is insensitive, for instance, to the fact that the individual's capacity to work is critically dependent on his or her position in the social division of labor, and that it would be vastly more limited without the existence of that division. We will see that this view of individual capacities was to become one of the central vulnerabilities of the liberal ideology of individual rights, for if the capacity to produce is potentially infinite *because of* the economies of scale inherent in the division of labor, it can hardly be seen as conferring rights that are independent of that division of labor. Third, although Hobbes had a naturalistic theory of needs – one that would be dubbed "paternalistic" by many a contemporary liberal – the fact that he equated indispensable needs with inessential wants in his account of desires as psychological imperatives together with his view that the true nature of these desires is determined behaviorally, by what people actually do, destroyed the possibility for any thoroughgoing distinction between needs and other sorts of desires. Although Hobbes did not propound a theory of revealed preference, his account of desires as inclusive of needs and wants, as subjectively identified, as potentially infinite, and as expressed and valued through the market, was an account that contained all the key elements of the modern individual preference function. This preference function became a standard axiom in classical and neo-classical theories of demand and in liberal theories of distributive justice. While Hobbes's remarks about wants and needs fall short of a full theory of effective demand, we will see in the next chapter that by the later part of the seventeenth century views remarkably like his would be incorporated into the systematic explorations of market behavior by Barbon, Locke, and their contemporaries.

A final ideological consequence of Hobbes's discussion concerns the nature and functions of the state. Although Hobbes conceived of the power of the state as absolute, he regarded the functions that the state will in fact perform as regulative of the private relationships that constitute his negative libertarian society. This is true not only in the economic sphere, where the state performs only those regulative functions necessary for the market to work, but in social life generally where, as we saw, rights have the same structure as private property rights of exclusive dominion. Action in general is considered private, and the sphere of negative liberty, guaranteed by the silence of the law, is expected to comprise the vast majority of social life.

It is often argued that Hobbes's investiture of the state with absolute power is at odds with the liberal view of man's relationship with the state and even that it has strong authoritarian implications. It is true that for Hobbes the power of the state is absolute, but it is important to notice that the powers Hobbes ascribes to the state are basically those which most liberals, too, regard as nonnegotiable: the guarantee of property rights and the rule of law, of territorial integrity and a workable currency system, the enforcement of contract and basic criminal sanctions, and the raising of taxes for these limited purposes. In liberal-capitalist societies the power that the state has to perform *these* functions *is* seen as absolute, as a condition for the civil freedoms liberals cherish. Note that Hobbes regards it as essential for the survival of any society that there *be* a decisive and absolute sovereign power, but this has nothing to do with the conduct of government which may be monarchical, aristocratic, or democratic (1968:239–51). His point is that without the existence of a decisive authoritative power that can enforce the rules and norms essential for social interaction, society will collapse into chaos. "*Take away the Civill Law,*" he tells us, "*and no man knows what is his own, and what another mans*" (1968:296). In a society where negative libertarian economic and social practices are firmly established and have an air of permanence, these powers of the state tend to be latent and invisible, at least until threatened. They are present nonetheless as must be obvious to anyone who reflects on what would happen, in contemporary Britain or America, if the state ceased forthwith to enforce contracts, protect individual property rights, or regard itself as responsible for territorial integrity.

A closely related implication concerns the activities that regulation of a negative libertarian society will entail in practice. I have already noted that a regulative state is not necessarily minimal in the modern sense of entailing relative inaction. If the state's goal is to regulate a society based on private relationships, the policies and practices it will have to adopt to achieve this end will vary greatly with historical circumstances. The idea of a regulative state would only entail the existence of a minimal state from liberal premises for the comparatively brief period between the rise of equilibrium theory and the definitive discovery by Keynes that there is no tendency toward efficient equilibrium in capitalist markets.[44] Hobbes wrote in a period of extensive social, economic, and political dislocation, when national markets in basic commodities such as land, corn, and labor were still establishing themselves, when the legal nature of property was in a process of extensive redefinition, when the state had for over a century been playing a central role in the redistribution of feudal wealth as transmissible property, when the very existence of private property and of a legally ordered society was seriously threatened by civil war. In such a period the goal of regulating a negative libertarian society would require a state that was in many respects interventionist. It would have to create the conditions in which a negative libertarian society could exist. These facts were reflected in much contemporary economic and political writing. Despite the presence of many elements of classical economic thinking there was no notion that the economy, let alone the rest of society, could be *self-regulating*, no assumption that it is a system with inertial self-equilibrating tendencies. On the contrary, the evidence of the past century would have suggested to contemporaries that secular, not cyclical, changes characterized the basic socioeconomic structure, and the evidence of the past several decades suggested to writers like Hobbes that without decisive social and political authority resting in the hands of the state, chaos and destruction, rather

44 Keynes was not the first to discover this. It had concerned economists in liberal and radical traditions such as Marx, Hobson, Kalecki, and others, before Keynes wrote. The idea achieved orthodoxy in the liberal consciousness, however, in association with Keynes's theory of consumption functions and in particular his argument that the diminishing marginal propensity to consume creates a permanent tendency toward disequilibrium, or at least an inefficient equilibrium, as a result of the insufficient aggregate demand it generates.

than the harmonious hum of a self-equilibrating social mechanism, would result. The myth of the minimal state could only arise once the social and legal institutions necessary for the functioning of a negative libertarian society had become so deeply entrenched that they would seem to be part of the natural order of things, and thus to function independently of the state. By its inaction the state would then preserve a status quo that its activism in an earlier period had been instrumental in creating.

Seen in this light, Hobbes's rejection, on the one hand, of all feudal definitions of property and right for the modern idea of exclusive dominion and its corresponding "spherical" and negative notion of individual privacy, and his insistence, on the other, that all civil rights, including property rights, are distributed by and exist on sufferance from the state, must be seen as ironically paradoxical. Hobbes *does* embrace a bourgeois conception of property rights, he *does* see all social relationships as essentially private, and he *does* see the role of the state as basically regulative of those private relationships; in short he *does* articulate a negative libertarian view of society. Yet he sees no contradiction between this and advocating a state that has both absolute power and no fixed limits to the extent to which it may intervene in society. On the contrary, he sees such a state as essential to the creation and preservation of this type of society. The key to this apparent paradox lies largely in comprehending it historically, in understanding the imperatives for the institution of a negative libertarian society in mid-seventeenth-century England. Part of the key, however, is logical, and is to be sought in Hobbes's characteristic tendency to pursue any argument to its logical extreme. He saw quite clearly that a society based on negative libertarian relationships, if it was to survive and remain stable, would have to be created and regulated by the state, and that this regulation would require different amounts and kinds of intervention in different historical circumstances. He had no ideological stake in pretending that the state did not perform these constitutive and regulative functions, or in pretending that in the areas decisive for the survival of a negative libertarian society the power of the state was not absolute. The myth of the minimal state would only arise in conjunction with the classical equilibrium model which was not present in the intellectual milieu in which Hobbes wrote, and had no application to his contemporary reality. This model was never very generally applicable, and certainly nowhere near as generally as it would be assumed to be in the axioms of classical and neo-classical economics, or in the mainstream of liberal ideology after John Stuart Mill. For this reason Hobbes supplies us with a more accurate and transparent account of the nature and role of the state in a negative libertarian society than do its subsequent defenders.

IV. CONCLUSION

In what sense is it accurate or useful from our point of view to regard Hobbes as a "bourgeois" theorist? Although there is much in the preceding analysis to confirm Macpherson's central contention that we discover at the heart of Hobbes's writing a "conception of the individual as essentially the proprietor of his own person or capacities, owing nothing to society for them" (1962:3), it also seems clear that Macpherson's analysis is seriously inadequate in three different respects. His possessive market model is historically inaccurate as a picture of the socioeconomic structure in England in the early to mid-seventeenth century, the view that Hobbes's account can be reduced to an articulation of the central normative propositions of that model is at best exegetically incomplete and more probably seriously misleading, and, most important from our point of view, Macpherson's simplistic reduction obscures some of the most subtle and important aspects of Hobbes's influence on the subsequent evolution of the liberal ideology of individual rights.

To begin with the historical viability of the model, for Macpherson a possessive market society is one in which there is an absence of an authoritative allocation of work or rewards, a presence of an authoritative enforcement of contracts, assumptions that individuals are rational utility maximizers, that land, natural resources, and labor are individually owned and alienable, that some individuals "want to increase their level of utilities or power," and that there is inequality of energy, skill, or possessions (Macpherson, 1962:53–4). This is contrasted with a "simple market society" which lacks alienable land, resources, and labor, unequal desires for power or utilities, and inequalities in energy, skill, and possessions, and with a "customary or status" society. Macpherson's claim is that

the model of a possessive market society, and no other, does correspond in essentials to modern competitive market societies, that each of its postulates is required to produce that correspondence, and that that model and no other does meet the essential requirements of Hobbes's society. (Ibid:61)

Passing over various difficulties that have been raised concerning the supposed exhaustiveness of these models and their coherence as distinct models of society,[45] the most serious historical difficulties with the possessive market model concern its inaccuracy as a picture of seventeenth-century England. It is one thing to hold that significant elements of the capitalist organization of society had begun to appear in England by the time of the Civil War, that those elements both influenced contemporary political writers and were causally important in the evolution of capitalist societies and the ideologies they spawned, and that an understanding of these causal connections will be helpful in analyzing the ideologies that prevail in our contemporary world. It is quite another to presume the applicability of this vague model to all "modern competitive market" societies and thereby ignore the vast significant differences between, for example, England in the 1640s and the United States in the late twentieth century. An argument of this generality lacks historical credibility and exposes Macpherson to endless objections from some historians as Hexter, Pocock, and others, who lump "Marxists and Straussians" together for their simplistic division between feudalism or traditionalism and "modernity," and their tendency to identify all that was said or done after about the time of Machiavelli as "contributing to" or "reflecting" either the rise of the bourgeois world or the decline of Western civilization.

Leaving aside the intrinsic difficulties with all such massive historical assertions, it is not at all clear that Macpherson's

45 For discussion of which see Letwin (1972).

model can very usefully be applied to seventeenth-century England. Although my analysis has confirmed the presence in this period of modern notions of contract, a growing wage labor force, and emerging national markets in various commodities, the overall picture is very much one of a society in transition.[46] For Macpherson to make the point that almost half the population of England consisted of wage-laborers invites the obvious retort from Letwin and others that over half did not, which clearly contradicts his assertion that England "approximated closely to a possessive market society in the seventeenth century" (1962:61). It may seem a little tendentious to make these points against Macpherson, especially if one is in sympathy with his general enterprise. His model is intended to be general and schematic, to make a few basic points about economic and social organization. But it is these basic points that are misleading, for they obscure the important transitions that were going on in England in this period. For this reason Macpherson's model provides no useful basis for an *historical* understanding of the political writings of the time.

A final historical weakness in this model is that it fails to take account of the central role played by the state in the transition to a capitalist society in England. Macpherson does acknowledge, elsewhere in his account, that the state played an important role in regulating trade, employment, and investment, and cites Barry Supple's important book on this subject,[47] but he appears to miss the more important point that during this period the state was actively creating many conditions for the functioning of a market society. Not only by its direct participation in the redistribution of feudal land, but also through the massive revolutions in public law, private law, and the relations between the two, the state was centrally in-

---

46 For a useful discussion of the historical literature, also concluding that seventeenth-century English society is best characterized as transitional between feudalism and capitalism, with certain sectors (notably agriculture) more advanced than others, see Wood (1983:7ff). The view that Hobbes's political theory should be understood in England's transitional socioeconomic context is also argued for by Thomas (1965:185–236), although he defends a more traditionally aristocratic view of Hobbes than that presented here.
47 Macpherson (1962:62); Supple (1959:225–53).

volved in instituting market relations in England. We might say with some plausibility that Macpherson is himself hoodwinked by the myth of the minimal state.[48]

Turning to the usefulness of Macpherson's model as a device for interpreting Hobbes's political theory, although his possessive market model has some affinities with the interpretation I have given, it is clear that Macpherson is plainly wrong on some exegetical questions, and that his discussion is so vague that it misses some of the key respects in which Hobbes articulates a negative libertarian ideology. Macpherson is wrong, for instance, in his discussion of Hobbes on inequality. A defining characteristic of the possessive market model is that there is basic inequality of energy, skill, and possessions (Macpherson, 1962:54). Yet it is a cardinal axiom of Hobbes's whole system that people are by nature equal in faculties of body and mind, that "though there bee found one man sometimes manifestly stronger in body, or of quicker mind then another; yet when all is reckoned together, the difference between man, and man, is not so considerable, as that one man can thereupon claim to himselfe any benefit" (1968:183). It is this basic natural equality that makes all men equally vulnerable in the state of nature and thus motivates their unanimous agreement. Macpherson tries to avoid this difficulty by asserting that, although Hobbes did not postulate any basic inequality, this is nonetheless required by what he takes to be Hobbes's conception of a possessive market society. A possessive market society, he says, requires substantial inequality of command over resources since such a society is divided between employers and employed, causing inequality of insecurity, the class of employed apparently being more insecure than that of employers. This generates the conclusion that Hobbes "failed to allow in his model for the inequality of insecurity which the other attributes of his model necessarily

48 It might be said in Macpherson's defense that since the huge scholarly interest in the role of the state in the transition from feudalism to capitalism occurred after his book was written, he cannot be taken to task for not considering the issues it raises. There is some truth to this, but it is worth pointing out that one of the most subtle and powerful accounts of this matter is still Polanyi's *The Great Transformation*, published in 1944, and that I am more interested in the viability of Macpherson's model than in making any judgment about his scholarship.

imply" (Macpherson, 1962:85). If ever there was a paradigm case of a non sequitur surely it is this: Macpherson begins by proposing a model that is held to explain Hobbes's theory; he then finds Hobbes asserting something in direct contradiction to one of the defining characteristics of his model, and so concludes by blaming Hobbes because he "failed to allow" for it.

For Macpherson to berate Hobbes for not having what amounts to Marx's concept of class is plainly absurd. By so doing he misses what is really most interesting in Hobbes's discussion of equality for the history of the liberal ideology of individual rights. Hobbes begins from radically egalitarian premises, produces an argument which appears to treat all men equally every step of the way, and nonetheless arrives at a conception of the social world that is very largely governed by market relations, as though such a view flows directly from man's natural equality. This is a device that would appear again and again in the subsequent history of liberalism. It turns on ascribing to presocial individuals a negative-libertarian conception of freedom and gearing social institutions to the preservation of that freedom. This is how a system that can generate enormous inequalities gets its egalitarian *gloss* and can be justified via an appeal to egalitarian principles. Hobbes was a theorist of mass, not class, society. This is precisely why the grammar of his account is more congenial to liberal ideology – in which social relationships are legitimated in universalist terms – than to class-based relationships that constitute liberal-capitalist practice. This appears to be lost on Macpherson in his eagerness to demonstrate that Hobbes "failed" to conform to the possessive market model.

Another serious inadequacy of Macpherson's model as an exegetical device for interpreting Hobbes is his vague assertion that individuals attempt to maximize "utilities or power." There are several important roots of utilitarianism in Hobbes's discussion, but this assertion is inaccurate and does not begin to get at them. Power, for Hobbes, is a relational concept denoting causal efficacy, a means for achieving goals. Utility, in the modern sense in which Macpherson wants to attribute it to Hobbes, is a measure of subjective satisfaction. Power may be a means

73

for maximizing subjective satisfactions, as Hobbes suggests in Chapter 10 of *Leviathan,* but it can be put to many other uses, at least some of them antithetical to this goal. Furthermore, there are other ways to maximize satisfactions than having power — such as living in accordance with the laws of nature. It is false to equate Hobbes's account of the desire for power with the desire to maximize utilities. Although Hobbes's account of the intrinsic insatiability of human desires generates a conception of human motivation that contains many key elements of the idea of a preference function, it is a misleading and unnecessary anachronism to attribute to him the whole utilitarian doctrine of human motivation. His central preoccupation with power and his axiom that man's primary psychological drive is fear mean that our claim about human motivation must be more partial than this if it is to be accurate.

Hobbes provided many of the conceptual tools for the utilitarian theory of human motivation — that people want more rather than less, that they define their own goals which vary across persons and time, and that these goals are conceived of and pursued independently of the activities of others. The vast gulf between his account and modern utilitarian accounts is that for Hobbes none of this is inconsistent with a theory of objective interests explicitly derived from a theory of human nature. It may be true, as intuitionists since G. E. Moore have claimed, that utilitarianism also rests on an implicit naturalism in its identification of utility with a natural human capacity. If this is so, however, it is a different and much weaker sense of naturalism than that implied by Hobbes's theory of objective interests, which rests on a view of ethics as a demonstrable science, perceivable with the absolute certainty of Euclidean geometry. In the context of Hobbes's theory of science [see section II(iii)], it made sense to hold *both* a "subjective" theory of rights, where individuals define their own goals in a kind of proto-emotivist fashion, *and* a theory of "objective" interests held to be unambiguously demonstrable and indubitably certain. What is worth emphasizing here is that the coexistence of these two theories was pegged to a view of science that was not destined to survive the eighteenth century. In the post-Humean era liberals would find themselves compelled to jettison all notions of objective interest, as values were separated from facts and ethics descended into the realm of the merely subjective. Once the view of science that had given Hobbes's theory its broad coherence fell into disrepute, his theory of rights became a basis for attacking the very idea of an objective interest. This development belongs to the era of neo-classical utilitarian theory; it is quite antithetical to Hobbes's view, as is it in fact to early versions of utilitarianism. Macpherson's desire for a model of ideological assumptions that is applicable to all "modern" market societies leads him to project values that he sees around him onto earlier periods for which they are inappropriate, or, perhaps more accurately, in which they were present in partial and embryonic forms. This in turn generates an unhistorical attempt to straitjacket arguments in accordance with his preconceived model, resulting in his stipulative identification of Hobbes's notion of power with subsequent conceptions of utility. Not only does his account lack plausibility as an interpretation of Hobbes, it also misses the more subtle, though nonetheless vital, developments in the history of the ideology he is concerned to analyze.

Macpherson's discussion of Hobbes on human motivation also misses one of the principal roots of modern utilitarianism in Hobbes's thought, one which is vital to the case Macpherson wants to make. This is Hobbes's transformation of the doctrine of natural law into what is essentially a brand of rule-utilitarianism. Hobbes radically transforms the idea of natural law from a system of divine injunctions from which rights are derived to a set of maxims that take rights as given and justified on the grounds that they are demonstrably rational. It is too simple to say that these maxims are reducible to man's "possessive individualism." It is Hobbes's view that if men are left to their own devices, to pursue their individual wants unregulated by law, they will *not* behave rationally. Their selfish pursuit of their passions will produce chaos, war, and death. The maxims embedded in the laws of nature are in principle rationally demonstrable to all and Hobbes takes great pains to demonstrate that they in fact function in the interests of all. This may, however, conflict with what a given individual in a given situation "possessively" regards as his interest. The law is there to force men

75

to behave rationally. For Hobbes, this means according to their true interest. This is the basis of Hobbes's command theory of law, which became central to utilitarianism in its major classical variants. The idea of rationality has been through several metamorphoses in the liberal tradition that have functioned to detach it from theories of objective interest and to identify it instead with simple maximization of exogenously determined goals. The criteria that are seen as relevant to identify a practice as rational have likewise varied, but utilitarian arguments for the legitimacy or illegitimacy of laws invariably resolve into claims that they are rational or irrational. If there is a single move in Hobbes's theory that links his account to that of Bentham and his followers, it is surely this redefinition of the whole epistemological basis for the law.

There are two separate roots of utilitarianism in Hobbes's account of individual rights. The first lies in his pluralist conception of the good according to which individuals identify, attach value to, and pursue their goals in relative isolation from one another, and are proprietors of their actions and thus own what they make or exchange. This is captured by Macpherson's possessive individualism thesis, although it is mistaken to imply that this entails anything like a doctrine of subjectivism. Such a doctrine would arise only in conjunction with the late eighteenth-century separation of facts from values which found its subsequent expression in utilitarianism in the neo-classical denial of the possibility of interpersonal comparisons of utility. The second source of utilitarianism in Hobbes's account is his rationalist theory of law that resolves into a version of rule-utilitarianism.

Macpherson's historically unviable model leads to misinterpretations of Hobbes's theory and prevents him from adducing some of the most effective arguments available in support of the thesis he wants to argue. It also leads him to miss one of Hobbes's most important contributions to the liberal ideology of individual rights which resides in his account of the nature and functions of the state. The anachronistic assumption built into Macpherson's application of his model of Hobbes's England—namely that market relations were already more or less fully established—leads him to ignore statements by Hobbes that seem incompatible with his model but that are pregnant with ideological significance for the early liberal-capitalist state. For Hobbes, the state distributes transmissible private property rights (and so rejects and undercuts feudal land law). It creates and enforces a system of bilateral recipro-cal contracts (and is thus by definition in opposition to large areas of medieval private law that still prevailed in Hobbes's England). It grants all individuals equal "negative" freedom where the law is silent (and thereby implies the illegitimacy of the obligations embedded in both feudal private law and abso-lutist public law, many of which were still in place well after the Civil War). Hobbes thus articulates a conception of the state which, when seen in the actual historical context of the transitions then occurring in English society, must be seen as innovative. None of this is reflected in a model that is derived from and portrays an established market system where the state plays a different role, but there is no reason for us to think that it should be so reflected.

Two aspects of Hobbes's account of the state that are of particular interest to us concern the nature, functions, and limits of its power and the moral justification for its existence. These go to the core of the enigmatic position of the state in the liberal ideological tradition and it will be useful to con-clude by summarizing my earlier discussion of them. First, the territorial state is granted power that is absolute, limited at any given time only in ways that the legitimate agent or agents of the state may deem appropriate. The property and other civil rights that it grants, as well as the laws it enacts, are inviolable injunctions applicable equally to all. But if the *power* of the state is absolute, its *purposes* are quite limited and resolve basi-cally into creating and regulating a negative libertarian society and within it a market-based economy. The expansion of the private sphere that followed the Reformation has been much commented on and needs little further discussion. The state divested first the church and then itself of direct responsibility for the spiritual and material well-being of its citizenry, and instead defined its responsibility as indirect, as creating and

77

maintaining a system in which individuals could take care of their own needs and wants, both spiritual and material. A language had been created that made this seem both morally desirable and practically efficient. It could seem morally desirable because it rested on a negative libertarian conception of freedom implied by the separation of right from law and the adoption of the spherical conception of the private rights of individuals as against one another. A merely regulative state could thus appear to be one that maximizes freedom. It could seem to be practically efficient in the context of emerging beliefs about the nature and production of wealth that came increasingly to be regarded as residing in the capacity to produce for exchange.

Although separate, these moral and practical justifications for the regulative state would become importantly related. As Locke was the first of many to point out, mere regulation of private relationships is not a sufficient condition for the preservation of even negatively defined freedom, unless it is accompanied by guarantees that some basic material needs will be filled, and that some of the actions the state is capable of performing can never be justified. The moral justification for the regulative state was shown to rest on factual assumptions about what mere regulation of the private sphere would actually result in. It was a short step from here to basing the moral argument *upon* the practical argument, to arguing that the regulative state is justified *because* it leads to the most efficient method of generating wealth. But this is to anticipate the argument. For the present I merely note that, although this regulative conception absolves the state from direct responsibility for the well-being of its citizens, its indirect responsibility significantly includes doing whatever is necessary for the efficient functioning of the market.

Second, despite the awesome power Hobbes gives to the regulative state, he provides the conceptual tools for perpetual attacks on it. Much of his account reinforces the liberal vision of the state as an intruder on the privacy of the individual. The equation of freedom with toleration and privacy from government rather than participation *in* it, the rejection of both feudal and traditional absolutist conceptions of public law, and the derivation of the legitimate authority of the state from the private-law rights of individuals, all served to make the legal and moral status of the state intrinsically question-able, on the grounds that it threatened the private-law rights whose protection had become its raison d'être.

3

The classical moment

I. INTRODUCTION

One would have to be ignorant, foolish, or both to suppose it now possible to give an entirely novel interpretation of Locke's role in the rise of Anglo-American liberalism. There are three ways, however, in which the account offered here is held to be distinctive. First, I will argue that the theory of rights articulated by Locke contributed to and rested on a conservative liberalism. This is not to invoke the view of Dunn, Tully, and others that Locke was basically a Christian writer, firmly rooted in the values of the sixteenth-century neo-Thomist revival. I think this interpretation, though partly correct, suffers serious inadequacies. Nor do I wish to deny that many of Locke's political and religious arguments, particularly in his later writings, were politically radical in the historical context in which he wrote, so much so that many of his Whig contemporaries distanced themselves from the argument of the *Two Treatises* after 1688. They found Locke's right to resist more radically threatening than had been required to get rid of James II, and certainly more radical than they were prepared to subscribe to thereafter.[1] These facts notwithstanding, I believe Locke's theory shaped the economically and socially conservative nature of liberalism as a political ideology in important and lasting ways, as capitalism began to establish itself and to advance. No text is inherently liberal, radical or conservative – the ideological functions of the same text vary greatly with historical circumstance and reader.[2] It is striking, however, that Locke's arguments provided many of the ideas that would become central to legiti-

---

1 This case is powerfully argued for by Franklin (1978:87–126). See also Ashcraft (1986), especially Chapters 8 and 9.
2 See Shapiro (1982:535–78).

mating capitalist economic practices, not by "transcending" natural law and claiming that the lower classes are incapable of rational behavior, as Macpherson and others have claimed, but by modifying the natural-law tradition to make it consistent with the economic and social practices capitalism would require, and doing this in universalist and egalitarian terms. Locke's radical politics did not generate much in the way of conceptual tools to challenge this emerging liberal capitalist view, in large part because of his central focus on toleration, admittedly the burning issue for radical politics in his day. It was an idea ripe for manipulation in a world in which toleration would increasingly come to connote toleration of capitalist social and economic practices by an attentive but subordinate state. From this point of view what was significantly missing from Locke's political vocabulary was a theory of democratic participation. In the one area where Locke's arguments had potentially more radical longer-term consequences – the labor theory of value and its political implications – his arguments were destined not to have a lasting influence in the liberal tradition.

Second, as with my interpretation of Hobbes, I offer an account of Locke's view of the nature and functions of the state that squares neither with Macpherson's nor with contemporary minimalist interpretations of the kind defended by Robert Nozick. By again taking account of the difference between a regulative and a minimal state, I argue that, although he equivocates a good deal, Locke does in fact sanction significant state intervention. Finally, in contrast to some who hold that Locke's theory was the first modern illustration of the liberal tendency to argue for the priority of the right over the good, and in contrast to others who see his rights as derived from a Thomist view of the good, I argue that Locke's rights rest on a theory of objective interests of a kind not uncommon in English political theory up to the time of Hume. Close attention to his view of the nature of moral knowledge and the possibility of an incontrovertible ethics reveals why Locke saw no contradiction between a theory of objective interests and a "subjective" theory of rights; he regarded these as entailing one another.

II. LOCKE'S THEORY OF RIGHTS

Traditionally, Locke, far more than Hobbes, has been regarded as the founder of modern liberal conceptions of individual human rights. He offers an account of natural rights
according to which every person, in virtue of the law of nature, is entitled to life, liberty, and property in order that he
may survive and thrive. Thus all property owners are entitled
to the protection of their property in virtue of their mutual
agreement to obey the law. Like Hobbes, Locke believed that
the state of nature was an actual historical condition which
still prevailed in parts of the world and to which civil societies
could, and did, in certain circumstances return,[3] but to Locke
its character and political implications were very different.
His contract did not generate a command theory of law as
did Hobbes's but rather a representational one, and his citizenry retained substantial rights of resistance against the
state. Whereas Hobbes's sovereign was never obligated to its
subjects because it never contracted with them, emerging instead as a byproduct of the citizens' mutual agreements one
with another, government for Locke is bound by a contract
with the people. If it violates its fiduciary trust the citizens'
natural right to revolution is activated, although just how this
process might occur is not entirely clear and has been the
subject of much exegetical dispute.[4]

The preceding is a fairly loose statement of Locke's view. As
will be seen, such central terms as "property," "owners," "consent," and "resistance" had vitally different meanings in the
context in which Locke wrote than do they for us today. To
illuminate the full significance of his account for the liberal
rights tradition, I now examine his argument in more detail.

i. The subject of rights

Although the state of nature, for Locke, is not necessarily a
state of war as it is for Hobbes, and although we do not find in

3 Some commentators have suggested that Locke's state of nature was not conceived
  of as an actual historical state, but impressive evidence to the contrary is adduced
  by Ashcraft (1968:898–915; 1986: Chapter 6).
4 For an extensive discussion of this see Ashcraft (1986:Chapter 8).

Locke's writings the same fear of the masses that permeates Hobbes's, there are several important parallels in their appeals to the interests of the masses as the ultimate justification for their political arguments. It is worth stressing that the kind of threat presented by the masses to the ruling classes was significantly different in Restoration England from that which had prevailed during the Civil War and Interregnum.[5] After 1660 the landowning class was secure from revolt from below. As England entered the mercantile revolution that was to open the way to the industrial revolution of the eighteenth century, social and economic conflict was more effectively managed within existing political structures. This was in part because of general improvement in the standard of living, there being general agreement among contemporaries by the mid-1670s that the country was prospering. The abundant harvests after mid-century reinforced this new social stability, in contrast to the social unrest generated by the terrible harvests of the 1640s. After a century of decline, real wages were rising and by the 1690s famine was perceived to be a thing of the past. The substitution of wheat for rye, the growth of large-scale market gardening and dairy farming, of intensive crop cultivation and stock breeding, all combined to improve living standards and weaken the pressure on the political system from below. The Restoration confirmed the defeat of popular democratic movements in London. By the 1680s industrial struggles had begun to assume their more modern forms of strikes, mutinies, and other combinations to secure higher wages. Although there were incidents of machine-breaking and rioting, what Hill refers to as the oligarchic political structure was essentially secure and, more important, widely perceived to be so.

The revolution of 1688 was a palace affair and even in their most radical moments in the early 1680s the Whigs never conceived of revolt as anything else. Hobbes had, understandably, regarded revolution as synonymous with a return to the state of nature and civil war. Locke, writing in the early 1680s, saw it as a return to the social community that stood between

5 The remainder of this paragraph is based on Hill (1961:200–8) and Appleby (1978:99–102).

the state of war in the state of nature and civil society, for the reestablishment of a government in conformity with the fiduciary trust that the community grants to the legislature (Locke, 1963:417–8).[6] If England's political structure after the Restoration was basically oligarchical, and if the Whig revolutionaries had no intention of altering that structure, it is nonetheless true that Locke like Hobbes, saw it essential to legitimate the state in universalist terms. All men are equally the subjects of natural rights that are both logically and temporally prior to civil society. Each man

is born with a double Right: *First, A Right of Freedom to his Person,* which no other Man has a Power over, but the free Disposal of it lies in himself. *Secondly, A Right,* before any other man, to *inherit,* with his Brethren, his Fathers Goods. (Locke, 1963:441)

When we look for the justification offered by Locke for this generalized individual natural right we find that there are several. Locke tends to shuffle perpetually among arguments from nature, reason and scripture–with important consequences as we will see. Sometimes he seems to regard all these terms as synonymous. Thus in the *Essays on the Laws of Nature,* written in 1660, the law of nature is identified as a decree of the Divine Will that reason does not establish but discovers as a law enacted by a superior power and "written in the hearts of men" (Locke, 1958:141ff). In the *Second Treatise,* however, published in 1690 (though probably written in 1681)[7] the Law of Nature is treated as synonymous with reason itself:

The *State of Nature* has a Law of Nature to govern it, which obliges everyone: And Reason, which is that Law, teaches all Mankind, who will but consult it, that being all equal and independent, no one

6 Whether or not this community is a transitional entity between the state of nature and civil society (so that revolution need not be synonymous with a return to the state of nature) has been much debated by Locke scholars. It is not an issue we need to resolve here. Recent scholarship has inclined to the view that Locke's "positive community" does exist in the state of nature; by definition a return to the former therefore involves a return to the latter. See Tully (1980:96–7, 125–6), Ashcraft (1986:Chapter 8).

7 For a review of the debate on dating Locke's *Second Treatise,* see Ashcraft (1980: 429–85). Ashcraft convincingly concludes that it was probably written in late 1681 or 1682.

ought to harm another in his Life, Health, Liberty, or Possessions. (Locke, 1963:311)[8]

In the *First Treatise* we find several attempts to identify reason with nature. A genuinely impartial observer, Locke argues,

will have little Reverence for the Practices which are in use and credit amongst Men, and will have Reason to think, that the Woods and Forests, where the irrational and untaught Inhabitants keep right by following Nature, are fitter to give us Rules, than Cities and Palaces, where those that call themselves Civil and Rational, go out of their way by Authority of Example. (Locke, 1963:219)

Locke's view is that man's originally sinful passions led him astray, but observation of nature can show him his natural and genuinely rational mode of existence. Two chapters later we find a further identification of nature and reason with scripture in the context of his rejection of Filmer's theory of inheritance:

God having made Man, and planted in him, as in other Animals, a strong desire of Self-preservation, and furnished the World with things fit for Food and Rayment and other Necessaries of Life, Subservient to his design, that Man should live and abide for some time upon the Face of the Earth, and not that so curious and wonderful a piece of Workmanship by its own Negligence, or want of Necessaries, should perish again, presently after a few moments continuance: God, I say . . . directed him by his Senses and Reason, as he did the inferior Animals by their Sense, and Instinct, which he had placed in them to that purpose, to the use of those things, which were serviceable for his Subsistence. (Ibid.:242)

What is natural is rational and is also God's will. Thus in the *First Treatise* Locke is at great pains to establish that Filmer's patriarchial theory of authority depends on misinterpretations of the scriptures *and* on arguments that lead to rational contradictions *and* on false assertions about nature.[9]

In his attempts to establish that all men are equally subjects

8 On this point note Dunn's (1969:193) observation that Locke affirmed "the existence of a perfect parallel between the calculus of rationally apprehended moral truths and the divinely furnished system of hedonic sanctions."

9 For attacks on Filmer's religious arguments, see Locke (1963:191–231), his rational arguments (ibid.:237–9), and his arguments from nature (ibid.:218–20).

of natural rights, Locke appeals to all three types of argument. To begin with the argument from reason, Locke, like Hobbes, argues that all men equally have a rational capacity for genuine knowledge and that sound political arguments must appeal to that capacity.[10] Thus at the outset of the *First Treatise* he claims that anyone who will "but think himself" will see the absurdity of Filmer's propositions. He sets himself the task of giving convincing reasons to anyone who is willing to listen, claiming that "[i]f anyone, concerned really for Truth, undertake the Confutation of my Hypothesis, I promise him either to recant my mistake, upon fair Conviction; or to answer his Difficulties." Like Hobbes in his attacks on the arguments from authority and the "insignificant speech" of the Schoolmen, Locke has nothing but contempt for Filmer's "proofs" of Adam's Royal authority, which are nothing but "often repeating it, which among some Men, goes for Argument" (Locke, 1963:176; 172–3; 175; 184. Cf. also 1959, I:37–8). Also reminiscent of Hobbes in this regard, Locke was quick to defuse arguments from authority by appealing to man's natural and unencumbered reasoning capacities. In his discussion of reason in Book IV of the *Essay* he notes:

[T]here are many men that reason exceedingly clear and rightly, who know not how to make a syllogism. He that will look into many parts of Asia and America, will find men reason there perhaps as acutely as himself, who yet never heard of a syllogism, nor can reduce any one argument to those forms. . . . God has not been so sparing to men to make them barely two-legged creatures, and left it to Aristotle to make them rational, i.e. those few of them that he could get so to examine the grounds of syllogisms. . . . God has been more bountiful to mankind than so. He has given them a mind that can reason, without being instructed in methods of syllogizing: the understanding is not taught to reason by these rules; it has a native faculty to perceive the coherence or incoherence of its ideas, and can range them right, without any such perplexing repetitions. (Locke, 1959, II:389–91)

---

10 I am here taking exception to Macpherson's "differential rationality" hypothesis, according to which the laboring classes were, for Locke, incapable of fully rational behavior and hence of full political membership. See Macpherson (1962:232–8). This issue is taken up in section IV of this chapter. For an extended critique of Macpherson on this point, see Ashcraft (1986:Chapters 7 and 9).

The view that sound political arguments must appeal to the universal innate capacity of human reason also infuses the argument of *A Letter Concerning Toleration*. Princes, Locke argues, may be born superior to other men in power, but in nature they are equal. "Neither the right nor the art of ruling does necessarily carry along with it the certain knowledge of other things" (Locke, 1979:189). As far as genuine knowledge is concerned "[i]t is only light and evidence that can work a change in men's opinions" (ibid.:174). In the *Second Treatise*, Locke avers that the laws of nature are more easily intelligible to men than positive laws, for "[a]s much as Reason is easier to be understood, than the Phansies and intricate Contrivances of Men . . ." In his discussion of the authority of parents, the whole basis of Locke's argument against Filmer is that their authority is temporary *because* all adults are equally capable of rational behavior. Thus are parents to "inform the Mind. and govern the Actions of their yet ignorant Nonage, till Reason shall take its place and ease them of that Trouble" (Locke, 1963:315–6; 348).

Locke's rationalist appeals were directed primarily toward a fairly small educated and reading public. It is doubtful that he gave much thought, in this connection, to the lower classes. What is significant from our point of view is that he framed these appeals in universalist terms, acknowledging an equal rational potential in all men; the differences he discerned among them were attributed to education and social circumstance.[11] Because all men are born equally rational, each had the "right of nature" to enforce the laws of nature in the absence of legitimate civil authority. For this reason civil society must be shown to be in the rational interests of every individual.

The religious argument for man's individual natural rights turns on the creationist view that Locke opposes to Filmer's Adamite theory of property and political authority – to the view, that is, that God gave the world to Adam and his heirs in virtue of their inheritance from him.[12] Filmer argued that par-

11 On this point, see Wood (1983:129–42).
12 This view, and its significance for understanding Locke's contrasting argument, has been discussed in some detail by Tully (1980:35ff) and Ashcraft (1986: Chapters 3 and 4). It is taken up in more detail in sections II(ii), II(iii), III, and IV of this chapter.

ents since Adam had absolute authority over their progeny because they created them. Locke claims that God creates all children and uses their parents for this purpose. Parents do not fashion the child and most commonly do not even intend to create it; they do so as a byproduct of the instinctive desires God has placed in them. The authority parents have over their children is thus provisional; it expires when the children attain the age of reason and therefore provides no legitimating model for patriarchal political authority. The implications of this creationist view will concern us in section II(iii) of this chapter. The central point to note at present is that all men are created equal as the children of God and this is the religious basis for their equal rights vis-à-vis one another in the state of nature (Locke, 1963:215–6, 231, 348).

Finally, to establish man's equal natural rights to self-preservation, Locke invokes arguments based on assertions about nature and human nature. These appeals are not altogether mutually consistent. Nature is at times considered instructive of how man ought to live, as when we are asked to observe the harmonious ways of the animal kingdom (1963:219). At other times Locke cites beast-like behavior as indicative of the depths to which man can fall if he fails to observe the law of nature (1963:307–8; 314–5; 319ff). But the naturalist appeal to how men behave in fact is at times critical to Locke's theory. In his discussion of resistance to prerogative power in the *Second Treatise,* for instance, Locke argues that the decisive test of when the executive has overstepped its rightful limits is when "the Majority *feel it,* and are weary of it, and find a necessity to have it amended," for "God *and Nature* never allowing a Man so to abandon himself, as to neglect his own preservation" must leave him with this final authority (1963: 427, emphases added). In *A Letter Concerning Toleration,* there is a similar descriptive appeal:

[I]f men enter into seditious conspiracies, *it is . . . their sufferings and oppressions* that make them willing to ease themselves. Just and moderate governments are everywhere quiet, everywhere safe; but oppression raises ferments and makes men struggle to cast off an uneasy and tyrannical yoke. . . . [F]rom *the common disposition of all mankind,* who when they groan under any heavy burthen endeavour

88

naturally to shake off the yoke that galls their necks. (Locke, 1979:215, emphasis added)

Despite his quickness to identify instances of the genetic fallacy in Filmer's argument (as when the latter asserts that the existence of such practices as slavery and child-selling in the world indicates their naturalness), and despite his rhetorical use of the argument that "when Fashion hath once Established, what Folly or Craft began, Custom makes it Sacred" (1963:219), Locke is thus not above appealing to what men and animals actually do, or appear to do, as evidence that these practices are both natural and justified, when it suits his purposes – whether these be to show biological grounds for monogamy, or to arrive at the particular view of resistance he wants to sustain (1963:363–4; 1979:215).

Locke's rationalist, naturalist, and religious arguments converge on the proposition that the prepolitical individual is the only legitimate subject of natural rights. Men are naturally equal and in general perceive themselves to be so; their equal rational capacities mark them as fundamentally opposed to traditional and patriarchal systems of political authority and their equality as children of God, their creator, assumes a fundamental moral equality among men. Since for Locke all civil rights arise from the institutions geared to the preservation of man's natural rights, this egalitarian view of the subject infuses his entire political theory.

ii. The substance of rights

What are there rights *to*? Locke answers this very broadly by saying that each man has a right to his life, liberty, and property; that in the state of nature he has a further right to enforce the law of nature for reasons of punishment, prevention of and compensation for injuries done to him, and that although this right to enforcement is renounced on entering civil society, man's other rights are grouped together under the single term property. Thus "no *Political Society* can be, nor subsist without having in it self the Power to preserve the Property . . ." for "the chief end [of civil society] . . . is the preservation of Property" (1963:367, 366). Property inheres quite generally in the capacity to do or make. It is in no way restricted to physical objects. We are proprietors of our *actions* and have exclusive rights over the freedoms and objects created as a result of those actions. Thus are slaves excluded from civil society not merely because they have no estates, but because they have "forfeited their Lives, and with it their Liberties." That is, they have given up their property in themselves. By comparable, if not entirely compatible, logic Locke holds, conversely, that absolute monarchy can never be justified because, by alienating their capacity for autonomous action, the subjects become slaves (Locke, 1963:366–8).

Unlike Hobbes, Locke regards the process of the creation of objects of entitlement as independent of government (although he expects government to facilitate and regulate it). He takes the more traditional view that the emergence of property rights is prior to, and, ultimately, served by the institutions of civil society. It is this aspect of his argument that has encouraged the view of Locke's state "as in effect a joint-stock company whose shareholders were the men of property" (Macpherson, 1962: 195). As Macpherson acknowledges, and as Tully, Ashcraft, and others have recently argued at some length, this view does justice neither to Locke's theory of property nor to the view of political authority generated by that theory. It will be useful to look at Tully's argument in some detail.

Tully's central claim is that at least two very different conceptions of right prevailed in seventeenth-century English and European political thought. Following Skinner (1978, II:138ff) and Tuck (1979:22–30, 46–7ff) he argues that on the one hand there was a "private" conception, adopted primarily by Grotius but also subscribed to by Hobbes, Filmer, and Pufendorf, and deriving ultimately from the Ockhamist "subjective" tradition. On the other there was a "common" conception deriving from the Thomist natural-law tradition that viewed individual property rights as functions of the individuation of the common, given by God to man for the preservation of human life, the first dicate of the law of nature.[13] In this tradition natural rights

13 There were differences of some importance among the writers comprising these traditions; Tully describes them in considerable detail (1980:53–94).

are not prior to natural law; on the contrary they are derived from it. Writers adhering to a "broad" conception of property, comprising common and private property, include Suarez, Selden, Cumberland, and Locke (Tully, 1980:64–79ff). The law of nature, for Locke, gives to all a theoretical inclusive use-right to the common – a right, that is, not to be excluded from it by others. The foundation of property is derived from this fact and from two characteristics of human beings. First, each individual is proprietor of his or her own person and, second, no one has a right to it other than that person. The individual qua natural being is God's property since God created us, but the individual qua person – that is, a being capable of intentional action – is not, and it is this latter individual that has the proprietorship of his or her own actions. In Locke's view, when God gave the earth to Adam, He was not giving him private dominion over it, He was giving it to mankind in common. We all therefore have an inclusive right (a right not to be excluded) to the common, but not an exclusive right (which is private dominion from which we can exclude others) to it. The former is *ius ad rem* (right to use a thing), the latter *ius in re* (right to a thing). This is the basic difference between Locke and Filmer on property. In the latter's Adamite conception, God gave Adam an unlimited right to property, passed on via inheritance to his heirs. The notion of use-rights to the common thus never arises. A similar view was held by Grotius, who claimed that all property is by definition private, and by Pufendorf, who embraced the notion of a "negative community" that exists before the introduction of private property and is merely an agreement that all things are free for any taker. Tully emphasizes that these notions all have much more in common with one another and with subsequent liberal conceptions of property than they do with Locke's Thomist conception of a positive community guaranteeing *ius ad rem* to all in common. This view, if correct, stands the conventional wisdom concerning the relationship between individualistic conceptions of property rights and liberal political theory on its head for "[t]he authors who adopt the private concept, Grotius, Filmer and Pufendorf, integrate it into the absolutist theories. The author who adheres to the common concept most emphatically is Locke" (Tully, 1980:79).[14]

There is no denying the plausibility of Tully's argument as an account of the different origins of these two types of theories of property. But how significant is it in overturning the conventional identification of Locke's theory with the classical liberal view of property rights as individual exclusive dominion against all takers? First, Locke's notion of positive community is not, strictly, a theory of common *property* at all. Tully claims that the "combination of a conditional use right in land, and an usufruct in the products of one's labor was the standard form of property" in England and was "available to Locke" as the basis for his theory of common property, modeled on the English Commons which were "called 'properties' " (ibid.:124–5). But Locke tells us repeatedly that the origin of property consists in the capacity to work, not in the land. Thus a hunter owns his catch because in laboring to remove it from the state of nature "wherein she was common" he "hath *begun a Property*" (Locke, 1963:331). God gave the world to mankind in common, but Locke refers to it as his "Waste," for " 'tis *Labour* indeed that *puts the difference of value* on every thing" and thus "*Labour*, in the Beginning, *gave a right of Property.*" Even in gathering food that has grown wild, "[t]hat labour put a distinciton between them and the common . . ." and thus became his private right. Tully himself quotes Locke as holding that if I dig ores from land that is part of the common, the "labour that was mine, removing them out of that common state, hath fixed my property in them." The act of removing them from the state of nature "*begins the property*" (ibid.:337; 338; 341; 330; Tully, 1980:124–5).

Locke is famously vague about the exact contributions of labor and nature to the *value* of property – although "*labour makes* the far greater part" (Locke, 1963:338) – but two points should be noted in this connection. First, the value of property is quite distinct from its ownership, and on this point Locke is in no way equivocal, empirically or morally. Second, in being unsure of how, precisely, to incorporate the value contributed

14 For further discussion of these and other seventeenth-century "inclusive" and "exclusive" theories, see Tully (1980:53–130).

by nature into a labor theory of value—recognizing that the capacity to work must comprise the vast majority but believing that nature must make some residual contribution—Locke was in the mainstream of the new economic orthodoxy, widespread among economic writers after Petty.[15] That Locke's view differs from Filmer's is undeniable, but it is in no sense a conservative reaffirmation of preabsolutist orthodoxies, as Tully asserts.

In support of his interpretation of Locke on common property Tully also has a good deal to say about the famous Lockean provisos that accumulation must not lead to waste and that "as much and as good" must be available to others in common. For Locke the problem of waste dissolves with the introduction of money which can be accumlated without deteriorating, but what of the "as much and as good" proviso? As Tully points out, every man has an inalienable right to subsistence [see section II(iv): subsistence is defined quite generously]. God gave the world to mankind in common to secure that right, but what does this mean? Remember that for Locke the source of the means of subsistence is almost exclusively the capacity to work, not nature. If this be so, all that is required for the fulfillment of the proviso is that people be enabled to work.[16] It seems most likely that Locke believed that in the kind of society he advocated, violations of the proviso would never in fact arise for precisely this reason, a view supported by his attitude toward enclosure and the unemployed.

Tully disputes Macpherson's claim that after the introduction of money the subsistence proviso of the law of nature became "transcended" because of increases in productivity (Tully, 1980:152; Macpherson, 1962:203; 211). He sees no supporting evidence for Macpherson's claim that accumulation generates increases in productivity which more than makes up for the lack of land available for others.

Locke explicitly states and repeats that, through increasing productivity, less land is used and more is left for others. He also specifies that this inverse ratio between increasing productivity and decreas-

---

15 See Chapter 2, section II(ii).
16 For further discussion of this point, see Isaac (1986).

ing amounts of land required to provide comfort and support, would ensure that even with double the present world population, appropriation could still take place in the natural manner without "prejudice [to] the rest of Mankind." (Tully, 1980:149)

Tully is confused here, however. Accumulation, in Locke's view, will generate increases in productivity such that in practice no one's subsistence rights will be violated. What Locke says is this:

[H]e who appropriates land to himself by his labour, does not lessen but increase the common stock of mankind. For the provisions serving to the support of humane life, produced by one acre of inclosed and cultivated land, are (to speak much within compasse) ten times more, than those, which are yielded by an acre of Land, of an equal richnesse, lyeing wast in common. And therefor he, that incloses Land and has a greater plenty of the conveniencys of life from ten acres, than he would have from an hundred left to Nature, may truly be said, to give ninety acres to Mankind. . . . I have here rated the improved land very low in making its product but as ten to one, when it is much nearer an hundred to one. (Locke, 1963:336)

It is clear that this justification turns on the increase in productivity of the enclosed land. There is no implication that it is desirable on the grounds that it functions indirectly to preserve other common land, nor does Locke suggest any theoretical or practical limit to the enclosure of land that would otherwise be "lyeing wast in common." Locke believed that the increase in productivity resulting from enclosed land would generate so much more wealth for all that man's natural use rights to the common would become moot. Though this argument may rest on questionable empirical beliefs about distribution and "trickle-down" assumptions that history would prove reluctant to substantiate, it clearly was Locke's view. His advocacy of enclosure for reasons of increased productivity refutes Tully's (1980:130) conclusion that "in the *Two Treatises,* Locke provides a justification, not of private property, but, rather, of the English Common." Locke's thesis about productivity, reminiscent of Petty's, implies that, although common-law rights are not in principle transcended, in practice claims

94

to them will never arise. Once money is instituted unlimited accumulation of *jus in re* is perfectly legitimate.[17] This is supported by Locke's well known view that the able-bodied unemployed should be put to work, since their unemployment was the result of their laziness and moral ineptitude. Although God gave the world to mankind in common "for their benefit, and the greatest Conveniencies of Life they were capable to draw from it," he gave it

> to the use of the Industrious and Rational, (and *Labour* was to be *his Title* to it;) not to the Fancy or Covetousness of the Quarrelsome and Contentious. He that has as good left for his Improvement, as was already taken up, needed not to complain, ought not to meddle with what was improved by another's Labour: If he did, 'tis plain he desired the benefit of another's Pains, which he had no right to. (Locke, 1963:333)

What God has given us in common we have no more than a right to "labour on" (ibid.). Locke's natural-law view of common property was thus quite consistent with the view that the able-bodied poor should be put to work.[18] In this, too, he was in the mainstream of economic thinking. Such writers as Petty, Fortrey, Reynell, and many others had criticized the policy of depopulating England through emigration, though they all simultaneously acknowledged the costly problem of high and growing unemployment. The belief that the capacity to work was the source of wealth, buttressed by the equally widespread view that a large population held down wages and encouraged internal trade, reinforced this analysis of the causes of unemployment and of the appropriate remedies (Appleby, 1978: 135–41; Coleman, 1956:280–95; Johnson, 1937:249ff).

This is not to say that Locke's conception of positive com-

---

17 Tully further asserts (1980:149) that Locke could not have been concerned with accumulation of capital because, following Keith Tribe, he holds there was no "independent category" of the "economy" of which land could be a part. My ultimate concern is with the fact that Locke's argument by its very terms could be used to justify capital accumulation (whether he intended this or not), but it is worth pointing out that Joyce Appleby's important (1978) study of seventeenth-century English economic theory and ideology (discussed later) creates a heavy burden of proof for anyone who wishes to adhere to the Tribe–Tully view.
18 For an extended discussion of the implications of these passages, see Isaac (1986).

munity is irrelevant to his theory of rights,[19] but he did have conventional views for his time of the origins of wealth, the desirability of enclosure from the point of view of productivity, and of treatment of the unemployed. He was not primarily interested in defending the English Common. The differences between Locke and his "adversaries" (the term Tully uses to denote Locke's various absolutist opponents, Filmer, Grotius, and Pufendorf)[20] should not obscure the fact that Locke's men create rights of exclusive dominion and that Locke expects these to be perfectly consistent with his natural-law proviso in practice.[21]

Tully is correct, however, in saying that Locke's account of the substance of rights derives from the workmanship metaphor. Although his principal interest is in Locke's theory of property rights, he points out that Locke applies this metaphor quite generally to all acts of doing and making. It is thus central, for instance, to his definition of privacy and his argument for toleration. The individual agent, capable of autonomous intentional action, is entitled to whatever that autonomous action legitimately can create. This idea is not without its ambiguities, but for the present we will restrict our attention to Locke's use of it. Although all men are the workmanship of God, "sent into the world by his order and about his business," in their actions vis-à-vis one another they are autonomous agents and may do as they like, within the limits imposed by the law of nature. Among other things this means that they must respect one another's autonomy qua rational intentional agents, so that no man may "harm another in his Life, Health, Liberty, or Possessions" (Locke, 1963:311). Man is thus born "with a Title to perfect Freedom, and an uncontrouled enjoyment of all the Rights and Privileges of the Law of Nature, equally with any other Man" (ibid.:366–7). For Locke, so long as man is not in violation of the laws of nature, his action is by definition his *own*, his private business. Although Locke is primarily concerned with religious toleration, when he comes to

19 It is discussed further in section II(iv).
20 Although, as Tully notes, on many key particulars the arguments of these writers differed from one another. See Tully (1980:64–80).
21 There is one minor exception to this, relating to the poor who are in "extream want," discussed in section III.

discuss the limits of the power of the magistrate, we find that he views religious action as paradigmatic of private action in general. Thus:

The care ... of every man's soul belongs unto himself, and is to be left unto himself. But what if he neglects the care of his soul? I answer: what if he neglects the care of his health or of his estate, which things are nearlier related to the government of the magistrate than the other? Will the magistrate provide by an express law that such a one shall not become poor or sick? Laws provide, as much as is possible, that the goods and health of subjects be not injured by the fraud and violence of others; they do not guard them from the negligence or ill-husbandry of the possessors themselves. (Locke, 1979:186–7)

The commonwealth is "a society of men constituted only for the procuring, preserving, and advancing their own civil interests" which are the "life, liberty, health, and indolency of body; and the possession of outward things such as money, lands, houses, furniture, and the like" (ibid.:172). It is the duty of the magistrate to secure these things, but that is all: "[A]ll civil power, right and dominion, is bounded and confined to the only care of promoting these things" (ibid.:172). Locke goes out of his way to make toleration in general not contingent on the truth or falsity of the belief to be tolerated. We are all subject to "the duties of peace and goodwill ... as well towards the erroneous as the orthodox" (ibid.:184).[22]

Locke was well aware that a perfectly unqualified principle of toleration will generate paradoxes, conflicting injunctions, and illiberal conclusions. He therefore imposed three kinds of limits on toleration. The first concerns toleration of practices inimical to the principle of toleration itself; that is, actions which, if tolerated, result in people being forced to do things that they would not otherwise do. "For all force (as has often been said) belongs only to the magistrate, nor ought any private persons at any time to use force, unless it is in self-

---

22 This exceptionally broad theory of religious toleration, and Locke's view that the ends of civil society are purely secular, are further reasons for questioning the interpretation of Locke as a conservative Thomist. For further discussion of Locke's religious radicalism in his later writings, see Ashcraft (1986:Chapters 1 and 2).

defence against unjust violence" (Locke, 1979:179). "Unjust violence" seems to mean direct violation of another's will, a refusal to tolerate another's private actions. Toleration requires intolerance of antitolerant acts: "[F]or who could be free when every other Man's Humor might domineer over him?" (Locke, 1963:348).

Second, in the *First Treatise*, Locke is unequivocal that because all people are bound by the laws of nature (whether these are divine injunctions, natural imperatives, or canons of rationality) they have an absolute liberty to act autonomously, but not a license to do as they please. Thus are children under the authority of parents until they are old enough to understand that law, and thus practices like cannibalism, sale of children, adultery, incest, and sodomy, all of which "cross the main intention of Nature" (ibid.:218–20), cannot be tolerated. Leaving aside how Locke expects us to know what is and is not against the main intention of nature, he clearly expects that the civil law will uphold this law and will not tolerate trangressions against it.

Finally, actions will not be tolerated which are prejudicial to the existence of the commonwealth. Thus atheists ought not to be tolerated, not because of the nature of their beliefs, but because those beliefs are threatening to the commonwealth. "Promises, covenants, and oaths, which are the bonds of human society, can have no hold upon an atheist" (Locke, 1979:212).[23] Papists and "Mahometans" ought not to be tolerated because they are bound to alien civil powers. "That church can have no right to be tolerated by the magistrate which is constituted upon such a bottom that all those who enter into it do thereby *ipso facto* deliver themselves up to the protection and service of another prince" (ibid.:212). It is difficult to know to what extent such beliefs were sincerely held by any writer in the political climate of Restoration and revolutionary England. On the question of atheism, Locke regarded questions about the existence of God as separate from questions about alternative religions. It is clear from the *Essay* that he believed in versions of

23 For an extended account of Locke's views on promising and trust, and their political implications, see Dunn (1984:279–301).

the cosmological proof and the argument from design.[24] In *A Letter Concerning Toleration* he seems to follow Hooker in invoking a version of the argument from common consent.[25] For whatever reason, Locke regarded the existence of God as self-evident and its denial as threatening to the life of the commonwealth. This was sufficient reason, as for those who acknowledge an alien civil power, to deny toleration.

In its essentials Locke's view of toleration was the standard Whig one of the 1680s, though more extreme than was typical. Since the Restoration Charles and James had been attempting to expand toleration of Catholics and nonconformists to undermine the religious and political power of the Anglican clergy. Charles's declaration for toleration in 1662 and his declaration for indulgence a decade later met with insurmountable political opposition, but James had considerably more success with his similar declaration in 1687. James's uneasy alliance with both Catholic and Protestant nonconformists was broken at the Revolution as a result of Anglican promises to tolerate nonconformists in the general interests of Protestantism. This was realized to some extent in the Toleration Act of 1689, although it did little more than exempt some narrowly defined groups of dissenters from some specific penalties. The Act achieved its purposes, however. It split Protestant from Catholic dissenters, the latter being excluded from toleration legislation for the rest of the Stuart period. Henceforth Catholicism could be regarded as treasonable as it was in the Act Against Popery of 1700, aimed at "preventing the further growth of popery and of such treasonable and execrable designs and conspiracies against his Majesty's person and government."[26] Locke's view was thus in the mainstream of Whig thinking on toleration that triumphed at the Revolution, which largely explains its contemporary influence. Its

24 See (1959, II:306–24). For commentary, see Tully (1980:38–43).
25 "All men know and acknowledge that God ought to be publicly worshipped; why otherwise do they compel one another unto the public assemblies? Men, therefore, constituted in this liberty are to enter into some religious society" (1979: 193).
26 The acts referred to in this paragraph are reprinted in Browning (1953:359–410).

influence on the subsequent evolution of the liberal ideology of individual rights derived from the negative libertarian view of the substance of rights that it presumed and sought to justify.

iii. The basis for rights

Locke's theory of natural rights is rooted in the triple appeal to reason, nature, and scripture behind his theory of natural law. If the exact relationships among these various appeals, and between them and his account of natural law, are not entirely clear, neither is the relationship between his natural law and his natural rights. In the *Essays on the Law of Nature* he rejected the traditional scholastic and Christian correlativities between right and law, a striking fact since in his earlier writings he adhered strongly to traditional natural-law views. In the *Essays,* however, we find him embracing the radically untraditional conceptual disjunction that we found in Chapter 14 of *Leviathan.*[27] Locke says:

[Natural Law] ought to be distinguished from natural right: for right is grounded in the fact that we have the free use of a thing, whereas law is what enjoins or forbids the doing of a thing. (Locke, 1958:111)

Right is thus categorially different from law, the former indicating a capacity for autonomous action, the latter externally imposed obligatory constraints. Thus Locke's view is not as easily categorized as Tully (1980:67–8) suggests. As Finnis (1980:206–8) points out, by following Hobbes and Pufendorf in distinguishing law from right in this way, Locke departed from the Thomist tradition, a departure rooted in Grotius's revival of the Roman law concept of a right as one's *suum,* a kind of moral power or *facultas* which every man has. This notion has its conceptual roots, as Skinner (1978, II:117, 176–8) has established, in the writings of Suarez, and ultimately Gerson and the conciliarist tradition. This "subjective" view of natural rights as "essentially something someone *has,* and above

27 For a useful account of the movement in Locke's political and moral thinking over his lifetime, see Ashcraft (1986:Chapter 1) and specifically on his changing conceptions of natural law, see Riley (1982:83–97).

all (or at least paradigmatically) a *power* or *liberty*" involved a
shift in perspective that carried the right-holder, and his right,
"altogether outside the juridical relationship which is fixed by
law (moral or posited) and which establishes *jus* in Aquinas's
sense: 'that which is just' [or fair]" (Finnis, 1980:207–8).

The categorial division between right and law required a
highly artificial distinction which does not withstand much
analysis. It has become a commonplace in the liberal tradition,
at least since Kant, that my right to X *is* your obligation to
respect that right, even if this is understood in the minimal
sense of a Hohfeldian "no-right" to respect my negatively defined liberty. Unless employed in the purely descriptive sense
of Hobbes's natural rights, which Locke clearly does not intend, an account of rights entails and is embedded in some
notion of law and obligation. Yet Locke's conceptual model
requires that natural rights are in some important sense basic
and prior to natural laws, a point that should not be lost sight
of in the face of recent Locke scholarship emphasizing the
centrality of Locke's theology to his politics.[28] Although he
equivocates a good deal, it is clear from the *Essay*, the *Second
Treatise*, and the *Reasonableness of Christianity*, as well as the
early natural-law writings, that Locke conceived of the natural
laws which bind human beings as being grounded in God's
capacity for autonomous action. They are expressions of His
will and are *His* natural rights.

This Cartesian view was theologically controversial and
Locke was never entirely comfortable with what he took to be
its implications.[29] It made the divine will basic to natural law –
and the capacity to will, by analogy, basic to all law as conceived of on this analytical model. This could be argued to
entail that there are no immutable laws of nature demonstrable with the certainty of mathematical proofs. Yet the demonstrability of ethics was an obsession that Locke was able
neither fully to reconcile with his view of natural law nor to
abandon.[30] If natural law was tied to the will of God, it was

---

28 The most important arguments on this point are made by Dunn (1969), Tully
(1980), and Ashcraft (1986).
29 For an account of Descartes' views, see Kenny (1979:16–22).
30 For further discussion of this tension in Locke's writings, see Riley (1982:87ff).

presumably alterable by that will, and not necessarily perceivable by human reason alone. Conversely, if natural laws were a body of rules in conformity with the rational nature of things, this could imply that God did not have the power to alter natural law by command, that natural law is binding even on God, or that it would be valid, as Grotius had argued, even if God did not exist.[31] Locke wanted to hold both to his celebrated view that morality and mathematics are parallel in that both are open to conclusive demonstration, and to his doctrine of theological voluntarism which made the will of God, and hence *His* natural right, basic to natural law from which what humans perceive as natural law is derived. Our natural law *is* God's natural right.

This generated profound tension in Locke's view of natural law (which intensified over his lifetime) between his voluntarist theology and theory of action, on the one hand, and his conviction that natural law was part of an immutable natural order on the other. Throughout his writings we find commitments to both these views and attempts to reconcile them. In the seventh *Essay on the Law of Nature* for instance, he argues that "certain duties arise out of necessity and cannot be other than they are." This is not because "nature or God (I should say more correctly) could not have created man differently." Rather the explanation is that

since man has been made such as he is, equipped with reason and his other faculties and destined for this mode of life, there necessarily result from his inborn constitution some definite duties for him, which cannot be other than they are. In fact it seems to me to follow just as necessarily from the nature of man that, if he is a man, he is bound to love and worship God and also to fulfil other things appropriate to the rational nature, i.e. to observe the law of nature, as it follows from the nature of a triangle that, if it is a triangle, its three angles are equal to two right angles, although perhaps very many men are so lazy and so thoughtless that for want of attention they are ignorant of both these truths, which are so manifest and certain that nothing can be plainer. (Locke, 1958:199–201)

31 For further discussion of these disputes, see von Leyden's introduction to Locke (1958:52ff).

It is beyond my immediate purpose to evaluate this and other attempts by Locke to reconcile his voluntarism with his theory of immutable natural law.[32] Ashcraft (1986: Chapter 2) suggests that Locke's resolution lies in holding that God has built into men instincts that make them perceive His intentions as intrinsically rational natural laws. It is possible that Locke believed such resolution followed from his argument from design for the existence of God. What is important is that Locke never abandoned the view that natural law was ultimately a function of the divine will, and the conviction that it could not have the force of *law* without being thus conceived. His theoretical machinations were geared to establishing that his naturalist and rationalist arguments were consistent with this view, but he never abandoned the basic commitment to the voluntarist theory. Locke's confusing and sometimes contradictory utterances on how the content of natural law is revealed to men, discovered by them, held to be synonymous with their rational capacities, or even to be those capacities, continue to be debated.[33] Beyond question, however, is that whatever else it is natural law is an expression of God's will. Locke's frequent appeals, so ably portrayed by Tully (1980:35ff), to metaphors of workmanship and watchmaking in the *Two Treatises* and elsewhere, make it fundamental that men are obliged to God because of his purposes in making them. Men are "the Workmanship of one Omnipotent, and infinitely wise Maker ... they are his Property, whose Workmanship they are, made to last during his, not one anothers Pleasure." Parents are thus obliged to provide for their children "not as their own Workmanship, but the

32 This issue is taken up at the end of the present section. For further discussion the reader is referred to Riley's (1982:63–91) useful analysis.

33 Von Leyden has argued with considerable plausibility that Locke does not supply a consistent account of man's knowledge of the content of natural law. Locke passes from "the recognition that man is rational to the assumption that man's reason, on the basis of sense-experience, leads to the discovery of moral truths, nay, if properly employed, to the discovery of one and the same set of moral truths, i.e. natural law ... to the belief that the truths discovered are divine commands binding on all men, and hence to the assertion that the validity of such commands can be proved, and even shown to be necessary in the same way as a geometrical proposition" (Locke, 1958:59, see also 43–60).

Workmanship of their own Maker, the Almighty, to whom they were to be accountable for them" (Locke, 1963:311, 347). Like Newton, Locke rejected the Aristotelian view that the world is uncreated, that matter must be eternal, on the grounds that it "denies one and the first great piece of his [God's] workmanship, the creation" (Locke, 1959, II:320).[34] God created the world and the creatures inhabiting it for a purpose, and that purpose is immanent in the fundamental imperatives guiding all human behavior.[35]

In the *Essay* Locke defines divine law as "that law which God has set to the actions of men, – whether promulgated to them by the light of nature, or the voice of revelation" (1959, I:475). Although there is some question as to how divine and natural law are related to one another,[36] as to how divine law is discovered by men or revealed to them as natural law, it is clear that the latter is either dependent on the former or comprises part of it. Natural law cannot bind men unless there is a superior power with the capacity to make that law, and hence the right to obligate them. Law always presupposes a lawmaker for Locke, a view which, once secularized, would be central to Bentham's jurisprudence. "That God has given a rule whereby men should govern themselves, I think there is nobody so brutish as to deny," Locke argues in the *Essay* and elaborates as follows:

He has a *right* to do it; we are his creatures: he has goodness and wisdom to direct our actions to that which is best: and he has power to enforce it by rewards and punishments of infinite weight and duration in another life; for nobody can take us out of his hands. This is the only true touchstone of moral rectitude; and, by comparing them to this law, it is that men judge of the most considerable moral good or evil of their actions. (Locke, 1959, I:475, emphasis added)

Riley is persuasive, then, that "Locke's final opinion appears to be that even a perfectly rational moral principle would not be a real law unless it were willed by a superior being who has a right, by virtue of having created everything, to govern his creation as he sees fit, and that even if reason helps us find

34 For further discussion, see Tully (1980:37).
35 For further discussion, see Dunn (1969:95).
36 See Riley (1982:85).

that law, it does not constitute that law" (1982:86. Cf. also Finnis, 1980:337). Locke did not think in terms of symmetrical correlativities of rights and obligations, but all obligations must nonetheless be grounded in rights, so that natural laws are rooted in what von Leyden sums up as "the natural right which the Creator has over His creation" (Locke, 1958:50), the right of ownership God has over what he makes.

There is a deep tension between the claim that both right and law are grounded in the capacity for autonomous willing (divine or human), and the argument that moral law has immutable moral content which is discoverable by human reason. Why did Locke fail to come to terms with this? Largely because, like Hobbes, he was committed to two incompatible assumptions about action, or, more accurately, to two assumptions that could only be rendered mutually compatible by a view of moral knowledge that was not destined to survive the eighteenth century. He was committed to a theory of interests by which man has certain modes of behavior appropriate to himself, resulting from his objective nature and embedded in the laws of nature. Locke was also committed to an essentially Cartesian idea of the individual human agent as the ultimate foundation of human knowledge and action, both morally and ontologically. There was a deep tension between Hobbes's moral account of man's free will and his psychological determinism. Locke's argument exhibits a different but analogous tension. He was convinced that there are moral imperatives that rational men must choose to live by, but it is indispensable to his ethics that the freedom to choose is theirs. This supplies the basis for his "subjective" view of rights, the view that makes individual consent central to the preservation of rights and to authentic knowledge of individual interests. Subjective certainty is the hallmark of genuine knowledge, and uncoerced individual assent the hallmark of legitimate action. This is the central idea that Locke seeks to capture with his notion of a right. Rights are not mere correlates of extrinsically determined obligations, they reflect the individual's capacity for autonomous intentional action.

Natural law may dictate that man is subject to divine, natural, or rational imperatives to live in certain ways, but two points should be noted in this regard. First, these are clearly conceived of as general negative constraints. Provided men do not violate natural law they may act as they please and create obligations to themselves by their own autonomous actions, ". . . for we are not bound to anything except what a law-maker in some way has made known and proclaimed as his will" (Locke, 1958:187). Where natural law is silent we cannot be bound. It is precisely because God has created man with free will and the capacity for autonomous action that men can create laws and obligations to themselves. If we were not free in this sense, we could not create obligations to ourselves. "[E]very man is put under a necessity, by his constitution as an intelligent being, to be determined in willing by his own thought and judgment what is best for him to do: else he would be under the determination of some other than him-self, which is want of liberty" (Locke, 1959, I:346). Within the limits set by the law of nature men may act, as Tully notes, in a Godlike fashion: "[m]an as maker . . . [has] analogous maker's knowledge of, and a natural right in his intentional actions" (Tully, 1980:109–10, 121).

The limits within which men may act autonomously are thus conceived of quite broadly. This is why, *pace* Barker and others, there is no fundamental tension between natural law and contractarianism even for the mature and more radical Locke, as Riley has recently pointed out. Natural law "defines only general moral goods and evils, only moral duties and sins; it cannot point out what is a crime, in the strict legal sense, in a commonwealth" (Riley, 1982:64). On the contrary, since natural law

neither appoints nor removes civil magistrates, neither creates nor pulls down particular political structures, consent and promise and contract must provide this appointing and removing and creating and pulling down. When natural law is used directly in politics, and not simply as a criterion of right, it will be in marginal or exceptional cases, such as those of aliens or of rulers who place themselves in a state of war with their subjects . . . the social contract, for Locke, is necessitated by natural law's inability to be literally "sovereign" on earth, by its incapacity to produce "one society." (Ibid.:69)

This is why men can only be obligated to commonwealths by their own intentional actions. "Nothing can make any Man so [obligated], but his actually entering into it by positive Engagement, and express Promise and Compact" (Locke, 1963:394; cf. also 318). Within the general limitations of the law of nature, man is free to act as he pleases precisely because God has created him with the capacity so to act. In this way Locke manages to ground his negative libertarian view of civil freedom in his voluntarist theology. God makes man, we are told in the *First Treatise, "in his own Image after his own Likeness,* makes him an intellectual Creature and so capable of *Dominion."* We are free agents because God gave us free will, it is His purpose that we should have it. "God having given Man an Understanding to direct his actions, has allowed him a freedom of Will" (Locke, 1963:197, 348). Thus we have a natural obligation to preserve our freedom as individuals, and to preserve mankind as far as possible (ibid.:311; Dunn, 1969:95ff). "The *Liberty of Man, in Society,* is to be under no other Legislative Power, but that established, by consent," and in civil society as outside it, unless there is legitimate law created either by voluntary human action or by God's commands, the negative libertarian view prevails. I have a natural liberty "to follow my own Will in all things, where the Rule prescribes not; and not to be subject to the inconstant, uncertain, unknown, Arbitrary Will of another Man. As *Freedom of Nature* is to be under no other restraint but the Law of Nature" (Locke, 1963:324).

The second point about the asymmetrical relation between law and right concerns its broader historical implications. Natural law, for Locke, is grounded in divine natural right, or God's will, a view that makes natural law derivative and secondary in Locke's system, dependent ultimately on the will and hence existence of God. Since God's natural right is thus basic, Locke was inadvertently opening the way for modern doctrines of the priority of right, though he himself only held this view in an unqualified form as it applied to God's actions, men being free only within the limits imposed by the law of nature or God's natural right. Once God came to be removed from the picture, however, this asymmetrical analytical model of the relationship between right and law imposed no constraints on us except our own autonomous wills. The fact that Locke offered no real argument concerning why the divine will is basic or why making confers ownership, left his view intrinsically open to manipulation. The notion of an autonomous will would become an axiom from which all political arrangements must consistently be derived. We can accept as conclusive much of the revision in Locke interpretation undertaken by Dunn, Tully, Riley, Ashcraft, and others and recognize with them the centrality of Locke's theology to his political writings.[37] The implications of this for Locke's place in the liberal tradition, however, are not so devastating to older conventional wisdom as Tully and others seem to suppose.[38] Although we now know that the "subjective" rights tradition has a genealogy much older than the seventeenth century, Locke is not so decisively separated from it in vocabulary or substance as Tully would have us believe.[39] For Locke, the theory of positive community and common property in the state of nature do not, in practice, prevent the emergence of conventional property rights of exclusive dominion.[40] These are "subjective" in the sense that they supply decisive authority to the right-holder for all significant economic, social, and political purposes. We can now see that this view has its philosophical foundations in Locke's voluntarist theology, and in particular in the theory of authentic action this theology presumed and reinforced. Locke's view of action is at the heart of subsequent liberal commitments to the priority of right over law which lies at the basis of modern doctrines of constitutionalism.[41]

37 Implicit in this reinterpretation is a rejection of Strauss's reading of Locke on natural law. For a good summary and critical discussion of Strauss's view, see Riley (1982:87–91).
38 To be exempted here is Ashcraft (1986). His central argument is that there is a fundamental tension in Locke's writings between a religious and political radicalism and a socioeconomic conservatism, a tension, he contends, fundamental to the liberal tradition of political theory. I do not accept that Locke's political ideas were as radical as Ashcraft claims, but, as further elaborated, the rest of his analysis is substantially compatible with my own.
39 Tully's claim rests in major part on his interpretation of Locke's theory of common property, taken up further in section IV of this chapter.
40 See section II(ii) of this chapter.
41 Contemporary debates concerning the relationship between the right and the good, and right and law, are taken up in Chapters 5 and 6.

At one level what Locke is confronting in his analysis of the relationship between right and law is the paradox of free will in Christianity. God made man in his own image with the capacity to behave in accordance with his will, but also with the freedom to choose not to. (It is never entirely clear how an omnipotent and perfectly good being can create the evil options available for men "freely" to consider.) This Protestant view, usefully summed up by Ryle (1949:159) as the belief that man had to be assumed to know "the moral state of his soul and the wishes of God without the aid of confessors and scholars," led the early Protestants to speak in terms "of the God-given 'light' of private conscience." It was central to the mature Locke's political and religious outlook. In *A Letter Concerning Toleration* he argued that the state may not force religious conformity on anyone, for "every church is orthodox to itself; [and] to others, erroneous or heretical." A church must therefore be a voluntary association of individuals which the magistrate both safeguards and limits, but may not try to regulate internally. "[T]he care of souls is not committed to the civil magistrate." His power consists in "outward force," but "true and saving religion consists in the inward persuasion of the mind" (Locke, 1979:181, 172, 173). Individual natural rights mark this capacity for individual persuasion.

The issue, however, is much larger than the question of free religious will. It goes to the heart of the tensions among Locke's arguments from nature, reason, and scripture. As with Hobbes, there is, prima facie, no conflict for Locke between the "subjective" theory of rights and the theory of objective interests embodied in the laws of nature, because he adheres to a view of knowledge by which moral truths can be known and demonstrated with certainty. The documentation of this fact is perhaps the most important contribution of Tully's book.[42] Overturning Laslett's view that the argument of the *Essay* is irrelevant to the *Two Treatises*, Tully points out that, like Grotius, Pufendorf, Cumberland, and Vico, Locke was convinced of the supremacy of the moral over the natural sciences. Locke made a basic distinction between "ec-

42 Although Tully does not accept that Locke had a "subjective" conception. See the discussion of common property in sections II(ii) and IV of this chapter.

type" and "archetype" ideas, the former being "[g]eneral ideas of substances" and the latter "in some sense, constructed by man" (Tully, 1980:9–12ff). This generated a radical disjunction between natural and conventional knowledge, underpinned by Locke's distinction between nominal and real essences. In substances that depend on the external world for their existence, only nominal essences can be known to man: the real essence is available only to the maker of the substance, God. In the case of archetypes, however, nominal and real essences are synonymous, so that real essences can by definition be known to man. Since social practices are always a function of archetype ideas, it follows that real social essences can be known to man, that he can have incontrovertible knowledge of his civil interests (ibid.:16–22). This kind of "maker's" or "constitution" theory of knowledge is identical to that of Hobbes.[43] Locke saw no difficulty in reconciling his "subjective" theory of rights with his account of objective interest. He thought he could demonstrate the latter with the kind of certainty that must command universal assent from rational beings. People might in fact be ignorant of the truths of morality or mathematics, but this is a function of their lack of education, laziness, or inattention – not a difficulty intrinsic to the discovery of such knowledge. At the outset of the *Essay* Locke makes this clear in his rejection of Descartes' epistemology. He plans to establish that men, "barely by the use of their natural faculties, may attain to all the knowledge they have, without the help of any innate impressions; and may arrive at certainty, without any such notions or principles [as innate ideas]" (Locke, 1959, I:38).

Locke's "maker's" view of knowledge, however, glosses over important ambiguities in his account of the basis for rights. The problem for Locke is twofold. He runs into difficulties concerning actions that men may take within the limits set by the law of nature, as well as when they violate, or are alleged to violate, fundamental natural law constraints. In the first and arguably less important case, it is clear that Locke's negative libertarian account of the substance of rights, and the voluntarist model of

43 See Chapter 2, section II(iii).

action derived from his theology, both presume and require that there are at least some significant areas of social and political life wherein natural law will either be silent or be consistent with alternative possible courses of action. Thus people might disagree over what to do in a particular case and not be helped by natural law. This must be true for his account of free human will to have any meaningful content whatsoever. Moreover, it is not an answer to this difficulty to say that here we are entering the realm of what Locke conceived of as prudential or practical knowledge, which is provisional and corrigible, gained primarily from the study of history, and more of the character of experiential generalizations than transcendental natural laws.[44] Locke's argument that we are free moral agents must entail the possibility of autonomous choice about moral questions, and hence the possibility of genuine moral disagreement. To this it might be responded that it is true but trivial, a possibility of which Locke took obvious account. The machinery of government Locke defends in the *Second Treatise*, with its emphasis on separation of powers and mechanisms of majority rule – as well as the individual rights defended from majoritarian and governmental tyranny in the letter on toleration – was designed with precisely this possibility in mind: that some moral disagreement is inevitable in society and political institutions must accommodate this fact. If Locke's natural law theory is interpreted in this way, however, an important implication is that natural law will be silent on – or indifferent to – many of the issues of distributive justice and social and political organization that have preoccupied writers in the liberal tradition since Locke, and that continue to dominate debates in contemporary liberal theory.

Locke's difficulty is more serious. It extends to the boundaries of legitimate political disagreement, to situations where there are alleged or actual transgressions of natural law. If natural laws are conceived of as divine commands implanted in us so that we feel them as instinctive imperatives, how are men to resolve disagreements about the content of natural law in particular cases? Locke's descriptive naturalism is neither

44 For analysis of these two types of knowledge and their respective roles in Locke's political theory, see Ashcraft (1986:Chapter 2).

internally consistent nor helpful in this regard, since the ways of the animal kingdom are sometimes appealed to as examples of what to do and at others they illustrate practices that men as higher creatures should avoid.[45] Locke's only alternative is to appeal to the rationality of natural law, and to man's alleged capacity to comprehend it and act on his comprehension of it. It is characteristic of man's natural condition that he has the capacity for free choice. Men differ from animals precisely in that they can suspend their instinctive desires and think critically about them before acting on them. "[D]uring this suspension of any desire, before the will be determined to action, and the action (which follows that determination) done, we have the opportunity to examine, view, and judge of the good or evil of what we are going to do . . . and it is not a fault, but a perfection of our nature, to desire, will, and act according to the last result of a fair examination" (Locke, 1959, I:345). Yet Locke was certainly aware that rational deliberation could result in conflicting judgments about the content of natural law. Part of Locke's critique of Filmer in the *First Treatise*, as Ashcraft (1986: Chapter 3) has pointed out, turns on the hermeneutical claim that because more than one interpretation of the Scriptures is sometimes possible, there can be no authoritative interpretation by ecclesiastical authorities. Individuals must rely on their commonsense and rational capacities to choose among contending interpretations. The tension is present here too, however, because Locke does not appear to doubt that there is a correct interpretation that reasonable people will rationally arrive at. He does not doubt that he can convince people that his literal reading of the Scriptures is consistent with their commonsense interpretations. Although God speaks with more truth and certainty than men, "when he vouchsafes to speak to Men [through the Scriptures], I do not think, he speaks differently from them, in crossing the Rules of language in use amongst them. This would not be to condescend to their Capacities, when he humbles himself to speak to them, but to lose his design in speaking, what thus spoken, they could not understand" (Locke, 1963:208–9). Common-

45 See section II(i) of this chapter.

sense readings of the Scriptures must, therefore, reveal their true meaning.[46]

Locke's assumption that people can always be brought to agree on fundamental moral and political questions was obviously at variance with his own political experience. He acknowledged this in the most Hobbesian of terms: "For though the Law of Nature be plain and intelligible to all rational Creatures," he tells us in his discussion of the aims of political society in the *Second Treatise*, "yet Men being biased by their Interest, as well as ignorant for want of study of it, are not apt to allow of it as a Law binding to them. . . . Men being partial to themselves, Passion and Revenge is very apt to carry them too far, and with too much heat, in their own Cases" (ibid.:396). It seems, here, that man's natural freedom is the problem, causing the inconveniences of the state of nature and necessitating the formation of civil society. For Hobbes this view could generate a command theory of law to force men to be rational; for Rousseau it would generate a Lawgiver to manipulate men to be "genuinely" free. Locke, however, takes the idea of individual consent too seriously to make an analogous move and he equivocates as a result. This is perhaps best illustrated by his discussion of prerogative power, the natural right of resistance, and the dissolution of government in the closing chapters of the *Second Treatise*.

The right of resistance defended in the *Second Treatise* was politically radical in England in the late 1680s. Locke placed himself at odds with the Whig establishment in 1689 by maintaining the Lawsonian view that when James left the throne what resulted was an entire dissolution of government. In violating the fiduciary trust placed in him James had, in Locke's view, created a situation in which he was in a direct state of war with the people. They thus had the right to resist him and to remove him as king.[47] The standard Whig view, in contrast, was that the Convention Parliament discovered that the throne had been vacated. The Whigs were unwilling to accept

---

46 For an extensive analysis of Locke's hermeneutical and methodological critique of Filmer's reading of the Scriptures in the *First Treatise*, on which I draw in this paragraph, see Ashcraft (1986:Chapter 3).

47 For an excellent discussion of Tory and Whig attitudes to resistance, and how they differed from Locke's view, see Franklin (1978:98–123) on which I rely here. See also Ashcraft (1986:Chapter 8).

that the indirect consequence of James's forfeiture was dissolution of the government, which would leave Parliament without the legal authority to install William and Mary on the
throne. It was not clear why such forfeiture should not be
seen as constructive abdication, as the Tories argued, in which
case James's daughter Mary would immediately succeed, assuming his infant son could be shown to have no legal claim.
Most Whigs accepted as part of the doctrine of a mixed constitution that the power of the monarchy was independent of
Parliament. Even if the crown might be shown to derive its
initial grant of authority from Parliament, this could not entail
a right by Parliament to tamper with the royal succession. The
Whigs, however, fearful of the radical consequences of the
Lockean position, held fast to their position that there had
been no general dissolution of government *and* that Parliament had inherent power to supply a royal vacancy.[48] The
Lockean view would entail not only that the king had been
justly removed from office, but also that the rule of law and
the legal authority of Parliament had been ended, necessitating a return of power to the general community. For fear of
these radical implications the Whigs paid a heavy price in
terms of logical consistency as Franklin (1978:116–7) has
noted and it may be true, as he claims, that the principal
reason Locke maintained the radical view was that he saw the
alternative as theoretically hopeless.

Whatever the reason, Locke's view was not without difficulties of its own. The most important concerns how and by
whom circumstances where resistance is justified are to be
determined. As Filmer had maintained against arguments for
limited and mixed monarchy alike, once the proposition is
granted that there is no final and authoritative judge within
the constitution, if the king is charged with tyranny neither

48 Since Locke kept his views and authorship of the *Second Treatise* secret, this was
not widely identified as his position. As Franklin (1978:87–126) has shown, however, the Whigs openly confronted and rejected this position while Locke was
revising the final chapters of the *Second Treatise*, for it was argued in several tracts
then in public currency. Franklin argues with considerable plausibility that this
view of the basis of political authority and its concomitant account of resistance
and dissolution was first formulated by George Lawson, and that Locke took it
over from him.

Parliament nor any court may settle the dispute. Locke tacitly accepted this position, as Franklin (1978:94–5) notes, but he never fully answered Filmer's charge that this would be an open invitation for continual resistance and even attempted revolution by anarchic individuals and groups disaffected by the actions of king or Parliament. It was precisely this consequence that the Whigs wanted to avoid. Locke tried to downplay these radical implications by holding that not every illegal act by the king justified revolution, "[i]t being safer for the Body, that some few private Men should be sometimes in danger to suffer, than that the head of the Republick should be easily, and upon slight occasions exposed." Unless a ruler actively places himself "into a State of War with his People, dissolve the Government, and leave them to that defence, which belongs to everyone in the State of Nature" he may not legitimately be resisted (Locke, 1963:450; Franklin, 1978:95). In the chapter on prerogative power Locke goes so far as to maintain that the independence of the ruler is such that there may be circumstances in which he may act where there is no law, and even in some cases "against the direct Letter of the Law" (Locke, 1963:424), provided this is for the public good. Wise and good princes will use this power well; others will misuse it. When Locke considers how to establish when prerogative power is being abused, he has no real answer:

Between an Executive Power in being, with such a Prerogative, and a Legislative that depends upon his will for their convening, there can be no *Judge on Earth*. As there can be none, between the Legislative, and the People, should either the Executive, or the Legislative, when they have got the Power in their hands, design, or go about to enslave, or destroy them. The People have no other remedy in this, as in all other cases when they have no Judge on Earth, but to *appeal to Heaven*. (Ibid.:425–6)

The appeal to heaven implies a resort to force, but this takes Locke uncomfortably close to the Hobbesian position that although a person cannot be blamed in certain circumstances for resisting legitimate authority, such resistance is not itself legitimate, and the person must hope that it will be recognized as valid in the life to come.

Locke clearly assumes that genuine cases of a prince's violation of his fiduciary trust will be obvious, but the only specific
elaboration in this regard is an appeal to majority opinion in
the community. The right to resist is held not to lay "a perpetual foundation for Disorder" on the grounds that it "operates
not, till the Inconvenience is so great, that the Majority feel it,
and are weary of it, and find a necessity to have it amended"
(ibid.:427). Locke has no institutional mechanism for dealing
with what would come to be known to nineteenth-century liberals as tyrannous majorities, or for preventing the systematic
violation of the rights of minorities by the king or his magistrates. In such circumstances all these groups can do is resort
to (presumably unsuccessful) force; in so doing the moral status of their actions remains deeply ambiguous. Locke maintains that in cases of alleged tyranny the people shall be the
judge, but he gives no account of how their opinions will be
consulted or their wills implemented, beyond this ill-defined
appeal to majority rule. Given the supreme importance he
attaches to personal consent as the final legitimating mark of
all political action and institutions, questions concerning
whether, and how, majority rule succeeds or fails in representing the personal assent or dissent of every individual necessarily force themselves onto the theoretical agenda.[49] Considering the sensitivity to these issues Locke exhibits in *A Letter
Concerning Toleration,* it is somewhat surprising that he says so
little on the subject of dealing institutionally with minority
opinions. He fails entirely to confront the (presumably typical)
case where there is strong disagreement over whether or not
the ruler has betrayed his fiduciary trust. Locke *predicts* that
people will be slow to resist in fact, that the right to resist, even
in circumstances of manifestly tyrannous acts, will frequently
not be exercised.

For if it reach no farther than some private Mens Cases, though they
have a right to defend themselves, and to recover by force, what by
unlawful force is taken from them; yet the Right to do so, will not
easily ingage them in a Contest, wherein they are sure to perish; it

49 For a useful discussion of the weaknesses in Locke's account of majority rule as a
mechanism for representing personal consent, see Riley (1982:93–7).

As we saw in section II(ii) above, in his argument in support of enclosure Locke claimed that individuals who attempt to maximize their wealth do mankind a service because of the productivity effects of their actions for the rest of society.

This practical identification of needs with wants also infuses Locke's economic writings. In the discussion of value in *Considerations of the Consequences of Lowering Interest* he claims again that "the intrinsic, natural worth of anything, consists in its fitness to supply the necessities, *or serve the conveniences* of human life; and the more necessary it is to our being, *or the more it contributes to our well-being*, the greater is its worth" (Locke, 1824, IV:42, emphasis added). Locke thus articulates, like Hobbes, a conception of the good that is essentially pluralist and utilitarian, although also as for Hobbes, this is ultimately limited by his theory of objective interests. Not only does Locke define man's private-law rights so broadly as to be potentially infinite in scope, but he also makes the primary purpose of social cooperation the preservation and expansion of those private-law rights. Political power, in Locke's view, is nothing but the right "of making Laws with Penalties of Death, and consequently all less Penalties, for the Regulating and Preserving of Property, and of employing the force of the Community in the Execution of such Laws" (1963:308).

It would be a mistake, however, to conclude that Locke conceived of social cooperation exclusively in atomistic terms. He thought of men as naturally sociable, and able to develop and flourish individually only in a society which fostered their sociality. "God, having designed man for a sociable creature," he avers at the outset of Book III of the *Essay*, he placed him "under a necessity to have fellowship with those on his own kind" and furnished him with a natural capacity to use language "which was to be the great instrument and common tie of society" (1959, II:3).[52] Locke thought social intercourse inevitable and his goal was to organize it along lines demonstrably rational. He believed that such organization could foster this sociality by providing for men's individual capacities for authentic action, by generating a productive system that would

52 For a useful discussion of Locke's views on man's natural sociability, see Wood (1983:109–48).

create plenty for all, by preserving, through toleration, freedom from political tyranny, and by encouraging self-development as the disciplined pursuit of happiness through hard individual work—a kind of proto-Protestant ethic of self-development as a condition for the fulfillment of man's social capacities and responsibilities.[53] Rather than attribute to Locke an Aristotelian view of community, which he clearly did not hold, it would perhaps be more accurate to equate his view of man's social condition with Oakeshott's conception of *societas:* an association of agents who "by choice or circumstance, are related to one another" and mutually bound not by "engagement in an enterprise to pursue a common substantive purpose or to promote a common interest," but by "loyalty to one another, the conditions of which may achieve the formality denoted by the kindred word 'legality'." It is "a formal relationship in terms of rules, not a substantive relationship in terms of common action . . . each [person] pursuing his own interests or even joined with some others in seeking common satisfactions, but related to one another in the continuous acknowledgement of the authority of rules of conduct indifferent to the pursuit or the achievement of any purpose" (Oakeshott, 1975:201–2, 245ff). Although there are tensions in Locke's view of the relation between men's individual drives and the demands of sociability, these were submerged in his rationalist account of natural law and his empirical belief that the system he advocated, and the plenty it would generate, could allow for the general development of the needs and wants of all. If Oakeshott's *societas* constitutes a midpoint between the radical social atomism we associate with modern libertarian writers, on the one hand, and substantive communitarian ideals on the other, it seems best to capture the kind of negative libertarian society Locke envisaged.

III. IDEOLOGICAL CONSEQUENCES OF LOCKE'S ARGUMENT

Locke believed, as did Hobbes, that the autonomous individual is the subject of all legitimate rights. He or she is the

53 For a useful discussion of this view of human nature as it emerges from the *Essay*, see Wood (1983:121–74).

subject of all natural rights and all civil rights must ultimately be a function of his or her personal assent. Thus are churches and other religious bodies voluntary associations of individuals with no more substantial powers than the constituting members confer upon them. Thus, ultimately, is the private individual the author of the system of public law and the state itself. The "pride of private judgement" that Hobbes feared, and acknowledged ambivalently as the paradigmatic basis of the politics of the future, was endorsed and even ennobled by Locke in his egalitarian view of reason as the basis for political life and as intrinsically available to all. Locke thought, with Hobbes, that all men have decisive epistemic and moral authority over their actions, but he was not a subjectivist in our sense. His "subjective" theory of rights was held to be compatible with—and indeed derived from—a theory of objective interests. For Hobbes this theory of interests was an egoistic psychology knowable with the certainty of geometry because rooted in intentional action. For Locke its roots are more ambiguous, the appeal being sometimes to nature, sometimes to reason, sometimes to scripture, and usually to some combination of these. Whether or not one of these appeals can ultimately be shown to be basic in that the others are derivable from it, it is certain that Locke, like Hobbes, thought the moral sciences superior to the natural sciences in that they depended on the constitutive intentional action invoked in the workmanship metaphor.

It is admittedly a substantial leap from this to Locke's intersubjective theory of objective interests, which requires not only that all men reason alike, but also that they will reason to the same substantive conclusions about how their interests can best be realized and preserved in civil society. This made sense only in terms of a view of scientific knowledge in which ethics was regarded much as analytical logic came to be regarded in the Western philosophical tradition from Kant to Quine: as proceeding from self-evident premises via incontrovertible chains of reasoning to apodictic conclusions. Locke believed that self-evident truths about human nature, perceivable by reflection, observation, and revelation, generate interests that can be known with certainty and therefore must rationally

123

govern man's intentional actions. We might sum up the tension internal to this claim by saying that for Locke men are free to choose to live according to the laws of nature, or – in secular terms – that Locke has no doubt as to what course rational men, on sound reflection, must inevitably choose. This view made sense only so long as the hallmark of genuine knowledge was subjective certainty of essences, and all people were regarded as having the same essences of which to be subjectively certain.

A second important ideological move was Locke's adoption of the Hobbesian tactic of separating rights from obligations, although Locke derived his view from his quite different voluntarist theology, which made God's will the fundamental natural right, basic to natural law. More than any other single factor this separates Locke's from traditional Christian discussions of right and law. Locke was never entirely clear about the exact status of his natural laws. It might be argued that his voluntarist theology presupposed a moral theory of why making confers ownership, an implicit moral theory in which God's natural right must ultimately be rooted. There are, however, two important respects in which Locke's account differed from the traditional Thomist one. First, Locke did not derive his rights from his view of natural law but regarded them instead as descriptive of man's capacity for autonomous intentional action, modeled on, if limited by, God's identical capacity. Second, although Locke identified natural law with the divine will, from the point of view of man's actions in civil society he much more crucially identified it with man's rational capacities. Locke failed, ultimately, to give a satisfactory account of how men are to know their rational interests in practice, or of how they are to resolve disagreements concerning the content of natural law and its application in concrete cases. His view nonetheless had significant implications for the utilitarian strand of the liberal tradition. Hobbes's natural laws became prudential and essentially utilitarian maxims for the realization of individual interests in the social world. Locke, too, saw reason, which in some of his formulations is identified with natural law and in others is a medium by which we discover its content, as enabling the individual most effectively to realize his private goals in the social world. Thus the requirement that positive law be comfortable to natural law was basically a requirement that it be rational, or, more accurately, that it appear to men to be rational, in the best interests of every individual subjectively understood. It was this rationalist formulation which could be secularized and which, ultimately, would lie at the heart of liberal doctrines of constitutionalism. Once it achieved centrality it brought to the theoretical foreground the concept of unanimity. The weaknesses already present in Locke's majoritarianism became increasingly and painfully evident.[54]

There is potential for powerful conflict between this rationalist view of law and a "subjective" view of rights, when individuals do not believe that the law is in their rational interest. Bentham evades this question by allowing only those rights that are consistent with and derived from his theory of positive law (thus subordinating the subjective theory of rights to the theory of law). Hobbes denies that such a conflict can arise by definition. Locke equivocates because of his genuine commitment to a concept of free human agency. He wants to hold that if the civil law in fact operates in the rational interests of all this type of conflict will not arise. As he acknowledges, however, whether or not this will be so may not always be entirely clear and at least at times will be in dispute. Although he never fully resolved these issues, in general he thought that illegitimate actions by some or all of the government would be manifest. For Locke this belief had ultimately to rest on the leap of faith that we perceive God's intentions as rational imperatives because He has constituted us so to perceive them, a position unavailable to the liberal establishment that subsequently appropriated his doctrine.

It is worth stressing that Locke believed such fundamental disagreement would be the exceptional case which need not, and typically would not, arise; in general the rule of law would be supreme. He has no real answer for the potential problems of tyrannous majorities, or for the situations wherein the law might systematically be manipulated to violate the rights of

54 Contemporary liberal preoccupation with the idea of unanimity will concern us in subsequent chapters.

minorities, or even of majorities, all of which might be sanctioned by his argument. He benevolently assumed that it is possible for the law to function impartially in the interests of all and expected that this would typically be the case. The ideological implications of this were substantial, for in it we find the beginnings of liberalism's attempt to disguise a limited moral and political pluralism as a very broad skepticism or relativism about people's moral and political values and goals. The law is presented as ideologically neutral, as guaranteeing those things that are in the rational interests of all even as it protects, and encourages by enclosure, the creation of a system of property ownership that dispossesses the vast majority. The law is presented as a neutral mechanism even as it denies toleration to those who would challenge the unjust practices of the law, and as it rules out various other practices – cannibalism, sale of children, slavery, sodomy, atheism, and Catholicism – which, because of prevailing mores and political imperatives, Locke regarded as rationally in the interest of all to prohibit. As the last three of these examples starkly illustrate today, such claims are intrinsically vulnerable to the charge that they are biased to a particular contestible conception of the good. Locke never embraced a doctrine of moral relativism or neutralism, but if his religious theory of natural law is abandoned and his rationalist jurisprudence retained, the impetus to take such positions seriously is difficult to escape. Once Locke's view of moral knowledge could no longer be sustained, liberal rights theorists would have to seek more opaque and surreptitious devices for constraining the freedoms of individuals to avoid the more obvious paradoxes of overdetermination that would otherwise result, and to produce the kind of economic and social organization they desired.

A third major consequence of Locke's argument concerns the definition of the substance of rights in terms of negative freedom. "Laws provide, as much as is possible, that the goods and health of subjects be not injured by the fraud and violence of others; they do not guard them from the negligence or ill-husbandry of the possessors themselves. No man can be forced to be rich or healthful whether he will or no" (Locke, 1979:187). We saw in section II(ii) that the origins of ownership in the waste of God notwithstanding, the paradigmatic form of action is private, inhering in the individual capacity for intentional agency. Locke grants everyone the right to the means of subsistence, but, contrary to appearances, the proviso functions as a negative libertarian constraint, because his generous definition of subsistence includes wants and needs. We are not required to care for others except in the exceptional cases of people suffering in extreme want or following the devastating effects of war. In normal circumstances the right to subsistence merely requires that a situation prevail where all can exercise their own private-law rights of dominion over themselves, their actions, and possessions, ideologically a very different proposition. This is all that the law must or may ensure. Note also that Locke believed the dispossessed should be put to work by the state, not given charity, and that he expected workers to live at physical subsistence. In the *Considerations of the Consequences of Lowering Interest* it is clear that he regards as perfectly natural a state of affairs wherein

the labourers, living generally but from hand to mouth; and, indeed, considered as labourers in order to trade, may well enough carry on their part, if they have but money enough to buy victuals, clothes, and tools: all which may very well be provided, without any great sum of money lying still in their hands. (Locke, 1824, IV:23–4)

Locke's proviso, therefore, does not generate a right to anything more than a negative libertarian constraint. The massive inequalities this view obviously sanctioned were acceptable to Locke because of his empirical belief that the productivity effects of enclosure and accumulation would be so great that violations of the proviso would not in fact arise. He believed it sufficient that everyone be enabled to preserve himself, and this is all the law must make possible. By making property rights and even rights of inheritance prior to and independent of the law (though the law must defend them), Locke sanctioned not only vast inequality, but the transmission of this inequality through generations and the cumulative destructive social and political impact of the division of labor on the laborers themselves.[55] Hobbes had charged the state with responsi-

55 This last was to become an important preoccupation of Adam Smith's (1937:733ff).

bility for creating a negative libertarian society. Locke treated it as part of the natural order of things.

An important political consequence of Locke's negative libertarianism was that it made the central ideal of a just polity toleration, not participation. Perhaps more than any other single factor, this gave the emerging ideology of individual rights its conservative political form. Hobbes spoke of freedom in terms of the residual of sovereign power, thus embracing this concept in an embryonic form. Locke turned the ideal of toleration into the centerpiece of his theology and his politics. By making all action by definition private and gearing the law to the protection of that action, Locke affirmed the paradigmatic liberal view of "genuine" freedom as freedom *from* politics: diversity is to be tolerated so long as it does not affect the basic structure and operation of political institutions. Historically this was reflected in the increasing conservatism of the Whig establishment after the compromise of 1688 and their opposition, after 1694, to anything that could plausibly be called a democratic politics. Once they had rid themselves of James and achieved supremacy within the oligarchic state, the Whig aristocracy began to strengthen, not restrict, monarchical authority, by opposing reduction of the standing army, supporting the Act of Union with Scotland, reducing the democratic franchise in London, and forcing through the Septennial Act (Goodwin, 1979:35ff).[56] Even Locke's more radical account of the right to resist provided nothing close to the kind of appeal to democratic participation and mass political education characteristic of radical leaders in the eighteenth century, the so-called "friends of liberty" of whom Albert Goodwin (1979:25ff) has so eloquently written. Locke occasionally spoke of law in terms of enabling conditions rather than mere restraints on natural freedom,[57] but in these pas-

56 For an account of the retreat of the Whigs from radical politics after 1688 see Dickinson (1976:28–45).
57 As in Chapter VI of the *Second Treatise* where he says that "[t]he end of law is not to abolish or restrain, but to preserve and enlarge freedom: for in all states of created beings capable of laws, where there is no law there is no freedom. For liberty is to be free from restraint and violence from others, which cannot be, where there is no law" (1963:347–8).

sages he was clearly arguing that the law should enlarge the private freedoms of the individual, to make sure that he is not " . . . subject to the arbitrary Will of another, but freely follow his own" (Locke, 1963:348). The egalitarianism in the liberal rights tradition was thus from its inception a gloss. It rationalized an oligarchic state and was never intended to have what we should recognize as substantive democratic consequences.

A fourth ideological consequence of Locke's discussion derived from his treatment of human desires. As we saw in section II(iv), Locke's broad definition of subsistence rested on an identification of wants with needs similar to that embodied in Hobbes's account of human desires. For Locke, as for Hobbes, this generated the proposition that the class of objects and actions to which there are private rights is potentially infinite. Hobbes and Locke thus supplied a theoretical foundation for the idea of effective demand that was coming to dominate contemporary economic thinking. There had been a number of implicit references to a postulate of demand during the sixteenth century, in, for example, the quantity theories of money formulated by Copernicus in the 1520s and Navarus in the 1550s,[58] but it was not until the seventeenth century that writers consciously concerned themselves with the phenomenon of effective demand. We find isolated references to this notion in the early seventeenth-century literature on trade – Misselden (1623:98), for example, asserts that while prices are determined by the "goodness" of money, they fluctuate "according to the occasions of both parties" – but it is in the literature on usury and wages that the concept first presents itself as a candidate for serious investigation.

The Ancient Hebraic and Aristotelian abhorrence of usury was affirmed in the Just Wage and Price doctrines of such Scholastic writers as Aquinas and Duns Scotus, and by Dante in *The Inferno* equated morally with blasphemy and sodomy. In the seventeenth century, however, discussions of usury began to center on the most desirable rate of interest for the economy rather than on the moral desirability or otherwise of usury as

58 For discussion of Copernicus' and Navarrus' theories, see Spiegel (1971:86–9).

such.[59] This general trend toward instrumental thinking about economic questions is manifestly the central concern of Locke's considerations on interest and money (Routh, 1975:29–30; Appleby, 1978:63–72). Appleby points out that, although much of the fifteenth- and sixteenth-century literature on usury had concentrated on the barrenness of money, the evident success of money-as-capital in generating increased agricultural productivity made criticisms of usury directed at its purported effects – such as the idleness of living off unearned income – less plausible. Some writers, such as Filmer, emphasized the difference between idleness and usury; some, such as Mun, defended the latter for its effects on productivity. "How many Merchants and Shop-keepers," asked Mun, "have begun with little or nothing of their own, and yet are grown very rich by trading with other men's money?" Usury is the means by which the rich and established merchants supply the opportunity for younger and poorer ones to establish themselves: "to the performance whereof, if they want means of their own, they may, and do, take it up at interest: so that our money lies not dead, it is still traded." Mun concluded that "contrary to those who affirm, that Trade decreaseth as Usury encreaseth . . . *they rise and fall together*" (Mun, 1954 [1623]:178–9).

Once economic writers began to concern themselves with the effects of usury on productivity, a series of related questions about money, value, and prices began to force their way to the top of the theoretical agenda. Writers became increasingly concerned with the determinants of the rate of interest, the cost of money on foreign exchanges, and the determinants of prices in general. None of these questions could be addressed without the articulation of a notion of effective demand, as can be seen, for example, in Petty's attempt to formulate a theory of prices. He argued that:

59 Tawney (1961:49) writes of the Scholastic accounts of usury: "These doctrines sprang as much from the popular consciousness of the plain facts of the economic situation as from the theorists who expounded them. The innumerable fables of the usurer who was prematurely carried to hell, or whose money turned to withered leaves in his strong box, or who (as the scrupulous recorder remarks) 'about the year 1240,' on entering a church to be married, was crushed by a stone figure falling from the porch, which proved by the grace of God to be a carving of another usurer and his money-bags being carried off by the devil, are more illuminating than the refinements of lawyers."

[F]orasmuch as almost all Commodities have their Substitutes or Succedanea, and that almost all uses may be answered several wayes; and for that novelty, surprize, example of Superiours, and opinion of unexaminable effects do adde or take away from the price of things, we must adde these contingent Causes to the permanent Causes [land and labor] abovementioned, in the judicious foresight and computation whereof lies the excellency of a Merchant. (Petty, 1899 [1672], I:90)

Petty is here trying to formulate a concept of effective demand by recognizing that, from the point of view of their economic effects, peoples' beliefs about their wants and needs are operationally equivalent to those wants and needs; that demand is an inherently subjective notion that nonetheless has objective effects. In *The Political Anatomy of Ireland* he applied this notion:

if a Picture-maker, suppose, make Pictures at 5L each; but then, find that more Persons would employ him at that rate than his time would extend to serve them in, it will certainly come to pass that this Artist will consider whether as many of those who apply to him at 5L each Picture, will give 6L as will take up his whole time to accommodate; and upon this Computation he pitcheth the Rate of his Work. (Petty, 1899 [1672], I:182)

For this reason "we make an Equation between Art and Opinion" (ibid.).

Petty's endeavor to grapple with the effect of demand on prices was followed by a series of more systematic attempts by Barbon, Houghton, Law, North, and Locke, all of whom rejected the notion of a "fixt price" holding that the value of commodities depended on their usefulness,[60] or, as Barbon (1690:20) put it, "things are worth just so much as they can be sold for."[61]

The debate on the determinants of interest rates and their effects on prices continued throughout the latter part of the

---

60 For discussion of these authors see Roll (1974:112–7) and Appleby (1978: 179–83).
61 Gregory King went further and formulated a demand law for the price of wheat which referred to deviations from an assumed norm and states that if the harvest falls below this norm by 1, 2, 3, 4, or 5 tenths the price will rise above its "constant" by 3, 8, 16, 28, or 445 tenths (Yule, 1915:296).

seventeenth century, continually bringing writers back to the elusive idea of effective demand. In their attempts to specify the role of demand in price formation, a number of these writers confronted the conundrum of reconciling the evident relevance of demand to price with their labor theories of value. None of them arrived at the classical (Smithean) solution, that demand determines long-run output and has only short-term effects on market price, which fluctuates around the "natural" price determined by labor. Barbon (1690:19–20) offered two ways of calculating prices: one from the costs of production and one from the price that would clear the market. Locke defended a theory of prices based on a law sensitive to different rates of elasticity of demand for different commodities:

By the like proportions, of increase and decrease, does the value of things, more or less convenient, rise and fall, in respect of money; only with this difference, that things absolutely necessary for life must be had at any rate; but things convenient will be had only as they stand in preference with other conveniences: and therefore in any one of these commodities, the value rises only as its quantity is less, and vent greater, which depends on its being preferred to other things, in its consumption. (Locke 1824, IV:31)

He thus defended his quantity theory of money against the mercantilist view that associated low interest rates with high prices. Regarding the demand theory of price he argued that the prices of all commodities, including money, were determined by the amount of money in circulation:

All things, that are bought and sold, raise and fall their price, in proportion as there are more buyers or sellers. Where there are a great many sellers to a few buyers, there use what art you will, the thing to be sold will be cheap. On the other side, turn the tables, and raise up a great many buyers for a few sellers, and the same thing will immediately grow dear. (Ibid.:39)

Another issue that led economic writers to pay closer attention to effective demand was wages. Although most seventeenth-century mercantilist writers favored low wages, there was a dissenting group of high-wages advocates who propounded the "Keynesian" (Wiles, 1968:113–26) view that high wages and a more equitable distribution of income are conducive to increased domestic trade and stimulate production. John Cary (1765 [1696]:96–102), for example, opposed low wages on the grounds that they would reduce the price of exports and cause workers to spend less on food, thereby reducing the income of landlords. Davenant and Defoe argued similarly defending a more equal distribution of income to the same end.[62] Many of Locke's contemporaries remarked that high wages were an indicator of a nation's prosperity and low wages of its opposite. Thomas Manley (1669:19) held this view, claiming that high wages could stimulate trade through their effect on demand. Similar assertions were made by Josiah Child (1693:ix), Davenant (1942 [1696]:72), and William Hodges (1696:20).[63] This type of reasoning is a direct consequence of viewing wealth as a capacity to produce rather than in intrinsic terms; once the matter is seen in this way attention must of necessity be directed toward the capacity to consume, hence the notion of effective demand. Distribution can be thought of as a positive-sum game because demand is perceived to be elastic and the "stock of the nation" is potentially infinite.

In addition to attacking the role of demand in the functioning of the economy, seventeenth-century writers began to treat the concept of demand itself in a more analytical way. In particular, they were confronted with the fact that once they were thinking of potentially infinite capacities for production and consumption, it was no longer possible to analyze production merely in terms of subsistence needs. From the functional point of view to which they found themselves increasingly attracted, needs and wants became synonymous terms. Petty had begun to equate these in his attempt to formulate a notion of effective demand, and as we saw Locke was able to assert that "the intrinsic, natural worth of any thing, consists in its fitness to supply the necessities, *or serve the conveniences* of human life; and the more necessary it is to our being, *or the more*

---

62 Grampp (1965, I:62–3) points out that the commitment to high wages conflicted with the general mercantilist predisposition toward high prices, often held to stimulate employment.
63 For detailed discussion of the "Keynesian" theorists, see Wiles (1968:113–26).

it contributes to our well-being, the greater is its worth" (Locke, 1824, IV:42, emphasis added).[64]

An important consequence of this assimilation of needs and wants was that it implied a new, utilitarian, theory of human psychology for the analysis of economic behavior. Writers concerned with sustaining demand as a means of stimulating production began to extol the virtues of prodigality and accumulation. Appleby (1978:190–1) notes that in contrast to much of the political writing in Restoration England, economic writers gave open endorsement to the Hobbist maxims of an infinite capacity for desire and the relentless pursuit of self-interest. Some, such as Josiah Child, actually cited Hobbes as an authority in this regard. The psychological thesis behind this was most systematically spelled out by Barbon in his *Discourse on Trade* (1690:13–15):

The Use of Things are to supply the Wants and Necessities of Man: There are Two General Wants that Mankind is born with; the Wants of the Body and the Wants of the Mind. . . . Wares that have their Value for supplying the wants of the Mind, are all such things that can satisfy Desire; Desire implies Want. It is the Appetite of the Soul, and is as natural to the Soul, as Hunger to the body. The Wants of the Mind are infinite, Man naturally Aspires, and as the Mind is elevated, his sense grow more refined, and more capable of Delight; his Desires are inlarged, and the Wants increase with his Wishes, which is for every thing that is rare, can gratify his Senses, adorn his Body, and provide the Ease, Pleasure, and Pomp of Life.

In *A Discourse Concerning Coining* (1696:1–3) Barbon repeats this argument, adding that "the greatest Number of them [commodities] have their value from supplying the wants of the mind," which leads him eventually to a theory of prices based on the relation between scarcity and effective demand (ibid.:3–11). Such theories required a philosophical identification of needs with wants of decisive importance for

64 Barbon employed the same reasoning to argue that the market is the best judge of value and Pufendorf (1710 [1672]:681–3) echoed this assimilation in his discussion of value in his *De Jure Natural et Gentium Libri* wherein he asserted that the "foundation of price in itself is the aptitude of a thing or action, by which it can either mediately or immediately contribute to the necessity of human life, *or to making it more advantageous or pleasant*" (emphasis added). For detailed discussion of this point, see Bowley (1963:128–34).

the subsequent evolution of the liberal ideology of individual rights, and lying at the heart of the modern doctrine of revealed preference. In identifying these two ideas and operationalizing them as effective demand, Locke and his contemporaries were – no doubt unwittingly – destroying the basis for the argument that the market might be satisfying the wants of some without satisfying the needs of others, let alone at the systematic expense of those needs. A necessary concomitant of attributing to man an infinite capacity to desire was the postulate of scarcity that would become axiomatized in classical political economy after the time of Say, and that was central to the neo-classical tradition that followed. If a man's capacity to consume is intrinsically insatiable, no matter how much can be produced there will still be scarcity in the technical sense that if people had the resources they would consume more, although, as Bentham and his successors argued, at a steadily diminishing rate. This new economic logic had no place for a concept of satiation.

A final ideological consequence of Locke's argument concerns his account of the economic functions of the state. In Chapter 2 we saw the importance of distinguishing a state geared to the regulation of the market from the modern idea of the minimal state. Locke's state is less interventionist than Hobbes's and Locke regarded property rights as prior to the state. Nevertheless Locke, like Hobbes, regarded regulation of the market by the state as involving active intervention. None of these writers had the concept of equilibrium or of the market as *self*-regulating, a concept first proposed by Mandeville at the turn of the eighteenth century and not systematically championed before Smith. Perhaps the clearest indication that Locke believed the state should regulate the market is in his *Considerations of the Consequences of Lowering Interest*. The thrust of his argument is that the state should enforce an interest rate conducive to expanded trade and manufacturing. In practice the state cannot enforce an artificial interest rate at variance with the rate dictated by the supply of and demand for money. Therefore, he argues, any attempt by the state to reduce the prevailing interest rate to four percent will fail, but this does not preclude the state from enforcing *a* rate of interest. In Locke's view, if this is not done serious consequences will follow for the market:

[I]n the present current of running cash, which now takes its course almost all to London, and is engrossed by a very few hands in comparison, young men, and those in want, might not too easily be exposed to extortion and oppression: and the dexterous and combining money-jobbers not have too great and unbounded a power, to prey upon the ignorance and necessity of borrowers. There would not be much danger of this, if money were more equally distributed into the several quarters of England, and into a greater number of hands, according to the exigencies of trade . . . But, when a kind of monopoly, by consent, has put this general commodity into a few hands, it may need regulation, though what the stated rate of interest should be, in the constant change of affairs, and flux of money, is hard to determine. (Locke, 1824, IV:64)

The point of Locke's quantity theory of money, and of the tortuous computations he thought it entailed, was to establish the *best* rate for the market which the state should then enforce:

[I]t should be within such bounds, as should not, on the one side, quite eat up the merchant's and tradesman's profit, and discourage their industry; nor, on the other hand, so low, as should hinder men from risquing their money in other men's hands, and so rather choose to keep it out of trade, than venture it upon so small profit. When it is too high, it so hinders the merchant's gain, that he will not borrow; when too low, it so hinders the monied-man's profit, that he will not lend; and both these ways it is an hinderance to trade. (Ibid.)

Locke's objection to a lowering of the interest rate is that it will not meet this criterion, not that the state should not regulate the rate of interest. The rate should be what is best for the market, but Locke has no belief that the market will necessarily generate and sustain that rate. This an unambiguous indication that, although he believed in the desirability of well functioning markets, he had no sense of the market as self-equilibrating. This is only one of several areas in which Locke favored active state regulation of market institutions. He also expected the state to regulate labor markets by forcing the able-bodied poor to work at subsistence and to support the extension of a market in land by legislating enclosures. The modern idea of the minimal state has therefore been incorrectly read into, and seen as justified by, Locke's argument, which rested on a recognition of the necessity for state intervention as and when required.

IV. CONCLUSION

Macpherson's interpretation of Locke is without question less problematical than his reading of Hobbes, but there are important difficulties with it analogous to those discussed in the preceding chapter. First, national market relations were more fully established, at least in some basic commodities, by Locke's time than when Hobbes wrote,[65] but the questions previously raised concerning the historical viability of Macpherson's excessively general interpretive model still raise serious issues. Second, Macpherson's central claim that Locke's entire argument presumes the existence of, and is intended to justify, a class-based organization of society is misleading. Macpherson avers that Locke's background assumption of a "class" society allows him to defend a state consisting of property owners and politically excluding the working class. The working class is presumed to be devoid of both property and rationality, incapable of consent and hence of full political membership (Macpherson, 1962:248–52; 232–3). Although laborers lived from hand to mouth Locke did not believe they were in principle less capable than others of rational behavior, as Macpherson claims, or that they did not own their capacities for autonomous action (ibid.:230).[66]

Neal Wood has recently attempted to revive a modified version of Macpherson's differential rationality thesis. It merits brief attention because it goes to the heart of the confusion attending accounts of the significance of Locke's argument for

---

65 For a useful account of the growth of markets in different commodities, see Thirsk (1978:158ff)

66 For an extended critique of Macpherson on this point, see Ashcraft (1986:Chapters 7 and 9).

bourgeois modes of thought. Wood distinguishes "moral" from "naturalistic" rationality in Locke's writing, holding that only the former is distributed universally, the latter being distributed along class lines. However, he finds (1983:115) no explicit textual basis for this claim and he qualifies it so heavily that it is difficult to discern any substantive content to it. He acknowledges that for Locke all men are born with equal rational potential, and that "differences in rationality among them stem largely from environment and education." Locke explicitly invoked an egalitarian theory of natural mental capacities in attacking the notion that American Indians have genetically inferior intellects to Europeans, arguing that primitive peoples are no less well endowed naturally than are civilized peoples (ibid.:116, 113–4). Given these qualifications it is hard to see in what sense this supposed differential rationality has a *natural* basis for Locke. Wood's broader argument, that we find at the heart of Locke's philosophy the ideal of a bourgeois man, a "self-directed individualist with a work ethic," in contrast to the traditional "war ethic" and its "gentlemanly" values, so that in Locke's vocabulary "labor, industry, perseverance, sobriety, and usefulness replaced aristocratic honor, pride, dignity, spirit and the non-utilitarian" (ibid.:121, 123, 148), seems to be at odds with the "natural" differential rationality thesis. It is surely because Locke presupposed and articulated this bourgeois conception (which Wood so ably documents) in universalist terms that he is a significant figure in the evolution of liberal ideology. The fact that Locke did hold that *all* men are the proprietors of their capacities, and intrinsically capable of rational judgment concerning their use made it possible to conceive of labor power as an alienable capacity exchangeable for any other in a voluntary transaction.

The whole issue of differential rationality that Macpherson raised is reminiscent of the confusion generated by his discussion of the senses in which Hobbes is supposed to have been a "bourgeois" thinker. Macpherson claimed that Locke was unaware of the "contradictions" deriving from Locke's alleged attempt to state in "universal (non-class) terms, rights and obligations which necessarily had a class content" (1962:251). It is difficult to see why Macpherson or Wood, if they so believed, should expect Locke to hold the assumptions about differential rationality that they attribute to him, and to charge Locke with a "contradiction" here seems absurd. If Macpherson wanted to establish that Locke did not have Marx's concept of class, so be it. It is hard to see why anyone would suppose that he did or be surprised that Marx's theories contradicted Locke's. Macpherson's underlying point, that Locke's account of rights contributed to the liberal egalitarian gloss of inegalitarian social relationships is valid. It requires, however, no differential rationality exegetical hypothesis (quite the contrary), and no anachronistic accusation of unperceived "contradictions."

A second aspect of Macpherson's thesis of interest to us concerns his claim that Locke regarded wage-labor relations as natural, that he "took it for granted, throughout his justification of the natural right to property, that labour was naturally a commodity and that the wage relationship which gives me the right to appropriate the produce of another's labour was a part of the natural order" (1962:220). This claim has drawn heavy fire from Locke commentators and Macpherson overstates it when he argues that Locke "was not confused about the class structure of his own England," which Macpherson suggests Locke intended to justify (ibid.:216). But my analysis establishes that the claim is fundamentally sound. One of the most comprehensive attempts to overturn Macpherson on this point, recently attempted by Tully, confirms this.

The famous "turfs" passage on which debate on this issue has focused, and on which Tully bases his argument, reads as follows:

[T]he Grass my Horse has bit; the turfs my Servant has cut; and the Ore I have digg'd in any place where I have a right to them in common with others, become my *Property*, without the assignation or consent of any body. The *labour* that was mine, removing them out of that common state they were in, hath *fixed* my *Property* in them. (Locke, 1963:330)

The issue is the sense in which my servant's labor is mine. Tully (1980:137) denies that Locke is concerned with the wage-labor relationship, claiming, "[s]ince it is a free man that makes himself a servant, the agreement must presuppose that the choice not to become a servant is available to him." This condition, Tully claims, is fulfilled by the availability of spontaneous products of labor and utilizable land on the English common, an institution that for Locke is inviolable: it is guaranteed in natural law. God gave the earth to men in common to ensure their subsistence. Each individual therefore has a right to live from the common, at least to meet his subsistence needs. Since he cannot be forced into a wage-labor relationship in order to meet these needs, Locke cannot be discussing such a relationship in the turfs passage. In support of this Tully cites the following passage from the *First Treatise:*

[A] man can no more justly make use of another's necessity, to force him to become his Vassal, by with-holding that Relief, God requires him to afford to the wants of his Brother, than he that has more strength can seize upon a weaker, master him to his Obedience, and with a Dagger at his Throat offer him Death for Slavery. (Locke, 1963:206)

According to Tully (1980:137–8) this makes it impossible for the capitalist to appear in Locke's theory: Locke actually stigmatizes the capitalist wage-labor relationship that Macpherson attributes to him. A final argument adduced by Tully is that Locke could not have been concerned with capitalist wage-labor relationships because they did not exist. "A social division of labour, in which a laborer is hired to do a complete service, was the dominant and non-capitalist mode of production in England until at least the late eighteenth century" (ibid.:140–2).

There are several difficulties with this view. First, exegetically Tully stretches our credulity in claiming that the turfs passage refers to a mode of production in which the laborer sold an entire craft. In support of this he cites the following passage:

[A] Free man makes himself a Servant to another, by selling him for a certain time, the Service he undertakes to do, in exchange for Wages he is to receive: And though this commonly puts him into the Family of his Master, and under the ordinary Discipline thereof; yet it gives the Master but a Temporary Power over him, and no greater, than what is contained in the *Contract* between 'em. (Locke, 1963:365–6)

This is taken as evidence that the capitalist wage-labor relationship does not concern Locke. If this be true of this passage (which is difficult to accept given the assumptions about time it obviously rests on, and the lack of any reference to the "complete service" to be performed during the period of employment), it is hard to see how it can be true of the turfs passage (which is what the argument is about) because in *that* passage no craft is being sold: a turf is being cut. A second difficulty for Tully concerns the voluntary character of the relationship between master and servant–"since it is a free man that makes himself a servant, the agreement must presuppose that the choice not to become a servant is available to him." This can be interpreted at two levels, a juridical one and a material one. If the claim is that the servant is legally free not to be a servant, it is wholly unconvincing as a criticism of the view that we are dealing with a capitalist relationship. Juridical freedom of this type is precisely characteristic of the capitalist wage-labor relationship.[67] Tully apparently wants to convince us that Locke did not have Marx's concept of wage-labor, but in attacking the straw man Macpherson created he is plainly missing the point. The claim must surely be that Locke had a view of wage-labor roughly akin to that of the classical economists of the eighteenth century–to which the ideology of the voluntary transaction between employer and employee was central, a conception subject to Marx's unrelenting scorn.[68] If it is Tully's claim, however, that the dictate of the law of nature to preserve mankind never allows us to force someone to work for another on pain of starvation, this re-

---

67 For further discussion of this point, see Isaac (1986).
68 To take one of a host of poignant illustrations, at the end of his analysis of exchange in volume 1 of *Capital*, Marx quips contemptuously: "This sphere that we are deserting [exchange], within those boundaries the sale and purchase of labour-power goes on, is in fact a very Eden of the innate rights of man. There alone rule Freedom, Equality, Property and Bentham. Freedom, because both buyer and seller of a commodity, say of labour-power, are constrained only by their own free will. . . . Equality, because . . . they exchange equivalent for equivalent. Property, because each disposes only of what is his own. And Bentham, because each looks only to himself. The only force that brings them together . . . is the selfishness, the gain and the private interests of each. Each looks to himself only, and no one troubles himself about the rest, and just because they do so, do they all, in accordance with the pre-established harmony of things, or under the auspices of an all-shrewd providence, work together to their mutual advantage, for the common weal and for the interest of all" (Marx, 1970, I:172).

solves into Locke's discussion of charity. The only obligation on those with plenty is to maintain those unemployables who are in "extream want" (and it is not clear that such a person has a right to anything more than work). Beyond this, as we saw in section II(ii) above, no obligations are entailed by natural-law rights to the common.[69]

We turn now to Tully's historical argument that Locke could not have been concerned with the wage-labor relationship of capitalism because such relationships did not exist. Tully cites a brace of authorities from (one side of) the transition debate and a passage from Marx's *Grundrisse* referring to a transitional organization of work that is "still half artistic, half end-in-itself etc., Mastery" (Marx, 1973:497), but offers no evidence in support of his claim that capitalist relations of production were absent until the late eighteenth century. This is a notoriously complex question, turning on how we differentiate the agrarian, commercial, industrial, and capitalist revolutions from one another. If we restrict our attention to the issue of wage-labor, however, it is clear from my review of the evidence in the last chapter that by mid-century wage-laborers constituted a very considerable proportion of the population. Locke was unquestionably writing in an environment in which wage-labor existed in significant quantities.

However we finally evaluate Locke's intentions in writing the "turfs" and "freeman" passages, preoccupation with internal analysis of the texts should not blind us to the fact that Locke is articulating a view of labor in which (1) x freely contracts (2) a capacity that becomes (3) y's for (4) a limited period of time to (5) perform a specified function that (6) creates wealth which (7) belongs to y. He thus states all the central ideas of the classical conception of wage-labor, whatever he subjectively intended. This formation undeniably contributed to the creation and reproduction of an ideology in which the

69 Thus while Dunn (1969:216) notes that Macpherson is incorrect in claiming that Locke *favored* unlimited accumulation, he also observes that "[t]here is every reason to believe that Locke supposed that a man in a non-political situation had a right to the whole produce of his labour. . . . There is every reason to suppose that he believed that the relations of capitalist production and monetary exchange provided the basis for the emergence of vast but altogether just differentials in the ownership of property."

commodification of individuals could appear both rational and desirable. It is in this sense that the spirit of Macpherson's argument is vindicated, albeit against a good deal of the letter of his own formulations.

Macpherson's account suffers from an additional inadequacy. His attempt to straitjacket Locke's argument to conform to his "possessive individualist" model leads him to miss some aspects of it significant for the subsequent history of liberalism. He misses the subtle way in which Locke gave the liberal ideology of individual rights its conservative flavor. No implicit denial of the rationality of the working class excluded that class from the political system. The double move of first charging the state with the responsibility of sustaining a negative libertarian society, and, second, of translating the ideal of liberty into the practice of toleration, a substantial (but by no means isolated) departure in the religious and political conflicts of Restoration England, effectively functioned in the long term to defuse the potentially much more radical idea of participatory democracy.[70] This negative libertarian view had the additional consequence of making it possible to conceive of all activities relating to the production, reproduction, and consumption of wealth as fundamentally private, engaged in for individual benefit, but with beneficial social consequences for all.

Macpherson's anachronistic model makes him insensitive to the special role played by the state in the commercial and early industrial revolutions, in fostering market practices at home and abroad, which Locke and his contemporaries took for granted. The full significance of this will become evident in Chapters 4 and 5, where we consider in more detail some of the changing realities behind the myth of the minimal state.

Macpherson, in his quickness to impute contradictions to Locke's argument without making an attempt to recover the intellectual context in which it was written, fails to perceive why Locke saw no contradiction between a rationalist theory of objective interests and a "subjective" theory of rights. These were reconciled, as for Hobbes, by a creationist view of

70 For an account of radical democratic movements in the Civil War and after, see Hill (1972).

knowledge pregnant with ideological significance. Once negative libertarian relationships have been portrayed as natural, embodied in and dictated by the laws of nature, a theory of objective interests requiring that the state be comfortable to those laws amounted to a rational imperative for the state to foster and maintain those social relationships. Locke, therefore, provided no less than a natural-law justification for a capitalist state.

Thus far I have sought to show in some detail the emergence and early consolidation of the liberal ideology of individual rights at the hands of the seventeenth-century English contract theorists. In examining the core components of their accounts of rights, I have tried to show how these ideas arose and what their consequences were for the emerging liberal rights tradition. They were yet to go through several metamorphoses, some of which we will examine, and other new ideas were yet to be incorporated. Much of this core, however, would prove to be very hardy and would shape the language of liberal politics of the future. It has been customary to argue that at the heart of this discourse was the idea of possessive individualism deriving from the innovative view of man as the proprietor of his capacities embodied in the workmanship metaphor. My analaysis has confirmed a modified version of this, although it is only a part of the story: it refers mainly to the *substance* of the rights defended by these writers. By way of summing up I conclude with some observations about the other three terms at the core of this political ideology.

There is an important respect in which the subject of rights, the idea of a person, embraced by these writers is a Cartesian idea. Since Hobbes and Locke were, for different reasons, hostile to substantial components of Descartes' philosophy, and since we are all taught as freshman philosophers that there is a basic division between the empiricism of Locke, Berkeley, and Hume and the rationalism of Descartes, Leibniz, and Spinoza, it will be necessary to specify this with some care. These writers' accounts are basically Cartesian in the commitment to the beliefs that the individual's will is the cause of his actions, and that every individual has decisive authority over his will because he has privileged access to the contents of

144

his own mind. The metaphor of "the ghost in the machine," attacked by Gilbert Ryle in *The Concept of Mind,* is an undeniable part of Locke's theory of rational individual reflection. Despite his mechanistic behaviorism and his opposition to Cartesian essentialism, Hobbes, too, embraced the Cartesian view of the subject of rights, as Ryle observed.[71] The model of action became intentional action and only the agent could be said to know his intentions with absolute certainty. Absolute certainty was the hallmark of genuine knowledge, an idea that also originates with Descartes.[72] Hobbes and Locke embraced this notion of the subject of rights for different reasons. Hobbes feared the masses and recognized that any viable political system would have to appeal to the interests of the "overmighty subject" who was to be the stuff of the politics of the future.[73] Such appeals could only be successful, however, if each individual could be convinced that the Leviathan would preserve his or her individual interests. For Locke the idea of privileged access has two sources. First there is his Protestant view of the relationship between man and God, which makes individual assent the defining characteristic of authentic religious experience. Hence the core of every man's soul "belongs unto himself" and "true and saving religion consists in the inward persuasion of the mind" (Locke, 1979:186–7; 173). Second, there is Locke's broader rationalist appeal to all to consent to his political arguments, on the grounds that these are rationally compelling. Thus, if anyone can reveal errors in his reasoning, "I promise him either to Recant my mistake, upon fair conviction; or to answer his Difficulties" (Locke, 1963:173ff).

Thus, for very different reasons, Hobbes and Locke defended egalitarian conceptions of rationality, generating contempt for authority and making the individual sovereign over

71 On Locke's absorption of the Cartesian view of the self, see Ryle (1949:159). For his account of the failure of Hobbes's argument to transcend the view of the mind as an internal theater inside the body, see ibid.(327–30).
72 For an account of the influence of these Cartesian ideas on early Enlightenment thought, see Rorty (1979:136ff).
73 In this regard it is interesting to note, with Tuck (1979:139–42), that despite Descartes' un-Hobbesian political psychology, several influential Dutch Cartesians adopted substantial elements of his political philosophy, and saw it as consistent with their radically voluntarist conceptions of free will.

his knowledge and actions. This view, with the workmanship model, gives individual rights their distinctively modern and secular character. It opens the way to retaining the basic workmanship metaphor that confers asymmetrical rights on the agent or maker, and shedding God from the picture. So long as rights were ultimately derived from man's relationship with God this could not be done. Once they became a function of intentional action, and it was additionally held that man is autonomously capable of such action, God became superfluous to the argument. Even for Locke the legitimacy of religious institutions was a function of the voluntary actions of individuals.

Although the consequences of this secularization were not worrisome to Hobbes, we saw that they were to Locke, who felt it necessary to place some limitations on the autonomy of individual action. This generated the proscription of various activities via the distinction between liberty and license, a deeply problematical move, reducing ultimately to an undefended assertion about man's rational natural interests. Locke wanted to say that man is free to act autonomously and so create entitlements for himself within the limits set by the law of nature or will of God. As God's creation, man cannot violate His intentions. Deciding what these are in practice, however, is arbitrary. Locke argues against Filmer in the *First Treatise,* for instance, that a father does not own his son because in the act of procreation it is God's intention that is critical – He merely uses adult human beings to achieve His ends. Yet in the act of making inanimate objects it is man's intention that is critical, conferring rights of exclusive dominion on the maker. This kind of assertion cannot withstand serious analysis. Obviously both procreation and, say, cutting turfs, can be done with varying degrees of intentionality. Locke argues that a father does not fashion the intricacies of the child, but simply acts out the sexual desire implanted in him by God, but it might equally be argued that in a complex division of labor any given agent, in making something, will employ tools and materials he did not and typically could not make himself. Some are the "waste" of God; others are made by other people with their specialized capacities and abilities. It is thus arbitrary to say that in this latter case the last human maker has a right of exclusive dominion but in the case of procreating he does not. One could easily construct an argument of the kind Locke constructs against Filmer's claim that parents own their children, showing that we do not in fact make the commodities we seem to make because our making them presumes the actions of others in the social division of labor. This is the standard socialist objection to liberal theories of individual ownership, a point worth noticing parenthetically. The principle "from each according to his ability to each according to his work" does not question the view that making confers ownership: it rests on a competing analysis of who "really" makes.[74] This may be one reason why the labor theory of value could not survive in its classical form in the mainstream of the liberal rights tradition. It made that tradition intrinsically vulnerable to immanent attack. Leaving aside Locke's arbitrary limitations to the making principle, Hobbes and Locke both clearly embrace it and regard the extra-political individual as the "basic unit of making" in all significant matters relating to wealth and politics in civil society. This view would become axiomatic to virtually all liberal rights talk in the future.

Hobbes and Locke also made decisively innovative moves as far as the basis for rights is concerned. Whatever else natural law is for them both, we have seen that it has a strong utilitarian component, generating maxims for the rational realization of exogenous goals by private individuals. In both their arguments law sheds its historical character (again, for very different reasons) and becomes a kind of prudential calculus for civil interaction. In my view, that classical utilitarianism has its roots in the seventeenth-century rights tradition in this way is the most important and perhaps least noticed argument in Macpherson's book, though he does misidentify its precise roots in their writings.

Both Hobbes and Locke rest their theories of the purposes of rights on a view of human desires which importantly equates wants with needs into an operational concept of effective demand. This provides the conceptual basis for a plural-

---

74 This is not true of Marx's vision of a utopian communist society that would function by the principle from each according to his ability to each according to his *need*.

ism of goals, but not a relativism of goals of the type prevailing in liberal ideology since the late eighteenth century. The
former could only be transformed into the latter after shedding the theory of objective interest embedded in early empiricist views of moral science, thus facilitating the rise of emotivism and the decline of subjective theories of rights into
"mere" subjectivism.

Part III
The modern arguments

4

The neo-classical moment

I. INTRODUCTION

John Rawls and Robert Nozick have been so discoursed upon that one might reasonably wonder whether everything worth saying about them has not been said. What justification can be offered for here devoting two chapters to their arguments? It is of considerable interest, however, that they have achieved such prominence in the liberal tradition. A major part of our enterprise is to understand the tenacity of the liberal ideology of individual rights, to explain its historical persistence despite the intellectual difficulties critics have found in its various formulations. If it is true that the arguments of Rawls and Nozick face serious difficulties that have long been known to attend rights-based contract theories, the question arises as to why they have been so influential. Not only have they provoked a massive secondary literature that has worked over virtually every aspect of their arguments, not only have they acted as catalysts for the propounding of alternative liberal theories of right and justice by Galston, Dworkin, Ackerman, Barry, Walzer, and many others, but both have been influential outside the academy on both sides of the Atlantic – a rare achievement for a living philosopher in any age. Rawls's theory is frequently invoked in jurisprudential argument[1] and Nozick has been hailed as the principal philosophical protagonist for conservative libertarianism.[2]

1 See, for instance, Parker (1979:269–95), and, for a comprehensive annotated bibliography of writings by and about Rawls, Wellbank et al. (1982). This has some 2511 entries covering all fields and gives brief summaries of the contents of each entry.
2 For examples of his influence outside the academy, see "The Inquisitive Robert Nozick," interview by Robert Asahina, *New York Times* (September 20, 1981), section 7; "If Inequality is Inevitable what can be Done About It?" Interview of Nozick, Bell, and Tobin by Anthony Lewis, *New York Times* (January 3, 1982), section 4; and

Although others, such as Friedrich Hayek, have for several decades advanced arguments similar to Nozick's on many particulars,[3] he has formulated a defense of this view unparalleled in its foundational comprehensiveness.

The novelty with which Rawls and Nozick formulate their arguments accounts to some extent for their influence. We will see, however, that many aspects of their claims are neither especially novel nor lucidly argued. (It is worth pointing out parenthetically that many brilliant works of political philosophy go unnoticed for centuries and some, presumably, forever.) The explanation I offer for their influence is that, Kantian arguments notwithstanding, their two theories lock into, make use of, and function to legitimate the two dominant socioeconomic views of our time. Nozick falls squarely into the tradition of neo-classical economics, which is traceable, via Adam Smith, to the English political and economic writers of the seventeenth century, but which takes on its modern form with the rise of marginalism and in particular Pareto's *Manual of Political Economy*. Nozick's ideological impact, I will argue, derives mainly from the fact that it appeals to, and offers what appears to be a cogent philosophical justification for, this tradition. The situation with Rawls is more complex and can be summed up by saying that his is the natural response of a liberal who has read Pigou and Keynes seriously. He appeals to those who believe in the desirability, efficiency, and justice of capitalist markets, recognize they may not always function well and may generate serious inequities for some, and want to find efficient ways of addressing those inequities without altering the essential nature of the system. The ambiguous moral status of Keynesianism and welfare economics has always inhered in the fact that they appeal to the short-term interests of the disadvantaged (such as unemployed workers and firms on the verge of bankruptcy

---

"Why R. Nozick is doing much better than K. Marx," *The Times* (London, January 25, 1978). Rawls and Nozick have been interviewed or discussed in many popular and semipopular weeklies including the *New York Review of Books*, the *New York Times Book Review*, the *Times Literary Supplement*, *The Economist*, the *Spectator*, *The Nation*, *New Republic*, *The Listener*, the *Washington Post*, *The Observer*, and many others. For these and further references see Daniels (1975:xi–xxxiv) and Paul (1981).

3 See, for instance, Hayek (1960).

during recessions) by ensuring subsistence, creating employment, and expanding credit, yet these policies are geared in the medium term to sustaining the system which generates those very disadvantages – hence the ironic force of Joan Robinson's quip that the one thing worse than being exploited is not being exploited at all.

The Keynesian and neo-classical views of the world share major elements in common, but they also exhibit striking differences. In common they share their origins in classical political economy, large components of which were already present in embryonic form in the intellectual context in which Hobbes wrote. Both are thus grounded in the liberal tradition broadly conceived and make extensive use of much of its economic, political, and moral vocabulary. Both also have similar long-term prescriptive goals in that they are geared toward well functioning capitalist markets, taken certainly to be desirable and often to be inevitable. Keynesian macroeconomics and Pigouvian welfare economics diverged from the mainstream of neo-classical economics over how to achieve these goals. The Keynesian consumption function entailed that "rational" individual economic behavior must generate permanent inertial tendencies toward weak demand and disequilibrium[4] for the system as a whole. Pigou based his challenge to the neo-classical orthodoxy on a distinction between private and social product. He argued that individually "rational" economic behavior would have by-products or "externalities," incidentally felicitous or infelicitous to others; thus the collective results of competitive individual self-interested behavior may not, and often will not, be socially optimal. Private enterprise, "even when it operates under conditions of simple competition, often leads to a distribution of resources less favorable to the national dividend than some other possible distributions" (Pigou, 1960:381).[5]

---

4 I avoid the issue of whether or not Keynes held there could be equilibria below full employment. For our purposes it is sufficient that he held there could not be full employment equilibrium.
5 For a useful discussion of the rise of welfare economics in opposition to neo-classical price theory, and the subsequent rise of modern public choice theory in opposition to welfare economics, see Furniss (1978:399–410). For a more detailed discussion of Pigou's argument, see Blaug (1978:409–10).

Both Keynesian macroeconomics and Pigouvian welfare economics were thus born of an acceptance of the goals of neoclassical equilibrium theory but a rejection (for different reasons) of its axiomatic assumption that competitive individual behavior would produce Pareto-optimal collective results in practice.[6] The claims of these newer orthodoxies seemed to many to be vindicated by the events of the Depression, the persistence of poverty with growth, and the seemingly congenital tendency toward periodic recession—the "boom-bust" model of growth—that appeared to prevail throughout the capitalist world between the wars. Furthermore, the countercyclical prescriptions of Keynesian macroeconomics seemed to work. The New Deal and Keynesian eras ushered in astonishing levels of growth that did not begin seriously to slow until the late 1960s. Beliefs that indicative management and "fine-tuning" could produce a permanent state of balanced growth abounded—beliefs that would not seriously be questioned until the 1970s brought serious economic stagnation throughout the advanced industrial world.

Keynesian demand management also brought renewed political optimism based on a new social-democratic consensus, because this new "managed capitalism" had a human face. A by-product of its fiscal policies was the welfare state and its safety net that redressed the worst diseconomies and externalities of capitalist competition. Thus the mixed economy with an active state, attentive but subordinte to the needs of the market, could seem to many to be morally desirable and practically efficient, to effect the rights-utility synthesis in the face of market failure. Rawls's argument naturally falls into this broadly Keynesian vision, which explains its inspirational appeal to so many liberals and the belief among many who perceive difficulties with his particular formulations, that something like it must nonetheless be true and salvageable.

The New Right that has emerged on both sides of the Atlantic in recent years embraces much of the philosophy Nozick espouses in opposition to these Keynesian orthodoxies. Although Nozick's book was written after *A Theory of Justice,* and

6 For a useful discussion of the Keynesian revolution and the impact of Pigouvian economics on that revolution, see Blaug (1978:665–96).

was in part a response to it, his argument is both historically and logically prior. It is historically prior in that the neo-classical tradition to which it appeals and which it seeks to render philosophically coherent is older than the one in which Rawls's argument is best located. It is logically prior in that the Keynesian tradition resulted from a reaction against the perceived inadequacies of neo-classical equilibrium theory, and sought to achieve its goals by alternative institutional mechanisms. It will therefore be heuristically useful to examine *Anarchy State and Utopia* first.

II. NOZICK'S THEORY OF RIGHTS

The fundamental project of *Anarchy State and Utopia* is to describe a form of government that can win the uncoerced assent of every person in society. In tackling this problem Nozick revives the idea of the state of nature employed by Locke, rejecting the utilitarian and legal positivist traditions that have dominated much Anglo-American moral and political philosophy in the nineteenth and twentieth centuries. His core argument is that individuals in a Lockean state of nature would form what he refers to as a minimal state, the "night-watchman state of classical liberal theory, limited to the functions of protecting all its citizens against violence, theft, and fraud, and the enforcement of contracts" (1974:26). This would be accomplished without violating the rights of any individual: it represents the most extensive state that can command the unanimous assent of the citizenry. Locke employed the working assumption that government is legitimate until a majority comes to feel it has violated its fiduciary trust. Nozick, however, begins with a paramount assumption that every individual has and retains inviolable rights of exclusive dominion, which can in no circumstances be breached without his consent. Thus all political institutions, conceived of as coercive by definition, must command the unanimous assent of the governed, or—what amounts to the same thing analytically for Nozick—they must be brought into existence purely by voluntary transactions. From this standpoint a theory of unanimous consent must form the bedrock of a political philosophy.

155

At the theoretical center of Nozick's argument is a modified version of Locke's account of the state of nature. Nozick argues that its inherent inconveniences, which he paradigmatically understands to be the costs to individuals of continually enforcing their own rights, would lead them to form "mutual protection associations" to function like insurance companies to protect and enforce their clients' rights. The force these associations must employ is such that, considered as a commodity, it is a natural monopoly. One of the associations would therefore eventually become dominant, as the result of an "invisible hand" process depending on wholly voluntary transactions. The only exceptions to this are "independents" who do not choose to join any protective association, preferring instead to fend for themselves. The independents would be forced to join the dominant protective association and would be fully compensated for the rights violations this entailed. No more extensive state than this would emerge by either voluntary or legitimate compensatory means. "Out of anarchy," Nozick argues, "pressed by spontaneous groupings, mutual-protection associations, division of labor, market pressures, economies of scale, and rational self-interest there arises something very much resembling a minimal state or a group of geographically distinct minimal states" (ibid.:16–17). Nozick conceives of this as the unique solution to the problem of legitimate government and his account is intended to have both causal-explanatory and moral force. The minimal state is the only state that would arise in such circumstances and the only one that can be morally justified. To this extent his voluntarist claim could be argued to rest on a naturalist foundation, although the hypothetical character of his argument militates against any very thoroughgoing naturalism.

The minimal state is not merely a satisficing solution to the problem of reconciling the existence of government with the preservation of individual rights. Nozick conceives of the kind of society that would result, were it fully implemented, as the utopian best of all possible worlds. Hence his impassioned conclusion: "How *dare* any state or group of individuals do more [than the minimal state]. Or less" (ibid.:334).

i. The subject of rights

Who are these individuals and what is their natural condition such that they must form the minimal state? In order to understand why Nozick describes them and their agreements as he does, we must first attend to his account of the state of nature. The principal reason Nozick finds Locke's state of nature to be heuristically useful is that it is relatively benign, differing—as it does—from Hobbes's treatment of it as synonymous with the state of war. Although inconvenient because each has the right and need to enforce his own rights (necessitating many ineconomies of smallness and unnecessary transactions costs) it is a situation in which "people generally satisfy moral constraints and generally act as they ought" (Nozick, 1974:5). This analytical move enables Nozick to present what is really an argument against extensive government as though it were an argument against anarchism. By starting from "the best anarchic situation one reasonably could hope for" without being "wildly optimistic" (ibid.) he builds into his premises a view of life without government as inherently desirable. This lends credence to the subsequent claim that the less government there is the more closely will this idyllic situation be replicated in civil society.

There are, however, several respects in which Nozick's state-of-nature explanation differs markedly from Locke's. To begin with it is a *hypothetical* explanation. Although Nozick claims that the process he conjectures "might have arisen if native Americans had not been forced off their land and if some had refused to affiliate with the surrounding society of the settlers" (ibid.:54), it is clearly not intended to have straightforward historical-descriptive force. It is what Nozick refers to as a "fundamental potential explanation." In *Anarchy State and Utopia* and in *Philosophical Explanations* Nozick argues that an explanation of a realm of reality can be genuinely illuminating, though false, providing it could in principle be true; it is in this sense that his explanation is a "potential" one (ibid.: 6–9, 18–22; 1981:571ff). An explanation is "fundamental" for Nozick if it makes use of explanatory variables beyond the realm of what is to be explained; a paradigm case would be the type of invisible hand explanation employed by Adam Smith. Such explanations are contrasted with "straightforward" explanations that do not venture outside this realm — such as hidden hand explanations like conspiracy theories. Fundamental explanations are "more satisfactory" since they yield "greater understanding" of the realm in question. Nozick regards his own state of nature explanation as fundamental in the relevant sense because it makes use of an invisible hand process to explain the emergence of political society in terms of "nonpolitical factors." As he elaborates:

The more fundamental the starting point (the more it picks out basic, important, and inescapable features of the human situation) and the less close it is or seems to its result (the less political or statelike it looks), the better. (Nozick, 1974:19, 6–7)

The idea of a "potential" explanation is taken over from Hempel as "what would be the correct explanation if everything mentioned in it were true and operated" (ibid.:7), but even if not true it can be useful: a fundamental potential explanation can be defective in three different ways and still be useful. It can be law-defective, where the explanatory model employed does not correspond to reality as it should; it can be fact-defective, where the initial conditions it assumes are false but could have been true; or it can be process-defective, where the "fundamental" process (the particular invisible hand process described, for instance) could have but did not occur. "State-of-nature explanations of the political realm *are* fundamental potential explanations of this realm and pack explanatory punch and illumination even if incorrect. We learn much by seeing how the state could have arisen, even if it didn't arise that way" (ibid.:7–9).

Although he does not say this, presumably Nozick assumes his explanation to be defective in all three respects: that the model was never instantiated, the initial conditions did not obtain, and the process did not occur. It is a purely hypothetical explanation of what might have happened (but did not) to people who might have been (but were not) via a process that could have occurred (but did not). Note too, that the realm to be "explained," the society governed by the minimal state, is also a hypothetical entity. This is an important, if unacknowledged, difference between Adam Smith's invisible hand explanation, or such explanations when employed, for instance, in biology, and his own account of the evolution of the minimal state. The former are explanations of actual entities (markets and organisms) which the scientist is trying to understand causally. Nozick's potential explanation is, however, of a potential entity as well. His interest is not in understanding how the actual American state or any other historical state developed, and there is thus a deep circularity to it. To say that state S would have arisen out of process P had it occurred, and then to describe process P as generating state S is to say nothing beyond the potential realm at all. Thus Nozick's state of nature has a very different ontological status than Locke's. Locke's was held to have been a condition that had existed historically, and to which men could return. This is not a surprising difference if we bear in mind the historical contexts in which these theories were constructed. Locke wrote at a time when the entire legal and political apparatus had collapsed once in his lifetime, was successfully declared to be illegal, and shaken from top to bottom a second time. In that context to consider a state of nature as an actual entity, relevant to understanding the political world, made a certain amount of sense. Developments of that political order are not on the agenda in the capitalist democracies in the late twentieth century, however. It is hardly surprising that the idea of the state of nature can only plausibly be revived in this hypothetical form.

If Nozick's state of nature is radically different from Locke's, so are the individuals who inhabit it. Nozick does not explain the emergence of individual property rights of exclusive dominion (which Locke derived from his labor theory of value and theory of positive community in the state of nature, both unavailable to Nozick). He takes these as axiomatic in his description of the state of nature as a flourishing (if comparatively inefficient) negative libertarian society, with a market-based division of labor, money, entrepreneurs, and businesses. Thus "[s]ome people will be *hired* to perform protective functions, and some entrepreneurs will go into the business of selling protective services" (ibid.:13). Nozick even takes Locke to task for claiming that any agreement was necessary for the institution of money (ibid.:18).

Isolated individuals in this state of nature are thus the subjects of all legitimate rights for Nozick. Isolated individuals are the subjects of all meaningful moral predicates:

[T]here is no *social entity* with a good that undergoes some sacrifice for its own good. There are only individual people, different individual people, with their own individual lives. Using one of these people for the benefit of others, uses him and benefits the others. Nothing more. (Ibid.:32–3)

Nozick acknowledges the inherently problematical status of natural law in traditional natural rights arguments and is cognizant of the difficulties attending the separation of right from law that we examined in Chapters 2 and 3. He nonetheless adopts a radical version of the negative libertarian view of rights as spheres surrounding individuals. "A line (or hyperplane) circumscribes an area in moral space around an individual" (ibid.:10, 56, 57), he argues, and there are no circumstances in which this line can be breached without the relevant individual's consent. This is his view of rights as "side constraints" on actions, as contrasted with the "end-state" or "patterned" conceptions embodied in conventional utilitarianism, all brands of egalitarianism, Rawls's difference principle, and the standard distributive principles employed in welfare economics. Any principle that declares some distribution in advance to be desirable is patterned in Nozick's sense, and such patterns can be—and typically will be—upset by the voluntary actions of individuals.[7] Patterns can thus only be implemented and sustained via redistributive actions that violate individual rights. Taxation, for instance, is illegitimate—it is a form of forced labor. Nozick's rights as side-constraints are held to be unique in that they specify no pattern or outcome and hence involve no redistribution and no rights-violations in any conceivable circumstances:

7 As in the Wilt Chamberlain example (ibid.:161–4).

The moral side constraints upon what we may do, I claim, reflect the fact of our separate existences . . . that no moral balancing act can take place among us; there is no moral outweighing of one of our lives by others so as to lead to a greater overall *social* good. There is no justified sacrifice of some of us for others. This root idea . . . underlies the existence of moral side constraints. (Ibid.:33)

Nozick rejects out of hand as "gimmicky" all possible attempts to restate his side-constraint view in end-state terms (ibid.:29n), although this claim is vulnerable in its own terms. The end-state formulation of Nozick's principle is that the class of distributions produced by voluntary transactions is the finite class of "legitimate" distributions. More strictly, given a distributive status quo *A*, distributions that are Pareto-indifferent, Pareto-superior or Pareto-optimal with respect to *A* are legitimate; distributions that are Pareto-undecidable or Pareto-inferior with respect to *A* are illegitimate. Without this "end-state" assumption his principles of compensation, retribution, and rectification of past injustices could not even be stated, because by definition they involve a move from a distribution not indifferent to or northeast of *A* to a distribution that is. Some implications of this will concern us in more detail when we examine Nozick's conception of free action in section II(iii) of this chapter. For the present note that, unlike Locke, Nozick offers no account of how and why these exclusive private rights exist. The question therefore arises as to why they should be conceived of in this way. On this point Nozick makes an intuitive appeal to a version of Kant's categorical imperative, claiming that his own view of rights as side-constraints is the only political principle that treats persons as ends rather than means (1974:30ff).

There are several difficulties with this and Nozick is clearly aware of some of them. It is not clear, to begin with, that his rights as side-constraints do preserve the categorical imperative.[8] There are many possible actions that do not violate Noz-

8 As has often been argued in relation to Rawls (see, for example, Wolff, 1977:112ff), it may be that no substantive political principle can be shown never to violate the categorical imperative. The implications of this more general point are taken up in Chapters 5 and 6.

ick's injunction but do violate any reasonable interpretation of Kant's dictum. The case Nozick considers is sexual leering. "In getting pleasure from seeing an attractive person go by," he asks rhetorically, "does one use that other solely as a means? Does someone so use an object of sexual fantasies?" (ibid.:32). There are some circumstances in which the answer would be affirmative, but to this possibility Nozick responds that it may not even be clear who is using whom (ibid.:337n3). This does not, however, bear on the question of whether or not violation of Nozick's injunction is a nonnecessary but sufficient condition for the violation of the categorical imperative, the most plausible reconstruction of his claim. His solution is to claim that "[t]hese and related questions raise very interesting issues for moral philosophy; but not, I think, for political philosophy. . . . Political philosophy is concerned only with *certain* ways that persons may not use others; primarily physically aggressing against them" (ibid.). It can be argued that such activities as sexual leering are intensely political, that they express and reinforce whole systems of power relationships that place women in subservient roles. In refusing to consider this sort of argument Nozick is adopting an exceedingly narrow implied definition of politics. Physical coercion is monopolized by the state and political activities are thus seen as those activities performed by or mediated through the state. Consequently, for Nozick, there can be no political relationships in the state of nature or in civil society beyond the legitimate purview of the state. Hence the "fundamental question of political philosophy . . . is whether there should be any state at all" (ibid.:4). All forms of economic and social and cultural coercion that are not the direct result of the repressive political apparatus of the state are assumed to be irrelevant to political theory. Even in the case where state action is at issue, it appears that only state actions, not failures to act, can be genuinely coercive to individuals. If the categorical imperative were to be taken seriously as a basis for a political theory, it would have to account for those political relationships exercised outside of – as well as through – the state, and for coercive powers exercised as a result of the state's failure to act in certain circumstances.

If politics is conceived this broadly, a principle like the categorical imperative, as Nozick interprets it, could not consistently be applied to political life. It is not obvious that we should therefore revise our conception of politics rather than abandon the categorical imperative. The categorical imperative is problematical for Nozick even within the limits of his own conception of politics. If political authority, unless assented to, is conceived of as violating individual autonomy by definition, it would seem to follow, as Robert Paul Wolff argues in *In Defense of Anarchism,* that no form of institutionalized political authority can be justified because it will inevitably violate the autonomy of some. Wolff contends that in principle unanimous direct democracy, wherein "every member of the society wills freely every law which is actually passed" (1970:22ff), is a solution to the conflict between authority and autonomy. This argument may appear to be similar in structure to Nozick's with the difference that Nozick could claim that every member of the society would "will freely" the institutions comprising the minimal state (leaving aside, for the present, the issue of how he might set about establishing this). Closer inspection of Wolff's formulation, however, reveals that a unanimity rule for passing legislation does not insure the Kantian autonomy of all will be preserved. On the contrary, it guarantees that the autonomy of some will be violated unless there is unanimous agreement among all members of society on every political issue. If a unanimous direct democracy were divided on whether or not to provide welfare payments to the indigent, for instance, in circumstances where the status quo is such that no welfare is provided, unanimity could not be respected. Once the welfare proposal was voted on, revealing the community's division, the unanimity rule would require that the proposal be rejected. This, too, however, violates unanimity because, as the vote has just indicated, there is no unanimity for not providing welfare either. This is a perfectly general result, in principle applicable no less to the writing of constitutions than to the provision of welfare or to any other legislation. Only by adopting a notion of "passing legislating" arbitrarily biased toward the status quo can Wolff, Buchanan and Tullock (1962), Nozick, and the other libertarian defenders of unanimity argue that it preserves individual autonomy. Unanimity *as a decision rule* has no unique properties as far as preserving Kantian autonomy is concerned, except under highly artificial assumptions about the difference between action and inaction. Moreover, these various libertarian formulations do clear violence to Kant's original argument. The categorical imperative does not hold that we should never use a person as a means (Kant rightly saw that we inevitably must). His "Formula of the End in Itself" reads: "[a]ct in such a way that you always treat humanity, whether in your own person or in the person of any other, never simply as a means, but always at the same time as an end" (Kant, 1948:96). We must never treat a person *exclusively* as a means, but always remember that he or she has an autonomous will – which is something quite different. It entails neither Nozick's thesis nor Wolff's claim that no political (or other power-wielding) institutions can be justified.

Nozick nonetheless holds that his version of the principle precludes treating peoples' abilities and talents as resources for others (1974:28–33ff). Why this injunction is held to capture the genuine character of human freedom and ought to be respected is not entirely clear and will be considered in detail in section II(iii) of this chapter. Nor is it clear that the means by which individuals attain their abilities and talents are not relevant to deciding on the senses in which they might legitimately own them. There is no sense in Nozick that individuals' capacities might be functions of the social division of labor, and even if they are, he would consider this morally irrelevant. The individual is proprietor of his capacities and hence the subject of asymmetrical rights of exclusive dominion, as he is for Locke, once society has advanced beyond subsistence and money has been introduced. Nozick's man, however, is not a possession as Locke's man is God's possession. Consequently, it is difficult to see how Nozick's men are constrained by any exogenous moral requirements, why they should, as Nozick claims, "satisfy moral constraints and generally act as they ought" (1974:5). From Nozick's premises, we should expect Hobbesian, not Lockean, natural men – at best indifferent to others and more likely hostile to them, bound by nothing except their own wills and desires.

ii. The substance of rights

In contrast to defenders of "patterned" conceptions of distributive justice, Nozick refuses to place any limitations other than Pareto superiority on distributive outcomes. The former are used to evaluate end-states, whereas he describes his own as historical: if the initial conditions are just and the procedures voluntary, the outcome is just by definition:

What each person gets, he gets from others who give it to him in exchange for something, or as a gift. In a free society, diverse persons control different resources, and new holdings arise out of the voluntary exchanges and actions of persons. There is no more a distributing or distribution of shares than there is a distributing of mates in a society in which persons choose whom they shall marry. . . . Whatever arises from a just situation by just steps is itself just. (Ibid.:149–51)

The intuitive idea behind this, familiar enough in the neo-classical tradition, is appealing because it appears to reconcile deontological considerations of right with utilitarian efficiency. Each individual's autonomy is preserved because his consent is necessary for every transaction involving his resources. The outcomes are held to be efficient on the grounds that people will engage in voluntary transactions with one another until a Pareto-optimal situation, where mutual benefits are no longer possible through exchange, has been reached.

Nozick divides his account of justice in holdings into three parts: an account of the original acquisition of holdings, a principle of justice in transfer, and a principle of rectification of injustice in holdings. A satisfactory account, he persuasively argues, must deal with all three of these.[9] He explicitly claims not to have developed a fully worked-out account of justice in holdings. He nonetheless has much to say concerning it that illuminates his core assumptions about the substance of rights.

On the subject of acquisition he returns to Locke's state of nature. Nozick is obviously uncomfortable with any labor the-

9 In any theory the third will in significant essentials be determined by the first two. Nozick's account of it (which generates ingenious ruminations about punishment and retribution) need not, therefore, detain us here.

ory of value and he has some fun at the expense of what he considers Locke's formulation of it (Nozick, 1974:174–5). He opts instead for what is actually a Grotian view of acquisition in a negative community in the state of nature, where everything in common is open to all takers. He nonetheless tacks on Locke's (second) proviso that there be enough and as good left in common for others, although it is not clear what basis he has for doing this once the remainder of Locke's theory of acquisition has been jettisoned. Nozick's (incorrect) interpretation of the proviso is that appropriation of an unowned object should not worsen the situation of others (ibid.:175).[10] As we saw in Chapter 3, Locke's second proviso requires only that no one actually starve. People may be made worse off in absolute or relative terms without the proviso being violated. In defining the proviso more robustly, and simultaneously maintaining that a market system will preclude its violation following the institution of conventional property, Nozick is making more extensive assumptions about the benign distributive effects of market exchanges than did Locke.

Nozick takes his formulation of the proviso as axiomatic. He acknowledges (ibid.:175–8) that establishing whether or not the proviso has been violated will involve (probably unverifiable) counterfactuals, but this in no way leads him to qualify his view that the road to its nonviolation is through unregulated markets:

Is the situation of persons who are unable to appropriate (there being no more accessible and useful unowned objects) worsened by a system allowing appropriation and permanent property? Here enter the various familiar social considerations favoring private property: it increases the social produce by putting means of production in the hands of those who can use them most efficiently (profitably); experimentation is encouraged, because with separate persons controlling resources, there is no one person or small group whom someone with a new idea must convince to try it out; private property enables people to decide on the pattern and types of risks they wish to bear, leading to specialized types of risk bearing; private property protects future persons by leading some to hold back re-

---

10 For a discussion of Nozick's misinterpretation of Locke's theory of property in general and of the proviso in particular, see Drury (1982:28–41).

sources from current consumption for future markets; it provides alternative sources of employment for unpopular persons who don't have to convince any one person or small group to hire them, and so on. (Ibid.:177)

This entire account of justice in acquisition rests on the empirical belief that the operation of capitalist markets is a sufficient condition for legitimate appropriation. "I believe that the free operation of a market system will not actually run afoul of the Lockean proviso. . . . Indeed, were it not for the effects of previous *illegitimate* state action, people would not think the possibility of the proviso's being violated as of more interest than any other logical possibility" (ibid.:182). Nozick acknowledges this to be an empirical claim, but does not appear to perceive this as entailing any need to present arguments or evidence in its defense. Thus we see that the benign assumptions about the productivity effects of private accumulation implicit in Locke's discussion of the substance of rights become explicit in Nozick's. Locke acknowledged the need to offer arguments and evidence in defense of the empirical views he held (the validity of his arguments being another matter). Nozick treats them as self-evident.

Nozick's account of "fundamental" explanations[11] arouses skepticism toward this standard neo-classical view, both as it relates to the preservation of individual rights and as it relates to efficient outcomes. Nozick's account of justice in holdings is what he referred to as a "straightforward" explanation (ibid.:18–22). By his own reasoning one might reasonably question whether there is not a "fundamental" explanation which would yield "greater understanding" of the realm of voluntary exchange. One might notice, for instance, that the voluntary actions of individuals can have consequences malicious for themselves, of which they may be unaware and which they may be unable to foresee. Individuals may inadvertently create a monopoly in a commodity for which there is high inelasticity of demand by buying, in the short term, only from the most efficient firm. Once this monopoly is established it may increase prices, and because capital-intensity in

11 Nozick (1974:6ff). This view is discussed in section II(i) of this chapter.

the relevant industry may well have increased to the point where entry costs are prohibitive, no other firm can enter the market. (Other exogenous factors could easily be imagined that would produce a comparable result.) A more "fundamental" and "satisfying" account would refer not merely to the voluntary decisions of individuals to buy the best product at the cheapest price in the initial situation; it would look "beyond the realm" being explained, in Nozick's terminology, at the process as a whole and the broader structural result, and evaluate that in terms of the initial situation – in this case the inadvertently frustrated goals of the original consumers. Presumably Nozick finds it unnecessary to consider this type of case because he believes that in practice unregulated markets do not generate monopolies. In his discussion of the monopoly of force necessary for the formation of the minimal state he argues that this commodity is unique in that the nature of the good requires that it be a monopoly. In other circumstances monopoly would not arise "without the government intervention that . . . creates and maintains it" (ibid.:17). This large assumption, contradicted by much empirical work on industrial concentration throughout the capitalist world,[12] reflects Nozick's benign assumption that unregulated capitalist markets function efficiently and in equilibrium. His empirical beliefs lead him to offer a "straightforward" explanation and to presume there is no more "fundamental" explanation that might lead us to question the justice in holdings achieved under the single constraint of voluntary exchange.

Nozick's account of justice in transfer is complicated because he must sanction a compensation principle that both gets the independents into the dominant protective association and ensures that no more extensive state than the minimal state can arise. Several commentators have observed it is dubious that Nozick achieves either of these goals and certain that he does not achieve both. His compensation argument inevitably involves an implicit interpersonal comparison of utilities (a

12 For a good review of the evidence on concentration in Western Europe, Japan, and the United States, see the recent report of the Committee of Experts on Restrictive Business Practices for the OECD (OECD, 1979). See also Shapiro and Kane (1983:13–19).

"paternalistic" judgment in violation of his side constraints). If we pass over this problem and grant the compensation principle, there is no compelling reason why it cannot be employed in defense of a considerably more extensive state than Nozick desires.[13] His quite elaborate discussion nonetheless merits a closer look, for it reveals much about his assumptions of interest from our point of view.

To begin with, why does the compensation principle concern Nozick? Why must he take the "independents" so seriously and thus make his whole argument evidently vulnerable? We have seen that the paradigm case of justice in transfer for Nozick is the (unanimous and voluntary) Pareto-superior exchange. He regards people in the state of nature as exclusive proprietors of their capacities and assets, as bearers of Lockean asymmetrical rights of exclusive proprietorship, without the natural-law constraints that for Locke both limited the scope of those rights and generated rational imperatives for the formation of civil society. An individual whose side constraints are overstepped thus requires consent. Nozick must therefore commit himself to a radical version of Pareto's non-comparable ordinal utilities.[14] Because his whole defense of the minimal state against a more extensive one turns on this view of free action, Nozick must take the independents seriously. He must show that they can be compensated into the dominant protective association, that they can be induced or otherwise made to join it without violations of their rights.

Nozick does not give a single exposition of his compensation argument, or indeed even a single argument. He offers several different arguments intended collectively to demonstrate that his view of compensation can be sustained.

The transactions costs argument. In Nozick's consideration of whether some apparent rights violations might be permissible on practical grounds he asks:

13 See for example Wolff (1981:77–104) and Holmes (1981:57–67).
14 It is true that Nozick says that his principle "uses measurement of utility on an interval scale" (1974:58), but he does not explain this. Presumably his rationale is that interval scales admit performance of arithmetic functions that he believes will be useful in his theory of punishment and might somehow be used to compare functions among individuals, but he nowhere explains how this can be done.

Shouldn't those who have not gotten their victim's prior consent (usually by purchase) [for a rights violation] be punished? The complication is that some factor may prevent obtaining this prior consent or make it impossible to do so. (Some factor other than the victim's refusing to agree.) It might be known who the victim will be, and exactly what will happen to him, but it might be temporarily impossible to communicate with him. Or it might be known that some person or other will be the victim of an act, but it might be impossible to find out which person. In each of these cases, no agreement gaining the victim's permission to do the act can be negotiated in advance. In some other cases it might be very costly, though not impossible, to negotiate an agreement. The known victim *can* be communicated with, but only by first performing a brain operation on him, or finding him in an African jungle, or getting him to cut short his six-month sojourn in a monastery where he has taken a vow of silence and abstinence from business affairs, and so on; all very costly. (Nozick, 1974:71–2)

Since unanimity is so critical for Nozick he must find a way around these issues. One would sometimes sanction violation with compensation, he argues, when communication with the relevant victim is impossible, because of "the great benefits of the act; it is worthwhile, ought to be done, and can pay its way." In the case where communication is not impossible but very costly, "the transaction costs of reaching a prior agreement" may be greater "than the costs of the posterior compensation process." Negotiated consent is unwise because it is inefficient: "Prohibiting such unconsented to acts would entail forgoing their benefits . . . [t]he most efficient policy forgoes the fewest net beneficial acts" (ibid.:72–3). The questions must necessarily present themselves: benefits for whom? Worthwhile for whom? Ought to be done for whom? Can pay its way at what price determined by whom? Nozick cannot appeal to the interests of society as a whole, for he has rejected the idea of an "overall social good," claiming without qualification that "no moral balancing act can take place . . . [t]here is no justified sacrifice of some of us for others" (ibid.:33). Efficient can only mean on at least as high an indifference curve for each party in the narrow Paretian sense. That cannot be deter-

mined, however, if one of the agents is not present. The doctrine of revealed preference cannot be applied if one of the
agents does not even know he or she is making an exchange,
or if the other does not even know who he or she is. Nozick
apparently presumes there *must be* rational solutions to these
transactions-costs problems. It may well be that unanimity
principles generate them willy nilly – that the problem is not
the man in the jungle but the principle of unanimity itself.[15] It
is a characteristic trait of contemporary deontological liberals
to believe that a just society is at least in principle possible, that
there has to be a theoretical solution to the problem of reconciling legitimate political authority with freedom or autonomy
as they understand it.[16]

The argument concerning productive and unproductive exchanges.
Nozick needs to distinguish compensation (unproductive)
from normal (productive) forms of exchange. He is most concerned with the individual who, by prior negotiation of the
rights violation might actually have raised his position on his
utility function somewhat, whereas if compensated without
such negotiations need only be restored to his original position. Let us say the state, to build a road, compulsorily pur-
chases my house for $80,000,[17] the minimal sum necessary to
make me at least as well off without the house. Had I known
these developments were imminent I might have negotiated a
sale for $85,000. In such cases the state should only pay
$80,000, Nozick argues, presumably to avoid the enormous
problems about counterfactuals he would otherwise confront
concerning what someone might have been able to do if he
were not moved down his utility function by the rights violation. Even if granted, however, this argument leaves unre-
solved all the critical questions that arose in relation to the
transaction costs argument as to how and by whom compensa-

---

15 Additional problems about unanimity are taken up in section II(iii) of this
chapter.
16 For an excellent illustration of this assumption at work, see Wolff (1970:77–8).
We will see the same presumption at work in Rawls's argument in Chapter 5, and
we will subject it to critical scrutiny in Chapter 6.
17 My example, not Nozick's.

tion is to be assessed. This distinction between productive and unproductive exchange is not without further difficulties.[18] Nozick believes a productive exchange is one wherein there is mutual gain or "market compensation;" an unproductive exchange leaves one party indifferent between the new situation and the old status quo and the other better off ("full compensation"). If *A* is planning a building that will block *B*'s view and *B* bribes him not to build it, that is a productive exchange, but if *A* merely pretends to plan the building in order to be bribed, it is unproductive. If a researcher discovers information harmful to another and is bribed not to publish it, this is unproductive and he "may not charge the best price he could get . . . [for] his silence" unless he happens to be someone "who *delights* in revealing secrets" in which case he "may charge differently" (ibid.:85–6n). Unless Nozick places some constraint on compensation he may face infinite demands from independents. There would be, however, immense difficulties in distinguishing the above cases from one another (he offers no procedure). Nor is the basic problem resolved of how to decide, and by what criteria, how much worse off the victim has been made and what would be required to restore him to his initial position.

The arguments from risk and fear. Nozick attempts, as a third strategy, to build an inertial bias toward compensation into his initial conditions by arguing that if the independents are *not* forced to join the dominant protective association, its members will pay a price in fear of the independents harming them or their property. If this argument is sustained, whatever other problems the compensation theory faces it would seem to be legitimate, for exogenous reasons, for the dominant protective association to force the independents to become members. Nozick argues:

Private wrongs are those where only the injured party need be compensated; persons who know they will be compensated fully do not

18 The history of classical and Marxian political economy from Smith down through the present is littered with unsuccessful attempts to distinguish productive from unproductive forms of economic activity. For useful, historically based accounts see Schumpeter (1978:628ff, and Dobb, 1973:42–43, 59ff, 60–61, 145).

fear them. Public wrongs are those people are fearful of, even though they know they may be compensated fully if and when the wrongs occur. Even under the strongest compensation proposal which compensates victims for their fear, some people (the nonvictims) will not be compensated for *their* fear. Therefore there is a legitimate public interest in eliminating these border-crossing acts. (Ibid.:67)

This argument shifts attention from the action performed by the dominant protective association in forcing the independent to join, with compensation, to the action performed by the independent in not joining. Its underlying logic requires some overriding public interest in not being fearful of independents, legitimating their forcible inclusion. The notion of uncompensated-for fear could otherwise quickly entail forcing people to do an infinite variety of things, once this negative definition of an action as not doing something that somebody else wants you to do is accepted. There can be no notion for Nozick of something being in the public interest unless it commands simple unanimity. He has already ruled out all theories of social entity and interest and clearly no principle of majority rule can be sanctioned by his rights-as-side-constraints. Unanimity is not at issue in this situation, however, where there is by definition at least one independent. In thus claiming that independents should forcibly be included Nozick is appealing to the concept of externality, which has far-reaching deleterious consequences for his argument. The idea that actions have external harmful consequences for others is unexceptionable, but it is impossible to argue from Nozick's neo-classical premises that the state should become involved in their mitigation, unless he gives up much else crucial for him to maintain. Elsewhere he explicitly rejects such appeals,[19] which cannot be surprising: the idea of externality requires not only interpersonal comparisons, but once appealed to it is

19 As in the section entitled "Having a say over what affects you" where it is explicitly claimed that "[o]thers have no right to a say in those decisions which importantly affect them that someone else . . . has the right to make," and that once such actions as stealing and physically assaulting others are excluded "[i]t is not clear that there are *any* decisions remaining about which even to raise the question of whether I have a right to a say in those that importantly affect me" (Nozick, 1974:270).

impossible either to hold that unregulated markets are by definition efficient, or to place merely "minimal" limits on the actions of the state. The extent of the state's redistributive actions will depend on the nature and extent of the real externalities it seeks to counteract. Pigou, for example, in adopting this notion in his *Economics of Welfare*, not only made utility comparisons to distinguish his private from social costs (the corollary of Nozick's private and public wrongs), but his analysis of "external" diseconomies resulted in injunctions for considerable redistribution via taxation and subsidies, to increase wage levels and employment.[20] Pigou's particular empirical analysis and the theory of social value on which it rested are not necessarily correct. However, if Nozick enters the realm of externalities in search of a workable theory of compensation, he is playing a different game by different rules and must give up much of the rest of his theory. Not only must he accept explicit interpersonal comparisons, he must also embrace all the troublesome implications of the view that unregulated markets do not produce Pareto-optimal outcomes. As it is, Nozick's selective use of the externality argument undermines many of his later empirical claims about the efficiency of unregulated markets.

The natural monopoly of force argument. Nozick attempts to justify compensation on the grounds that the commodity sold by the dominant protective agencies is a unique natural monopoly:

The worth of the product purchased, protection against others, is *relative*: it depends upon how strong the others are. Yet unlike other goods that are comparatively evaluated, maximal competing protective services cannot coexist; the nature of the service brings different agencies not only into competition for customers' patronage, but also into violent conflict with each other. Also, since the worth of the less than maximal product declines disproportionately with the number who purchase the maximal product, customers will not stably settle for the lesser good, and competing companies are caught in a declining spiral. (Nozick, 1974:17)

20 For discussion, see Blaug (1978:635ff).

The claim seems to be that the demand curve for purchasing protection is something like a step-function: unless everyone buys it from one company it has negligible value, but if they do, it suddenly becomes more valuable to those who value it. This also involves not only assumptions about the utility functions of all individuals being identical with respect to this good, but an additional "paternalistic" assumption that it is a good for everyone. It is presumably precisely this, however, that the hard-boiled anarchist, whom Nozick claims as his real protagonist, denies.[21] If it was a contingent truth that protection was both a natural monopoly and universally desired, this would raise a host of troublesome issues for Nozick concerning free riding. If everyone knew the contingent nature of this good, there would be massive incentives for not buying it, knowing full well that one could expect to be given it and paid into the bargain (at what price?). Nozick's few remarks about the free rider problem do not begin to address this issue.[22] It is difficult to see what he could say about it except that posturing and misrepresenting one's preferences are dishonest, and that people in the state of nature generally act as they ought. If this was the claim he would need a moral theory to back it up, which he does not supply. Nor is it intuitively evident that such a theory would mesh with the neo-classical theory of revealed preference via market transactions that Nozick invokes time and again against "paternalistic" theories.[23] The natural monopoly argument is thus self-defeating in that it requires interpersonal comparisons and raises a whole nest of problems related to the possibilities of free riding. It cannot therefore generate the kind of compensation argument Nozick requires.

Nozick recognizes that his various formulations of the compensation argument are less than watertight. In this connection he remarks that "we need not . . . state the principle exactly. We need only state the correctness of some principles,

---

21 For defense of this view against Nozick, see Holmes (1981:57–67).
22 These remarks (Nozick, 1974:94, 266–8) do not deal with the issue of compensation of independents.
23 I argue further, in section II(iv) of this chapter, that the theory of objective goods outlined in *Philosophical Explanations* cannot be used to this end either.

such as the principle of compensation" (ibid.:87). The question therefore arises whether there is perhaps some different compensation principle that *would* generate the result he requires.

Theories of compensation are of two principal kinds: those deriving from Paretian welfare economics that attempt to work only with ordinal utilities, and those deriving from Pigouvian welfare economics that explicitly employ intercomparable scales and distinctions between public and private costs and benefits. The first consists of a formidable series of theoretical attempts from Kaldor and Hicks to Samuelson to produce a principle that neither is self-contradictory nor introduces a hidden assumption of comparability. There is now a very wide consensus among welfare economists that this is not possible,[24] but we need not enter these thickets here. There is a clinching reason why, even if it could be done, it would not help Nozick. The issue addressed by the principles of Kaldor and Hicks, Scitovsky, and their progeny concerns hypothetical compensation. Their problem involved finding a way of discussing Pareto-undecidable outcomes that increased overall welfare. Intuitively: if an exchange occurs between A and B whereby A loses and B gains, but the gain to B is greater than the loss to A, it seemed plausible to say that the overall social product or welfare had increased. They wanted to do this, however, without invoking the whole Benthamite system of comparable additive utilities and its radically redistributive implications.[25] This felt need generated the claim that if B could compensate A for A's loss and still be better off than before the exchange, the total product had increased, even though no actual compensation occurred (otherwise we would be dealing with the normal case of productive exchange

24 An up-to-date and accessible discussion of these issues can be found in the chapter on general equilibrium and welfare economics in Blaug (1978:602–44).
25 If we commit both to comparability and to the principle of diminishing marginal utility, efficiency dictates radical downward distribution to absolute equality (Rae et al., 1981:136ff). Since it is basic to the entire neo-classical theory of marginal cost pricing that the principle of diminishing marginal utility be true, the only way out of this is to deny comparability. Other arguments against downward redistribution have been based on investment incentives, but these are notoriously difficult to apply and are, in any case, irrelevant to Nozick's argument for reasons that will be discussed.

covered by the Pareto principle). Now as Little and others have observed,[26] it is a curious notion of welfare that holds that if I take your assets, provided I could in principle (but do not in practice) pay you for them and still be better off, the welfare of both of us has increased. This is not a solution to Nozick's problem, since he requires that the independents actually receive "full compensation" (1974:84). Ordinalist welfare arguments are hypothetical by definition and cannot generate a theory of actual compensation. If Nozick went the whole way with the ordinalists he would have to embrace and justify this deeply implausible notion of welfare, as well as confront the formidable arguments of many economists showing that ordinalist compensation arguments do not work.

This leaves the Pigouvian theories that explicitly embrace some kind of cardinal scale. Whatever their theoretical difficulties and inevitable and explicit value-ladenness, it may be impossible for organized social and political life to proceed without them, as Furniss (1978:406–9) has persuasively argued. For Nozick, however, embracing the assumptions behind the Pigouvian notion of real external diseconomy would involve abandoning his account of rights-as-side-constraints, the centerpiece of his entire political theory. Once the Pigouvian notion is embraced there is no logical reason for stopping with the minimal state. A much more activist state than Nozick envisages could be justified on precisely the same grounds. Nozick needs something like Pigouvian conclusions from something like Paretian premises but the former are not entailed by the latter.

Nozick's account of justice in transfer, based on (strict neo-classical) productive exchange, undercuts his compensation argument and thus his invisible hand explanation of the rise of the minimal state.[27] Instead of confronting these difficulties and dealing with their implications, Nozick banks on the enormous prestige enjoyed by neo-classical microeconomics as the only "real" or "hard" social science. He can make it appear

26 Little (1950:84–116); Fishkin (1979:91–6).
27 It is worth adding here that none of these issues is addressed in *Philosophical Explanations*, and that in discussing his theory of punishment there he again invokes the notion of compensation, remarking parenthetically that the "details of the theory of compensation are not our concern here" (Nozick, 1981:363).

plausible to outline a rough argument and claim that the economists out there will sort out the details. Nozick embraces a radical version of the view of the substance of rights as the exclusive dominion of individuals. He fails to supply an account of compensation consistent both with his rights-as-side-constraints and the rise of the minimal state. The fact that he devotes so much theoretical energy to trying to render these diverse commitments mutually compatible underscores the extent of his commitment to the negative libertarian view. Nozick treats this view as axiomatic. In this he differs markedly from Locke. Locke's theory of conventional property presupposed a theory of positive community in the state of nature, a labor theory of value, and a theory of natural law. None of these is available to Nozick.

iii. The basis for rights

Nozick's rights, as were Locke's, are grounded in a conception of free action. Nozick recognizes, however, that in the absence of a doctrine of natural law, an ethics and politics based on the concept of freedom requires some account of its nature. Formulating a coherent account of the concept of free will must be a central task for Nozick. He remarks in *Philosophical Explanations* that he has "spent more time thinking about the problem of free will . . . than about any other philosophical topic except perhaps the foundations of ethics" (1981:293). The project of that work is largely devoted to rescuing the concept of free will from the various determinisms—evolutionary, sociobiological, physical, and psychological—that seem to Nozick most seriously to threaten it.[28] Nozick's conception of "the problem" of free will is itself revealing from our point of view. His concern is to rescue the idea of individual freedom from its "enemies" who "think it important to deny, for instance,

---

28 I do not claim to do full justice to all the intricacies of this very dense book; my attention is restricted to those arguments that shed light on his theory of rights. It is worth recording, however, that Nozick refers in it to *Anarchy State and Utopia* but does not reject or qualify any of the central arguments made there. He clearly intends his discussions of free will and the foundations of ethics to provide the moral foundations of his political theory, although he acknowledges that he has not made the connections explicit and that there might be some difficulties in trying to do so (Nozick, 1981:498–9n).

that we have free will, that we can do something because it is right, that we know reality, that we are anything other than a congery of physiochemical processes and properties" (ibid.: 444). Nozick defines an action as "an intentional doing arising out of a process of choice among alternatives" (ibid.: 304). His central question about freedom of action, which he repeats many times, is: how can a person freely perform an action "if his doing it was causally determined, eventually by factors originating before his birth, and hence outside his control?" (ibid.:291). He solves this problem by embracing an antireductionist view of explanation grounded in the claim that, just as the truth or falsity of a proposition is not itself a function of the causes which lead it to be asserted, so the fact that there may be true causal explanations of the genesis of our capacity to choose does not in itself entail that we cannot make genuinely free choices:

The question is not whether there will be evolutionary explanations of how consciousness, language, and self-consciousness arise and are selected for. The question is whether once these do arise by a blind process, they then operate and lead to some things unblindly. (Do percepts with concepts *stay* blind?) That there is an invisible hand explanation of our having our cognitive capacities does not mean there is an invisible hand explanation of my writing the contents of this book. (Ibid.:347)

The advent of consciousness opens up new possibilities in Nozick's view. It introduces the possibility that we may be able to comprehend the causal mechanisms that lead us to act as we do, and make decisions based on this knowledge as a result. This is reminiscent of Locke's claim, in Book 2, Chapter 11, of the *Essay,* that man's freedom lies in his capacity to suspend desire before the performance of an action, and that "during this suspension of any desire, before the will be determined to action, and the action . . . done, we have opportunity to examine, view, and judge of the good or evil of what we are going to do." For Locke "it is not a fault, but a perfection of our nature, to desire, will and act according to the last result of a fair examination" (1959, I:345). For Nozick, too, a free action "withstands knowledge of its own causes" (1981:349).

179

These considerations lead Nozick to a definition of free action in terms of self-conscious choice:

Let us say an act is in disequilibrium for a person if (a) he does (or wants to do) it, yet (b) if he knew the causes of his doing or wanting to do it, this knowledge would lead him not to do it, or not to want to. . . . When condition *a* is satisfied but *b* is not, the act is in equilibrium. . . . [I]f he knew the causes of his doing or wanting to do the act then he still would (want to) do it as much. (Ibid.:349)

Notice, however, that Nozick limits this account of free action severely by his narrow definition of an action as an intentional choice among alternatives. Leaving aside the many conceptual difficulties attaching to such notions of action,[29] in focusing exclusively on actions as choices among alternatives Nozick is bypassing the one kind of determinism he most needs to deal with. Those with misgivings about his view that free actions are best realized in capitalist markets, are not really concerned that a sociobiological explanation might show why a particular consumer made a particular choice q out of the class of options $\{p, q\}$. What is pregnant politically about the freedom or unfreedom of the choice is whether there might be some realistic alternative arrangement of society where his class of options in the relevantly similar situation might be $\{p, q, r, s\}$ such that he would, say, choose r over q. The agent might well know all this (as well as much other relevant causal information) and still want to pick q over p. His choice of q would satisfy Nozick's subjunctive condition for acting in equilibrium, but we may well (and so may the relevant agent) want to say that he did not choose q freely. Presumably this is the logic we have in mind when we wonder if an unemployed black who chooses a job as a bus-boy for half the minimum wage is really acting freely.[30] Hence a (non-trivial) unfree act may well "withstand knowledge of its causes."

It is undeniable that all meaningful choices are among options (it is doubtful that we can even make sense of the idea of

29 See, for instance, my discussion in Shapiro (1982:542–63).
30 Of course there are many additional complexities here concerning what counts as a realistic alternative array of options, whether *A* is aware of all his possible options, and if not, why not (and if so, why), and so on. But these are different issues.

definitions of "freedom" and "coercion" involve counterfactual reasoning when applied to specific instances, he can legitimately choose the one that suits his purposes, since competing views will face comparable difficulties. This is true only if we seek such general definitions to begin with, a point taken up in section III of this chapter. Without the assumption that the normal course of events is not itself coercive Nozick's rights-as-side-constraints cannot get off the ground. It amounts to less than an argument to hold this, however, on the grounds that it is too complicated to show it is not true, not least when it appears from the same premises it is equally too complicated to show it is.[32]

If this is Nozick's account of freedom, how might it give rise to the individual rights he defends? For Nozick, one necessary condition for attaining the good for humans, or "tracking best-ness," is acting in equilibrium. The other major necessary condition for any organism or entity is maximizing its "degree of organic unity," discussion of which is deferred to the next section. The notion of acting in equilibrium leads to accounts of "ethical push" and "ethical pull" that take account of man's capacity to act in equilibrium, to be a "self-choosing being." This is intended to generate an account having the force of the categorical imperative, if a somewhat different content. Because each person is a "value-seeking I" (that is, each person individually wants to track bestness by acting in equilibrium), the fundamental ethical principle is: "Treat someone (who is a value-seeking I) as a value-seeking I" (1981:462). More fully:

> The theory of the moral pull and the moral push come together in this way. Someone else's basic moral characteristic, being a value-seeking I, exerts a pull on me, a moral claim. I am to treat him as a value-seeking I, cueing and shaping my behavior to his being one, thereby responding to him qua value-seeking I. However, the only way I can respond to his basic moral characteristic in this way is by exercising my own. Responding to his characteristic and to the moral pull it exerts, draws upon my being a value-seeking I and the capacities associated with this. Lower capacities just cannot do an adequately subtle and nuanced job of response. (Nozick, 1981:517–8)

32 For more general discussion of related difficulties about status quo assumptions in public choice and welfare economics, see Rae (1975a).

For Nozick this "value-seeking I" is the unique solution to the tension between free will and objectively valid ethical judgments. Nozick's difficulty with Kant's deontology is that if genuine freedom consists in acting only out of reverence for the moral law, it is not clear in what sense our actions can really be free. " . . . [W]hy doesn't reverence for the moral law also show us to be passively bound? If because it reflects or encapsulates our nature, cannot that too bind us? In any case, couldn't one act equally autonomously from another motive?" (ibid.:355). Thus even if the moral law reflects our true nature, since we may not like our nature, or may not for other reasons want to act from it, observing the categorical imperative is inconsistent with genuine free choice.[33]

Nozick nonetheless argues that free will is objectively desirable and ought to be preserved. Thus the

> moral law must not only be given to ourselves and so chosen, it must be given by something that itself is chosen. Only what arises from a chosen essence will not bind. But if that essence is chosen, in what way is it inescapable? Can we have our cake and choose it too? There is one essence that would not bind: being a self-chooser. The fullest autonomy is had only by a being whose essense is self-choosing. (Ibid.:355)

A value-seeking I is someone who chooses to be self-choosing. Nozick avers that we must choose *this* with the force of a categorical imperative if we are *really* to be free. He makes the Sartrean point that since choosing not to choose is itself a choice, everyone chooses willy nilly to be a self-choosing being: we cannot escape our freedom because trying to do so is another manifestation of its presence.

Can this argument do the theoretical work Nozick requires of it? That we are constrained to choose does not necessarily entail that we should maximize this capacity, acknowledge it in others, or turn it into the basis of political organization. Nozick claims this is part of what being a self must require, for a "self-choosing being," he argues, "would choose to be a self" (ibid.:359). A genuinely self-choosing being, in Nozick's sense,

---

33 This seems to me to miss the force that the injunction "ought entails can" is intended to have in Kant's argument, but I cannot pursue this here.

however, might choose a whole range of things (otherwise it would not be capable of genuine choice), and, specifically, it might or might not choose to acknowledge others in any particular way. That we are constrained to make choices does not, by itself, entail *any* moral and political principles or program, or even that choosing is valuable. Sartre struggled with this problem for most of his life. Nozick offers some independent reasons why choosing is inherently valuable that are considered in section II(iv) of this chapter. For the present I concentrate on how this neo-Kantian view might generate Nozick's rights.

The connection between this ethics and the side-constraint theory of rights apparently inheres in the claim that a "constraint on treating everything in accordance with its value is your own value" (ibid.:523). Realizing that this will involve conflicts, Nozick adds that a "due sense of proportion" is to be maintained. Thus:

I do not think others should be taxed to support my research, and hence do not apply for or accept government research funds; I do not want to participate in this system, even as a way of receiving back unjustly taken tax payments. Yet I do not try to disengage myself completely from all government activities that I wish would not take place, such as mail delivery and public transportation. I am not required to sacrifice a normal life or normal activities in order to avoid all contact with illegitimate activities. (Ibid.)

The "normal and expected course of events" rears its head once more. Although Nozick remarks that "each of us will judge others by where they draw the lines" (ibid.) he fails to confront the fact that people's capacities to draw different lines frequently differ for reasons not of their own choosing; that no "normal life of normal activities" for an individual can be specified independently of the reasons why he or she has the capacities to live the life he or she does.

In another attempt to resolve this issue Nozick remarks that the domain of individual autonomy "must include a range of important and significant choices (such as religious practice, place of residence, choice of mate and lifestyle, choice of occupation), as well as a vast range of trivial choices which go to make up the daily texture of our lives" (ibid.:501). Nozick does not explain why these particular activities are so central (rather than, for instance, being assured of employment and a living wage) except to say "[t]he choices that are viewed as significant and central to a person's life and self-definition may vary from culture to culture . . . the domain of autonomy might [in a different culture] be demarcated differently" (ibid.:501–2). But this is a version of the Austinian fallacy, supposing that what is taken to be legitimate "by a culture" is for that reason legitimate. This view ignores the (presumably typical) case in a culture where different people have different views of what constitutes the legitimate domain, and of what that entails in practice. It is difficult to see a way out of this for Nozick except through an appeal to the market; this is in fact his fundamental appeal, as we will now see.

Because Nozick believes there are objective goods that can be known, he must take seriously the claim that sometimes people do not strive for them. Otherwise this assertion would be empty. He cannot therefore accept the doctrine of revealed preference as a sufficient condition for an agent's having performed a good/desirable action, since agents may do bad/undesirable things in their voluntary transactions one with another. Hence:

The mechanism of the market lures one to serve the wants of others, but does not lure one to serve their highest capacities or their harmonious hierarchical development, except insofar as others express their desire for this within the market. Nor need working in the market draw directly upon our own highest capacities and motivations . . . [T]he market mechanism does not especially reward us for satisfying those desires. (Nozick, 1981:514)

Although a market is not a sufficient condition for "tracking bestness"[34] it is necessary, because a necessary condition of tracking bestness, for Nozick, is obeying his subjunctive condition to act in equilibrium. This, he believes, can only be achieved via a market. Thus the fact that the market satisfies mere wants "is not a criticism of the market our fellows can

34 This is a modification of Nozick's position in *Anarchy State and Utopia*, where his discussion of markets implies that it is sufficient (Nozick, 1974:17, 248–50).

make; the market serves them no worse than they choose to be served" (ibid.). Any other mechanism might also satisfy our desires, "whatever they happen to be . . . [but] such a mechanism sometimes would lower us even as it got to raise others, and it would merely reinforce *our* acting on already existing desires" (ibid.). Thus, although Nozick avoids the claim that everyone can, or even if they can, will, realize their highest capacities via the market, he does hold that without the market they will not, for without it they cannot act in equilibrium. This assumes that the market is a necessary condition for acting in equilibrium, which Nozick does not establish. As I argued via the bus-boy example, an action being a market transaction can in certain circumstances be a sufficient condition for its being coerced.

Nozick's account of the basis for rights thus rests on a combination of his subjunctive conditional for acting in equilibrium and his leap of faith that people will want to "track bestness." On the second of these he believes that philosophy has nothing to say;[35] the first is assumed, ultimately without argument, to be guaranteed exclusively by the market.

iv. The purposes of rights

Apparently rejecting the doctrine of the priority of right propounded in *Anarchy State and Utopia,* in *Philosophical Explanations* Nozick presents an account of objective goods for all entities (plants, animals, humans, even solar systems) in terms of maximizing the "degree of organic unity" of the relevant entity. For humans this consists of a process of self-improvement or "harmonious hierarchical development," variously likened to stages in the Platonic hierarchy of the soul, to the Aristotelian notion of potential, and to the experiences of (usually unidentified) mystics. It is difficult to discuss this view without caricaturing it, especially since *Philosophical Explanations* begins with a homily on the vices of "coercive philosophy," the traditional (argumentative) mode that tries to "force" conclusions on people with "powerful" "knockdown" arguments (1981:4–11). Rather, Nozick argues, philosophy should illuminate with ex-

35 See Nozick (1981:410–11). This issue is taken up in Section II(iv) of this chapter.

planations, it should be motivated by "puzzlement, curiosity, [and] a desire to understand." Philosophers should not be "thought-police" (ibid.:13). This may sound disingenuous coming from the author of one of the most explicitly argumentative and ideological books of philosophy to achieve prominence in many years, but it would be churlish not to recognize that *Philosophical Explanations* is written in a quite different and much more speculative mood.

Apart from the doubtful plausibility of his distinction between coercive and noncoercive philosophy, the question arises whether Nozick practices what he preaches. The ethics presented in *Philosophical Explanations* is clearly intended, inter alia, to provide a moral foundation for the argument of *Anarchy State and Utopia*. When he mentions the earlier book, he makes no attempt to qualify its "coercive" doctrine. In this book Nozick clearly attempts to establish an argument about the existence of free will and a particular conception of the good, both being best realized in practice in unregulated capitalist markets. He outlines and argues for a position with substantive philosophical and political implications. His arguments therefore invite critical scrutiny.

Nozick's theory of objective good in terms of "degree of organic unity" is spelled out as follows: organic unity is "the common strand of value across different realms" of existence. Although there may be other things with particular values for entities, "degree of organic unity" accounts for at least "90 percent of the variance in intrinsic value." It is the "basic dimension of intrinsic value, accounting for almost all differences in intrinsic value" (ibid.:418–9). What is valuable for an entity is that which maximizes its degree of organic unity; what is disvaluable is that which tends to destroy this unity. Nozick takes a broad evolutionary view of entities striving always to act by this principle of unifying diversity. Thus he relates, from the *Book of Genesis*, "everything was formless and void and God then structured it and saw it was very good, whereas the parts were only said to be good." And, "[a]ccording to *Meshech Chachmah*, there was new goodness in the whole, greater than the sum of the parts" (ibid.:424–5n). More technically, for Nozick:

The value of X is the sum of its degree of organic unity plus the values of each of its parts. Since by hypothesis each of these parts has zero value, the second term will be zero. However, since X does have some degree of organic unity greater than zero, its value will be greater than zero, and equal to $O(X)$. Thus, the view that organic unity gives rise to new value allows value creation *ex nihilo:* the creation of intrinsic value out of nothing of intrinsic value. There need not be atoms of value, since there can be valuable molecules composed of valueless atoms. (Ibid.:423–4)

Although he reduces this statement to a formal equation, he supplies no dimension for measuring this degree of organic unity: the idea is the intuitive claim that values arise out of the objective structuring of the world, and goods are those things either conducive to the viability of existing structures, or leading to the creation of new unified structures.

The sense in which these structures are held to exist in the world is difficult to get at, but they appear to be something like noumenal entities.[36] Nozick is aware that any given entity (or action) admits of many true descriptions and that an explanation is always an explanation under some description. Because concepts without percepts are blind, however,[37] he must postulate objective structures "out there" that nonetheless form the basis of knowledge and value. Hence the following metaphor:

It is not impossible that there be beings who experience phonograph records differently, whose vision registers the microscopic contours of the grooves, the intricate relationships exhibited there; for them, the record itself is a visual art form. In this case, the spatial features (isomorphic to the relations among sounds and tones) would have important weight for them, and be crucial to (their view of) the identity of the object as the kind of thing it was. Here we would expect further relationships also to be salient to them, such as relations of adjacency between grooves (for instance, lying on the same radius from the center); these would make further unities possible, whereas the "corresponding" uniformly changing temporal relations among the musical sounds would not be a unifying mode for the

36 Nozick does not himself draw this comparison.
37 Again, this is not Nozick's phrase in this context.

music. Similarly one could imagine the record as a tactile art form, with its own salient organizing relationships. (Ibid.:426)

His claim seems to be that underlying all these different possible valuable experiences of the record is its basic "brute" structure which is, or stands in isomorphic correspondence to, its intrinsic value. Leaving aside the well known difficulties with such noumenal theories (such as how we can say anything about them at all, even identify them, if they are genuinely noumenal, and what the causal relationship between them and phenomenal entities is), note Nozick's claims not only that organic unity is desirable, but the greater the diversity that is unified the better. Thus he gives his pluralism its transcendental gloss. The more diversity an "ontologically unified structure" encompasses the more valuable it is. The degree of organic unity is a function of both the diversity and the degree of unifiedness. Even accepting all the rest, this is by no means intuitively obvious from Nozick's premises. For instance, the old AJS 500cc single-cylinder motorcycle was tremendously simple by contemporary standards. Do we say that a 1985 four-cylinder Honda 1000cc has more intrinsic value because it has three more pistons, extra wing-mirrors, electric starter . . . more diversity? Degree of organic unity does not necessarily entail greater value for more rather than less united diversity.

There also seem to be serious difficulties about the entities to which these value-predicates attach. Although degree of organic unity is the basic dimension of intrinsic value across different realms, this "does not mean that we can make value rankings across realms as well as within them" (ibid.:419). The nature of the structured diversity will be different in different cases, but Nozick does want to generalize to the extent of saying that whatever is conducive to the preservation of an organic unity is valuable. This obviously becomes problematical if unities are conceived so generally, because unities in nature and social life destroy one another, as he notes:

Some destroyers of organic unity are themselves highly organized unities, for example, concentration camps. Someone might say that therefore these are intrinsically valuable, though instrumentally disvaluable. The latter they certainly are, but I am reluctant to see them as at all instrinsically valuable. For their purpose, their *telos,* is an important component of their unity; indeed, it is their central unifying factor. Since this purpose is destructive of organic unity, it itself is disvaluable and infects with disvalue the unity that it animates. (Ibid.:419)

This solution, however, is fraught with difficulties, some of which Nozick half acknowledges in a footnote.[38] By this logic a cancer-killing drug must be held to disvaluable, for instance. Nozick may not like concentration camps, but at this level of abstraction, they are no different than cancer-killing drugs.

To avoid these difficulties this argument would have to specify – at a much lower level of generality – the nature of the entity concerned, the conditions for its survival, the implications of those conditions for other entities, their imperatives for survival, and, above all, why some entities are valuable while others are disvaluable. Nozick's answers to these questions are at best implicit, as can be seen as soon as he applies this doctrine to political and economic life. Thus:

Is the most valuable society a tightly organized centrally controlled hierarchical society of fixed hereditary status, termed by some theorists an "organic society"? Although it would have a high degree of unity, it would not encompass the same vast diversity as a free and open society. A far-flung system of voluntary cooperation unifies diverse parts in an intricate structure of changing equilibria, and also unifies these parts in a way that takes account of their degree of organic unity. Enlisting a person's voluntary cooperation or participation takes account of his degree of organic unity to a greater extent than commanding him. (Ibid.:421)

Granting the unity/diversity thesis, the objective structure thesis, the value/disvalue thesis, this is an additional undefended empirical claim, not even intuitively plausible to boot. A cor-

---

38 "[W]e must take into account the alternative possibilities of what the organic unity can do, and whether destruction is a central aim of the entity. . . . Are people less valuable because they eat animals, which are organic unities? However if these animals eat plants, are they not destructive, so that it is better to eat them than to eat (innocent) plants? Yet to eat only animals who eat plants is to bask in the good fortune that there are such destructive entities, so that one does not have to eat (the less valuable because having a lesser degree of organic unity) plants oneself, and so one is a parasite on the disvalue of others. These animals themselves have no other alternatives, and so on" (Nozick, 1981:420). The implications of these observations for his more general argument are not considered by Nozick.

poratist society of the kind envisioned by Plato could conceiva-
bly be just as complex, have just as many interlocking but
independent constituent parts, as the most complex market
society imaginable; it might have more components than many
actual market societies. Alternatively, there are cases of markets destroying diversity through monopoly, or by promoting
mediocrity as Mill and Tocqueville feared. One might compare British and American television, for instance, where the
very much greater number of channels organized on a market
basis in America results in significantly inferior output. It is by
no means obvious that American television has greater intrinsic value, or even that it contains more genuine diversity,
though the market-based system may generate a greater number of channels.

It should by now be clear that Nozick's philosophical theory
of objective goods is quite irrelevant to his substantive claims
about objective value. These rest on little more than faith in the
utopian consequences held to flow from unregulated markets.
At no time does he explain why we should value the unification
of diversity which, he claims without evidential support, this
process generates. Thus he argues that "in my value ranking I
place people higher in instrinsic value than animals which are
higher than plants which are higher than rocks. There are
distinctions in value within these categories, as well as some
overlap; for example, I do not rank a mouse higher than an
800-year-old redwood" (1981:415). Two pages later, however,
he has attributed these idiosyncratic rankings to the rest of us:
"Thus the ranking of organisms in accordance with degree of
organic unity [complexity of unified diversity] matches *our*
value ranking of them, with people above other animals above
plants above rocks" (ibid.:417, emphasis added). In his list of
the valuable characteristics a self-choosing being would select in
order to be valuable, he feels "little doubt" that these include:
having free will, conscious, self-conscious, able to do something
because it is right, able to recognize value, able to guide behavior in accord with recognition of value, self-choosing. "You
would want your child to have these characteristics," he says
(ibid.:445). Perhaps one would, but perhaps one might think
other characteristics just as (or more) important, such as com-

passion for others, or a critical mind. One might even think too much self-consciousness a bad thing in some people, if it immobilizes them, for instance. We seek, not to debate general characteristics with Nozick, but to establish that he offers no reasons for the ones he prefers, nor does he remotely prove that they will effectively be realized via unregulated markets.

What of the big question confronting all who want to hold both a subjective theory of rights and an objective theory of goods: how are they to be mutually reconciled? Either they must be shown to entail one another (or at least not to generate mutually incompatible injunctions), or one must ultimately be held to be prior.[39] Hobbes and Locke believed they reconciled them in a view of science and an ontology not available to Nozick. What is his solution? He tries to side-step this question by arguing that if there is objective value its "allure" will be such that people will in fact strive for it.

Is it humanocentric to think that value must inspire us? Couldn't we be so sunk in sloth and darkness (original sin?) that we would not choose the good even under good conditions? Isn't it possible for some selves to be in that unfortunate state? Perhaps it is us. However, we are not sunk absolutely low, since we quest for value, and we are attracted to some things *qua* valuable. Since questing for value is itself valuable, it is a sign that we are not thoroughly bad; moreover, if questing for value also falls under the same dimension that allures us, that is a sign that the dimension itself is valuable. (Ibid.:439)

If we accept Nozick's claim that people strive for what they take to be valuable for them, this need not entail that they will strive for the particular things Nozick enumerates, nor exemplify his theory of individual "harmonious hierarchical development," as he is aware:

[D]o we believe that all selves who are attracted by anything in the peaceful contest will be attracted by the same thing? Leaving aside other beings described in science fiction novels, there is some evidence that every person will be attracted most by the same thing, once they encounter it. . . . Mystics report their experiences as over-

39 Leaving aside the nature of this priority: absolute, conditional, lexical, or some other.

whelmingly valuable and powerful in impact; certain types of these experiences not only transform the person's view of what the world contains, they also transform the person. If all those who experience it agree in their response and in the nature of their transformation, and no additional experience of anything else damps down this response, isn't this a sign that it is an objective response to value? (Ibid.:439–40)

It must be the apotheosis of implausibility to maintain there is objective value because there is consensus among mystics. This aside, it is still unclear why people should strive for the objectively valuable. "Is the thought," Nozick wonders "overly optimistic that underlies all this, namely, that value will inspire (under good conditions) more strongly than disvalue or non-value?" (ibid.). This is the crux of the question as far as rights are concerned. The closest Nozick comes to confronting it is the following:

If there is objective value, we should expect it sometimes to be divorced from a person's actual motivations, while being none the less valuable for that. Surely, some adverse biographical conditions, or even moods, can lead a person not to care about value. . . . "But if under some conditions value is divorced from a person's motivation, that person may lack (sufficient) motivation to behave morally; what then can we do?" There is much we can do in society, ranging from attempts at persuasion to punishment of the person who does not behave morally, by connecting sanctions to motivations he does have. There is no guarantee he will not be able to avoid our institutional network. However, it is not the task of philosophy to plug this gap and provide motivation for people. At any rate, that is not our task here. I want to understand how a person is worse off being immoral, not to convince the immoral person that he is worse off. "But he might just dig in his heels and refuse to be convinced without a knock down argument." When he digs in his heels and lives accordingly, his choice has the effect of determining the value of his life, whether or not he realizes this. What he needs is not a philosopher but inspiration. (Ibid.:410–11)

Thus it seems that ultimately the rights must be prior to the objectively valuable since the latter is critically dependent on the agent *choosing* to act in accordance with value. If he does not, so much the worse for him; but since a necessary condition for acting valuably is acting in equilibrium, individual choice must be prior. The rest of the theory of objective goods is irrelevant to the argument. The purpose of rights is for people to treat one another as self-choosing beings. This is Nozick's philosophical defense of the market, although we saw that it is riddled with arbitrary assertions and unsubstantiated empirical claims.

III. IDEOLOGICAL CONSEQUENCES OF NOZICK'S ARGUMENT

The force of Nozick's argument clearly derives from the neo-classical view of the world that it both invokes and seeks to justify. The neo-Kantian foundations supplied for this theory of rights are neither Kantian nor generative of his conclusions. Locke adumbrated a modified natural-law theory to give his rights their transhistorical force, but Nozick appeals to a modified version of the categorical imperative to give his rights their objective and transcendental gloss. Nozick's main appeal is to the liberal language of individual rights discussed in the last two chapters, although this language had, since its early formulations, been strongly influenced by the rise of equilibrium theory, the shedding of labor theories of value, and the impact of modern utilitarianism on its evolution. It remains to consider the ideological consequences of this appeal in detail.

Nozick believes, with Locke, that the isolated individual is the subject of asymmetrical rights of exclusive dominion, but now in a much more radical form. He takes over Locke's doctrine of the individual as proprietor of his capacities and possessions with two important modifications. First, God is removed from the picture, destroying the possibility of exogenous binding moral constraints on individual behavior. In *Anarchy State and Utopia* he claims that people in the state of nature "generally act as they ought," but we saw that this was (implicitly) circularly defined to mean respecting one another's rights. In *Philosophical Explanations* Nozick holds that people will "track bestness" to avoid what he sees as the nihilistic moral implications of not holding this. His strong attachment to the priority of right over good, however, and his claim that if there is an objective good the priority of right – necessary for acting "in equilibrium" – must be a necessary condition for its attainment, both preclude sanction of any exogenous constraints on individuals at all. There is Lockean liberty but no Lockean license for Nozick. For ideological reasons, he needs the conclusion that no redistribution by the state can ever be justified. He is thus forced to embrace a radical version of Pareto's noncomparable ordinal utilities, ruling out all "moral balancing acts" and "paternalistic judgments" that might limit the realm of individual autonomy. The workmanship model of intentional action as the source of all moral imperatives, together with the Cartesian privileged-access thesis, are thus neatly adapted to the neo-classical view of rights, stripped of their theological baggage.

Not merely is Locke's argument from scripture unavailable to Nozick; the arguments from reason and nature were embedded in a view of science to which he does not subscribe. His individuals are thus subject to no exogenous constraints at all. In making these moves Nozick is neither original nor alone: he falls squarely into the neo-classical tradition as adapted to politics by the modern discipline of public choice.[40] Second, although for Nozick the individual is proprietor of his actions, this entails no labor theory of value as it did for Locke, again in keeping with the neo-classical revolution against classical political economy. Neo-classical theory takes all property rights as given and explains value in terms of returns on the factors of production – land, labor and capital. A standard criticism of this has always been that to assume this is to assume much that is controversial. The standard reply, that questions about the original endowment of property rights are the proper concern of historians, not economists, is not especially convincing. Perhaps out of

40 For similar views that noncomparable utility functions are necessary for respecting individual rights, see Buchanan and Tullock (1962) and Arrow (1973). It might be argued that a comparable thesis is embedded in Mill's claim that "the sole end for which mankind are warranted, individually or collectively, in interfering with the liberty of action of any of their number is . . . to prevent harm to others. His own good, either physical or moral, is not a sufficient warrant. He cannot rightfully be compelled to do or to forbear because it will be better for him to do so, because it will make him happier, because, in the opinion of others, to do so would be wise, or even right" (Mill, 1975:15).

awareness of this Nozick acknowledges the need to have an account of justice in acquisition, although once he has jettisoned Locke's labor theory of value it is unclear why his particular (Grotian) theory, with a modified version of Locke's second proviso tacked on, should necessarily be chosen. Nozick avoids the issue of justice in acqusition by holding that even his more demanding version of the proviso will never be violated under capitalist market conditions, because of the productivity and other congenial effects of capitalist production and exchange. These factual claims are never defended and might easily be challenged, both as claims about long-term efficiency and productivity and as claims that the proviso will not be violated for any given individual. Thus, despite many internal difficulties with his formulations of it, Nozick uses the asymmetrical model of individual proprietorship to justify capitalist markets.

Nozick remains firmly in the tradition of Locke and Hobbes in separating right from law, and making individual private rights prior to civil law from which this latter is derived. For Nozick the issue is not to explain the relationship between public and private law in terms of private-law contracts; it is to deny that there can be *any* public law other than simple unanimity. There is no sense of a public sphere operating for different purposes and by different rules than the private. This logical outgrowth of the arguments of Hobbes and Locke is vastly more extreme than theirs. Hobbes's sovereign, once created, had very great (autonomous) powers. Locke's state, too, could act autonomously in the public interest, though this power was conditioned and dependent on its fiduciary trust. For Nozick, there is no public sphere; the market rules that Hobbes and Locke restricted to the private sphere are directly applied to politics. Thus can the state in all seriousness be conceived of as a business run by entrepreneurs, an insurance company from which clients buy a service for a fee. If this sounds implausible, note that Nozick is firmly anchored to the public-choice tradition that has made use of similar assumptions since the 1950s. In one of its formative works, for instance, Downs (1957) treats political parties as firms trying to maximize votes (the analogue of profits); and at least since

Buchanan and Tullock (1962) this entire school has treated voting preferences as utility functions, and the search for "equilibrium" in the political "market" as an exact parallel of the neo-classical conception of the economic market, based on voluntary transactions, Pareto-superior trades, and "stable" efficient outcomes. The Nobel Prize-winning Arrow theorem could not even be stated without embracing this whole view of the political world.[41]

The ideological implications of this are doubly ironic. First, there is the simple fact of this "ecomorphism" of the political, this view of politics as a simple extension of the market, and therefore governed by the same assumptions, rules, and procedures as the market. Ideology is never entirely at odds with reality, and, particularly in the United States (where public choice has had its greatest impact), these developments to a considerable extent reflect the expansion of the market system into all walks of life – most notably politics. Politicians do, to a greater extent than ever before, sell a commodity as entrepreneurs, employ agencies to "package" their products for advertising, and gear those products to what they believe the market demands.[42] Even in England, where two decades ago such practices would have been inconceivable, professional political managers, consulting firms, and advertising agencies have made substantial inroads into the political process. However much this ecomorphism clashes with more traditional conceptions of politics and the public sphere, it would be a mistake to think it has no grounding in contemporary political practices. To the extent that the ideology strikes us as quaintly extreme this is a reflection of the degree to which political concerns have actually come to be dominated by, and mimic, those of the market.

41 For good recent summaries of the public choice literature with many illustrations of these assumptions, see Mueller (1979) and Ordeshook and Shepsle (1982).
42 For a discussion of one significant illustration of this, see Mayhew (1974:1–77), where it is shown that the most important factor affecting the behavior of U.S. Congressmen in office is their set of beliefs about what will get them reelected, and how other considerations are tailored to this end. I skirt the issue of whether they actually do what they believe their potential electorate wants done, or whether they try to describe what they do in terms that make it seem they are doing what their potential electorate wants done; not always, needless to say, the same thing.

The second ironic aspect of these developments concerns this wholesale importation of neo-classical equilibrium theory into political theory, which added much fuel to pretentions toward scienticity and value neutrality,[43] taking hold just as it was dawning on economists that traditional neo-classical (competitive) models bore scant relationship to the actual structure of contemporary capitalist markets. The much vaunted predictive prowess of neo-classical price theory was reduced to impotence as these economies entered sustained periods of combined low growth, high unemployment, and continuous inflation (even during periods of recession), from which they have yet successfully to emerge. The neo-classical price mechanism bore no readily discernible relationship to contemporary price behavior and many economists began to cast about for alternative models.[44] That in this situation the neo-classical model, seen as scientifically sound, as tried and tested by generations of economists since Marshall, should be adapted to political theory is thus deeply ironic. The myth of the political market was now built atop the myth of the economic market. Neo-classical price theory still retains tremendous prestige and influence among dominant intellectual elites, but it masks a quite different reality in the highly concentrated economies of the advanced capitalist world. Without these prevailing beliefs Nozick's modeling of the state on the firm, his presumption of the validity and adaptability of the axioms of (macro and micro) neo-classical theory to politics, could never get off the ground, let alone win him pride of place as a champion of contemporary libertarianism.

Closely related to this is his negative libertarianism, which falls into the classical mold discussed in the last chapter, but takes on much more extreme dimensions in its neo-classical form. Nozick's side-constraint view of rights, which literally

---

43 For one of many possible illustrations: "Since this theory [of Pareto-optimal equilibrium] admits prediction of an equilibrium and since the actual occurrences of numerous predicted equilibria [in economics] have been verified, the prestige of this theory is higher, I believe, than that of any other theory in the social sciences. Indeed, it seems to me that this success alone (i.e., predictions from the theory of price) elevates the science of economics above all other social sciences" (Riker, 1982:6).

44 See Shapiro and Kane (1983:6–28).

invokes the metaphor of a line or "hyperplane" in moral space surrounding an individual, wholly ignores the social and economic relationships that place people in the "moral spaces" they occupy, just as the Pareto system ignores the (determinants of) the initial conditions of the distributions to which it is applied. The neo-classical tradition denies the possibility of interpersonal comparisons of utility for fear of the distributive consequences that may result. The effect of this postulate on Nozick's formulation is to make the isolation of individuals from one another absolute. Small wonder that the view of the "meaning of life" at the end of *Philosophical Explanations* is so romantically individualistic, concerned with the "harmonious hierarchical development" of the individual soul, lapsing into appeals to mystical experiences, and at times almost autistic in tone. This is the logical outcome of taking deadly seriously a view of social life as constituted by a scatter of unrelated entities (or entities whose relatedness extends no further than acknowledging their mutual separateness), each spending its time running up and down its utility function, impervious to the activities of others except insofar as those activities might enhance or impede its own advancement.

Nozick is in the mainstream of classical and neo-classical tradition, too, in viewing the class of objects and actions to which there are private rights as potentially infinite. There is not the hint of a distinction between wants and needs in any of his writings. He openly embraces the empirical belief that unfettered capitalist production will lead to continuous productive growth. It is worth saying a word here about Nozick's utilitarian assumptions, because the claim that the productivity effects of capitalist production will be such that the proviso will not be violated smacks of traditional utilitarian consequentialism. Nozick explicitly rejects utilitariansim as an "end-state" principle. He also rejects the weaker "utilitarianism of rights" where the "total (weighted) amount of violations of rights is built into the desirable end-state to be achieved" (1974:28) – a kind of rule-utilitariansim. Nozick employs precisely this procedure, however, when he argues that in certain cases it is not worth getting an individual's consent to a rights violation because the transactions costs are too great. The logic of this claim is that of a rule-utilitarian maxim to minimize some weighted measure of rights violations. In addition, Nozick imports the whole (neo-classical) theory of value into his account of the substance of rights. He is content to refer to individual utilities, indifference curves, and utility maximization; the whole discussion of compensation obviously presumes the neo-classical utilitarian theory of value. In what sense is his account antiutilitarian? It is an attempt at the kind of synthesis of rights and utility undertaken by Mill in *On Liberty*, which has always resolved into either a restatement of rights in rule-utilitarian terms or a (consequentialist) claim that utilitarian efficiency will be best served by respecting individual rights. Nozick attempts both these strategies of argument at different times. His argument would not have the surface plausibility it does if it did not implicitly attempt this synthesis.

Nozick's account of the nature and functions of the state falls squarely into the classical tradition as modified by the rise of equilibrium theory. His reading of the minimal state into Locke involved an anachronistic misreading of Locke and a misleading conflation of minimalism with regulation. Nozick exemplifies the libertarian tendency to look back at what is taken to be a classical liberal past, when the state really was minimal, and the market was permitted to function unimpeded. The era of this supposed Golden Age is never clearly specified by Nozick or others who ritually invoke it, but we know from Polanyi, Supple, and others that classical laissez-faire capitalism lasted briefly in nineteenth-century England and was never fully adopted elsewhere, and that the creation of capitalist markets required a massively interventionist state. My analysis of the views on the state held by Hobbes and Locke confirmed that, although both thought the state should regulate a negative libertarian society, this in no way entailed minimalism. These writers, I argued, had no notion of equilibrium. When Nozick appeals to the neo-classical system he is appealing to the belief that capitalist economies can be efficiently self-regulating, an empirical claim for which little evidence has ever been supplied.

Nozick's belief that such self-regulating systems would emerge naturally has no basis in fact. A state would be (and in fact was) required to create the particular systems of property rights, contracts, torts, and other legal arrangements necessary to their preservation and reproduction. Once these are established the power of the state becomes latent and its inactivity will be sought by those desirous of preserving the broad socio-economic status quo. The idea of the minimal state has always been a myth, not least today when it is invoked by the New Right on both sides of the Atlantic as a means for restoring the "traditional" competitive structure of these economies. In fact, deregulation has resulted in greater concentration of capital and less competition than ever before.[45] That Nozick invokes it is a primary reason for the ideological appeal of his work. It is the institutional manifestation of the conservatism inherent in a liberal tradition in which to be free is to be free above all from politics: the government that governs least governs best.

IV. CONCLUSION

A recent attempt by Jeffrey Paul to explain the impact of *Anarchy State and Utopia* sees it as a paradox:

In contrast to the moderate and conventional ideological stance of John Rawls's *A Theory of Justice,* its distinguished predecessor in political philosophy, Nozick's work announced a thesis so out of joint with its times that the critical acclaim accorded it by many of its reviewers must have astounded its author as much as it baffled its critics. That a treatise extolling the virtues of eighteenth-century individualism and nineteenth-century laissez-faire capitalism should not have elicited either hostility or silence, is both a puzzling and gratifying phenomenon; puzzling because its themes run counter to the *Zeitgeist* and gratifying because it is a work of considerable philosophical acuity. (Paul, 1978:1)

Paul's solution to this is to invoke the Kuhnian notion of a paradigm shift with Nozick at its center, which explains "why *Anarchy State and Utopia* was able to replicate the enthusiastic welcome accorded to Rawls's work only three years earlier." Rawls's work was written partly to restore the "impaired foun-

---

45 See OECD (1979) and Shapiro and Kane (1983:13–19).

dations of the current ideological paradigm," but Nozick's book "struck at the conceptual underpinnings of both contemporary Western society and its totalitarian adversaries in the East" (ibid.:2–3).

If the analysis offered in this chapter is broadly correct, Paul's assessment could not be further from the truth. Nozick's argument falls squarely into the well established traditions of neo-classical economics and conservative liberalism which are both rooted in classical liberalism and have always comprised a powerful strand of modern liberal thought. From Pareto to Friedman in economics, from Hayek to the modern discipline of public choice, these ideas have substantial twentieth-century intellectual pedigrees, apart from the earlier influences I have sought to establish. They are also deeply embedded in contemporary liberal culture, constituting a substantial part of the prevailing *Zeitgeist*. The metaphor of a paradigm shift could not be more misleading.

5

The Keynesian moment

I. INTRODUCTION

Rawls employs a hypothetical contract, like Nozick, but its structure and explanatory status are very different.[1] Nozick's appeal was to a modified version of Locke's state of nature, but Rawls sees himself as building on the work of Rousseau and especially Kant, who "sought to give a philosophical foundation to Rousseau's idea of the general will" (Rawls, 1971:264). His principal concern is comparable to Nozick's in that he is seeking to establish unanimity for the fundamental social contract. His aim is to argue for a theory of justice by convincing the reader that the principles he advocates would be chosen by imaginary persons in a hypothetical state of nature (or "original position"), ignorant of all "particular facts" about themselves and their actual lives in society that might impair their impartiality. From behind this veil of ignorance, Rawls argues, it would be rational for all persons to choose his two principles of justice over several other common candidates, notably intuitionism, two types of utilitarianism, perfectionism, and various combinations of these. The two principles chosen would constitute the basic social structure, as well as shape constitutional, legal,

---

1 It is in the nature of a book as long as *A Theory of Justice,* written over an extensive period and circulated in manuscript form for many years, that its central doctrines have been subtly qualified and modified at many points, to the degree that it is sometimes difficult to discover what the argument is, as Barry (1973:1–3), among others, has noted. This is complicated by the fact that, since its publication, Rawls has published several articles in response to critics, further clarifying and in some cases modifying his position. In this chapter I will take *A Theory of Justice* as the definitive statement of Rawls's view, referring to subsequent writings only where they decisively affect my argument. This seems defensible to me, first, because none of the central doctrines has been given up, and, second, because I am primarily concerned with the influence of Rawls's argument – and this undoubtedly derives from the central doctrines of the book, not the subsequent qualifications.

economic, and political practices. He sums up the essential impartiality of the conditions under which the principles are chosen in the phrase "justice as fairness." The principles are also held to be procedural expressions of the categorical imperative – to acknowledge and preserve our sense of justice and our essential nature *qua* autonomous beings capable of free choice. They are public in that everyone understands, acknowledges, and agrees to them, and permanent in that all subsequent decisions will be made in accordance with them and they are understood as applying to future generations as well as present.

II. RAWLS'S THEORY OF RIGHTS

Rawls often uses the words "right" and "just" interchangeably, but his considered view is that an account of right must be embedded in a theory of justice, that it is consequently on the question of justice that individuals in the original position must agree first and foremost. He argues that these individuals will first agree on a general conception of justice which rules out inequalities that are not to the benefit of all. More specifically, they will agree that "All social values – liberty and opportunity, income and wealth, and the bases of self-respect – are to be distributed equally unless an unequal distribution of any, or all, of these values is to everyone's advantage" (Rawls, 1971:62).

As a "special case" of this general view of justice Rawls formulates his two principles which, in their final form, read as follows:

First Principle
Each person is to have an equal right to the most extensive total system of equal basic liberties compatible with a similar system of liberty for all.
Second Principle
Social and economic inequalities are to be arranged so that they are both:
(a) to the greatest benefit of the least advantaged, . . . and
(b) attached to offices and positions open to all under conditions of fair equality of opportunity (ibid.:302).

These principles are "lexically" ordered, with the first prior to the second, and, within the second, (b) prior to (a).[2] Thus for Rawls a liberty protected by the first principle can never be sacrificed for improvements in economic well-being, no matter how extensive they may be or how minor the infraction of the relevant liberty. The only justifiable basis for sacrificing a liberty in whole or in part would be to "strengthen the total system of liberty shared by all" (ibid.).

Once the principles have been chosen under the relevant conditions of ignorance, the veil of ignorance is gradually lifted in a four-stage process. Individuals are given the information necessary to agree on more specific economic, political, and legal institutions, always in conformity with the two "constitutional" principles which, once established, constitute the permanent basis of social organization. Although this four-stage sequence is "suggested by the United States Constitution and its history" (ibid.:196n), the choice problem is conceived of as hypothetical, on the level of so-called "ideal theory." Once the principles have been justified in this way, however, they are held to be applicable to the real world, as a goal for which to strive and a yardstick for establishing the relative justice of extant institutions. They are conceived of quite generally[3] as applicable wherever the "circumstances of justice" (the most important of which is conflicting claims for scarce resources) obtain, and are discussed in relation to historical and contemporary societies. They are held to be applicable in both capitalist and socialist societies, although the only case Rawls considers in any detail is that of a "property-owning democracy" (ibid.: 274).

i. The subject of rights

Who are these persons in the original position, and what is the nature of their agreement? Although Rawls's individuals are hypothetical, they are intended to correspond to actual per-

2 A principle higher in a lexical ranking must always be given priority over a lower one, and can never be sacrificed for a lower one should conflicts arise.

3 There is a proviso that their strict application requires a certain level of economic development, but even in the case where this condition is not met, they are held to become increasingly relevant as economic development advances.

sons in all essentials relevant to questions of justice. The denial of particular information in the original position is justified by reasons that clearly presuppose a theory of human nature. The problems of partiality to one's particular goals, free ridership, and intolerance are all seen as features of the human condition needing to be controlled for in setting up the original position. In this respect, Rawls's purpose can be likened to that of Rousseau, who states in the opening sentence of *The Social Contract* that he proposes "taking men as they are and laws as they might be" to "consider if, in political society, there can be any legitimate and sure principle of government" (Rousseau, 1968:49).[4]

Rawls offers little by way of justification for the particular view of human nature to which he subscribes, except to say that it rests on weak assumptions that are widely shared. (He never attempts to establish the truth of this claim, for which he has been heavily criticized.)[5] Most of his energy is devoted to showing that if his assumptions *are* granted the persons in the original position must rationally choose his two principles. This contention has often been challenged[6] but for now we will concentrate on the assumptions themselves, and the view of human nature they presuppose.

For Rawls, mutually disinterested apolitical individuals behind a veil of ignorance are the subjects not only of all rights and principles of justice, but also of all "requirements" and "permissions" of social behavior – indeed of all moral predicates with the possible exception of those relating to the law of nations (which he mentions but does not discuss) (1971:108). They have no natural rights in the traditional sense. Their rights are restricted to those that would be chosen unanimously in the original position. The principles are those "that free and rational persons concerned to further their own interests would accept in an initial position of equality as defining the fundamental terms of their association" (ibid.:11). Their equality is forced on them by their universal ignorance,

---

4 Rawls does not compare his enterprise to Rousseau's in this respect.
5 See, for instance, Wolff (1977:208ff).
6 See, for instance, Barry (1973:116ff); Fishkin (1975:615–29); Lyons (1975:141–67); Wolff (1977:119–91); and Mueller (1979:227–46).

which also forces them to reason in general terms. Rawls distances himself from the view that human nature is not shaped in important ways by social institutions, by asserting that in fact it is. He even supplies knowledge of this fact to the contractors in the original position, but this is not fully convincing. He clearly believes that he can strip his individuals of natural and social "contingencies" that are "arbitrary" from "the moral point of view," and retain what is essential – his modified view of Kant's noumenal self. This noumenal self is conceived of as making the original agreement in order to "express" and preserve itself. The original position is "the point of view from which noumenal selves see the world" (ibid.:255ff).

What are the natures of these contracting agents? We are told they have no knowledge of "particular facts" about themselves, of their place in society, class position, social status, natural assets and abilities, or "special psychological propensities" (ibid.:12). Rawls does allow them, however, knowledge of the "general facts" of social life, they "understand political affairs and the principles of economic theory; they know the basis of social organization and the laws of human psychology" (ibid.:137). In fact they know a good deal more, and we know a good deal more about their motivation, but before getting onto these issues it will be useful to examine this account of the contracting agents with particular attention to the distinction between general and particular facts, and to the criteria by which Rawls imparts to, and excludes information from, individuals in the original position.

The principles chosen in the original position, Rawls tells us, must be general. That is, "it must be possible to formulate them without the use of what would be intuitively recognized as proper names, or rigged definite descriptions" (ibid.:131). Rawls does not define the term "rigged definite description." He acknowledges that it might be potentially problematical, but contends that in "presenting a theory of justice one is entitled to avoid the problem of defining general properties and relations and to be guided by what seems reasonable" (ibid.). This begs the question, for Rawls employs many definite descriptions in his characterization of the original position and they are "rigged" to produce precisely the conclusions he requires. Indeed, it is difficult to imagine a different interpretation, given the repeated claims he makes to the effect that "[w]e want to define the original position so that we get the desired solution" (ibid.:141).[7] There seems to be an ambiguity in Rawls's account between the requirement that the principles themselves embody no definite descriptions and the requirement that the information available to the parties in the original position contain no definite descriptions. The first of these might be plausible although it in no way requires the device of the veil of ignorance. Many principles (utilitarianism, for instance) are general and require no definite descriptions in (what seems to be) the relevant sense.[8] The second is clearly false. The fact that an empirical description makes no reference to an individual has no bearing on its definiteness or lack of it. Rawls's aim in ruling out reference to individuals is to achieve *impartiality* among the various parties in the original position. Justice-as-fairness is held to be impartial because the ignorance of the parties rules out their acting from motives of personal gain. The extent to which this procedure achieves impartiality is dubious, however, as we will see.

Rawls claims in many places that a substantive theory of justice need not concern itself with questions of ontology and epistemology. He also rejects out of hand any attempt at a purely a priori ethics, holding that some factual assumptions are essential for the conduct of moral theory (ibid.:51). He must be aware, however, that particular events, entities, and actions admit of multiple true descriptions, that explanations and justifications always presume one of several descriptions of an event, entity, or action, and that the process of description is itself inevitably loaded as a result. Yet Rawls asserts that relying on commonly accepted assumptions "implies no particular metaphysical doctrine or theory of knowledge. For this criterion appeals to what everyone can accept." This is blatantly false, as Hare (1975:86ff) and others have argued. Even

7 For similar assertions, see Rawls (1971:19, 26ff). For extended criticism of Rawls on this score, see Hare (1975:81–107).
8 I will argue in section II(ii) of this chapter, however, that what surface plausibility Rawls's difference principle has assumes a number of definite descriptions of reality that are certainly not uncontroversial.

if Rawls did show (which he never attempts to do) that any or all of the factual assumptions he builds into the original position were widely accepted, this would not demonstrate their truth or their impartiality without the added assumptions of a consensus theory of truth and the possibility of neutral principles of social organization.[9]

Rawls's individuals behind the veil of ignorance have a good deal of quite specific information presumably derived from their knowledge of the "laws" of economics and psychology and the "general facts" about society.[10] They understand and accept Rawls's theory of so-called primary social goods. These are "the things that every rational man is presumed to want" whatever else he or she wants. These include "rights and liberties, powers and opportunities, [and] income and wealth."[11] Rawls supplies the contractors yet more specific "general information." He argues that it would be irrational, given their ignorance, to make probabilistic calculations about their position once the veil is lifted. He claims their conceptions of the good are such that they care greatly about being the worst-off member of society, but care little about the increasing payoffs of being above this lower limit:

[T]he person choosing has a conception of the good such that he cares very little, if anything, for what he might gain above the minimum stipend that he can, in fact, be sure of by following the maximin rule [i.e. inequalities must maximize the position of the worst-off]. It is not worthwhile for him to take a chance for the sake of a

9 The alleged neutrality of Rawls's argument is taken up in section II(iii) of this chapter. The implications of his and Nozick's characteristically liberal failure to come to terms with the problems for political theory raised by multiple and competing true descriptions are taken up in Chapter 6.

10 For further discussion of Rawls's arbitrary uses of information in the original position, see Wolff (1977:119–32) and Mueller (1979:239ff).

11 In this discussion of his general conception of justice Rawls includes "the bases of self-respect" as a primary good. He also acknowledges there are other primary goods, including "health and vigor, [and] intelligence and imagination." These, however, are "natural goods" because "although their possession is influenced by the basic structure, they are not so directly under its control" (Rawls, 1971:62). The three main "social" primary goods are clearly intended to correspond to the principles and to be similarly lexically ordered. It is not entirely clear where the "social bases of self-respect" are to be ranked (with respect to the other goods), how they are to be measured, and by what specific principle(s) they are to be distributed, although Rawls clearly intends them to be very prominent. For discussion of some of the difficulties associated with the relationship between self-respect and the other primary goods, see Michelman (1975:340ff).

further advantage, especially when it may turn out that he loses much that is important to him. . . . The situation involves grave risks. (ibid.:154)

Their preferences thus constitute identical step-functions, which is why they will be partial to the difference principle. By the principle of insufficient reason all are equally likely to be the worst-off, and, given the nature of their preferences, they must devote prime concern to this eventuality. Rawls rejects the notion that individuals under conditions of ignorance would choose the principle of average utility, as Edgeworth argued, because it involves risks, and "[t]he essential thing is not to allow the principles chosen to depend on special attitudes toward risk" (ibid.:172).[12]

Neglecting the question of what makes an attitude toward risk "special," Rawls's description of the preferences (as step-functions at the position of the worst-off stratum) seems arbitrary. The various positions have no necessary material correlates (as they do, for instance, in Shue's (1981:13–87) account of "basic rights" or Barrington Moore's (1978:3–48ff) account of universal human needs). The worst-off position is defined relationally, purely by reference to the other positions to which it is compared. It is worth considering why this claim can seem plausible to Rawls.

There seems to be a general (Pigouvian) assumption in his argument that an efficiently functioning economic system may not function optimally for all, particularly the worst-off. It is therefore rational for the contractors to ensure that inequalities work to the benefit of the least-advantaged and to charge the state with responsibility for this. The strict neo-classical view would be that all inequalities that arise in a market system are efficient (else they would not arise), and necessary for investment incentives, and that the benefits will eventually trickle down to the worst off. Rawls is fearful of this assumption, arguing instead for a "trickle up" theory, discussed in detail in section II(ii) of this chapter. For the present, note only that Rawls must consider the position of the worst-off

---

12 For a critical discussion of Rawls's assumptions about risk-aversion, see Barber (1975:296ff).

because he acknowledges that market systems can generate very serious inequities, no matter how fast they grow, how much wealth they contain, or how well functioning they are in terms of technical efficiency. Apart from this problem of the worst-off (as well as some reservations relating to externalities and monopolies) Rawls is in general well disposed toward unregulated markets. Thus:

[O]nce a suitable minimum is provided by transfers, it may be perfectly fair that the rest of total income be settled by the price system, assuming that it is moderately efficient and free from monopolistic restrictions, and unreasonable externalities have been eliminated. Moreover, this way of dealing with the claims of need would appear to be more effective then trying to regulate income by minimum wage standards, and the like. (Rawls, 1971:277)

Rawls does not reveal who will decide, and on what basis, which externalities are unreasonable, but his view that the market requires state management to prevent its worst inequities is clearly at the root of his desire to build the "grave risks" assumption into the original position, thereby generating a predisposition toward the difference principle on the part of the contracting agents. This is close to explicit in the following:

Suppose that law and government act effectively to keep markets competitive, resources fully employed, property and wealth (especially if private ownership of the means of production is allowed) widely distributed by the appropriate forms of taxation, or whatever, and *to guarantee a reasonable social minimum.* Assume also that there is fair equality of opportunity underwritten by education for all; and that the other equal liberties are secured. *Then it would appear that the resulting distribution of income and the pattern of expectations will tend to satisfy the difference principle.* In this complex of institutions, *which we think of as establishing social justice in the modern state,* the advantages of the better situated improve the condition of the least favored. Or when they do not, they can be adjusted to do so, for example, by setting the social minimum at the appropriate level. (Ibid.:87, emphases added)

Rawls evidently assumes that the most important economic factor in making market systems just is providing a "reasonable social minimum," and to predispose his contracting agents to a state which ensures this, the "grave-risks" assumption is built into the original position.

Rawls's account of his "thin theory of the good," those minimal assumptions about rational life plans on which individuals would allegedly agree behind the veil of ignorance, is also empirically and ontologically loaded, as has been observed by several critics.[13] One of Rawls's primary concerns is to show that his principles would be chosen over various types of utilitarianism. His main objection to utilitarianism is that it is a teleological theory; it specifies the good independently of and prior to the right, the latter being "defined as that which maximizes the good" (ibid.:24). In classical utilitarianism the good is regarded as the sum of satisfactions across all individuals; in aggregate utilitarianism it is the average social satisfaction that has to be maximized. In both these cases "there is no reason in principle why the greater gains of some should not compensate for the lesser losses of others; or more importantly, why the violation of the liberty of a few might not be made right by the greater good shared by many" (ibid.:26). Rawls repeats this standard objection to classical utilitarianism many times. It parallels Nozick's objection that utilitarianism involves "moral balancing" of the interests of some against the interests of others. Like Nozick, Rawls wants to argue for the priority of right over good to avoid this, but the kind of solution Nozick adopts is not available to him, for two reasons. First, he is aware that the market may not preserve the interests of all, and that it cannot be appealed to, a priori, as the preserver of individual rights. Second, Rawls does want to make some comparisons among persons. He wants to do this, however, without violating the priority of right and so collapsing into the kind of teleology that, for him, makes utilitarianism objectionable. "A competitive price system," he writes, "gives no consideration to needs and therefore it cannot be the sole device of distribution" (ibid.:276). Statements of this kind presume a theory of needs. It is to the solution of this problem that his "thin theory" and "primary goods" are directed.

13 For one recent discussion, see Galston (1983:625ff). See also Hare (1975:81–107).

Rawls argues that there is a plurality of conceptions of the good, but that they all require certain things, namely his primary goods. Thus he can have his cake and eat it, too, for he can have a theory of objective needs without falling into teleology. What is the nature and extent of this theory of needs? Rawls attempts to downplay the interpersonal comparisons involved in it, holding that an attraction of his difference principle is that it requires only that we identify the worst-off member in any distribution. He claims that the difference principle "meets some of the difficulties in making interpersonal comparisons" because, "as long as we can identify the least advantaged representative man, only ordinal judgments of well-being are required from then on." The "further difficulties of cardinal measurement" allegedly do not arise because no further interpersonal comparisons are necessary. If we can determine whether a change in the basic structure makes the worst-off individual better or worse off, according to Rawls, we can determine his best situation.

We do not have to know how much he prefers one situation to another. The difference principle, then, asks less of our judgments of welfare. We never have to calculate a sum of advantages involving a cardinal measure. While qualitative interpersonal comparisons are made in finding the bottom position, for the rest the ordinal judgments of one representative man suffice. . . . The only index problem that concerns us is that for the least advantaged group. The primary goods enjoyed by other representative individuals are adjusted to raise this index, subject of course to the usual constraints. It is unnecessary to define weights for the more favored position in any detail, as long as we are sure that they are more favored. (Ibid.:91–4)

This is very murky. All interpersonal comparisons require at the very least a definition of the dimension along which individuals are to be compared and the criteria for ranking all relevant individuals along that dimension. To identify the worst-off individual we must compare every individual with every other individual along the relevant dimension. If we had a bag of marbles and wanted to know which was the most scratched, we should have to compare every marble with every other marble in this respect.[14] In regard to Rawls's primary goods, too, we need to have them sufficiently well defined to compare all individuals along the relevant dimension. (The one application of his principle on pages 153–4 assumes that primary goods can be given dollar values, although it is by no means obvious that this is feasible given their very broad definition and the range of situations to which this principle is meant to be applicable, but I will pass over this issue here.)[15]

Once the worst-off individual has been identified, what of Rawls's claim that we can proceed to ordinal meaures? How will we know that the individual's situation *has* been improved on an ordinal scale? Ask her? What if we give her a million dollars and she replies in the negative? Give her another million and see what she says then? Surely not.[16] How can we know, without reverting to cardinal scales, whether she still *is* the worst-off individual? After any distributional change we should again have to compare every individual with every other along the relevant cardinal dimension to know who was now the worst-off. Thus Rawls's weak cardinality turns out on closer inspection not to be so weak. If it is a full-blown cardinal system, however, as it seems that it must be, Rawls is

14 We could take some shortcuts in this process by assuming various transitivity rules, but it would be a mistake to think that this in any way (in this context) reduces the comparisons involved. A transitivity rule is only a form of shorthand – it entails comparisons of all the entities covered by it.

15 Arrow (1973:254) has noted that so long as there is more than one primary good there is an index-number problem in commensurating the different goods, in principle just as difficult as the interpersonal comparisons problem. Little (1950) and others have argued with some force that as soon as ordinal utilities are given a dollar value they implicitly become cardinal.

16 Rawls (1982:164) avoids some of these difficulties by retreating to the claim that "the least advantaged are defined as those who have the lowest index of primary goods, when their prospects are viewed over a complete life. . . . The two principles of justice allow for social mobility through the principle of fair equality of opportunity: it is not a primary good to be weighted in the index." This move creates new difficulties of its own. It certainly weakens the already weak egalitarian component of the difference principle (discussed later in this section), since this now requires only actions that improve the situation of the worst-off but do not alter their situation *as* worst-off. Given Rawls's assumptions about grave risks and risk-aversion this would seem to make the difference principle even less attractive to the parties in the original position. These issues aside, this move does nothing to mitigate the difficulties involved in identifying the worst-off and deciding what would benefit them sufficiently to satisfy the difference principle, without interpersonal comparability.

clearly in danger of collapsing into precisely the kind of teleology he finds so objectionable in utilitarianism.[17]

His only real bastion against this is his additional claim that primary goods "are things which it is supposed a rational man wants whatever else he wants. Regardless of what an individual's rational plans are in detail, it is assumed that there are various things which he would prefer more of rather than less" (ibid.:92). This must be true if the principles are to be neutral between different conceptions of the good as Rawls claims:

Justice as fairness . . . does not look behind the use which persons make of the rights and opportunities available to them in order to measure, much less to maximize, the satisfactions they achieve. Nor does it try to evaluate the relative merits of different conceptions of the good. Instead, it is assumed that the members of society are rational persons able to adjust their conceptions of the good to their situation. There is no necessity to compare the worth of the conceptions of different persons *once it is supposed they are compatible with the principles of justice.* (Ibid.:94, emphasis added)

This is a big supposition and by no means intuitively self-evident. It is clearly an empirical claim, yet Rawls seems to regard it as a logical requirement. That all persons would agree that it would be rational always to want more rather than less of his primary goods is not self-evident, particularly when the

---

17 More recently, in response to Arrow's criticisms, Rawls has acknowledged that his theory requires explicit interpersonal comparisons. He has retreated to the view that I termed Pigouvian in the last chapter: that interpersonal comparisons are unavoidable in a theory of just distribution. Thus to "an economist concerned with social justice and public policy an index of primary goods may seem merely *ad hoc* patchwork." For a moral theory, however, the "use of primary goods is not a makeshift which a better theory can replace, but a reasonable social practice which we try to design so as to achieve the workable agreement required for effective and willing social cooperation" (1982:184–5). Plausible as this might be as a point about the inevitability of interpersonal comparisons, it leaves Rawls with the problem of defining an index for comparison not teleological in what he takes to be the relevant objectionable sense. In this paper he does not define such an index, and primary goods are again "estimated in terms of income and wealth." This is problematical, as he acknowledges, since it is not at all clear, for instance, that such primary goods as the social bases of self-respect can be so estimated, and if so, how it will be done (ibid.:162–3). If the bases of self-respect are taken seriously as primary goods, this is likely to involve many things that cannot be measured in this way (cf. Walzer, 1983). Problems of index-definition aside, Rawls offers here no new concrete reasons why his particular primary goods, in their particular lexical order, are to be preferred.

primary goods are so loosely defined. Kane (1982:249–52) has mentioned the case of religious sects that may eschew worldly wealth as well as religious toleration for other groups. Without going to such extremes we might well imagine, for example, someone holding with good reason that the desire for income and wealth beyond a certain limit becomes self-destructive and/or socially destructive. It has thus been a standard objection to Rawls's argument that the values he claims everyone can accept are in fact those of a relatively small group of liberal intellectuals. Rawls nonetheless takes his theory of motivation as axiomatic.[18] In his discussion of toleration, for instance, he holds that it is legitimate to be intolerant of conceptions of the good incompatible with the two principles (Rawls, 1971:216–7ff), if circumstances arise in which they become threatening to social stability.[19] If the two principles are held to be nonteleological, however, as neutral among different conceptions of the good, they cannot be used as a basis for rejecting a particular conception of the good on the grounds that it violates the two principles, unless it is held a priori that only conceptions of the good consistent with the two principles are rational. If *this* is the claim, Rawls's argument is irreducibly teleological.

The criteria employed by Rawls to characterize the original position and the motivation of, and information available to, the contracting agents seem thus quite arbitrary. They are clearly geared to producing the conclusions he desires, yet he feels no compunction to argue for many of the factual claims he makes or presupposes along the way. The closest he comes to a justification of his procedures is the following:

[I]t is obviously impossible to develop a substantive theory of justice founded solely on truths of logic and definition. The analysis of moral concepts and the a priori, however traditionally understood, is too slender a basis. Moral philosophy must be free to use contingent

---

18 For further discussion of the arbitrariness of Rawls's theory of primary goods see Fishkin (1979:105–20).

19 Rawls makes the empirical claim that this is unlikely to be a problem in practice because initial toleration of the intolerant "may persuade them to a belief in freedom" so that an intolerant sect will "tend to lose its intolerance and accept liberty of conscience" (Rawls, 1971:219). This is wishful thinking, however, based on his (undemonstrated) claim that just institutions will tend to be stable.

assumptions and general facts as it pleases. . . . This is the conception of the subject adopted by most classical British writers down through Sidgwick. I see no reason to depart from it. (Ibid.:51)

It is one thing to claim that a substantive theory of justice must make factual assumptions, and quite another to say that it is licensed to do so "as it pleases." We saw in earlier chapters that seventeenth-century writers in the tradition to which Rawls refers felt it incumbent upon themselves to demonstrate their empirical claims, insofar as they were able, and to argue for their assumptions about knowledge and reality. This was also true in varying degrees of writers such as Bentham, Hume, and Mill. Only under the extreme division of labor prevailing in the academy today can a writer like Rawls simply ignore issues clearly relevant to his enterprise, and make factual claims about the world that suit his theory, leaving the validation of those claims to others whose job it is held to be within the academic division of labor.

ii. The substance of rights

Rawls's first principle grants everyone the most extensive system of basic liberties "compatible with a like liberty for all," and his second principle requires, first, that all offices be open to everyone under "conditions of fair equality of opportunity," and, second, that inequalities be arranged for the benefit of the least advantaged. These requirements must be satisfied in the order stated, an injunction lower on the list always giving way to a higher one.

Notice first that these principles presuppose that it is possible to consider issues of liberty independently of issues of equality. As Rawls puts it:

As their formulation suggests, these principles presuppose that the social structure can be divided into two more or less distinct parts, the first principle applying to the one, the second to the other. They distinguish between those aspects of the social system that define and secure the equal liberties of citizenship and those that specify and establish social and economic inequalities. (Ibid.:61)

It is an exceedingly large assumption to hold that parties in the original position would make a division of this kind, particularly knowing that in the society in which they will be living, being the poorest individual would involve "grave risks." It might be argued with some force that from the point of view of the worst-off individual (which the principle of insufficient reason, according to Rawls, requires us to take),[20] eligibility for public office, voting, and so on should be seen as secondary to ensuring that some basic economic guarantees are fulfilled. What good is the right to run for President to someone who is dying of starvation? The response to this – that the parties to the agreement know conditions of "moderate scarcity" and a certain "level" of economic development obtain – does not suffice to meet this objection. Rawls's objections to utilitarian efficiency and his "grave risks" argument require the contracting agents to assume that, even if the level of economic development is considerable and the wealth in a society extensive, this does not ensure the situation of the worst-off will not be precarious. Whatever the average per capita income there may be bag ladies living out of railway station lockers, and we might be them.

It is more than a little naive to suppose that the political and economic spheres of society are distinct in the way Rawls suggests, governed by different principles of organization. Not only does Rawls regard the first principle as morally prior, in the sense that it should take precedence should conflicts arise; he seems to think that it can be specified independently of, and somehow temporally prior to, the principles governing the economic organization of society:

The first principle of equal liberty is the primary standard for the constitutional convention. Its main requirements are that the fundamental liberties of the person and liberty of conscience and freedom of thought be protected and that the political process as a whole be a just procedure. . . . The second principle comes into play at the stage of the legislature. It dictates that social and economic policies be aimed at maximizing the long-term expectations of the least advantaged under conditions of fair equality of opportunity, subject to the equal liberties being maintained. *At this point* the full range of general economic and social facts is brought to bear. (Ibid.:199, emphasis added)

20 See Rawls (1971:167–73)

It is surely possible, without buying into any very rigid determinism, to wonder whether this makes much sense; whether the forms of political organization in medieval Europe had not something to do with feudal methods of production and exchange; whether the forms of political organization in the contemporary capitalist world have not something to do with market-based industrialization; whether the forms of political organization in the communist countries have not something to do with late planned industrialization in a capitalist world economy; whether the forms of political authoritarianism that prevail in such third world countries as Brazil have not something to do with the economic conditions under which industrial modernization is taking place there. Yet Rawls seems blithely unaware of such considerations; so, too, are the parties in the original position – for all their knowledge of the "general facts" of social life and the "laws" of economic and psychological theory.

What is this "most extensive system of basic liberties compatible with a like liberty for all" required by the first principle? What is a liberty for Rawls? This is not entirely clear. Despite the fact that he endorses MacCallum's analysis of freedom as a triadic relation[21] (Rawls, 1971:201–3; MacCallum, 1972:174–93), he takes little or no account of it in his subsequent discussion of freedom, which is littered with phrases like "the standpoint of liberty itself," "the priority of liberty," and "the principle of equal liberty" (Rawls, 1971: 207; 211). The point of MacCallum's analysis, however, was to show it is meaningless to speak of freedom or liberty in these ways. If Rawls were to take that analysis seriously as a basis for talking about freedom, he would always need to describe his freedoms relationally, specifying which agents were to be free from which constraints to perform which actions. It seems highly unlikely, on this view, that one could formulate a general principle guaranteeing freedom that "holds unconditionally, that is, whatever the circumstances or state of society" (ibid.:125). Further, it could certainly not be specified independently of the principles governing social

21 For discussion of MacCallum's view, see notes 11 and 14 to Chapter 1.

and economic organization. Once the term "freedom" is held to entail reference to constraints, enabling conditions, and actions, we cannot talk sensibly about freedom without reference to substantive questions concerning economy and society, which so obviously determine the nature of many constraints on, and enabling conditions for, actions, and indeed the class of actions available to a given individual.

Rawls sometimes seems aware of these complications, making one attempt to sidestep them via a distinction between "liberty" and "the worth" of liberty:

The inability to take advantage of one's rights and opportunities as a result of poverty and ignorance, and a lack of means generally, is sometimes counted among the constraints definitive of liberty. I shall not, however, say this, but rather I shall think of these things as affecting the worth of liberty, the value to individuals of the rights that the first principle defines. . . . Thus liberty and the worth of liberty are distinguished as follows: liberty is represented by the complete system of the liberties of equal citizenship, while the worth of liberty to persons and groups is proportional to their capacity to advance their ends within the framework the system defines. Freedom as equal liberty is the same for all; the question of compensating for a lesser than equal liberty does not arise. But the worth of liberty is not the same for everyone. Some have greater authority and wealth, and therefore greater means to achieve their aims. (Ibid.:204)

Inequalities in the *worth* of liberty are to be governed by the difference principle. They are secondary to, and can never dictate any changes in, the definition of the liberties themselves. No affirmative action could be justified, for Rawls, if it involved the mildest infraction of the equal liberty of the most advantaged.[22]

22 I will not discuss in detail Rawls's argument for fair equality of opportunity – the weaknesses of which have been well explored by Fishkin (1975:623ff). Suffice it to note that the issues discussed in the last two paragraphs and the next arise in that connection also: the priority of very generally defined liberties seriously limits the possibility for achieving meaningful equality of opportunity. As Williams (1962: 110–131) has shown, and as Rawls seems at times to be aware (e.g., 1971: 74ff), the notion of equality of opportunity, if taken seriously, is potentially highly radical. I would argue that in the cases where it began to make significant differences to the social structure, it would be rendered inactive by the general provisions of the first principle.

Rawls defines "freedom" here quite independently of the uses to which it is put, a definition clearly at odds with Mac-Callum's formula which analytically requires reference to the action performed and the means for performing it as part of the meaning of statements about freedom. If we grant Rawls his distinction between "liberty" and its "worth," it seems implausible that the individuals in the original position would only be concerned with unconditional guarantees concerning the former. Knowing that having a liberty entailed nothing about having the capacity to exercise it—as in the old saying that the poor are equally free to dine at the Ritz—is an insufficient guarantee to our risk-averse contractors who view the situation from the point of view of the worst-off.[23]

Rawls's definition of freedom is the standard negative libertarian one that we have encountered, in one form or another, in each of the last three chapters. It is no accident that the first kind of liberty he discusses in any detail is religious toleration, or that he takes this as his basic model of substantive freedom. Thus the "reasoning in this case [of religious toleration] can be generalized to apply to other freedoms" (ibid.:206). He begins by arguing that "equal liberty of conscience is the only principle that the persons in the original position can acknowledge." They cannot "take chances with their liberty by permitting the dominant religious or moral doctrine to persecute or suppress others if it wishes." To do so "would show that one did not take one's religious or moral convictions seriously, or highly value the liberty to examine one's beliefs" (ibid.:207). Rawls acknowledges (ibid.:208) that these remarks may not be consistent with all views of religion. He nonetheless maintains it is the only rational view to adopt. This surely begs the question, since it is often in the nature of religious conviction precisely to deny the kind of ethical pluralism that these remarks presuppose. On reading them one cannot help but think of the English statesman whose solution to the Middle East conflict was that Jews and Arabs should settle their differences in a

---

23 For a more elaborate discussion of this issue, see Daniels (1975:253–81), who avers that if Rawls's argument for equal liberty is to be accepted it must entail an argument for equal worth of liberty, and that Rawls implicitly makes such an appeal in his arguments for equal liberty of conscience.

Christian fashion. Rawls's view of toleration derives from the standard Protestant view of the importance of individual conscience, and the centrality of the personal relationship between man and God. It is inconsistent with crusading religions such as Islam (or Medieval Catholicism), and with the doctrines of the present-day Catholic Church – which still include Papal infallibility and the acceptance of doctrine as interpreted by the church hierarchy whatever one's individual convictions happen to be. Rawls holds that the contracting agents must regard religious obligations as "self-imposed" (ibid.:206); to ensure this the parties must acknowledge pluralism and require toleration.

We confront here the same type of circularity we encountered in relation to the thin theory of the good. Religious toleration is held to be a good because it is the only means of ensuring that one can be free to practice one's religion. Religions incompatible with the doctrine of toleration are ruled out since they are inconsistent with this principle. It may be that religious toleration is a social good, but if Rawls is to be convincing on this score he must supply some independent reasons why this is so. The claim that the doctrine of toleration is neutral among different religions is false – it is neutral only among the (historically and geographically) few religions that embrace it. The tactic of defining acceptable religions as those which acknowledge (or at least do not threaten) the principle of toleration is as unconvincing as that of defining acceptable conceptions of the good as those which conform to the thin theory.

Rawls nonetheless takes this doctrine of toleration as paradigmatic for the freedoms guaranteed by the first principle.

Justice as fairness provides, as we have now seen, strong arguments for an equal liberty of conscience. *I shall assume that these arguments can be generalized in suitable ways to support the principle of equal liberty.* Therefore the parties have good grounds for adopting this principle. *It is obvious that these considerations are also important in making the case for the priority of liberty.* (Ibid.:211, emphases added)

The "basic liberties" of citizens are thus defended by Rawls through an appeal to the conventional negative libertarian arguments of Locke, and oft repeated by Mill, Berlin, Nozick, Dworkin, and many others.[24]

Leaving aside, for now, questions that have been raised by Hart (1975: 230–52) and others concerning the coherence of Rawls's idea of "the most extensive system of basic liberties" and his apparently arbitrary translation of this into the standard liberal freedoms of the right to vote and be eligible for public office, freedom of speech, assembly, conscience, and thought, and the right to hold personal property and to be free from arbitrary arrest, notice that these freedoms are purely formal and procedural. Questions about their substantive content, or "worth," are treated as of secondary import, and protected from serious discussion by the a priori commitment to pluralist conceptions of the good. It might be argued that Rawls's attachment to the negative libertarian notion of rights as spheres surrounding individuals is even stronger than Nozick's. In outlining why his account of rights is not vulnerable to Sen's paradox of the Paretian liberal,[25] Rawls likens his position to Nozick's, asserting that the "basic liberties are, in effect, unalienable and therefore can neither be waived nor limited by any agreements made by citizens, nor overridden by shared collective preferences" (1982:171n). These liberties are conceived of as on a higher plane than preferences, and can therefore not be part of the pairwise comparisons that generate Sen's paradox. Rawls notes that this is actually a stronger claim for inviolability than Nozick's (for whom rights can be traded by agreement or compensation, as we saw). In justice as fairness, by contrast:

... any undertakings to waive or to infringe them [basic liberties] are *void ab initio*; citizens' desires in this respect have no legal force and

24 If we forget for a moment Locke's arguments for the suppression of atheists and Papists (though, as we saw in Chapter 3, his reasoning for this is very Rawlsish) his defense of toleration could be straight out of *A Letter Concerning Toleration*. All the main ingredients are present: the view of religious and other freedoms as rights to privacy, the view of religious groups as voluntary associations whose internal activities should never be interfered with unless they violate an individual's freedom, and the view of the state as reserving the right to regulate these associations in the interests of "public order and security," but remaining otherwise neutral with respect to different religions (Rawls, 1971:211–2).

25 Which purports to demonstrate that the Pareto principle is incompatible with the most minimal assignment of individual rights, given some very weak conditions (Sen, 1970:82ff).

should not affect these rights. Nor should the desires of however many others to deny or limit a person's equal basic liberties have any weight. Preferences which would have this effect never, so to speak, enter into the social calculus. . . . Both the agreements and preferences of citizens in society are counted as hierarchically subordinate to these [highest-order] interests, and this is the ground of the priority of liberty.

The metaphor of a sphere in moral space is almost too weak to capture this: Rawls's view of man *qua* moral being seems almost monadic. If this is a more internally consistent statement of the negative libertarian view than Nozick's, it still remains to be shown why this highest-order interest in absolute inviolability would rationally be agreed on in the original position, something by no means self-evident.

Rawls is a liberal who has read Keynes and welfare economics seriously. He therefore feels compelled to enter the thickets of substantive conceptions of the good, although he tries to downplay this, and of the active regulation of economy and society by the state. His assumptions on these counts are even more clearly apparent in his second principle, as I will now argue.

In its final formulation the difference principle postulates that inequalities can only be justified if they work to the advantage of the worst-off. It is important to note, however, that Rawls has changed his formulation (in both the general and special conceptions). In its first (and much less contentious) form the difference principle held that inequalities are justified only if they can reasonably be expected to work to *everyone's* advantage (ibid.:60–2). He often writes as though these two injunctions are synonymous. They clearly are not, without the addition of extremely powerful empirical assumptions concerning the multiplier effects on the welfare of every stratum above the worst-off, and on the economy as a whole, of increasing welfare at the bottom. Not only must such increases improve the welfare of every stratum, but they must somehow generate the expansion necessary to make this possible (otherwise at least one stratum must be less well off by definition). The only attempt Rawls makes at justifying this assumption is his very brief discussion of "chain connection" and "close-knitness" (Rawls, 1971:80–3).

Rawls makes two distinct empirical claims in this regard: first that the application of the difference principle generates a tendency toward equality; second, that it can be expected to increase the welfare of all social strata. Taking the second of these first, he claims that inequalities in expectations are chain connected: "if an advantage has the effect of raising the expectations of the lowest position, it raises the expectations of all positions in between." Thus, for Rawls, "if the greater expectations for entrepreneurs benefit the unskilled worker, they also benefit the semiskilled." Furthermore, he argues, "expectations are close-knit: that is, it is impossible to raise or lower the expectation of any representative man without raising or lowering the expectation of every other representative man, especially that of the least advantaged." Under these empirical assumptions, Rawls concludes, "there is a sense in which everyone benefits when the difference principle is satisfied. For the representative man who is better off in any two-way comparison gains by the advantages offered him, and the man who is worse off gains from the contributions which these inequalities make" (ibid.:80–2). These are powerful empirical assumptions, not obviously warranted. In this connection Rawls remarks:

I shall not examine how likely it is that chain connection and close-knitness hold. The difference principle is not contingent on these relations being satisfied. However, one may note that when the contributions of the more favored positions spread generally throughout society and are not confined to particular sectors, it seems plausible that if the least advantaged benefit so do others in between. (Ibid.)

What is the force of this claim? Rawls's position appears to be that, although he does not know to what extent chain connection holds in the actual world, in a just society it would hold most of the time, and it therefore rests on "natural assumptions" (ibid.:80). He is aware, however, that in cases where this is so there will be no difference between the practical results of his principle and of classical utilitarianism. If this is taken to be the typical case it surely undercuts the effectiveness of his objection to utilitarianism, as has been

Table 1 *The difference principle without chain connection for distributional changes where the sum of advantages remains constant, with three representative individuals*

Individuals ranked by possession of primary goods	Distributions				
	Status quo	Departures from status quo			
		D_1	D_2	D_3	D_4
A	90	90	89	91	6
B	7	6	8	5	90
C	3	4	3	4	4

observed by several commentators.[26] Rawls offers no evidence that chain connection occurs in the world to any significant extent, and as Barry (1973:111ff), Rae (1975b:641), and others have noted, it is a highly unwarranted assumption. Rawls sidesteps this issue by claiming his principle does not *require* that chain connection holds, but if the intuitive force of the principle is not contingent on chain connection, why talk about it at all? The truth is that it *is* so contingent, as can be seen when we consider the distributive possibilities without chain connection. There are three main types of cases: where the sum of advantags remains constant, where it is increasing, and where it is decreasing.[27]

Where the sum of advantages remains constant, some examples of which are given in Table 1, it can *never* be true that the difference principle works to everyone's advantage (therefore, strictly, chain connection cannot hold), since improving the position of C requires worsening the position of someone else, either A (as in the move from the status quo to D_4) or B (as in the move from the status quo to D_1). Rawls's argument does not prevent improvement in the position of the worst-off

26 See especially Rae (1975b:635–41); see also Fishkin (1975:625–6).
27 Some of the examples presented in the following paragraphs are logically analogous to those discussed by Rae (1975b). They are all special cases of a more general rule demonstrated by Rae et al. (1981) in Chapter 6, "Relative equalities," especially pp. 110–23. Some implications of Rae's discussion are taken up in the next chapter.

Table 2 *The difference principle without chain connection for distributional changes where the sum of advantages decreases, with three representative individuals*

Individuals ranked by possession of primary goods	status quo	Distributions			
		Departures from status quo			
		D_1	D_2	D_3	D_4
A	90	10	7	4	4
B	7	7	4	4	5
C	3	4	4	4	4

member at the expense of the middle strata, while either leaving the most well-off as they were before (as in the move from the status quo to D_1) or improving their situation (as in moving from the status quo to D_3). The difference principle sanctions both these moves from the status quo.[28] These anomalous results, and others, can also be produced if the difference principle is applied when the sum of advantages is decreasing, as can be seen from Table 2.

Rawls never discusses the implications of his principle for a contracting economy, but it is a case he must confront if only because of the standard conservative argument that planned downward distribution has precisely this contracting result, due to its long-run effects on investment incentives. In this case it is obvious that improving the situation of the least advantaged does not improve that of all. By definition the sum of advantages is decreasing, thus again chain connection cannot strictly hold.[29] Notice that by the difference principle we would prefer all four departures from the status quo in Table 2, though they are radically different distributions, ranging from perfect equality in D_3, to D_1 where the best-off individ-

28 For further discussion of why the difference principle would be unacceptable to the middle classes, see Rae (1975b:635ff).
29 If we enter the realm of counterfactuals, more complexities arise concerning what would have occurred had the distributional change not taken place, and the extent to which the change is responsible for overall expansion and contraction. Rawls never considers these issues, but surely any general principle of distribution that claims such broad application as Rawls's would have to deal with them.

Table 3 *The difference principle with and without chain connection for distributional changes where the sum of advantages is increasing, with three representative individuals*

Individuals ranked by possession of primary goods	Distributions				
	Status quo	Departures from status quo			
		D_1	D_2	D_3	D_4
A	90	90	90	6,000	6,000
B	7	7	6	10	6
C	3	7	5	4	4

ual has two and a half times as many primary goods as the worst-off, to D_4 where the middle stratum actually replaces the top stratum. All these moves constitute chronic reductions in overall wealth for the sake of very minor increases for the worst-off.[30] From these considerations it can be seen that the difference principle is highly undetermined, that many of its possible injunctions violate many intuitive notions of rational distribution, and that it will in all likelihood remain silent on many, if not most, controversial questions about distribution.

Where the sum of advantages is increasing, both with and without chain connection, many of these anomalies remain and others arise. In Table 3, again, all four departures are preferred to the status quo; D_1 is preferred to D_2, which is preferred to D_3, which is preferred to D_4. It is by no means intuitively obvious, however, that we should prefer D_1 to D_3, for instance, or D_3 to the status quo. The move from the status quo to D_3 (where chain connection holds) is highly inegalitarian and could be shown to embody the logic of the distributive consequences of across-the-board percentage-based tax cuts of the type implemented by the Reagan administration during the early 1980s. The even more inegalitarian move from the status quo to D_4 (where there is no chain connection) would be sanctioned by the difference principle.

30 More generally, Rae (1979) has shown that the difference principle can militate against both equality and efficiency at the same time.

From these examples it is clear that if the chain connection assumption is relaxed many additional absurd distributive consequences can result. The difference principle can work to the benefit of all only if we assume a continuously expanding economy, and even in this case (with or without chain connection) it can produce highly inegalitarian results. In short, there are few rational grounds for embracing the difference principle as a general principle for distributing income and wealth. It takes so little information into account, either about the impacts of its application on other social strata or about the circumstances in which it is applied, that it would be unwise to embrace it under conditions of ignorance as the only and permanent principle of social distribution. Whether the sum of advantages is constant, decreasing, or increasing, there are circumstances in which there are at least prima facie reasons for rejecting it. Finally, it is simply false that there is any necessary egalitarian tendency in the principle as Rawls and many of his conservative critics have claimed.[31] The principle is based on such sparse information that, although it can sanction some distributional changes that increase equality (somehow defined), it can sanction many which obviously either have no significant distributional impact or have an inegalitarian impact.

Only if it is packed with Keynesian assumptions about the multiplier effects of increasing the position of the worst-off can this argument make intuitive sense. This would further require the postulate that the effects on aggregate demand of applying the difference principle will be such as to increase investment, production, output, and wealth for all. Such logic is compatible with the one concrete illustration Rawls gives of his principle (1971:153–4) wherein the sum of advantages is greatest in the distribution favored by the difference principle.[32] There are no

31 For further discussion of the weakness of Rawls's claims about equality in relation to the difference principle, see Fishkin (1975:624–5). For a conservative attack on Rawls's supposed egalitarianism, see Bloom (1975).
32 It is not clear, however, whether or not chain connection holds in this example. It does not hold in his three "decisions" as compared with one another, but since Rawls fails to describe the status quo from which the decisions are considered, it is unclear whether moving from the status quo to D_3 improves the situation of each stratum above the worst-off.

special reasons for thinking this is the typical case, however, and Rawls never supplies us with any. He does make the empirical claim that in a society governed by his principles very substantial inequalities will not arise. The difference principle "relies on the idea that in a competitive economy (with or without private ownership) with an open class system excessive inequalities will not be the rule. Given the distribution of natural assets and the laws of motivation, great disparities will not long persist" (ibid.:158). By way of justification for these assumptions Rawls continues:

Now the point to stress here is that there is no objection to resting the choice of first principles upon the general facts of economics and psychology. As we have seen, the parties in the original position are assumed to know the general facts about human society. Since this knowledge enters into the premises of their deliberations, their choice of principles is relative to these facts. What is essential, of course, is that these premises be true and sufficiently general. (Ibid.)

Rawls, however, supplies no reasons for us to suppose that his premises are true or sufficiently general. He is here not appealing to the "general facts" of any society: one thing we know with little doubt is that competitive market systems generate massive inequalities, always have done, and perhaps even require them – or so many (defenders and critics) would claim.[33] Rawls is appealing here not to any generally accepted facts or laws, but to his own highly speculative account of economic systems in Chapter 5 of *A Theory of Justice*, wherein he claims that his principles can apply equally to capitalist and socialist economies, and that "there is no essential tie between the use of free markets and private ownership of the instruments of production" (ibid.:271ff). Contentious empirical claims, at the least, yet Rawls feels no compulsion to descend to the realms of evidence to establish either of them. He makes one reference to the fact that markets predate capitalism (although what he should show is that they predate private ownership of the means of production). He pays no attention to the immense differences between medieval markets and national and international markets today, or to the huge

33 See, for example, Parkin (1971:163ff).

difficulties encountered by socialist countries such as Poland and Hungary that have attempted to conjoin socialist institutions with competitive market practices in some areas.[34]

For two reasons it is difficult to make much sense of his claim that his principles can apply to both capitalist and socialist societies. First, he offers no account of what the socialist institutional manifestations of his principles would be. Many of our intuitive notions of socialism are in tension, to say the least, with his account of the priority of liberty and his insistence on plural conceptions of the good. Second, his assumptions about market systems are so lacking in evidential support it is difficult to imagine *any* system conforming to the one he describes. The assumptions about chain connection and the absence of substantial inequality are two cases in point. Questions could also be raised concerning the efficiency and viability of a distributive system based solely on the difference principle, assuming it could be implemented, and about the lack of any thoroughgoing account of how, in the absence of substantial inequalities, investment incentives will be maintained.

Rawls's application of his principles in a "property owning democracy" presumes a highly benign view of how competitive markets operate. He claims that a market-based system, if fully competitive, just happens to be consistent with the first two of his three lexically ordered principles:

A . . . significant advantage of a market system is that, given the requisite background institutions, it is consistent with equal liberties and fair equality of opportunity. Citizens have a free choice of careers and occupations. There is no reason at all for the forced and central direction of labor. Indeed, in the absence of some differences in earnings as these arise in a competitive scheme, it is hard to see how, under ordinary circumstances anyway, certain aspects of a command society inconsistent with liberty can be avoided. Moreover, a system of markets decentralizes the exercise of economic power. (Ibid.:272)

On this basis Rawls feels justified in claiming that market arrangements constitute the only way "that the problem of dis-

---

34 I have argued elsewhere that, at least with respect to Poland, the attempt to introduce market-price systems where there is no private ownership seems to run into intractable difficulties (Shapiro, 1981:469–502).

tribution can be handled as a case of pure procedural justice" and that this has the additional advantage of "efficiency" and leaves us able to "protect the important liberty of free choice of occupation" (ibid.:274). Leaving aside the claim that the market system is held to be neutral between capitalist and socialist worlds, leaving aside the claims that market systems decentralize the exercise of economic power or that they give everyone the freedom to work to begin with, let alone in the occupation of their choice (again, no evidence is offered for any of this), it is clear from his discussion of "exploitation" that Rawls has an essentially benign view of markets:

It may be objected ... that a perfectly competitive economy can never be realized. Factors of production never in fact receive their marginal products, and under modern conditions anyway industries soon come to be dominated by a few large firms. Competition is at best imperfect and persons receive less than the value of their contribution, and in this sense they are exploited. The reply to this is first that in any case the conception of a suitably regulated competitive economy with the appropriate background institutions is an ideal scheme which shows how the two principles of justice might be realized. It serves to illustrate the content of these principles, and brings out one way in which either a private-property economy or a socialist regime can satisfy this conception of justice. Granting that existing conditions always fall short of the ideal assumptions, we have some notion of what is just. Moreover we are in a better position to assess how serious the existing imperfections are and to decide upon the best way to approximate the ideal. (Ibid.:309)

We have to patch up the market and approximate the ideal as best we can. This whole argument assumes that "exploitation" only arises under "imperfect" market conditions, a view that Rawls takes from Pigou (ibid.:309).

This benign notion of exploitation is not, strictly, available to Rawls. Pigou's notion of exploitation turned on his concept of external diseconomy which, as we saw in Chapter 4 and as Pigou never thought of denying, in turn requires a full-blown cardinal utilitarian system and interpersonal judgments of social utility. This was anything but a minimal commitment for Pigou. As even the most cursory reading of his chapter on unfair wages (Pigou, 1960:549–71) will reveal, he thought

233

substantive judgments about unfairnesses worked by the market due to the low mobility of labor, ignorance of workers, power of employers, and the weak bargaining position of certain sectors – notably women – could and should be made. This is a far cry from Marx's notion of exploitation, which turned on the claim that under an advanced division of labor human labor-power produces more fresh exchange-value than is required to produce it (and more, therefore, than the worker can command in wages). Pigou's is, however, unquestionably a teleological theory in Rawls's sense, requiring independent judgments concerning the "most advantageous" distribution of resources. Rawls explicitly rejects it in his discussion of classical utilitarianism (Rawls, 1971:32ff). It is difficult to see how part of it can be invoked without implicitly accepting the system in its entirety, with all its uncomfortable teleological implications. As with his account of the identification of the most disadvantaged for the difference principle, and with the discussion of the thin theory of the good, Rawls here equivocates concerning the interpersonal comparisons he is prepared to sanction, understating the extent to which they are required by the arguments he endorses. The overarching commitment is to the notion that the market system can be made fair and efficient when "suitably regulated," although criteria for suitability are nowhere expressly laid out.

iii. The basis for rights

What is the force of Rawls's argument that his principles would be chosen unanimously in the original position? Strictly speaking, it is not the hypothetical unanimity that is decisive, but our agreement that unanimity for his principles would occur under the relevant conditions. To understand fully this claim, we must examine Rawls's views on the nature of moral theory.

Rawls holds that we "should strive for a kind of moral geometry with all the rigor which this name connotes" and says that his eventual aim is to produce a theory of justice that is "strictly deductive" (ibid.:121). He rejects out of hand, however, all attempts at a priori ethical systems, arguing that empirical considerations must inevitably be part of the subject matter of moral philosophy. Rawls's method is difficult to characterize. He rejects "Cartesian" views of moral justification which presume "that first principles can be seen to be true, even necessarily so; [and] deductive reasoning then transfers this conviction from premises to conclusion," as well as so-called naturalist attempts to derive moral conclusions from alleged facts about the human condition. These two methods of justification, he holds, are the two main ways philosophers have sought to justify moral arguments, and both are unsuccessful (ibid.:577–8). "[W]e do better," he argues, "to regard a moral theory just as any other theory" (ibid.:578) and model it on scientific explanation. Rawls has long been concerned with giving an account of ethical justification analogous to (his understanding of) scientific justification. In his "Outline of a Decision Procedure for Ethics" (1951:177–97) he argued that just as the objectivity of the sciences turns on the reliability of their methods, so an objectively justifiable ethics must be founded on a reliable method. At a minimum this must include a procedure for isolating the relevant set of facts, a procedure for formulating a set of principles that would satisfactorily "explicate" the relevant facts, and an account of the reasons why the principles formulated are held to be rationally justifiable (ibid.:177–97).

Applying these notions to *A Theory of Justice,* we may say that the procedure for isolating the relevant set of moral facts is the veil of ignorance. The relevant moral facts to be "explicated" are the principles of justice that hypothetical individuals in the original position would choose as the permanent basis for the organization of their society. The procedure by which the choice of these principles is validated is a "thought experiment" the reader is asked to conduct, by imagining the persons in the original position, and considering whether the principles for which Rawls argues are not in closer agreement with our "considered judgments" in "reflective equilibrium" (the moral convictions we hold after careful consideration of the choice problem Rawls constructs) than a limited class of alternatives.[35] Hence:

35 For a discussion of the influence of Rawls's early methodological writings on *A Theory of Justice,* see Delaney (1977:153).

By going back and forth, sometimes altering the conditions of the contractual circumstances, at others withdrawing our judgments and conforming them to principle, I assume that eventually we shall find a description of the initial situation that both expresses reasonable conditions and yields principles which match our considered judgments duly pruned and adjusted. (Rawls, 1971:20)

Before examining these arguments in detail, it is worth pointing out that the claim that these procedures in any significant sense parallel the procedures of science is highly questionable. Kane (1982:232–40) has argued with some force that, although the practitioners of science must strive for impartiality, this is not typically achieved by enforcing ignorance on them in the manner Rawls advocates. In addition to this general difference between Rawls's procedures and those regarded as relevant to the pursuit of objectivity and impartiality, several questions arise concerning his more specific claims for his procedures.

First there is the sense in which he appeals to "our" considered judgments. Rawls intends the idea of reflective equilibrium to capture the "Socratic" element in moral philosophy, the sense in which we might "want to change our present considered judgments once their regulative principles are brought to light" (1971:49). Whether or not this is accurate, it does not entail that the process or results of reflective equilibrium will be the same for everyone, at least not without the addition of several other substantial premises. Rawls is aware of this complication, but his attempt to deal with it is not unproblematical:

I shall not even ask whether the principles that characterize one person's considered judgments are the same as those that characterize another's. *I shall take for granted that these principles are either approximately the same for persons whose judgments are in reflective equilibrium, or if not, that their judgments divide along a few main lines represented by the family of traditional doctrines that I shall discuss.* (Ibid.:50, emphasis added)

This procedure is held to be justified by analogy to Chomsky's theory of linguistics, in terms of which Rawls claims, "if we can describe one person's sense of grammar we shall surely know many things about the general structure of language. Similarly, if we should be able to characterize one (educated) person's sense of justice, we would have a good beginning toward a theory of justice." We can assume that everyone has "the whole form of a moral conception," so that "the views of the reader and the author are the only ones that count" (ibid.). This appeal to linguistic rules rests, however, on a misleading conflation of levels of abstraction. Earlier Rawls says more fully:

A useful comparison here is with the problem of describing the sense of grammaticalness that we have for the sentences of our native language. In this case the aim is to characterize the ability to recognize well-formed sentences by formulating clearly expressed principles which make the same discriminations as the native speaker. This is a difficult undertaking which, although still unfinished, is known to require theoretical constructions that far outrun the ad hoc precepts of our explicit grammatical knowledge. *A similar situation presumably holds in moral philosophy.* There is no reason to assume that our sense of justice can be adequately characterized by familiar common sense precepts, or derived from the more obvious learning principles. A correct account of moral capacities will certainly involve principles and theoretical constructions which go much beyond the norms and standards cited in everyday life; it may eventually require fairly sophisticated mathematics as well. (Ibid.:47, emphasis added)

It is one thing to claim that the use of moral terms, like other terms, involves the invocation of (often highly complex and implicit) rules of grammar and reference, and that such rules might (perhaps even necessarily) be the same for all users of a particular language. It is quite another thing to move to the view that peoples' substantive judgments will be in agreement, that a "moral grammar" will thus yield universal substantive moral judgments. The fact that a group of persons knows and agrees on the correct usages of the terms "good" and "conduct" in no way entails that they will agree on which conduct is good. They could not debate the issue without agreement on the meanings of the terms, and the correct use of those terms may well presuppose highly complex grammatical rules speakers could not typically articulate. No amount of analysis of the

logic of those meanings and rules, however, would be sufficient to produce agreement in their substantive judgments.
There is no reason to suppose that the views of a particular
reader in Rawlsian reflective equilibrium might constitute gen-
eralizable substantive judgments, certainly not for the reasons
Rawls offers.

Second, it might plausibly be wondered what the particular
significance of "educated" persons is for views generalizing
about substantive questions of justice. Perhaps only intellectuals with nothing better to do will be properly equipped and
have time to engage in Rawls's thought experiments. It is difficult to see why this gives them any special claim to make
substantive moral judgments for others. In this respect Rawls's
appeal to the assent of the reader is arbitrary.

Perhaps this is to miss the force of Rawls's claim. His appeal is not strictly (at least at first sight) to the reader's assent
to his substantive propositions, but to his assent that those
proposals would be chosen unanimously in the original position. The difficulty with this formulation is that it throws us
back on Rawls's highly speculative descriptivism, on what he
takes to be the "general facts of society," the "laws" of economics and psychology, and the "facts of everyday life." We
are invited to agree with these and to suppose that the individuals in the original position agree with them as well, and
to conclude that these persons would unanimously choose his
two principles of justice. Since he has devoted so much attention to defining the so-called laws and facts in such a way
that they generate (he believes) his conclusions, and since he
openly admits he would change them if they did not, this
argument can have little force for anyone who does not
agree with Rawls's conclusions in advance. There is a basic
appeal to a consensus theory of truth implicit in Rawls's argument: even if it could be shown that some of Rawls's assumptions were widely believed, this would demonstrate
nothing about their truth or the rational basis for thinking
about justice. Should Rawls, as he claims, "avoid introducing"
any "controversial ethical elements" into his account (ibid.:14)
this would in itself be no justification. At different times
there has been wide consensus on the flatness of the earth,

the divine right of kings, and the rationality of slavery.[36] Rawls does not even begin to establish that there is (or would be in the original position) consensus on many of his critical propositions. The assumptions behind his appeal to consensus thus need not concern us here, although this question will inevitably arise in Section III of this chapter.[37]

The whole battery of theoretical devices relating to the thought experiment Rawls proposes has one end: to achieve impartiality or fairness in the original position. The least convincing and most criticized aspects of this are Rawls's tactical uses of "knowledge" and "ignorance" in pursuit of this goal. Note, however, that Rawls's paradigm case of a fair decision in no way necessarily involves the use of ignorance. The example he uses to illustrate his "pure procedural justice" is that of the fair division of a cake; the aim is to devise a procedure that makes it rational for the cake-cutter to divide it equally. The obvious solution is to have the cutter get the last piece, since, by hypothesis, he "wants as large a piece as he can get" (ibid.:85). Yet what is the nature of the impartiality generated here? There is certainly no ignorance involved. Given Rawls's maximizing notion of rationality ("standard in economic theory"), the potential cutter can presumably predict exactly who will take which pieces for all possible ways of dividing the cake as soon as he knows the order in which they will choose, and indeed the logic of the example requires this knowledge. The "impartiality" or "fairness" seems to lie in devising a set of procedures that will produce an outcome we intuitively regard as fair *on wholly independent*

36 For further discussion of Rawls's appeal to consensus, see Hare (1975:81–107).
37 In the Dewey lectures Rawls retreats slightly from this consensus theory to the rather Millian claim that the principles must rest on "common knowledge and on shared practices of inquiry" and that the "parties must reason only from general beliefs that are suitably common," not on the grounds that these are necessarily true, but because there is no justifiable alternative. Indeed, he notes, in a democratic society "there is no settled and enduring agreement on these matters;" they are part of the "subjective circumstances of justice" that at best rest on "part of the truth" (1980:540ff). Despite this, neither in *A Theory of Justice* nor in his subsequent clarifications, does Rawls ever try to establish that the particular factual assumptions and "laws" of economics and psychology *are* widely shared. Even if a particular belief were shown to be widely held, this would not be a sufficient reason for basing an argument for political principles on it, without first investigating why it is widely held, with a sharp eye out for any ideological uses to which it might likely be put. This issue is taken up in detail in the next chapter.

grounds, assuming only self-interested behavior on the part of the relevant agents.[38]

To the extent that this is the logic of Rawls's enterprise, two (related) questions arise. First, can the argument for the two principles be made without appeal to the problem-ridden device of the original position, and, second, what independent justification can be given for the notion of fairness embodied in the two principles? As in the cake-cutting example, the desired distributive result must be desirable on grounds independent of the procedures that produce it, if the procedures are to be defended because they produce the desired result.[39] Rawls must tell us why the fair way to divide a cake *is* to divide it equally before we can evaluate his proffered account of pure procedural justice. He must also tell us why his two principles are a desirable basis for institutions of social justice before we can evaluate his claims that mutually disinterested persons, acting in accordance with some exogenously determined rules (in this case the relevant conditions of ignorance), would choose these principles.

What are the grounds on which the two principles and the priority of right *are* held to be desirable? Rawls has two basic types of response. First he claims that his principles are desirable because they are neutral among different conceptions of the good. His primary goods supply people with the wherewithal to achieve their goals and the priority of liberty gives them the freedom to do this. We have seen, however, that these claims are fallacious, partly because his principles are not neutral among different conceptions of the good (rather they arbitrarily *define* one class of conceptions as acceptable), and partly because his principles need not generate either the freedom or the wherewithal as Rawls claims. The distinction between freedom and its "worth" places Rawls in the standard negative-

---

38 The fact that Rawls's account of the original position presupposes an independent criterion of fairness has been noted by several commentators, including Sen (1970:135) and Mueller (1979:229ff).

39 In this connection notice Gewirth's (1982:44) observation that Rawls's doctrine "that if persons were to choose the constitutional structure of their society from behind a veil of ignorance ... they would provide that each person must have certain basic rights" becomes a circular argument if viewed as an answer to the question "whether human beings have equal moral rights."

libertarian mold, and entails that in most significant essentials peoples' lives will be governed by the difference principle. This principle is so ill-specified, however, and compatible with so many different distributive arrangements, that it cannot be evaluated as a principle of social distribution. Once Rawls comes to discuss the application of his principles he takes great pains to show they are compatible with competitive markets, duly regulated to get rid of problems of monopoly, externality, and free-ridership. He further claims that his principles, as now expressed via "the price system," have the additional advantage of promoting "efficiency." He grows increasingly ambiguous, however, between this claim and the claim that the market system is desirable because it embodies his principles, as in the claim that market arrangements are efficient and preserve the important liberties required by the first principle (ibid.: 274ff). Indeed, although Rawls often claims to eschew arguments from efficiency (1971:276; 1980:562), at times he moves teeteringly close to precisely these. In one more recent formulation of the reasons for departing from equality in the original position, for instance, this is quite explicit:

Now since we are regarding citizens as free and equal moral persons . . . the obvious starting point is to suppose that all other social primary goods [beyond those covered by the first principle], and in particular income and wealth, should be equal: everyone should have an equal share. *But society must take organizational requirements and economic efficiency into account. So it is unreasonable to stop at an equal division.* The basic structure should allow inequalities so long as they improve everyone's situation. (1979:15, emphasis added)

This sounds suspiciously like another attempt at the good old rights-utility synthesis via the market, since the difference principle is being justified by a direct appeal to efficiency.

Thus Rawls explicitly rejects, in general, appeals to efficiency or utility as justifications for principles, but he avers that his principles (which are just for other reasons) happen to be compatible with a distributive system designed to maximize efficiency. If these are not grounds for holding that the principles are justifiable, why mention them? Why get involved in contentious and controversial arguments about the compatibility or otherwise of competitive markets and market-based price systems with socialist economic and political institutions, if these considerations are irrelevant to the justification of his principles? The truth is that they are not irrelevant at all. He assumes, for instance, that although market institutions are "riddled with grave injustices," there "presumably are ways of running them compatible with their basic design and intention so that the difference principle is satisfied consistent with the demands of liberty and fair equality of opportunity" (1971:87). *This* assumption, I submit, is intended to give his argument its intuitive appeal. It "underlies our assurance that these [market] arrangements can be made just" (ibid.).

If this is so, Rawls's appeal is ultimately an intuitionist one to the complex of liberal moral commitments behind the rights-utility synthesis. Despite his oft repeated antipathy to intuitionism, this conclusion seems inescapable. By Rawls's own account the force of his argument depends not on the claim that the individuals in the original position would choose his principles under the specified conditions, but on the claim that the principles themselves are fair, just as in the cake-cutting example the primary question must be: is an equal division fair? The appeal is to "our considered judgments" about the justice of the principles themselves and the institutions they entail. Once the question is cast in this light we are left only with Rawls's many assertions about what "seems reasonable," what is "desirable" and what is "plausible."[40]

The only other attempt at an independent justification for the principles is Rawls's much commented upon, but nonetheless very brief, "Kantian interpretation" of his two principles (1971:251–7), which he has since (1980:515–72) elaborated on as a form of "Kantian constructivism." If we consider the problem of justice, Rawls argues, from the point of view of Kant's noumenal self, the two principles are what this autonomous being would rationally choose. They are thus a procedural "interpretation" of the categorical imperative and the Kant-

---

40 It has been argued at some length by Hare (1975:83ff) that Rawls provides very little argument on these points and that the appeal is almost invariably to intuition, something which Rawls himself in several places grudgingly acknowledges.

ian conception of autonomy, since they express and preserve our nature as "free and equal rational beings with a liberty to choose" (1971:256).

The central difficulty that Rawls confronts in relation to his Kantian interpretation parallels that confronted by Nozick. Rawls wants a principle with the force of the categorical imperative, but he wants to alter its content to suit his own purposes. He wants to say that the only justifiable principles of justice are those which are freely chosen, but he then wants to constrain the class of principles and load the choice problem so that it "must" be rational to choose his principles. As Sidgwick objected to Kant (in Rawls's view decisively), however, if one takes seriously the notion of free will as Kantian autonomy, the possibility has to be accepted that people may choose evil over good, or irrational over rational. Either the right is derived from the good or it is not. To try to escape this via the "thin theory" is a red herring, for this amounts to no more than saying the priority of right is (a part of) the good. The question remains as to whether this is held to be the case because it is chosen or because it conforms to some exogenously determined conception of the good (whether this is based on natural law, intuition, "reflective equilibrium," or anything else).

Like Nozick, Rawls wants to attach Archimedean significance to individual choice in legitimating the principles which regulate human behavior, but also, like Nozick, he cannot live with the subjectivist consequences of holding this. Therefore he attempts to rig the choice that "autonomous" individuals would make, to ensure that the principles chosen conform to what he intuitively takes to be "reasonable" values. The discussions of his "Kantian conception of equality" in "A Well Ordered Society" (1979:6–20) and of "Kantian constructivism" in the Dewey lectures (1980:515–72) do not begin to meet this difficulty, because in both these discussions Rawls's primary concern is to elaborate the claim that his Kantian conception of equality is embodied in the theoretical device of the original position. He advances no new substantive arguments for his particular theory of primary goods or for the particular assumptions he makes about "general facts" and "laws" of society, all of which are needed to generate the claim that, in the original position, his principles would "freely" be chosen over the various alternatives. Thus even if his neo-Kantian conceptions of equality and autonomy are accepted, this does not generate a justification for the specific principles constituting his theory of justice. Such a justification requires additional assumptions about economics, psychology, and society that are problematical quite independently of the view we take on the desirability or usefulness of Kant's theory of moral autonomy. The concept of the original position, therefore, does not resolve Sidgwick's objection to Kant, as Rawls claims it does, because by itself it does not show "which principles, if any, free and equal rational persons would choose," or that these principles are "applicable in practice" (1971:255).

Rawls's departures from Kant's ethics in both method and content are so extensive it is difficult to see how anything resembling a genuine Kantian foundation could be given his theory of justice. First, as Rawls (ibid.:256–7) acknowledges, it is one thing to require individuals to act as though the principles guiding their actions are to become universal laws, or always to treat others as ends as well as means to your own ends, and quite another to say that such injunctions can be turned into principles of collective choice and as such will yield the same substantive principles for all. We have no better reasons for saying this than for saying if it is rational for each individual to maximize his total utility then it is rational for society to maximize *its* total utility, a view that can quickly be shown to generate paradoxes and absurdities. Kant's argument, it bears repeating, does not generate any substantive principles for collective welfare decisions. Kant was unequivocal about this, although at times he ignored some of its implications. In *The Contest of the Faculties,* for instance, in a discussion of the role of government in providing for the welfare of the citizenry, he squarely asserts that:

[W]elfare does not have any ruling principle, either for the recipient or for the one who provides it, for each individual will define it differently. It depends, in fact, upon the will's *material* aspect, *which*

244

is empirical and thus incapable of becoming a universal rule. (Kant, 1970:183–4n, second emphasis added)

If Rawls wanted to claim that his principles, if implemented, would never violate the categorical imperative, this would be something different, but he would have to show this – something he never attempts to do. Many would take issue with such a claim. It might be argued, for instance, that the distinction between liberty and its "worth," and the massive inequalities that can be sanctioned by the difference principle, might well generate situations where given individuals are not in any convincing sense respected as ends.

A second major departure from Kant, which Rawls also acknowledges but attempts to downplay (ibid.:257), is his free use of empirical considerations, so-called empirically established laws of human behavior, facts of society, and so on – huge quantities of material Kant would have regarded as "anthropological" and irrelevant therefore to questions of moral philosophy. Rawls's eventual goal is for a "strictly deductive" ethics. It is unclear, however, what this is supposed to rest on, given his hostility to what he calls "Cartesian" views of ethics purporting to rest on self-evident premises – unless he seriously believes the empirical claims he makes or presupposes in describing the original position have been established with sufficient certainty to generate a deductive ethics. If this was his view it is difficult to see how it avoids being a kind of naturalism, since it would rest ultimately on the claims that since all men naturally reason alike, and since all men naturally require certain things, they must rationally choose his principles. It is clear that Rawls's views on the nature of moral philosophy differ markedly from Kant's. Kant must represent one of the most extreme cases in the history of philosophy of what Rawls refers to as a "Cartesian" theory, based on supposedly self-evident premises, perceivable by introspection and transcendental reasoning, in no way dependent for their truth or plausibility on considerations "borrowed from" experience.

Finally, Rawls differs from Kant in that much of his mode of thought and argument is heavily consequentialist. The specific sense in which Rawls endorses consequentialism is not entirely clear.[41] In his appeals to the market as embodying his principles, he makes many consequentialist claims about efficiency and the priority of right being preserved by the market. His objections to utilitarianism, too, are generally consequentialist in nature: he imagines specific situations in which application of the utility principle might have deleterious consequences for a given individual. He explicitly defends a kind of limited consequentialism, saying that although it is the virtue of institutions that determines their justness, "other things equal, one conception of justice is preferable to another when its broader consequences are more desirable" (ibid.:6). This view may well have much to commend it and it may be unavoidable given the empirical premises in Rawls's argument. It is, however, unquestionably anything but Kantian: Kant notoriously held that the only relevant factor in evaluating the moral worth of an action is the motive with which it is performed.

Given these difficulties, Kant's ethics obviously cannot provide a moral foundation for Rawls's principles of justice. They rest, in fact, on no more than an intuitive appeal to what "seems reasonable" to the reader, and much of that appeal is to a reader already predisposed to the empirical beliefs and substantive moral judgments Rawls is interested in establishing.

iv. The purposes of rights

The underlying purpose of the rights embodied in Rawls's principles is that mutually disinterested individuals may most effectively realize their individual conceptions of the good. He also claims, however, that a society organized to achieve this is desirable in the broader sense that it conforms to "our" considered judgment about what is socially optimal. Prudential and moral rationality are intended to coincide at this point. Thus a just society is a "social union of social unions" ranging from individuals through families, friendships, and larger associations (1971:563); it is an objectively fair and rational arrangement in which individual conceptions of the good can "endure and flourish" (1975:554). These individual concep-

41 This matter is taken up more fully in Chapter 6.

tions of the good are conceived of as essentially private, embodied in the "rational life plans" of persons. In describing these purposes in detail in *A Theory of Justice* and subsequently, Rawls invokes the metaphor of religious toleration:

[T]he notion of a well-ordered society is an extension of the idea of religious toleration. Consider a pluralistic society, divided along religious, ethnic, or cultural lines in which the various groups have reached a firm understanding on the scheme of principles to regulate their fundamental institutions. While they have deep differences about other things, there is public agreement on this framework of principles and citizens are attached to it. (Rawls, 1979:8)

A well ordered society is thus one in which people institutionalize agreement on what is possible and sensibly regulate conflict over what is not, in the interests of a flourishing plurality of individual achievement. The pursuit of this latter provides the overriding purpose of their cooperation.

For Rawls, where social cooperation is possible, its basic purpose remains individual private gain – it is geared to each "disinterested" individual's realization of his rational life plan. Like Hobbes, Rawls defines "good" relationally and argues that it is determined, for a given individual, by his rational life plan. The definition of the term "good," in his descriptivist account, is presented as morally neutral (ibid.:401–7ff). Thus, for instance, he takes over the standard neo-classical definition of public goods (from Buchanan) as being essentially public only in the sense of being indivisible (such as national defense). Public goods are thus implicitly defined as things individuals want which, for one of several contingent reasons, cannot be individually attained, and which therefore necessitate state action to provide them. "Many of the traditional activities of government, insofar as they can be justified, can be accounted for in this way" (1971:267–8ff). This is a negative definition of public goods in the sense that the need for them only arises with the breakdown (or potential for breakdown) of private market arrangements.

Rawls, then, has the standard negative libertarian view of mutual cooperation for individual advancement. Even the groupings that constitute social unions are no more than

Lockean voluntary associations. We might, therefore, conceive of Rawls's view of human association in terms of Oakeshott's notion of *societas*. The purpose of social organization, for Rawls, consists primarily in the preservation of individual freedom which consists in turn of two things. First, it consists in mutual acknowledgment of each individual as the "self-originating source of [moral] claims," which translates in practice into "not requiring the parties to justify the claims they wish to make." Second, it consists in acknowledging in all persons the "moral power to have a conception of the good" which generates "the right to view their persons as independent and not identified with any particular system of ends" (1980:544ff).[42] This freedom is held to be compatible with, and required by, our moral equality, inhering in our capacity to act in compliance with the public conception of justice (1980:546ff).

Despite Rawls's use of the term "social union of social unions," and his various assertions that mutual cooperation is inevitable, desirable, and even that "the self is realized in the activities of many selves" (1971:565), as well as more recent attempts to deemphasize his individualistic assumptions (1975: 539–47), it is difficult, as Sandel (1982:151ff) has persuasively argued, to discover much content behind these phrases. I will suggest later that there is some ideological significance to these quasi-liberal corporatist assertions, but in terms of substantive intellectual content they appear to be entirely lacking. Whatever the surface attraction of Rawls's account of the mutual reinforcement of freedom and equality in a well ordered society, he does not begin to establish that this will occur in the actual world as organized in accordance with his principles of justice. I have argued that there is no necessary sense in which these are egalitarian, and that they might well function – particularly when instantiated via "the price system" – to the serious detriment of the autonomy of some, as Rawls understands this term.

---

42 A third "aspect" of freedom is that citizens are responsible for their ends in the sense of being authoritative in adjusting and revising their conceptions of the good (Rawls, 1980:544).

Rawls's blithe political optimism[43] is compounded here by his failure to consider seriously the likely obstacles to his social union of social unions. It might be argued, for instance, that although economic growth is a good which serves everyone's interest, there may be no system of achieving this neutrally, and different systems will distribute the benefits and burdens in different ways. Rawls misses this because he makes an implicit distinction between the *type of economic system* and the *level of economic development,* disallowing knowledge of the former, but not of the latter, to individuals in the original position. Implicit in the idea of the consensus at the contractual stage is the view that once a certain level of economic development has been reached there *is* a just or fair distributive principle to which all might agree (once sufficient account has been taken of their basic liberties): namely maximize the position of the worst-off. It may be argued that there are causal links between the type of economic system and the level of economic development such that the achievement and maintenance of "moderate scarcity" requires the systematic impoverishment of certain groups. History has surely not disconfirmed this view. The distributional status quo is at least in part a function of the type of economic system prevailing in a society. Whether or not a single distributive principle can be found "rationally" and equally dictated by the interests of all will depend on whether or not the constant reproduction of the level of economic development (moderate scarcity plus) effectively divides society into different groups whose needs and interests conflict with one another.[44]

Rawls seems to assume that the economic system can work in some kind of neutral way, if not to the benefit of all at least to the detriment of none. No historical society has worked in this way. It is precisely this assumption, however, which, for Rawls, generates consensus on one distributive rule for all. Rawls fails to understand that, although there may be social goals universal in the sense that everyone needs them, this in

43 On which Barber (1975:310ff) has commented in some detail.
44 On this subject, see Miller (1975:206–30).

no way entails that there are neutral means of distributing the costs necessary to produce them. Aspects of social life may be inherently cooperative, but they nonetheless involve activities which are inherently conflictual.[45]

Rawls never addresses these questions because he conceives of economic problems as problems of distribution, without giving serious attention to the production of what is to be distributed. Thus in the original position we assume a certain level of development, the availability of certain quantities of primary goods, and the instrumental rationality of the parties; the problem then becomes how to distribute these goods most rationally in accordance with the relevant constraints. The question of how these goods are produced in the first place is never considered and presumably held to be irrelevant to the initial decision. Yet the implicit distinction between type and level of development is deeply artificial. One wonders, given the different possible ways of producing wealth to the required level of "moderate scarcity," whether our initial contractors might not want some assurances about the mode of production to be employed.[46] It is a measure of his lack of attention to questions about production that Rawls can believe once a certain level of economic development has been achieved his principles can be neutral between capitalism and socialism, and applicable equally to both.

The social union of social unions, in which "everyone's conception of the good as given by his rational plan is a subplan of the larger comprehensive plan that regulates the community" (ibid.:563) requires a highly benign view of the world. It

45 When Rawls (1979:6ff) notes that some aspects of life are conflictual and others amenable to cooperation he does not answer this point, because this truism does not address the issue of the unequally distributed *costs* of cooperative, mutually beneficial, activities.

46 The few remarks Rawls does make relating to production seem to presuppose a conventional view of investment incentives in competitive markets. Thus inequalities are adjudged rational when "as we raise the expectations of the more advantaged the situation of the worst off is continuously improved. Each such increase is in the latter's interest . . . For the greater expectations of the more favored presumably cover the costs of training and encourage better performance thereby contributing to the general advantage" (Rawls, 1971:158). Although he asserts that his principles are applicable under socialism as well as a "property owning democracy," he never explains how production there would occur; presumably his notion of incentives in competitive markets could not be applied.

is almost as if Rawls perceives a well functioning ecosystem, with the difference that no organism ever gets eaten. He does not begin to show, however, that this would be generated by his principles, or that it could ever be exemplified in the actual world.

III. IDEOLOGICAL CONSEQUENCES OF RAWLS'S ARGUMENT

The ideological force of Rawls's argument derives mainly from his appeal to and legitimation of the Keynesian values and assumptions outlined in Chapter 4. Rawls presents his argument as a deontological alternative to what he takes to be the dominant teleological mode of political theory. He sees his contractarian account of justice as an alternative to utilitarianism in all its unsatisfactory forms. Nevertheless, these claims obscure as much as they reveal; like other canonized writers in the liberal tradition, Rawls offers an account of the rights-utility synthesis via the market. His views of what market practices entail, what their limitations are, and how they are best managed and regulated, all powerfully shape the particular account of the synthesis he offers, as we will see by examining the ideological consequences of his argument in more detail.

For Rawls, as for Nozick, the isolated individual is the subject of all political rights and his voluntary actions are decisive in legitimating all political practices. The principles are what mutually disinterested individuals would rationally choose unanimously. Although Rawls argues that his principles are desirable on other grounds – most important that they are held to conform to "our considered judgments" and to preserve a Kantian notion of individual freedom – what makes them legitimate, he claims, is that they would be freely chosen in the original position.

The whole idea of the original position assumes that moral and political questions can be considered independently of man's social relationships. In this respect there is an important affinity between Rawls's procedures and Hobbes's resolutive-compositive method, specifically in the assumption that the most profound way to understand the nature of social relationships is to reduce them to their individual component parts. Claims to the contrary notwithstanding, this generates a powerful atomistic bias in Rawls's argument. The closest he ever comes to defending it is the following:

The essential idea [of justice as fairness] is that we want to account for the social values, for the intrinsic good of institutional, community, and associative activities, by a conception of justice that in its theoretical basis is individualistic. For reasons of clarity among others, we do not want to rely on an undefined concept of community, or to suppose that society is an organic whole with a life of its own distinct from and superior to that of all its members in their relations with one another. Thus the contractual conception of the original position is worked out first. It is reasonably simple and the problem of rational choice that it poses is relatively precise. From this conception, however individualistic it might seem, we must eventually explain the value of community. (Ibid.:264–5)

There is no reason why beginning with assumptions about individuals, and a denial that societies are in any significant sense more than the sum of their (individual) constituent parts, is in any way conducive to greater "clarity" than beginning with (arguably more accurate) assumptions about man's natural sociality and about societies as irreducibly complex structures. The extent to which such assumptions are clear will depend on how well defined they are, and the extent to which they are useful in understanding questions of justice will depend on their accuracy and their relevance to the problem at hand. Rawls pays scant attention to these issues. It is a measure of the powerful hold atomistic assumptions about man and society have over the mainstream of contemporary political theory that he is able to rely on such vacuous off-the-cuff assertions, in lieu of serious argument, for the position he holds. The whole cluster of ideas relating to the original position and the veil of ignorance can be thought of as generating rigor and clarity only against a particular view of moral philosophy, one that sees moral imperatives as timeless universals predicated of isolated individuals, whatever their social and political circumstances. It is precisely because this view cannot be applied to substantive political and moral issues that Rawls is forced, as we have seen, to smuggle in panoplies of unsub-

252

stantiated empirical and consequentialist assumptions about the actual structure of the political and economic world.

Rawls's appeal to simplicity is ideologically loaded in a similar way. He frequently appeals to the notion of simplicity, either in a direct claim that simpler principles are preferred to complex ones, or merely to make his problem workable at all. Thus he refuses to consider the notion that different substantive principles of justice might be justifiable in different cultural and historical circumstances, on the grounds (among others) that if views of this kind were added to the list of principles to be chosen from in the original position, "our problem would become very complicated if not unmanageable." He therefore considers only universal principles "to keep things simple" (ibid.:125). An appeal to theoretical simplicity, holding that we should always seek out ways to cut out redundant theoretical entities, would be one thing but Rawls's claim is quite different. He constructs a highly artificial procedure (not notable for its theoretical economy) for choosing among alternative principles of justice. He then rules out of consideration principles many would regard as plausible on the grounds that it is too complicated to apply them under the procedure as he has defined it (presumably because different substantive principles of justice that might be required in different historical circumstances could only be considered in light of factual knowledge not available behind the veil of ignorance). One might, at this point, reasonably anticipate some reconsideration of the adequacy of his procedure for evaluating alternative principles of justice. On the contrary, Rawls regards this as *grounds* for ignoring complex principles of various types. There is no more reason to expect the best justifiable substantive principles of justice in one society to be theoretically simple than there is to assume that all societies beyond a certain level of economic development are governed by the same principles. That Rawls assumes there *must be* a solution to the choice problem he has constructed is equally clear in the Dewey lectures, where "Kantian constructivism" is conceived of as follows: "[I]t starts by allowing the parties no information and then adds just enough so that they can make a rational agreement." The contracting agents are endowed with "sufficiently specific desires that their rational deliberations reach a definite result" (1980:549; 525). It seems more likely, however, given the difficulties we and others have encountered in his internal reasoning, that this artificial device will yield no "definite result." Certainly there is no noncircular sense in which the agreement reached can be termed "rational."

These various simplifying assumptions seem plausible to Rawls, I think, because, despite the very broad claims he makes for his theory, the only alternative that he takes at all seriously is utilitarianism. He considers and rejects versions of intuitionism, perfectionism, egoism, and various "mixed" conceptions, but his discussion of these is quite cursory. A close reading of *A Theory of Justice* reveals that most of Rawls's critical argument is devoted to attacking utilitarianism in what he takes to be its most influential forms, and to showing his own argument avoids its most serious weaknesses. Rawls clearly regards utilitarianism as the most serious alternative to contract theory.[47] This may explain why the limitations of his procedures seem acceptable to him. If one's view of the class of serious substantive moral positions is restricted to rights-based contract theories and utilitarianism, so long as one's procedures allow consideration of these they will seem reasonably all-encompassing (particularly if they can be shown to allow consideration for one or two other positions as well). It is a measure of the extent to which contemporary political theory is dominated by the so-called choice between rights and utility that such arbitrary limitations can seem intuitively plausible.

Hare (1975:83ff), among others, has argued that Rawls's argument rests on a disguised subjectivism rooted in his appeal to consensus in validating moral claims. Rawls very much wants to avoid this position, but he does make the basic subjectivist move, as Kane (1982:249–52ff) has pointed out, of identifying the good with what is desired (so that primary goods

---

47 This should not be taken to imply that Rawls is not influenced by the various other doctrines mentioned, particularly intuitionism. As I follow Hare (1975:83ff) in arguing, his appeal to "our considered judgments" is essentially intuitionist, proclamations to the contrary notwithstanding.

are held to be such on the contingent grounds that all persons *want* them, whatever else they *want*). Rawls (1971:406–7) acknowledges that his argument may be consistent with emotivism. He also defends something of a rationalist theory of interests, but what does this amount to? He defends a notion of "goodness as rationality," according to which a person's plan of life is held to be rational if and only if:

(1) it is one of the plans that is consistent with the principles of rational choice when these are applied to all the relevant features of his situation, and (2) it is that plan among those meeting this condition which would be chosen by him with full deliberative rationality, that is, with full awareness of the relevant facts and after a careful consideration of the consequences. (Ibid.:408)

The first part of this definition hearkens back to his earlier one (ibid.:142–50ff) of rationality in purely instrumental terms as the most effective means to a given end ("standard in economic theory"). The second part, referring to "full deliberative rationality," is notable for its similarity to Nozick's account of acting in equilibrium discussed in the last chapter. Leaving aside the various difficulties raised there in connection with this notion (how full awareness of the relevant facts is established in practice, and how choices can be designated free in some "open" sense – without reference to the determinants of the options among which choices are made), this move does seem to confirm the case for a kind of moral subjectivism at the heart of Rawls's account. The ultimate appeal, in validating his claims that certain courses of action are rational and others not, is to what individuals would want to *choose* under some (not very well specified) optimal conditions. There is no room here for a notion that what is good for an individual may (in a nontrivial sense) conflict with what he desires, since the good is derived from an idealized notion of desire. Therefore, Rawls, like Nozick must devote much attention to proving that voluntary unanimity is theoretically possible at the constitutional stage: voluntary individual assent is necessary and sufficient for validating moral claims.

A second (connected) consequence of Rawls's argument concerns his account of the relationship between the right and the good, which in an important respect parallels the traditional liberal distinction between right and law. Rawls's central reason for attacking utilitarianism, it will be remembered, is its teleological character. Specifically, what Rawls objects to is that "the good is defined independently from the right, and then the right is defined as that which maximizes the good" (ibid.:24). This is a misleading formulation. It suggests that he objects to the independence thesis itself, whereas in fact he objects to the priority of the good. This is obvious as soon as we reflect that Rawls's argument for the priority of right must rest on the converse of the independence thesis he identifies in "teleological" theories: he defines the right independently of the good and the good as that which maximizes the right. It might be objected that Rawls's account of the priority of right is derived from his "thin" theory of the good, but we saw that if *this* is his position it is teleological in exactly the sense that he regards as objectionable.

Rawls descends into incoherence on this point, on the one hand because his powerful attachment to the notion of individual choice impels him to reject teleology and argue for the priority of right, on the other because his fear of the consequences of subjectivism makes him want somehow to constrain this priority. He needs something like a theory of Lockean license, but in the absence of a philosophy adjuring us to obey the injunctions of our creator because he created us, or a naturalist or rationalist theory of the imperatives for human survival, this is not readily forthcoming. Rawls's way out of this conundrum is to assert that the priority of right *is* the good and that his particular definition and ranking of primary goods, and his particular account of pluralism, are neutral among all possible rational conceptions of the good.[48] These

48 In "Fairness to Goodness" he appears to retreat somewhat on this position, saying he is not holding that the original position is neutral "in the sense that its description uses no moral concepts." He even acknowledges that it might favor some conceptions of the good (Rawls, 1975:539ff). He retains his "thin theory" unmodified, however, and still argues that questions of right can be "bracketed" and considered separately from issues about substantive conceptions of the good. The negative libertarian model remains: "[W]e want to work out principles of accommodation between different moralities much as a constitution insuring liberty of conscience and freedom of thought contains principles of accommodation between different religions" (ibid.:539).

claims do not withstand much scrutiny, but it is of greater significance for us that Rawls feels constrained to make them. Like Nozick, Rawls evaluates actions partly in terms of their consequences. Unlike Nozick, he does not pretend not to be doing this. He addresses gross injustice and inequity as he perceives it. He will not rely on an a priori appeal to the market *qua* preserver of the priority of right (although he does hold that market relationships can be made just). Rawls lacks a theory of needs on which to base his alternative claims, largely because his strong commitment to a subjectivist conception of persons requires identification of the good with what is desired. This makes it impossible to distinguish clearly between wants and needs, or to have any basis for moving away from a theory of revealed preference. A theory of needs would have to be argued for on the basis of evidence and claims about interests, all of which would be objectionable to Rawls as forms of naturalism and teleology.

The limitations on, and limited character of, his attempts to avoid the weaknesses of traditional accounts of the priority of right are even more clearly evident in the negative libertarian account of freedom. The freedoms guaranteed by the first principle are, we saw, wholly formal and dealt with independently of (and prior to) questions concerning their substantive worth. In addition, the fact that Rawls models his discussion of liberty on religious toleration generates an exceedingly limited view of political participation. He is mainly concerned, in his brief discussion of this latter subject (ibid.:228–34), with the traditional liberal problem of defining constitutional checks to limit problems of tyrannous majorities. His exclusive concern, however, is with the formal liberties enumerated under his first principle; questions about their "worth," or about peoples' capacities to exercise those liberties, receive no attention in the procedural guarantees of political participation.[49] Again we find broad endorsement of the standard liberal view of procedural democracy as sufficient to guarantee democratic participation in its important forms. Rawls's claim (ibid.:230) that

---

49 "[P]rocedural constraints are said to mitigate the defects of the majority principle. The justification appeals to a greater equal liberty. At no point is there a reference to compensating economic and social benefits" (Rawls, 1971:229).

those "who place a higher worth on the principle of participation will be prepared to take greater risks with the freedoms of the person, say, in order to give political liberty a larger place" hardly meets this point. First, political liberty as he defines it is purely procedural. Second, even if it were not, this argument would have the force of a claim that if workers valued owning the factories in which they worked, they would go out and buy them. The point is that the disadvantaged may not have the capacity to participate.

Regarding the difference principle, the only coherent account of it is in terms of a Keynesian view of capitalist markets that can make sense of the assumptions of "chain connection" and "close-knitness," and consequently the move from what benefits the worst-off to what benefits everyone. Even with these strong assumptions, not borne out by the experience of the capitalist democracies over the past fifteen years at least,[50] the difference principle is not without its difficulties, largely because it supplies so little of the information one would want to consider in judging the justness of particular distributions.

A further consequence of Rawls's discussion of distributive justice concerns his assumption that such questions can be considered in isolation from questions about production. This is a weakness for which Nozick takes him to task, arguing with some force that an adequate account of distributive justice must include an account of justice in acquisition. Having raised this question, Nozick proceeds to avoid it via the simple assertion that market-based acquisitions are just by definition. Rawls never even considers it. In this he is in the mainstream of the reaction against classical economics which rested primarily on the rejection of labor theories of value and the relegation of questions about the genesis of property rights to disciplines outside economics. This development was of considerable ideological importance in the evolution of liberalism: it placed limits on the extent to which the workmanship metaphor could be invoked to criticize relations of private property. The last remaining vestiges of radicalism in Locke's argument were cast off with this reaction, since issues of the origin of rights of

---

50 See Shapiro and Kane (1983:5–39).

private property were removed from the agenda of serious political debate.

Once the labor theory of value had been jettisoned, all questions of history could be seen as quite irrelevant to moral and political philosophy. This, in turn, is in significant part responsible for the speculative rationalism, "ideal theory," and moral philosophy based on hypothetical examples and counterexamples dominating so much of the discipline today, and exemplified in the work of Nozick and Rawls. I will have more to say about so-called ideal theory in Chapter 6. Note for now that Rawls's exclusive focus on distributive outcomes is one of the main sources of the deep conservatism in his argument. His evident indifference to so many questions relevant to issues of distributive justice places serious limits on the extent to which his arguments might be used critically to evaluate existing economic institutions. This is hardly surprising since, as we have seen, Rawls has little desire to do this. He clearly believes that, provided the worst problems of externality, free ridership, and monopoly are dealt with and the weak requirements of the difference principle are satisfied, capitalist markets are just distributive mechanisms that function simultaneously to preserve the priority of right and economic efficiency.

Rawls's account of rights falls into the traditional liberal mold, as well, in that the class of objects to which there are entitlements is potentially infinite, so long as the difference principle is satisfied. The difference principle functions like Locke's second proviso and can generate monumental inequalities for the same reasons as can the proviso. There is some lack of clarity in Rawls's conception of the worst-off. He begins by defining them purely relationally (in terms of the difference principle), but in discussing the functions of the "transfers" department of government, he clearly intends physical subsistence to be guaranteed. Neither of these views, however, entails anything about the relative equality in the systems as a whole. Rawls argues (not very coherently as we saw) that once the worst-off have been identified we can work with ordinal utilities for all other purposes. Thus, beyond identification of the worst-off, statements about relative inequality cannot, strictly, even be made.

It should not be thought that my claim that the difference principle can justify serious inequality rests on theoretically possible but empirically unlikely eventualities. I pointed out in section II(ii) that the benefits of the Reagan administration's tax cuts in the early 1980s, highly regressive in their overall effect, were in perfect conformity with the difference principle.[51] It could be argued, with reference to the postwar experience in the United States, that welfare policies improving the position of the worst-off have coexisted with virtually no change in the relative inequalities in the system as a whole on several measures, even with increased inequality on some measures.[52] Similar claims could be made about many of the so-called socialist economies in the post-Stalinist era. I have argued elsewhere that in Poland, for instance, the economic position of industrial workers has improved since the 1950s but inequality in the system as a whole has increased (Shapiro 1981:469–502). Rae et al. (1981:104–29) have shown more generally that the difference principle is one of a whole class of distributive mechanisms that can be more and less egalitarian depending on the circumstances, most particularly on whether the economy expands, contracts, or remains constant. The view that welfare policies geared to providing sustenance for the worst-off are in any necessary sense egalitarian is a highly influential myth, of which Rawls is both a victim and a perpetrator.

Rawls's use of utility functions in identifying the worst-off raises the broader question of the extent to which his argument is at odds with utilitarianism in all its forms as he so often claims. There is a strawmanish quality to Rawls's discussions of utilitarianism, deriving from the fact that he takes Sidgwick's classical statement of it as paradigmatic. Although he considers several variants of this, as well as the so-called doctrine of "average" utility, he never considers the strict neoclassical version based on noncomparable ordinal utilities. Whatever the difficulties with this doctrine (and they are

---

51 I refer here only to the actual reductions in income tax rate schedules. No doubt if we took into account the additional losses in services and welfare benefits suffered by those at the bottom of the income scale, and calculated the overall changes in the position of the worst-off social stratum, we might find its position had in fact declined.

52 For an illuminating discussion of evidence on this question, see Cameron (1978).

many), it is not, strictly speaking, vulnerable to Rawls's stock objection to utilitarianism. By denying the legitimacy of inter-personal comparisons of utility, it does not permit the sacrifice of some for the benefit of others.

To the extent that Rawls invokes ordinal utilities he might be said to be appealing to a version of this argument. Like Mill, however, he wants to add some ground-floor guarantees. Rawls's attack on Mill's utilitarianism (ibid.:562ff) focuses pri-marily on the notorious "proof," but it is in *On Liberty* that Mill argues that a single system can be created that both preserves individual rights and maximizes utilitarian efficiency. Rawls's claim is strikingly similar. It is frustratingly difficult to pin him down to a precise view on this question because he constantly shifts his ground depending on the particular claim he is try-ing to establish. Thus, when trying to minimize his "paternal-ism," he makes his claims for weak cardinality and ordinality once the worst-off is identified, but when discussing primary goods and needs he makes vastly more extensive interpersonal claims. In making his argument for the priority of right his thin theory is held to be confined to characteristics contin-gently shared by different conceptions of the good, but when he comes to argue against particular conceptions of the good to which he objects, the thin theory begins to thicken.

Whatever Rawls's final position on these questions, his argu-ment clearly imports much of the method and substance of neo-classical utilitarianism. His instrumental definition of ra-tionality, the psychology of his persons as mutually disinter-ested and always wanting more means to the good than less, the very idea of the radical separation of means and ends embodied in the theory of primary goods, the unquestioning use of the theoretical paraphernalia of utilitarianism (includ-ing utility functions), individuals engaged in acting out indi-vidually conceived "rational life plans," the identification of the good with what is desired, and the claim that his system is in general conducive to utilitarian efficiency, all these are indi-cations that the utilitarianism he rejects has left its indelible stamp on his argument. The main difference between Rawls and Nozick on this count is that Rawls recognizes that need for some limited state action if his version of the rights-utility synthesis is to be achieved, whereas Nozick does not. Rawls's view of the role of the state is remarkably similar to what students of comparative politics refer to as a liberal corporatist one.

The image of a corporate state is associated primarily with the fascist and Nazi states of the 1920s and 1930s. The idea of liberal corporatism is linked to these, stripped, however, of its violently coercive and statist implications.[53] Instead of being seen as an arena of class conflict, or as a plurality of groups striving on behalf of their own interests with the state providing a passive "aggregating" function, society is construed as an organic unity in which each group has its essential function to perform, the true interest of each being found within the general interest of the whole organism. The state actively negotiates a consensus between different social groups, most important business, labor, and its own representatives via liberal-democratic forms. It takes ultimate responsibility for the efficient functioning of the system, and can require sacrifices from particular groups, via taxation and prices and incomes policies, for instance, in what is held to be the interest of the system as a whole. The state is decisively reliant on the private economy for its existence, and its actions are geared toward this latter's efficient functioning. There is no presumption, however, that left to its own devices the private economy will be naturally efficient or that it can deal with all questions of social justice. The liberal corporatist state derives its legitimacy from taking responsibility for those matters. It works actively for agreement between business and labor, ensures mass support by guaranteeing the basic social and economic mechanisms of the welfare state, and by making government publicly responsible for full employment, price stability, and growth. It seeks support from business by promising a workable investment climate, beneficial currency and tariff arrangements, and, above all, the orderly integration of labor. The liberal corporatist state is held to be nonpartisan with respect to internal constituent members, enforcing rules essential to the survi-

---

53 For a useful discussion of liberal corporatism, see Panitch (1977:66ff).

val of the system as a whole and consequently to the individual interests of all members.

Rawls's account of social justice in a well ordered society appeals to all the main elements of this view. This is particularly clear in his account of the activities to be performed by the state. In the only case he considers in detail he assumes a "properly organized democratic state that allows private ownership of capital and natural resources" (ibid.:275), and then ascribes to the state four main functions.[54] First, the "allocation" branch "is to keep the price system workably competitive and to prevent the formation of unreasonable market power . . . [which] does not exist as long as markets cannot be made more competitive consistent with the requirements of efficiency and the facts of geography and the preferences of households" (ibid.: 275–6). This branch also strives (via taxes and subsidies) to ensure that the price system reflects actual social costs and benefits (although the criteria by which such decisions will be made are not described). Next there is a "stabilization" branch which "strives to bring about reasonably full employment in the sense that those who want work can find it and the free choice of occupation and the deployment of finance are supported by strong effective demand" (ibid.:276). These first two branches are thus concerned with the efficiency of the system. The other two, the "transfer" and "distributive" branches, deal with questions of distributive justice, ensure the preservation of basic liberties and equality of opportunity, the social minimum, tax and savings structures, and regulate inheritance of wealth (which "is no more inherently unjust than the unequal inheritance of intelligence"), all in accordance with the difference principle (ibid.:276–8).

These institutions are sufficient to ensure that capitalist markets will be both just and efficient. By enforcing a view of justice aiming to "reduce disagreements and to bring divergent convictions more in line" (ibid.:53), the state maintains a negotiated consensus and a social system that is relatively

---

54 There is a fifth function discussed separately (Rawls, 1971:282ff), dealing with the expansion of expenditure on public goods when unanimously agreed on. This is taken up in section IV of this chapter.

stable over time. Since exploitation is held to derive from inefficiencies and malfunctions of the market, there is no sense that the two goals of promoting efficiency and distributive justice might systematically conflict; indeed the presumption clearly is that they will be mutually reinforcing. By "policing the conduct of firms and private associations and by preventing the establishment of monopolistic restrictions" (ibid.:275), the state ensures that free equality of opportunity is maintained. Demand management is implied to generate employment (ibid.:276). Welfare payments to the worst-off are presumed to benefit all because of the multiplier effects of chain connection. In short, something very like a liberal corporatist state, in pursuit of social justice in a market society via something very like Keynesian economic policies, appears to constitute Rawls's view of the legitimate role of the state in a well ordered society. The intuitive appeal of Rawls's "social union of social unions" inheres in the fact that it invokes this view of the nature and purposes of the state. The appeal to liberal corporatism, however, as Panitch (1977: 61–90) and others have argued, is essentially an ideological one under conditions of capitalist markets, since it invokes a picture of an internally complex but intrinsically harmonious social structure to describe relationships in reality that are profoundly opposed.

IV. CONCLUSION

Enough has been said to establish the case outlined at the outset of the last chapter. As with Nozick, for Rawls the appeal to a Kantian ethics as the basis for his political theory is seriously misleading. In both structure and content Rawls's argument differs so markedly from Kant's it is difficult to know in what precise sense it is supposed to be Kantian. Rawls does not begin to establish his case that his principles constitute procedural expressions of the categorical imperative and Kant's notion for autonomy. Like Nozick, Rawls is especially attracted to this latter notion because it seems to embody what he intuitively understands as the priority of liberty; it seems to attach prime importance, in the formulation of a moral position, to the decisive validating function of free individual choice. It has the further attraction of seeming to offer a way of attaching primary importance to these notions without falling victim to the bugbear of modern liberalism, subjectivism, since it purports to have some objective basis and universalist tendencies. Thus pluralism need not be based on indifference to alternative moral positions, or on a claim that all moral positions are equally (in)valid. It can appear to have some more robust philosophical status.

Wherein this robustness lies is deeply problematical for Rawls, because of his antipathy for what he takes to be teleological modes of philosophical argument. This prevents his arguing for a pluralist society on the grounds that it is a good idea, reducing him instead to the claim that his particular brand of pluralism is neutral among all rational substantive conceptions of the good. This claim is either false or tautologically true from Rawls's definition of rationality, in which case it is teleological in precisely the sense that he takes to be objectionable.

Rawls does not even try to establish that his principles would, in practice, preserve the categorical imperative or Kant's notion of autonomy. This claim could easily be challenged with reference to the difference principle alone, not to mention the considerations about the "worth" of liberty mentioned earlier. This principle ensures that the worst-off individual is not used exclusively to others' advantage; it says nothing, however, about the use of other strata for the benefit of the worst-off, or of one another. The only case in which observing the difference principle would ensure conformity to the categorical imperative would be the case where benefiting the worst-off really did benefit all, which requires both an expanding economy and strict chain connection throughout the system. Rawls does not even try to establish that these empirical circumstances typically prevail. Were he to do so, this would show only that, several very benign empirical conditions happening to hold in the world, Kant's categorical imperative would not be violated if we acted by Rawls's principles. This would be true of many principles in these circumstances, including utilitarianism, as Rae (1975b: 630–647) has shown. Something has clearly gone awry here, however, since the categorical imperative supposedly holds quite independently of empirical considerations. If the two principles are held to be "procedural expressions" of it, so, too, should they.

If Rawls replied that all distributive principles make empirical assumptions, one could agree but this must inevitably raise two further questions: first, to what extent is Rawls's argument really based on Kant's ethics, and, second, what grounds does Rawls offer for thinking that the particular empirical assumptions embodied in his principles in fact hold (or might hold) in the actual world to a significant extent? The decisive answers to these questions are, we have seen, not much and not many. His appeal is principally an intuitionist one to a hodgepodge of normative and empirical beliefs I have broadly designated as Keynesian. The three most important of these beliefs are, first, that stimulating income at the bottom will have beneficial multiplier effects throughout the economy – which presumes a particular thesis about the causes and consequences of weak demand; second, that market systems are only exploitative when they malfunction – which presumes a Pigouvian analysis of exploitation; and, third, that actions necessary to make the system more just will tend to make it more efficient – which is not strictly held to be a justification but is clearly held out as bait to ensnare the reader on his or her prejudices.

A somewhat different assessment of Rawls's argument has recently been offered by DiQuattro (1983:53–78) and it will be useful to conclude by considering his claims in light of the analysis offered here. DiQuattro's main aim is to demonstrate that Rawls's "left critics" (by which he means principally Brian Barry, C. B. Macpherson and Kai Nielson) have misunderstood both the spirit and the letter of *A Theory of Justice*, which not only can accommodate all the serious criticisms they make of it, but actually rules out a capitalist organization of production and exchange; although it does not require socialism, it would be consistent with it. This is a strong claim. It requires that Rawls be mistaken about the political implications of his argument (not in principle impossible), since, in his discussion of just political institutions, Rawls presumes a "state that allows private ownership of capital and natural resources" (1971:275).

DiQuattro's thesis rests on two arguments. First, he claims that since Rawls does not have a Marxist concept of class he does not have a Marxist concept of exploitation:

If Rawls meant by "class" what Marxists mean, who wouldn't share Macpherson's befuddlement over Rawls's presumed attempt to reconcile an egalitarian theory of justice with class divisions and their inherent exploitative mechanisms? ... [H]e could not consistently claim that the existence of social classes is compatible with a theory of justice if he believed that class division entailed exploitation of one class by another. (DiQuattro, 1983:54–55)

Leaving aside the extent to which Rawls's theory of justice is genuinely egalitarian (which there are serious grounds for questioning), what is the force of this? DiQuattro's point is that since Rawls uses the term "class" much as contemporary social scientists use the term "stratum," and defines classes in terms of their relative shares of primary goods, he is not sanctioning exploitative relationships. If class relationships under capitalism are inherently exploitative (which DiQuattro implies is his own view), they cannot be sanctioned by Rawls's argument. This is more than a little like Tully's claim (discussed in Chapter 3) that since Locke does not have Marx's concept of wage labor, he cannot be considered as legitimating capitalist wage–labor relationships. DiQuattro's claim is fallacious as Tully's is and for a parallel reason. Tully misses the point when he says that for Locke employment relationships are not coercive because they are voluntary. DiQuattro misses the point when he says that since Rawls is opposed to exploitation, his argument cannot sanction exploitative relationships. Tully attacks a strawman in countering Macpherson's proposition that Locke had Marx's concept of wage labor (when, in actuality he had something like Smith's). DiQuattro seems to think this question turns on whether Rawls has Marx's concept of exploitation (when *the point is* he has something like Pigou's).

When DiQuattro says the "principles of justice (and the entire argument backing them) *plus* the truth of the Marxian account [of exploitation] rule out capitalism as just" (DiQuattro, 1983:69) he is saying no more than if Rawls had a different (arguably more accurate) theory of how capitalist markets operate, and if Rawls took a different (arguably more plausible) view of what constitutes exploitation, he would have made a different argument, one which specifically denied the justness of capitalism. Hence Rawls's argument rules out capitalism. This is plainly absurd. It misses the fact that the ideological force of Rawls's argument derives precisely from his belief that capitalist markets can be "made just" since exploitation only arises when they malfunction. Largely because his theory is thought to provide a moral basis for this view has it been as influential as it has. If the first page of *A Theory of Justice* had stated that one of the implications of the argument would be that capitalism can never be justified, this book would not have had the impact it has had. Much of the ideological force of Rawls's argument derives precisely from the fact that it can legitimate the managed capitalism of the Keynesian state.

DiQuattro's second strategy of argument (not obviously consistent with his first) is to follow Rawls through his tortuous claims about the compatibility of markets with socialist political institutions (as Rawls understands these terms). DiQuattro notes that Rawls distinguishes allocative from distributive functions of markets and argues that under socialism the market might be employed for the former but not the latter. Whether or not this is true, it is clearly not Rawls's view since he regards the distributive functions of markets as their raison d'être, as DiQuattro is well aware (ibid.:69–70). Rawls's discussion at the level of "ideal theory" makes "considerable use of market arrangements. It is only in this way . . . that the problem of *distribution* can be handled as a case of pure procedural justice" (Rawls, 1971:274, emphasis added). It is, however, DiQuattro's view that "how capitalism fares under the difference principle depends [in part] on Rawls's distinction between ideal and nonideal normative theory" (DiQuattro, 1983:67). With this in mind he proceeds to Rawls's discussion of economic systems, noting that Rawls employs a conventional definition of public goods as those things which are uniquely public, essentially indivisible, and goods and services that are particularly vulnerable to problems of externality and free ridership. He argues, too, that for Rawls the notion of a public good must inherently be so limited (whether in the production or the consumption of goods) "because of the distributional consequences of its [the market's] allocative function" (ibid.:70–1). He follows Rawls in arguing that, although the class of goods that is *necessarily* public is limited, there is no reason why it cannot be expanded by the voluntary agreements of persons, should they unanimously agree to make their society more communitarian or socialistic.

In this sense socialism is an open question for Rawls's principles: it could justly be instituted in varying degrees without violating his theory of justice, provided this was done in accordance with Wicksell's "unanimity criterion" which requires near-unanimous approval on the public financing of collective goods. Beyond this, Rawls's position is that (provided the market-based distributive status quo is just, a large and pregnant assumption) "[t]here is no more justification for using the state apparatus to compel some citizens to pay for unwanted benefits that others desire than there is to force them to reimburse others for their private expenses" (ibid.:72; Rawls, 1971:283ff). This Nozickian language betrays the limited extent to which Rawls takes the concept of public goods seriously. It seems difficult to reconcile it with the proposition that Rawls's argument is compatible with, let alone requires, socialist political institutions.

Much of what Rawls has said militates against this conclusion. Most significant is that his open embrace of the view that individuals have rights of exclusive dominion over all objects of value except neo-classically defined public goods misses the social character of production on which arguments for the public control of means to "the good" are usually based. When socialists argue that the fruits of the division of labor should be publicly controlled, they appeal to the fact that our capacity to own the things we do own is critically dependent on the actions of others. Thus they are maintaining (perhaps, often, implicitly) that all goods beyond what an isolated individual could produce absolutely unassisted *are* public goods; it is therefore illegitimate to suppose that individuals can have rights of exclusive dominion over them.

The claim that an expanded (perhaps even comprehensive) public sector might legitimately emerge from bilateral agreements among all members of a society based on private ownership is a quite different *moral* claim (not to mention its being palpably unlikely). It presumes the existence of legitimate individual rights of exclusive dominion over parts of the social product, which any intelligent defender of socialism would not grant to begin with. The claim that Rawls's principles are neutral between "property owning democracies" and "socialism" on the grounds that they do not rule out individuals choosing to finance as extensive a public sector as they can unanimously agree to presumes that the market-based status quo can be made just (something Rawls never establishes since he never explains the origins of individual rights of private property). It also presumes that justifications of social institutions must appeal to the voluntary consent of every individual, a key liberal assumption which, I will suggest in the next chapter, we have grounds for questioning. For the present I conclude that by allowing these theoretical possibilities (empirically so unlikely that no one need worry about them) Rawls, DiQuattro, and others can pretend (possibly even to themselves) that they are agnostic about socialist political institutions. We have seen that the only socialist institutions Rawls could accept are those that maintain the integrity of well functioning capitalist markets.

Part IV
Conclusion

6

The liberal ideology of individual rights

I. HISTORICAL SUMMARY

The case I have sought to establish is that there is a distinctive way of conceiving of individual rights that has been central to the Anglo-American liberal tradition of political theory since the mid-seventeenth century, and that is very much alive in it today. Elements of this view have important roots in Renaissance and medieval European political thought, and in Roman law, but the seventeenth-century contract theorists combined these elements in new ways, thereby constructing a view of rights that formed the armature of modern liberal ideology. This view is so deeply embedded that it infects not only explicit rights theories, but is presupposed in the most influential traditional liberal alternative to these, utilitarianism in its major historical forms. Although my focus has been on rights-based theories, enough has been said to indicate that, just as these have always co-existed with powerful utilitarian commitments, a history of utilitarianism could be written that would bring out its reciprocal dependence on the evolving language of individual rights. The whole idea that liberals somehow face a choice between rights and utility[1] assumes misleading accounts of the concept of a right and of the goals of liberal writers, historical and contemporary. The nature of the term "right" is such that reference to the substance and purposes of

1 See, for instance, H.L.A. Hart's (1979:77) assertion that the philosophy of government in England and America has, for much of this century, been based on a "widely accepted old faith that some form of utilitarianism, if only we could discover the right form, *must* capture the essence of political morality." According to Hart, however, this old faith is finally being replaced by a "new faith" which is "that the truth must lie not with a doctrine that takes the maximisation of aggregate or average general welfare for its goal, but with a doctrine of basic human rights, protecting specific basic liberties and interests of individuals, if only we could find some sufficiently firm foundation for such rights to meet some long familiar objections."

rights is inevitably entailed by its use. Defenders of rights *theories* have typically focused their attention on the subject of and basis for rights (sometimes exclusively on the first of these), but their treatments of the other terms in the relation reveal much of the utilitarian conceptions of value and ends, both individual and collective. A more accurate picture of their endeavor, both historically and conceptually, portrays it as the search for a synthesis of rights and utility.[2]

The liberal view of rights has not gone unchanged historically. Rather than argue that there is some family resemblance, or even weaker relationship, among the various views discussed, I have presented the liberal view of rights as an internally complex set of evolving doctrines, theories, beliefs, and assumptions. This has advantages over the view argued for by Macpherson, that a single unit idea, "possessive individualism," triumphed after the Reformation and has governed all our philosophical and political preconceptions ever since, or MacIntyre's arguably comparable account of "the emotivist self," and also over general categories of traditionalism and modernity for which Marxists and Straussians are often summarily derided by historians. I have tried to preserve, without overstating, the elements of truth in these views, recognizing a core structure to all assertions about rights, and tracing the doctrines that constitute the liberal view of rights through several incarnations: transitional, classical, neo-classical, and Keynesian. These categories are very broad and might usefully be further subdivided in a more comprehensive study, although they seem to me to capture at least some of the most significant "moments" in its evolution. In contrast to the writers just mentioned, I have emphasized the

---

2 It would take a different book to argue this case in detail from the point of view of the history of utilitarianism, but note that even Bentham, who rejected all doctrines of natural law and natural right out of hand, made central use of the language of individual rights and the negative libertarian view of freedom we have been examining. A poignant illustration of this can be found in his *Principles of the Civil Code*, where he argues that "[l]aw does not say to man, *Labour, and I will reward you*, but it says: *Labour, and I will assure to you the enjoyment of the fruits of your labour – that natural and sufficient recompense which without me you cannot preserve, I will insure it by arresting the hand which may seek to ravish it from you. If industry creates, it is law which preserves*" (reprinted in Macpherson, 1978:50, emphases added). On this subject, see Long (1977:3ff); see also Rosenblum (1978:58–9, 71, 152).

internally complex evolving nature of the liberal view of individual rights, the particular philosophical conception of the subject (to which they devote almost exclusive attention) being one (evolving) part of it. It remains to consider the liberal conception of the subject, as well as the other evolving parts of this ideology, in more detail.

i. The subject of rights

The view of the subject of rights embraced by the seventeenth-century contract theorists is usefully termed Cartesian. It assumes that the individual will is the cause of all actions, individual and collective; it ascribes decisive epistemic and hence moral authority to the individual over his actions, on the grounds that he has privileged access to the contents of his own mind. For this reason individual consent becomes vital to the whole idea of political activity. The doctrine of individual consent was not, however, synonymous with that of individual right for the seventeenth-century writers, because it was embedded in and limited by explicit theories of objective interests. For Hobbes this turned on his view of science, and in particular on his belief in the possibility of a deductive ethics, intersubjectively demonstrable with the certainty of Euclidean geometry. For Locke the creationist view of knowledge took a more explicitly religious form, but produced a moral theory similar in structure if not in content. Neither writer seriously doubted that there *were* rational rules of social organization that could be demonstrated so to be, and that must, as a result, be chosen freely by rational persons acting in their genuine interests, and neither doubted that true interests could be known – such was their faith in the possibility of an objective science of morality. Thus the importance they ascribed to the subject of rights and individual consent was not seen as threatening to their beliefs in objective standards of value and interest. Hobbes's relational theory of the good and Locke's account of toleration did generate doctrines of pluralism, but these were circumscribed by definite and explicit limits: in Hobbes's case by the rule of law as imposed by the sovereign in accordance with the laws of nature, and in Locke's by a more limited view of the rule of law and more complex appeals to the distinction between liberty and license and the imperatives for social stability. Neither writer took seriously for a minute the possibility that liberal writers since Hume have been attempting to escape: that the centrality ascribed to the will and convictions of the isolated subject would undercut their natural-law constraints, so that their limited moral pluralism might collapse into the kind of ethical relativism that seems to many to be entailed by emotivism in its dominant contemporary forms. Hobbes and Locke were transforming the natural-law tradition from within. The extent of the transformation was obscured, I argued, by their attachment to a view of science not destined to survive the eighteenth century.

Contemporary liberals face the consequences of this longer-term transformation. Their primary concern has been to find a way to hold onto the ontological conception of the individual of the seventeenth-century writers, but simultaneously to find some alternative moral basis that both acknowledges the centrality of his freedom and limits his power to act in any way he pleases. This has been attempted principally by embracing a version of Kant's ethics that appears both to acknowledge the centrality of the autonomous individual and to generate universal moral injunctions. The great difficulty this faces, embodied in Sidgwick's objection to Kant, lies in showing that the autonomous Kantian agent must choose any particular substantive moral or political principles. Even the injunction that he must act rationally, however defined, or consistently, appears to undercut the freedom of the individual contemporary liberals feel compelled to defend in a radical form. The Cartesian agent is given a centrality in the modern theories it lacked in the earlier ones: it trumps all other considerations.

ii. The substance of rights

The negative libertarian view of the substance of rights has been an integral part of the liberal conception of individual rights since its inception. It, too, has been through several metamorphoses. In Hobbes's argument it is literally defined negatively, as a residual, by the silence of the law, and although it constitutes "the greatest liberty of subjects," it exists at the sovereign's pleasure and can be invaded by him at his will. The rights of subjects vis-à-vis one another, however, are inviolable. These rights constitute the modern notion of exclusive proprietorship that was eventually to be turned against the state, as the system of public law shed its independent foundation and came to rest on the evolving system of private law. The notion of private-law rights of exclusive dominion having force against the state first achieved currency with Locke and the Whigs during their radical phase in the early 1680s. Ashcraft (1980:429–34ff) points out that it was they who adapted the metaphor of invasion from the nation to the individual, in order to argue that the king had invaded the liberties of his subjects. This was an important move because it entailed a separation of the concept of the public interest from that of the ruler, and because it meant that the rights of "the people" were reducible to, and perhaps even derived from, rights of individuals.[3] These ideological changes paralleled changes in public law, private law, and the relations between the two that were then in process.

This view of man's negative freedom, of a private sphere surrounding him that cannot be entered (first by other individuals and eventually by the state) without his consent, became the standard view of freedom in the liberal tradition, interlocking neatly with the Cartesian view of the person. We saw that it takes on extreme proportions with Nozick, that he

3 Skinner (1978, II: 239–348; 1980:309–30), as part of his concern to overturn Walzer's thesis in *Revolution of the Saints* that the modern notions of resistance originated with the Calvinists, traces a number of key components of the secular theory of resistance articulated in Locke's later writings, and of the Calvinist and Huguenot theories of resistance, to the Lutheran Reformation and in particular the Conciliarist writers of the early sixteenth century, Almain and Mair. As he points out, however, Locke's account is distinctive in that, first, the right to resist is held to be inalienable; second, the possibility of resistance in cases of tyrannical government is treated as a straightforward right, and, third, "the right of resistance is treated as the possession of each individual citizen, and hence of the whole body of the people viewed as a legal entity." These features distinguish Locke's theory "from a number of earlier and less radical strands of revolutionary thought, and at the same time license us to describe it as having a wholly secular and populist character." Thus for Locke in the state of nature each individual "has a right to punish the transgressors of that Law [of Nature] to such a Degree, as may hinder its Violation" (Locke, 1963:312).

is even prepared to jeopardize the coherence of large parts of his argument to maintain it intact. It requires his tortuous compensation arguments, his arbitrary definition of acting in "equilibrium," and his whole "side-constraint" theory of rights. Although Rawls claims to take a different, relational, view of freedom, his need to maintain the content of the negative libertarian view leads him to model his definition of freedom on a version of Locke's account of religious toleration, to distinguish liberty from its "worth," and to argue for the priority of the former, all hallmarks of the standard negative libertarian view. Leaving aside the vagueness of the difference principle, its injunctions are secondary to, and can never override, the priority of liberty understood in this negative libertarian form. In these various formulations private individuals are thus conceived of as having exclusive proprietorship over their capacities and actions, the latter constituting, in Nozick's phrase, a sphere in "moral space" surrounding them. This sphere can never be entered by other individuals with (formally) equal rights, except by consent.

The only exceptions to this in Rawls's argument consist in limitations on liberty for the protection of "liberty itself," a view most famously associated with Mill's harm principle, but also present in all its essentials in *A Letter Concerning Toleration*. Since Locke wrote, this view has been conceived of as holding equally against the state and against other individuals, with the difference that the state ceases to have the rights of a legal person, descending eventually in status in modern doctrines of constitutionalism to the role of "servant of the people." In this context Nozick can argue that the state has no rights beyond those unanimously conferred on it by the citizens. Rawls can limit its activities to those necessary when the mechanism for conferring consent (the market) breaks down – as in the case of public goods where problems of free ridership arise – or when the market breaks down for other reasons of externality or monopoly. The essential idea of preserving spheres surrounding individuals remains, however. Individuals conceive of and execute their "plans of life" separately, are indifferent to one another, and, above all, Rawls feels it incumbent upon himself to show, would unanimously consent to his prin-

278

ciples at the constitutional stage, the assumption being that anything less would illegitimately violate the rights of some. This is built into the so-called Kantian conception of equality that guarantees everyone a *"right* to view their persons as independent and not identified with any particular system of ends" (Rawls, 1980:544, emphasis added). Rawls's "social union of social unions" consists essentially of Lockean voluntary associations. To the extent that the state has a more active role than mere aggregator of the interests of these various groups, I argued that this is best understood in terms of the ideology of liberal corporatism.

iii. The basis for rights

The two main changes that ushered in the modern liberal view of the basis for rights were the collapse of history and precedent as modes of political justification and the radically diminished possibilities of religious justification of political principles. The first of these, I followed Pocock (1957) in arguing, was an indirect by-product of the discovery by Spelman and the common lawyers that English law was largely feudal in content and German in origin. This decisively laid to rest the myth that its legitimacy lay in an Ancient Constitution, lost in the mists of time. Pocock held that Locke was something of an exception to anti-Royalist writers of his time in not attempting to argue for a version of the Ancient Constitution. I suggested, however, that this was a decisive reason for his longer-term influence in the liberal tradition. Locke shifted the basis of antiabsolutist conceptions of political legitimacy away from history and toward a moral justification based on an appeal to reason. Despite the tremendous differences in their substantive arguments and their politics, Locke shares this mode of argument with Hobbes. Both sought to show that a political constitution could be justified when and only when it functioned in the rational individual interests of each citizen. Whatever other religious and anthropological force their laws of nature were intended to have, it is in this that their longer-term influence is to be found.

The decline in religious bases for political legitimacy and

the growth of secularism have been so often discussed it would be superfluous to rehearse the arguments here. Two points are worth noting, however. First, religious skepticism on the part of Hobbes or Locke was not critical to their contributions to the secularization of liberal conceptions of political legitimacy. (The nature and extent of both their religious views remain controversial.) Both succeeded in making religious considerations largely irrelevant to their arguments. Locke did rely at times on his arguments from scripture and it may be impossible to establish the distinction between liberty and license, one of the mechanisms by which he limits the scope of his individual rights, without some such appeal. Precisely this aspect of his argument, however, was destined to be ignored in the dominant strand of the liberal tradition, as we saw in Chapter 4. Had Locke not offered an alternative rationalist construction of his argument it is doubtful he could have achieved the sustained prominence he did in that tradition.

Second, whatever the particular religious views of Hobbes and Locke, their Cartesian views of genuine knowledge in the moral sciences as subjective certainty of essences, undercut the possibility of religious, and indeed all forms of, extrinsic moral justification. Hobbes's railings against arguments from authority (religious and secular) and his appeals to the individual convictions of his readers, Locke's heady rationalism and his Protestant view of the sanctity of the individual conscience all militated against forms of justification based on anything other than individual assent. Neither writer perceived the potential implications of this because of their intense convictions that people could be decisively convinced of the truth of their arguments. It is arguable that even within their own terms of reference these contentions were vulnerable, and that both writers played on the ambiguity in the workmanship metaphor between one's having essential knowledge of what one makes, and holding that all persons will and/or should make the same things. The latter claims involve very strong additional assumptions not only that all men reason alike, but that they have identical (but separate) interests that can be preserved by an act of common consent. Neither of these assumptions would have seemed implausible to seventeenth-century writers, who had no ideological stake in denying interpersonal comparability or in holding that a concept of human nature grounded in a theory of objective interests was unavoidable in a full account of legitimate rights. Nonetheless, these assumptions could be, and eventually were, challenged by appeal to the very Cartesian conception of the self these writers had articulated, and on which both had, in different ways, relied.

Hobbes and Locke abandoned historical and religious modes of justification and sought instead for universal principles of rational social organization. They did not, however, strive for *afactual* theories in the post-Kantian sense that pervades the writings of contemporary rights theorists. The whole idea of the contract was, for the earlier writers, intended to have a basis in (their understanding of) actual political events. This is entirely lacking in the hypothetical arguments of Nozick and Rawls, as well as those of other contemporary liberal theorists, most notably Ackerman (1980).[4] The whole notion of "ideal theory,"[5] according to which concrete principles of justice are worked out in purely abstract terms and then applied to the "second best" situations of the actual world, would never have occurred to the earlier writers. This is a further reason, perhaps, why they perceived no significant tension between their "subjective" account of the subject of rights and emphasis on free choice, on the one hand, and their objective theories of the good, on the other. Although they thought that people must choose freely in some significant sense if their rights are to be respected, they never really doubted what people should choose, or that substantive, partly empirical, conceptions of the good could be argued over in terms of evidence and reason. I have argued that this is unavoidable in fact, and that the contemporary writers also presume substantive, partly empirical, conceptions of the good. They do so, however, as Rawls puts it,

---

4 Aspects of Ackerman's account are taken up in section III of this chapter.
5 His particular account of ideal theory is arguably one of Rawls's most influential innovations. Thus, for instance, Galston (1980:13), who is critical of much of Rawls's argument asserts that: "[o]ne of the main virtues of Rawls' *Theory of Justice* is his reliance on the concept of 'ideal theory'." The mere fact that so much of the Rawls literature consists of derivations of similar principles, and arguments over whether his initial conditions generate different conclusions than he claims, testifies to the degree to which is mode of moral argument has been influential.

"as they please," with little attention to the truth or plausibility of the empirical assumptions they make. There is thus an air of unrealism to contemporary arguments which the earlier ones lacked. This partly explains the tendency of contemporary liberal political theory to feed off its own controversies, since it is largely unconstrained by anything else.

iv. The purposes of rights

At the heart of the liberal conception of the purposes of rights in all its formulations is a pluralist account of the good. The nature of, and limits to, this pluralism have varied, as have the practical injunctions believed necessary to sustain it. Taking the second of these first, we saw that a critical development in the liberal tradition was the emergence of classical equilibrium theory in the eighteenth century. Before this Hobbes, and to a lesser extent Locke, saw no conflict between a pluralist view of human goods and a highly interventionist state: the Mandevillian belief that radical egoism would work for the benefit of all would only arise in conjunction with the view that the market system could be self-equilibrating. Although Hobbes recognized, somewhat equivocally, the inevitability of market relationships in large areas of social life, and although Locke openly endorsed such relationships, both believed they would have to be actively regulated, and in some critical areas even created, by the state.

This view went into decline with the rise of classical equilibrium theory, in terms of which the state appeared to be unnecessary for market regulation. The inherently vulnerable position of the state created by the changes in public law previously mentioned was exacerbated by this development. The regulative state became identified with the minimal state in the neo-classical revival, although it has been anachronistically read back into the views of earlier liberals by writers such as Nozick. The principal departure in the Keynesian tradition articulated by Rawls derives from a questioning of the equilibrium assumptions of neo-classical economics, generating a liberal corporatist view of the state geared to a managed capitalist economy. The equation of regulation with minimalism is given up, but the primary role of the state – to regulate a negative libertarian society and a market-based private economy – remains. The nature and content of Rawls's primary goods, and the empirical assumptions behind the difference principle, reveal both to be geared toward this end. The writers examined all see the purpose of political organization generally, and the civil rights constituted by it in particular, as being to preserve a negative libertarian society in which individuals can pursue their different individual goals unimpeded. The institutional manifestations of this, however, have varied greatly with external circumstances, and with related assumptions about the driving causal mechanisms of market societies.

An important difference between the pluralism of Hobbes and Locke and that argued for by Rawls and Nozick is that the former did not argue that pluralism was in any sense a morally neutral doctrine. This is one of the most problematical claims in the contemporary arguments. It is worth considering why it is defended at all. The central reason is the fear of "paternalism" and "teleology" that permeates their writings; dictated by their Cartesian view of the self trumping all other considerations. Many elements of the modern doctrine of subjectivism were present in the seventeenth-century arguments, but not all were. Perhaps more important, although Hobbes and Locke subscribed to a Cartesian view of the self, their view of the nature of moral knowledge meant that this Cartesian self was not inevitably subjectivist, where this is understood to entail that moral imperatives are statements of "mere" appetites and aversions. They believed that objective moral knowledge was both possible and necessary, thus were not forced to make the claim that pluralism was desirable because of its putative neutrality among different individual conceptions of the good. They held that it was a necessary and desirable method of social organization, a view for which they adduced both arguments and evidence, however internally problematical these might be revealed to be. The modern writers, fearful of the broader implications of substantive assertions about the good, fall back on neutrality as a (not very convincing) way out of this dilemma. We saw this most clearly in our discussions of Nozick's claim that his argument presupposes no "end state" or "patterned" theory of distribution, and of Rawls's "thin theory" of the good.[6]

II. PROBLEMS OF COHERENCE

Many of the internal difficulties confronted in the arguments discussed derive from a tension between the negative libertarian view of freedom, to some formulation of which these writers all subscribe in their accounts of the subject and substance of rights, and other moral positions they feel impelled to hold. More precisely, the Cartesian self with decisive authority over its private sphere as the basis for political life, and to whom all political arrangements must be shown to be justifiable, and even causally reducible, militates against other sentiments to which these writers are powerfully attached. It is for this reason that the modern writers particularly try to disguise these sentiments, claiming that they are somehow entailed by the negative libertarian view. Thus what is actually a quite limited form of pluralism is presented by Rawls and Nozick as a much more extensive form of moral neutralism, a claim for which, ironically, liberals have sometimes been strongly criticized.[7] Although this tension is present in an embryonic form in the early arguments, it does not become manifest until after the time of Hume. In its contemporary form it leaves liberal writers running from subjectivism with nowhere to go. This fact is at the root of the search for a Kantian basis for their arguments, in the hope that the radical notion of free choice embodied in Kant's conception of autonomy can somehow itself constitute an Archimedean point. This amounts to a complex restatement of the problem, however, rather than a solution to it.

An important substantive consequence of this tension is that

6 It is true that Rawls (1975:536–54) has more recently added some qualifications to his neutrality claim, but they do not in any essentials alter his accounts of primary goods being necessary for all rational conceptions of the good, the "thin theory," or of the possibility of coherently "bracketing" questions of the right from questions of the good. The considerable attention Rawls devotes to attempting to make a (suitably qualified) version of his claim to neutrality plausible underscores the importance he attaches to this question.

7 See, for instance, Bloom (1975:648–62) on Rawls, and more generally Strauss's indictment of this aspect of modernism in *Natural Right and History* (1953:9–80).

the liberal state is presented as a neutral arbiter or aggregator of different individual interests. Even in Rawls's liberal corporatist account the state's raison d'être is to enable individuals to pursue their individual conceptions of the good. He differs from Nozick only in his account of how this is to be achieved and what it entails in practice. Both writers view the (legitimate) state as neutral among citizens, performing essentially regulative functions. The liberal state, however, is no more neutral than the conception of the good on which it rests. This is not a sufficient reason for rejecting it, but it is sufficient for claiming that, if it is to be advocated in the contemporary world, some reasons must be given other than the fallacious claim that it is neutral among different conceptions of the good, and hence enables everyone freely to achieve his or her individual goals. The modern rights theorists, however, are prevented from formulating independent justifications of this kind by their attachment to the negative libertarian conception of freedom, and their concomitant need to show that it is preserved by the liberal state.

This negative libertarian view of freedom is conceptually problematical, in that it rests on a misunderstanding of the relational character of the term "freedom." The whole idea that persons can in some general sense be free, either because they are surrounded by a "sphere" in "moral space" or because they have some formal guarantees that are specifiable independently of their "worth," misses the point that freedoms are of agents from constraints to perform actions. The notion that we may be free to perform actions we are unable to perform, that both writers must take seriously, rests on this politically pregnant confusion. If the claim were that formal guarantees are an insufficient necessary condition for most significant substantive freedoms, this would be one thing. But Nozick regards the formal guarantees as necessary and sufficient, and although Rawls acknowledges difficulties with the "worth" of liberty, these are conceived of as secondary to liberty "itself" (whatever that is) and governed by different principles.

A second major internal difficulty with the liberal conception of individual rights in its dominant contemporary forms is that its proclaimed opposition to utilitarianism is fundamentally bogus. From its first formulations it has embodied what were to become utilitarian assumptions concerning individual rationality, preference valuation, and the justification for mutually cooperative behavior. Liberal rights theorists underestimate the degree to which utilitarian assumptions are incorporated into their arguments largely because they fail to consider (or, in Rawls's case, take seriously) the relational character of assertions about freedom, right, and justice.[8] Many of their utilitarian assumptions about value and ends are therefore suppressed, and obscured by the false claim that they do not make "paternalistic" or "teleological" claims about these matters. These claims are, however, present implicitly, in many places appealed to as back-door intuitive justifications for their arguments.

The most obvious of these, we saw, concerned claims of Rawls and Nozick (supposedly irrelevant to their arguments) that their proposals would work to maintain utilitarian efficiency. In addition, both adopt much else of the theoretical paraphernalia of neo-classical utilitarianism including ordinal utility functions (again dictated by the negative libertarian definition of freedom), mutual disinterestedness, and instrumental rationality. Both obscure this fact by rejecting classical utilitarianism for its teleology, at the same time appealing to a version of the neo-classical brand of this doctrine, widely believed to be antiteleological because based on ordinal noncomparable utilities. Although both writers implicitly employ cardinal (and hence uncontroversially teleological) measures (Nozick in his compensation argument and Rawls in his "thin theory" and the application of the difference principle), both attempt to downplay this and present themselves as relying principally, if not exclusively, on ordinal noncomparable measures.[9] This is done, I argued, out of the (false) conviction

---

8 Although I did not argue for a relational account of the term "justice" in Chapter 1 this could be done, as Rawls (1979:6) makes clear when he says: "[w]hen fully articulated, any conception of justice expresses a conception of the person, of the relations between persons, and of the general structure and ends of social co-operation."

9 Although I noted that Rawls (1982) has more recently retreated from this position to something more like a Pigouvian account of the inevitability of interpersonal comparisons.

that if it can be consistently achieved, what is intuitively useful in utilitarianism can be incorporated without "moral balancing" to maximize some exogenously defined conception of the good. Both avoid admitting that they embrace substantive conceptions of the good of any kind, including utilitarian, because they perceive this to be at variance with their subjectivist assumptions about persons that invariably trump. Because, however, an account of rights is more than an account of persons they find themselves willy nilly with substantive accounts of value and ends that are largely utilitarian in content.

Closely related to the tensions between the account of a free person embraced by the neo-Kantian writers and others of their substantive moral commitments, is the importance they attach to abstract doctrines of individual consent. Some notion of the consent of the citizenry has played a part in arguments for political legitimacy in the West since the Renaissance at least,[10] but the doctrine of individual consent as it has evolved in the contractarian tradition since Hobbes is distinctive in that it has become steadily more abstract and individualist. Hobbes's emphasis on a political regime needing to appeal to the subjective assent of the people was grounded in a fear of the masses quite common and perfectly understandable among the English ruling classes in the early and mid-seventeenth century. Hobbes's analysis rested, at least in part, on the descriptive thesis that unless the sovereign could command the assent of the citizenry it would not long survive, a view quite understandable historically. Locke's critique of Hobbes rested in part on a disputation of Hobbes's empirical claim that the state of nature might not be worth returning to in certain circumstances, and that the principal impetus for leaving it was its "inconvenience." Locke's claim, obviously felicitous for the Whigs in the early 1680s, has since supplied the basis for vastly more abstract theories of consent in the post-Kantian liberal tradition, where the "normal" or "essential" human condition *in* civil society is conceived of as both asocial and apolitical.

The increasing abstractness of the anthropological claim for the necessity for individual consent to all political arrange-

10 See Skinner (1978:Vol I).

ments is closely bound up with the radical transformation of the moral claim that individual consent forms the basis of political legitimacy. Hobbes's materialism resulted in a fusion of the anthropological and moral arguments via a deterministic psychology. From Locke on, however, influential writers in the liberal tradition have avoided this view, or at least been deeply uncomfortable with its implications. It was natural that Locke should give the moral doctrine of consent greater critical bite than Hobbes, since he was concerned with a theory of legitimate resistance to a corrupted sovereign – an oxymoronic notion for Hobbes. The historical legacy of Locke's discussion of consent has been complex and many sided. One aspect of it is of particular interest. It supplied the conceptual foundation for modern negative libertarianism, since it made the activities of the state intrinsically vulnerable to the charge that they lacked the consent of all or some of the governed and were by definition illegitimate as a result.[11] Locke's aim had been to specify conditions under which it could be legitimate to resist the supremacy of the rule of law. His argument also supplied the conceptual tools for questioning the legitimacy of the law itself. Instead of asking in what circumstances resistance might be justified (assuming that in general it was not), the question would become: in what circumstances is government justified? Thus Nozick, at the logical extreme of this conceptual transformation, defines his task with the casual assertion that the "fundamental question" of political theory is whether there ought to be a state at all (1974:4). For Rawls, too, except in cases of indivisible public goods, or where the market breaks down, the only criterion for expanded state action is Wicksell's unanimity criterion.

So deeply embedded have negative libertarian conceptions of freedom become that the sheer absurdity of this view escapes many people. If someone said that the fundamental question of dental theory is whether people should have teeth at all, no one would take him seriously for a minute. Yet if the existence of politics and states are an inevitable part of social life – which the weight of the evidence surely

---

11 Hence the liberal preoccupation, also since Locke, with the deeply problematic notion of tacit consent.

suggests – Nozick's question and many of the assumptions behind the negative libertarian conception of freedom are no less absurd. At the heart of the negative libertarian ideal is the notion that the state *presence or action* needs to be justified, not state *absence or inaction*. This assumes, fallaciously, some "normal" or "expected course of events," in Nozick's terminology, morally benign or at worst morally neutral. It takes as its model of "normal" human interaction a view of simple voluntary transactions among isolated persons, unmediated by external authority structures and power relations, that has never prevailed anywhere in human history, is unimaginable in practice, and even in theory.[12] Thus the negative libertarian conceptions of freedom defended by these writers are inevitably loaded ideologically. They clearly presume many of the latent power structures and relationships that in fact prevail in contemporary market societies in their accounts of their "prepolitical" initial conditions. This is quite blatant with Nozick but Rawls, too, holds that unless they malfunction markets are essentially neutral mechanisms that preserve individual freedom. He seems unaware that market systems require particular legal and political institutions and definitions of property and contract that do not prevail everywhere, had to be created historically, and have to be reproduced if they are to survive. His assertion that markets predate capitalism is not remotely sufficient to deal with this problem and is, in any case, irrelevant to the question of their moral neutrality. The myth of the minimal state could only arise once these market relations were established. Thus the ideological force of negative libertarianism in the contemporary world derives from the fact that, to the extent that new state action or initiatives are held to be illegitimate, the power relations embedded in the existing market system can function unimpeded.

Closely connected to the arbitrary distinction between action and inaction is the view of all social relationships as nothing more than relationships among individuals, to be evaluated by the same sorts of criteria by which we typically evaluate indi-

12 See the discussion of the theoretical breakdown of unanimity rules in Chapter 4, section II(i).

vidual actions. This view is fundamentally inappropriate to theorizing about questions of political right and social justice, that by their nature involve complex structures that condition and shape individual actions, and the options available to individuals, in ways often directly intended by no one, even when they are understood. Thus the enterprise of normative theorizing about questions of distributive justice must be a heavily descriptive and consequentialist endeavor. This makes the problems of political philosophy vastly more difficult, because it implies coming to terms with hotly contested and ideologically loaded competing descriptions of the actual social world and the causes of its problems, and this in turn often necessitates counterfactual empirical argument that may be impossible to settle definitively. I have sought to establish that even the deontological liberals engage in these activities – proclamations to the contrary notwithstanding. The descriptive choices they make, most often by assumption, predetermine their normative conclusions. They seem blithely unaware that there may be true alternative descriptions with competing claims to relevancy, or even that their own descriptions are controversial. In this connection Elizabeth Anscombe (1969:175–95) has argued with some force that one of the greatest weaknesses of English (and, we might certainly add, American) moral philosophy since Sidgwick is its inability to come to terms with the problems entailed by multiple descriptions that she, Davidson, and others have identified.[13] Anscombe's explanation of this is that it has been dominated by consequentialism, necessarily a "shallow philosophy" (ibid.:187). Without wishing to take issue with Anscombe's general assessment of modern moral philosophy, I should like to suggest that it is not consequentialism as a doctrine that is problem-ridden, but rather the particular naive version of it that dominates the tradition we have been examining.

Neither Nozick nor Rawls regards himself as a consequentialist in the classical sense. Nozick's "historical" entitlement theory is expressly opposed to "patterned" theories that focus on a particular outcome of an action in evaluating its moral

---

13 See Davidson (1968:79–94) and Anscombe (1969:175–95, 1958:69–72).

worth. Rawls explicitly embraces only a very limited form of consequentialism resting heavily on *ceteris paribus* clauses that invoke other (deontological) requirements. Both appeal to Kant's concept of autonomy in validating moral claims that would seem to be radically anticonsequentialist. There is an important sense, however, in which these appeals are only skin-deep; much of both their modes of argument is implicitly consequentialist in character; not only in their intuitive appeals to the consequences of enacting their principles, but in their back-door appeals to efficiency and in the logic of their objections to classical utilitarianism. In short, some assumptions about utilitarian efficiency seem to be quite close to the center of the modern liberal's metaphorical Quinean field, and to do some surreptitious trumping of their own.

I do not take issue with the fact of appealing to consequences. This is inevitable in substantive moral argument. My objection is that they do not look hard at or far enough into the consequences of actions, almost never beyond their intended consequences.[14] They tend to take the agent's conception of what he is doing at face value and commit what I once described as the *meaning-of-the-act* fallacy as a result. This is the fallacy of assuming that an agent's intentional description of an action he performs is the only, or the primary, relevant description of that action (Shapiro, 1982:546–7ff). Perhaps the paradigmatic instance of this occurs in a recent book by Bruce Ackerman in which he takes the "ideal theory" approach to political philosophy to its logical extreme, shifting the constitutional choice problem to an imaginary planet discovered by a spaceship. Ackerman argues for three principles that must govern all arguments over the distribution of power, which he takes to be the basic problem of politics. First, persons are constrained to argue rationally, that is "the power holder must respond not by suppressing the questioner but by giving a reason that explains why he is more entitled to the resource than the questioner is." Second, arguments must be

14 The exceptions are Nozick's use of "fundamental" explanations that he arbitrarily switches on and off to suit his purposes, and Rawls's acknowledgment that in certain cases individual actions will have unintended "externalities" needing to be rectified by the state. Such cases are seen as exceptional, however.

consistent in that the "reason advanced by a power wielder on one occasion must not be inconsistent with the reasons he advances to justify his other claims to power." Third, all dialogue is to be constrained by the principle of neutrality, requiring that no reason is a good reason if the power holder must assert either that his "conception of the good is better than that asserted by any of his fellow citizens" or that he is "intrinsically superior" to them. By conducting "constrained power talk" in accordance with these requirements, Ackerman argues, the inhabitants will govern themselves via a liberal state as he understands it (Ackerman, 1980:3–30).

It is beyond the scope of this discussion to consider Ackerman's spirited and often ingenious arguments for his particular version of social justice in the liberal state. The only point I wish to establish is that it never seems to occur to him in setting up his constraints on dialogue that some of the most important disagreements about politics and political power arise not out of assertions about intrinsic superiority or the refusal to supply reasoned arguments, but out of conflicting depictions of the relevant situation itself. He seems to think there will be no intractable questions about this. All three of Ackerman's constraints presume it is clear who in fact wields the relevant power, over whom it is wielded, and what the power consists in. The problem is conceived of as how to justify this neutrally, rationally, and consistently. He does not consider the case where A maintains that B has power over her and B denies this – that is, they have competing descriptions of the situation and both supply what they take to be reasonable answers. It is in this sense, I think, that Ackerman's assumptions about neutral discourse exemplify the liberal tendency to ignore the difficulties of competing descriptions; this is what constitutes shallowness in Anscombe's sense. Some of the most difficult and important questions of right and justice arise from such competing descriptions. The route to their resolution, if there is one, will lie in arguing over the nature of the situation itself, which will no doubt rapidly lead to complicated factual disputes about what is causally relevant to its characterization. To ignore these questions by assuming that there is an accurate consensus on the nature of the situation is palpably question-begging.

In addition to the difficulties that arise (for evaluating issues of social justice) out of the liberal predisposition toward the *meaning-of-the-act* fallacy, the fact that modern liberals view social relationships as essentially additive of individual intentional actions, to which social relationships are reducible, means they ignore the senses in which it might be justifiable and necessary to make moral judgments about social relationships quite independently of (and sometimes even in conflict with) moral judgments about individuals. A strong case can be made, for instance, for intentions being centrally relevant to the assessment of individual culpability, although I would follow Anscombe (1969:175–95) in placing some limits on this where a person acts in ignorance of consequences of which we might reasonably expect him to be cognizant. I would distinguish between the case where no harm is intended by an agent out of complete ignorance of the consequence of his actions, and the case where he does not intend the harm but is aware of the causal consequences.[15] There are exceedingly complex issues involved in evaluating these kinds of actions, and they depend on a great many factors. However we finally resolve these issues concerning the evaluation of individual moral actions, assuming that we can, they are separate from those relating to judgments concerning the justice or otherwise of social institutions and relationships, which must be evaluated in terms of different, and almost always wholly consequentialist, criteria. In this sense the deontological appeal to some hypothetical consent of individuals rests on a category mistake. Nozick's "acting in equilibrium" and Rawls's similar appeal to "what would be chosen" by individuals with "full deliberative rationality" (assuming these notions could be made sense of and applied – which I argue is not so) are typically irrelevant to evaluating the justness of social institutions and relationships. Although social relationships are partly produced and reproduced via the voluntary actions of persons, the relations

15 There are, no doubt, a great many further pertinent distinctions to be made in a thorough account of individual culpability.

among the various levels of relevant descriptions of such actions are seldom, and certainly not typically, transparent or direct. Leaving aside all the other difficulties of hypothetical contracts, speculation about what imaginary individuals would freely choose in imaginary conditions thus should not be expected to generate the relevant criteria for evaluating the justness of existing social institutions and relationships.

Trying to pin down what these criteria should be is extremely difficult, and very likely impossible at the scale of comprehensiveness to which writers in the modern liberal tradition aspire. We should expect this for two main reasons. First we should be suspicious of the claim that there are *any* neutral principles of social organization for a given society— let alone all historical and imaginary societies. Which social groups are hurt and which benefit from the operation of a particular principle are often determined by exogenous empirical conditions that vary greatly and often in unpredictable ways. The mere fact that all persons have a common interest in a particular good does not entail there is a neutral way of providing it. Moreover, the relevant empirical conditions presumed in arguments for different principles often (perhaps invariably) depend on counterfactual assumptions that are themselves ideologically loaded. For example, the move in Locke's argument from a positive community in which everyone has inclusive use-rights to the common to private individual rights of exclusive dominion requires there be no violation of the second proviso (that "as much and as good" be available to others). I have not defended Macpherson's view, for which there seems to be no textual evidence, that the nature of productivity is such that the proviso rapidly becomes "transcended" for Locke, but it is clear that Locke believed the productivity effects of enclosure and labor under conditions of private ownership would be such that the proviso would not be violated in practice. As our discussion of Nozick's account of justice in acquisition revealed, any argument for private property making use of Locke's arguments assumes some variant of this causal descriptive thesis, however implicitly.

Many would question this empirical assumption on the

grounds that capitalist economies based on private ownership of the means of production necessarily generate unemployment, thus there will always be some for whom the proviso is violated. If accepted, this argument might generate a Lockean case for a welfare state, or perhaps even for some sort of socialism, but many would not accept it. They might argue that unemployment results from the laziness of the poor, that it would be worse under any of the feasible alternatives, that in the long run there will be no unemployment, or that unemployment is not generated by the market system but by state intervention in it, to name a few common candidates. Leaving aside whether or not such questions will ever be settled decisively, the view taken of them is clearly pregnant ideologically, since it decisively shapes what the Lockean argument requires in practice. To adopt one or another establishment view of such questions may win a writer recognition from that establishment. It is likely, however, to weaken his credibility among others to whom he will appear to be peddling that establishment's values. This is, to a significant extent, what he will inevitably be doing – just because his counterfactual assumptions will be ideologically pregnant. This problem of inevitably loaded counterfactuals arises independently of the problem of inevitably loaded multiple descriptions. The latter no doubt compounds it in practice so they become mutually reinforcing in ideological debate.

A second, related, reason prompting suspicion toward the comprehensive theories to which writers in the liberal tradition aspire is that the kind of empirical knowledge necessary for the formulation of principles with so general a range is almost certainly beyond the capacity of a single person, if it is available at all. If political theorists are going to make use of empirical assumptions and theories about the workings of the societies to which their principles apply (which, it seems, they inevitably must), they are going to have to grapple with difficult and controversial causal questions and arguments about the possibilities available in a given situation. This is a monumental task for someone interested in formulating a general theory of distributive justice.

From this vantage point the debate between proponents of

the Kantian liberalism we have been examining and the "new communitarians" such as Michael Sandel, Alasdair MacIntyre, and Richard Rorty, is cast in a somewhat different light. These and other writers have increasingly argued in recent years that the major fault of the neo-Kantians is their failure to offer an adequate account of political community. This is an obvious (and acknowledged) source of the renewed interest in Aristotelianism we find in the writings of William Galston and MacIntyre, of Michael Walzer's attempt to give substantive content to the ideal of a liberal community, and of the growing interest in Hegelian political philosophy.[16] Several of these writers make much of the fact that substantive moral judgments about politics require acceptance of some notion of the good community as their basis. There is a blossoming debate between them and Kantian liberals over "community" versus "no community" in liberal theory.[17] This is no more, however, than a beguiling opposition of gross concepts. Of course substantive judgments about how communities ought to be organized and governed assumes accounts of how they are formed and reproduced, of what their goals and purposes might be, and of how they should limit community action, both internally, with respect to the individual actions of members, and externally, with respect to the needs and resources of other communities. We can no more make substantive judgments about politics without reference to the purposes of political life and the nature of political communities than can we make substantive judgments about food without reference to the purposes of eating. Because this is so, and writers in the deontological liberal tradition in all its variants have always made such assumptions, the argument should not be over whether community, but rather over what sort.

Many of the new communitarian writers appear to assume that community is synonymous with republican community,

---

16 Sandel (1982, 1984:81–96), Galston (1980), MacIntyre (1981), Walzer (1983, 1984:315–30), Rorty (1983:583–9, 1984a:1–19, 1984b:32–44), Charvet (1981), and Taylor (1979). For other examples of the revival of interest in the concept of political community, see Newell (1984:775–84), Beer (1984:361–86), Kateb (1984:331–60), Hirsch (1984), and Yack (1985:92–112), and, for a semi-popular account, Bellah, et al. (1985).

17 For one recent illustration, see Hirsch (1984).

and that this notion should be opposed, at a very high level of generality, to the neo-Kantian liberalism of Rawls, Nozick, and their progeny. Advocates of this view should keep in mind, however, that republicanism as an ideology has also proven itself serviceable to social and political repression, both historically and in the contemporary world, and that to embrace it as an abstract ideal is to say little useful from the point of view of articulating a viable alternative political ideology. Those interested in advancing this debate should shift it to a lower level of abstraction and seek to supply substantive content to the various communitarian proposals they advocate. They should consider how these are to be implemented in the capitalist economies of the late twentieth century, with their powerfully entrenched centralized bureaucratic states, and their seemingly inevitable participation in an ever more mutually interdependent international political and economic order. If these arrangements are seen as compatible with the various communitarian notions these authors defend, they must take seriously the burden of justifying them, and of dealing with the massive injustices they are thought by many to generate. If not, some account of how the new communitarian proposals might be implemented must be offered, in light of what we appear to know about the extraordinary stability of the centralized national states of the advanced industrial world.[18] Attractive as various romantic appeals to Aristotelian virtue, local communities, and republican conceptions of citizenship might be, if they are simply new variants of "ideal theory" they will turn out to be, on closer inspection, as vulnerable as the alternatives embraced by their opponents. If we want to avoid the inadequacies attending neo-Kantian answers, we have to refrain from asking neo-Kantian questions.

It is not my argument that critical thinking about general moral principles of social organization is avoidable or even ought to be avoidable. If it is going to be done intelligently it will require a range of sensitivity to empirical questions so difficult to achieve that it must inevitably limit the scope of our general moral claims. For instance, when Rawls asserts at

18 See Skocpol (1979:284ff).

the outset of *A Theory of Justice* that for his purposes society is viewed as a "closed system isolated from other societies," or in the Dewey lectures that a well ordered society is "a self-sufficient association of human beings which, like a nation-state, controls a connected territory" (1971:8; 1980:536), he is revealing what many would regard as so chronic a lack of awareness of how the world economy operates today, of how domestic policies concerning employment, growth, and wages are often, perhaps even typically for most countries, determined in large part by external events, of how even what Rawls conceives of as "primary" political liberties are often likewise overdetermined, it is difficult to see how a theory of justice based on his "isolation" and "self-sufficiency" assumptions can have much application to the problems of right and justice emerging in the actual world. There are many complex and ideologically loaded factual issues in international trade, for instance, concerning whether or not endemic problems of underconsumption in the metropolitan capitalist economies generate dependent relationships between themselves and third world countries, that in turn prevent in the latter balanced industrial growth, and in some cases all industrial growth: the so-called "development of underdevelopment" at the periphery as a condition for prosperity at the center.[19] Issues about the nature, causes, and consequences of this dependence are so controversial and so tremendously complicated, that someone professing to formulate a theory of distributive justice with some relevance to the contemporary world cannot ignore them by definitional fiat and expect to convince anyone who did not agree with him in advance.[20] To keep adding simplifying assumptions to a problem until it is theoretically "manageable" is all very well, but as these assumptions retreat from reality so, too, do the injunctions entailed by the theoretical model.

19 See, for instance, Baran and Sweezy (1965), Emmanuel (1972), Amin (1974), Cardoso and Faletto (1977), and Evans (1979) for pertinent discussions of these issues.

20 I am not suggesting that no liberal writers devote attention to questions of international justice. Beitz (1979), Shue (1981), and Barry (1982) exemplify something of a trend in this direction that cannot be evaluated here. For a review of recent liberal writing on this subject, see Dagger (1983).

It might be said that all arguments make assumptions and these writers could not be expected both to make their arguments and to establish all their assumptions, empirical and theoretical. So far as theories of right and justice are involved, the difficulty is that the assumptions are themselves inevitably loaded morally and politically, and largely determine the substantive results of the arguments based on them. To the extent that a writer constructs a model generating injunctions favorable to a particular establishment he will no doubt win recognition from that establishment and appear to others as an ideologue for it. This he will be, whether he intends it, as one suspects with Nozick, or not, as one suspects with Rawls, because he is presenting what is in fact an ideologically loaded and controversial model as a reasonable set of assumptions with a sound basis in the solid discoveries of psychologists and economists.

It might be thought that this attack on scientism is at variance with the realist view of social science I have outlined elsewhere,[21] but two points should be noted in this regard. First, the claim that the causal mechanisms constituting the social world are in principle discoverable must be distinguished from the claims of existing social scientists to have discovered the mechanisms they claim to have discovered. The realist claim is that the concept dependent nature of the social world does not make it in principle impossible to study scientifically, but the methodological problems arising in attempting to do so can be considerable, possibly even insurmountable. We assume there are causal mechanisms operating and try to discover their nature; of course we must expect the results to be at least variable and frequently unsuccessful. The methodological limitations inherent in studying causal mechanisms in the "open systems"[22] that constitute the social world

---

21 Shapiro (1982:563–78). For a comprehensive defense of this view, see Bhaskar (1978) and especially Bhaskar (1979).
22 This is Roy Bhaskar's term, intended to contrast the task normally faced by the social scientist with the experimental closure typical in most natural sciences (with the obvious exceptions of such sciences as astronomy, meteorology, and aspects of archeology, geology, and evolutionary biology). See Bhaskar (1978:64ff). For a summary of Bhaskar's views and those of other realist writers as they relate to the natural versus the human sciences, see Shapiro (1982:563–70).

are very great. I hold that there are good reasons for being skeptical of many of the proclaimed discoveries of the social sciences, particularly economics. The critical scientific attitude to the world consists in evaluating arguments and evidence, not in accepting the claims of proclaimed experts on faith alone. Complexities of technology and the inevitable constraints imposed on us by the intellectual division of labor severely limit the capacities of any given individual in this regard. This is no reason to turn blind faith in received opinion into a virtue.

Second, the realist makes an important distinction between the truth or falsity of a belief and its ideological function in the legitimation or delegitimation of relationships of power and authority. False beliefs can function ideologically as often as true beliefs, precisely because their ideological content is defined in terms of their function and not their truth content. Whatever the truth, assuming we can eventually discover it, about capitalist markets and productivity, different public assumptions about it will benefit different groups differently, and these assumptions will be used successfully to legitimate, or attack, various social practices relating to it.

This is not to say that questions about the truth of a proposition will be irrelevant to questions about its ideological function. I doubt that there are general rules concerning the relationship between them, but there usually is some relationship. Ideologies typically derive their persuasive appeal from the fact that they do make straightforward sense of some realm of experience, as suggested in Chapter 1. Once we suspect that claims about the productivity of capitalist markets serve a particular ideological end we become interested in their truth or falsity for two reasons. First, discovery of the ways in which a claim might be false, partly false, misleading, or misapplied may tell us more about its ideological force and why it is held to be true. We thus find ourselves grappling with the actual causal claim willy nilly. Second, to the extent that we might have an interest in criticizing a particular causal claim we think we have reasons for regarding as ideological, questions about alternatives to it inevitably arise. These force us to consider the substantive causal questions involved *as* causal questions. If establishment claims about the productivity of unregulated

capitalist markets obviously serve certain establishment interests and are simultaneously questionable empirically, questions
inevitably arise concerning the alternatives to them, whose interests they would serve, and whether they are viable. Thus
even though, in the realist view, there is no general or necessary relationship between the truth content and the ideological
function of propositions, it is unlikely we can understand the
latter without seriously studying the former.

III. CONCLUSION

I have argued that the liberal conception of individual rights
constitutes the skeleton of liberal political theory as it has
evolved in its dominant forms in the modern Anglo-American
tradition. I have treated this conception as an internally complex structure, and tried to sketch an account of the evolution
of its major component parts both historically sensitive and
useful for understanding its dominant contemporary forms.
Perhaps the greatest danger of this type of evolutionary explanation of contemporary ideas is that the whole process takes
on a teleological air many will find objectionable. There is a
vast difference, however, between the use of teleological explanations, in biology for instance, for heuristic reasons, and
the epistemologically loaded teleological view of history we
find in the writings of Hegel, and, in some interpretations,
Marx. In these latter there is a pregnant directed causal necessity inherent in events, a motor of history, that is driving in a
certain direction, if not predetermined at least inevitable. The
former type of teleological explanation makes no such assumption. Although later events are shown as evolving causally from earlier ones, and in that sense being determined by
them, there is no necessary sense in which they *had* so to
evolve. If some critical events had been different they might
have evolved differently. Biology offers good examples of
this: evolutionary biologists regularly employ teleological explanations as heuristic devices, yet this requires no questioning
of their assumption that biological evolution depends critically
on random events, or that organisms might have evolved differently than they have. The nature of the organism, its need

for survival, and the nature of its environment all place limits on the possibilities of adaptive change available to the relevant organism, but these are contingent limits that will vary with both organisms and circumstance.

The only sense in which the explanation offered here is teleological is in this weaker heuristic sense. This is not inherently implausible. It might be argued that all causal historical explanations are teleological in this sense. In claiming that the liberal view of rights evolved via processes of adaptive change importantly conditioned by, and functional to, the evolution of capitalist markets, I am not holding that this had to be the case, or that things might not have been significantly different, though this is difficult for us to imagine. Whether or not they could have is an empirical matter that could never be established with much certainty for obvious methodological reasons. We can speculate and argue, in terms of counterfactuals, about such questions. There are, further, conditional observations: the requirements of capitalist markets may be such that unless people in significant numbers hold certain moral and political beliefs, those markets will not be able to function. True conditionals of this form do not entail any necessary determinism, either in the sense that "since" capitalist markets "had" to function the relevant beliefs would become widespread (whether or not capitalist markets were bound to emerge and survive is a different, and also contingent, historical question), or in the sense that, if the conditional is true, the existence of capitalist markets "caused" the beliefs to be held. The actual causal process must have been vastly more complex, depending on mutually reciprocal mechanisms, elective affinities, and by-products of other historically parallel causal processes. A general theory of historical change which could tell us in advance how all causal mechanisms will operate is in my view unlikely to be forthcoming and certainly has not yet been discovered.

I have sought to show that the principal reasons for the tenacity of the liberal conception of individual rights, problems and all, are ideological: its Cartesian view of the subject of rights, its negative libertarian view of the substance of rights, its view of individual consent as the legitimate basis for rights, and its essentially pluralist and utilitarian conception of the purposes of rights have, in their various formulations, combined to express a view of politics that is required by and legitimates capitalist market practices. As the needs of those markets have evolved so this ideology (in its most influential forms) has evolved with it, generating rationalizations for its imperatives and legitimating the particular institutional structures it has required.

The historical anthropology we have been engaged in has been an anthropology of establishment values. I have tried to show how the radical conservatism of Hobbes and Locke's liberal constitutionalism have been pressed into the service of the emerging liberal establishment and modified with the needs of that establishment. In pointing out the conservative tendencies (in this proestablishment sense) of this ideology from its inception and showing how, in its establishment forms, this doctrine has been stripped of potentially radical ideas such as thoroughgoing notions of participation, democratic community, and the labor theory of value, I have arguably downplayed the critical possibilities of some of the ideas discussed. Flatham (1976:184ff) has argued, for instance, that the widely shared assumptions about rights in liberal societies entail quite robust communitarian relationships. The practice of rights assumes shared rules and judgments, acceptance of common authority, and relationships of reciprocal dependence, so that individual rights presuppose "patterned interrelationships and interdependencies." From a different point of view Sandel (1982:133–83) has argued that if liberalism is to make good on its promise of a theory of justice acceptable to liberal sentiments, it must develop a stronger and more dominant notion of community than that offered either by Rawls's deontology or conventional utilitarian alternatives. From still a different point of view Walzer (1983) has undertaken an immanent critique of pluralism and tried to show that if adhered to consistently this doctrine entails conclusions many establishment liberals would, one suspects, regard as unacceptably radical.

This is not the place to pass judgment on these various arguments. Despite the reservations expressed earlier I certainly do not reject them out of hand. No set of substantive political principles, I have argued, is intrinsically radical or conservative: radical ideas in one context become conservative in another and sometimes vice versa. It may be that there is potential for very extensive internal criticism of liberalism; many of the arguments of the last four chapters might even be conceived of as such. My primary aim has been to show in as much detail as possible how conventional liberal values have come to function, and continue to function, conservatively in today's world, how they legitimate the two principal establishment ideologies of our time. I have also suggested that if these are to be questioned seriously, not only must we question the standard Cartesian conception of the subject, but also negative libertarianism and the view of individual and social action it presupposes, the artificial doctrine of individual consent on which liberal conceptions of legitimacy rest, and the pluralist and utilitarian view of social ends based on the identification of the good with the desired. We must recognize, as Galston, MacIntyre, and others have done, that morality is inevitably in part teleological, and that substantive conceptions of the good cannot be avoided in arguments of right and justice.[23] Unlike those writers, however, we must acknowledge that a theory of the good is inevitably in significant part empirical. This entails a more general injunction to come off the terrain of "ideal theory" and get involved in factual arguments about the causal structure of the social world which is where problems of social justice arise.

I have not argued that if all factual questions were resolved no moral questions would remain, but I do claim first that sensitivity to factual questions is a necessary condition for pertinent moral theorizing, and, second, that it is unavoidable in knowing what is possible. The one injunction from Kant that we really need to take seriously is that ought entails can. To engage seriously in moral argument within these constraints would, I think, produce a kind of moral philosophy substantially different from that examined in part III. It would be less ambitious in that it would try to answer fewer all-encompassing

23 For a more detailed discussion of this point, see Kane (1982:180–252).

moral questions. Indeed, it would be skeptical of the very possibility of general theories of right and justice. It would be more ambitious, however, in that it would require those theorizing about substantive questions of right and justice to involve themselves seriously in vast areas of the social sciences currently left to other experts in the intellectual division of labor.

Bibliography

Ackerman, B. A. (1980), *Social Justice in the Liberal State* (New Haven: Yale University Press).

Amin, S. (1974), *Accumulation on a World Scale: A Critique of the Theory of Underdevelopment* (New York and London: Monthly Review).

Anderson, P. (1974), *Lineages of the Absolutist State* (Norfolk: Verso).

Anscombe, G.E.M. (1958), "On Brute Facts," *Analysis*, vol. 18, no. 3, pp. 69–72.

 (1969). "Modern Moral Philosophy," W. D. Hudson, ed., *The Is-Ought Question* (London: Macmillan Press), pp. 175–95.

Appleby, J. O. (1978), *Economic Thought and Ideology in Seventeenth Century England* (Princeton: Princeton University Press).

Arendt, H. (1958), *The Human Condition* (Chicago: University of Chicago Press).

Arrow, K. J. (1963), *Social Choice and Individual Values* (New Haven: Yale University Press).

 (1973), "Some Ordinalist-Utilitarian Notes on Rawls' Theory of Justice," *The Journal of Philosophy*, vol. 70, no. 9, pp. 245–63.

Ashcraft, R. (1968), "Locke's State of Nature: Historical Fact or Moral Fiction?" *American Political Science Review*, vol. 62, no. 3, pp. 898–915.

 (1978), "Ideology and Class in Hobbes's Political Theory," *Political Theory*, vol. 6, pp. 27–62.

 (1980), "Revolutionary Politics and Locke's *Two Treatises of Government:* Radicalism and Lockean Political Theory," *Political Theory*, vol. 8, no. 4, pp. 429–86.

 (1986), *Locke's Two Treatises of Government* (London: Allen & Unwin, in press).

Baran, P., and Sweezy, P. (1965), *Monopoly Capital* (London: Monthly Review).

Barber, B. (1975), "Justifying Justice: Problems of Psychology, Politics and Measurement in Rawls," N. Daniels, ed., *Reading Rawls: Critical Studies of A Theory of Justice* (Oxford: Blackwell), pp. 292–319.

Barbon, N. (1690), *A Discourse of Trade* (London).

(1696), *A Discourse Concerning Coining the New Money Lighter* (London).

Barry, B. (1973), *The Liberal Theory of Justice* (Oxford: Oxford University Press [Clarendon Press]).

(1982), "Humanity and Justice in Global Perspective," R.J. Pennock and J. W. Chapman, eds., *Nomos 24: Ethics, Economics and the Law* (New York: New York University Press).

Beer, S. (1984), "Liberty and Union: Walt Whitman's Idea of the Nation," *Political Theory,* vol. 12, no. 3, pp. 361–86.

Beitz, C. S. (1979), *Political Theory and International Relations* (Princeton: Princeton University Press).

Bellah, R. N., R. Madsen, W.M. Sullivan, A. Swidler, and S.M. Tipto. (1985), *Habits of the Heart: Individualism and Commitment in American Life* (Berkeley and Los Angeles: University of California Press).

Berlin, I. (1969), "Two Concepts of Liberty," I. Berlin, *Four Essays on Liberty* (Oxford: Oxford University Press), pp. 118–72.

Bhaskar, R. (1978), *A Realist Theory of Science* (Sussex: Harvester & Humanities Press).

(1979), *The Possibility of Naturalism* (Sussex: Harvester & Humanities Press).

Blackstone, W. (1979), *Commentaries on the Laws of England,* 4 vols. (Chicago: University of Chicago Press).

Blaug, M. (1978), *Economic Theory in Retrospect,* 3d ed., (Cambridge: Cambridge University Press).

Bloom, A. (1975), "Justice: John Rawls vs. The Tradition of Political Philosophy," *American Political Science Review,* vol. 69, no. 2, pp. 648–62.

Bloor, D. (1983), *Wittgenstein: A Social Theory of Knowledge* (New York: Columbia University Press).

Bowden, P. (1967), "Agricultural Prices, Farm Profits and Rents," J. Thirsk, ed., *The Agrarian History of England and Wales,* vol. 4, (Cambridge: Cambridge University Press), pp. 593–695.

Bowley, M. (1963), "Some Seventeenth Century Contributions to the Theory of Value," *Economica,* vol. 30, new series, no. 118, pp. 122–39.

Brenner, R. (1973), "The Civil War Politics of London's Merchant Community," *Past and Present,* no. 58, pp. 53–107.

Browning, A. (1953), ed., *English Historical Documents 1660–1714,* vol. 8 (London: Eyre & Spottiswoode).

Buchanan, J., and G. Tullock. (1962), *The Calculus of Consent: Logical Foundations of Constitutional Democracy* (Michigan: Ann Arbor Paperbacks).

Cameron, D. (1978), "Economic Inequality in the United States," paper presented at the annual meeting of the Midwest Political Science Association (Chicago, April, 1978).

Cardoso, F. H., and E. Faletto. (1977), *Dependency and Development in Latin America* (Berkeley: University of California Press).

Cary, J. ([1765] 1696), *A Discourse on Trade and Other Matters Relative to It* (London).

Chappell, V. (1966), ed., *Hume: A Collection of Critical Essays* (London: Macmillan).

Charvet, J. (1981), *A Critique of Freedom and Equality* (Cambridge: Cambridge University Press).

Child, A. (1953), "Making and Knowing in Hobbes, Vico and Dewey," G. Adams, ed., *University of California Publications in Philosophy*, vol. 16 (Berkeley and Los Angeles: University of California Press), pp. 271–310.

Claude, R. P. (1976), *Comparative Human Rights* (Baltimore: Johns Hopkins University Press).

Coleman, D. C. (1956), "Labor in the English Economy in the Seventeenth Century," *Economic History Review*, 2d series, vol. 8, no. 3, pp. 280-95.

Daniels, N. (1975), ed., *Reading Rawls: Critical Studies of A Theory of Justice* (Oxford: Blackwell).

Dagger, R. (1983), "Rights, Boundaries and the Bonds of Community," paper presented at 1983 annual meeting of the American Political Science Association in Chicago, Ill. (September 1983).

Davenant, C. (1696), *A Memorial Concerning Credit*, reprinted in G.H.J. Evans, ed., *A Reprint of Economic Tracts* (Baltimore, 1942).

Davidson, D. (1968), "Actions, Reasons & Causes," A. R. White, ed., *The Philosophy of Action* (Oxford: Oxford University Press), pp. 79–94.

Delaney, C.F. (1977), "Rawls on Method," K. Nielson and R. Shiner, eds., *New Essays on Contract Theory, Canadian Journal of Philosophy*, sup. vol. 3, pp. 153–61.

Dickenson, H. T. (1976), "The Eighteenth Century Debate on the 'Glorious Revolution'," *History*, vol. 61, no. 201, pp. 28–45.

DiQuattro, A. (1983), "Rawls and Left Criticism," *Political Theory*, vol. 11, no. 1, pp. 53–78.

Dobb, M. (1973), *Theories of Value and Distribution since Adam Smith: Ideology and Economic Theory* (Cambridge: Cambridge University Press).

Downs, A. (1957), *An Economic Theory of Democracy* (New York: Harper & Row).

Drury, S. B. (1982), "Locke and Nozick on Property," *Political Studies*, vol. 30, no. 1, pp. 28–41.

Dunn, J. (1969), *The Political Thought of John Locke* (Cambridge: Cambridge University Press).

   (1984), "The concept of 'trust' in the politics of John Locke," R. Rorty, J. B. Schneewind, and Q. Skinner, eds., *Philosophy in History: Essays on the Historiography of Philosophy* (Cambridge: Cambridge University Press) pp. 279–301.

Dworkin, G. (1975), "Non-Neutral Principles," N. Daniels ed., *Reading Rawls: Critical Studies of A Theory of Justice* (Oxford: Blackwell), pp. 124–41.

Dworkin, R. (1977), *Taking Rights Seriously* (Cambridge, Mass.: Harvard University Press).

Emmanuel, A. (1972), *Unequal Exchange: A Study of the Imperialism of Trade* (New York and London: Monthly Review).

Evans, P. (1979), *Dependent Development: The Alliance of Multinational, State and Local Capital in Brazil* (Princeton: Princeton University Press).

Everitt, A. (1967), "Farm Labourers," J. Thirsk, ed., *The Agrarian History of England and Wales*, vol. 4 (Cambridge: Cambridge University Press), pp. 396–454.

Farer, T. J. (1981), ed., *The International Bill of Human Rights* (California: Entwhistle Books).

Finnis, J. (1980), *Natural Law and Natural Rights* (Oxford: Oxford University Press [Clarendon Press]).

Fishkin, J. (1975), "Justice and Rationality: Some Objections to the Central Arguments in Rawls' Theory," *American Political Science Review*, vol. 69, no. 2, pp. 615–29.

   (1979), *Tyranny and Legitimacy: A Critique of Political Theories* (Baltimore: Johns Hopkins University Press).

Flathman, R. (1976), *The Practice of Rights* (Cambridge: Cambridge University Press).

Franklin, J. H. (1978), *John Locke and the Theory of Sovereignty* (Cambridge: Cambridge University Press).

Furniss, N. (1978), "The Political Implications of the Public Choice–Property Rights School," *American Political Science Review*, vol. 72, no. 2, pp. 399–410.

Gallie, W. B. (1956), "Essentially Contested Concepts," *Proceedings of the Aristotelian Society*, vol. 56, pp. 167–98.

Galston, W. A. (1980), *Justice and The Human Good* (Chicago: University of Chicago Press).

——— (1983), "Defending Liberalism," *American Political Science Review*, vol. 76, no. 3, pp. 621–29.

Gardiner, S. R. (1889), *The Constitutional Documents of the Puritan Revolution*, 2d ed. (Oxford: Oxford University Press [Clarendon Press]).

Gewirth, A. (1982), *Human Rights: Essays on Justification and Applications* (Chicago: University of Chicago Press).

Giddens, A. (1976), *New Rules of Sociological Method* (New York: Basic Books).

Gierke, O. (1934), *Natural Law and the Theory of Society*, 2 vols. (Cambridge: Cambridge University Press).

Goodwin, A. (1979), *The Friends of Liberty: The English Democratic Movement in the Age of the French Revolution* (Cambridge, Mass.: Harvard University Press).

Grafstein, R. (1983), "Taking Dworkin to Hart: A Positivist Conception of Institutional Rules," *Political Theory*, vol. 11, no. 2, pp. 244–65.

Graham, K. (1977), *J. L. Austin: A Critique of Ordinary Language Philosophy* (Sussex: Harvester).

Grampp, W. D. (1965), *Economic Liberalism*, 2 vols. (New York: Random House).

Hare, R. M. (1975), "Rawls' Theory of Justice," N. Daniels, ed., *Reading Rawls: Critical Studies of A Theory of Justice* (Oxford: Blackwell), pp. 81–107.

Hart, H.L.A. (1961), *The Concept of Law* (Oxford: Oxford University Press).

——— (1975), "Rawls on Liberty and its Priority," N. Daniels, ed., *Reading Rawls: Critical Studies of A Theory of Justice* (Oxford: Blackwell), pp. 230–53.

——— (1979), "Between Rights and Utility," A. Ryan, ed., *The Idea of Freedom: Essays in Honour of Isaiah Berlin* (Oxford: Oxford University Press).

Hayek, F. A. (1960), *The Constitution of Liberty* (Chicago: University of Chicago Press).

——— (1976), *Law Legislation and Liberty*, vol. II, *The Mirage of Social Justice* (Chicago: University of Chicago Press).

Hexter, J. H. (1979), "The Myth of the Middle Class in Tudor England," J. H. Hexter, *Reappraisals in History: New Views on His-*

tory and Society in Early Modern Europe, 2d ed. (Chicago: University of Chicago Press), pp. 71–116.

Hill, C. (1961), *The Century of Revolution: 1603–1714* (New York and London: W. W. Norton).

(1968), "The Many-Headed Monster in Late Tudor and Early Stuart Political Thinking," in G.H. Carter, ed., *From the Renaissance to the Counter-Reformation: Essays in Honor of Garrett Mattingly* (London), pp. 296–324.

(1972), *The World Turned Upside Down* (Harmondsworth: Pelican).

Hirsch, H. N. (1984), "The Threnody of Liberalism: Constitutional Liberty and the Renewal of Community," paper presented at the annual meeting of the American Political Science Association, The Washington Hilton, September 1984.

Hobbes, T. (1966), *The English Works of Thomas Hobbes*, XI vols. (London: John Bohn).

(1968), *Leviathan*, C.B. Macpherson, ed. (London: Pelican Books).

(1972), *De Homine*, C.T. Wood, T.S.K. Scott-Craig, and B. Gert, ed. & trans., *Man and Citizen* (New York: Anchor).

Hodges, W. (1696), *The Groans of the Poor* (London).

Hohfeld, W. (1923), *Fundamental Legal Conceptions as Applied to Juridical Reasoning and Other Essays* (New Haven: Yale University Press).

Holdsworth, W. (1956–72), *A History of English Law*, 17 vols. (London: Methuen & Co.).

Holmes, R. L. (1981), "Nozick on Anarchism," J. Paul, ed., *Reading Nozick: Essays on Anarchy State and Utopia* (Totowa, N.J.: Rowman & Littlefield), pp. 57–67.

Isaac, J. (1986), "Was John Locke a Bourgeois Theorist? A Critical Appraisal of Macpherson and Tully," *Canadian Journal of Political and Social Theory*, vol. 10, no. 3 (in press).

Johnson, E.A.J. (1937), *Predecessors of Adam Smith* (New York: Prentice-Hall).

Johnston, D. C. (1981), The New Sovereign and the Modern Subject: An Interpretation of Hobbes's Political Theory (Unpublished Ph.D. thesis, Princeton University).

(1986), *The Rhetoric of Leviathan: Thomas Hobbes and the Politics of Cultural Transformation* (Princeton: Princeton University Press, in press).

Kane, J. (1982), Justice and the Good: The Logical Priority of Conceptions of the Good in Arguments of Right and Justice (Unpublished Ph.D. thesis, London School of Economics).

Kant, I. (1948), *Groundwork of the Metaphysic of Morals*, H. J. Paton, trans. as *The Moral Law* (London: Hutchinson University Library).

(1970), *Kant's Political Writings*, H. Reiss, ed., H. B. Nisbet, trans. (Cambridge: Cambridge University Press).

Kateb, G. (1984), "Democratic Individuality and the Claims of Politics," *Political Theory*, vol. 12, no. 3, pp. 331–60.

Kenny, A. (1979), *The God of the Philosophers* (New York: Oxford University Press).

Krook, D. (1956), "Thomas Hobbes's doctrine of meaning and truth," *Philosophy*, vol. 31, no. 116, pp. 3–22.

Landes, D. (1969), *The Unbounded Prometheus: Technological Change and Industrial Development in Western Europe from 1750 to the Present* (Cambridge: Cambridge University Press).

Letwin, W. (1972), "The Economic Foundations of Hobbes' Politics," M. Cranston and R. S. Peters, eds., *Hobbes and Rousseau: A Collection of Critical Essays* (New York: Doubleday), pp. 143–64.

Little, I.M.D. (1950), *A Critique of Welfare Economics* (Oxford: Oxford University Press).

Locke, J. (1824), *The Works of John Locke*, 12th ed., IX vols. (London: Baldwin).

(1958), *Essays on the Law of Nature*, W. Von Leiden, ed. (Oxford: Oxford University Press [Clarendon Press]).

(1959), *An Essay Concerning Human Understanding*, 2 vols. (New York: Dover).

(1963), *Two Treatises of Government*, P. Laslett, ed. (Cambridge: Cambridge University Press).

(1979), *Treatise of Civil Government and A Letter Concerning Toleration*, C.L. Sherman, ed. (New York: Irvington [1685]).

Long, D.G. (1977), *Bentham on Liberty: Jeremy Bentham's Idea of Liberty in Relation to his Utilitarianism* (Toronto: University of Toronto Press).

Lukes, S. (1977), "Relativism: Cognitive and Moral," S. Lukes, *Essays in Social Theory* (London: Macmillan), pp. 154–74.

Lyons, D. (1975), "Nature and Soundness of the Contract and Coherence Arguments," N. Daniels, ed., *Reading Rawls: Critical Studies of A Theory of Justice* (Oxford: Blackwell), pp. 141–67.

MacCallum, J. R., Jr. (1972), "Negative and Positive Freedom," P. Laslett, W. G. Runciman, and Q. Skinner, eds., *Philosophy, Politics and Society*, 4th series (Oxford: Blackwell), pp. 174–93.

MacIntyre, A. (1981), *After Virtue* (Notre Dame: University of Notre Dame Press).

Macpherson, C.B. (1962), *The Political Theory of Possessive Individualism: Hobbes to Locke* (Oxford: Oxford University Press).

(1965), "Hobbes' Bourgeois Man," K. Brown, ed., *Hobbes Studies* (Cambridge, Mass.: Harvard University Press), pp. 169–83.

(1973a), *Democratic Theory: Essays in Retrieval* (Oxford: Oxford University Press).

(1973b), "Rawls' Models of Man and Society," *Philosophy of the Social Sciences*, vol. 3, no. 4, pp. 341–7.

(1978), ed., *Property: Mainstream and Critical Positions* (Toronto: University of Toronto Press).

Maitland, F. W. (1920), *The Constitutional History of England* (Cambridge: Cambridge University Press).

Manley, T. (1669), *Usury at Six Percent Examined* (London).

Marx, K. (1969), *Theories of Surplus Value*, III vols. (Moscow: Progress Publishers).

(1973), *Grundrisse* (London: Pelican Books).

(1976), *Capital*, vol. I (Middlesex: Penguin Books).

Mayhew, D. R. (1974), *Congress: The Electoral Connection* (New Haven: Yale University Press).

Michelman, F. (1975), "Constitutional Welfare Rights and *A Theory of Justice*," N. Daniels, ed., *Reading Rawls: Critical Studies of A Theory of Justice* (Oxford: Blackwell), pp. 319–47.

Mill, J. S. (1950), *Mill on Bentham and Coleridge* (London: Chatto & Windus).

(1962), *Utilitarianism* (London: Collins).

(1974), *On Liberty* (London: Pelican Books).

(1975), *Three Essays: On Liberty, Representative Government, The Subjugation of Women* (New York: Oxford University Press).

Miller, R. (1975), "Rawls and Marxism," N. Daniels, ed., *Reading Rawls: Critical Studies of A Theory of Justice* (Oxford: Blackwell), pp. 206–30.

Minogue, K. R. (1972), "Hobbes and the Just Man," M. Cranston and R. S. Peters, eds., *Hobbes and Rousseau: A Collection of Critical Essays* (New York: Doubleday), pp. 66–84.

Misselden, E. (1632), *The Circle of Commerce or the Balance of Trade, in Defence of Free Trade* (London).

Moore, B., Jr. (1978), *Injustice: The Social Bases of Obedience and Revolt* (White Plains, N.Y.: M. E. Sharpe).

Mueller, D. C. (1979), *Public Choice* (Cambridge: Cambridge University Press).

Mun, T. (1623), *England's Treasure by Foreign Trade*, reprinted in J. R.

McCullock, ed., *Early English Tracts on Commerce* (Cambridge: Cambridge University Press, 1954), pp. 121–209.

Nasmith, D. (1875), *The Institutes of English Private Law: Book II – Things* (London: Butterworths).

Newell, W.R. (1984), "Heidegger on Freedom and the Community: Some Political Implications of his Early Thought," *American Political Science Review*, vol. 78, no. 3, pp. 775–84.

Nozick, R. (1972), "Coercion," P. Laslett, W.G. Runciman, and Q. Skinner, eds., *Philosophy, Politics and Society*, 4th series (Oxford: Blackwell), pp. 101–35.

(1974), *Anarchy State and Utopia* (Oxford: Blackwell).

(1981), *Philosophical Explanations* (Cambridge, Mass.: Harvard University Press).

Oakeshott, M. (1975), *On Human Conduct* (Oxford: Oxford University Press [Clarendon Press]).

OECD (1979), *Concentration and Competition Policy*, report of the committee of experts on restrictive business practices (Paris: OECD).

Ollman, B. (1971), *Alienation: Marx's Concept of Man in Capitalist Society* (Cambridge: Cambridge University Press).

Ordeshook, P. C., and K. A. Shepsle. (1982), eds., *Political Equilibrium* (Boston: Kluwer-Nijhof).

Outhwaite, R. B. (1969), *Inflation in Tudor and Early Stuart England* (London: Macmillan).

Panitch, L. (1977), "The Development of Corporatism in Liberal Democracies," *Comparative Political Studies* (April, 1977), pp. 61–90.

Parent, W.A. (1974), "Some Recent Work on the Concept of Liberty," *American Philosophical Quarterly*, vol. 11, no. 3, pp. 149–67.

Pareto, V. (1970), *Manual of Political Economy*, A.S. Schwier, trans., A.S. Schwier and A.M. Page, eds., (New York: Augustus Kelly).

Parker, R. B. (1979), "The Jurisprudential Uses of John Rawls," J. R. Pennock and J.W. Chapman, eds., *Constitutionalism* (New York: New York University Press).

Parkin, F. (1971), *Class, Inequality and Political Order*, (London: Praeger).

Paul, J. (1981), ed., *Reading Nozick: Essays on Anarchy State and Utopia* (Totowa, N.J.: Rowman & Littlefield).

Pennock, J. R. (1965), "Hobbes's Confusing 'Clarity' – The Case of 'Liberty'," K.C. Brown, ed., *Hobbes Studies* (Cambridge, Mass.: Harvard University Press), pp. 101–16.

Petty, W. (1899), *The Economic Writings of Sir William Petty together with the Observations upon the Bills of Mortality More Probably by John Grant*, C.H. Hull, ed., 2 vols. (Cambridge: Cambridge University Press).

Pigou, A. (1960), *Economics of Welfare* (London: Macmillan).

Pitkin, H. F. (1972), *Wittgenstein and Justice: On the Significance of Ludwig Wittgenstein for Social and Political Thought* (Berkeley and Los Angeles: University of California Press).

Plamenatz, J. (1965), "Mr. Warrender's Hobbes," K.C. Brown, ed., *Hobbes Studies* (Cambridge, Mass.: Harvard University Press), pp. 73–87.

Pocock, J.G.A. (1957), *The Ancient Constitution and the Feudal Law* (Cambridge: Cambridge University Press).

(1975), *The Machiavellian Moment* (Princeton: Princeton University Press).

(1981), "Virtues, Rights and Manners: A Model for Historians of Political Thought," *Political Theory*, vol. 9, no. 3, pp. 353–68.

(1984), "Verbalizing a Political Act: Toward a Politics of Speech," M.J. Shapiro, ed., *Language and Politics* (Oxford: Blackwell).

Polanyi, K. (1944), *The Great Transformation: The Political and Economic Origins of Our Time* (Boston: Beacon).

Pufendorf, S. von. (1710 [1672]), *De Jure Naturae et Gentium Libri Octo* (Lund, Sweden), B. Kennett, trans., as *Of the Law of Nature and Nations* (London).

Quine, W.V. (1953), "Two Dogmas of Empiricism," W.V. Quine, *From a Logical Point of View: Logico-Philosophical Essays* (New York: Harper Torchbooks), pp. 20–46.

Rae, D. (1975a), "The Limits of Consensual Decision," *American Political Science Review*, vol. 69, pp. 1270–94.

(1975b), "Maximin Justice and an Alternative Principle of General Advantage," *American Political Science Review*, vol. 69, no. 2, pp. 630–47.

(1979), "A Principle of Simple Justice," P. Laslett and J. Fishkin, eds., *Philosophy Politics and Society*, 5th series (Oxford: Blackwell), pp. 134-54.

Rae, D., D. Yates, J. Hochschild, J. Morone, and C.M. Fessler. (1981), *Equalities* (Cambridge, Mass.: Harvard University Press).

Ramsey, P. (1965), *Tudor Economic Problems* (London: Gollancz).

Rawls, J. (1951), "Outline of a Decision Procedure for Ethics," *Philosophical Review*, no. 60, pp. 177–97.

(1971), *A Theory of Justice* (Oxford: Oxford University Press).

(1975), "Fairness to Goodness," *Philosophical Review*, vol. 84, pp. 536–54.

(1979), "A Well-Ordered Society," P. Laslett and J. Fishkin, eds., *Philosophy Politics and Society*, 5th series (Oxford: Blackwell), pp. 6–20, originally published as "A Kantian Conception of Equality," *The Cambridge Review* (1975), pp. 94–9.

(1980), "Kantian Constructivism in Moral Theory," *The Journal of Philosophy*, vol. 77, no. 9, pp. 515–72.

(1982), "Social Unity and Primary Goods," A. Sen and B. Williams, eds., *Utilitarianism and Beyond* (Cambridge: Cambridge University Press), pp. 159–85.

Reik, M. M. (1977), *The Golden Lands of Thomas Hobbes* (Detroit: Wayne State University Press).

Riker, W. H. (1982), "Implications from the Disequilibrium of Majority Rule for the Study of Institutions," P.C. Ordeshook and K. Shepsle, eds., *Political Equilibrium* (Boston: Kluwer-Nijhof).

Riley, P. (1982), *Will and Political Legitimacy: A Critical Exposition of Social Contract Theory in Hobbes, Locke, Rousseau, Kant, and Hegel* (Cambridge, Mass.: Harvard University Press).

Roll, E. (1974), *A History of Economic Thought* (Homewood, Ill.: Irwin).

Rorty, R. (1979), *Philosophy and the Mirror of Nature* (Princeton: Princeton University Press).

(1980), "A Reply to Dreyfus and Taylor," *Review of Metaphysics*, no. 34, pp. 39–55.

(1983), "Postmodernist Bourgeois Liberalism," *The Journal of Philosophy*, vol. 80, no. 10, pp. 583–9.

(1984a), "Solidarity or Objectivity?" *Nanzan Review of American Studies*, vol. 4, pp. 1–19.

(1984b), "Habermas and Lyotard on Post-modernity," *Praxis International*, vol. 6, no. 1, pp. 32–44.

Rosenblum, N. L. (1978), *Bentham's Theory of the Modern State* (Cambridge, Mass.: Harvard University Press).

Rousseau, J-J. (1968), *The Social Contract* (Aylesbury: Penguin Books).

Routh, G. (1975), *The Origin of Economic Ideas* (London: Macmillan).

Ryle, G. (1949), *The Concept of Mind* (London: Hutchinson).

Sandel, M. J. (1982), *Liberalism and the Limits of Justice* (Cambridge: Cambridge University Press).

(1984), "The Procedural Republic and the Unencumbered Self," *Political Theory*, vol. 12, no. 1, pp. 81–96.

Sartre, J-P. (1969), *Being and Nothingness* (London: Methuen).

Schumpeter, J. A. (1978), *History of Economic Analysis* (Oxford: Oxford University Press).

Sen, A. K. (1970), *Collective Choice and Social Welfare* (London: Oliver & Boyd).

(1975), "Rawls versus Bentham: An Axiomatic Examination of the Pure Distribution Problem," N. Daniels, ed., *Reading Rawls: Critical Studies of A Theory of Justice* (Oxford: Blackwell), pp. 283–92.

Shapiro, I. (1981), "Fiscal Crisis of the Polish State," *Theory and Society*, vol. 10, no. 4, pp. 469–502.

(1982), "Realism in the Study of the History of Ideas," *History of Political Thought*, vol. 3, no. 3, pp. 535–78.

Shapiro, I., and J. Kane. (1983), "Stagflation and the New Right," *Telos*, no. 56, pp. 5–39.

Shue, H. (1981), *Basic Rights* (Princeton: Princeton University Press).

Sigmund, P. E. (1971), *Natural Law in Political Thought* (Cambridge, Mass.: Winthrop).

Skinner, Q. (1972), "The Context of Hobbes' Theory of Political Obligation," in M. Cranston and R. S. Peters, eds., *Hobbes and Rousseau: A Collection of Critical Essays* (New York: Doubleday), pp. 109–42.

(1978), *The Foundations of Modern Political Thought*, 2 vols., vol. I: *The Renaissance;* vol. II: *The Age of Reformation* (Cambridge: Cambridge University Press).

(1980), "The Origins of the Calvinist Theory of Revolution," B.C. Malament, ed., *After the Reformation: Essays in Honor of H. J. Hexter* (Philadelphia: University of Pennsylvania Press), pp. 309–30.

Skocpol, T. (1979), *States and Social Revolutions: A Comparative Analysis of France, Russia and China* (Cambridge: Cambridge University Press).

Smith, A. (1937), *An Inquiry into the Nature and Causes of The Wealth of Nations* (New York: The Modern Library).

Spiegel, H. W. (1971), *The Growth of Economic Thought* (Englewood Cliffs, N.J.: Prentice-Hall).

Stone, L. (1965), *The Crisis of the Aristocracy: 1558–1641* (Oxford: Oxford University Press).

Strauss, L. (1953), *Natural Right and History* (Chicago: University of Chicago Press).

(1963), *The Political Philosophy of Hobbes: Its Basis and Its Genesis* (Chicago: University of Chicago Press).

Stroud, B. (1977), *Hume* (London: Routledge & Kegan Paul).

Supple, B. E. (1959), *Commercial Crisis and Change in England: 1600–42* (Cambridge: Cambridge University Press).

Tawney, R. H. (1961), *Religion and the Rise of Capitalism* (New York: New American Library).

Taylor, A. E. (1965), "The Ethical Doctrine of Hobbes," K.C. Brown, ed., *Hobbes Studies* (Cambridge, Mass.: Harvard University Press), pp. 35–55.

Taylor, C. (1979), *Hegel and Modern Society* (Cambridge: Cambridge University Press).

Thirsk, J. (1978), *Economic Policy and Projects: The Development of a Consumer Society in Early Modern England* (Oxford: Oxford University Press [Clarendon Press]).

Thomas, K. (1965), "The Social Origins of Hobbes' Political Thought," K. Brown, ed., *Hobbes Studies* (Cambridge, Mass.: Harvard University Press), pp. 185–236.

Tigar, M., and M. Levy. (1977), *Law and the Rise of Capitalism* (New York: Monthly Review).

Tocqueville, A. de. (1981), *Democracy in America* (New York: Doubleday).

Tribe, K. (1978), *Land, Labour and Economic Discourse* (London: Routledge & Kegan Paul).

Tuck, R. (1979), *Natural Rights Theories: Their Origin and Development* (Cambridge: Cambridge University Press).

Tully, J. (1980), *A Discourse on Property: John Locke and His Adversaries* (Cambridge: Cambridge University Press).

Walzer, M. (1965), *The Revolution of the Saints: A Study in the Origins of Radical Politics* (Cambridge, Mass.: Harvard University Press).

(1983), *Spheres of Justice: A Defense of Pluralism and Equality* (New York: Basic Books).

(1984), "Liberalism and the Art of Separation," *Political Theory*, vol. 12, no. 3, pp. 315–30.

Warrender, H. (1957), *The Political Philosophy of Hobbes: His Theory of Obligation* (Oxford: Oxford University Press [Clarendon Press]).

Wellbank, J. H., D. Snook, and D.T. Mason. (1982), *John Rawls and his Critics: An Annotated Bibliography* (New York: Garland).

Wernham, A. G. (1965), "Liberty and Obligation in Hobbes," K.C. Brown, ed., *Hobbes Studies* (Cambridge, Mass.: Harvard University Press), pp. 117–39.

Wiles, R. C. (1968), "The Theory of Wages in Later English Mercantilism," *Economic History Review*, 2d series, no. 21, pp. 113–26.

Williams, B. (1962), "The Idea of Equality," P. Laslett and W. G.

Runciman, eds., *Philosophy, Politics and Society*, 2d series (Oxford: Blackwell, 1962), pp. 110–31.

Winch, D. (1980), *Adam Smith's Politics: An Essay in Historiographic Revision* (Cambridge: Cambridge University Press).

Wittgenstein, L. (1958), *Philosophical Investigations*, G.E.M. Anscombe, trans. (Oxford: Blackwell).

Wolff, R. P. (1970), *In Defense of Anarchism* (New York: Harper & Row).

(1977), *Understanding Rawls: A Reconstruction and Critique of A Theory of Justice* (Princeton: Princeton University Press).

(1981), "Robert Nozick's Derivation of the Minimal State," in J. Paul, ed., *Reading Nozick: Essays on Anarchy State and Utopia* (Totowa, N.J.: Rowman and Littlefield).

Wood, N. (1981), "Thomas Hobbes and the Crisis of the English Aristocracy," *History of Political Thought*, vol. 1, no. 3, pp. 437–52.

(1983), *The Politics of Locke's Philosophy: A Social Study of "An Essay Concerning Human Understanding,"* (Berkeley: University of California Press).

Yack, B. (1985), "Community and Conflict in Aristotle's Political Philosophy," *The Review of Politics*, vol. 47, no. 1, pp. 92–112.

Yule, G. U. (1915), "Crop Production and Prices," *Journal of the Royal Statistical Society*, vol. 78, pp. 296–8.

Index

321

THE WORLD'S CLASSICS

THE DUKE'S CHILDREN

ANTHONY TROLLOPE (1815–82), the son of a failing London barrister, was brought up an awkward and unhappy youth amidst debt and privation. His mother maintained the family by writing, but Anthony's own first novel did not appear until 1847, when he had at length established a successful Civil Service career in the Post Office, from which he retired in 1867. After a slow start, he achieved fame, with 47 novels and some 16 other books, and sales sometimes topping 100,000. He was acclaimed an unsurpassed portraitist of the lives of the professional and landed classes, especially in his perennially popular *Chronicles of Barsetshire* (1855–67), and his six brilliant Palliser novels (1864–80). His fascinating *Autobiography* (1883) recounts his successes with an enthusiasm which stems from memories of a miserable youth. Throughout the 1870s he developed new styles of fiction, but was losing critical favour by the time of his death.

HERMIONE LEE is a Lecturer in English at York University. She is the author of *The Novels of Virginia Woolf* (1977), *Elizabeth Bowen: An Estimation* (1981), *Philip Roth* (1982) and of introductions for Virago and Faber, and editor of *Stevie Smith: A Selection* (1983). She reviews fiction for the *Observer*, reviews regularly for the *TLS*, and has recently presented Channel Four's books programme, *Book Four*.

THE CENTENARY EDITION OF
ANTHONY TROLLOPE'S
PALLISER NOVELS

General Editor: W. J. Mc Cormack

CAN YOU FORGIVE HER? (1864–5)

Introduced by Kate Flint and edited by Andrew Swarbrick,
with a Preface by Norman St. John-Stevas

PHINEAS FINN (1869)

Introduced and edited by Jacques Berthoud

THE EUSTACE DIAMONDS (1873)

Introduced and edited by W. J. Mc Cormack

PHINEAS REDUX (1874)

Introduced by F. S. L. Lyons and edited by John C. Whale

THE PRIME MINISTER (1876)

Introduced by John McCormick and edited by Jennifer Uglow

THE DUKE'S CHILDREN (1880)

Introduced and edited by Hermione Lee

THE WORLD'S CLASSICS

===

ANTHONY TROLLOPE
The Duke's Children

===

EDITED WITH AN INTRODUCTION BY

HERMIONE LEE

WITH ILLUSTRATIONS BY CHARLES MOZLEY

Oxford   New York

OXFORD UNIVERSITY PRESS

Oxford University Press, Walton Street, Oxford OX2 6DP

Oxford New York Toronto
Delhi Bombay Calcutta Madras Karachi
Petaling Jaya Singapore Hong Kong Tokyo
Nairobi Dar es Salaam Cape Town
Melbourne Auckland

and associated companies in
Berlin Ibadan

Oxford is a trade mark of Oxford University Press

Foreword and Chronology © W. J. McCormack 1982
Introduction, Bibliography and Notes © Hermione Lee 1983

This edition first published 1983 as a World's Classics paperback
Reprinted 1985, 1986, 1987, 1989, 1990

British Library Cataloguing in Publication Data

Trollope, Anthony
The Duke's Children.—(The World's classics)
I. Title   II. Lee, Hermione
823'.8[F]   PR5684.D/
ISBN 0–19–281586–5

Library of Congress Cataloging in Publication Data

Trollope, Anthony, 1815–1882.
The Duke's children.
(The Centenary edition of Anthony Trollope's Palliser novels) (The World's classics)
Bibliography: p.
I. Lee, Hermione. II. Title. III. Series: Trollope,
Anthony, 1815–1892. Palliser novels.
PR 5684.D7 1983   823'.8 83–6295
ISBN 0–19–281586–5 (pbk.)

Printed in Great Britain by
BPCC Hazell Books
Aylesbury, Bucks

CONTENTS

CONTENTS

FOREWORD

THE CENTENARY EDITION OF
ANTHONY TROLLOPE'S PALLISER NOVELS

ANTHONY TROLLOPE died in 1882, and in his centenary year Oxford University Press is launching a new edition of the six political novels commonly (if rather misleadingly) called the Palliser novels. Trollope has always been popular, but the 1970s and '80s have seen a renewed and distinctive interest in his work. Instead of seeing Trollope as a quaint Victorian second-ranker who offered the hard-pressed twentieth-century reader scenes of clerical life, a new generation has decided that Trollope is a serious moralist, a consistent political thinker, a conscious artist.

The writers who introduce and annotate this Centenary Edition reflect this revaluation, but not passively nor with one voice. The Preface to *Can You Forgive Her?* is by a distinguished senior member of the British Tory Party, and is complemented by a feminist critique of Trollope's sexual politics; *The Eustace Diamonds* is annotated by an Irish Marxist. Hermione Lee relates *The Duke's Children* to America rather than Barchester, and Jacques Berthoud compares Trollope to Flaubert and Turgenev. Such diversity is not a fashionable pluralism, but directly springs from my conviction that the literature of the past has no immutable or indestructible value. Generation after generation *we* participate in the creation of that 'past' literature in a process which crucially involves a historical perspective. The critic who refuses to concede that *The Prime Minister* is a political novel nevertheless reads the character of Lopez and the anti-semitism which gathers round him in the hideous light of twentieth-century history. It is true that the recent Trollope industry has appropriated the novelist to the conservative cause, but the dynamics of his fiction are such that it can illustrate other ideological interpretations also.

At this point the Old Trollopian is feeling decidedly uneasy. He fears that the genial anachronisms he has mentally fondled for years are now about to be ridiculed in scholarly notes or—worse still—dragooned into some unseemly systematization. Certainly the Centenary Edition provides the most copious annotation of the Palliser novels ever published; certainly the editors marshal their critical arguments with precision and vigour. But the result contains a paradox which may both reassure the Old Trollopian and reveal something genuinely radical about the business of criticism. First of all, Trollope is a great deal more attentive, perceptive, and accurate than many of his admirers realize; second, the novels thus scrutinized offer a counter-narrative to that of the traditionalist plots, in the form of material traces which question and challenge the enfolding legitimation of liberal Tory values which were officially Trollope's.

The Brave New Critics cannot be opposed to the Old Trollopians in any simple-minded way. If the recent revival of interest is in part an exercise in extending that insidious form of social control represented by institutionalized literature, the other side of the coin shows Trollope as particularly popular during the Second World War. In June 1945 Elizabeth Bowen broadcast a playlet in which a serving soldier and his uncle (born 1882) debate the function of literature at a time of world crisis . . . 'there must be *something* about any writer who lives twice'. Of course it is not some mystical genius or individual trait of the biographical Trollope which sanctions this renewed interest in the Palliser novels; it is the multiple potentiality of literature as produced in the contradictory world of nineteenth-century Britain.

In 1882 the book trade was flourishing. The three-decker novel had not yet been unseated, and Mudie's circulating library simultaneously maintained the high price of the novel and distributed it to a public much larger than that which could afford to pay the retail price. It need hardly be said that today the book trade is in quite a different state, virtually ousted from the list of significant modes of cultural entertainment. Film and television, recorded music, ritualized sport even, have supplanted the book as our primary experience of art. Television has long ago taken the Palliser novels and turned them into 'The Pallisers', thereby giving an age which is materially and spiritually unstable illusory access to past opulence. What the book uniquely retains, however, is precisely the physical presence of history. The Centenary Edition acknowledges both the Trollope of the 1880s and the market of our decade. It has not entered into the fabulously expensive business of establishing new texts which, with bombinating minutiae, often retards or replaces the reader's engagement with literary history. The texts are those of the Oxford Trollope, published between 1948 and 1954 under the general editorship of Michael Sadleir and Frederick Page. Together with fresh Introductions and extensive annotations, this represents a solution of which Trollope himself might have been proud.

W. J. Mc CORMACK

INTRODUCTION

ENGLISH CODES AND AMERICAN INFLUENCES

I

The Duke's Children has two shapes, or actions: it closes a circle, and opens outwards. From the first sentence of the novel, which abruptly lets us know of Glencora's death and of the loneliness of 'our old friend' the Duke of Omnium, an affectionate familiarity with these characters is assumed. The reader of the last of the Palliser novels is meant to know the earlier books, to be shocked at the loss of Glencora and concerned for the Duke in his widowed state. But *The Duke's Children*'s dependence on the earlier books is not a sentimental or a lazy one, cosily inviting the reader's sympathy. Its relation to past history is, rather, ironic and disturbing. Palliser's attempt to prevent his daughter Mary from marrying Tregear, 'a commoner without an income', and to arrange an aristocratic match for her instead, re-enacts the circumstances of his own arranged marriage to Glencora in *Can You Forgive Her?* That Glencora, before her death, should have encouraged the handsome Frank Tregear, seems to Palliser a 'posthumous infidelity'[1] which bitterly recalls to him her own romantic, renounced love for Burgo Fitzgerald. Mary's resistance (stronger than Glencora's) to pressure and parental authority forces Palliser to reinterpret his own marriage. He is made to ask himself whether Glencora had always loved Burgo, and whether she might not have been happier had she married him. Trollope's great strength is his authenticity of characterization, and this is particularly so with the slowly, soundly developing presentation of Palliser. The psychological details of his response to Mary's rebellion—for instance that his retrospective jealousy makes him more cruel to her than his official, social reasons for disliking Tregear seem to

[1] Juliet MacMaster, *Trollope's Palliser Novels*, Macmillan, 1978, p. 125.

warrant,[2] or that he transfers his anger at Glencora, 'with the full weight of his mind', to Mrs. Finn (who understands this better than he does himself)—are marvellously acute and convincing.

The Duke's difficulties with one of his children thus takes us back full circle to the first of the Palliser novels, and much of the charm and pathos of the book arise from its echoes and reminders. But the novel is also about altera- tion, compromise, and adapting. In a counterpoint more complicated than Trollope's bland, relaxed manner would suggest, he plays a process of re-enactment against a process of change. Mary's 'modern' firmness about her right to choose a husband, and Tregear's assumption that he is her equal, are threats to 'those rules as to birth and position by which he [the Duke] thought his world was kept straight'. Meanwhile, the Duke is trying to inculcate these very rules into his son and heir, Silverbridge (and to a less important extent into the younger brother Gerald) so that a silly 'mooncalf' playboy may turn into the responsible heir to the Omnium line and to the English Liberal tradition. Silverbridge's social, political and amatory follies, though different in kind, are all equally disappointing to the Duke. That his son should be sent down from Oxford for painting the Dean's house red, give all his time to horses, racing companions and shooting, 'plunge' heavily on a race, stand for the family borough on the Conservative side (under the influence of Mary's impertinent suitor) and reject an English lord's daughter in favour of an 'American beauty' are, to the Duke, interrelated signs that Silverbridge is unequal to the duties of an aristocrat and a gentleman. But if Palliser is disappointed he is also forgiving and generous: a large sum of money has been set aside in case the sons run into debt. The novel's particularly tender quality comes from the combination of disapproval and affection in

[2] This aspect of the novel is best dealt with in *'The Duke's Children*: Trollope's psychological masterpiece', by John H. Hagan, *Nineteenth Century Fiction*, Vol. 13, 1958–9, pp. 1–21.

Palliser (answered in his sons by a mixture of guilt and respect), very nicely displayed in the scene at the club where the Duke, having made sure that he and Silverbridge are alone, 'put out his hand and gently stroked the young man's hair', or at 'the family breakfast-table' where he lectures his two hungry sons on the uses of wealth and the value of work, while they get through a plateful of broiled salmon and stewed kidneys.

The Duke's repeated attempts 'to indoctrinate his children with the ideas by which his own mind was fortified and controlled' involve, as in that breakfast scene, a comedy of mismatching languages. Personally, Palliser is inarticulate (with his children as once with Glencora). ' "He never talks to any of us" ', Silverbridge tells Lady Mabel. And so he does not know them: 'He had never found out anything in reference to his daughter's character.' His communication with his children takes the form of lectures or Ciceronian letters. When he is moved to 'indoctrinate' them, his rhetoric becomes official and statesmanlike, a mark of his difficulty (which is one of the novel's central subjects) in making a proper and coherent relationship between the public and the private arena.

In the course of this novel the Duke expresses to his children (more fully than ever before in the Palliser novels) the codes of behaviour which have shaped his life. He loves justice, duty and honour; he believes that a political career is a service to the country, not a means of self-advancement, or a sport. The politician should be loyal, should know with equal thoroughness all the unglamorous branches of his job, and should despise false rhetoric. Happiness consists in hard work; money is the reward of labour; luxury and riches (the incentives of the gambler) are to be seen in proportion, not as necessities. The leaders of the country should not merely obey the law, but should be guided by the higher requirements of 'patriotism, philanthropy, self-abnegation, public service, purity of purpose, devotion to the needs of others'.

There is no doubt that these codes, personally vouched for in Trollope's *Autobiography*, are much admired (Sir Timothy Beeswax provides the example of a more disreputable kind of English politician, referred to in the *Autobiography* as 'the clever conjurers, to whom politics is simply such a game as is billiards or rackets') and that the language with which Palliser's sons respond to his lessons is, by contrast, comically inferior. The linguistic generation gap[3] is a running joke in the novel, from the Duke's corrections of his sons' awful slang (' "I am awfully sorry" ... "There is no occasion for awe," said the Duke') to his critique of Silverbridge's letter about the election (' "It was beastly work!" The Duke made another memorandum to instruct his son that no gentleman above the age of a schoolboy should allow himself to use such a word in such a sense.') or to Gerald's translation of 'the governor's' lecture against gambling (' "It cannot be that a rational being should consent to risk the money he has himself" ') into his own easygoing modern idioms (' " What is a fellow to get by playing high—a fellow like you and me?" ').

But though Silverbridge and Gerald are less eloquent and disciplined than their father, and will evidently never be as committed politicians, the Duke's codes do not always make him right. The novel's interest lies in the closing of the gap between his personal obtuseness and prejudice, and his public high-mindedness. Palliser's Liberalism has not been reconciled with his inborn aristocratic conservatism. Politically, he believes in 'a drawing-nearer of the classes', but also in 'the maintenance of an aristocracy that shall be of the very best'. He wants Silverbridge to stand as a Liberal candidate, but he no more wants him to marry the American granddaughter of a Dutch dock-worker than he wants his daughter to marry a commoner (even one whose political beliefs, in a nice Trollopian irony, are much more conservative than the Duke's). 'There was an inner feeling

[3] See George Watson, 'Trollope's Forms of Address', *Critical Quarterly*, 15, 1973, pp. 219–30.

in his bosom as to his own family, his own name, his own children, and his own personal self, which was kept altogether apart from his grand political theories. It was a subject on which he never spoke.'

That unexpressed dichotomy between personal and political codes is paralleled by the gap between his moral standards and his understanding of individuals. It is all very well to lecture Silverbridge about duty, but he is, after all, not a bit like Lord Buttercup ('as constant at his office, or during a session on the Treasury Bench, as though there were not a pack of hounds or a card-table in Great Britain') and Lord Popplecourt is, personally, a ridiculous substitute-lover for Tregear. Though Palliser does not alter his principles, he does have to adapt them to the more spontaneous 'codes of conduct and honour' which Mary asserts in keeping faith with her chosen lover; to a more flexible recognition of individual needs within the social order (delicately and persuasively argued by Mrs. Finn in Chapter LXVI); and to the democratization, which Silverbridge's transatlantic alliance presages, of one of the grand old Whig governing families, no longer to make its matches exclusively among 'the Upper Ten Thousand' so as to ensure the upkeep of the English constitution by 'an aristocracy of the very best'. That Palliser's education, in middle age, should keep pace with his elder son's, is the novel's subtlest enterprise.

II

One of the novel's earlier titles was *Lord Silverbridge* (the others were *The Duke and his Children* and *The Ex-Prime Minister*) and the heir's acquisition of 'age and flavour' is given as much weight as Palliser's difficulties in widowhood. Silverbridge, whose simplicity and attractiveness Trollope makes pleasantly evident, is exactly the sort of handsome English aristocrat described by Henry James in 'An International Episode' (1878–9), the story of an English lord who fails to marry a Bostonian girl. Lord

Lambeth's appearance, like Silverbridge's, 'proclaimed that to be a nobleman, an athlete, and an excellent fellow, was a sufficiently brilliant combination of qualities.' Like Lord Lambeth, Silverbridge is not 'tremendously clever', but in the course of the novel he acquires a threefold education, political, social and sexual. In each area, Silverbridge is guided as much by his personal feelings (naturally 'gentlemanly') as by 'rules as to birth and position'. He makes less division between private and public life than his father, and is swayed by the dictates of the heart rather than by traditional codes. (Evidently the novel proposes a reconciliation between these two standards of behaviour.) Politically, his defection into the Conservative ranks, undertaken as a matter of personal conviction (' "I've got my own ideas" ') is corrected not so much by his father's sense that it is a betrayal for a Palliser not to be a Liberal as by Silverbridge's personal distaste for the character of Sir Timothy Beeswax. Socially, Silverbridge puts his Beargarden, horse-racing, gambling pursuits behind him, and gives up the friendship of the shabby-genteel Major Tifto. Tifto's passionate language of the turf, his 'high-mounting heart' and quickness to take offence, his arrangements for making ends meet, his vacillations between tearful self-justification and boastful attempts at wordliness, show how well Trollope manages men of a particular profession and men on the edges of good society. The Major's conversation with Captain Green at Egham (Chapter XXXVI) and his self-conscious importuning of 'his pal' Silverbridge when he is with his father at the club (Chapter XXVII) are two of the novel's most exact, socially authentic scenes. Characteristically, as the latter scene shows, Silverbridge breaks with Tifto out of personal embarrassment rather than a sense of social duty.

Tifto's desire for intimacy with Silverbridge, his rejection (not a friend 'for home use'), his revenge after being slighted, and his eventual acceptance of an 'annual pension' from his 'former noble partner' have the air of courtship, marital quarrel, divorce, and maintenance arrangements. The sporting partnership thus connects with the central educative choice which Silverbridge has to make between Lady Mabel Grex and Isabel Boncassen. The choice is not just between two girls, one English and one American, each of whom Trollope is careful to make as beautiful and potent as the other. It is also a choice between two kinds of inheritance for 'the future Dukes of Omnium'. Though the Duke is to a comical extent inflexible and emotional about his children's marriages, he is right, Trollope suggests, to feel an anxiety about them which is public as well as personal. It is an anxiety about how the Liberal aristocracy, which should be governing England, shall perpetuate itself—more especially at a time when 'the world is bewigging itself', 'buckram' and 'deportment' are the order of the day, grand old Whig noblemen like the Duke of St. Bungay have gone out to grass, the sons of peers spend their time at cards and races, and (as Major Tifto has noticed) 'men had abandoned the idea of squareness'. Trollope provides a choice for the ex-Prime Minister's heir between two different dynasties and civilizations. It is a mark of his narrative dexterity and discretion that the rivals for Silverbridge's love are so sharply individualized, while carrying the weight of this historical significance.

That Lady Mabel's story begins *'in medias res'*, that she has renounced the man she loves before the novel starts, that she is always being thought of as older than she is: these things[4] are all of a piece with her family history. Lord Grex, a Conservative peer of an 'ancient family' who has wasted his fortunes, and spends his life at cards and racing trying to win them back, is, though he makes few appearances in the novel, a powerful and significant character. His shambling, bad-tempered, brutal cynicism about politics, his squalid financial squabbles with his son (a 'beast' who ruthlessly takes large sums of money from

---

[4] Juliet MacMaster makes the point at length: *op. cit.*, pp. 141–5.

Gerald at cards), his savagery to his children even on his death-bed, provide a strong 'off-stage' contrast to Palliser's treatment of his sons and daughter. Grex illustrates Palliser's dilemma about the maintenance of the aristocracy. The Duke knows that he is 'a wretched unprincipled old man' and that if 'many of his order should become as was now Lord Grex' then his order had better 'go to the wall'. But Lord Grex has the 'blue blood' he wants for his heirs. It is a mark of Palliser's uneasy negotiation between public and personal needs that he is prepared to contemplate Grex as a father-in-law for his son, just as he is prepared to consider the doltish Lord Popplecourt as a husband for his daughter because he has a large 'unencumbered' estate and 'a barony of an old date'.

Lady Mabel, however, for all Palliser's courtly encouragement, is bound for 'a great shipwreck' and not a great marriage. This personal tragedy is affecting: Mabel's wit and spirit under duress, her self-destructive moments when 'her feelings completely got the better of her' or when she 'worked herself into such a state of mind that she hardly knew what to do', her angry eloquence about her position (' "You can flirt with any woman you please. I must wait till somebody comes,—and put up with it if nobody does come" ') are very expressive. Nevertheless, it is made clear that in marrying her, Silverbridge would be marrying into a stale, decayed line. She is 'a manufactured article', her gaiety is not spontaneous but is 'the work of her life', and she is the victim of an unalterably wasteful situation: ' "The thing has been going on so long that one is used to it." ' Mabel's unsuitability for Silverbridge is best suggested by her love for Grex, the mouldering, melancholy old family seat in Westmoreland, where, always companioned by the reactionary and pessimistic Miss Cassowary, she broods over the past. Like a number of Trollope's thwarted women characters—Lady Laura Kennedy in *Phineas Redux*, or Emily Trevelyan in *He Knew He Was Right*—Mabel is doomed to a fixed existence, locked in a defunct English past which Silverbridge can rejuvenate by marrying an American.

III

Henry James is affable, if pernickety, about Trollope's treatment of his own speciality, the American girl in Europe.

The American girl was destined sooner or later to make her entrance into British fiction, and Trollope's treatment of this complicated being is full of good humour and of that fatherly indulgence, that almost motherly sympathy, which characterizes his attitude throughout towards the youthful feminine. He has not mastered all the springs of her delicate organism, nor sounded all the mysteries of her conversation. . . . 'I got to be thinking if any one of them should ask me to marry him', words attributed to Miss Boncassen in *The Duke's Children*, have much more the note of English American than of American English.[5]

Trollope's interest in, and 'fatherly indulgence' for the type has several sources. It can partly be attributed to his love for Kate Field, the American feminist, twenty-five years his junior, whom he met in Florence in 1860 and to whom he pays an emotional tribute in the *Autobiography* (1883), which was completed in April 1876, a few days before *The Duke's Children* was begun. It is probably sentimental to assume that Palliser's half-fatherly susceptibility for Isabel reflects the emotion felt for Kate Field,[6] but her influence certainly accounts for the marked resemblance between his American heroines. Historically, Trollope's interest in Anglo-American marriages is, like James's, easy to explain.[7] A caustic mother in James's 'The Point of View' (1882) reminds her daughter 'that scarcely a day passes that a foreigner, usually of distinction, doesn't select an American

[5] Henry James, 'Anthony Trollope', *The Century Magazine*, July 1883, reprinted in *Partial Portraits*, Macmillan, 1888.

[6] This is suggested by C. P. Snow in *Trollope*, Macmillan, 1975, p. 121.

[7] John Halperin gives a full account of Trollope's American theme. *Trollope and Politics*, Macmillan, 1977, pp. 245–54.

bride'. Lord Randolph Churchill's marriage in 1874 to Jennie Jerome of New York City, and Lord Randolph's nephew's later marriage to Consuela Vanderbilt, were only the most spectacular examples of such alliances, which were growing more frequent from the 1870s onwards.

The character of 'the American beauty' (which is how Isabel is first described, as though it were a standard classification) who might make such a match, had long been of sociological interest to Trollope. Like his mother Frances, whose *Domestic Manners of the Americans* (1832) included, in its notoriously critical account of her American experience, a brisk look at 'the everywhere privileged class of very young ladies', Trollope, on his visits to the States in 1861, '68, '72 and '75, was struck by the effects of those privileges on American manners. In *North America* (1862) his response is divided. The American woman who pushes on to street cars wearing a huge crinoline, and who accepts chivalric attentions as her due without acknowledging them, is anathema to him. But the others are admired for their exceptional 'brightness, beauty, grace, and sweetness', which makes them 'the aristocracy of the land'. The double image is reflected in James: Winterbourne's 'cynical compatriot' in *Daisy Miller* (1878) calls American women 'at once the most exacting in the world and the least endowed with a sense of indebtedness', and the matter is summed up in 'The Point of View':

If a girl is a very nice girl, the American method brings her to great completeness,—makes all her graces flower; but if she isn't nice, it makes her exceedingly disagreeable,—elaborately and fatally perverts her.[8]

Trollope's fiction incorporates both his distaste and nervousness at American feminist aggression, which can do without chivalry (a valuable and integral part, for Trollope, of the English gentleman's inheritance) and his pleasure in

Henry James, 'The Point of View' (first published 1882, reprinted in *Siege of London*, 1883), *The Complete Tales*, ed. Leon Edel, Vol. 4, p. 290.

the sweet, bright, innocent, 'very nice' kind of American girl, who responds enthusiastically and gratefully to the chivalric approach. Ophelia Gledd (in *Lotta Schmidt and Other Stories*, 1867) and Caroline Spalding (in *He Knew He Was Right*, 1869), equally energetic, attractive, eloquent Bostonians who marry into the English aristocracy, are to be set against Mrs. Hurtle, Paul Montague's embittered American mistress in *The Way We Live Now* (1875) and Wallachia Petrie, Caroline's feminist poetess friend in *He Knew He Was Right*. Wallachia, who 'hates chivalry', rank, riches and English aristocrats, and lectures the future Lord Peterborough ferociously on social and sexual equality, grotesquely illustrates a scornful attitude to nineteenth-century American idealism to be found in works as different as *Martin Chuzzlewit* and *The Bostonians*. Wallachia's feminism, ridiculous though it is made to seem, is only one element in her American zeal. She shares the button-holing, pompous quality of Trollope's chauvinist American public men, Elias Gotobed (in *The American Senator*, 1877), and Jonas Spalding, the 'American minister' in *He Knew He Was Right*.

Trollope's versions of 'the American girl' can usefully be compared to James's. It is surely a coincidence that Isabel Boncassen has the same name as Isabel Archer (*The Portrait of a Lady* was written in the spring and summer of 1880, *The Duke's Children* started publication in June of that year), but the friendship between Isabel Archer and Henrietta Stackpole might well owe something to *He Knew He Was Right*. Henrietta (' "Gracious, there's that Lord" ') often sounds like Wallachia (' "I believe that in London the titled aristocrats do hang pretty much together" '), just as Miss Birdseye, in *The Bostonians* (1886), is strikingly like the short-skirted feminist in *Is He Popenjoy?* (1878). Physically, James's slim American girls are very like Trollope's. Daisy's 'constantly moving' lips and eyes, her 'soft, slender, agreeable voice' and 'decidedly sociable' tone; Diana Belfield's 'frank, quick glance, and her rapid, gliding step'

INTRODUCTION

in 'Longstaff's Marriage' (1878), Bessie Alden's graceful gravity in 'An International Episode' (1878–9), and Isabel's 'light slim figure' whose 'very pliancy' seems to mock at 'poor Lord Warburton', make them of the same type as Ophelia Gledd and Isabel Boncassen, whose dominant quality is their 'vitality'. And the problems for James's American girls in Europe are similar. Like Ophelia Gledd, who is 'the very girl for Boston' but might not have 'the gait of going that would suit London', they find that the freedoms allowed in Boston or Schenectady are liable to misinterpretation in Rome or England. Like Wallachia, they find much to dismay them in the politics of the English aristocracy: Bessie Alden refuses Lord Lambeth because of his lack of political commitment and idealism as a 'hereditary legislator'.

But James's version of the confrontation is more complex and sombre (and develops more) than Trollope's. His American girls of the '70s and '80s refuse their aristocratic English suitors because, for all their 'picturesqueness', they represent a constricted world: Isabel sees in the eyes of Lord Warburton's sister 'the peace, the kindness, the honour, the possessions, a deep security and a great exclusion'. The only Anglo-American union he finds possible is made on a death-bed, in 'Longstaff's Marriage' (another odd coincidence of names, since Isabel Boncassen's rejected aristocratic suitor is Dolly Longstaff). The substitution of death-bed for marriage-bed is, later, at the heart of *The Wings of the Dove* (1902), in which Lord Mark's unsuccessful pursuit of Milly repeats the earlier theme more sinisterly. Daisy's death, Isabel's incarceration, Milly's betrayal, are James's ever more ambivalent versions of the dangers to American innocence and freedom in the Old World.

Trollope's interest in the confrontation is, characteristically, much more to do with social self-consciousness and personal pride. Isabel, Ophelia Gledd and Caroline Spalding all have the same feelings: they are proud of their classless American inheritance (though 'allured' by the

xxii

charm of English gentility), they want to be treated as
equals, and they are anxious not be condescended to by the
families of the man they love. (James is perfectly alert to
these factors too, as the visit of Lord Lambeth's mother to
Bessie and her sister demonstrates in 'An International
Episode', and as a letter about *Daisy Miller* shows: 'It didn't
at all suit them that a little unknown American girl should
marry their coveted kinsman. Such a consummation
certainly does not suit English duchesses and countesses in
general. . .'[9]) ' "What would the Baronet's wife say to me
with all my sharp Boston notions?" ' asks Ophelia Gledd.
' "Can't you see her looking at me over the length of the
drawing room? And can't you fancy how pert I should
be?" ' Isabel, similarly anxious not to be thought a 'pert
poppet', sums up the argument with a typical romantic
flourish: she wants to ' "walk out of our republic into your
aristocracy with my head erect, with the stars and stripes
waving proudly round me till I had been accepted into the
shelter of the Omnium griffins." '

That Isabel achieves this ambition provides a climax to
Trollope's treatment (very much more positive than
James's) of these Anglo-American alliances. He is careful,
in *The Duke's Children*, to make Isabel as much of a 'natural'
aristocrat as Silverbridge is a 'natural' gentleman, and to
suppress the tedious side of Republicanism (though
Gotobed makes a brief comic appearance, with a splendidly
Whitmanesque American poet, and Isabel's mother, not
unlike Daisy Miller's is a stout lady who was really
interested with the cooking apparatus and the wash-houses'
at Carlton Terrace). Isabel has no awful feminist friend,
and only a very slight nasal twang, and her rich scholarly
father, a possible future President, is fit company for Dukes.
Though much is made of her dock-working grandfather and
of her having danced with bank clerks, she is perfectly

---

[9] Henry James, *Letters*, 21 March 1879, ed. Leon Edel, Vol. II, p. 221,
Harvard, 1975.

suited to the Omnium griffins, and Lady Mabel's spite misfires when she calls her 'a convict's granddaughter'. It is for her freshness and vigour, rather than her republicanism, that Isabel is necessary to the Pallisers, and Trollope makes her energies attractively felt in, for instance, her 'high opinion' of herself (very similar to the other Isabel's), her commitment to 'the present moment', her wanting 'to walk about the room for half an hour and stamp my feet' when she is cross, her passion for the new game of lawn-tennis, and her play at going to church 'with her foot stuck out before her, with her chin in the air, and one arm akimbo.'

Like the other girls in the novel, she is impatient at the restrictions suffered by women. All three speak of this with the same voice:

(Isabel): '[Young men] become men some day, whereas we must only be women to the end.'
(Mary): 'He does not suffer as I do. . . A man can never be like a girl.'
(Mabel): 'You are not a woman, and do not understand how women are trammelled.'

Trollope's sympathy for such feelings (at odds with his satires on feminism and his statements about womens' rights in *North America* and 'The Higher Education of Women' (1868)) do not allow for any solution other than a happy marriage. Isabel is the opposite of Wallachia; like James's Bessie Alden recognizing that Lord Lambeth is 'handsomer and more splendid than anything I have ever seen', she hero-worships Silverbridge as the flower of his civilization.

But Isabel's acceptance into the Omnium family (sealed by the gift of Glencora's ring from the Duke, which balances Mabel's messy refusal of Silverbridge's ring) does mean a necessary alteration in that civilization. This is succinctly suggested by the references to the medieval ancestor of all the Pallisers, Sir Guy, whose legless statue stands in the ruins of, and whose look-out dominates, Matching Priory.

Sir Guy (whose part in the Palliser history was cynically recounted by Glencora in Chapter XXII of *Can You Forgive Her?*) overlooks Silverbridge's scenes with Isabel and with Mabel, and, at the end, Silverbridge's wedding. Mary, setting herself doggedly against aristocratic codes, never 'troubles herself' about Sir Guy; Mabel, with her feeling for the past, thinks his 'look-out' 'a lovely spot'; Isabel, hearing from Silverbridge of Sir Guy's having 'run off with half-a-dozen heiresses', responds: ' "Nobody should have run away with me. I have no idea of going on such a journey except on terms of equality." ' The Duke's reluctant double acceptance of a commoner and an American for his children marks the very end of Sir Guy's era: historically, the old Liberal aristocracy's coming to terms with the future; personally, a compromise (painful and not altogether satisfactory) between codes of duty and natural feelings.

NOTE ON THE TEXT

The Duke's Children was written between 2 May 1876 and 29 October 1876. Trollope planned to publish it in twelve monthly parts and in four volumes in book form, but the disappointing reception of *The Prime Minister* (1875–6) led him to set aside the manuscript of the new novel. Before its eventual publication, it had to be cut—presumably on the advice of his publishers. Serialized in *All the Year Round* from 4 October 1879 to 24 July 1880, *The Duke's Children* was published in three volumes by Chapman & Hall in 1880.

The manuscript with its corrections and cuts is in the Beinecke Rare Book and Manuscript Library at Yale University; it has not been published in its original form. In *Trollope's Palliser Novels* (1978), Juliet MacMaster gives several examples of the kinds of cuts which Trollope made. These included, for instance, a lengthy reference to Alice Vavasor (the heroine of *Can You Forgive Her?* and now Mrs. Grey) originally intended 'presumably to remind his readers of the close connection between the two novels' (MacMaster, p. 229). A passage about the Duke's suspicions of Madame Max (Mrs. Finn) is cut: 'She had been in some degree mysterious, and in the same degree, objectionable.' The first description of Tregear in Chapter III originally included, in connection with Tregear's rejection of a number of professions, these three sentences: 'He did not, he said, like the duplicity. He did not, in truth, like the labour. He liked to be a gentleman at large.' A comment on Silverbridge's defection to the Conservatives is cut from Chapter VII: 'No doubt the conservative party would like it, and in order to seduce from his allegiance the heir of the Duke of Omnium would take care that arrangements should be made so that the family borough of Silverbridge should help him to his apostasy.' Chauncy B. Tinker, in his introduction to the *Oxford Trollope* edition of the novel in 1973, comments on the 'smooth movement' with which Trollope eradicated evidence of the many cuts he had made: 'the published book betrays no signs of this.'

The present edition follows that first published under the general editorship of Michael Sadleir and Frederick Page in 1954 as part of *The Oxford Trollope* series, and reissued in 1973.

SELECT BIBLIOGRAPHY

Trollope's *Autobiography* (1883) is an essential companion to *The Duke's Children*. In general, the student of Trollope still needs to read Michael Sadleir's *Trollope: A Commentary* (1927), and will find *Trollope: The Critical Heritage* (1969), edited by Donald Smalley, of great interest. For *The Duke's Children* in particular, John Halperin's *Trollope and Politics* (1977) and Juliet MacMaster's *Trollope's Palliser Novels* (1978) provide useful material and commentary. Ruth Ap Roberts's *Trollope: Artist and Moralist* (1971) is excellent on the relation of Trollope's ideas to Cicero's, and Shirley Robin Letwin's *The Gentleman in Trollope: Individuality and Moral Conduct* (1982) is a useful study. There are helpful sections on *The Duke's Children* in Robert Tracy's *Trollope's Later Novels* (1978), James Kincaid's *The Novels of Anthony Trollope* (1977) (which deals very well with the 'different kinds of language' in the novel) and in P. D. Edwards's *Anthony Trollope: His Art and Scope* (1978), who writes sensibly about the novel's political references.

Henry James's essay ('Anthony Trollope', 1883, reprinted in *Partial Portraits*, 1888) is essential reading; Asa Briggs's 'Trollope, Bagehot, and the English Constitution' (in *Victorian People*, 1955) is the best essay on Trollope's political beliefs. All essays on *The Duke's Children* owe a debt to John Hagan's '*The Duke's Children*: Trollope's psychological masterpiece' (*Nineteenth Century Fiction*, 13, 1958–9, pp. 1–21). John Halperin's 'Trollope, James, and the International Theme' (*Yearbook of English Studies*, 7, January 1977, pp. 141–7) parallels his treatment of *The Duke's Children* in his book; other less persuasive articles on the same theme are George Butte's 'Ambivalence and Affirmation in *The Duke's Children*' (*Studies in English Literature*, 17, Autumn 1977, pp. 709–27) and 'The Two Isabels: A Study in Distortion' by Blair Gates Kenney (*Victorian Newsletter*, 25, 1964, pp. 15–17). There is a good essay by George Watson on 'Trollope's Forms of Address', *Critical Quarterly*, 15, 1973, pp. 219–230, and an excellent account of Trollope's developing treatment of Palliser in Stephen Wall's Introduction to the Penguin *Can You Forgive Her?* (1972).

A CHRONOLOGY OF
ANTHONY TROLLOPE

Virtually all Trollope's fiction appeared first in serial form, with book production timed to coincide with the final instalment of the serial. In this chronology the titles are dated as on the title-page of the first book edition. On a very few occasions the book edition appeared in December of the year previous to that indicated on the title-page, so as to catch the Christmas sales.

1815   (24 Apr.) Born at 6 Keppel Street, Bloomsbury, the fourth son of Thomas and Frances Trollope.

1822   To Harrow as a day-boy.

1825   To a private school at Sunbury.

1827   To school at Winchester.

1830   Removed from Winchester and returned to Harrow.

1834   The family move to Bruges.
       (Autumn) He accepts a junior clerkship in the General Post Office.

1841   (Aug.) Deputy Postal Surveyor at Banagher, King's County, Ireland.

1843   (Autumn) Begins work on his first novel, *The Macdermots of Ballycloran*.

1844   (11 June) Marries Rose Heseltine.
       Transferred to Clonmel, County Tipperary.

1845   Promoted to the office of Surveyor, and transferred to Mallow, County Cork.

1845–7   Famine and epidemic throughout Ireland, especially the south and west with which Trollope was familiar.

1847   *The Macdermots of Ballycloran*, published in 3 vols. (Newby).

1848   Rebellion in Ireland, concentrated in Cork and Tipperary. *The Kellys and the O'Kellys; or Landlords and Tenants* 3 vols. (Colburn).

1850   Writes *The Noble Jilt* (published 1923).
       La Vendée; an Historical Romance 3 vols. (Colburn).

1851   Transferred to England.

1853   Returns to Ireland; completes *The Warden* (the first of the Barsetshire novels) in Belfast.

1854   (Autumn) Leaves Belfast and settles outside Dublin at Donnybrook.

1855   *The Warden* 1 vol. (Longman).

1857   *Barchester Towers* 3 vols. (Longman).
        (Sept.) Visits his mother in Florence.

1858   *Doctor Thorne* 3 vols. (Chapman & Hall).
        The Three Clerks 3 vols. (Bentley).
        (Feb.) Departs for Egypt on Post Office business.
        (Mar.) Removes from Egypt to Palestine.
        (Apr.–May) Returns via Malta, Gibraltar and Spain.
        (May–July) Visits Scotland and north of England on business.
        (Aug.–Oct.) At home in Ireland.
        (Nov.) On Post Office business in the West Indies.

1859   *The Bertrams* 3 vols. (Chapman & Hall).
        The West Indies and the Spanish Main 1 vol. (Chapman & Hall).
        (Sept.) Holiday in the Pyrenees.
        (Dec.) Leaves Ireland; settles at Waltham Cross.

1860   *Castle Richmond* 3 vols. (Chapman & Hall).
        (Oct.) With his wife he visits his mother and brother in Florence; makes the acquaintance of Kate Field, a beautiful twenty-year-old American with whom he falls in love.

1861   *Framley Parsonage* 3 vols. (Smith, Elder).
        Tales of All Countries—first series, 1 vol. (Chapman & Hall).
        (Spring) Elected a member of the Garrick Club; some two years later is elected to the committee to fill the vacancy caused by Thackeray's death.
        (Aug.) To America on official business.

1862   *Orley Farm* 2 vols. (Chapman & Hall).
        North America 2 vols. (Chapman & Hall).
        The Struggles of Brown, Jones and Robinson; by One of the Firm 1 vol. (New York, Harper—an American piracy).
        (Spring) Returns home from America.

1863   *Rachel Ray* 2 vols. (Chapman & Hall).
        Tales of All Countries—second series 1 vol. (Chapman & Hall).
        (6 Oct.) Death of his mother, Mrs. Frances Trollope.
        (Dec.) Death of W. M. Thackeray.

1864   *The Small House at Allington* 2 vols. (Smith, Elder).
        Can You Forgive Her? 2 vols. (Chapman & Hall).
        (Summer) Elected a member of the Athenaeum Club.

1865   *Miss Mackenzie* 1 vol. (Chapman & Hall).
        Hunting Sketches 1 vol. (Chapman & Hall).

1866   *The Belton Estate* 3 vols. (Chapman & Hall).

Travelling Sketches 1 vol. (Chapman & Hall).
Clergymen of the Church of England 1 vol. (Chapman & Hall).

1867   *Nina Balatka* 2 vols. (Blackwood).
The Last Chronicle of Barset 2 vols. (Smith, Elder).
The Claverings 2 vols. (Smith, Elder).
Lotta Schmidt and Other Stories 1 vol. (Strahan).
(1 Sept.) Resigns from the Civil Service.

1868   *Linda Tressel* 2 vols. (Blackwood).
(Mar.) Leaves London for the United States on business involving
copyright, in touch again with Kate Field.
(July) Returns from America.
(Nov.) Stands unsuccessfully as Liberal candidate for Beverley,
Yorkshire, losing £2,000 in the enterprise.

1869   *Phineas Finn; the Irish Member* 2 vols. (Virtue & Co.).
He Knew He was Right 2 vols. (Strahan).
Did He Steal It? A Comedy in Three Acts—a version of *The Last Chronicle of
Barset* 1 vol. (printed by Virtue & Co.).

1870   *The Vicar of Bullhampton* 1 vol. (Bradbury, Evans).
An Editor's Tales 1 vol. (Strahan).
The Commentaries of Caesar 1 vol. (Blackwood).

1871   *Sir Harry Hotspur of Humblethwaite* 1 vol. (Hurst & Blackett).
Ralph the Heir 3 vols. (Hurst & Blackett).
(Apr.) Gives up house at Waltham Cross.
(May) Sails to Australia to visit his son.
(20 July) Arrives at Melbourne.

1872   *The Golden Lion of Granpere* 1 vol. (Tinsley).
(Jan.–Oct.) Travelling in Australia and New Zealand.
(Apr.) A dramatized (and pirated) version of *Ralph the Heir* produced
by Charles Reade.
(Dec.) Returns via the United States, and settles in Montagu Square,
London.

1873   *The Eustace Diamonds* 3 vols. (Chapman & Hall).
Australia and New Zealand 2 vols. (Chapman & Hall).
(Winter) Hunting actively.

1874   *Phineas Redux* 2 vols. (Chapman & Hall).
Lady Anna 2 vols. (Chapman & Hall).
Harry Heathcote of Gangoil; a Tale of Australian Bush Life 1 vol. (Samp-
son Low).

1875   *The Way We Live Now* 2 vols. (Chapman & Hall).
(Feb.) Travels to Ceylon via Brindisi and the Suez Canal, once again
on the way to Australia.
(Mar.–Apr.) In Ceylon.

(June) Arrives in Australia.
(Aug.–Oct.) Sailing homewards.
(Oct.) Begins work on his *Autobiography*.

1876   *The Prime Minister* 4 vols. (Chapman & Hall).

1877   *The American Senator* 3 vols. (Chapman & Hall).
Christmas at Thompson Hall 1 vol. (New York, Harper)
(June) Leaves London for South Africa.
(Dec.) Sails for home.

1878   *Is He Popenjoy?* 3 vols. (Chapman & Hall).
South Africa 2 vols. (Chapman & Hall).
How the 'Mastiffs' Went to Iceland 1 vol. (Virtue & Co.).
(June–July) Travels to Iceland in the yacht 'Mastiff'.

1879   *An Eye for an Eye* 2 vols. (Chapman & Hall).
John Caldigate 3 vols. (Chapman & Hall).
Cousin Henry 2 vols. (Chapman & Hall).
Thackeray 1 vol. (Macmillan).

1880   *The Duke's Children* 3 vols. (Chapman & Hall).
(July) Settles at Harting Grange, near Petersfield.

1881   *Dr. Wortle's School* 2 vols. (Chapman & Hall).
Ayala's Angel 3 vols. (Chapman & Hall).

1882   *Why Frau Frohmann Raised Her Prices; and Other Stories* 1 vol. (Isbister).
Kept in the Dark 2 vols. (Chatto & Windus).
Marion Fay 3 vols. (Chapman & Hall).
The Fixed Period 2 vols. (Blackwood).
Palmerston 1 vol. (Isbister).
(May) Visits Ireland to collect material for a new Irish novel.
(Aug.) Returns to Ireland a second time.
(Sept.) Moves to London for the winter.
(6 Dec.) Dies in London.

1883   *Mr. Scarborough's Family* 3 vols. (Chatto & Windus).
The Landleaguers (unfinished) 3 vols. (Chatto & Windus).
An Autobiography 2 vols. (Blackwood).

1884   *An Old Man's Love* 2 vols. (Blackwood).

1923   *The Noble Jilt* (a play) 1 vol. (Constable).

1927   *London Tradesmen* 1 vol. (Elkin Mathews).

1972   *The New Zealander* 1 vol. (Oxford University Press.)

CONTENTS

CONTENTS

CONTENTS

CONTENTS

CHAPTER I

When the Duchess was Dead

No one, probably, ever felt himself to be more alone in the world than our old friend,*the Duke of Omnium, when the Duchess died. When this sad event happened he had ceased to be Prime Minister. During the first nine months after he had left office he and the Duchess remained in England. Then they had gone abroad, taking with them their three children. The eldest, Lord Silverbridge, had been at Oxford, but had had his career there cut short by some more than ordinary youthful folly, which had induced his father to agree with the college authorities that his name had better be taken off the college books,—all which had been cause of very great sorrow to the Duke. The other boy was to go to Cambridge; but his father had thought it well to give him a twelvemonth's run on the Continent, under his own inspection. Lady Mary, the only daughter,*was the youngest of the family, and she also had been with them on the Continent. They remained the full year abroad, travelling with a large accompaniment of tutors, lady's-maids, couriers, and sometimes friends. I do not know that the Duchess or the Duke had enjoyed it much; but the young people had seen something of foreign courts and much of foreign scenery, and had perhaps perfected their French. The Duke had gone to work at his travels with a full determination to create for himself occupation out of a new kind of life. He had studied Dante, and had striven to arouse himself to ecstatic joy amidst the loveliness of the Italian lakes.* But through it all he had been aware that he had failed. The Duchess had made no such resolution,—had hardly, perhaps, made any attempt; but, in truth, they had both sighed to be back among the war-trumpets. They had both suffered much among the trumpets, and yet they longed to return. He told himself from day to day, that though he had been banished* from the House of Commons, still, as a peer, he had a seat in Parliament; and that, though he was no longer a minister,

1

still he might be useful as a legislator. She, in her career as a leader of fashion, had no doubt met with some trouble,— with some trouble but with no disgrace; and as she had been carried about among the lakes and mountains, among the pictures and statues, among the counts and countesses, she had often felt that there was no happiness except in that dominion which circumstances had enabled her to achieve once, and might enable her to achieve again—in the realms of London society.

Then, in the early spring of 187–,*they came back to England, having persistently carried out their project, at any rate in regard to time. Lord Gerald, the younger son, was at once sent up to Trinity. For the eldest son a seat was to be found in the House of Commons, and the fact that a dissolution of Parliament was expected served to prevent any prolonged sojourn abroad. Lady Mary Palliser was at that time nineteen, and her entrance into the world was to be her mother's great care and great delight. In March they spent a few days in London, and then went down to Matching Priory.*When she left town the Duchess was complaining of cold, sore throat, and debility. A week after their arrival at Matching she was dead.

Had the heavens fallen and mixed themselves with the earth, had the people of London risen in rebellion with French ideas of equality, had the Queen persistently declined to comply with the constitutional advice of her ministers, had a majority in the House of Commons lost its influence in the country,—the utter prostration of the bereft husband could not have been more complete. It was not only that his heart was torn to pieces, but that he did not know how to look out into the world. It was as though a man should be suddenly called upon to live without hands or even arms. He was helpless, and knew himself to be helpless. Hitherto he had never specially acknowledged to himself that his wife was necessary to him as a component part of his life. Though he had loved her dearly, and had in all things consulted her welfare and happiness, he had at times been inclined to think that in the

2

exuberance of her spirits she had been a trouble rather than a support to him. But now it was as though all outside appliances were taken away from him. There was no one of whom he could ask a question.

For it may be said of this man that, though throughout his life he had had many Honourable and Right Honourable friends, and that though he had entertained guests by the score, and though he had achieved for himself the respect of all good men and the thorough admiration of some few who knew him, he had hardly made for himself a single intimate friend—except that one who had now passed away from him. To her he had been able to say what he thought, even though she would occasionally ridicule him while he was declaring his feelings. But there had been no other human soul to whom he could open himself. There were one or two whom he loved, and perhaps liked; but his loving and his liking had been exclusively political. He had so habituated himself to devote his mind and his heart to the service of his country, that he had almost risen above or sunk below humanity. But she, who had been essentially human, had been a link between him and the world.

There were his three children, the youngest of whom was now nearly nineteen, and they surely were links! At the first moment of his bereavement they were felt to be hardly more than burdens. A more loving father there was not in England, but nature had made him so undemonstrative that as yet they had hardly known his love. In all their joys and in all their troubles, in all their desires and all their disappointments, they had ever gone to their mother. She had been conversant with everything about them, from the boys' bills and the girl's gloves to the innermost turn in the heart and the disposition of each. She had known with the utmost accuracy the nature of the scrapes into which Lord Silverbridge had precipitated himself, and had known also how probable it was that Lord Gerald would do the same. The results of such scrapes she, of course, deplored; and therefore she would give good counsel, pointing out how imperative it was that such evildoings

3

should be avoided; but with the spirit that produced the scrapes she fully sympathised. The father disliked the spirit almost worse than the results; and was therefore often irritated and unhappy.

And the difficulties about the girl were almost worse to bear than those about the boys. She had done nothing wrong. She had given no signs of extravagance or other juvenile misconduct. But she was beautiful and young. How was he to bring her out into the world? How was he to decide whom she should or whom she should not marry? How was he to guide her through the shoals and rocks which lay in the path of such a girl before she can achieve matrimony?

It was the fate of the family that, with a world of acouaintance, they had not many friends. From all close connection with relatives on the side of the Duchess they had been dissevered by old feelings at first, and afterwards by want of any similitude in the habits of life. She had, when young, been repressed by male and female guardians*with an iron hand. Such repression had been needed, and had been perhaps salutary, but it had not left behind it much affection. And then her nearest relatives were not sympathetic with the Duke. He could obtain no assistance in the care of his girl from that source. Nor could he even do it from his own cousins' wives, who were his nearest connections on the side of the Pallisers. They were women to whom he had ever been kind, but to whom he had never opened his heart. When, in the midst of the stunning sorrow of the first week, he tried to think of all this, it seemed to him that there was nobody.

There had been one lady, a very dear ally, staying in the house with them when the Duchess died. This was Mrs. Finn,* the wife of Phineas Finn, who had been one of the Duke's colleagues when in office. How it had come to pass that Mrs. Finn and the Duchess had become singularly bound together has been told elsewhere. But there had been close bonds,— so close that when the Duchess on their return from the Continent had passed through London on her way to Matching, ill at the time and very comfortless, it had been almost a thing

4

of course, that Mrs. Finn should go with her. And as she had
sunk, and then despaired, and then died, it was this woman
who had always been at her side, who had ministered to her,
and had listened to the fears and the wishes and hopes she had
expressed respecting the children.

At Matching, amidst the ruins of the old Priory,*there is
a parish burying-ground, and there, in accordance with her
own wish, almost within sight of her own bedroom-window,
she was buried. On the day of the funeral a dozen relatives
came, Pallisers and M'Closkies,*who on such an occasion were
bound to show themselves, as members of the family. With
them and his two sons the Duke walked across to the grave-
yard, and then walked back; but even to those who stayed the
night at the house he hardly spoke. By noon on the following
day they had all left him, and the only stranger in the house
was Mrs. Finn.

On the afternoon of the day after the funeral the Duke and
his guest met, almost for the first time since the sad event.
There had been just a pressure of the hand, just a glance of
compassion, just some murmur of deep sorrow,—but there
had been no real speech between them. Now he had sent for
her, and she went down to him in the room in which he
commonly sat at work. He was seated at his table when she
entered, but there was no book open before him, and no pen
ready to his hand. He was dressed of course in black. That,
indeed, was usual with him, but now the tailor by his funereal
art had added some deeper dye of blackness to his appearance.
When he rose and turned to her she thought that he had at
once become an old man. His hair was grey in parts, and he
had never accustomed himself to use that skill in managing
his outside person by which many men are able to preserve
for themselves a look, if not of youth, at any rate of freshness.
He was thin, of an adust complexion, and had acquired a habit
of stooping which, when he was not excited, gave him an
appearance of age. All that was common to him: but now it
was so much exaggerated that he who was not yet fifty might
have been taken to be over sixty.

He put out his hand to greet her as she came up to him. 'Silverbridge,' he said, 'tells me that you go back to London to-morrow.'

'I thought it would be best, Duke. My presence here can be of no comfort to you.'

'I will not say that anything can be of comfort. But of course it is right that you should go. I can have no excuse for asking you to remain. While there was yet a hope for her——' Then he stopped, unable to say a word further in that direction, and yet there was no sign of a tear and no sound of a sob.

'Of course I would stay, Duke, if I could be of any service.'

'Mr. Finn will expect you to return to him.'

'Perhaps it would be better that I should say that I would stay were it not that I know that I can be of no real service.'

'What do you mean by that, Mrs. Finn?'

'Lady Mary should have with her at such a time some other friend.'

'There was none other whom her mother loved as she loved you—none, none.' This he said almost with energy.

'There was no one lately, Duke, with whom circumstances caused her mother to be so closely intimate. But even that perhaps was unfortunate.'

'I never thought so.'

'That is a great compliment. But as to Lady Mary, will it not be as well that she should have with her, as soon as possible, someone,—perhaps someone of her own kindred if it be possible, or, if not that, at least one of her own kind?'

'Who is there? Whom do you mean?'

'I mean no one. It is hard, Duke, to say what I do mean, but perhaps I had better try. There will be,—probably there have been,—some among your friends who have regretted the great intimacy which chance produced between me and my lost friend. While she was with us no such feeling would have sufficed to drive me from her. She had chosen for herself, and if others disapproved her choice that was nothing to me. But as regards Lady Mary, it will be better, I think, that from the beginning she should be taught to look for friendship and

6

guidance to those—to those who are more naturally connected with her.'

'I was not thinking of any guidance,' said the Duke.

'Of course not. But with one so young, where there is intimacy there will be guidance. There should be somebody with her. It was almost the last thought that occupied her mother's mind. I could not tell her, Duke, but I can tell you, that I cannot with advantage to your girl be that somebody.'

'Cora wished it.'

'Her wishes, probably, were sudden and hardly fixed.'

'Who should it be, then?' asked the father, after a pause.

'Who am I, Duke, that I should answer such a question?'

After that there was another pause, and then the conference was ended by a request from the Duke that Mrs. Finn would stay at Matching for yet two days longer. At dinner they all met,—the father, the three children, and Mrs. Finn. How far the young people among themselves had been able to throw off something of the gloom of death need not here be asked; but in the presence of their father they were sad and sombre, almost as he was. On the next day, early in the morning, the younger lad returned to his college, and Lord Silverbridge went up to London, where he was supposed to have his home.

'Perhaps you would not mind reading these letters,' the Duke said to Mrs. Finn, when she again went to him, in compliance with a message from him asking for her presence. Then she sat down and read two letters, one from Lady Cantrip,* and the other from a Mrs. Jeffrey Palliser,*each of which contained an invitation for his daughter, and expressed a hope that Lady Mary would not be unwilling to spend some time with the writer. Lady Cantrip's letter was long, and went minutely into circumstances. If Lady Mary would come to her, she would abstain from having other company in the house till her young friend's spirits should have somewhat recovered themselves. Nothing could be more kind, or proposed in a sweeter fashion. There had, however, been present to the Duke's mind as he read it a feeling that a proposition to a bereaved husband to relieve him of the society of an only daughter, was not one which would usually be made to a father. In such a position a child's company would probably be his best solace. But he knew,—at this moment he painfully remembered,—that he was not as are other men. He acknowledged the truth of this, but he was not the less grieved and irritated by the reminder. The letter from Mrs. Jeffrey Palliser was to the same effect, but was much shorter. If it would suit Mary to come to them for a month or six weeks at their place in Gloucestershire, they would both be delighted.

'I should not choose her to go there,' said the Duke, as Mrs. Finn refolded the latter letter. 'My cousin's wife is a very good woman, but Mary would not be happy with her.'

'Lady Cantrip is an excellent friend for her.'

'Excellent. I know no one whom I esteem more than Lady Cantrip.'

'Would you wish her to go there, Duke?'

There came a wistful piteous look over the father's face. Why should he be treated as no other father would be treated? Why should it be supposed that he would desire to send his girl away from him? But yet he felt that it would be better that she should go. It was his present purpose to remain at Matching through a portion of the summer. What could he do to make a girl happy? What comfort would there be in his companionship?

'I suppose she ought to go somewhere,' he said.

'I had not thought of it,' said Mrs. Finn.

'I understood you to say,' replied the Duke, almost angrily, 'that she ought to go to someone who would take care of her.'

'I was thinking of some friend coming to her.'

'Who would come? Who is there that I could possibly ask? You will not stay.'

'I certainly would stay, if it were for her good. I was thinking, Duke, that perhaps you might ask the Greys*to come to you.'

'They would not come,' he said, after a pause.

'When *she* was told that it was for her sake, she would come, I think.'

8

Then there was another pause. 'I could not ask them,' he said; 'for his sake I could not have it put to her in that way. Perhaps Mary had better go to Lady Cantrip. Perhaps I had better be alone here for a time. I do not think that I am fit to have any human being here with me in my sorrow.'

CHAPTER II
Lady Mary Palliser

IT may as well be said at once that Mrs. Finn knew something of Lady Mary which was not known to the father, and which she was not yet prepared to make known to him. The last winter abroad had been passed at Rome, and there Lady Mary Palliser had become acquainted with a certain Mr. Tregear,—Francis Oliphant Tregear. The Duchess, who had been in constant correspondence with her friend, had asked questions by letter as to Mr. Tregear, of whom she had only known that he was the younger son of a Cornish gentleman, who had become Lord Silverbridge's friend at Oxford. In this there had certainly been but little to recommend him to the intimacy of such a girl as Lady Mary Palliser. Nor had the Duchess, when writing, ever spoken of him as a probable suitor for her daughter's hand. She had never connected the two names together. But Mrs. Finn had been clever enough to perceive that the Duchess had become fond of Mr. Tregear, and would willingly have heard something to his advantage. And she did hear something to his advantage,— something also to his disadvantage. At his mother's death this young man would inherit a property amounting to about fifteen hundred a year.*'And I am told,' said Mrs. Finn, 'that he is quite likely to spend his money before it comes to him.' There had been nothing more written specially about Mr. Tregear; but Mrs. Finn had feared not only that the young man loved the girl, but that the young man's love had in some imprudent way been fostered by the mother.

Then there had been some fitful confidence during those

9

few days of acute illness. Why should not the girl have the man if he were lovable? And the Duchess referred to her own early days*when she had loved, and to the great ruin which had come upon her heart when she had been severed from the man she had loved. 'Not but that it has been all for the best,' she had said. 'Not but that Plantagenet has been to me all that a husband should be. Only if she can be spared what I suffered, let her be spared.' Even when these things had been said to her, Mrs. Finn had found herself unable to ask questions. She could not bring herself to inquire whether the girl had in truth given her heart to this young Tregear. The one was nineteen and the other as yet but two-and-twenty! But though she asked no questions she almost knew that it must be so. And she knew also that the father, as yet, was quite in the dark on the matter. How was it possible that in such circumstances she should assume the part of the girl's confidential friend and monitress? Were she to do so she must immediately tell the father everything. In such a position no one could be a better friend than Lady Cantrip, and Mrs. Finn had already almost made up her mind that, should Lady Cantrip occupy the place, she would tell her ladyship all that had passed between herself and the Duchess on the subject.

Of what hopes she might have, or what fears, about her girl, the Duchess had said no word to her husband. But when she had believed that the things of the world were fading away from her, and when he was sitting by her bedside,— dumb, because at such a moment he knew not how to express the tenderness of his heart,—holding her hand, and trying so to listen to her words, that he might collect and remember every wish, she had murmured something about the ultimate division of the great wealth*with which she herself had been endowed. 'She had never,' she said, 'even tried to remember what arrangements had been made by lawyers, but she hoped that Mary might be so circumstanced, that if her happiness depended on marrying a poor man, want of money need not prevent it.' The Duke suspecting nothing, believing this to be a not unnatural expression of maternal interest, had assured her that Mary's fortune would be ample.

Mrs. Finn made the proposition to Lady Mary in respect to Lady Cantrip's invitation. Lady Mary was very like her mother, especially in having exactly her mother's tone of voice, her quick manner of speech, and her sharp intelligence. She had also her mother's eyes, large and round, and almost blue, full of life and full of courage, eyes which never seemed to quail, and her mother's dark brown hair, never long but very copious in its thickness. She was, however, taller than her mother, and very much more graceful in her movement. And she could already assume a personal dignity of manner which had never been within her mother's reach. She had become aware of a certain brusqueness of speech in her mother, a certain aptitude to say sharp things without thinking whether the sharpness was becoming to the position which she held, and, taking advantage of the example, the girl had already learned that she might gain more than she would lose by controlling her words.

'Papa wants me to go to Lady Cantrip,' she said.

'I think he would like it,—just for the present, Lady Mary.'

Though there had been the closest possible intimacy between the Duchess and Mrs. Finn, this had hardly been so as to the intercourse between Mrs. Finn and the children. Of Mrs. Finn it must be acknowledged that she was, perhaps fastidiously, afraid of appearing to take advantage of her friendship with the Duke's family. She would tell herself that though circumstances had compelled her to be the closest and nearest friend of a Duchess, still her natural place was not among dukes and their children, and therefore in her intercourse with the girl she did not at first assume the manner and bearing which her position in the house would have seemed to warrant. Hence the 'Lady Mary.'

'Why does he want to send me away, Mrs. Finn?'

'It is not that he wants to send you away, but that he thinks it will be better for you to be with some friend. Here you must be so much alone.'

11

'Why don't you stay? But I suppose Mr. Finn wants you to be back in London.'

'It is not that only, or, to speak the truth, not that at all. Mr. Finn could come here if it were suitable. Or for a week or two he might do very well without me. But there are other reasons. There is no one whom your mother respected more highly than Lady Cantrip.'

'I never heard her speak a word of Lady Cantrip.'

'Both he and she are your father's intimate friends.'

'Does papa want to be—alone here?'

'It is you, not himself, of whom he is thinking.'

'Therefore I must think of him, Mrs. Finn. I do not wish him to be alone. I am sure it would be better that I should stay with him.'

'He feels that it would not be well that you should live without the companionship of some lady.'

'Then let him find some lady. You would be the best, because he knows you so well. I, however, am not afraid of being alone. I am sure he ought not to be here quite by himself. If he bids me go, I must go, and then of course I shall go where he sends me; but I won't say that I think it best that I should go, and certainly I do not want to go to Lady Cantrip.' This she said with great decision, as though the matter was one on which she had altogether made up her mind. Then she added, in a lower voice: 'Why doesn't papa speak to me about it?'

'He is thinking only of what may be best for you.'

'It would be best for me to stay near him. Whom else has he got?'

All this Mrs. Finn repeated to the Duke as closely as she could, and then of course the father was obliged to speak to his daughter.

'Don't send me away, papa,' she said at once.

'Your life here, Mary, will be inexpressibly sad.'

'It must be sad anywhere. I cannot go to college, like Gerald, or live anywhere just as I please, like Silverbridge.'

'Do you envy them that?'

12

'Sometimes, papa. Only I shall think more of poor mamma by being alone, and I should like to be thinking of her always.' He shook his head mournfully. 'I do not mean that I shall always be unhappy, as I am now.'

'No, my dear; you are too young for that. It is only the old who suffer in that way.'

'You will suffer less if I am with you; won't you, papa? I do not want to go to Lady Cantrip. I hardly remember her at all.'

'She is very good.'

'Oh yes. That is what they used to say to mamma about Lady Midlothian.*Papa, pray do not send me to Lady Cantrip.'

Of course it was decided that she should not go to Lady Cantrip at once, or to Mrs. Jeffrey Palliser, and, after a short interval of doubt, it was decided also that Mrs. Finn should remain at Matching for at least a fortnight. The Duke declared that he would be glad to see Mr. Finn, but she knew that in his present mood the society of any one man to whom he would feel himself called upon to devote his time, would be a burden to him, and she plainly said that Mr. Finn had better not come to Matching at present. 'There are old associations,' she said, 'which will enable you to bear with me as you will with your butler or your groom, but you are not as yet quite able to make yourself happy with company.' This he bore with perfect equanimity, and then, as it were, handed over his daughter to Mrs. Finn's care.

Very quickly there came to be close intimacy between Mrs. Finn and Lady Mary. For a day or two the elder woman, though the place she filled was one of absolute confidence, rather resisted than encouraged the intimacy. She always remembered that the girl was the daughter of a great duke, and that her position in the house had sprung from circumstances which would not, perhaps, in the eyes of the world at large, have recommended her for such friendship. She knew— the reader may possibly know*—that nothing had ever been purer, nothing more disinterested than her friendship. But she knew also,—no one knew better,—that the judgment of men and women does not always run parallel with facts. She entertained, too, a conviction in regard to herself, that hard words and hard judgments were to be expected from the world,—were to be accepted by her without any strong feeling of injustice,—because she had been elevated by chance to the possession of more good things than she had merited. She weighed all this with a very fine balance, and even after the encouragement she had received from the Duke, was intent on confining herself to some position about the girl inferior to that which such a friend as Lady Cantrip might have occupied. But the girl's manner, and the girl's speech about her own mother, overcame her. It was the unintentional revelation of the Duchess's constant reference to her,—the way in which Lady Mary would assert that 'Mamma used always to say this of you; mamma always knew that you would think so and so; mamma used to say that you had told her.' It was the feeling thus conveyed, that the mother who was now dead had in her daily dealings with her own child spoken of her as her nearest friend, which mainly served to conquer the deference of manner which she had assumed.

Then gradually there came confidences,—and at last absolute confidence. The whole story about Mr. Tregear was told. Yes; she loved Mr. Tregear. She had given him her heart, and had told him so.

'Then, my dear, your father ought to know it,' said Mrs. Finn.

'No; not yet. Mamma knew it.'

'Did she know all that you have told me?'

'Yes; all. And Mr. Tregear spoke to her, and she said that papa ought not to be told quite yet.'

Mrs. Finn could not but remember that the friend she had lost was not, among women, the one best able to give a girl good counsel in such a crisis.

'Why not yet, dear?'

'Well, because——. It is very hard to explain. In the first place, because Mr. Tregear himself does not wish it.'

'That is a very bad reason; the worst in the world.'

'Of course you will say so. Of course everybody would sa,

14

so. But when there is one person whom one loves better than all the rest, for whom one would be ready to die, to whom one is determined that everything shall be devoted, surely the wishes of a person so dear as that ought to have weight.'

'Not in persuading you to do that which is acknowledged to be wrong.'

What wrong? I am going to do nothing wrong.'

'The very concealment of your love is wrong, after that love has not only given but declared. A girl's position in such matters is so delicate, especially that of such a girl as you!'

'I know all about that,' said Lady Mary, with something almost approaching to scorn in her tone. 'Of course I have to be——delicate. I don't quite know what the word means. I am not a bit ashamed of being in love with Mr. Tregear. He is a gentleman, highly educated, very clever, of an old family, —older, I believe, than papa's. And he is manly and handsome; just what a young man ought to be. Only he is not rich.'

'If he be all that you say, ought you not to trust your papa? If he approve of it, he could give you money.'

'Of course he must be told; but not now. He is nearly broken-hearted about dear mamma. He could not bring himself to care about anything of that kind at present. And then it is Mr. Tregear that should speak to him first.'

'Not now, Mary.'

'How do you mean not now?'

'If you had a mother you would talk to her about it.'

'Mamma knew.'

'If she were still living she would tell your father.'

'But she didn't tell him though she did know. She didn't mean to tell him quite yet. She wanted to see Mr. Tregear here in England first. Of course I shall do nothing till papa does know.'

'You will not see him?'

'How can I see him here? He will not come here, if you mean that.'

'You do not correspond with him?' Here for the first time

15

the girl blushed. 'Oh, Mary, if you are writing to him your father ought to know it.'

'I have not written to him; but when he heard how ill poor mamma was, then he wrote to me—twice. You may see his letters. It is all about her. No one worshipped mamma as he did.'

Gradually the whole story was told. These two young persons considered themselves to be engaged, but had agreed that their engagement should not be made known to the Duke till something had occurred, or some time had arrived, as to which Mr. Tregear was to be the judge. In Mrs. Finn's opinion nothing could be more unwise, and she said much to induce the girl to confess everything to her father at once. But in all her arguments she was opposed by the girl's reference to her mother. 'Mamma knew it.' And it did certainly seem to Mrs. Finn as though the mother had assented to this imprudent concealment. When she endeavoured, in her own mind, to make excuse for her friend, she felt almost sure that the Duchess, with all her courage, had been afraid to propose to her husband that their daughter should marry a commoner without an income. But in thinking of all that, there could now be nothing gained. What ought she to do—at once? The girl, in telling her, had exacted no promise of secrecy, nor would she have given any such promise; but yet she did not like the idea of telling the tale behind the girl's back. It was evident that Lady Mary had considered herself to be safe in confiding her story to her mother's old friend. Lady Mary no doubt had had her confidences with her mother,—confidences from which it had been intended by both that the father should be excluded; and now she seemed naturally to expect that this new ally should look at this great question as her mother had looked at it. The father had been regarded as a great outside power, which could hardly be overcome, but which might be evaded, or made inoperative by stratagem. It was not that the daughter did not love him. She loved him and venerated him highly,—the veneration perhaps being stronger than the love. The Duchess, too, had loved him dearly,—more dearly in late years than in her early life. But her husband to her had

16

always been an outside power which had in many cases to be evaded. Lady Mary, though she did not express all this, evidently thought that in this new friend she had found a woman whose wishes and aspirations for her would be those which her mother had entertained.

But Mrs. Finn was much troubled in her mind, thinking that it was her duty to tell the story to the Duke. It was not only the daughter who had trusted her, but the father also; and the father's confidence had been not only the first but by far the holier of the two. And the question was one so important to the girl's future happiness! There could be no doubt that the peril of her present position was very great.

'Mary,' she said one morning, when the fortnight was nearly at an end, 'your father ought to know all this. I should feel that I had betrayed him were I to go away leaving him in ignorance.'

'You do not mean to say that you will tell?' said the girl, horrified at the idea of such treachery.

'I wish that I could induce you to do so. Every day that he is kept in the dark is an injury to you.'

'I am doing nothing. What harm can come? It is not as though I were seeing him every day.'

'This harm will come; your father of course will know that you became engaged to Mr. Tregear in Italy, and that a fact so important to him has been kept back from him.'

'If there is anything in that, the evil has been done already. Of course poor mamma did mean to tell him.'

'She cannot tell him now, and therefore you ought to do what she would have done.'

'I cannot break my promise to him.' 'Him' always meant Mr. Tregear. 'I have told him that I would not do so till I had his consent, and I will not.'

This was very dreadful to Mrs. Finn, and yet she was most unwilling to take upon herself the part of a stern elder, and declare that under the circumstances she must tell the tale. The story had been told to her under the supposition that she was not a stern elder, that she was regarded as the special

17

friend of the dear mother who was gone, that she might be trusted to assist against the terrible weight of parental authority. She could not endure to be regarded at once as a traitor by this young friend who had sweetly inherited the affection with which the Duchess had regarded her. And yet if she were to be silent how could she forgive herself? 'The Duke certainly ought to know at once,' said she, repeating her words merely that she might gain some time for thinking, and pluck up courage to declare her purpose, should she resolve on betraying the secret.

'If you tell him now, I will never forgive you,' said Lady Mary.

'I am bound in honour to see that your father knows a thing which is of such vital importance to him and to you. Having heard all this I have no right to keep it from him. If Mr. Tregear really loves you'—Lady Mary smiled at the doubt implied by this suggestion—'he ought to feel that for your sake there should be no secret from your father.' Then she paused a moment to think. 'Will you let me see Mr. Tregear myself, and talk to him about it?'

To this Lady Mary at first demurred, but when she found that in no other way could she prevent Mrs. Finn from going at once to the Duke and telling him everything, she consented. Under Mrs. Finn's directions she wrote a note to her lover, which Mrs. Finn saw, and then undertook to send it, with a letter from herself, to Mr. Tregear's address in London. The note was very short, and was indeed dictated by the elder lady, with some dispute, however, as to certain terms, in which the younger lady had her way. It was as follows:

'DEAREST FRANK,

'I wish you to see Mrs. Finn, who, as you know, was dear mamma's most particular friend. Please go to her, as she will ask you to do. When you hear what she says I think you ought to do what she advises.

'Yours for ever and always,
'M. P.'

This Mrs. Finn sent enclosed in an envelope, with a few words from herself, asking the gentleman to call upon her in Park Lane, on a day and at an hour fixed.

CHAPTER III

Francis Oliphant Tregear

Mr. FRANCIS OLIPHANT TREGEAR was a young man who might not improbably make a figure in the world, should circumstances be kind to him, but as to whom it might be doubted whether circumstances would be sufficiently kind to enable him to use serviceably his unquestionable talents and great personal gifts. He had taught himself to regard himself as a young English gentleman of the first water, qualified by his birth and position to live with all that was most noble and most elegant; and he could have lived in that sphere naturally and gracefully were it not that the part of the 'sphere' which he specially affected requires wealth as well as birth and intellect. Wealth he had not, and yet he did not abandon the sphere. As a consequence of all this, it was possible that the predictions of his friends as to that figure which he was to make in the world might be disappointed.

He had been educated at Eton, from whence he had been sent to Christ Church; and both at school and at college had been the most intimate friend of the son and heir of a great and wealthy duke. He and Lord Silverbridge had been always together, and they who were interested in the career of the young nobleman had generally thought he had chosen his friend well. Tregear had gone out in honours,* having been a second-class man. His friend Silverbridge, we know, had been allowed to take no degree at all; but the terrible practical joke by which the whole front of the Dean's house had been coloured scarlet in the middle of the night, had been carried on without any assistance from Tregear. The two young men had then been separated for a year; but immediately after taking his degree, Tregear, at the invitation of Lord Silverbridge, had gone to Italy, and had there completely made good his footing with the Duchess,—with what effect on another member of the Palliser family the reader already knows.

The young man was certainly clever. When the Duchess found that he could talk without any shyness, that he could speak French fluently, and that after a month in Italy he could chatter Italian, at any rate without reticence or shame: when she perceived that all the women liked the lad's society and impudence, and that all the young men were anxious to know him, she was glad to find that Silverbridge had chosen so valuable a friend. And then he was beautiful to look at,— putting her almost in mind of another man*on whom her eyes had once loved to dwell. He was dark, with hair that was almost black, but yet was not black; with clear brown eyes, a nose as regular as Apollo's, and a mouth in which was ever to be found that expression of manliness, which of all characteristics is the one which women love the best. He was five feet ten in height. He was always well dressed, and yet always so dressed as to seem to show that his outside garniture had not been matter of trouble to him. Before the Duchess had dreamed what might take place between this young man and her daughter she had been urgent in her congratulations to her son as to the possession of such a friend.

For though she now and then would catch a glimpse of the outer man, which would remind her of that other beautiful one whom she had known in her youth, and though, as these glimpses came, she would remember how poor in spirit and how unmanly that other one had been, though she would confess to herself how terrible had been the heart-shipwreck which that other one had brought upon herself; still she was able completely to assure herself that this man, though not superior in external grace, was altogether different in mind and character. She was old enough now to see all this and to appreciate it. Young Tregear had his own ideas about the politics of the day, and they were ideas with which she sympathised, though they were antagonistic to the politics of her life. He had his ideas about books too, as to manners of life, as to art, and even ethics. Whether or no in all this there was not much that was superficial only, she was not herself deep enough to discover. Nor would she have been deterred from admiring him had she been told that it was tinsel. Such were the acquirements, such the charms, that she loved. Here was a young man who dared to speak, and had always something ready to be spoken; who was not afraid of beauty, nor daunted by superiority of rank; who, if he had not money, could carry himself on equal terms among those who had. In this way he won the Duchess's heart, and having done that, was it odd that he should win the heart of the daughter also?

His father was a Cornwall squire of comfortable means, having joined the property of his wife to his own for the period of his own life. She had possessed land also in Cornwall, supposed to be worth fifteen hundred a year, and his own paternal estate at Polwenning was said to be double that value. Being a prudent man, he lived at home as a country gentleman, and thus was able in his county to hold his head as high as richer men. But Frank Tregear was only his second son; and though Frank would hereafter inherit his mother's fortune, he was by no means now in a position to assume the right of living as an idle man. Yet he was idle. The elder brother, who was considerably older than Frank, was an odd man, much addicted to quarrelling with his family, and who spent his time chiefly in travelling about the world. Frank's mother, who was not the mother of the heir also, would sometimes surmise, in Frank's hearing, that the entire property must ultimately come to him. That other Tregear, who was now supposed to be investigating the mountains of Crim Tartary,*would surely never marry. And Frank was the favourite also with his father, who paid his debts at Oxford with not much grumbling; who was proud of his friendship with a future duke; who did not urge, as he ought to have urged, that vital question of a profession; and who, when he allowed his son four hundred pounds a year, was almost content with that son's protestations that he knew how to live as a poor man among rich men, without chagrin and without trouble.

Such was the young man who now, in lieu of a profession, had taken upon himself the responsibility of an engagement with Lady Mary Palliser. He was tolerably certain that, should he be able to overcome the parental obstacles which he would no doubt find in his path, money would be forthcoming sufficient for the purposes of matrimonial life. The Duke's wealth was fabulous, and as a great part of it, if not the greater, had come from his wife, there would probably be ample provision for the younger children. And when the Duchess had found out how things were going, and had yielded to her daughter, after an opposition which never had the appearance even of being in earnest, she had taken upon herself to say that she would use her influence to prevent any great weight of trouble from pecuniary matters. Frank Tregear, young and bright, and full of hearty ambitions, was certainly not the man to pursue a girl simply because of her fortune; nor was he weak enough to be attracted simply by the glitter of rank; but he was wise enough with worldly wisdom to understand thoroughly the comforts of a good income, and he was sufficiently attached to high position to feel the advantage of marrying a daughter of the Duke of Omnium.

When the Duchess was leaving Italy, it had been her declared purpose to tell her husband the story as soon as they were at home in England. And it was on this understanding that Frank Tregear had explained to the girl that he would not as yet ask her father for his permission to be received into the family as a suitor. Everyone concerned had felt that the Duke would not easily be reconciled to such a son-in-law, and that the Duchess should be the one to bell the cat.*

There was one member of the family who had hitherto been half-hearted in the matter. Lord Silverbridge had vacillated between loyalty to his friend and a certain feeling as to the impropriety of such a match for his sister. He was aware that something very much better should be expected for her, and still was unable to explain his objections to Tregear. He had not at first been admitted into confidence, either by his sister or by Tregear, but had questioned his friend when he saw what was going on. 'Certainly I love your sister,' Tregear had said; 'do you object?' Lord Silverbridge was the weaker of the two, and much subject to the influence of his friend; but he could on occasion be firm, and he did at first object. But he did not object strongly, and allowed himself at last to be content with declaring that the Duke would never give his consent.

While Tregear was with his love, or near her, his hopes and fears were sufficient to occupy his mind; and immediately on his return, all the world was nothing to him, except as far as the world was concerned with Lady Mary Palliser. He had come back to England somewhat before the ducal party, and the pleasures and occupations of London life had not abated his love, but enabled him to feel that there was something in life over and beyond his love; whereas to Lady Mary, down at Matching, there had been nothing over and beyond her love—except the infinite grief and desolation produced by her mother's death.

Tregear, when he received the note from Mrs. Finn, was staying at the Duke's house in Carlton Terrace. Silverbridge was there, and, on leaving Matching, had asked the Duke's permission to have his friend with him. The Duke at that time was not well pleased with his son as to a matter of politics, and gave his son's friend credit for the evil counsel which had produced this displeasure. But still he had not refused his assent to this proposition. Had he done so, Silverbridge would probably have gone elsewhere; and though there was a matter in respect to Tregear of which the Duke disapproved, it was not a matter, as he thought, which would have justified him in expelling the young man from his house. The young man was a strong Conservative; and now Silverbridge had declared his purpose of entering the House of Commons, if he did enter it, as one of the Conservative party.*

This had been a terrible blow to the Duke; and he believed that it all came from this young Tregear. Still he must do his duty, and not more than his duty. He knew nothing against Tregear. That a Tregear should be a Conservative was perhaps natural enough—at any rate, was not disgraceful; that he should have his political creed sufficiently at heart to be able to persuade another man, was to his credit. He was a gentleman, well educated, superior in many things to Silverbridge himself. There were those who said that Silverbridge had redeemed himself from contempt—from that sort of contempt which might be supposed to await a young nobleman who had painted scarlet the residence of the Head of his college—by the fact of his having chosen such a friend. The Duke was essentially a just man; and though, at the very moment in which the request was made, his heart was half crushed by his son's apostasy, he gave the permission asked.

'You know Mrs. Finn?' Tregear said to his friend one morning at breakfast.

'I remember her all my life. She used to be a great deal with my grandfather.* I believe he left her a lot of diamonds and money, and that she wouldn't have them. I don't know whether the diamonds are not locked up somewhere now, so that she can take them when she pleases.'

'What a singular woman!'

'It was odd; but she had some fad about it. What makes you ask about Mrs. Finn?'

'She wants me to go and see her.'

'What about?'

'I think I have heard your mother speak of her as though she loved her dearly,' said Tregear.

'I don't know about loving her dearly. They were intimate, and Mrs. Finn used to be with her very much when she was in the country. She was at Matching just now, when my poor mother died. Why does she want to see you?'

'She has written to me from Matching. She wants to see me——'

'Well?'

'To tell you the truth, I do not know what she has to say to me; though I can guess.'

24

'What do you guess?'

'It is something about your sister.'

'You will have to give that up, Tregear.'

'I think not.'

'Yes, you will; my father will never stand it.'

'I don't know what there is to stand. I am not noble, nor am I rich; but I am as good a gentleman as he is.'

'My dear fellow,' said the young lord, 'you know very well what I think about all that. A fellow is not any better to me because he has got a title, nor yet because he owns half a county. But men have their ideas and feelings about it. My father is a rich man, and of course he'll want his daughter to marry a rich man. My father is noble, and he'll want his daughter to marry a nobleman. You can't very well marry Mary without his permission, and therefore you had better let it alone.'

'I haven't even asked his permission as yet.'

'Even my mother was afraid to speak to him about it, and I never knew her to be afraid to say anything else to him.'

'I shall not be afraid,' said Tregear, looking grimly.

'I should. That's the difference between us.'

'He can't very well eat me.'

'Nor even bite you;—nor will he abuse you. But he can look at you, and he can say a word or two which you will find it very hard to bear. My governor is the quietest man I know, but he has a way of making himself disagreeable when he wishes, that I never saw equalled.'

'At any rate, I had better go and see your Mrs. Finn.' Then Tregear wrote a line to Mrs. Finn, and made his appointment.

CHAPTER IV

Park Lane

From the beginning of the affair Tregear had found the necessity of bolstering himself up inwardly in his great attempt by mottoes, proverbs, and instigations to courage addressed to himself. 'None but the brave deserve the fair.'* 'De l'audace, et encore de l'audace, et toujours de l'audace.'* He was a man naturally of good heart in such matters, who was not afraid of his brother-men, nor yet of women, his sisters. But in this affair he knew very much persistence would be required of him, and that even with such persistence he might probably fail, unless he should find a more than ordinary constancy in the girl. That the Duke could not eat him, indeed that nobody could eat him as long as he carried himself as an honest man and a gentleman, was to him an inward assurance on which he leaned much. And yet he was conscious, almost with a feeling of shame, that in Italy he had not spoken to the Duke about his daughter because he was afraid lest the

26

Duke might eat him. In such an affair he should have been careful from the first to keep his own hands thoroughly clean. Had it not been his duty as a gentleman to communicate with the father, if not before he gained the girl's heart, at any rate as soon as he knew he had done so? He had left Italy thinking that he would certainly meet the Duchess and her daughter in London, and that then he might go to the Duke as though this love of his had arisen from the sweetness of those meetings in London. But all these ideas had been dissipated by the great misfortune of the death of Lady Mary's mother. From all this he was driven to acknowledge to himself that his silence in Italy had been wrong, that he had been weak in allowing himself to be guided by the counsel of the Duchess, and that he had already armed the Duke with one strong argument against him.

He did not doubt but that Mrs. Finn would be opposed to him. Of course he could not doubt but that all the world would now be opposed to him,—except the girl herself. He would find no other friend so generous, so romantic, so unworldly as the Duchess had been. It was clear to him that Lady Mary had told the story of her engagement to Mrs. Finn, and that Mrs. Finn had not as yet told it to the Duke. From this he was justified in regarding Mrs. Finn as the girl's friend. The request made was that he should at once do something which Mrs. Finn was to suggest. He could hardly have been so requested, and that in terms of such warm affection, had it been Mrs. Finn's intention to ask him to desist altogether from his courtship. This woman was regarded by Lady Mary as her mother's dearest friend. It was therefore incumbent on him now to induce her to believe in him as the Duchess had believed.

He knocked at the door of Mrs. Finn's little house in Park Lane a few minutes before the time appointed, and found himself alone when he was shown into the drawing-room. He had heard much of this lady though he had never seen her, and had heard much also of her husband. There had been a kind of mystery about her. People did not quite understand

27

how it was that she had been so intimate with the Duchess, nor why the late Duke had left to her an enormous legacy,* which as yet had never been claimed. There was supposed, too, to have been something especially romantic in her marriage with her present husband. It was believed also that she was very rich. The rumours of all these things together had made her a person of note, and Tregear, when he found himself alone in the drawing-room, looked round about him as though a special interest was to be attached to the belongings of such a woman. It was a pretty room, somewhat dark, because the curtains were almost closed across the windows, but furnished with a pretty taste, and now, in these early April days, filled with flowers.

'I have to apologise, Mr. Tregear, for keeping you waiting,' she said as she entered the room.

'I fear I was before my time.'

'I know that I am after mine,—a few minutes,' said the lady.

He told himself that though she was not a young woman, yet she was attractive. She was dark, and still wore her black hair in curls, such as are now seldom seen with ladies. Perhaps the reduced light of the chamber had been regulated with some regard to her complexion and to her age. The effect, however, was good, and Frank Tregear felt at once interested in her.

'You have just come up from Matching?' he said.

'Yes; only the day before yesterday. It is very good of you to come to me so soon.'

'Of course I came when you sent for me. I am afraid the Duke felt his loss severely.'

'How should he not, such a loss as it was? Few people knew how much he trusted her, and how dearly he loved her.'

'Silverbridge has told me that he is awfully cut up.'

'You have seen Lord Silverbridge then?'

'Just at present I am living with him, at Carlton Terrace.'

'In the Duke's house?' she asked, with some surprise.

'Yes; in the Duke's house. Silverbridge and I have been very intimate. Of course the Duke knows that I am there. Is there any chance of his coming to town?'

'Not yet, I fear. He is determined to be alone. I wish it were otherwise, as I am sure he would better bear his sorrow, if he would go about among other men.'

'No doubt he would suffer less,' said Tregear. Then there was a pause. Each wished that the other should introduce the matter which both knew was to be the subject of their conversation. But Tregear would not begin. 'When I left them all at Florence,' he said, 'I little thought that I should never see her again.'

'You had been intimate with them, Mr. Tregear?'

'Yes; I think I may say I have been intimate with them. I had been at Eton and at Christ Church with Silverbridge, and we have always been much together.'

'I have understood that. Have you and the Duke been good friends?'

'We have never been enemies.'

'I suppose not that.'

'The Duke, I think, does not much care about young people. I hardly know what he used to do with himself. When I dined with them, I saw him, but I did not often do that. I think he used to read a good deal, and walk about alone. We were always riding.'

'Lady Mary used to ride?'

'Oh yes; and Lord Silverbridge and Lord Gerald. And the Duchess used to drive. One of us would always be with her.'

'And so you became intimate with the whole family?'

'So I became intimate with the whole family.'

'And especially so with Lady Mary?' This she said in her sweetest possible tone, and with a most gracious smile.

'Especially so with Lady Mary,' he replied.

'It will be very good of you, Mr. Tregear, if you endure and forgive all this cross-questioning from me, who am a perfect stranger to you.'

'But you are not a perfect stranger to her.'

'That is it, of course. Now, if you will allow me, I will explain to you exactly what my footing with her is. When the Duchess returned, and when I found her to be so ill as she

29

passed through London, I went down with her into the country,—quite as a matter of course.'

'So I understand.'

'And there she died,—in my arms. I will not try to harass you by telling you what those few days were; how absolutely he was struck to the ground, how terrible was the grief of the daughter, how the boys were astonished by the feeling of their loss. After a few days they went away. It was, I think, their father's wish that they should go. And I too was going away, —and had felt, indeed, directly her spirit had parted from her, that I was only in the way in his house. But I stayed at his request, because he did not wish his daughter to be alone.'

'I can easily understand that, Mrs. Finn.'

'I wanted her to go to Lady Cantrip who had invited her, but she would not. In that way we were thrown together in the closest intercourse, for two or three weeks. Then she told me the story of your engagement.'

'That was natural, I suppose.'

'Surely so. Think of her position, left as she is without a mother! It was incumbent on her to tell someone. There was, however, one other person in whom it would have been much better that she should have confided.'

'What person?'

'Her father.'

'I rather fancy that it is I who ought to tell him.'

'As far as I understand these things, Mr. Tregear,— which, indeed, is very imperfectly,—I think it is natural that a girl should at once tell her mother when a gentleman has made her understand that he loves her.'

'She did so, Mrs. Finn.'

'And I suppose that generally the mother would tell the father.'

'She did not.'

'No; and therefore the position of the young lady is now one of great embarrassment. The Duchess has gone from us, and we must now make up our minds as to what had better be done. It is out of the question that Lady Mary should be allowed to consider herself to be engaged, and that the father should be kept in ignorance of her position.' She paused for his reply, but as he said nothing, she continued: 'Either you must tell the Duke, or she must do so, or I must do so.'

'I suppose she told you in confidence.'

'No doubt. She told it me presuming that I would not betray her; but I shall,—if that be a betrayal. The Duke must know it. It will be infinitely better that he should know it through you, or through her, than through me. But he must be told.'

'I can't quite see why,' said Tregear.

'For her sake,—whom I suppose you love.'

'Certainly I love her.'

'In order that she may not suffer. I wonder you do not see it, Mr. Tregear. Perhaps you have a sister.'

'I have no sister as it happens.'

'But you can imagine what your feelings would be. Should you like to think of a sister as being engaged to a man without the knowledge of any of her family?'

'It was not so. The Duchess knew it. The present condition of things is altogether an accident.'

'It is an accident that must be brought to an end.'

'Of course it must be brought to an end. I am not such a fool as to suppose that I can make her my wife without telling her father.'

'I mean at once, Mr. Tregear.'

'It seems to me that you are rather dictating to me, Mrs. Finn.'

'I owe you an apology, of course, for meddling in your affairs at all. But as it will be more conducive to your success that the Duke should hear this from you than from me, and as I feel that I am bound by my duty to him and to Lady Mary to see that he be not left in ignorance, I think that I am doing you a service.'

'I do not like to have a constraint put upon me.'

'That, Mr. Tregear, is what gentlemen, I fancy, very often feel in regard to ladies. But the constraint of which you speak

31

is necessary for their protection. Are you unwilling to see the Duke?'

He was very unwilling, but he would not confess so much. He gave various reasons for delay, urging repeatedly that the question of his marriage was one which he could not press upon the Duke so soon after the death of the Duchess. And when she assured him that this was a matter of importance so great, that even the death of the man's wife should not be held by him to justify delay, he became angry, and for awhile insisted that he must be allowed to follow his own judgment. But he gave her a promise that he would see the Duke before a week was over. Nevertheless he left the house in dudgeon, having told Mrs. Finn more than once that she was taking advantage of Lady Mary's confidence. They hardly parted as friends, and her feeling was, on the whole, hostile to him and to his love. It could not, she thought, be for the happiness of such a one as Lady Mary that she should give herself to one who seemed to have so little to recommend him.

He, when he had left her, was angry with his own weakness. He had not only promised that he would make his application to the Duke, but that he would do so within the period of a week. Who was she that she should exact terms from him after this fashion, and prescribe days and hours? And now, because this strange woman had spoken to him, he was compelled to make a journey down to the Duke's country house, and seek an interview in which he would surely be snubbed!

This occurred on a Wednesday, and he resolved that he would go down to Matching on the next Monday. He said nothing of his plan to anyone, and not a word passed between him and Lord Silverbridge about Lady Mary during the first two or three days. But on the Saturday Silverbridge appeared at breakfast with a letter in his hand. 'The governor is coming up to town,' he said.

'Immediately?'

'In the course of next week. He says that he thinks he shall be here on Wednesday.'

It immediately struck Tregear that this sudden journey must have some reference to Lady Mary and her engagement. 'Do you know why he is coming?'

'Because of these vacancies in Parliament.'

'Why should that bring him up?'

'I suppose he hopes to be able to talk me into obedience. He wants me to stand for the county*—as a Liberal, of course. I intend to stand for the borough as a Conservative, and I have told them so down at Silverbridge. I am very sorry to annoy him, and all that kind of thing. But what the deuce is a fellow to do? If a man has got political convictions of his own, of course, he must stick to them.' This the young Lord said with a good deal of self-assurance, as though he, by the light of his own reason, had ascertained on which side the truth lay in political contests of the day.

'There is a good deal to be said on both sides of the question, my boy.' At this particular moment Tregear felt that the Duke ought to be propitiated.

'You wouldn't have me give up my convictions!'

'A seat in Parliament is a great thing.'

'I can probably secure that, whichever side I take. I thought you were so devilish hot against the Radicals.'*

'So I am. But then you are, as it were, bound by family allegiance.'

'I'll be shot if I am. One never knows how to understand you nowadays. It used to be a great doctrine with you, that nothing should induce a man to vote against his political opinions.'

'So it is,—if he has really got any. However, as your father is coming to London, I need not go down to Matching.'

'You don't mean to say that you were going to Matching.'

'I had intended to beard the lion in his country den; but now the lion will find me in his own town den, and I must beard him here.'

Then Tregear wrote a most chilling note to Mrs. Finn, informing her with great precision, that, as the Duke of

Omnium intended to be in town one day next week, he would postpone the performance of his promise for a day or two beyond the allotted time.

CHAPTER V

'It is impossible'

Down at Matching Lady Mary's life was very dull after Mrs. Finn had left her. She had a horse to ride, but had no one to ride with her. She had a carriage in which to be driven, but no one to be driven with her, and no special places whither to go. Her father would walk daily for two hours, and she would accompany him when he encouraged her to do so; but she had an idea that he preferred taking his walks alone, and when they were together there was no feeling of confidence between them. There could be none on her part, as she knew that she was keeping back information which he was entitled to possess. On this matter she received two letters from Mrs. Finn, in the first of which she was told that Mr. Tregear intended to present himself at Matching within a few days, and was advised in the same letter not to endeavour to see her lover on that occasion; and then, in the second she was informed that this interview with her father was to be sought not at Matching but in London. From this latter letter there was of course some disappointment, though some feeling of relief. Had he come there she might possibly have seen him after the interview. But she would have been subjected to the immediate sternness of her father's anger. That she would now escape. She would not be called on to meet him just when the first blow had fallen upon him. She was quite sure that he would disapprove of the thing. She was quite sure that he would be very angry. She knew that he was a peculiarly just man, and yet she thought that in this he would be unjust. Had she been called upon to sing the praises of her father she would have insisted above all things on the absolute integrity of his mind, and yet, knowing as she did that he would be opposed to her marriage with Mr. Tregear, she assured herself every day and every hour that he had no right to make any such objection. The man she loved was a gentleman, and an honest man, by no means a fool, and subject to no vices. Her father had no right to demand that she should give her heart to a rich man, or to one of high rank. Rank! As for rank, she told herself that she had the most supreme contempt for it. She thought that she had seen it near enough already to be sure that it ought to have no special allurements. What was it doing for her? Simply restraining her choice among comparatively a few who seemed to her by no means the best endowed of God's creatures.

Of one thing she was very sure, that under no pressure whatsoever would she abandon her engagement with Mr. Tregear. That to her had become a bond almost as holy as matrimony itself could be. She had told the man that she loved him, and after that there could be no retreat. He had kissed her, and she had returned his caress. He had told her that she was his, as his arm was round her; and she had acknowledged that it was so, that she belonged to him, and could not be taken away from him. All this was to her a compact so sacred that nothing could break it but a desire on his part to have it annulled. No other man had ever whispered a word of love to her, of no other man had an idea entered her mind that it could be pleasant to join her lot in life with his. With her it had been all new and all sacred. Love with her had that religion which nothing but freshness can give it. That freshness, that bloom, may last through a long life. But every change impairs it, and after many changes it has perished for ever. There was no question with her but that she must bear her father's anger, should he be angry; put up with his continued opposition, should he resolutely oppose her; bear all that the countesses of the world might say to her; —for it was thus that she thought of Lady Cantrip now. Any retrogression was beyond her power.

She was walking with her father when she first heard of his intended visit to London. At that time she had received

Mrs. Finn's first letter, but not the second. 'I suppose you'll see Silverbridge,' she said. She knew then that Frank Tregear was living with her brother.

'I am going up on purpose to see him. He is causing me much annoyance.'

'Is he extravagant?'

'It is not that—at present.' He winced even as he said this, for he had in truth suffered somewhat from demands made upon him for money, which had hurt him not so much by their amount as by their nature. Lord Silverbridge had taken upon himself to 'own a horse or two,' very much to his father's chagrin, and was at this moment part pro-prietor of an animal supposed to stand well for the Derby. The fact was not announced in the papers with his lordship's name, but his father was aware of it, and did not like it the better because his son held the horse in partnership with a certain Major Tifto, who was well known in the sporting world.

'What is it, papa?'

'Of course he ought to go into Parliament.'

'I think he wishes it himself.'

'Yes, but how? By a piece of extreme good fortune, West Barsetshire is open to him. The two seats are vacant together. There is hardly another agricultural county in England that will return a Liberal, and I fear I am not asserting too much in saying that no other Liberal could carry the seat but one of our family.'

'You used to sit for Silverbridge, papa.'

'Yes, I did. In those days the county returned four Con-servatives. I cannot explain it all to you, but it is his duty to contest the county on the Liberal side.'

'But if he is a Conservative himself, papa?' asked Lady Mary, who had had some political ideas suggested to her own mind by her lover.

'It is all rubbish. It has come from that young man Tregear, with whom he has been associating.'

'But, papa,' said Lady Mary, who felt that even in this

matter she was bound to be firm on what was now her side of the question, 'I suppose it is as—as—as respectable to be a Conservative as a Liberal.'

'I don't know that at all,' said the Duke angrily.

'I thought that—the two sides were——'

She was going to express an opinion that the two parties might be supposed to stand as equal in the respect of the country, when he interrupted her. 'The Pallisers have always been Liberal. It will be a blow to me, indeed, if Silverbridge deserts his colours. I know that as yet he himself has had no deep thoughts on the subject, that unfortunately he does not give himself much to thinking, and that in this matter he is being talked over by a young man whose position in life has hardly justified the great intimacy which has existed.'

This was very far from being comfortable to her, but of course she said nothing in defence of Tregear's politics. Nor at present was she disposed to say anything as to his position in life, though at some future time she might not be so silent. A few days later they were again walking together, when he spoke to her about herself. 'I cannot bear that you should be left here alone while I am away,' he said.

'You will not be long gone, I suppose?'

'Only for three or four days now.'

'I shall not mind that, papa.'

'But very probably I may have to go into Barsetshire. Would you not be happier if you would let me write to Lady Cantrip, and tell her that you will go to her?'

'No, papa, I think not. There are times when one feels that one ought to be almost alone. Don't you feel that?'

'I do not wish you to feel it, nor would you do so long if you had other people around you. With me it is different. I am an old man, and cannot look for new pleasures in society. It has been the fault of my life to be too much alone. I do not want to see my children follow me in that.'

'It is so very short a time as yet,' said she, thinking of her mother's death.

'But I think that you should be with somebody,—with some woman who would be kind to you. I like to see you with books, but books alone should not be sufficient at your age.' How little, she thought, did he know of the state either of her heart or mind! 'Do you dislike Lady Cantrip?'

'I do not know her. I can't say that I dislike a person whom I don't think I ever spoke to, and never saw above once or twice. But how can I say that I like her?' She did, however, know that Lady Cantrip was a countess all over, and would be shocked at the idea of a daughter of a Duke of Omnium marrying the younger son of a country squire. Nothing further was then said on the matter, and when the Duke went to town Lady Mary was left quite alone; with an understanding that if he went into Barsetshire he should come back and take her with him.

He arrived at his own house in Carlton Terrace about five o'clock in the afternoon, and immediately went to his study, intending to dine and spend the evening there alone. His son had already pleaded an engagement for that afternoon, but had consented to devote the following morning to his father's wishes. Of the other sojourner in his house the Duke had thought nothing; but the other sojourner had thought very much of the Duke. Frank Tregear was fully possessed of that courage which induces a man who knows that he must be thrown over a precipice, to choose the first possible moment for his fall. He had sounded Silverbridge about this change in his politics, and had found his friend quite determined not to go back to the family doctrine. Such being the case, the Duke's ill-will and hardness and general severity would probably be enhanced by his interview with his son. Tregear, therefore, thinking that nothing could be got by delay, sent his name in to the Duke before he had been an hour in the house, and asked for an interview. The servant brought back word that his Grace was fatigued, but would see Mr. Tregear if the matter in question was one of importance. Frank's heart quailed for a moment, but only for a moment. He took up a pen and wrote a note.

'My dear Duke of Omnium,

'If your Grace can spare a moment, I think you will find that what I have to say will justify the intrusion.

'Your very faithful servant,

'F. O. Tregear.'

Of course the Duke admitted him. There was but one idea in his head as to what was coming. His son had taken this way of making some communication to him respecting his political creed. Some overture or some demand was to be preferred through Tregear. If so, it was proof of a certain anxiety as to the matter on his son's part which was not displeasing to him. But he was not left long in this mistake after Tregear had entered the room. 'Sir,' he said, speaking quite at once, as soon as the door was closed behind him, but still speaking very slowly, looking beautiful as Apollo as he stood upright before his wished-for father-in-law—'Sir, I have come to you to ask you to give me the hand of your daughter.' The few words had been all arranged beforehand, and were now spoken without any appearance of fear or shame. No one hearing them would have imagined that an almost penniless young gentleman was asking in marriage the daughter of the richest and greatest nobleman in England.

'The hand of my daughter!' said the Duke, rising from his chair.

'I know how very great is the prize,' said Frank, 'and how unworthy I am of it. But—as she thinks me worthy——'

'She! What she?'

'Lady Mary.'

'She think you worthy!'

'Yes, your Grace.'

'I do not believe it.' On hearing this, Frank simply bowed his head. 'I beg your pardon, Mr. Tregear. I do not mean to say that I do not believe you. I never yet gave the lie to a gentleman, and I hope I never may be driven to do so. But there must be some mistake in this.'

'I am complying with Lady Mary's wishes in asking your

permission to enter your house as her suitor.' The Duke stood for a moment biting his lips in silence. 'I cannot believe it,' he said at last. 'I cannot bring myself to believe it. There must be some mistake. My daughter! Lady Mary Palliser!' Again the young man bowed his head. 'What are your pretensions?'

'Simply her regard.'

'Of course it is impossible. You are not so ignorant but that you must have known as much when you came to me.'

There was so much scorn in his words, and in the tone in which they were uttered, that Tregear in his turn was becoming angry. He had prepared himself to bow humbly before the great man, before the Duke, before the Crœsus,*before the late Prime Minister, before the man who was to be regarded as certainly one of the most exalted of the earth; but he had not prepared himself to be looked at as the Duke looked at him. 'The truth, my Lord Duke, is this,' he said, 'that your daughter loves me, and that we are engaged to each other,— as far as that engagement can be made without your sanction as her father.'

'It cannot have been made at all,' said the Duke.

'I can only hope,—we can both of us only hope that a little time may soften——'

'It is out of the question. There must be an end of this altogether. You must neither see her, nor hear from her, nor in any way communicate with her. It is altogether impossible. I believe, sir, that you have no means?'

'Very little at present, Duke.'

'How did you think you were to live? But it is altogether unnecessary to speak of such a matter as that. There are so many reasons to make this impossible, that it would be useless to discuss one as being more important than others. Has any other one of my family known of this?' This he added, wishing to ascertain whether Lord Silverbridge had disgraced himself by lending his hand to such a disposition of his sister.

'Oh yes,' said Tregear.

40

'Who has known it?'

'The Duchess, sir. We had all her sympathy and approval.'

'I do not believe a word of it,' said the Duke, becoming extremely red in the face. He was forced to do now that which he had just declared that he had never done in his life,—driven by the desire of his heart to acquit the wife he had lost of the terrible imprudence, worse than imprudence, of which she was now accused.

'That is the second time, my Lord, that you have found it necessary to tell me that you have not believed direct assertions which I made you. But, luckily for me, the two assertions are capable of the earliest and most direct proof. You will believe Lady Mary, and she will confirm me in the one and the other.'

The Duke was almost beside himself with emotion and grief. He did know,—though now at this moment he was most loath to own to himself that it was so,—that his dear wife had been the most imprudent of women. And he recognised in her encouragement of this most pernicious courtship, —if she had encouraged it,—a repetition of that romantic folly by which she had so nearly brought herself to shipwreck in her own early life. If it had been so,—even whether it had been so or not,—he had been wrong to tell the man that he did not believe him. And the man had rebuked him with dignity. 'At any rate it is impossible,' he repeated.

'I cannot allow that it is impossible.'

'That is for me to judge, sir.'

'I trust that you will excuse me when I say that I also must hold myself to be in some degree a judge in the matter. If you were in my place, you would feel——'

'I could not possibly be in your place.'

'If your Grace were in my place you would feel that as long as you were assured by the young lady that your affection was valued by her you would not be deterred by the opposition of her father. That you should yield to me, of course I do not expect; that Lady Mary should be persistent in her present feelings, when she knows your mind, perhaps I have no right to hope; but should she be so persistent as to make you feel that her happiness depends, as mine does, on our marriage, then I shall believe that you will yield at last.'

'Never!' said the Duke. 'Never! I shall never believe that my daughter's happiness can be assured by a step which I should regard as disgraceful to her.'

'Disgraceful is a violent word, my Lord.'

'It is the only word that will express my meaning.'

'And one which I must be bold enough to say you are not justified in using. Should she become my wife to-morrow, no one in England would think she had disgraced herself. The Queen would receive her on her marriage. All your friends would hold out their hands to us,—presuming that we had your goodwill.'

'But you would not have it.'

'Her disgrace would not depend upon that, my Lord. Should your daughter so dispose of herself, as to disgrace herself,—which I think to be impossible,—your countenance could not set her right. Nor can the withdrawal of your countenance condemn her before the world if she does that with herself which any other lady might do and remain a lady.'

The Duke, when he heard this, even in the midst of his wrath, which was very violent, and in the midst of his anger, which was very acute, felt that he had to deal with a man,— with one whom he could not put off from him into the gutter, and there leave as buried in the mud. And there came, too, a feeling upon him, which he had no time to analyse, but of which he was part aware, that this terrible indiscretion on the part of his daughter and of his late wife was less wonderful than it had at first appeared to be. But not on that account was he the less determined to make the young man feel that his parental opposition would be invincible.

'It is quite impossible, sir. I do not think that I need say anything more.' Then, while Tregear was meditating whether to make any reply, the Duke asked a question which had better have been left unasked. The asking of it diminished somewhat from that ducal, grand-ducal, quasi-archducal, almost godlike superiority which he had assumed, and showed the curiosity of a mere man. 'Has anybody else been aware of this?' he said, still wishing to know whether he had cause for anger against Silverbridge in the matter.

'Mrs. Finn is aware of it,' answered Tregear.

'Mrs. Finn!' exclaimed the Duke, as though he had been stung by an adder.

This was the woman whom he had prayed to remain awhile with his daughter after his wife had been laid in her grave, in order that there might be someone near whom he could trust! And this very woman whom he had so trusted,—whom, in his early associations with her, he had disliked and distrusted, but had taught himself both to like and to trust because his wife had loved her,—this woman was the she-Pandarus*who had managed matters between Tregear and his daughter! His wife had been too much subject to her influence. That he had always known. And now, in this last act of her life, she had allowed herself to be persuaded to give up her daughter by the baneful wiles of this most pernicious woman. Such were the workings of the Duke's mind when the young man told him that Mrs. Finn was acquainted with the whole affair. As the reader is aware, nothing could have been more unjust.

'I mentioned her name,' said Tregear, 'because I thought she had been a friend of the family.'

'That will do, sir. I have been greatly pained as well as surprised by what I have heard. Of the real state of the case I can form no opinion till I see my daughter. You, of course, will hold no further intercourse with her.' He paused as though for a promise, but Tregear did not feel himself called upon to say a word in one direction or in the other. 'It will be my care that you shall not do so. Good-morning, sir.'

Tregear, who during the interview had been standing, then bowed, turned upon his heel, and left the room.

The Duke seated himself, and, crossing his arms upon his chest, sat for an hour looking up at the ceiling. Why was it that, for him, such a world of misery had been prepared? What wrong had he done, of what imprudence had he been guilty, that, at every turn of life, something should occur so grievous as to make him think himself the most wretched of men? No man had ever loved his wife more dearly than he had done; and yet now, in that very excess of tenderness which her death had occasioned, he was driven to accuse her of a great sin against himself, in that she had kept from him her knowledge of this affair;—for, when he came to turn the matter over in his mind, he did believe Tregear's statement as to her encouragement. Then, too, he had been proud of his daughter. He was a man so reticent and undemonstrative in his manner that he had never known how to make confidential friends of his children. In his sons hitherto he had not taken pride. They were gallant, well-grown, handsome boys, with a certain dash of cleverness,—more like their mother than their father; but they had not as yet done anything as he would have had them do it. But the girl, in the perfection of her beauty, in the quiescence of her manner, in the nature of her studies, and in the general dignity of her bearing, had seemed to be all that he had desired. And now she had engaged herself, behind his back, to the younger son of a little county squire!

But his anger against Mrs. Finn was hotter than his anger against anyone in his own family.

CHAPTER VI

Major Tifto

MAJOR TIFTO had lately become a member of the Beargarden Club,* under the· auspices of his friend Lord Silverbridge. It was believed, by those who had made some inquiry into the matter, that the Major had really served a campaign as a volunteer in the Carlist army*in the north of Spain. When, therefore, it was declared by someone that he was not a major at all, his friends were able to contradict the assertion, and to impute it to slander. Instances were brought up,—declared by these friends to be innumerable, but which did, in truth, amount to three or four,—of English gentlemen who had come home from a former Carlist war, bearing the title of colonel, without any contradiction or invidious remark. Had this gallant officer appeared as Colonel Tifto, perhaps less might have been said about it. There was a little lack of courage in the title which he did choose. But it was accepted at last, and, as Major Tifto, he was proposed, seconded, and elected at the Beargarden.

But he had other points in his favour besides the friendship of Lord Silverbridge,—points which had probably led to that friendship. He was, without doubt, one of the best horsemen in England. There were some who said that, across country, he was the very best, and that, as a judge of a hunter, few excelled him. Of late years he had crept into credit as a betting-man. No one supposed that he had much capital to work with; but still, when he lost a bet he paid it.

Soon after his return from Spain, he was chosen as Master of the Runnymede Fox-Hounds, and was thus enabled to write the letters M.F.H.*after his name. The gentlemen who rode with the Runnymede were not very liberal in their terms, and had lately been compelled to change their Master rather more frequently than was good for that quasi-suburban hunt; but now they had fitted themselves well. How he was to hunt the country five days a fortnight, finding servants and horses, and feeding the hounds, for eight hundred pounds a year, no one could understand. But Major Tifto not only undertook to do it, but did it. And he actually succeeded in obtaining for the Runnymede a degree of popularity which for many years previous it had not possessed. Such a man,—even though no one did know anything of his father or mother, though no one had ever heard him speak of a brother or a sister, though it was believed that he had no real income,—was felt by many to be the very man for the Beargarden; and when his name was brought up at the committee, Lord Silverbridge was able to say so much in his favour that only two blackballs*were given against him. Under the mild rule of the club, three would have been necessary to exclude him; and therefore Major Tifto was now as good a member as anyone else.

He was a well-made little man, good-looking for those who like such good looks. He was light-haired and blue-eyed, with regular and yet not inexpressive features. But his eyes were small and never tranquil, and rarely capable of looking at the person who was speaking to him. He had small well-trimmed, glossy whiskers, with the best-kept moustache, and the best-kept tuft on his chin which were to be seen anywhere. His face still bore the freshness of youth, which was a marvel to many, who declared that, from facts within their knowledge, Tifto must be far on the wrong side of forty. At a first glance you would hardly have called him thirty. No doubt, when, on close inspection, you came to look into his eyes, you could see the hand of time. Even if you believed the common assertion that he painted,—which it was very hard to believe of a man who passed the most of his time in the hunting-field or on a race-course,—yet the paint on his cheeks would not

46

enable him to move with the elasticity which seemed to belong to all his limbs. He rode flat races and steeple chases,*—if jump races may still be so called; and with his own hounds and with the Queen's did incredible things on horseback. He could jump over chairs too,—the backs of four chairs in a dining-room after dinner,—a feat which no gentleman of forty-five could perform, even though he painted himself ever so.

So much in praise of Major Tifto honesty has compelled the present chronicler to say. But there were traits of character in which he fell off a little, even in the estimation of those whose pursuits endeared him to them. He could not refrain from boasting,—and especially from boasting about women. His desire for glory in that direction knew no bounds, and he would sometimes mention names, and bring himself into trouble. It was told of him that at one period of his life, when misfortune had almost overcome him, when sorrow had produced prostration, and prostration some expression of truth, he had owned to a friend his own conviction that could he have kept his tongue from talking of women, he might have risen to prosperity in his profession. From these misfortunes he had emerged, and no doubt, had often reflected on what he himself had then said. But we know that the drunkard, though he hates drunkenness, cannot but drink,—that the gambler cannot keep from the dice. Major Tifto still lied about women, and could not keep his tongue from the subject. He would boast, too, about other matters,—much to his own disadvantage. He was, too, very 'deep', and some men, who could put up with his other failings, could not endure that. Whatever he wanted to do he would attempt round three corners. Though he could ride straight, he could do nothing else straight. He was full of mysteries. If he wanted to draw Charter Wood he would take his hounds out of the street at Egham* directly in the other direction. If he had made up his mind to ride Lord Pottlepot's horse for the great Leamington handicap,* he would be sure to tell even his intimate friends that he was almost determined to take the 'baronet's' offer of a mount. This he would do even where there was no possible turn in the betting to be affected by such falsehood. So that his companions were apt to complain that there was no knowing where to have Tifto. And then, they who were old enough in the world to have had some experience in men, had perceived that peculiar quality of his eyes, which never allowed him to look anyone in the face.

That Major Tifto should make money by selling horses was, perhaps, a necessity of his position. No one grumbled at him because he did so, or thought that such a pursuit was incompatible with his character as a sporting gentleman. But there were some who considered that they had suffered unduly under his hands, and in their bargains with him had been made to pay more than a proper amount of tax for the advantages of his general assistance. When a man has perhaps made fifty pounds by using a 'straight tip'*as to a horse at Newmarket,* in doing which he had of course encountered some risks, he feels he ought not to be made to pay the amount back into the pockets of the 'tipper,' and at the same time to find himself saddled with the possession of a perfectly useless animal. In this way there were rocks in the course through which Tifto was called on to steer his bark. Of course he was anxious, when preying upon his acquaintances, to spare those who were useful friends to him. Now and again he would sell a serviceable animal at a fair price, and would endeavour to make such sale in favour of someone whose countenance would be a rock to him. He knew his business well, but yet there would be mistakes.

Now, at this very moment, was the culmination of the Major's life. He was Master of the Runnymede Hounds, he was partner with the eldest son of a Duke in the possession of that magnificent colt, the Prime Minister, and he was a member of the Beargarden. He was a man who had often been despondent about himself, but was now disposed to be a little triumphant. He had finished his season well with the Runnymede, and were it not that, let him work as he would, his expenses always exceeded his means, he would have been fairly comfortable.

At eight o'clock Lord Silverbridge and his friend met in the dining-room of the Beargarden. 'Have you been here before?' asked the Lord.

'Not in here, my Lord. I just looked in at the smoking-room last night. Glasslough and Nidderdale were there. I thought we should have got up a rubber, but they didn't seem to see it.'

'There is whist here generally. You'll find out all about it before long. Perhaps they are a little afraid of you.'

'I'm the worst hand at cards, I suppose, in England. A dash at loo* for about an hour, and half-a-dozen cuts at blind hookey,*—that's about my form. I know I drop more than I pick up. If I knew what I was about I should never touch a card.'

'Horses; eh, Tifto?'

'Horses, yes. They've pretty good claret, here, eh, Silverbridge?' He could never hit off his familiarity quite right. He had my-Lorded his young friend at first, and now brought out the name with a hesitating twang, which the young nobleman appreciated. But then the young nobleman was quite aware that the Major was a friend for club purposes, and sporting purposes, and not for home use.

'Everything of that kind is pretty good here,' said the Lord.

'You were saying—horses.'

'I dare say you do better with them than with cards.'

'If I didn't I don't know where I should be, seeing what a lot pass through my hands in the year. Anyone of our fellows who has a horse to sell thinks that I am bound to buy him. And I do buy 'em. Last May I had forty-two hunters on my hands.'

'How many of them have you got now?'

'Three. Three of that lot,—though a goodish many have come up since. But what does it amount to? When I have anything that is very good, some fellow that I like gets him from me.'

'After paying for him.'

'After paying for him! Yes; I don't mean that I make

49

a fellow a present. But the man who buys has a deal the best of it. Did you ever get anything better than that spotted chestnut in your life?'

'What, old Sarcinet?'

'You had her for one hundred and sixty pounds. Now, if you were on your oath, what is she worth?'

'She suits me, Major, and of course I shouldn't sell her.'

'I rather think not. I knew what that mare was, well enough. A dealer would have had three hundred and fifty pounds for her. I could have got the money easily if I had taken her down into the shires, and ridden her a day or two myself.'

'I gave you what you asked.'

'Yes, you did. It isn't often that I take less than I ask. But the fact is, about horses, I don't know whether I shouldn't do better if I never owned an animal at all but those I want for my own use. When I am dealing with a man I call a friend, I can't bear to make money of him. I don't think fellows give me all the credit they should do for sticking to them.'

The Major, as he said this, leaned back in his chair, put his hand up to his moustache, and looked sadly away into the vacancy of the room, as though he was meditating sorrowfully on the ingratitude of the world.

'I suppose it's all right about Cream Cheese?' asked the Lord.

'Well; it ought to be.' And now the Major spoke like an oracle, leaning forward on the table, uttering his words in a low voice, but very plainly, so that not a syllable might be lost. 'When you remember how he ran at the Craven with 9 st. 12 lb. on him, that it took Archbishop all he knew to beat him with only 9 st. 2 lb., and what the lot at Chester*are likely to be, I don't think that there can be seven to one against him. I should be very glad to take it off your hands, only the figures are a little too heavy for me.'

'I suppose Sunflower'll be the best animal there?'

'Not a doubt of it, if he's all right, and if his temper will stand. Think what a course Chester is for an ill-conditioned brute like that! And then he's the most uncertain horse in training. There are times he won't feed. From what I hear, I shouldn't wonder if he don't turn up at all.'

'Solomon*says he's all right.'

'You won't get Solomon to take four to one against him, nor yet four and a half. I suppose you'll go down, my Lord?'

'Well, yes; if there's nothing else doing just then. I don't know how it may be about this electioneering business. I shall go and smoke upstairs.'

At the Beargarden there were,—I was going to say, two smoking-rooms; but in truth the house was a smoking-room all over. It was, however, the custom of those who habitually played cards, to have their cigars and coffee upstairs. Into this sanctum Major Tifto had not yet been introduced, but now he was taken there under Lord Silver-bridge's wing. There were already four or five assembled, among whom was Mr. Adolphus Longstaff,*a young man of about thirty-five years of age, who spent very much of his time at the Beargarden. 'Do you know my friend Tifto?' said the Lord. 'Tifto, this is Mr. Longstaff, whom men within the walls of this asylum sometimes call Dolly.' Whereupon the Major bowed and smiled graciously.

'I have heard of Major Tifto,' said Dolly.

'Who has not?' said Lord Nidderdale,* another middle-aged young man, who made one of the company. Again the Major bowed.

'Last season I was always intending to get down to your country and have a day with the Tiftoes,' said Dolly. 'Don't they call your hounds the Tiftoes?'

'They shall be called so if you like,' said the Major. 'And why didn't you come?'

'It always was such a grind.'

'Train down from Paddington every day at half-past ten.'

'That's all very well if you happen to be up. Well, Silver-bridge, how's the Prime Minister?'

'How is he, Tifto?' asked the noble partner.

'I don't think there's a man in England just at present

51

enjoying a very much better state of health,' said the Major pleasantly.

'Safe to run?' asked Dolly.

'Safe to run! Why shouldn't he be safe to run?'

'I mean sure to start.'

'I think we mean him to start, don't we, Silverbridge?' said the Major.

There was something perhaps in the tone in which the last remark was made which jarred a little against the young lord's dignity. At any rate he got up and declared his purpose of going to the opera. He should look in, he said, and hear a song from Mdlle Stuffa.*Mdlle Stuffa was the nightingale of the season, and Lord Silverbridge, when he had nothing else to do, would sometimes think that he was fond of music. Soon after he was gone Major Tifto had some whisky-and-water, lit his third cigar, and began to feel the glory of belonging to the Beargarden. With Lord Silverbridge, to whom it was essentially necessary that he should make himself agreeable at all times, he was somewhat overweighted as it were. Though he attempted an easy familiarity, he was a little afraid of Lord Silverbridge. With Dolly Longstaff he felt that he might be comfortable,—not, perhaps, understanding that gentleman's character. With Lord Nidderdale he had previously been acquainted, and had found him to be good-natured. So, as he sipped his whisky, he became confidential and comfortable.

'I never thought so much about her good looks,' he said. They were talking of the singer, the charms of whose voice had carried Lord Silverbridge away.

'Did you ever see her off the stage?' asked Nidderdale.

'Oh dear yes.'

'She does not go about very much, I fancy,' said someone.

'I dare say not,' said Tifto. 'But she and I have had a day or two together, for all that.'

'You must have been very much favoured,' said Dolly.

'We've been pals ever since she has been over here,' said Tifto, with an enormous lie.

'How do you get on with her husband?' asked Dolly,—in the simplest voice, as though not in the least surprised at his companion's statement.

'Husband!' exclaimed the Major; who was not possessed of sufficient presence of mind to suppress all signs of his ignorance.

'Ah,' said Dolly; 'you are not probably aware that your pal has been married to Mr. Thomas Jones for the last year and a half.' Soon after that Major Tifto left the club,—with considerably enhanced respect for Mr. Longstaff.

CHAPTER VII

Conservative Convictions

LORD SILVERBRIDGE had engaged himself to be with his father the next morning at half-past nine, and he entered the breakfast-room a very few minutes after that hour. He had made up his mind as to what he would say to his father. He meant to call himself a Conservative, and to go into the House of Commons under that denomination. All the men among whom he lived were Conservatives. It was a matter on which, as he thought, his father could have no right to control him. Down in Barsetshire, as well as up in London, there was some little difference of opinion in this matter. The people of Silverbridge declared that they would prefer to have a Conservative member,* as indeed they had one for the last session. They had loyally returned the Duke himself while he was a commoner, but they had returned him as being part and parcel of the Omnium appendages. That was all over now. As a constituency they were not endowed with advanced views, and thought that a Conservative would suit them best. That being so, and as they had been told that the Duke's son was a Conservative, they fancied that by electing him they would be pleasing everybody. But, in truth, by so doing they would by no means please the Duke. He had told them on previous occasions that they might elect whom they pleased, and felt no anger because they had elected a Conservative. They might send up to Parliament the most antediluvian old Tory they could find in England if they wished, only not his son, not a Palliser as a Tory or Conservative. And then, though the little town had gone back in the ways of the world, the county, or the Duke's division of the county, had made so much progress, that a Liberal candidate recommended by him would almost certainly be returned. It was just the occasion on which a Palliser should show himself ready to serve his country. There would be an expense, but he would think nothing of expense in such a matter. Ten thousand pounds spent on such an object would not vex him. The very contest would have given him new life. All this Lord Silverbridge understood, but had said to himself and to all his friends that it was a matter in which he did not intend to be controlled.

The Duke had passed a very unhappy night. He had told himself that any such marriage as that spoken of was out of the question. He believed that the matter might be so represented to his girl as to make her feel that it was out of the question. He hardly doubted but that he could stamp it out. Though he should have to take her away into some further corner of the world, he would stamp it out. But she, when this foolish passion of hers should have been thus stamped out, could never be the pure, the bright, the unsullied, unsoiled thing, of the possession of which he had thought so much. He had never spoken of his hopes about her even to his wife, but in the silence of his very silent life he had thought much of the day when he would give her to some noble youth, —noble with all gifts of nobility, including rank and wealth, —who might be fit to receive her. Now, even though no one else should know it,—and all would know it,—she would be the girl who had condescended to love young Tregear.

His own Duchess, she whose loss to him now was as though he had lost half his limbs,—had not she in the same way loved a Tregear, or worse than a Tregear, in her early days? Ah yes! And though his Cora had been so much to him, had he not often felt, had he not been feeling all his days, that Fate had robbed him of the sweetest joy that is given to man, in that she had not come to him loving him with her early spring of love, as she had loved that poor ne'er-do-well? How infinite had been his regrets. How often had he told himself that, with all that Fortune had given him, still Fortune had been unjust to him because he had been robbed of that. Not to save his life could he have whispered a word of this to anyone, but he had felt it. He had felt it for years. Dear as she had been, she had not been quite what she should have been but for that. And now this girl of his, who was so much dearer to him than anything else left to him, was doing exactly as her mother had done. The young man might be stamped out. He might be made to vanish as that other young man had vanished. But the fact that he had been there, cherished in the girl's heart,—that could not be stamped out.

He struggled gallantly to acquit the memory of his wife. He could best do that by leaning with the full weight of his mind on the presumed iniquity of Mrs. Finn. Had he not known from the first that the woman was an adventuress? And had he not declared to himself over and over again that between such a one and himself there should be no intercourse, no common feeling? He had allowed himself to be talked into an intimacy, to be talked almost into an affection. And this was the result!

And how should he treat this matter in his coming interview with his son;—or should he make an allusion to it? At first it seemed as though it would be impossible for him to give his mind to that other subject. How could he enforce the merits of political Liberalism, and the duty of adhering to the old family party, while his mind was entirely preoccupied with his daughter? It had suddenly become almost indifferent to him whether Silverbridge should be a Conservative or a Liberal. But as he dressed he told himself that, as a man, he ought to be able to do a plain duty, marked out for him as this had been by his own judgment, without regard to personal suffering. The hedger and ditcher must make his hedge and clean his ditch even though he be tormented by rheumatism. His duty by his son he must do, even though his heart were torn to pieces.

During breakfast he tried to be gracious, and condescended to ask his son a question about Prime Minister. Racing was an amusement*to which English noblemen had been addicted for many ages, and had been held to be serviceable rather than disgraceful, if conducted in a noble fashion. He did not credit Tifto with much nobility. He knew but little about the Major. He would much have preferred that his son should have owned a horse alone, if he must have anything to do with ownership. 'Would it not be better to buy the other share?' asked the Duke.

'It would take a deal of money, sir. The Major would ask a couple of thousand, I should think.'

'That is a great deal.'

'And then the Major is a very useful man. He thoroughly understands the turf.'

'I hope he doesn't live by it?'

'Oh no; he doesn't live by it. That is, he has a great many irons in the fire.'

'I do not mind a young man owning a horse, if he can afford the expense,—as you perhaps can do; but I hope you don't bet.'

'Nothing to speak of.'

'Nothing to speak of is so apt to grow into that which has to be spoken of.' So much the father said at breakfast, hardly giving his mind to the matter discussed,—his mind being on other things. But when their breakfast was eaten, then it was necessary that he should begin. 'Silverbridge,' he said, 'I hope you have thought better of what we were talking about as to these coming elections.'

'Well, sir;—of course I have thought about it.'

'And you can do as I would have you?'

'You see, sir, a man's political opinion is a kind of thing he can't get rid of.'

'You can hardly as yet have any very confirmed political

opinion. You are still young, and I do not suppose that you have thought much about politics.'

'Well, sir; I think I have. I've got my own ideas. We've got to protect our position as well as we can against the Radicals and Communists.'*

'I cannot admit that at all, Silverbridge. There is no great political party in this country anxious either for Communism or for revolution. But, putting all that aside for the present, do you think that a man's political opinions should be held in regard to his own individual interests, or to the much wider interests of others, whom we call the public?'

'To his own interest,' said the young man with decision.

'It is simply self-protection then?'

'His own and his class. The people will look after themselves, and we must look after ourselves. We are so few and they are so many, that we shall have quite enough to do.'

Then the Duke gave his son a somewhat lengthy political lecture, which was intended to teach him that the greatest benefit of the greatest number*was the object to which all political studies should tend. The son listened to it with attention, and when it was over, expressed his opinion that there was a great deal in what his father had said. 'I trust, if you will consider it,' said the Duke, 'that you will not find yourself obliged to desert the school of politics in which your father has not been an inactive supporter, and to which your family has belonged for many generations.'

'I could not call myself a Liberal,' said the young politician.

'Why not?'

'Because I am a Conservative.'

'And you won't stand for the county on the Liberal interest?'

'I should be obliged to tell them that I should always give a Conservative vote.'

'Then you refuse to do what I ask?'

'I do not know how I can help refusing. If you wanted me to grow a couple of inches taller I couldn't do it, even though I should be ever so anxious to oblige you.'

'But a very young man, as you are, may have so much deference for his elders as to be induced to believe that he has been in error.'

'Oh yes; of course.'

'You cannot but be aware that the political condition of the country is the one subject to which I have devoted the labour of my life.'

'I know that very well; and, of course, I know how much they all think of you.'

'Then my opinion might go for something with you?'

'So it does, sir; I shouldn't have doubted at all only for that little. Still, you see, as the thing is,—how am I to help myself?'

'You believe that you must be right,—you, who have never given an hour's study to the subject!'

'No, sir. In comparison with a great many men, I know that I am a fool. Perhaps it is because I know that, that I am a Conservative. The Radicals are always saying that a Conservative must be a fool. Then a fool ought to be a Conservative.'

Hereupon the father got up from his chair and turned round, facing the fire, with his back to his son. He was becoming very angry, but endeavoured to restrain his anger. The matter in dispute between them was of so great importance, that he could hardly be justified in abandoning it in consequence of arguments so trifling in themselves as these which his son adduced. As he stood there for some minutes thinking of it all, he was tempted again and again to burst out in wrath and threaten the lad,—to threaten him as to money, as to his amusements, as to the general tenure of his life. The pity was so great that the lad should be so stubborn and so foolish! He would never ask his son to be a slave to the Liberal party, as he had been. But that a Palliser should not be a Liberal,—and his son, as the first recreant Palliser,—was wormwood to him! As he stood there he more than once clenched his fist in eager desire to turn upon the young man; but he restrained himself, telling himself that in justice he should not be angry for such offence as this. To become a Conservative, when the path to Liberalism was so fairly open, might be the part of a fool, but could not fairly be imputed as a crime. To endeavour to be just was the study of his life, and in no condition of life can justice be more imperatively due than from a father to his son.

'You mean to stand for Silverbridge?' he said at last.

'Not if you object, sir.'

This made it worse. It became now still more difficult for him to scold the young man.

'You are aware that I should not meddle in any way.'

'That was what I supposed. They will return a Conservative at any rate.'

'It is not that I care about,' said the Duke sadly.

'Upon my word, sir, I am very sorry to vex you; but what would you have me do? I will give up Parliament altogether, if you say that you wish it.'

'No; I do not wish that.'

'You wouldn't have me tell a lie?'

'No.'

'What can I do then?'

'Learn what there is to learn from some master fit to teach you.'

'There are so many masters.'

'I believe it to be that most arrogant ill-behaved young man who was with me yesterday who has done this evil.'

'You mean Frank Tregear?'

'I do mean Mr. Tregear.'

'He's a Conservative, of course; and of course he and I have been much together. Was he with you yesterday, sir?'

'Yes, he was.'

'What was that about?' asked Lord Silverbridge, in a voice that almost betrayed fear, for he knew very well what cause had produced the interview.

'He has been speaking to me——' When the Duke had got so far as this he paused, finding himself to be hardly able to declare the disgrace which had fallen upon himself and his family. As he did tell the story, both his face and his voice were altered, so that the son, in truth, was scared. 'He has been speaking to me about your sister. Did you know of this?'

'I knew there was something between them.'

'And you encouraged it?'

'No, sir; just the contrary. I have told him that I was quite sure it would never do.'

'And why did you not tell me?'

'Well, sir; that was hardly my business, was it?'

'Not to guard the honour of your sister?'

'You see, sir, how many things have happened all at once.'

'What things?'

'My dear mother, sir, thought well of him.' The Duke uttered a deep sigh and turned again round to the fire. 'I always told him that you would never consent.'

'I should think not.'

'It has come so suddenly. I should have spoken to you about it as soon as——as soon as——' He had meant to say as soon as the husband's grief for the loss of his wife had been in some degree appeased, but he could not speak the words. The Duke, however, perfectly understood him. 'In the meantime, they were not seeing each other.'

'Nor writing?'

'I think not.'

'Mrs. Finn has known it all.'

'Mrs. Finn!'

'Certainly. She has known it all through.'

'I do not see how it can have been so.'

'He told me so himself,' said the Duke, unwittingly putting words into Tregear's mouth which Tregear had never uttered. 'There must be an end of this. I will speak to your sister. In the meantime, the less, I think, you see of Mr. Tregear the better. Of course it is out of the question he should be allowed to remain in this house. You will make him understand that at once, if you please.'

'Oh, certainly,' said Silverbridge.

CHAPTER VIII

'He is a Gentleman'

THE Duke returned to Matching an almost broken-hearted man. He had intended to go down into Barsetshire, in reference to the coming elections;—not with the view of interfering in any unlordly, or rather unpeerlike fashion, but thinking that if his eldest son were to stand for the county in a proper constitutional spirit, as the eldest son of so great a county magnate ought to do, his presence at Gatherum Castle,* among his own people, might probably be serviceable, and would certainly be gracious. There would be no question of entertainment. His bereavement would make that impossible. But there would come from his presence a certain savour ot proprietorship, and a sense of power, which would be beneficial to his son, and would not, as the Duke thought, be contrary to the spirit of the constitution. But all this was now at an ·end. He told himself that he did not care how the elections might go;—that he did not care much how anything might go. Silverbridge might stand for Silverbridge if he so pleased. He would give neither assistance nor obstruction, either in the county or in the borough. He wrote to this effect to his agent, Mr. Morton;—but at the same time desired that gentleman to pay Lord Silverbridge's electioneering expenses, feeling it to be his duty as a father to do so much for his son.

But though he endeavoured to engage his thoughts in these parliamentary matters, though he tried to make himself believe that this political apostasy was the trouble which vexed him, in truth that other misery was so crushing, as to make the affairs of his son insignificant. How should he express himself to her? That was the thought present to his mind as he went down to Matching. Should he content himself with simply telling her that such a wish on her part was disgraceful, and that it could never be fulfilled; or should he argue the matter with her, endeavouring as he did so to persuade her gently that she was wrong to place her affections so low, and so to obtain from her an assurance that the idea should be abandoned?

The latter course would be infinitely the better,—if only he could accomplish it. But he was conscious of his own hardness of manner, and was aware that he had never succeeded in establishing confidence between himself and his daughter. It was a thing for which he had longed,—as a plain girl might long to possess the charms of an acknowledged beauty;—as a poor little fellow, five feet in height, might long to have a cubit added to his stature.

Though he was angry with her, how willingly would he take her into his arms and assure her of his forgiveness! How anxious he would be to make her understand that nothing should be spared by him to add beauty and grace to her life! Only, as a matter of course, Mr. Tregear must be abandoned. But he knew of himself that he would not know how to begin to be tender and forgiving. He knew that he would not know how not to be stern and hard.

But he must find out the history of it all. No doubt the man had been his son's friend, and had joined his party in Italy at his son's instance. But yet he had come to entertain an idea that Mrs. Finn had been the great promoter of the sin, and he thought that Tregear had told him that that lady had been concerned with the matter from the beginning. In all this there was a craving in his heart to lessen the amount of culpable responsibility which might seem to attach itself to the wife he had lost.

He reached Matching about eight, and ordered his dinner to be brought to him in his own study. When Lady Mary came to welcome him, he kissed her forehead and bade her come to him after his dinner. 'Shall I not sit with you, papa, whilst you are eating it?' she asked; but he merely told her that he would not trouble her to do that. Even in saying this he was so unusually tender to her that she assured herself that her lover had not as yet told his tale.

The Duke's meals were not generally feasts for a Lucullus.* No man living, perhaps, cared less what he ate, or knew less what he drank. In such matters he took what was provided for him, making his dinner off the first bit of meat that was brought, and simply ignoring anything offered to him afterwards. And he would drink what wine the servant gave him, mixing it, whatever it might be, with seltzer water. He had never been much given to the pleasures of the table; but this habit of simplicity had grown on him of late, till the Duchess used to tell him that his wants were so few that it was a pity he was not a hermit, vowed to poverty.

Very shortly a message was brought to Lady Mary, saying that her father wished to see her. She went at once, and found him seated on a sofa, which stood close along the bookshelves on one side of the room. The table had already been cleared, and he was alone. He not only was alone, but had not even a pamphlet or newspaper in his hand.

Then she knew that Tregear must have told the story. As this occurred to her, her legs almost gave way under her. 'Come and sit down, Mary,' he said, pointing to the seat on the sofa beside himself.

She sat down and took one of his hands within her own. Then, as he did not begin at once, she asked a question. 'Will Silverbridge stand for the county, papa?'

'No, my dear.'

'But for the town?'

'Yes, my dear.'

'And he won't be a Liberal?'

'I am afraid not. It is a cause of great unhappiness to me; but I do not know that I should be justified in any absolute opposition. A man is entitled to his own opinion, even though he be a very young man.'

'I am so sorry that it should be so, papa, because it vexes you.'

'I have many things to vex me;—things to break my heart.'

'Poor mamma!' she exclaimed.

'Yes; that above all others. But life and death are in God's hands, and even though we may complain we can alter nothing. But whatever our sorrows are while we are here, we must do our duty.'

'I suppose he may be a good Member of Parliament, though he has turned Conservative.'

'I am not thinking about your brother. I am thinking about you.' The poor girl gave a little start on the sofa. 'Do you know—Mr. Tregear?' he added.

'Yes, papa; of course I know him. You used to see him in Italy.'

'I believe I did; I understand that he was there as a friend of Silverbridge.'

'His most intimate friend, papa.'

'I dare say. He came to me, in London yesterday, and told me——! Oh Mary, can it be true?'

'Yes, papa,' she said, covered up to her forehead with blushes, and with her eyes turned down. In the ordinary affairs of life she was a girl of great courage, who was not given to be shaken from her constancy by the pressure of any present difficulty; but now the terror inspired by her father's voice almost overpowered her.

64

'Do you mean to tell me that you have engaged yourself to that young man without my approval?'

'Of course you were to have been asked, papa.'

'Is that in accordance with your idea of what should be the conduct of a young lady in your position?'

'Nobody meant to conceal anything from you, papa.'

'It has been so far concealed. And yet this young man has the self-confidence to come to me and to demand your hand as though it were a matter of course that I should accede to so trivial a request. It is, as a matter of course, quite impossible. You understand that; do you not?' When she did not answer him at once, he repeated the question. 'I ask you whether you do not feel that it is altogether impossible?'

'No, papa,' she said, in the lowest possible whisper, but still in such a whisper that he could hear the word, and with so much clearness that he could judge from her voice of the obstinacy of her mind.

'Then, Mary, it becomes my duty to tell you that it is quite impossible. I will not have it thought of. There must be an end of it.'

'Why, papa?'

'Why! I am astonished that you should ask me why.'

'I should not have allowed him, papa, to go to you unless I had,—unless I had loved him.'

'Then you must conquer your love. It is disgraceful and must be conquered.'

'Disgraceful!'

'Yes. I am sorry to use such a word to my own child, but it is so. If you will promise to be guided by me in this matter, if you will undertake not to see him any more, I will,—if not forget it,—at any rate pardon it, and be silent. I will excuse it because you were young, and were thrown imprudently in his way. There has, I believe, been someone at work in the matter with whom I ought to be more angry than with you. Say that you will obey me, and there is nothing within a father's power that I will not do for you, to make your life happy.' It was thus that he strove not to be stern. His heart, indeed, was tender enough, but there was nothing tender in the tone of his voice or in the glance of his eye. Though he was very positive in what he said, yet he was shy and shame-faced even with his own daughter. He, too, had blushed when he told her that she must conquer her love.

That she should be told that she had disgraced herself was terrible to her. That her father should speak of her marriage with this man as an event that was impossible made her very unhappy. That he should talk of pardoning her, as for some great fault, was in itself a misery. But she had not on that account the least idea of giving up her lover. Young as she was, she had her own peculiar theory on that matter, her own code of conduct and honour, from which she did not mean to be driven. Of course she had not expected that her father would yield at the first word. He, no doubt, would wish that she should make a more exalted marriage. She had known that she would have to encounter opposition, though she had not expected to be told that she had disgraced herself. As she sat there she resolved that under no pretence would she give up her lover;—but she was so far abashed that she could not find words to express herself. He, too, had been silent for a few moments before he again asked her for her promise.

Will you tell me, Mary, that you will not see him again?'

'I don't think that I can say that, papa.'

'Why not?'

'Oh papa, how can I, when of all the people in the world I love him the best?'

It is not without a pang that anyone can be told that she who is of all the dearest has some other one who to her is the dearest. Such pain fathers and mothers have to bear; and though, I think, the arrow is never so blunted but that it leaves something of a wound behind, there is in most cases, if not a perfect salve, still an ample consolation. The mother knows that it is good that her child should love some man better than all the world beside, and that she should be taken away to become a wife and a mother. And the father, when that delight of his eyes ceases to assure him that he is her nearest

and dearest, though he abandon the treasure of that nearest-
ness and dearestness with a soft melancholy, still knows that
it is as it should be. Of course that other 'him' is the person
she loves the best in the world. Were it not so how evil a
thing it would be that she should marry him! Were it not so
with reference to some 'him', how void would her life be!
But now, to the poor Duke the wound had no salve, no consolation. When he was told that this young Tregear was the
owner of his girl's sweet love, was the treasure of her heart,
he shrank as though arrows with sharp points were pricking
him all over. 'I will not hear of such love,' he said.

'What am I to say, papa?'

'Say that you will obey me.'

Then she sat silent. 'Do you not know that he is not fit to
be your husband?'

'No, papa.'

'Then you cannot have thought much either of your position or of mine.'

'He is a gentleman, papa.'

'So is my private secretary. There is not a clerk in one of
our public offices who does not consider himself to be a
gentleman. The curate of the parish is a gentleman, and the
medical man who comes here from Bradstock. The word is
too vague to carry with it any meaning that ought to be
serviceable to you in thinking of such a matter.'

'I do not know any other way of dividing people,' said she,
showing thereby that she had altogether made up her mind as
to what ought to be serviceable to her.

'You are not called upon to divide people. That division
requires so much experience that you are bound in this matter
to rely upon those to whom your obedience is due. I cannot
but think you must have known that you were not entitled to
give your love to any man without being assured that the
man would be approved of by—by—by me.' He was going
to say, 'your parents,' but was stopped by the remembrance of
his wife's imprudence.

She saw it all, and was too noble to plead her mother's

authority. But she was not too dutiful to cast a reproach upon him, when he was so stern to her. 'You have been so little with me, papa.'

'That is true,' he said, after a pause. 'That is true. It has been a fault, and I will mend it. It is a reason for forgiveness, and I will forgive you. But you must tell me that there shall be an end to this.'

'No, papa.'

'What do you mean?'

'That as I love Mr. Tregear, and as I have told him so, and as I have promised him, I will be true to him. I cannot let there be an end to it.'

'You do not suppose that you will be allowed to see him again?'

'I hope so.'

'Most assuredly not. Do you write to him?'

'No, papa.'

'Never?'

'Never since we have been back in England.'

'You must promise me that you will not write.'

She paused a moment before she answered him, and now she was looking him full in the face. 'I shall not write to him. I do not think I shall write to him; but I will not promise.'

'Not promise me,—your father!'

'No, papa. It might be that—that I should do it.'

'You would not wish me so to guard you that you should have no power of sending a letter but by permission?'

'I should not like that.'

'But it will have to be so.'

'If I do write I will tell you.'

'And show me what you write?'

'No, papa; not that; but I will tell you what I have written.'

Then it occurred to him that this bargaining was altogether derogatory to his parental authority, and by no means likely to impress upon her mind the conviction that Tregear must be completely banished from her thoughts. He began already to find how difficult it would be for him to have the charge of such a daughter,—how impossible that he should conduct such a charge with sufficient firmness, and yet with sufficient tenderness! At present he had done no good. He had only been made more wretched than ever by her obstinacy. Surely he must pass her over to the charge of some lady,—but of some lady who would be as determined as was he himself that she should not throw herself away by marrying Mr. Tregear.

'There shall be no writing,' he said, 'no visiting, no communication of any kind. As you refuse to obey me now, you had better go to your room.'

CHAPTER IX

'In medias res'*

PERHAPS the method of rushing at once 'in medias res' is, of all the ways of beginning a story, or a separate branch of a story, the least objectionable. The reader is made to think that the gold lies so near the surface that he will be required to take very little trouble in digging for it. And the writer is enabled,—at any rate for a time, and till his neck has become, as it were, warm to the collar,—to throw off from him the difficulties and dangers, the tedium and prolixity, of description. This rushing 'in medias res' has doubtless the charm of ease. 'Certainly, when I threw her from the garret window to the stony pavement below, I did not anticipate that she would fall so far without injury to life or limb.' When a story has been begun after this fashion, without any prelude, without description of the garret or of the pavement, or of the lady thrown, or of the speaker, a great amount of trouble seems to have been saved. The mind of the reader fills up the blanks,— if erroneously, still satisfactorily. He knows, at least, that the heroine has encountered a terrible danger, and has escaped from it with almost incredible good fortune; that the demon of the piece is a bold demon, not ashamed to speak of his own iniquity, and that the heroine and the demon are so far united that they have been in a garret together. But there is the drawback on the system,—that it is almost impossible to avoid the necessity of doing, sooner or later, that which would naturally be done at first. It answers, perhaps, for half-a-dozen chapters;—and to carry the reader pleasantly for half-a-dozen chapters is a great matter!—but after that a certain nebulous darkness gradually seems to envelope the characters and the incidents. 'Is all this going on in the country, or is it in town, —or perhaps in the Colonies? How old was she? Was she tall? Is she fair? Is she heroine-like in her form and gait? And, after all, how high was the garret window?' I have always found that the details would insist on being told at last, and that by rushing 'in medias res' I was simply presenting the cart before the horse. But as readers like the cart the best, I will do it once again,—trying it only for a branch of my story, —and will endeavour to let as little as possible of the horse be seen afterwards.

'And so poor Frank has been turned out of heaven?' said Lady Mabel Grex to young Lord Silverbridge.

'Who told you that? I have said nothing about it to anybody.'

'Of course he told me himself,' said the young beauty. I am aware that, in the word beauty, and perhaps, also, in the word young, a little bit of the horse is appearing; and I am already sure that I shall have to show his head and neck, even if not his very tail. 'Poor Frank! Did you hear it all?'

'I heard nothing, Lady Mab, and know nothing.'

'You know that your awful governor won't let him stay any longer in Carlton Terrace?'

'Yes, I know that.'

'And why not?'

'Would Lord Grex allow Percival to have his friends living here?' Earl Grex was Lady Mabel's father, Lord Percival was the Earl's son;—and the Earl lived in Belgrave Square. All these are little bits of the horse.

'Certainly not. In the first place, I am here.'

'That makes a difference, certainly.'

'Of course it makes a difference. They would be wanting to make love to me.'

'No doubt. I should, I know.'

'And therefore it wouldn't do for you to live here; and then papa is living here himself. And then the permission never has been given. I suppose Frank did not go there at first without the Duke knowing it.'

'I daresay that I had mentioned it.'

'You might as well tell me all about it. We are cousins, you know.' Frank Tregear, through his mother's family, was second cousin to Lady Mabel; as was also Lord Silverbridge, one of the Grexes having, at some remote period, married a Palliser. This is another bit of the horse.

'The governor merely seemed to think that he would like to have his own house to himself—like other people. What an ass Tregear was to say anything to you about it.'

'I don't think he was an ass at all. Of course he had to tell us that he was changing his residence. He says that he is going to take a back bedroom somewhere near the Seven Dials.'*

'He has got very nice rooms in Duke Street.'

'Have you seen him, then?'

'Of course I have.'

'Poor fellow! I wish he had a little money; he is so nice. And now, Lord Silverbridge, do you mean to say that there is not something in the wind about Lady Mary?'

'If there were I should not talk about it,' said Lord Silverbridge.

'You are a very innocent young gentleman.'

'And you are a very interesting young lady.'

'You ought to think me so, for I interest myself very much about you. Was the Duke very angry about your not standing for the county?'

'He was vexed.'

'I do think it is so odd that a man should be expected to be this or that in politics because his father happened to be so before him! I don't understand how he should expect that

71

you should remain with a party so utterly snobbish and down in the world as the Radicals. Everybody that is worth anything is leaving them.'

'He has not left them.'

'No, I don't suppose he could; but you have.'

'I never belonged to them, Lady Mab.'

'And never will, I hope. I always told papa that you would certainly be one of us.' All this took place in the drawing-room of Lord Grex's house. There was no Lady Grex alive, but there lived with the Earl a certain elderly lady, reported to be in some distant way a cousin of the family, named Miss Casseway, who, in the matter of looking after Lady Mab, did what was supposed to be absolutely necessary. She now entered the room with her bonnet on, having just returned from church. 'What was the text?' asked Lady Mab at once.

'If you had gone to church, as you ought to have done, my dear, you would have heard it.'

'But as I didn't?'

'I don't think the text alone will do you any good.'

'And probably you forget it.'

'No, I don't, my dear. How do you do, Lord Silverbridge?'

'He is a Conservative, Miss Cass.'

'Of course he is. I am quite sure that a young nobleman of so much taste and intellect would take the better side.'

'You forget that all you are saying is against my father and my family, Miss Cassewary.'

'I dare say it was different when your father was a young man. And your father, too, was, not very long since, at the head of a government which contained many Conservatives.* I don't look upon your father as a Radical, though perhaps I should not be justified in calling him a Conservative.'

'Well; certainly not, I think.'

'But now it is necessary that all noblemen in England should rally to the defence of their order.' Miss Cassewary was a great politician, and was one of those who are always fore-seeing the ruin of their country. 'My dear, I will go and take my bonnet off. Perhaps you will have tea when I come down.'

72

'Don't you go,' said Lady Mabel, when Silverbridge got up to take his departure.

'I always do when tea comes.'

'But you are going to dine here?'

'Not that I know of. In the first place, nobody has asked me. In the second place, I am engaged. Thirdly, I don't care about having to talk politics to Miss Cass; and fourthly, I hate family dinners on Sunday.'

'In the first place, I ask you. Secondly, I know you were going to dine with Frank Tregear, at the club. Thirdly, I want you to talk to me, and not to Miss Cass. And fourthly, you are an uncivil young—young,—young,—I should say cub if I dared, to tell me that you don't like dining with me any day of the week.'

'Of course you know what I mean is, that I don't like troubling your father.'

'Leave that to me. I shall tell him you are coming, and Frank too. Of course you can bring him. Then he can talk to me when papa goes down to his club, and you can arrange your politics with Miss Cass.' So it was settled, and at eight o'clock Lord Silverbridge reappeared in Belgrave Square with Frank Tregear.

Earl Grex was a nobleman of very ancient family, the Grexes having held the parish of Grex, in Yorkshire, from some time long prior to the Conquest. In saying all this, I am, I know, allowing the horse to appear wholesale;—but I find that he cannot be kept out. I may as well go on to say that the present Earl was better known at Newmarket and the Beaufort,*—where he spent a large part of his life in playing whist,—than in the House of Lords. He was a grey-haired, handsome, worn-out old man, who through a long life of pleasure had greatly impaired a fortune which, for an earl, had never been magnificent, and who now strove hard, but not always successfully, to remedy that evil by gambling. As he could no longer eat and drink as he had used to do, and as he cared no longer for the light that lies in a lady's eye, there was not much left to him in the world but cards and racing.

Nevertheless he was a handsome old man, of polished manners, when he chose to use them; a staunch Conservative and much regarded by his party, for whom in his early life he had done some work in the House of Commons.

'Silverbridge is all very well,' he had said; 'but I don't see why that young Tregear is to dine here every night of his life.'

'This is the second time since he has been up in town, papa.'

'He was here last week, I know.'

'Silverbridge wouldn't come without him.'

'That's d—— nonsense,' said the Earl. Miss Casseway gave a start,—not, we may presume, because she was shocked, for she could not be much shocked, having heard the same word from the same lips very often; but she thought it right always to enter a protest. Then the two young men were announced.

Frank Tregear, having been known by the family as a boy, was Frank to all of them,—as was Lady Mabel, Mabel to him, somewhat to the disgust of the father and not altogether with the approbation of Miss Cass. But Lady Mabel had declared that she would not be guilty of the folly of changing old habits. Silverbridge, being Silverbridge to all his own people, hardly seemed to have a Christian name;—his godfathers and godmothers had indeed called him Plantagenet;—but having only become acquainted with the family since his Oxford days he was Lord Silverbridge to Lady Mabel. Lady Mabel had not as yet become Mabel to him, but, as by her very intimate friends she was called Mab, had allowed herself to be addressed by him as Lady Mab. There was thus between them all considerable intimacy.

'I'm deuced glad to hear it,' said the Earl when dinner was announced. For, though he could not eat much, Lord Grex was always impatient when the time of eating was at hand. Then he walked down alone. Lord Silverbridge followed with his daughter, and Frank Tregear gave his arm to Miss Cassewary. 'If that woman can't clear her soup better than that, she might as well go to the d——,' said the Earl;—upon which

74

remark no one in the company made any observation. As there were two men-servants in the room when it was made the cook probably had the advantage of it. It may be almost unnecessary to add that though the Earl had polished manners for certain occasions he would sometimes throw them off in the bosom of his own family.

'My Lord,' said Miss Cassewary—she always called him 'My Lord'—'Lord Silverbridge is going to stand for the Duke's borough*in the Conservative interest.'

'I didn't know the Duke had a borough,' said the Earl.

'He had one till he thought it proper to give it up,' said the son, taking his father's part.

'And you are going to pay him off for what he has done by standing against him. It's just the sort of thing for a son to do in these days. If I had a borough Percival would go down and make radical speeches there.'

'There isn't a better Conservative in England than Percival,' said Lady Mabel, bridling up.

'Nor a worse son,' said the father. 'I believe he would do anything he could lay his hand on to oppose me.' During the past week there had been some little difference of opinion between the father and the son as to the signing of a deed.

'My father does not take it in bad part at all,' said Silverbridge.

'Perhaps he's ratting himself,'*said the Earl. 'When a man lends himself to a coalition he is as good as half gone.'

'I do not think that in all England there is so thorough a Liberal as my father,' said Lord Silverbridge. 'And when I say that he doesn't take this badly, I don't mean that it doesn't vex him. I know it vexes him. But he doesn't quarrel with me. He even wrote down to Barsetshire to say that all my expenses at Silverbridge were to be paid.'

'I call that very bad politics,' said the Earl.

'It seems to me to be very grand,' said Frank.

'Perhaps, sir, you don't know what is good or what is bad in politics,' said the Earl, trying to snub his guest.

But it was difficult to snub Frank. 'I know a gentleman

when I see him, I think,' he said. 'Of course Silverbridge is right to be a Conservative. Nobody has a stronger opinion about that than I have. But the Duke is behaving so well that if I were he I should almost regret it.'

'And so I do,' said Silverbridge.

When the ladies were gone the old Earl turned himself round to the fire, having filled his glass and pushed the bottles away from him, as though he meant to leave the two young men to themselves. He sat leaning with his head on his hand, looking the picture of woe. It was now only nine o'clock, and there would be no whist at the Beaufort till eleven. There was still more than an hour to be endured before the brougham* would come to fetch him. 'I suppose we shall have a majority,' said Frank, trying to rouse him.

'Who does "We" mean?' asked the Earl.

'The Conservatives, of whom I take the liberty to call myself one.'

'It sounded as though you were a very influential member of the party.'

'I consider myself to be one of the party, and so I say "We."'

Upstairs in the drawing-room Miss Cassewary did her duty loyally. It was quite right that young ladies and young gentlemen should be allowed to talk together, and very right indeed that such a young gentleman as Lord Silverbridge should be allowed to talk to such a young lady as Lady Mabel. What could be so nice as a marriage between the heir of the house of Omnium and Lady Mabel Grex? Lady Mabel looked indeed to be the elder,—but they were in truth the same age. All the world acknowledged that Lady Mabel was very clever and very beautiful and fit to be a Duchess. Even the Earl, when Miss Cassewary hinted at the matter to him, grunted an assent. Lady Mabel had already refused one or two not ineligible offers, and it was necessary that something should be done. There had been at one time a fear in Miss Cassewary's bosom lest her charge should fall too deeply in love with Frank Tregear;—but Miss Cassewary knew that whatever danger there might have been in that respect had passed away. Frank was willing to talk to her, while Mabel and Lord Silverbridge were in a corner together.

'I shall be on tenterhooks now till I know how it is to be at Silverbridge,' said the young lady.

'It is very good of you to feel so much interest.'

'Of course I feel an interest. Are not you one of us? When is it to be?'

'They say that the elections will be over before the Derby.'

'And which do you care for the most?'

'I should like to pull off the Derby, I own.'

'From what papa says, I should think the other event is the more probable.'

'Doesn't the Earl stand to win on Prime Minister?'

'I never know anything about his betting. But,—you know his way,—he said you were going to drop a lot of money like a—— I can't quite tell you what he likened you to.'

'The Earl may be mistaken.'

'You are not betting much, I hope.'

'Not plunging. But I have a little money on.'

'Don't get into a way of betting.'

'Why:—what difference does it make,—to you?'

'Is that kind, Lord Silverbridge?'

'I meant to say that if I did make a mess of it you wouldn't care about it.'

'Yes, I should. I should care very much. I dare say you could lose a great deal of money and care nothing about it.'

'Indeed I could not.'

'What would be a great deal of money to me. But you would want to get it back again. And in that way you would be regularly on the turf.'

'And why not?'

'I want to see better things from you.'

'You ought not to preach against the turf, Lady Mab.'

'Because of papa? But I am not preaching against the turf. If I were such as you are I would have a horse or two myself. A man in your position should do a little of everything. You

77

should hunt and have a yacht, and stalk deer and keep your own trainer at Newmarket.'

'I wish you'd say all that to my father.'

'Of course I mean if you can afford it. I like a man to like pleasure. But I despise a man who makes a business of his pleasures. When I hear that this man is the best whist-player in London, and that man the best billiard-player, I always know that they can do nothing else, and then I despise them.'

'You needn't despise me, because I do nothing well,' said he, as he got up to take his leave.

'I do so hope you'll get the seat,—and win the Derby.'

These were her last words to him as she wished him good-night.

CHAPTER X

'Why not like Romeo if I feel like Romeo?'

'THAT's nonsense, Miss Cass, and I shall,' said Lady Mabel. They were together, on the morning after the little dinner-party described in the last chapter, in a small back sitting-room which was supposed to be Lady Mabel's own, and the servant had just announced the fact that Mr. Tregear was below.

'Then I shall go down too,' said Miss Cassewary.

'You'll do nothing of the kind. Will you please to tell me what it is you are afraid of? Do you think that Frank is going to make love to me again?'

'No.'

'Or that if I chose that he should I would let you stop me? He is in love with somebody else,—and perhaps I am too. And we are two paupers.'

'My lord would not approve of it.'

'If you know what my lord approves of and what he disapproves you understand him a great deal better than I do. And if you mind what he approves or disapproves, you care

78

for his opinion a great deal more than I do. My cousin is here now to talk to me,—about his own affairs, and I mean to see him,—alone.' Then she left the little room, and went down to that in which Frank was waiting for her, without the company of Miss Cassewary.

'Do you really mean,' she said after they had been together for some minutes, 'that you had the courage to ask the Duke for his daughter's hand?'

'Why not?'

'I believe you would dare do anything.'

'I couldn't very well take it without asking him.'

'As I am not acquainted with the young lady I don't know how that might be.'

'And if I took her so, I should have to take her empty-handed.'

'Which wouldn't suit;—would it?'

'It wouldn't suit for her,—whose comforts and happiness are much more to me than my own.'

'No doubt! Of course you are terribly in love.'

'Very thoroughly in love, I think, I am.'

'For the tenth time, I should say.'

'For the second only. I don't regard myself as a monument of constancy, but I think I am less fickle than some other people.'

'Meaning me!'

'Not especially.'

'Frank, that is ill-natured, and almost unmanly,—and false also. When have I been fickle? You say that there was one before with you. I say that there has never really been one with me at all. No one knows that better than yourself. I cannot afford to be in love till I am quite sure that the man is fit to be, and will be, my husband.'

'I doubt sometimes whether you are capable of being in love with anyone.'

'I think I am,' she said very gently. 'But I am at any rate capable of not being in love till I wish it. Come, Frank; do not quarrel with me. You know,—you ought to know,—that

I should have loved you had it not been that such love would have been bad for both of us.'

'It is a kind of self-restraint I do not understand.'

'Because you are not a woman.'

'Why did you twit me with changing my love?'

'Because I am a woman. Can't you forgive as much as that to me?'

'Certainly. Only you must not think that I have been false because I now love her so dearly.'

'I do not think you are false. I would do anything to help you if there were anything I could do. But when you spoke so like a Romeo of your love——'

'Why not like a Romeo, if I feel like a Romeo?'

'But I doubt whether Romeo talked much to Rosaline of his love for Juliet.* But you shall talk to me of yours for Lady Mary, and I will listen to you patiently and encourage you, and will not even think of those former vows.'

'The former vows were foolish.'

'Oh,—of course.'

'You at least used to say so.'

'I say so now, and they shall be as though they had been never spoken. So you bearded the Duke in his den, and asked him for Lady Mary's hand,—just as though you had been a young Duke yourself and owned half a county?'

'Just the same.'

'And what did he say?'

'He swore that it was impossible.—Of course I knew all that before.'

'How will it be now? You will not give it up?'

'Certainly not.'

'And Lady Mary?'

'One human being can perhaps never answer for another with perfect security.'

'But you feel sure of her?'

'I do.'

'He, I should think, can be very imperious.'

'And so can she. The Pallisers are all obstinate.'

'Is Silverbridge obstinate?' she asked.

'Stiff-necked as a bull if he takes it into his head to be so.'

'I shouldn't have thought it.'

'No;—because he is so soft in his manner, and often finds it easier to be led by others than to direct himself.'

Then she remained silent for a few seconds. They were both thinking of the same thing, and both wishing to speak of it. But the words came to her first. 'I wonder what he thinks of me.' Whereupon Tregear only smiled. 'I suppose he has spoken to you about me?'

'Why do you ask?'

'Why!'

'And why should I tell you? Suppose he should have said to me in the confidence of friendship that he thinks you ugly and stupid.'

'I am sure he has not said that. He has eyes to see and ears to hear. But, though I am neither ugly nor stupid, he needn't like me.'

'Do you want him to like you?'

'Yes, I do. Oh yes; you may laugh; but if I did not think that I could be a good wife to him I would not take his hand even to become Duchess of Omnium.'

'Do you mean that you love him, Mabel?'

'No; I do not mean that. But I would learn to love him. You do not believe that?' Here he smiled again and shook his head. 'It is as I said before, because you are not a woman, and do not understand how women are trammelled. Do you think ill of me because I say this?'

'No, indeed.'

'Do not think ill of me if you can help it, because you are almost the only friend that I can trust. I almost trust dear old Cass, but not quite. She is old-fashioned and I shock her. As for other women, there isn't one anywhere to whom I would say a word. Only think how a girl such as I am is placed; or indeed any girl. You, if you see a woman that you fancy, can pursue her, can win her and triumph, or lose her and gnaw your heart;—at any rate you can do something.

You can tell her that you love her; can tell her so again and again even though she should scorn you. You can set yourself about the business you have taken in hand and can work hard at it. What can a girl do?'

'Girls work hard too sometimes.'

'Of course they do;—but everybody feels that they are sinning against their sex. Of love, such as a man's is, a woman ought to know nothing. How can she love with passion when she should never give her love till it has been asked, and not then unless her friends tell her that the thing is suitable? Love such as that to me is out of the question. But, as it is fit that I should be married, I wish to be married well.'

'And you will love him after a fashion?'

'Yes;—after a very sterling fashion. I will make his wishes my wishes, his ways my ways, his party my party, his home my home, his ambition my ambition,—his honour my honour.' As she said this she stood up with her hands clenched and head erect, and her eyes flashing. 'Do you not know me well enough to be sure that I should be loyal to him?'

'Yes;—I think that you would be loyal.'

'Whether I loved him or not, he should love me.'

'And you think that Silverbridge would do?'

'Yes, I think that Silverbridge would do. You, no doubt, will say that I am flying high?'

'Not too high. Why should you not fly high? If I can justify myself, surely I cannot accuse you.'

'It is hardly the same thing, Frank. Of course, there is not a girl in London to whom Lord Silverbridge would not be the best match that she could make. He has the choice of us all.'

'Most girls would think twice before refusing him.'

'Very few would think twice before accepting him. Perhaps he wishes to add to his wealth by marrying richly,—as his father did.'

'No thought on that subject will ever trouble him. That will be all as it happens. As soon as he takes a sufficient fancy to a girl he will ask her straight off. I do not say that he might not change afterwards, but he would mean it at the time.'

'If he had once said the word to me, he should not change. But then what right have I to expect it? What has he ever said about me?'

'Very little. But had he said much I should not tell you.'

'You are my friend,—but you are his too; and he, perhaps, is more to you than I am. As his friend it may be your duty to tell him all that I am saying. If so, I have been wrong.'

'Do you think that I shall do that, Mabel?'

'I do not know. Men are so strong in their friendships.'

'Mine with you is the older, and the sweeter. Though we may not be more than friends, I will say that it is the more tender. In my heart of hearts I do not think that Silverbridge could do better.'

'Thanks for that, Frank.'

'I shall tell him nothing of you that can set him against you.'

'And you would be glad to see me his wife?' she said.

'As you must be somebody's wife, and not mine.'

'I cannot be yours, Frank; can I?'

'And not mine,' he repeated, 'I will endeavour to be glad. Who can explain his feelings in such a matter? Though I most truly love the girl I hope to marry, yet my heart goes back to former things and opens itself to past regrets.'

'I know it all,' she whispered.

'But you and I must be too wise to permit ourselves to be tormented by such foolish melancholy.' As he said this he took her hand, half with the purpose of bidding her good-bye, but partly with the idea of giving some expression to the tenderness of his feelings. But as he did so, the door was opened, and the old Earl shambled into the room.

'What the deuce are you doing here?' he said.

'I have been talking to Lady Mabel.'

'For about an hour.'

'Indeed I do not know for how long.'

'Papa, he is going to be married.' When she said this Frank Tregear turned round and looked at her almost in anger.

'Going to be married, is he? Who is the fortunate woman?'

'I don't think he will let me tell you.'

'Not yet, I think,' said Frank gloomily. 'There is nothing settled.'

The old Earl looked puzzled, but Lady Mabel's craft had been successful. If this objectionable young second-cousin had come there to talk about his marriage with another young woman, the conversation must have been innocent. 'Where is Miss Cassewary?' asked the Earl.

'I asked her not to come down with me because Frank wished to speak to me about his own affairs. You have no objection to his coming, papa?'

There had been objections raised to any intimacy with Frank Tregear; but all that was now nearly two years since. He had been assured over and over again by Miss Cassewary that he need not be afraid of Frank Tregear, and had in a sort of way assented to the young man's visits. 'I think he might find something better to do with his time than hanging about here all day.' Frank, shrugging his shoulders, and having shaken hands both with the daughter and father, took his hat and departed. 'Who is the girl?' asked the Earl.

'You heard him say that I was not to tell.'

'Has she got money?'

'I believe she will have a great deal.'

'Then she is a great fool for her pains,' said the Earl, shambling off again.

Lady Mabel spent the greater part of the afternoon alone, endeavouring to recall to her mind all that she had said to Frank Tregear, and questioning herself as to the wisdom and truth of her own words. She had intended to tell the truth,— but hardly perhaps the whole truth. The life which was before her,—which it was necessary that she should lead,—seemed to her to be so difficult! She could not clearly see her way to be pure and good and feminine, and at the same time wise. She had been false now;—so far false that she had told her friend that she had never been in love. But she was in love;—in love with him, Frank Tregear She knew it as thoroughly as it was possible for her to know anything;—and had acknowledged it to herself a score of times.

But she could not marry him. And it was expected, nay, almost necessary that she should marry someone. To that someone, how good she would be! How she would strive by duty and attention, and if possible by affection, to make up for that misfortune of her early love!

And so I hope that I have brought my cart in to its appointed place in the front, without showing too much of the horse.

CHAPTER XI

'*Cruel*'

FOR two or three days after the first scene between the Duke and his daughter,—that scene in which she was forbidden either to see or to write to her lover,—not a word was said at Matching about Mr. Tregear, nor were any steps taken towards curtailing her liberty of action. She had said she would not write to him without telling her father, and the Duke was too proud of the honour of his family to believe it to be possible that she should deceive him. Nor was it possible. Not only would her own idea of duty prevent her from writing to her lover, although she had stipulated for the right to do so in some possible emergency,—but, carried far beyond that in her sense of what was right and wrong, she felt it now incumbent on her to have no secret from her father at all. The secret, as long as it had been a secret, had been a legacy from her mother,—and had been kept, at her lover's instance, during that period of mourning for her mother in which it would, she thought, have been indecorous that there should be any question of love or of giving in marriage. It had been a burden to her, though a necessary burden. She had been very clear that the revelation should be made to her father, when it was made, by her lover. That had been done,—and now it was open to her to live without any secrecy,—as was her nature.

She meant to cling to her lover. She was quite sure of that. Nothing could divide her from him but his death or hers,—or falseness on his part. But as to marriage, that would not be possible till her father had assented. And as to seeing the man,—ah, yes, if she could do so with her father's assent! She would not be ashamed to own her great desire to see him. She would tell her father that all her happiness depended upon seeing him. She would not be coy in speaking of her love. But she would obey her father.

She had a strong idea that she would ultimately prevail,— an idea also that that 'ultimately' should not be postponed to some undefined middle-aged period of her life. As she intended to belong to Frank Tregear, she thought it expedient that he should have the best of her days as well as what might be supposed to be the worst; and she therefore resolved that it would be her duty to make her father understand that though she would certainly obey him, she would look to be treated humanely by him, and not to be made miserable for an indefinite term of years.

The first word spoken between them on the subject,—the first word after that discussion,—began with him and was caused by his feeling that her present life at Matching must be sad and lonely. Lady Cantrip had again written that she would be delighted to take her;—but Lady Cantrip was in London and must be in London, at any rate when Parliament should again be sitting. A London life would perhaps, at present, hardly suit Lady Mary. Then a plan had been prepared which might be convenient. The Duke had a house at Richmond, on the river, called The Horns.*That should be lent to Lady Cantrip, and Mary should there be her guest. So it was settled between the Duke and Lady Cantrip. But as yet Lady Mary knew nothing of the arrangement.

'I think I shall go up to town to-morrow,' said the Duke to his daughter.

'For long?'

'I shall be gone only one night. It is on your behalf that I am going.'

86

'On my behalf, papa?'

'I have been writing to Lady Cantrip.'

'Not about Mr. Tregear?'

'No;—not about Mr. Tregear,' said the father with a mixture of anger and solemnity in his tone. 'It is my desire to regard Mr. Tregear as though he did not exist.'

'That is not possible, papa.'

'I have alluded to the inconvenience of your position here.'

'Why is it inconvenient?'

'You are too young to be without a companion. It is not fit that you should be so much alone.'

'I do not feel it.'

'It is very melancholy for you, and cannot be good for you. They will go down to The Horns, so that you will not be absolutely in London, and you will find Lady Cantrip a very nice person.'

'I don't care for new people just now, papa,' she said. But to this he paid but little heed; nor was she prepared to say that she would not do as he directed. When therefore he left Matching, she understood that he was going to prepare a temporary home for her. Nothing further was said about Tregear. She was too proud to ask that no mention of his name should be made to Lady Cantrip. And he when he left the house did not think that he would find himself called upon to allude to the subject.

But when Lady Cantrip made some inquiry about the girl and her habits,—asking what were her ordinary occupations, how she was accustomed to pass her hours, to what she chiefly devoted herself,—then at last with much difficulty the Duke did bring himself to tell the story. 'Perhaps it is better you should know it all,' he said as he told it.

'Poor girl! Yes, Duke; upon the whole it is better that I should know it all,' said Lady Cantrip. 'Of course he will not come here.'

'Oh dear; I hope not.'

'Nor to The Horns.'

'I hope he will never see her again anywhere,' said the Duke.

'Poor girl!'

'Have I not been right? Is it not best to put an end to such a thing at once?'

'Certainly at once, if it has to be put an end to,—and can be put an end to.'

'It must be put an end to,' said the Duke, very decidedly. 'Do you not see that it must be so? Who is Mr. Tregear?'

'I suppose they were allowed to be together.'

'He was unfortunately intimate with Silverbridge, who took him over to Italy. He has nothing; not even a profession.' Lady Cantrip could not but smile when she remembered the immense wealth of the man who was speaking to her;—and the Duke saw the smile and understood it. 'You will understand what I mean, Lady Cantrip. If this young man were in other respects suitable, of course I could find an income for them. But he is nothing; just an idle seeker for pleasure without the means of obtaining it.'

'That is very bad.'

'As for rank,' continued the Duke energetically, 'I do not think that I am specially wedded to it. I have found myself as willing to associate with those who are without it as with those who have it. But for my child, I would wish her to mate with one of her own class.'

'It would be best.'

'When a young man comes to me who, though I believe him to be what is called a gentleman, has neither rank, nor means, nor profession, nor name, and asks for my daughter, surely I am right to say that such a marriage shall not be thought of. Was I not right?' demanded the Duke persistently.

'But it is a pity that it should be so. It is a pity that they should ever have come together.'

'It is indeed, indeed to be lamented,—and I will own at once that the fault was not hers. Though I must be firm in this, you are not to suppose that I am angry with her. I have myself been to blame.' This he said with a resolution that,—

as he and his wife had been one flesh,—all faults committed by her should, now that she was dead, be accepted by him as his faults. 'It had not occurred to me that as yet she would love any man.'

'Has it gone deep with her, Duke?'

'I fear that all things go deep with her.'

'Poor girl!'

'But they shall be kept apart! As long as your great kindness is continued to her they shall be kept apart!'

'I do not think that I should be found good at watching a young lady.'

'She will require no watching.'

'Then of course they will not meet. She had better know that you have told me.'

'She shall know it.'

'And let her know also that anything I can do to make her happy shall be done. But, Duke, there is but one cure.'

'Time, you mean.'

'Yes; time; but I did not mean time.' Then she smiled as she went on. 'You must not suppose that I am speaking against my own sex if I say that she will not forget Mr. Tregear till someone else has made himself agreeable to her. We must wait till she can go out a little into society. Then she will find out that there are others in the world besides Mr. Tregear. It so often is the case that a girl's love means her sympathy for him who has chanced to be nearest to her.'

The Duke as he went away thought very much of what Lady Cantrip had said to him;—particularly of those last words. 'Till some one else has made himself agreeable to her.' Was he to send his girl into the world in order that she might find a lover? There was something in the idea which was thoroughly distasteful to him. He had not given his mind much to the matter, but he felt that a woman should be sought for,—sought for and extracted, cunningly, as it were, from some hiding-place, and not sent out into a market to be exposed as for sale. In his own personal history there had been a misfortune,—a misfortune, the sense of which he could

never, at any moment, have expressed to any ears, the memory
of which had been always buried in his own bosom,—but
a misfortune in that no such cunning extraction on his part
had won for him the woman to whose hands had been confided
the strings of his heart. His wife had undergone that process
of extraction before he had seen her, and his marriage with
her had been a matter of sagacious bargaining. He was now
told that his daughter must be sent out among young men in
order that she might become sufficiently fond of some special
one to be regardless of Tregear. There was a feeling that in
doing so she must lose something of the freshness of the
bloom of her innocence. How was this transfer of her love to
be effected? Let her go here because she will meet the heir
of this wealthy house who may probably be smitten by her
charms; or there because that other young lordling would
make a fit husband for her. Let us contrive to throw her into
the arms of this man, or put her into the way of that man.
Was his girl to be exposed to this? Surely that method of
bargaining to which he had owed his own wife would be better
than that. Let it be said,—only he himself most certainly could
not be the person to say it,—let it be said to some man of
rank and means and fairly good character: 'Here is a wife for
you with so many thousand pounds, with beauty, as you can
see for yourself, with rank and belongings of the highest; very
good in every respect;—only that as regards her heart she
thinks she has given it to a young man named Tregear. No
marriage there is possible; but perhaps the young lady might
suit you?' It was thus he had been married. There was an
absence in it of that romance which, though he had never
experienced it in his own life, was always present to his
imagination. His wife had often ridiculed him because he could
only live among figures and official details; but to her had
not been given the power of looking into a man's heart and
feeling all that was there. Yes;—in such bargaining for a wife,
in such bargaining for a husband, there could be nothing of
the tremulous delicacy of feminine romance; but it would be
better than standing at a stall in the market till the sufficient

purchaser should come. It never occurred to him that the delicacy, the innocence, the romance, the bloom might all be preserved if he would give his girl to the man whom she said she loved. Could he have modelled her future course according to his own wishes, he would have had her live a gentle life for the next three years, with a pencil perhaps in her hand or a music-book before her;—and then come forth, cleaned as it were by such quarantine from the impurity to which she had been subjected.

When he was back at Matching he at once told his daughter what he had arranged for her, and then there took place a prolonged discussion both as to his view of her future life and as to her own. 'You did tell her then about Mr. Tregear?' she asked.

'As she is to have charge of you for a time I thought it best.'

'Perhaps it is. Perhaps—you were afraid.'

'No; I was not afraid,' he said angrily.

'You need not be afraid. I shall do nothing elsewhere that I would not do here, and nothing anywhere without telling you.'

'I know I can trust you.'

'But, papa, I shall always intend to marry Mr. Tregear.'

'No!' he exclaimed.

'Yes;—always. I want you to understand exactly how it is. Nothing you can do can separate me from him.'

'Mary, that is very wicked.'

'It cannot be wicked to tell the truth, papa. I mean to try to do all that you tell me. I shall not see him, or write to him,—unless there should be some very particular reason. And if I did see him or write to him I would tell you. And of course I should not think of—of marrying without your leave. But I shall expect you to let me marry him.'

'Never!'

'Then I shall think you are—cruel; and you will break my heart.'

'You should not call your father cruel.'

'I hope you will not be cruel.'

91

'I can never permit you to marry this man. It would be altogether improper. I cannot allow you to say that I am cruel because I do what I feel to be my duty. You will see other people.'

'A great many perhaps.'

'And will learn to,—to,—to forget him.'

'Never! I will not forget him. I should hate myself if I thought it possible. What would love be worth if it could be forgotten in that way?' As he heard this he reflected whether his own wife, this girl's mother, had ever forgotten her early love for that Burgo Fitzgerald whom in her girlhood she had wished to marry.

When he was leaving her she called him back again. 'There is one other thing I think I ought to say, papa. If Lady Cantrip speaks to me about Mr. Tregear, I can only tell her what I have told you. I shall never give him up.' When he heard this he turned angrily from her, almost stamping his foot upon the ground, when she quietly left the room.

Cruel! She had told him that he would be cruel, if he opposed her love. He thought he knew of himself that he could not be cruel,—even to a fly, even to a political opponent. There could be no cruelty without dishonesty, and did he not always struggle to be honest? Cruel to his own daughter!

CHAPTER XII

At Richmond

THE pity of it!* The pity of it! It was thus that Lady Cantrip looked at it. From what the girl's father had said to her she was disposed to believe that the malady had gone deep with her. 'All things go deep with her,' he had said. And she too from other sources had heard something of this girl. She was afraid that it would go deep. It was a thousand pities! Then she asked herself whether the marriage ought to be regarded as impossible. The Duke had been very positive,— had declared again and again that it was quite impossible, had

so expressed himself as to make her aware that he intended
her to understand that he would not yield whatever the sufferings of the girl might be. But Lady Cantrip knew the world
well and was aware that in such matters daughters are apt to
be stronger than their fathers. He had declared Tregear to
be a young man with very small means, and intent on such
pleasures as require great means for their enjoyment. No
worse character could be given to a gentleman who had proposed himself as a son-in-law. But Lady Cantrip thought it
possible that the Duke might be mistaken in this. She had
never seen Mr. Tregear, but she fancied that she had heard his
name, and that the name had been connected with a character
different from that which the Duke had given him.

Lady Cantrip, who at this time was a young-looking
woman, not much above forty, had two daughters, both of
whom were married. The younger about a year since had
become the wife of Lord Nidderdale, a middle-aged young
man who had been long about town, a cousin of the late
Duchess, the heir to a marquisate, and a Member of Parliament. The marriage had not been considered to be very
brilliant; but the husband was himself good-natured and
pleasant, and Lady Cantrip was fond of him. In the first place
she went to him for information.

'Oh yes, I know him. He's one of our set at the Beargarden.'

'Not your set, now, I hope,' she said laughing.

'Well;—I don't see so much of them as I used to do.
Tregear is not a bad fellow at all. He's always with Silverbridge. When Silverbridge does what Tregear tells him, he
goes along pretty straight. But unfortunately there's another
man called Tifto, and when Tifto is in the ascendant then
Silverbridge is apt to get a little astray.'

'He's not in debt, then?'

'Who?—Tregear? I should think he's the last man in the
world to owe a penny to any one.'

'Is he a betting man?'

'Oh dear no; quite the other way up. He's a severe, sarcastic bookish sort of fellow,—a chap who knows everything and turns up his nose at people who know nothing.'

'Has he got anything of his own?'

'Not much, I should say. If he had had any money he would have married Lady Mab Grex last year.'

Lady Cantrip was inclined from what she now learned to think that the Duke must be wrong about the young man. But before Lady Mary joined her she made further inquiry. She too knew Lady Mabel, and knowing Lady Mabel, she knew Miss Cassewary. She contrived to find herself alone with Miss Cassewary, and asked some further questions about Mr. Tregear. 'He is a cousin of my Lord's,' said Miss Cass.

'So I thought. I wonder what sort of a young man he is. He is a good deal with Lord Silverbridge.'

Then Miss Cassewary spoke her opinion very plainly. 'If Lord Silverbridge had nobody worse about him than Mr. Tregear he would not come to much harm.'

'I suppose he's not very well off.'

'No;—certainly not. He will have a property of some kind, I believe, when his mother dies. I think very well of Mr. Tregear;—only I wish that he had a profession. But why are you asking about him, Lady Cantrip?'

'Nidderdale was talking to me about him and saying that he was so much with Lord Silverbridge. Lord Silverbridge is going into Parliament now, and, as it were, beginning the world, and it would be a thousand pities that he should get into bad hands.' It may, however, be doubted whether Miss Cassewary was hoodwinked by this little story.

Early in the second week in May the Duke brought his daughter up to The Horns, and at the same time expressed his intention of remaining in London. When he did so Lady Mary at once asked whether she might not be with him, but he would not permit it. The house in London would, he said, be more gloomy even than Matching.

'I am quite ashamed of giving you so much trouble,' Lady Mary said to her new friend.

'We are delighted to have you, my dear.'

'But I know that you have been obliged to leave London because I am with you.'

'There is nothing I like so much as this place, which your father has been kind enough to lend us. As for London, there is nothing now to make me like being there. Both my girls are married, and therefore I regard myself as an old woman who has done her work. Don't you think this place very much nicer than London at this time of the year?'

'I don't know London at all. I had only just been brought out when poor mamma went abroad.'

The life they led was very quiet, and must probably have been felt to be dull by Lady Cantrip, in spite of her old age and desire for retirement. But the place itself was very lovely. May of all the months of the year is in England the most insidious, the most dangerous, and the most inclement. A greatcoat cannot be endured, and without a greatcoat who can endure a May wind and live? But of all months it is the prettiest. The grasses are then the greenest, and the young foliage of the trees, while it has all the glory and all the colour of spring vegetation, does not hide the form of the branches as do the heavy masses of the larger leaves which come in the advancing summer. And of all villas near London The Horns was the sweetest. The broad green lawn swept down to the very margin of the Thames, which absolutely washed the fringe of grass when the tide was high. And here, along the bank, was a row of flowering ashes, the drooping boughs of which in places touched the water. It was one of those spots which when they are first seen make the beholder feel that to be able to live there and look at it always would be happiness enough for life.

At the end of the week there came a visitor to see Lady Mary. A very pretty carriage was driven up to the door of The Horns, and the servant asked for Lady Mary Palliser. The owner of that carriage was Mrs. Finn. Now it must be explained to the reader that there had never been any friendship between Mrs. Finn and Lady Cantrip, though the ladies had met each other. The great political intimacy which had existed between the Duke and Lord Cantrip had created some intimacy also between their wives. The Duchess and Lady Cantrip had been friends,—after a fashion. But Mrs. Finn had never been cordially accepted by those among whom Lady Cantrip chiefly lived. When therefore the name was announced, the servant expressly stating that the visitor had asked for Lady Mary, Lady Cantrip, who was with her guest, had to bethink herself what she would do. The Duke, who was at this time very full of wrath against Mrs. Finn, had not mentioned this lady's name when delivering up the charge of his daughter to Lady Cantrip. At this moment it occurred to her that not improbably Mrs. Finn would cease to be included in the intimacies of the Palliser family from the time of the death of the Duchess,—that the Duke would not care to maintain the old relations, and that he would be as little anxious to do it for his daughter as for himself. If so, could it be right that Mrs. Finn should come down here, to a house which was now in the occupation of a lady with whom she was not on inviting terms, in order that she might thus force herself on the Duke's daughter? Mrs. Finn had not left her carriage, but had sent in to ask if Lady Mary could see her. In all this there was considerable embarrassment. She looked round at her guest, who had at once risen from her chair. 'Would you wish to see her?' asked Lady Cantrip.

'Oh yes; certainly.'

'Have you seen her since,—since you came home from Italy?'

'Oh dear, yes! She was down at Matching when poor mamma died. And papa persuaded her to remain afterwards. Of course I will see her.' Then the servant was desired to ask Mrs. Finn to come in;—and while this was being done Lady Cantrip retired.

Mrs. Finn embraced her young friend, and asked after her welfare, and after the welfare of the house in which she was staying,—a house with which Mrs. Finn herself had been well acquainted,—and said half-a-dozen pretty little things in her

96

own quiet pretty way, before she spoke of the matter which had really brought her to The Horns on that day.

'I have had a correspondence with your father, Mary.'

'Indeed.'

'And unfortunately one that has been far from agreeable to me.'

'I am sorry for that, Mrs. Finn.'

'So am I, very sorry. I may say with perfect truth that there is no man in the world, except my own husband, for whom I feel so perfect an esteem as I do for your father. If it were not that I do not like to be carried away by strong language I would speak of more than esteem. Through your dear mother I have watched his conduct closely, and have come to think that there is perhaps no other man at the same time so just and so patriotic. Now he is very angry with me,—and most unjustly angry.'

'Is it about me?'

'Yes;—it is about you. Had it not been altogether about you I would not have troubled you.'

'And about——?'

'Yes;—about Mr. Tregear also. When I tell you that there has been a correspondence I must explain that I have written one long letter to the Duke, and that in answer I have received a very short one. That has been the whole correspondence. Here is your father's letter to me.' Then she brought out of her pocket a note, which Lady Mary read,—covered with blushes as she did so. The note was as follows:

'The Duke of Omnium understands from Mrs. Finn's letter that Mrs. Finn, while she was the Duke's guest at Matching, was aware of a certain circumstance affecting the Duke's honour and happiness,—which circumstance she certainly did not communicate to the Duke. The Duke thinks that the trust which had been placed in Mrs. Finn should have made such a communication imperative. The Duke feels that no further correspondence between himself and Mrs. Finn on the matter could lead to any good result.'

'Do you understand it?' asked Mrs. Finn.

'I think so.'

'It simply means this,—that when at Matching he had thought me worthy of having for a time the charge of you and of your welfare, that he had trusted me, who was the friend of your dear mother, to take for a time in regard to you the place which had been so unhappily left vacant by her death; and it means also that I deceived him and betrayed that trust by being privy to an engagement on your part, of which he disapproves, and of which he was not then aware.'

'I suppose he does mean that.'

'Yes, Lady Mary; that is what he means. And he means further to let me know that as I did so foully betray the trust which he had placed in me,—that as I had consented to play the part of assistant to you in that secret engagement,—therefore he casts me off as altogether unworthy of his esteem and acquaintance. It is as though he had told me in so many words that among women he had known none more vile or more false than I.'

'Not that, Mrs. Finn.'

'Yes, that;—all of that. He tells me that, and then says that there shall be no more words spoken or written about it. I can hardly submit to so stern a judgment. You know the truth, Lady Mary.'

'Do not call me Lady Mary. Do not quarrel with me.'

'If your father has quarrelled with me, it would not be fit that you and I should be friends. Your duty to him would forbid it. I should not have come to you now did I not feel that I am bound to justify myself. The thing of which I am accused is so repugnant to me, that I am obliged to do something and to say something, even though the subject itself be one on which I would so willingly be silent.'

'What can I do, Mrs. Finn?'

'It was Mr. Tregear who first told me that your father was angry with me. He knew what I had done and why, and he was bound to tell me in order that I might have an opportunity of setting myself right with the Duke. Then I wrote and

explained everything,—how you had told me of the engagement, and how I had then urged Mr. Tregear that he should
not keep such a matter secret from your father. In answer
to my letter I have received—that.'

'Shall I write and tell papa?'

'He should be made to understand that from the moment
in which I heard of the engagement I was urgent with you
and with Mr. Tregear that he should be informed of it. You
will remember what passed.'

'I remember it all.'

'I did not conceive it to be my duty to tell the Duke myself,
but I did conceive it to be my duty to see he should be told.
Now he writes as though I had known the secret from the
first, and as though I had been concealing it from him at the
very moment in which he was asking me to remain at Matching on your behalf. That I consider to be hard,—and unjust.
I cannot deny what he says. I did know of it while I was at
Matching, for it was at Matching that you told me. But he
implies that I knew it before. When you told me your story
I did feel that it was my duty to see that the matter was not
kept longer from him;—and I did my duty. Now your father
takes upon himself to rebuke me,—and takes upon himself
at the same time to forbid me to write to him again!'

'I will tell him all, Mrs. Finn.'

'Let him understand this. I do not wish to write to him
again. After what has passed I cannot say I wish to see him
again. But I think he should acknowledge to me that he has
been mistaken. He need not then fear that I shall trouble him
with any reply. But I shall know that he has acquitted me of
a fault of which I cannot bear to think I should be accused.'
Then she took a somewhat formal though still an affectionate
farewell of the girl.

'I want to see papa as soon as possible,' said Lady Mary
when she was again with Lady Cantrip. The reason for her
wish was soon given, and then the whole story told. 'You do
not think that she should have gone to papa at once?' Lady
Mary asked. It was a point of moral law on which the elder

woman, who had had girls of her own, found it hard to give an immediate answer. It certainly is expedient that parents should know at once of any engagement by which their daughters may seek to contract themselves. It is expedient that they should be able to prevent any secret contracts. Lady Cantrip felt strongly that Mrs. Finn having accepted the confidential charge of the daughter could not, without gross betrayal of trust, allow herself to be the depositary of such a secret. 'But she did not allow herself,' said Lady Mary, pleading for her friend.

'But she left the house without telling him, my dear.'

'But it was because of what she did that he was told.'

'That is true; but I doubt whether she should have left him an hour in ignorance.'

'But it was I who told her. She would have betrayed me.'

'She was not a fit recipient for your confidence, Mary. But I do not wish to accuse her. She seems to be a high-minded woman, and I think that your papa has been hard upon her.'

'And mamma knew it always,' said Mary. To this Lady Cantrip could give no answer. Whatever cause for anger the Duke might have against Mrs. Finn, there had been cause for much more against his wife. But she had freed herself from all accusation by death.

Lady Mary wrote to her father, declaring that she was most particularly anxious to see him and talk to him about Mrs. Finn.

CHAPTER XIII

The Duke's Injustice

No advantage whatever was obtained by Lady Mary's interview with her father. He persisted that Mrs. Finn had been untrue to him when she left Matching without telling him all that she knew of his daughter's engagement with Mr. Tregear. No doubt by degrees that idea which he at first entertained was expelled from his head,—the idea that she had been cognisant of the whole thing before she came to Matching; but even this was done so slowly that there was no moment at which he became aware of any lessened feeling of indignation. To his thinking she had betrayed her trust, and he could not be got by his daughter to say that he would forgive her. He certainly could not be got to say that he would apologise for the accusation he had made. It was nothing less that his daughter asked; and he could hardly refrain himself from anger when she asked it. 'There should not have been a moment,' he said, 'before she came to me and told me all.' Poor Lady Mary's position was certainly uncomfortable enough. The great sin,—the sin which was so great that to have known it for a day without revealing it was in itself a damning sin on the part of Mrs. Finn,—was Lady Mary's sin. And she differed so entirely from her father as to think that this sin of her own was a virtue, and that to have spoken of it to him would have been, on the part of Mrs. Finn, a treachery so deep that no woman ought to have forgiven it! When he spoke of a matter which deeply affected his honour, —she could hardly refrain from asserting that his honour was quite safe in his daughter's hands. And when in his heart he declared that it should have been Mrs. Finn's first care to save him from disgrace, Lady Mary did break out. 'Papa, there could be no disgrace.' 'That for a moment shall be laid aside,' he said, with that manner by which even his peers in council had never been able not to be awed, 'but if you communicate with Mrs. Finn at all you must make her understand that I regard her conduct as inexcusable.'

Nothing had been gained, and poor Lady Mary was compelled to write a few lines which were to her most painful in writing.

'MY DEAR MRS. FINN,

'I have seen papa, and he thinks that you ought to have told him when I told you. It occurs to me that that would have been a cruel thing to do, and most unfair to Mr. Tregear, who was quite willing to go to papa, and had only put off doing so because of poor mamma's death. As I had told mamma, of course it was right that he should tell papa. Then I told you, because you were so kind to me! I am so sorry that I have got you into this trouble; but what can I do?

'I told him I must write to you. I suppose it is better that I should, although what I have to say is so unpleasant. I hope it will all blow over in time, because I love you dearly. You may be quite sure of one thing,—that I shall never change.' In this assurance the writer was alluding not to her friendship for her friend but her love for her lover,—and so the friend understood her. 'I hope things will be settled some day, and then we may be able to meet.

'Your very affectionate Friend,
'MARY PALLISER.'

Mrs. Finn, when she received this, was alone in her house in Park Lane. Her husband was down in the North of England. On this subject she had not spoken to him, fearing that he would feel himself bound to take some steps to support his wife under the treatment she had received. Even though she must quarrel with the Duke, she was most anxious that her husband should not be compelled to do so. Their connection had been political rather than personal. There were many reasons why there should be no open cause of disruption between them. But her husband was hot-headed, and, were all this to be told him and that letter shown to him which the Duke had written, there would be words between him and the Duke which would probably make impossible any further connection between them.

It troubled her very much. She was by no means not alive to the honour of the Duke's friendship. Throughout her intimacy with the Duchess she had abstained from pressing herself on him, not because she had been indifferent about him, but that she had perceived that she might make her way with him better by standing aloof than by thrusting herself forward. And she had known that she had been successful. She could tell herself with pride that her conduct towards him had been always such as would become a lady of high spirit and fine feeling. She knew that she had deserved well of him, that in all her intercourse with him, with his uncle, and with his wife, she had given much and had taken little. She was the last woman in the world to let a word on such a matter pass her lips; but not the less was she conscious of her merit towards him. And she had been led to act as she had done by sincere admiration for the man. In all their political troubles, she had understood him better than the Duchess had done. Looking on from a distance she had understood the man's character as it had come to her both from his wife and from her own husband.

That he was unjust to her,—cruelly unjust, she was quite sure. He accused her of intentional privity*as to a secret which it behoved him to know, and of being a party to that secrecy. Whereas from the moment in which she had heard the secret she had determined that it must be made known to him. She felt that she had deserved his good opinion in all things, but in nothing more than in the way in which she had acted in this matter. And yet he had treated her with an imperious harshness which amounted to insolence. What a letter it was that he had written to her! The very tips of her ears tingled with heat as she read it again to herself. None of the ordinary courtesies of epistle-craft had been preserved either in the beginning or in the end. It was worse even than if he had called her, Madam without an epithet. 'The Duke understands——' 'The Duke thinks——' 'The Duke feels——' feels that he should not be troubled with either letters or conversation; the upshot of it all being that the Duke declared her to have shown herself unworthy of being treated like a lady! And this after all that she had done!

She would not bear it. That at present was all that she could say to herself. She was not angry with Lady Mary. She did not doubt but that the girl had done the best in her power to bring her father to reason. But because Lady Mary had failed she, Mrs. Finn, was not going to put up with so grievous an injury. And she was forced to bear all this alone! There was none with whom she could communicate;—no one from whom she could ask advice. She would not bring her husband into a quarrel which might be prejudicial to his position as a member of his political party. There was no one else to whom she would tell the secret of Lady Mary's love. And yet she could not bear this injustice done to her.

Then she wrote as follows to the Duke:

'Mrs. Finn presents her compliments to the Duke of Omnium. Mrs. Finn finds it to be essential to her that she should see the Duke in reference to his letter to her. If his Grace will let her know on what day and at what hour he will be kind enough to call on her, Mrs. Finn will be at home to receive him.

'*Park Lane. Thursday, 12th May, 18—.*'

CHAPTER XIV

The New Member for Silverbridge

LORD SILVERBRIDGE was informed that it would be right that he should go down to Silverbridge a few days before the election, to make himself known to the electors. As the day for the election drew near it was understood that there would be no other candidate. The Conservative side was the popular side among the tradesmen of Silverbridge. Silverbridge had been proud to be honoured by the services of the heir of the house of Omnium, even while that heir had been a Liberal,—had regarded it as so much a matter of course that the borough should be at his disposal that no question as to politics had ever arisen while he retained the seat. And had the Duke chosen to continue to send them Liberals, one after another, when he went into the House of Lords, there would have been no question as to the fitness of the man or men so sent. Silverbridge had been supposed to be a Liberal as a matter of course, —because the Pallisers were Liberals. But when the matter was remitted to themselves,—when the Duke declared that he would not interfere any more, for it was thus that the borough had obtained its freedom;—then the borough began to feel Conservative predilections. 'If his Grace really does mean us to do just what we please ourselves, which is a thing we never thought of asking from his Grace, then we find, having turned the matter over among ourselves, that we are upon the whole Conservative.' In this spirit the borough had elected a certain Mr. Fletcher; but in doing so the borough had still a shade of fear that it would offend the Duke. The house of Palliser, Gatherum Castle, the Duke of Omnium, and this special Duke himself, were all so great in the eyes of the borough, that the first and only strong feeling in the borough was the one of duty. The borough did not altogether enjoy being enfranchised. But when the Duke had spoken once, twice, and thrice, then with a hesitating heart the borough returned Mr. Fletcher. Now Mr. Fletcher was wanted elsewhere, having been persuaded to stand for the county, and it was a comfort to the borough that it could resettle itself beneath the warmth of the wings of the Pallisers.

So the matter stood when Lord Silverbridge was told that his presence in the borough for a few hours would be taken as a compliment. Hitherto no one knew him at Silverbridge. During his boyhood he had not been much at Gatherum Castle, and had done his best to eschew the place since he had ceased to be a boy. All the Pallisers took a pride in Gatherum Castle, but they all disliked it. 'Oh yes; I'll go down,' he said to Mr. Morton, who was up in town. 'I needn't go to the great barrack I suppose.' The great barrack was the Castle. 'I'll put up at the Inn.' Mr. Morton begged the heir to come to his own house; but Silverbridge declared that he would prefer the Inn, and so the matter was settled. He was to meet sundry politicians,—Mr. Sprugeon and Mr. Sprout and Mr. Du Boung,*—who would like to be thanked for what they had done. But who was to go with him? He would naturally have asked Tregear, but from Tregear he had for the last week or two been, not perhaps estranged, but separated. He had been much taken up with racing. He had gone down to Chester with

Major Tifto, and under the Major's auspicious influences had won a little money;—and now he was very anxiously preparing himself for the Newmarket Second Spring Meeting. He had therefore passed much of his time with Major Tifto. And when this visit to Silverbridge was pressed on him he thoughtlessly asked Tifto to go with him. Tifto was delighted. Lord Silverbridge was to be met at Silverbridge by various well-known politicians from the neighbourhood, and Major Tifto was greatly elated by the prospect of such an introduction into the political world.

But no sooner had the offer been made by Lord Silverbridge than he saw his own indiscretion. Tifto was very well for Chester or Newmarket, very well perhaps for the Beargarden, but not very well for an electioneering expedition. An idea came to the young nobleman that if it should be his fate to represent Silverbridge in Parliament for the next twenty years, it would be well that Silverbridge should entertain respecting him some exalted estimation,—that Silverbridge should be taught to regard him as a fit son of his father and a worthy specimen of the British political nobility. Struck by serious reflections of this nature he did open his mind to Tregear. 'I am very fond of Tifto,' he said, 'but I don't know whether he's just the sort of fellow to take down to an election.'

'I should think not,' said Tregear very decidedly.

'He's a very good fellow, you know,' said Silverbridge. 'I don't know an honester man than Tifto anywhere.'

'I dare say. Or rather, I don't dare say. I know nothing about the Major's honesty, and I doubt whether you do. He rides very well.'

'What has that to do with it?'

'Nothing on earth. Therefore I advise you not to take him to Silverbridge.'

'You needn't preach.'

'You may call it what you like. Tifto would not hold his tongue, and there is nothing he could say there which would not be to your prejudice.'

'Will you go?'

'If you wish it,' said Tregear.

'What will the governor say?'

'That must be your look-out. In a political point of view I shall not disgrace you. I shall hold my tongue and look like a gentleman,—neither of which is in Tifto's power.'

And so it was settled, that on the day but one after this conversation Lord Silverbridge and Tregear should go together to Silverbridge. But the Major, when on the same night his noble friend's altered plans were explained to him, did not bear the disappointment with equanimity. 'Isn't that a little strange?' he said, becoming very red in the face.

'What do you call strange?' said the Lord.

'Well;—I'd made all my arrangements. When a man has been asked to do a thing like that, he doesn't like to be put off.'

'The truth is, Tifto, when I came to think of it, I saw that, going down to these fellows about Parliament and all that sort of thing, I ought to have a political atmosphere, and not a racing or a betting or a hunting atmosphere.'

'There isn't a man in London who cares more about politics than I do;—and not very many perhaps who understand them better. To tell you the truth, my Lord, I think you are throwing me over.'

'I'll make it up to you,' said Silverbridge, meaning to be kind. 'I'll go down to Newmarket with you and stick to you like wax.'

'No doubt you'll do that,' said Tifto, who, like a fool, failed to see where his advantage lay. 'I can be useful at Newmarket, and so you'll stick to me.'

'Look here, Major Tifto,' said Silverbridge; 'if you are dissatisfied, you and I can easily separate ourselves.'

'I am not dissatisfied,' said the little man, almost crying.

'Then don't talk as though you were. As to Silverbridge, I shall not want you there. When I asked you I was only thinking what would be pleasant to both of us; but since that I have remembered that business must be business.' Even this did not reconcile the angry little man, who as he turned away declared within his own little bosom that he would 'take it out of Silverbridge for that.'

Lord Silverbridge and Tregear went down to the borough together, and on the journey something was said about Lady Mary,—and something also about Lady Mabel. 'From the first, you know,' said Lady Mary's brother, 'I never thought it would answer.'

'Why not answer?'

'Because I knew the governor would not have it. Money and rank and those sort of things are not particularly charming to me. But still things should go together. It is all very well for you and me to be pals, but of course it will be expected that Mary should marry some——'

'Some swell?'

'Some swell, if you will have it.'

'You mean to call yourself a swell?'

'Yes I do,' said Silverbridge, with considerable resolution. 'You ought not to make yourself disagreeable, because you understand all about it as well as anybody. Chance has made me the eldest son of a Duke and heir to an enormous fortune. Chance has made my sister the daughter of a Duke, and an heiress also. My intimacy with you ought to be proof at any rate to you that I don't on that account set myself up above other fellows. But when you come to talk of marriage, of course it is a serious thing.'

'But you have told me more than once that you have no objection on your own score.'

'Nor have I.'

'You are only saying what the Duke will think.'

'I am telling you that it is impossible, and I told you so before. You and she will be kept apart, and so——'

'And so she'll forget me.'

'Something of that kind.'

'Of course I have to trust to her for that. If she forgets me, well and good.'

'She needn't forget you. Lord bless me! you talk as though the thing were not done every day. You'll hear some morning

108

that she is going to marry some fellow who has a lot of money and a good position; and what difference will it make then whether she has forgotten you or not?' It might almost have been supposed that the young man had been acquainted with his mother's history.

After this there was a pause, and there arose conversation about other things, and a cigar was smoked. Then Tregear returned once more to the subject. 'There is one thing I wish to say about it all.'

'What is that?'

'I want you to understand that nothing else will turn me away from my intention but such a marriage on her part as that of which you speak. Nothing that your father can do will turn me.'

'She can't marry without his leave.'

'Perhaps not.'

'That he'll never give,—and I don't suppose you look forward to waiting till his death.'

'If he sees that her happiness really depends on it he will give his leave. It all depends on that. If I judge your father rightly, he's just as soft-hearted as other people. The man who holds out is not the man of the firmest opinion, but the man of the hardest heart.'

'Somebody will talk Mary over.'

'If so, the thing is over. It all depends on her.' Then he went on to tell his friend that he had spoken of his engagement to Lady Mabel. 'I have mentioned it to no soul but to your father and to her.'

'Why to her?'

'Because we were friends together as children. I never had a sister, but she has been more like a sister to me than anyone else. Do you object to her knowing it?'

'Not particularly. It seems to me now that everybody knows everything. There are no longer any secrets.'

'But she is a special friend.'

'Of yours,' said Silverbridge.

'And of yours,' said Tregear.

'Well, yes;—in a sort of way. She is the jolliest girl I know.'

'Take her all round, for beauty, intellect, good sense, and fun at the same time, I don't know anyone equal to her.'

'It's a pity you didn't fall in love with her.'

'We knew each other too early for that. And then she has not a shilling. I should think myself dishonest if I did not tell you that I could not afford to love any girl who hadn't money. A man must live,—and a woman too.'

At the station they were met by Mr. Sprugeon and Mr. Sprout, who, with many apologies for the meanness of such entertainment, took them up to the George and Vulture, which was supposed for the nonce to be the Conservative hotel in the town. Here they were met by other men of importance in the borough, and among them by Mr. Du Boung. Now Mr. Sprout and Mr. Sprugeon were Conservatives, but Mr. Du Boung was a strong Liberal.

'We are, all of us, particularly glad to see your Lordship among us,' said Mr. Du Boung.

'I have told his Lordship how perfectly satisfied you are to see the borough in his Lordship's hands,' said Mr. Sprugeon.

'I am sure it could not be in better,' said Mr. Du Boung. 'For myself I am quite willing to postpone any peculiar shade of politics to the advantage of having your father's son as our representative.'

This Mr. Du Boung said with much intention of imparting both grace and dignity to the occasion. He thought that he was doing a great thing for the house of Omnium, and that the house of Omnium ought to know it.

'That's very kind of you,' said Lord Silverbridge, who had not read as carefully as he should have done the letters which had been sent to him, and did not therefore quite understand the position.

'Mr. Du Boung had intended to stand himself,' said Mr. Sprout.

'But retired in your Lordship's favour,' said Mr. Sprugeon.

'In doing which I considered that I studied the interest of the borough,' said Mr. Du Boung.

'I thought you gave it up because there was hardly a footing for a Liberal,' said his Lordship, very imprudently.

'The borough was always Liberal till the last election,' said Mr. Du Boung, drawing himself up.

'The borough wishes on this occasion to be magnanimous,' said Mr. Sprout, probably having on his mind some confusion between magnanimity and unanimity.

'As your Lordship is coming among us, the borough is anxious to sink politics altogether for the moment,' said Mr. Sprugeon. There had no doubt been a compact between the Sprugeon and Sprout party and the Du Boung party in accordance with which it had been arranged that Mr. Du Boung should be entitled to a certain amount of glorification in the presence of Lord Silverbridge.

'And it was in compliance with that wish on the part of the borough, my Lord,' said Mr. Du Boung,—'as to which my own feelings were quite as strong as that of any other gentleman in the borough,—that I conceived it to be my duty to give way.'

'His Lordship is quite aware how much he owes to Mr. Du Boung,' said Tregear. Whereupon Lord Silverbridge bowed.

'And now what are we to do?' said Lord Silverbridge.

Then there was a little whispering between Mr. Sprout and Mr. Sprugeon. 'Perhaps, Mr. Du Boung,' said Sprugeon, 'his Lordship had better call first on Dr. Tempest.'*

'Perhaps,' said the injured brewer, 'as it is to be a party affair after all I had better retire from the scene.'

'I thought all that was to be given up,' said Tregear.

'Oh, certainly,' said Sprout. 'Suppose we go to Mr. Walker* first?'

'I'm up to anything,' said Lord Silverbridge; 'but of course everybody understands that I am a Conservative.'

'Oh dear yes,' said Sprugeon.

'We are all aware of that,' said Sprout.

111

'And very glad we've all of us been to hear it,' said the landlord.

'Though there are some in the borough who could have wished, my Lord, that you had stuck to the old Palliser politics,' said Mr. Du Boung.

'But I haven't stuck to the Palliser politics. Just at present I think that order and all that sort of thing should be maintained.'

'Hear, hear!' said the landlord.

'And now, as I have expressed my views generally, I am willing to go anywhere.'

'Then we'll go to Mr. Walker first,' said Sprugeon. Now it was understood that in the borough, among those who really had opinions of their own, Mr. Walker the old attorney stood first as a Liberal, and Dr. Tempest the old rector first as a Conservative.

'I am glad to see your Lordship in the town which gives you its name,' said Mr. Walker, who was a hale old gentleman with silvery-white hair, over seventy years of age. 'I proposed your father for this borough on, I think, six or seven different occasions. They used to go in and out then whenever they changed their offices.'

'We hope you'll propose Lord Silverbridge now,' said Mr. Sprugeon.

'Oh; well;—yes. He's his father's son, and I never knew anything but good of the family. I wish you were going to sit on the same side, my Lord.'

'Times are changed a little perhaps,' said his Lordship.

'The matter is not to be discussed now,' said the old attorney. 'I understand that. Only I hope you'll excuse me if I say that a man ought to get up very early in the morning if he means to see further into politics than your father.'

'Very early indeed,' said Mr. Du Boung, shaking his head.

'That's all right,' said Lord Silverbridge.

'I'll propose you, my Lord. I need not wish you success, because there is no one to stand against you.'

Then they went to Dr. Tempest, who was also an old man.

'Yes, my Lord, I shall be proud to second you,' said the rector. 'I didn't think that I should ever do that to one of your name in Silverbridge.'

'I hope you think I've made a change for the better,' said the candidate.

'You've come over to my school of course, and I suppose I am bound to think that a change for the better. Nevertheless I have a kind of idea that certain people ought to be Tories and that other certain people ought to be Whigs. What does your father say about it?'

'My father wishes me to be in the House, and that he has not quarrelled with me you may know by the fact that had there been a contest he would have paid my expenses.'

'A father generally has to do that whether he approves of what his son is about or not,' said the caustic old gentleman.

There was nothing else to be done. They all went back to the hotel, and Mr. Sprugeon with Mr. Sprout and the landlord drank a glass of sherry at the candidate's expense, wishing him political long life and prosperity. There was no one else whom it was thought necessary that the candidate should visit, and the next day he returned to town with the understanding that on the day appointed in the next week he should come back again to be elected.

And on the day appointed the two young men again went to Silverbridge, and after he had been declared duly elected, the new Member of Parliament made his first speech. There was a meeting in the town-hall and many were assembled anxious to hear,—not the lad's opinions, for which probably nobody cared much,—but the tone of his voice and to see his manner. Of what sort was the eldest son of the man of whom the neighbourhood had been so proud? For the county was in truth proud of their Duke. Of this son whom they had now made a Member of Parliament they at present only knew that he had been sent away from Oxford,—not so very long ago,—for painting the Dean's house scarlet. The speech was not very brilliant. He told them that he was very much obliged to them for the honour they had done him. Though he could not follow exactly his father's political opinions,—he would always have before his eyes his father's political honesty and independence. He broke down two or three times and blushed, and repeated himself, and knocked his words a great deal too quickly one on the top of another. But it was taken very well, and was better than was expected. When it was over he wrote a line to the Duke.

'MY DEAR FATHER,

'I am Member of Parliament for Silverbridge,—as you used to be in the days which I can first remember. I hope you won't think that it does not make me unhappy to have differed from you. Indeed it does. I don't think that anybody has ever done so well in politics as you have. But when a man does take up an opinion I don't see how he can help himself. Of course I could have kept myself quiet;—but then you wished me to be in the House. They were all very civil to me at Silverbridge, but there was very little said.

'Your affectionate Son,
'SILVERBRIDGE.'

CHAPTER XV

The Duke receives a Letter,—and writes One

THE DUKE, when he received Mrs. Finn's note, demanding an interview, thought much upon the matter before he replied. She had made her demand as though the Duke had been no more than any other gentleman, almost as though she had a right to call upon him to wait upon her. He understood and admired the courage of this;—but nevertheless he would not go to her. He had trusted her with that which of all things was the most sacred to him, and she had deceived him! He wrote to her as follows:

'The Duke of Omnium presents his compliments to Mrs. Finn. As the Duke thinks that no good could result either to

Mrs. Finn or to himself from an interview, he is obliged to say that he would rather not do as Mrs. Finn has requested.

'But for the strength of this conviction the Duke would have waited upon Mrs. Finn most willingly.'

Mrs. Finn when she received this was not surprised. She had felt sure that such would be the nature of the Duke's answer; but she was also sure that if such an answer did come she would not let the matter rest. The accusation was so bitter to her that she would spare nothing in defending herself,— nothing in labour and nothing in time. She would make him know that she was in earnest. As she could not succeed in getting into his presence she must do this by letter,—and she wrote her letter, taking two days to think of her words.

'May 18, 18—.

'MY DEAR DUKE OF OMNIUM,

'As you will not come to me, I must trouble your Grace to read what I fear will be a long letter. For it is absolutely necessary that I should explain my conduct to you. That you have condemned me I am sure you will not deny;—nor that you have punished me as far as the power of punishment was in your hands. If I can succeed in making you see that you have judged me wrongly, I think you will admit your error and beg my pardon. You are not one who from your nature can be brought easily to do this; but you are one who will certainly do it if you can be made to feel that by not doing so you would be unjust. I am myself so clear as to my own rectitude of purpose and conduct, and am so well aware of your perspicuity, that I venture to believe that if you will read this letter I shall convince you.

'Before I go any further I will confess that the matter is one,—I was going to say almost of life and death to me. Circumstances, not of my own seeking, have for some years past thrown me so closely into intercourse with your family that now to be cast off, and to be put on one side as a disgraced person,—and that so quickly after the death of her who loved me so dearly and who was so dear to me,—is such an affront

as I cannot bear and hold up my head afterwards. I have come
to be known as her whom your uncle trusted and loved, as her
whom your wife trusted and loved,—obscure as I was before;
—and as her whom, may I not say, you yourself trusted? As
there was much of honour and very much of pleasure in this,
so also was there something of misfortune. Friendships are
safest when the friends are of the same standing. I have always
felt there was danger, and now the thing I feared has come
home to me.

'Now I will plead my case. I fancy, that when first you
heard that I had been cognisant of your daughter's engagement, you imagined that I was aware of it before I went to
Matching. Had I been so, I should have been guilty of that
treachery of which you accuse me. I did know nothing of it
till Lady Mary told me on the day before I left Matching.
That she should tell me was natural enough. Her mother had
known it, and for the moment,—if I am not assuming too
much in saying so,—I was filling her mother's place. But, in
reference to you, I could not exercise the discretion which
a mother might have used, and I told her at once, most decidedly, that you must be made acquainted with the fact.

'Then Lady Mary expressed to me her wish,—not that
this matter should be kept any longer from you, for that it
should be told she was as anxious as I was myself,—but that
it should be told to you by Mr. Tregear. It was not for me to
raise any question as to Mr. Tregear's fitness or unfitness,—
as to which indeed I could know nothing. All I could do was
to say that if Mr. Tregear would make the communication
at once, I should feel that I had done my duty. The upshot
was that Mr. Tregear came to me immediately on my return
to London, and agreeing with me that it was imperative that
you be informed, went to you and did inform you. In all of
that, if I have told the story truly, where has been my offence?
I suppose you will believe me, but your daughter can give
evidence as to every word that I have written.

'I think that you have got it into your mind that I have be-
friended Mr. Tregear's suit, and that, having received this

impression, you hold it with the tenacity which is usual to you. There never was a greater mistake. I went to Matching as the friend of my dear friend;—but I stayed there at your request, as your friend. Had I been, when you asked me to do so, a participator in that secret I could not have honestly remained in the position you assigned to me. Had I done so, I should have deserved your ill opinion. As it is I have not deserved it, and your condemnation of me has been altogether unjust. Should I not now receive from you a full withdrawal of all charge against me, I shall be driven to think that after all the insight which circumstances have given me into your character, I have nevertheless been mistaken in the reading of it.

'I remain,

'Dear Duke of Omnium,

'Yours truly,

'M. FINN.

'I find on looking over my letter that I must add one word further. It might seem that I am asking for a return of your friendship. Such is not my purpose. Neither can you forget that you have accused me,—nor can I. What I expect is that you should tell me that you in your conduct to me have been wrong and that I in mine to you have been right. I must be enabled to feel that the separation between us has come from injury done to me, and not by me.'

He did read the letter more than once, and read it with tingling ears, and hot cheeks, and a knitted brow. As the letter went on, and as the woman's sense of wrong grew hot from her own telling of her own story, her words became stronger and still stronger, till at last they were almost insolent in their strength. Were it not that they came from one who did think herself to have been wronged, then certainly they would be insolent. A sense of injury, a burning conviction of wrong sustained, will justify language which otherwise would be unbearable. The Duke felt that, and though his ears were tingling and his brow knitted, he could have forgiven the language, if only he could have admitted the argument. He understood every word of it. When she spoke of tenacity she intended to charge him with obstinacy. Though she had dwelt but lightly on her own services she had made her thoughts on the matter clear enough. 'I, Mrs. Finn, who am nobody, have done much to succour and assist you, the Duke of Omnium; and this is the return which I have received!' And then she told him to his face that unless he did something which it would be impossible that he should do, she would revoke her opinion of his honesty! He tried to persuade himself that her opinion about his honesty was nothing to him;—but he failed. Her opinion was very much to him. Though in his anger he had determined to throw her off from him, he knew her to be one whose good opinion was worth having.

Not a word of overt accusation had been made against his wife. Every allusion to her was full of love. But yet how heavy a charge was really made! That such a secret should be kept from him, the father, was acknowledged to be a heinous fault; —but the wife had known the secret and had kept it from him, the father! And then how wretched a thing it was for him that anyone should dare to write to him about the wife that had been taken away from him! In spite of all her faults her name was so holy to him that it had never once passed his lips since her death, except in low whispers to himself,—low whispers made in the perfect, double-guarded seclusion of his own chamber. 'Cora, Cora,' he had murmured, so that the sense of the sound and not the sound itself had come to him from his own lips. And now this woman wrote to him about her freely, as though there were nothing sacred, no religion in the memory of her.

'It was not for me to raise any question as to Mr. Tregear's fitness.' Was it not palpable to all the world that he was unfit? Unfit! How could a man be more unfit? He was asking for the hand of one who was second only to royalty—who was possessed of everything, who was beautiful, well-born, rich, who was the daughter of the Duke of Omnium, and he had absolutely nothing of his own to offer.

But it was necessary that he should at last come to the consideration of the actual point as to which she had written to him so forcibly. He tried to set himself to the task in perfect honesty. He certainly had condemned her. He had condemned her and had no doubt punished her to the extent of his power. And if he could be brought to see that he had done this unjustly, then certainly must he beg her pardon. And when he considered it all, he had to own that her intimacy with his uncle and his wife had not been so much of her seeking as of theirs. It grieved him now that it should have been so, but so it was. And after all this,—after the affectionate surrender of herself to his wife's caprices which the woman had made,— he had turned upon her and driven her away with ignominy. That was all true. As he thought of it he became hot, and was conscious of a quivering feeling round his heart. These were bonds indeed; but they were bonds of such a nature as to be capable of being rescinded and cut away altogether by absolute bad conduct. If he could make it good to himself that in a matter of such magnitude as the charge of his daughter she had been untrue to him and had leagued herself against him, with an unworthy lover, then, then—all bonds would be rescinded! Then would his wrath be altogether justified! Then would it have been impossible that he should have done aught else than cast her out! As he thought of this he felt sure that she had betrayed him! How great would be the ignominy to him should he be driven to own to himself that she had not betrayed him! 'There should not have been a moment,' he said to himself over and over again,—'not a moment!' Yes;— she certainly had betrayed him.

There might still be safety for him in that confident assertion of 'not a moment'; but had there been anything of that conspiracy of which he had certainly at first judged her to be guilty? She had told her story, and had then appealed to Lady Mary for evidence. After five minutes of perfect stillness,— but five minutes of misery, five minutes during which great beads of perspiration broke out from him and stood upon his brow, he had to confess to himself that he did not want any evidence. He did believe her story. When he allowed himself to think she had been in league with Tregear he had wronged her. He wiped away the beads from his brow, and again repeated to himself those words which were now his only comfort, 'There should not have been a moment;—not a moment!'

It was thus and only thus that he was enabled to assure himself that there need be no acknowledgment of wrong done on his part. Having settled this in his own mind he forced himself to attend a meeting at which his assistance had been asked as to a complex question on Law Reform. The Duke endeavoured to give himself up entirely to the matter; but through it all there was the picture before him of Mrs. Finn waiting for an answer to her letter. If he should confirm himself in his opinion that he had been right, then would any answer be necessary? He might just acknowledge the letter, after the fashion which has come up in official life, than which silence is an insult much more bearable. But he did not wish to insult, nor to punish her further. He would willingly have withdrawn the punishment under which she was groaning could he have done so without self-abasement. Or he might write as she had done,—advocating his own cause with all his strength, using that last one strong argument,—'there should not have been a moment.' But there would be something repulsive to his personal dignity in the continued correspondence which this would produce. 'The Duke of Omnium regrets to say, in answer to Mrs. Finn's letter, that he thinks no good can be attained by a prolonged correspondence.' Such, or of such kind, he thought must be his answer. But would this be a fair return for the solicitude shown by her to his uncle, for the love which had made her so patient a friend to his wife, for the nobility of her own conduct in many things? Then his mind reverted to certain jewels,—supposed to be of enormous value,—which were still in his possession though they were the property of this woman. They had been left to her by his uncle, and she had obstinately refused to take them. Now they were lying packed in the cellars of certain bankers,—but still they were in his custody. What should he now do in this matter? Hitherto, perhaps once in every six months, he had notified to her that he was keeping them as her curator, and she had always repeated that it was a charge from which she could not relieve him. It had become almost a joke between them. But how could he joke with a women with whom he had quarrelled after this internecine fashion?

What if he were to consult Lady Cantrip? He could not do so without a pang that would be very bitter to him,—but any agony would be better than that arising from a fear that he had been unjust to one who had deserved well of him. No doubt Lady Cantrip would see it in the same light as he had done. And then he would be able to support himself by the assurance that that which he had judged to be right was approved of by one whom the world would acknowledge to be a good judge on such a matter.

When he got home he found his son's letter telling him of the election at Silverbridge. There was something in it which softened his heart to the young man,—or perhaps it was that in the midst of his many discomforts he wished to find something which at least was not painful to him. That his son and his heir should insist on entering political life in opposition to him was of course a source of pain; but, putting that aside, the thing had been done pleasantly enough, and the young member's letter had been written with some good feeling. So he answered the letter as pleasantly as he knew how.

'My dear Silverbridge,

'I am glad that you are in Parliament and am glad also that you should have been returned by the old borough; though I would that you could have reconciled yourself to adhering to the politics of your family. But there is nothing disgraceful in such a change, and I am able to congratulate you as a father should a son and to wish you long life and success as a legislator.

'There are one or two things*I would ask you to remember; —and firstly this, that as you have voluntarily undertaken certain duties you are bound as an honest man to perform them as scrupulously as though you were paid for doing them. There was no obligation in you to seek the post;—but having sought it and acquired it you cannot neglect the work attached to it without being untrue to the covenant you have made. It is necessary that a young member of Parliament should bear this in his mind, and especially a member who has not worked his way up to notoriety outside the House, because to him there will be great facility for idleness and neglect.

'And then I would have you always remember the purport for which there is a Parliament elected in this happy and free country. It is not that some men may shine there, that some may acquire power, or that all may plume themselves on being the elect of the nation. It often appears to me that some members of Parliament so regard their success in life,—as the fellows of our colleges do too often, thinking that their fellowships were awarded for their comfort and not for the furtherance of any object as education or religion. I have known gentlemen who have felt that in becoming members of Parliament they had achieved an object for themselves instead of thinking that they had put themselves in the way of achieving something for others. A member of Parliament should feel himself to be the servant of his country,—and like every other servant, he should serve. If this be distasteful to a man he need not go into Parliament. If the harness gall him he need not wear it. But if he takes the trappings, then he should draw the coach. You are there as the guardian of your fellow-countrymen,—that they may be safe, that they may be prosperous, that they may be well governed and lightly burdened, —above all that they may be free. If you cannot feel this to be your duty, you should not be there at all.

'And I would have you remember also that the work of a member of Parliament can seldom be of that brilliant nature which is of itself charming; and that the young member should think of such brilliancy as being possible to him only at a distance. It should be your first care to sit and listen so that the forms and methods of the House may as it were soak into you gradually. And then you must bear in mind that speaking in the House is but a very small part of a member's work, perhaps that part which he may lay aside altogether with the least strain on his conscience. A good member of Parliament will be good upstairs in the Committee Rooms, good downstairs to make and to keep a House, good to vote, for his party if it may be nothing better, but for the measures also which he believes to be for the good of his country.

'Gradually, if you will give your thoughts to it, and above all your time, the theory of legislation will sink into your mind, and you will find that there will come upon you the ineffable delight of having served your country to the best of your ability.

'It is the only pleasure in life which has been enjoyed without alloy by your affectionate father,

'OMNIUM.'

The Duke in writing this letter was able for a few moments to forget Mrs. Finn, and to enjoy the work which he had on hand.

CHAPTER XVI

'Poor Boy'

THE new member for Silverbridge, when he entered the House to take the oath, was supported on the right and left by two staunch old Tories. Mr. Monk*had seen him a few minutes previously,—Mr. Monk who of all Liberals was the firmest and than whom no one had been more staunch to the Duke,—and had congratulated him on his election, expressing at the same time some gentle regrets. 'I only wish you could have come among us on the other side,' he said.

'But I couldn't,' said the young Lord.

'I am sure nothing but a conscientious feeling would have separated you from your father's friends,' said the old Liberal. And then they were parted, and the member for Silverbridge was bustled up to the table between two staunch Tories.

Of what else was done on that occasion nothing shall be said here. No political work was required from him, except that of helping for an hour or two to crowd the Government benches. But we will follow him as he left the House. There were one or two others quite as anxious as to his political career as any staunch old Liberal. At any rate one other. He had promised that as soon as he could get away from the House he would go to Belgrave Square and tell Lady Mabel Grex all about it. When he reached the square it was past seven, but Lady Mabel and Miss Cassewary were still in the drawing-room.

'There seemed to be a great deal of bustle, and I didn't understand much about it,' said the member.

'But you heard the speeches?' These were the speeches made on the proposing and seconding of the address.

'Oh, yes;—Lupton did it very well. Lord George didn't seem to be quite so good. Then Sir Timothy Beeswax*made a speech, and then Mr. Monk. After that I saw other fellows going away, so I bolted too.'

'If I were a member of Parliament I would never leave it while the House was sitting,' said Miss Cassewary.

'If all were like that there wouldn't be seats for them to sit upon,' said Silverbridge.

'A persistent member will always find a seat,' continued the positive old lady.

'I am sure that Lord Silverbridge means to do his duty,' said Lady Mabel.

'Oh yes;—I've thought a good deal about it, and I mean to try. As long as a man isn't called upon to speak I don't see why it shouldn't be easy enough.'

'I'm so glad to hear you say so! Of course after a little time you will speak. I should so like to hear you make your first speech.'

'If I thought you were there, I'm sure I should not make it at all.'

Just at this period Miss Cassewary, saying something as to the necessity of dressing, and cautioning her young friend that there was not much time to be lost, left the room.

'Dressing does not take me more than ten minutes,' said Lady Mabel.

Miss Cassewary declared this to be nonsense, but she nevertheless left the room. Whether she would have done so if Lord Silverbridge had not been Lord Silverbridge, but had been some young man with whom it would not have been expedient that Lady Mabel should fall in love, may perhaps be doubted. But then it may be taken as certain that under such circumstances Lady Mabel herself would not have remained. She had quite realised the duties of life, had had her little romance,—and had acknowledged that it was foolish.

'I do so hope that you will do well,' she said, going back to the parliamentary duties.

'I don't think I shall ever do much. I shall never be like my father.'

'I don't see why not.'

'There never was anybody like him. I am always amusing myself, but he never cared for amusement.'

'You are very young.'

'As far as I can learn he was just as he is now at my age. My mother has told me that long before she married him he used to spend all his time in the House. I wonder whether you would mind reading the letter he wrote me when he heard of my election.'

Then he took the epistle out of his pocket and handed it to Lady Mabel.

'He means all that he says.'

'He always does that.'

'And he really hopes that you will put your shoulder to the wheel;—even though you must do so in opposition to him.'

'That makes no difference. I think my father is a very fine fellow.'

'Shall you do all that he tells you?'

'Well;—I suppose not;—except that he advises me to hold my tongue. I think that I shall do that. I mean to go down there, you know, and I daresay I shall be much the same as others.'

'Has he talked to you much about it?'

'No;—he never talks much. Every now and then he will give me a downright lecture, or he will write me a letter like that; but he never talks to any of us.'

'How very odd.'

'Yes; he is odd. He seems to be fretful when we are with him. A good many things make him unhappy.'

'Your poor mother's death.'

'That first;—and then there are other things. I suppose he didn't like the way I came to an end at Oxford.'

'You were a boy then.'

'Of course I was very sorry for it,—though I hated Oxford. It was neither one thing nor another. You were your own master and yet you were not.'

'Now you must be your own master.'

'I suppose so.'

'You must marry, and become a lord of the Treasury. When I was a child I acted as a child.*You know all about that.'

'Oh yes. And now I must throw off childish things. You mean that I mustn't paint any man's house? Eh, Lady Mab.'

'That and the rest of it. You are a legislator now.'

'So is Popplecourt, who took his seat in the House of Lords two or three months ago. He's the biggest young fool I know out. He couldn't even paint a house.'

'He is not an elected legislator. It makes all the difference. I quite agree with what the Duke says. Lord Popplecourt can't help himself. Whether he's an idle young scamp or not, he must be a legislator. But when a man goes in for it himself, as you have done, he should make up his mind to be useful.'

'I shall vote with my party of course.'

'More than that; much more than that. If you didn't care for politics you couldn't have taken a line of your own.' When she said this she knew that he had been talked into what he had done by Tregear,—by Tregear, who had ambition, and intelligence, and capacity for forming an opinion of his own. 'If you do not do it for your own sake, you will for the sake of those who,—who,—who are your friends,' she said at last, not feeling quite able to tell him that he must do it for the sake of those who loved him.

'There are not very many I suppose who care about it.'

'Your father.'

'Oh yes,—my father.'

'And Tregear.'

'Tregear has got his own fish to fry.'

'Are there none others? Do you think we care nothing about it here?'

'Miss Cassewary?'

'Well;—Miss Cassewary! A man might have a worse friend than Miss Cassewary;—and my father.'

'I don't suppose Lord Grex cares a straw about me.'

'Indeed he does,—a great many straws. And so do I. Do you think I don't care a straw about it?'

'I don't know why you should.'

'Because it is my nature to be earnest. A girl comes out into the world so young that she becomes serious, and steady as it were, so much sooner than a man does.'

'I always think that nobody is so full of chaff as you are, Lady Mab.'

'I am not chaffing now in recommending you to go to work in the world like a man.'

As she said this they were sitting on the same sofa, but with some space between them. When Miss Cassewary had left the room Lord Silverbridge was standing, but after a little he had fallen into the seat, at the extreme corner, and had gradually come a little nearer to her. Now in her energy she put out her hand, meaning perhaps to touch lightly the sleeve of his coat, meaning perhaps not quite to touch him at all. But as she did so he put out his hand and took hold of hers.

She drew it away, not seeming to allow it to remain in his grasp for a moment; but she did so, not angrily, or hurriedly, or with any flurry. She did it as though it were natural that he should take her hand and as natural that she should recover it.

'Indeed I have hardly more than ten minutes left for dressing,' she said, rising from her seat.

'If you will say that you care about it, you yourself, I will do my best.' As he made this declaration blushes covered his cheeks and forehead.

'I do care about it,—very much; I myself,' said Lady Mabel, not blushing at all. Then there was a knock at the door, and Lady Mabel's maid putting her head in, declared that my Lord had come in and had already been some time in his dressing-room. 'Good-bye, Lord Silverbridge,' she said quite gaily, and rather more aloud than would have been necessary, had she not intended that the maid also should hear her.

'Poor boy!' she said to herself as she was dressing. 'Poor boy!' Then, when the evening was over she spoke to herself again about him. 'Dear sweet boy!' And then she sat and thought. How was it that she was so old a woman, while he was so little more than a child? How fair he was, how far removed from conceit, how capable of being made into a man— in the process of time! What might not be expected from him if he could be kept in good hands for the next ten years! But in whose hands? What would she be in ten years, she who already seemed to know the town and all its belongings so well? And yet she was as young in years as he. He, as she knew, had passed his twenty-second birthday,—and so had she. That was all. It might be good for her that she should marry him. She was ambitious. And such a marriage would satisfy her ambition. Through her father's fault, and her brother's, she was likely to be poor. This man would certainly be rich. Many of those who were buzzing around her from day to day, were distasteful to her. From among them she knew that she could not take a husband, let their rank and wealth be what it might. She was too fastidious, too proud, too prone to think that things should be with her as she liked them! This last was in all things pleasant to her. Though he was but a boy, there was a certain boyish manliness about him. The very way in which he had grasped at her hand and had then blushed ruby-red at his own daring, had gone far with her. How gracious he was to look at! Dear sweet boy! Love him? No;— she did not know that she loved him. That dream was over. She was sure however that she liked him.

But how would it be with him? It might be well for her to become his wife, but could it be well for him that he should become her husband? Did she not feel that it would be better for him that he should become a man before he married at all? Perhaps so;—but then if she desisted would others desist? If she did not put out her bait would there not be other hooks, —others and worse? Would not such a one, so soft, so easy, so prone to be caught and so desirable for the catching, be sure to be made prey of by some snare?

But could she love him? That a woman should not marry a man without loving him, she partly knew. But she thought she knew also that there must be exceptions. She would do her very best to love him. That other man should be banished from her very thoughts. She would be such a wife to him that he should never know that he lacked anything. Poor boy! Sweet dear boy! He, as he went away to his dinner, had his thoughts also about her. Of all the girls he knew she was the jolliest,—and of all his friends she was the pleasantest. As she was anxious that he should go to work in the House of Commons he would go to work there. As for loving her! Well; —of course he must marry someone, and why not Lady Mab as well as anyone else?

CHAPTER XVII

The Derby

An attendance at the Newmarket Second Spring Meeting* had unfortunately not been compatible with the Silverbridge election. Major Tifto had therefore been obliged to look after the affair alone. 'A very useful mare,' as Tifto had been in the habit of calling a leggy, thoroughbred, meagre-looking brute named Coalition, was on this occasion confided to the Major's sole care and judgment. But Coalition failed, as coalitions always do, and Tifto had to report to his noble patron that they had not pulled off the event. It had been a match for four hundred pounds, made indeed by Lord Silver-bridge, but made at the suggéstion of Tifto;—and now Tifto wrote in a very bad humour about it. It had been altogether his Lordship's fault in submitting to carry two pounds more* than Tifto had thought to be fair and equitable. The match had been lost. Would Lord Silverbridge be so good as to pay the money to Mr. Green Griffin and debit him, Tifto, with the share of his loss?

We must acknowledge that the unpleasant tone of the Major's letter was due quite as much to the ill-usage he had received in reference to that journey to Silverbridge, as to the loss of the race. Within that little body there was a high-mounting heart, and that heart had been greatly wounded by his lordship's treatment. Tifto had felt himself to have been treated like a servant. Hardly an excuse had even been made. He had been simply told that he was not wanted. He was apt sometimes to tell himself that he knew on which side his bread was buttered. But perhaps he hardly knew how best to keep the butter going. There was a little pride about him which was antagonistic to the best interests of such a trade as his. Perhaps it was well that he should inwardly suffer when in-jured. But it could not be well that he should declare to such men as Nidderdale, and Dolly Longstaff, and Popplecourt that he didn't mean to put up with that sort of thing. He certainly should not have spoken in this strain before Tregear. Of all men living he hated and feared him the most. And he knew that no other man loved Silverbridge as did Tregear. Had he been thinking of his bread-and-butter, instead of giving way to the mighty anger of his little bosom, he would have hardly declared openly at the club that he would let Lord Silverbridge know that he did not mean to stand any man's airs. But these extravagances were due perhaps to whisky-and-water, and that kind of intoxication which comes to certain men from momentary triumphs. Tifto could always be got to make a fool of himself when surrounded by three or four men of rank who, for the occasion, would talk to him as an equal. He almost declared that Coalition had lost his match because he had not been taken down to Silverbridge.

'Tifto is in a deuce of a way with you,' said Dolly Longstaff to the young member.

'I know all about it,' said Silverbridge, who had had an interview with his partner since the race.

'If you don't take care he'll dismiss you.'

Silverbridge did not care much about this, knowing that words of wisdom did not ordinarily fall from the mouth of Dolly Longstaff. But he was more moved when his friend Tregear spoke to him. 'I wish you knew the kind of things that fellow Tifto says behind your back.'

'As if I cared!'

'But you ought to care.'

'Do you care what every fellow says about you?'

'I care very much what those say whom I choose to live with me. Whatever Tifto might say about me would be quite indifferent to me, because we have nothing in common. But you and he are bound together.'

'We have a horse or two in common; that's all.'

'But that is a great deal. The truth is he's a nasty, brawling, boasting, ill-conditioned little reptile.'

Silverbridge of course did not acknowledge that this was true. But he felt it, and almost repented of his trust in Tifto. But still Prime Minister*stood very well for the Derby. He was second favourite, the odds against him being only four to one.*The glory of being part owner of a probable winner of the Derby was so much to him that he could not bring himself to be altogether angry with Tifto. There was no doubt that the horse's present condition was due entirely to Tifto's care. Tifto spent in these few days just before the race the greatest part of his time in the close vicinity of the horse, only running up to London now and then, as a fish comes up to the surface, for a breath of air. It was impossible that Lord Silverbridge should separate himself from the Major,—at any rate till after the Epsom meeting.

He had paid the money for the match without a word of reproach to his partner, but still with a feeling that things were not quite as they ought to be. In money matters his father had been liberal, but not very definite. He had been told that he ought not to spend above two thousand pounds a year, and had been reminded that there was a house for him to use both in town and in the country. But he had been given to understand also that any application made to Mr. Morton, if not very unreasonable, would be attended with success. A solemn promise had been exacted from him that he would have no dealings with money-lenders;*—and then he had been set afloat. There had been a rather frequent correspondence with Mr. Morton, who had once or twice submitted a total of the money paid on behalf of his correspondent. Lord Silverbridge, who imagined himself to be anything but extravagant, had wondered how the figures could mount up so rapidly. But the money needed was always forthcoming, and the raising of objections never seemed to be carried back beyond Mr. Morton. His promise to his father about the money-lenders had been scrupulously kept. As long as ready money can be made to be forthcoming without any charge for interest, a young man must be very foolish who will prefer to borrow it at twenty-five per cent.

Now had come the night before the Derby, and it must be acknowledged that the young Lord was much fluttered by the greatness of the coming struggle. Tifto, having seen his horse conveyed to Epsom, had come up to London in order that he might dine with his partner and hear what was being said about the race at the Beargarden. The party dining there consisted of Silverbridge, Dolly Longstaff, Popplecourt, and Tifto. Nidderdale was to have joined them, but he told them on the day before, with a sigh, that domestic duties were too strong for him. Lady Nidderdale,—or if not Lady Nidderdale herself, then Lady Nidderdale's mother,—was so far potent over the young nobleman as to induce him to confine his

Derby jovialities to the Derby Day. Another guest had also been expected, the reason for whose non-appearance must be explained somewhat at length. Lord Gerald Palliser, the Duke's second son, was at this time at Cambridge,—being almost as popular at Trinity as his brother had been at Christ Church. It was to him quite a matter of course that he should see his brother's horse run for the Derby. But, unfortunately, in this very year a stand was being made by the University pundits*against a practice which they thought had become too general. For the last year or two it had been considered almost as much a matter of course that a Cambridge undergraduate should go to the Derby as that a Member of Parliament* should do so. Against this three or four rigid disciplinarians had raised their voices,—and as a result, no young man up at Trinity could get leave to be away on the Derby pretext.

Lord Gerald raged against the restriction very loudly. He at first proclaimed his intention of ignoring the college authorities altogether. Of course he would be expelled. But the order itself was to his thinking so absurd,—the idea that he should not see his brother's horse run was so extravagant, —that he argued that his father could not be angry with him for incurring dismissal in so excellent a cause. But his brother saw things in a different light. He knew how his father had looked at him when he had been sent away from Oxford, and he counselled moderation. Gerald should see the Derby, but should not encounter that heaviest wrath of all which comes from a man's not sleeping beneath his college roof. There was a train which left Cambridge at an early hour, and would bring him into London in time to accompany his friends to the racecourse;—and another train, a special, which would take him down after dinner, so that he and others should reach Cambridge before the college gates were shut.

The dinner at the Beargarden was very joyous. Of course the state of the betting in regard to Prime Minister was the subject generally popular for the night. Mr. Lupton came in, a gentleman well known in all fashionable circles, parliamentary, social, and racing, who was rather older than his company on this occasion, but still not so much so as to be found to be an incumbrance. Lord Glasslough too, and others joined them, and a good deal was said about the horse. 'I never keep these things dark,' said Tifto. 'Of course he's an uncertain horse.'

'Most horses are,' said Lupton.

'Just so, Mr. Lupton. What I mean is, the Minister has got a bit of temper. But if he likes to do his best I don't think any three-year-old*in England can get his nose past him.'

'For half a mile he'd be nowhere with the Provence filly,' said Glasslough.

'I'm speaking of a Derby distance, my Lord.'

'That's a kind of thing nobody really knows,' said Lupton.

'I've seen him 'ave his gallops,' said the little man, who in his moments of excitement would sometimes fall away from that exact pronunciation which had been one of the studies of his life, 'and have measured his stride. I think I know what pace means. Of course I'm not going to answer for the 'orse. He's a temper, but if things go favourably, no animal that ever showed on the Downs*was more likely to do the trick. Is there any gentleman here who would like to bet me fifteen to one in hundreds against the two events,—the Derby and the Leger?'*The desired odds were at once offered by Mr. Lupton, and the bet was booked.

This gave rise to other betting, and before the evening was over Lord Silverbridge had taken three-and-a-half to one against his horse to such an extent that he stood to lose twelve hundred pounds. The champagne which he had drunk, and the news that Quousque, the first favourite, had so gone to pieces that now there was a question which was the first favourite, had so inflated him that, had he been left alone, he would almost have wagered even money on his horse. In the midst of his excitement there came to him a feeling that he was allowing himself to do just that which he had intended to avoid. But then the occasion was so peculiar! How often can it happen to a man in his life that he shall own a favourite for the Derby? The affair was one in which it was almost necessary that he should risk a little money.

Tifto, when he got into his bed, was altogether happy. He had added whisky-and-water to his champagne, and feared nothing. If Prime Minister should win the Derby he would be able to pay all that he owed, and to make a start with money in his pocket. And then there would be attached to him all the infinite glory of being the owner of a winner of the Derby. The horse was run in his name. Thoughts as to great successes crowded themselves upon his heated brain. What might not be open to him? Parliament! The Jockey Club!*The mastership of one of the crack shire packs!*Might it not come to pass that he should some day become the great authority in England upon races, racehorses, and hunters? If he could be the winner of a Derby and Leger he thought that Glasslough and Lupton would snub him no longer, that even Tregear would speak to him, and that his pal the Duke's son would never throw him aside again.

Lord Silverbridge had bought a drag*with all its appendages. There was a coach, the four bay horses, the harness, and the two regulation grooms. When making this purchase he had condescended to say a word to his father on the subject. 'Everybody belongs to the four-in-hand club now,' said the son.

'I never did,' said the Duke.

'Ah,—if I could be like you!'

The Duke had said that he would think about it, and then had told Mr. Morton that he was to pay the bill for this new toy. He had thought about it, and had assured himself that driving a coach and four was at present regarded as a fitting amusement for young men of rank and wealth. He did not understand it himself. It seemed to him to be as unnatural as though a gentleman should turn blacksmith and make horseshoes for his amusement. Driving four horses was hard work. But the same might be said of rowing. There were men, he knew, who would spend their days standing at a lathe, making little boxes for their recreation. He did not sympathise with it. But the fact was so, and this driving of coaches was regarded with favour. He had been a little touched by that word his son had spoken. 'Ah,—if I could be like you!' So he had given the permission; the drag, horses, harness, and grooms had come into the possession of Lord Silverbridge; and now they were put into requisition to take their triumphant owner and his party down to Epsom. Dolly Longstaff's team was sent down to meet them half-way. Gerald Palliser, who had come up from Cambridge that morning, was allowed to drive the first stage out of town to compensate him for the cruelty done to him by the University pundits. Tifto, with a cigar in his mouth, with a white hat and a blue veil, and a new light-coloured coat, was by no means the least happy of the party.

How that race was run, and how both Prime Minister and Quousque were beaten by an outsider named Fishknife, Prime Minister, however, coming in a good second, the present writer having no aptitude in that way, cannot describe. Such, however, were the facts, and then Dolly Longstaff and Lord Silverbridge drove the coach back to London. The coming back was not so triumphant, though the young fellows bore their failure well. Dolly Longstaff had lost a 'pot of money', Silverbridge would have to draw upon that inexhaustible Mr. Morton for something over two thousand pounds,—in regard to which he had no doubt as to the certainty with which the money would be forthcoming, but he feared that it would give rise to special notice from his father. Even the poor younger brother had lost a couple of hundred pounds, for which he would have to make his own special application to Mr. Morton.

But Tifto felt it more than anyone. The horse ought to have won. Fishknife had been favoured by such a series of accidents that the whole affair had been a miracle. Tifto had these circumstances at his fingers' ends, and in the course of the afternoon and evening explained them accurately to all who would listen to him. He had this to say on his own behalf,—that before the party had left the course their horse stood first favourite for the Leger. But Tifto was unhappy as he came back to town, and in spite of the lunch, which had been very glorious, sat moody and sometimes even silent within his gay apparel.

'It was the unfairest start I ever saw,' said Tifto, almost getting up from his seat on the coach so as to address Dolly and Silverbridge on the box.

'What the —— is the good of that?' said Dolly from the coach-box. 'Take your licking and don't squeal.'

'That's all very well. I can take my licking as well as another man. But one has to look to the causes of these things. I never saw Peppermint ride so badly. Before he got round the Corner I wished I'd been on the horse myself.'

'I don't believe it was Peppermint's fault a bit,' said Silverbridge.

'Well;—perhaps not. Only I did think that I was a pretty good judge of riding.'

Then Tifto again settled down into silence.

But though much money had been lost, and a great deal of disappointment had to be endured by our party in reference to the Derby, the most injurious and most deplorable event in the day's history had not occurred yet. Dinner had been ordered at the Beargarden at seven,—an hour earlier than would have been named had it not been that Lord Gerald must be at the Eastern Counties Railway Station at nine P.M. An hour and a half for dinner and a cigar afterwards, and half an hour to get to the railway station would not be more than time enough.

But of all men alive Dolly Longstaff was the most unpunctual. He did not arrive till eight. The others were not there before half-past seven, and it was nearly eight before any of them sat down. At half-past eight Silverbridge began to be very anxious about his brother, and told him that he ought to start without further delay. A hansom cab*was waiting at the door, but Lord Gerald still delayed. He knew, he said, that the special would not start till half-past nine. There were a lot of fellows who were dining about everywhere, and they would never get to the station by the hour fixed. It became apparent to the elder brother that Gerald would stay altogether unless he were forced to go, and at last he did get up and pushed the young fellow out. 'Drive like the very devil,' he said to the cabman, explaining to him something of the circumstances. The cabman did do his best, but a cab cannot be made to travel from the Beargarden, which as all the world knows is close to St. James's Street, to Liverpool Street in the City in ten minutes. When Lord Gerald reached the station the train had started.

At twenty minutes to ten the young man reappeared at the club. 'Why on earth didn't you take a special for yourself?' exclaimed Silverbridge.

'They wouldn't give me one.' After that it was apparent to all of them that what had just happened had done more to ruffle our hero's temper than his failure and loss at the races.

'I wouldn't have had it happen for any money you could name,' said the elder brother to the younger, as he took him home to Carlton Terrace.

'If they do send me down, what's the odds?' said the younger brother, who was not quite as sober as he might have been.

'After what happened to me it will almost break the governor's heart,' said the heir.

CHAPTER XVIII

One of the Results of the Derby

On the following morning at about eleven Silverbridge and his brother were at breakfast at an hotel in Jermyn Street. They had slept in Carlton Terrace, but Lord Gerald had done so without the knowledge of the Duke. Lord Silverbridge, as he was putting himself to bed, had made up his mind to tell the story to the Duke at once, but when the morning came his courage failed him. The two young men therefore slunk out of the house, and as there was no breakfasting at the Beargarden they went to this hotel. They were both rather gloomy, but the elder brother was the more sad of the two. 'I'd give anything I have in the world,' he said, 'that you hadn't come up at all.'

'Things have been so unfortunate!'

'Why the deuce wouldn't you go when I told you?'

'Who on earth would have thought that they'd have been so punctual? They never are punctual on the Great Eastern. It was an infernal shame. I think I shall go at once to Harnage and tell him all about it.' Mr. Harnage was Lord Gerald's tutor.

'But you've been in ever so many rows before.'

'Well,—I've been gated,*and once when they'd gated me I came right upon Harnage on the bridge at King's.'

'What sort of a fellow is he?'

'He used to be good-natured. Now he has taken ever so many crotchets into his head. It was he who began all this about none of the men going to the Derby.'

'Did you ask him yourself for leave?'

'Yes. And when I told him about your owning Prime Minister he got savage and declared that was the very reason why I shouldn't go.'

'You didn't tell me that.'

'I was determined I would go. I wasn't going to be made a child of.'

At last it was decided that the two brothers should go down to Cambridge together. Silverbridge would be able to come back to London the same evening, so as to take his drag down to the Oaks*on the Friday,—a duty from which even his present misery would not deter him. They reached Cambridge at about three, and Lord Silverbridge at once called at the Master's lodge and sent in his card. The Master of Trinity is so great that he cannot be supposed to see all comers, but on this occasion Lord Silverbridge was fortunate. With much trepidation he told his story. Such being the circumstances, could anything be done to moderate the vials of wrath which must doubtless be poured out over the head of his unfortunate brother?

'Why come to me?' said the Master. 'From what you say yourself, it is evident that you know that this must rest with the College tutor.'

'I thought, sir, if you would say a word.'

'Do you think it would be right that I should interfere for one special man, and that a man of special rank?'

'Nobody thinks that would count for anything. But——'

'But what?' asked the Master.

'If you knew my father, sir!'

'Everybody knows your father;—every Englishman I mean. Of course I know your father,—as a public man, and I know how much the country owes to him.'

'Yes, it does. But it is not that I mean. If you knew how this would,—would,—would break his heart.' Then there came a tear into the young man's eye,—and there was something almost like a tear in the eye of the old man too. 'Of course it was my fault. I got him to come. He hadn't the slightest intention of staying. I think you will believe what I say about that, sir.'

'I believe every word you say, my Lord.'

'I got into a row at Oxford. I daresay you heard. There never was anything so stupid. That was a great grief to my father,—a very great grief. It is so hard upon him because he never did anything foolish himself.'

'You should try to imitate him.' Silverbridge shook his head. 'Or at least not to grieve him.'

'That is it. He has got over the affair about me. As I'm the eldest son I've got into Parliament, and he thinks perhaps that all has been forgotten. An eldest son may, I fancy, be a greater ass than his younger brother.' The Master could not but smile as he thought of the selection which had been made of a legislator. 'But if Gerald is sent down, I don't know how he'll get over it.' And now the tears absolutely rolled down the young man's face, so that he was forced to wipe them from his eyes.

The Master was much moved. That a young man should pray for himself would be nothing to him. The discipline of the college was not in his hands, and such prayers would avail nothing with him. Nor would a brother praying simply for a brother avail much. A father asking for his son might be resisted. But the brother asking pardon for the brother on behalf of the father was almost irresistible. But this man had long been in a position in which he knew that no such prayers

141

should ever prevail at all. In the first place it was not his
business. If he did anything, it would only be by asking a
favour when he knew that no favour should be granted;—and
a favour which he of all men should not ask, because to him
of all men it could not be refused. And then the very altitude
of the great statesman whom he was invited to befriend,—
the position of this Duke who had been so powerful and might
be powerful again, was against any such interference. Of himself he might be sure that he would certainly have done this as
readily for any Mr. Jones as for the Duke of Omnium; but
were he to do it it would be said of him that it had been done
because the man was Duke of Omnium. There are positions
exalted beyond the reach of benevolence, because benevolence
would seem to be self-seeking. 'Your father, if he were here,'
said he, 'would know that I could not interfere.'

'And will he be sent down?'

'I do not know all the circumstances. From your own showing the case seems to be one of great insubordination. To tell
the truth, Lord Silverbridge, I ought not to have spoken to
you on the subject at all.'

'You mean that I should not have spoken to you.'

'Well; I did not say so. And if you have been indiscreet I
can pardon that. I wish I could have served you; but I fear
that it is not in my power.' Then Lord Silverbridge took his
leave, and going to his brother's rooms waited there till Lord
Gerald had returned from his interview with the tutor.

'It 's all up,' said he, chucking down his cap, striving to be
at his ease. 'I may pack up and go—just where I please. He
says that on no account will he have anything more to do
with me. I asked him what I was to do, and he said that the
Governor had better take my name off the books of the college.
I did ask whether I couldn't go over to Maclean.'

'Who is Maclean?'

'One of the other tutors. But the brute only smiled.'

'He thought you meant it for chaff.'

'Well;—I suppose I did mean to show him that I was
not going to be exterminated by him. He will write to

the Governor to-day. And you will have to talk to the Governor.'

Yes! As Lord Silverbridge went back that afternoon to London he thought very much of that talking to the Governor! Never yet had he been able to say anything very pleasant to 'the Governor.' He had himself been always in disgrace at Eton, and had been sent away from Oxford. He had introduced Tregear into the family, which of all the troubles perhaps was the worst. He had changed his politics. He had spent more money than he ought to have done, and now at this very moment must ask for a large sum. And he had brought Gerald up to see the Derby, thereby causing him to be sent away from Cambridge! And through it all there was present to him a feeling that by no words which he could use would he be able to make his father understand how deeply he felt all this.

He could not bring himself to see the Duke that evening, and the next morning he was sent for before he was out of bed. He found his father at breakfast with the tutor's letter before him. 'Do you know anything about this?' asked the Duke very calmly.

'Gerald ran up to see the Derby, and in the evening missed the train.'

'Mr. Harnage tells me that he had been expressly ordered not to go to these races.'

'I suppose he was, sir.'

Then there was silence between them for some minutes. 'You might as well sit down and eat your breakfast,' said the father. Then Lord Silverbridge did sit down and poured himself out a cup of tea. There was no servant in the room, and he dreaded to ring the bell. 'Is there anything you want?' asked the Duke. There was a small dish of fried bacon on the table, and some cold mutton on the sideboard. Silverbridge, declaring that he had everything that was necessary, got up and helped himself to the cold mutton. Then again there was silence, during which the Duke crunched his toast and made an attempt at reading the newspaper. But, soon pushing that aside, he again took up Mr. Harnage's letter. Silverbridge watched every motion of his father as he slowly made his way through the slice of cold mutton. 'It seems that Gerald is to be sent away altogether.'

'I fear so, sir.'

'He has profited by your example at Oxford. Did you persuade him to come to these races?'

'I am afraid I did.'

'Though you knew the orders which had been given?'

'I thought it was meant that he should not be away the night.'

'He had asked permission to go to the Derby and had been positively refused. Did you know that?'

Silverbridge sat for some moments considering. He could not at first quite remember what he had known and what he had not known. Perhaps he entertained some faint hope that the question would be allowed to pass unanswered. He saw, however, from his father's eye that that was impossible. And then he did remember it all. 'I suppose I did know it.'

'And you were willing to imperil your brother's position in life, and my happiness, in order that he might see a horse, of which I believe you call yourself part owner, run a race?'

'I thought there would be no risk if he got back the same night. I don't suppose there is any good in my saying it, but I never was so sorry for anything in all my life. I feel as if I could go and hang myself.'

'That is absurd,—and unmanly,' said the Duke. The expression of sorrow, as it had been made, might be absurd and unmanly, but nevertheless it had touched him. He was severe because he did not know how far his severity wounded. 'It is a great blow,—another great blow! Races! A congregation of all the worst blackguards in the country mixed with the greatest fools.'

'Lord Cantrip was there,' said Silverbridge; 'and I saw Sir Timothy Beeswax.'

'If the presence of Sir Timothy be an allurement to you, I

pity you indeed. I have nothing further to say about it. You have ruined your brother.' He had been driven to further anger by this reference to one man whom he respected, and to another whom he despised.

'Don't say that, sir.'

'What am I to say?'

'Let him be an attaché,* or something of that sort.'

'Do you believe it possible that he should pass any examination? I think that my children between them will bring me to the grave. You had better go now. I suppose you will want to be—at the races again.' Then the young man crept out of the room, and going to his own part of the house shut himself up alone for nearly an hour. What had he better do to give his father some comfort? Should he abandon racing altogether, sell his share of Prime Minister and Coalition, and go in hard and strong for committees, debates, and divisions? Should he get rid of his drag, and resolve to read up parliamentary literature? He was resolved upon one thing at any rate. He would not go to the Oaks that day. And then he was resolved on another thing. He would call on Lady Mab Grex and ask her advice. He felt so disconsolate and insufficient for himself that he wanted advice from someone whom he could trust.

He found Tifto, Dolly Longstaff, and one or two others at the stables, from whence it was intended that the drag should start. They were waiting, and rather angry because they had been kept waiting. But the news, when it came, was very sad indeed. 'You wouldn't mind taking the team down and back yourself; would you, Dolly?' he said to Longstaff.

'You aren't going!' said Dolly, assuming a look of much heroic horror.

'No;—I am not going to-day.'

'What's up?' asked Popplecourt.

'That's rather sudden; isn't it?' asked the Major.

'Well; yes; I suppose it is sudden.'

'It's throwing us over a little, isn't it?'

'Not that I see. You've got the trap and the horses.'

'Yes;—we've got the trap and the horses,' said Dolly, 'and I vote we make a start.'

'As you are not going yourself, perhaps I'd better drive your horses,' said Tifto.

'Dolly will take the team,' said his Lordship.

'Yes;—decidedly. I will take the team,' said Dolly. 'There isn't a deal of driving wanted on the road to Epsom, but a man should know how to hold his reins.' This of course gave rise to some angry words, but Silverbridge did not stop to hear them.

The poor Duke had no one to whom he could go for advice and consolation. When his son left him he turned to his newspaper, and tried to read it—in vain. His mind was too ill at ease to admit of political matters. He was greatly grieved by this new misfortune as to Gerald, and by Lord Silverbridge's propensity to racing.

But though these sorrows were heavy, there was a sorrow heavier than these. Lady Cantrip had expressed an opinion almost in favour of Tregear—and had certainly expressed an opinion in favour of Mrs. Finn. The whole affair in regard to Mrs. Finn had been explained to her, and she had told the Duke that, according to her thinking, Mrs. Finn had behaved well! When the Duke, with an energy which was by no means customary with him, had asked that question, on the answer to which so much depended, 'Should there have been a moment lost?' Lady Cantrip had assured him that not a moment had been lost. Mrs. Finn had at once gone to work, and had arranged that the whole affair should be told to him, the Duke, in the proper way. 'I think she did,' said Lady Cantrip, 'what I myself should have done in similar circumstances.'

If Lady Cantrip was right, then must his apology to Mrs. Finn be ample and abject. Perhaps it was this feeling which at the moment was most vexatious to him.

CHAPTER XIX

'No; my Lord, I do not'

BETWEEN two and three o'clock Lord Silverbridge, in spite of his sorrow, found himself able to eat his lunch at his club. The place was deserted, the Beargarden world having gone to the races. As he sat eating cold lamb and drinking soda-and-brandy he did confirm himself in certain modified resolutions, which might be more probably kept than those sterner laws of absolute renunciation to which he had thought of pledging himself in his half-starved morning condition. His father had spoken in very strong language against racing, —saying that those who went were either fools or rascals. He was sure that this was exaggerated. Half the House of Lords and two-thirds of the House of Commons were to be seen at the Derby; but no doubt there were many rascals and fools, and he could not associate with the legislators without finding himself among the fools and rascals. He would,—as soon as he could,—separate himself from the Major. And he would not bet. It was on that side of the sport that the rascals and the fools showed themselves. Of what service could betting be to him whom Providence had provided with all things wanted to make life pleasant? As to the drag, his father had in a certain measure approved of that, and he would keep the drag, as he must have some relaxation. But his great effort of all should be made in the House of Commons. He would endeavour to make his father perceive that he had appreciated that letter. He would always be in the House soon after four, and would remain there,—for, if possible, as long as the Speaker sat in the chair. He had already begun to feel that there was a difficulty in keeping his seat upon those benches. The half-hours there would be so much longer than elsewhere! An irresistible desire of sauntering out would come upon him. There were men the very sound of whose voices was already odious to him. There had come upon him a feeling in regard to certain orators, that when once they had begun there was no reason why they should ever stop. Words of some sort were always forthcoming, like spiders' webs. He did not think that he could learn to take a pleasure in sitting in the House; but he hoped that he might be man enough to do it, though it was not pleasant. He would begin to-day, instead of going to the Oaks.

But before he went to the House he would see Lady Mabel Grex. And here it may be well to state that in making his resolutions as to a better life, he had considered much whether it would not be well for him to take a wife. His father had once told him that when he married, the house in Carlton Terrace should be his own. 'I will be a lodger if you will have me,' said the Duke; 'or if your wife should not like that, I will find a lodging elsewhere.' This had been in the sadness and tenderness which had immediately followed the death of the Duchess. Marriage would steady him. Were he a married man, Tifto would of course disappear. Upon the whole he thought it would be good that he should marry. And, if so, who could be so nice as Lady Mabel? That his father would be contented with Lady Mab, he was inclined to believe. There was no better blood in England. And Lady Mabel was known to be clever, beautiful, and, in her peculiar circumstances, very wise.

He was aware, however, of a certain drawback. Lady Mabel as his wife would be his superior, and in some degree his master. Though not older she was wiser than he,—and not only wiser but more powerful also. And he was not quite sure but that she regarded him as a boy. He thought that she did love him,—or would do so if he asked her,—but that her love would be bestowed upon him as on an inferior creature. He was already jealous of his own dignity, and fearful lest he should miss the glory of being loved by this lovely one for his own sake,—for his own manhood, and his own gifts and his own character.

And yet his attraction to her was so great that now in the day of his sorrow he could think of no solace but what was to be found in her company.

148

'Not at the Oaks!' she said as soon as he was shown into the drawing-room.

'No;—not at the Oaks. Lord Grex is there, I suppose?'

'Oh yes;—that is a matter of course. Why are you a recreant?'

'The House sits to-day.'

'How virtuous! Is it coming to that,—that when the House sits you will never be absent?'

'That's the kind of life I'm going to lead. You haven't heard about Gerald?'

'About your brother?'

'Yes—you haven't heard?'

'Not a word. I hope there is no misfortune.'

'But indeed there is,—a most terrible misfortune.' Then he told the whole story. How Gerald had been kept in London, and how he had gone down to Cambridge,—all in vain; how his father had taken the matter to heart, telling him that he had ruined his brother; and how he, in consequence, had determined not to go to the races. 'Then he said,' continued Silverbridge, 'that his children between them would bring him to his grave.'

'That was terrible.'

'Very terrible.'

'But what did he mean by that?' asked Lady Mabel, anxious to hear something about Lady Mary and Tregear.

'Well; of course what I did at Oxford made him unhappy; and now there is this affair of Gerald's.'

'He did not allude to your sister?'

'Yes he did. You have heard of all that. Tregear told you.'

'He told me something.'

'Of course my father does not like it.'

'Do you approve of it?'

'No,' said he—curtly and sturdily.

'Why not? You like Tregear.'

'Certainly I like Tregear. He is the friend, among men, whom I like the best. I have only two real friends.'

'Who are they?' she asked, sinking her voice very low.

149

'He is one;—and you are the other. You know that.'

'I hoped that I was one,' she said. 'But if you love Tregear so dearly, why do you not approve of him for your sister?'

'I always knew it would not do.'

'But why not?'

'Mary ought to marry a man of higher standing.'

'Of higher rank you mean. The daughters of Dukes have married commoners before.'

'It is not exactly that. I don't like to talk of it in that way. I knew it would make my father unhappy. In point of fact he can't marry her. What is the good of approving of a thing that is impossible?'

'I wish I knew your sister. Is she—firm?'

'Indeed she is.'

'I am not so sure that you are.'

'No,' said he, after considering awhile; 'nor am I. But she is not like Gerald or me. She is more obstinate.'

'Less fickle perhaps.'

'Yes, if you choose to call it fickle. I don't know that I am fickle. If I were in love with a girl I should be true to her.'

'Are you sure of that?'

'Quite sure. If I were really in love with her I certainly should not change. It is possible that I might be bullied out of it.'

'But she will not be bullied out of it?'

'Mary? No. That is just it. She will stick to it if he does.'

'I would if I were she. Where will you find any young man equal to Frank Tregear?'

'Perhaps you mean to cut poor Mary out.'

'That isn't a nice thing for you to say, Lord Silverbridge. Frank is my cousin,—as indeed you are also; but it so happens that I have seen a great deal of him all my life. And, though I don't want to cut your sister out, as you so prettily say, I love him well enough to understand that any girl whom he loves ought to be true to him.' So far what she said was very well, but she afterwards added a word which might have been wisely omitted. 'Frank and I are almost beggars.'

'What an accursed thing money is,' he exclaimed, jumping up from his chair.

'I don't agree with you at all. It is a very comfortable thing.'

'How is anybody who has got it to know if anybody cares for him?'

'You must find that out. There is such a thing I suppose as real sympathy.'

'You tell me to my face that you and Tregear would have been lovers only that you are both poor.'

'I never said anything of the kind.'

'And that he is to be passed on to my sister because it is supposed that she will have some money.'

'You are putting words into my mouth which I never spoke, and ideas into my mind which I never thought.'

'And of course I feel the same about myself. How can a fellow help it? I wish you had a lot of money, I know.'

'It is very kind of you;—but why?'

'Well;—I can't explain myself,' he said, blushing as was his wont. 'I daresay it wouldn't make any difference.'

'It would make a great difference to me. As it is, having none, and knowing as I do that papa and Percival are getting things into a worse mess every day, I am obliged to hope that I may some day marry a man who has got an income.'

'I suppose so,' said he, still blushing, but frowning at the same time.

'You see I can be very frank with a real friend. But I am sure of myself in this,—that I will never marry a man I do not love. A girl needn't love a man unless she likes it, I suppose. She doesn't tumble into love as she does into the fire. It would not suit me to marry a poor man, and so I don't mean to fall in love with a poor man.'

'But you do mean to fall in love with a rich one?'

'That remains to be seen, Lord Silverbridge. The rich man will at any rate have to fall in love with me first. If you know of any one you need not tell him to be too sure because he has a good income.'

151

'There's Popplecourt. He's his own master, and, fool as he is, he knows how to keep his money.'

'I don't want a fool. You must do better for me than Lord Popplecourt.'

'What do you say to Dolly Longstaff?'

'He would be just the man, only he never would take the trouble to come out and be married.'

'Or Glasslough?'

'I'm afraid he is cross, and wouldn't let me have my own way.'

'I can only think of one other;—but you would not take him.'

'Then you had better not mention him. It is no good crowding the list with impossibles.'

'I was thinking of——myself.'

'You are certainly one of the impossibles.'

'Why, Lady Mab?'

'For twenty reasons. You are too young, and you are bound to oblige your father, and you are to be wedded to Parliament,—at any rate for the next ten years. And altogether it wouldn't do,—for a great many reasons.'

'I suppose you don't like me well enough?'

'What a question to ask! No; my Lord, I do not. There; that's what you may call an answer. Don't you pretend to look offended, because if you do, I shall laugh at you. If you may have your joke surely I may have mine.'

'I don't see any joke in it.'

'But I do. Suppose I were to say the other thing. Oh, Lord Silverbridge, you do me so much honour! And now I come to think about it, there is no one in the world I am so fond of as you. Would that suit you?'

'Exactly.'

'But it wouldn't suit me. There's papa. Don't run away.'

'It's ever so much past five,' said the legislator, 'and I had intended to be in the House more than an hour ago. Good-bye. Give my love to Miss Cassewary.'

'Certainly. Miss Cassewary is your most devoted friend. Won't you bring your sister to see me some day?'

'When she is in town I will.'

'I should so like to know her. Good-bye.'

As he hurried down to the House in a hansom he thought over it all, and told himself that he feared it would not do. She might perhaps accept him, but if so, she would do it simply in order that she might become Duchess of Omnium. She might, he thought, have accepted him then, had she chosen. He had spoken plainly enough. But she had laughed at him. He felt that if she loved him, there ought to have been something of that feminine tremor, of that doubting, hesitating half-avowal of which he had perhaps read in novels, and which his own instincts taught him to desire. But there had been no tremor nor hesitating. 'No; my Lord, I do not,' she had said when he asked her to her face whether she liked him well enough to be his wife. 'No; my Lord, I do not.' It was not the refusal conveyed in these words which annoyed him. He did believe that if he were to press his suit with the usual forms she would accept him. But it was that there should be such a total absence of trepidation in her words and manner. Before her he blushed and hesitated and felt that he did not know how to express himself. If she would only have done the same, then there would have been an equality. Then he could have seized her in his arms and sworn that never, never, never would he care for any one but her.

In truth he saw everything as it was only too truly. Though she might choose to marry him if he pressed his request, she would never subject herself to him as he would have the girl do whom he loved. She was his superior, and in every word uttered between them showed that it was so. But yet how beautiful she was;—how much more beautiful than any other thing he had ever seen!

He sat on one of the high seats behind Sir Timothy Beeswax and Sir Orlando Drought,* listening, or pretending to listen, to the speeches of three or four gentlemen respecting sugar,* thinking of all this till half-past seven;—and then he went to dine with the proud consciousness of having done his duty. The forms and methods of the House were, he flattered himself, soaking into him gradually,—as his father had desired. The theory of legislation was sinking into his mind. The welfare of the nation depended chiefly on sugar. But he thought that, after all, his own welfare must depend on the possession of Mab Grex.

CHAPTER XX

'Then he will come again'

LADY MABEL, when her young lover left her, was for a time freed from the necessity of thinking about him by her father. He had returned from the Oaks in a very bad humour. Lord Grex had been very badly treated by his son, whom he hated worse than any one else in the world. On the Derby Day he had won a large sum of money, which had been to him at the time a matter of intense delight,—for he was in great want of money. But on this day he had discovered that his son and heir had lost more than he had won, and an arrangement had been suggested to him that his winnings should go to pay Percival's losings. This was a mode of settling affairs to which the Earl would not listen for a moment, had he possessed the power of putting a veto upon it. But there had been a transaction lately between him and his son with reference to the cutting off a certain entail under which money was to be paid to Lord Percival. This money had not yet been forthcoming, and therefore the Earl was constrained to assent. This was very distasteful to the Earl, and he came home therefore in a bad humour, and said a great many disagreeable things to his daughter. 'You know, papa, if I could do anything I would.' This she said in answer to a threat, which he had made often before and now repeated, of getting rid altogether of the house in Belgrave Square. Whenever he made this threat he did not scruple to tell her that the house had to be kept up solely for her welfare. 'I don't see why the deuce you don't get married. You'll have to do it sooner or later.' That was not a pleasant speech for a daughter to hear from her father. 'As to that,' she said, 'it must come or not as chance will have it. If you want me to sign anything I will sign it;'—for she had been asked to sign papers, or in other words to surrender rights;—'but for that other matter it must be left to myself.' Then he had been very disagreeable indeed.

They dined out together,—of course with all the luxury that wealth can give. There was a well-appointed carriage to take them backwards and forwards to the next square, such as an Earl should have. She was splendidly dressed, as became an Earl's daughter, and he was brilliant with some star which had been accorded to him by his sovereign's grateful minister in return for staunch parliamentary support. No one looking at them could have imagined that such a father could have told such a daughter that she must marry herself out of the way because as an unmarried girl she was a burden.

During the dinner she was very gay. To be gay was the habit,—we may almost say the work,—of her life. It so chanced that she sat between Sir Timothy Beeswax, who in these days was a very great man indeed, and that very Dolly Longstaff, whom Silverbridge in his irony had proposed to her as a fitting suitor for her hand.

'Isn't Lord Silverbridge a cousin of yours?' asked Sir Timothy.

'A very distant one.'

'He has come over to us, you know. It is such a triumph.'

'I was so sorry to hear it.' This, however, as the reader knows, was a fib.

'Sorry!' said Sir Timothy. 'Surely Lord Grex's daughter must be a Conservative.'

'Oh yes;—I am a Conservative because I was born one. I think that people in politics should remain as they are born,— unless they are very wise indeed. When men come to be statesmen and all that kind of thing, of course they can change backwards and forwards.'

'I hope that is not intended for me, Lady Mabel.'

'Certainly not. I don't know enough about it to be personal.'

155

That, however, was again not quite true. 'But I have the greatest possible respect for the Duke, and I think it a pity that he should be made unhappy by his son. Don't you like the Duke?'

'Well;—yes;—in a way. He is a most respectable man; and has been a good public servant.'

'All our lot are ruined, you know,' said Dolly, talking of the races.

'Who are your lot, Mr. Longstaff?'

'I'm one myself.'

'I suppose so.'

'I'm utterly smashed. Then there's Percival.'

'I hope he has not lost much. Of course you know he's my brother.'

'Oh laws;—so he is. I always put my foot in it. Well;—he has lost a lot. And so have Silverbridge and Tifto. Perhaps you don't know Tifto.'

'I have not the pleasure of knowing Mr. Tifto.'

'He is a major. I think you'd like Major Tifto. He's a sort of racing coach to Silverbridge. You ought to know Tifto. And Tregear is pretty nearly cleared out.'

'Mr. Tregear! Frank Tregear!'

'I'm told he has been hit very heavy. I hope he's not a friend of yours, Lady Mabel.'

'Indeed he is;—a very dear friend and a cousin.'

'That's what I hear. He's very much with Silverbridge you know.'

'I cannot think that Mr. Tregear has lost money.'

'I hope he hasn't. I know I have. I wish someone would stick up for me, and say that it was impossible.'

'But that is not Mr. Tregear's way of living. I can understand that Lord Silverbridge or Percival should lose money.'

'Or me?'

'Or you, if you like to say so.'

'Or Tifto?'

'I don't know anything about Mr. Tifto.'

'Major Tifto.'

156

'Or Major Tifto;—what does it signify?'

'No;—of course. We inferior people may lose our money just as we please. But a man who can look as clever as Mr. Tregear ought to win always.'

'I told you just now that he was a friend of mine.'

'But don't you think that he does look clever?' There could be no question but that Tregear, when he disliked his company, could show his dislike by his countenance; and it was not improbable that he had done so in the presence of Mr. Adolphus Longstaff. 'Now tell the truth, Lady Mabel; does he not look conceited sometimes?'

'He generally looks as if he knew what he was talking about, which is more than some other people do.'

'Of course he is a great deal more clever than I am. I know that. But I don't think even he can be so clever as he looks. "Or you so stupid," that's what you ought to say now.'

'Sometimes, Mr. Longstaff, I deny myself the pleasure of saying what I think.'

When all this was over she was very angry with herself for the anxiety she had expressed about Tregear. This Mr. Longstaff was, she thought, exactly the man to report all she had said in the public room at the club. But she had been annoyed by what she had heard as to her friend. She knew that he of all men should keep himself free from such follies. Those others had, as it were, a right to make fools of themselves. It had seemed so natural that the young men of her own class should dissipate their fortunes and their reputations by every kind of extravagance! Her father had done so, and she had never even ventured to hope that her brother would not follow her father's example. But Tregear, if he gave way to such follies as these, would soon fall headlong into a pit from which there would be no escape. And if he did fall, she knew herself well enough to be aware that she could not stifle, nor even conceal, the misery which this would occasion her. As long as he stood well before the world she would be well able to assume indifference. But were he to be precipitated into some bottomless misfortunes then she could only throw herself

157

after him. She could see him marry, and smile,—and perhaps even like his wife. And while he was doing so, she could also marry, and resolve that the husband whom she took should be made to think that he had a loving wife. But were Frank to die,—then must she fall upon his body as though he had been known by all the world to be her lover. Something of this feeling came upon her now, when she heard that he had been betting and had been unfortunate. She had been unable so to subdue herself as to seem to be perfectly careless about it. She had begun by saying that she had not believed it;—but she had believed it. It was so natural that Tregear should have done as the others did with whom he lived! But then the misfortune would be to him so terrible,—so irremediable! The reader, however, may as well know at once that there was not a word of truth in the assertion.

After the dinner she went home alone. There were other festivities to be attended, had she pleased to attend them; and poor Miss Cassewary was dressed ready to go with her as chaperone;—but Miss Cassewary was quite satisfied to be allowed to go to bed in lieu of Mrs. Montacute Jones's great ball. And she had gone to her bedroom when Lady Mabel went to her. 'I am glad you are alone,' she said, 'because I want to speak to you.'

'Is anything wrong?'

'Everything is wrong. Papa says he must give up this house.'

'He says that almost always when he comes back from the races, and very often when he comes back from the club.'

'Percival has lost ever so much.'

'I don't think my Lord will hamper himself for your brother.'

'I can't explain it, but there is some horrible money complication. It is hard upon you and me.'

'Who am I?' said Miss Cassewary.

'About the dearest friend that ever a poor girl had. It is hard upon you,—and upon me. I have given up everything,— and what good have I done?'

'It is hard, my dear.'

158

'But after all I do not care much for all that. The thing has been going on so long that one is used to it.'

'What is it then?'

'Ah;—yes;—what is it? How am I to tell you?'

'Surely you can tell me,' said the old woman, putting out her hand so as to caress the arm of the younger one.

'I could tell no one else; I am sure of that. Frank Tregear has taken to gambling,—like the rest of them.'

'Who says so?'

'He has lost a lot of money at these races. A man who sat next me at dinner,—one of those stupid do-nothing fools that one meets everywhere,—told me so. He is one of the Beargarden set, and of course he knows all about it.'

'Did he say how much?'

'How is he to pay anything? Of all things that men do this is the worst. A man who would think himself disgraced for ever if he accepted a present of money will not scruple to use all his wits to rob his friend of everything that he has by studying the run of cards or by watching the paces of some brutes of horses! And they consider themselves to be fine gentlemen! A real gentleman should never want the money out of another man's pocket;—should never think of money at all.'

'I don't know how that is to be helped, my dear. You have got to think of money.'

'Yes; I have to think of it, and do think of it; and because I do so I am not what I call a gentleman.'

'No;—my dear; you're a lady.'

'Psha! you know what I mean. I might have had the feelings of a gentleman as well as the best man that ever was born. I haven't; but I have never done anything so mean as gambling. Now I have got something else to tell you.'

'What is it? You do frighten me so when you look like that.'

'You may well be frightened,—for if this all comes round I shall very soon be able to dispense with you altogether. His Royal Highness Lord Silverbridge——'

'What do you mean, Mabel?'

159

'He's next door to a Royal Highness at any rate, and a much more topping man than most of them. Well then;—His Serene Highness the heir of the Duke of Omnium has done me the inexpressible honour of asking me—to marry him.'

'No!'

'You may well say, No. And to tell the truth exactly, he didn't.'

'Then why do you say he did?'

'I don't think he did quite ask me, but he gave me to understand that he would do so if I gave him any encouragement.'

'Did he mean it?'

'Yes;—poor boy! He meant it. With a word;—with a look, he would have been down there kneeling. He asked me whether I liked him well enough. What do you think I did?'

'What did you do.'

'I spared him;—out of sheer downright Christian charity! I said to myself "Love your neighbours." "Don't be selfish." "Do unto him as you would he should do unto you,"—that is, think of his welfare. Though I had him in my net, I let him go. Shall I go to heaven for doing that?'

'I don't know,' said Miss Casseawry, who was so much perturbed by the news she had heard as to be unable to come to any opinion on the point just raised.

'Or mayn't I rather go to the other place? From how much embarrassment should I have relieved my father! What a friend I should have made for Percival! How much I might have been able to do for Frank! And then what a wife I should have made him!'

'I think you would.'

'He'll never get another half so good; and he'll be sure to get one before long. It is a sort of tenderness that is quite inefficacious. He will become a prey, as I should have made him a prey. But where is there another who will treat him so well?'

'I cannot bear to hear you speak of yourself in that way.'

'But it is true. I know the sort of girl he should marry. In the first place she should be two years younger, and four years fresher. She should be able not only to like him and love him, but to worship him. How well I can see her! She should have fair hair, and bright green-gray eyes, with the sweetest complexion, and the prettiest little dimples;—two inches shorter than me, and the delight of her life should be to hang with two hands on his arm. She should have a feeling that her Silverbridge is an Apollo upon earth. To me he is a rather foolish, but very, very sweet-tempered young man;—anything rather than a god. If I thought that he would get the fresh young girl with the dimples then I ought to abstain.'

'If he was in earnest,' said Miss Cassewary, throwing aside all this badinage and thinking of the main point, 'if he was in earnest he will come again.'

'He was quite in earnest.'

'Then he will come again.'

'I don't think he will,' said Lady Mabel. 'I told him that I was too old for him, and I tried to laugh him out of it. He does not like being laughed at. He has been saved, and he will know it.'

'But if he should come again?'

'I shall not spare him again. No;—not twice. I felt it to be hard to do so once, because I so nearly love him! There are so many of them who are odious to me, as to whom the idea of marrying them seems to be mixed somehow with an idea of suicide.'

'Oh, Mabel!'

'But he is as sweet as a rose. If I were his sister, or his servant, or his dog, I could be devoted to him. I can fancy that his comfort and his success and his name should be everything to me.'

'That is what a wife ought to feel.'

'But I could never feel him to be my superior. That is what a wife ought in truth to feel. Think of those two young men and the difference between them! Well;—don't look like that at me. I don't often give way, and I dare say after all I shall live to be the Duchess of Omnium.' Then she kissed her friend and went away to her own room.

CHAPTER XXI

Sir Timothy Beeswax

THERE had lately been a great Conservative reaction*in the country, brought about in part by the industry and good management of gentlemen who were strong on that side;—but due also in part to the blunders and quarrels of their opponents. That these opponents should have blundered and quarrelled, being men active and in earnest, was to have been expected. Such blunderings and quarrellings have been a matter of course since politics have been politics, and since religion has been religion. When men combine to do nothing, how should there be disagreement? When men combine to do much, how should there not be disagreement? Thirty men can sit still, each as like the other as peas. But put your thirty men up to run a race, and they will soon assume different forms. And in doing nothing, you can hardly do amiss. Let the doers of nothing have something of action forced upon them, and they, too, will blunder and quarrel.

The wonder is that there should ever be in a reforming party enough of consentaneous action to carry any reform. The reforming or Liberal party in British politics had thus stumbled,—and stumbled till it fell. And now there had been a great Conservative reaction! Many of the most Liberal constituencies in the country had been untrue to their old political convictions. And, as the result, Lord Drummond was Prime Minister in the House of Lords,—with Sir Timothy Beeswax acting as first man in the House of Commons.

It cannot be denied that Sir Timothy had his good points as a politician. He was industrious, patient, clear-sighted, intelligent, courageous, and determined. Long before he had had a seat in the House, when he was simply making his way up to the probability of a seat by making a reputation as an advocate, he had resolved that he would be more than an Attorney-General, more than a judge,—more, as he thought it, than a Chief Justice; but at any rate something different.

This plan he had all but gained,—and it must be acknowledged that he had been moved by a grand and manly ambition. But there were drawbacks to the utility and beauty of
Sir Timothy's character as a statesman. He had no idea as to
the necessity or non-necessity of any measure whatever in
reference to the well-being of the country. It may, indeed, be
said that all such ideas were to him absurd, and the fact that
they should be held by his friends and supporters was an inconvenience. He was not in accord with those who declare that
a Parliament is a collection of windbags which puff, and blow,
and crack to the annoyance of honest men. But to him Parliament
was a debating place, by having a majority in which, and by
no other means, he,—or another,—might become the great
man of the day. By no other than parliamentary means could
such a one as he come to be the chief man. And this use of
Parliament, either on his own behalf or on behalf of others,
had been for so many years present to his mind, that there
seemed to be nothing absurd in an institution supported for
such a purpose. Parliament was a club so eligible in its nature
that all Englishmen wished to belong to it. They who succeeded were acknowledged to be the cream of the land. They
who dominated in it were the cream of the cream. Those two
who were elected to be the chiefs of the two parties had more
of cream in their composition than any others. But he who
could be the chief of the strongest party, and who therefore,
in accordance with the prevailing arrangements of the country,
should have the power of making dukes, and bestowing garters
and appointing bishops, he who by attaining the first seat
should achieve the right of snubbing all before him, whether
friends or foes, he, according to the feelings of Sir Timothy,
would have gained an Elysium of creaminess not to be found
in any other position on the earth's surface. No man was more
warmly attached to parliamentary government than Sir
Timothy Beeswax; but I do not think that he ever cared
much for legislation.

Parliamentary management was his forte. There have been
various rocks on which men have shattered their barks in

their attempts to sail successfully into the harbours of parliamentary management. There is the great Senator who declares to himself that personally he will have neither friend nor foe. There is his country before him and its welfare. Within his bosom is the fire of patriotism, and within his mind the examples of all past time. He knows that he can be just, he teaches himself to be eloquent, and he strives to be wise. But he will not bend;—and at last, in some great solitude, though closely surrounded by those whose love he had neglected to acquire,—he breaks his heart.

Then there is he who seeing the misfortune of that great one, tells himself that patriotism, judgment, industry, and eloquence will not suffice for him unless he himself can be loved. To do great things a man must have a great following, and to achieve that he must be popular. So he smiles and learns the necessary wiles. He is all for his country and his friends,—but for his friends first. He too must be eloquent and well instructed in the ways of Parliament, must be wise and diligent; but in all that he does and all that he says he must first study his party. It is well with him for a time;—but he has closed the door of his Elysium too rigidly. Those without gradually become stronger than his friends within, and so he falls.

But may not the door be occasionally opened to an outsider, so that the exterior force be diminished? We know how great is the pressure of water; and how the peril of an overwhelming weight of it may be removed by opening the way for a small current. There comes therefore the Statesman who acknowledges to himself that he will be pregnable. That, as a Statesman, he should have enemies is a matter of course. Against moderate enemies he will hold his own. But when there comes one immoderately forcible, violently inimical, then to that man he will open his bosom. He will tempt into his camp with an offer of high command any foe that may be worth his purchase. This too has answered well; but there is a Nemesis. The loyalty of officers so procured must be open to suspicion. The man who has said bitter things against you will never sit at your feet in contented submission, nor will

your friend of old standing long endure to be superseded by
such converts.

All these dangers Sir Timothy had seen and studied, and
for each of them he had hoped to be able to provide an anti-
dote. Love cannot do all. Fear may do more. Fear acknowledges a superior. Love desires an equal. Love is to be created
by benefits done, and means gratitude, which we all know to
be weak. But hope, which refers itself to benefits to come, is
of all our feelings the strongest. And Sir Timothy had parliamentary doctrines concealed in the depths of his own bosom
more important even than these. The Statesman who falls is
he who does much, and thus injures many. The Statesman
who stands the longest is he who does nothing and injures
no one. He soon knew that the work which he had taken in
hand required all the art of a great conjuror. He must be
possessed of tricks so marvellous that not even they who sat
nearest to him might know how they were performed.

For the executive or legislative business of the country he
cared little. The one should be left in the hands of men who
liked work;—of the other there should be little, or, if possible,
none. But Parliament must be managed,—and his party. Of
patriotism he did not know the meaning;—few, perhaps, do,
beyond a feeling that they would like to lick the Russians,*or
to get the better of the Americans*in a matter of fisheries
or frontiers. But he invented a pseudo-patriotic conjuring
phraseology which no one understood but which many admired. He was ambitious that it should be said of him that he
was far-and-away the cleverest of his party. He knew himself
to be clever. But he could only be far-and-away the cleverest
by saying and doing that which no one could understand. If
he could become master of some great hocus-pocus system
which could be made to be graceful to the ears and eyes of
many, which might for awhile seem to have within it some
semi-divine attribute, which should have all but divine power
of mastering the loaves and fishes, then would they who followed him believe in him more firmly than other followers
who had believed in their leaders. When you see a young

165

woman read a closed book placed on her dorsal vertebræ,—
if you do believe that she so reads it, you think that she is
endowed with a wonderful faculty! And should you also be
made to believe that the same young woman had direct communication with Abraham, by means of some invisible wire,
you would be apt to do a great many things as that young
woman might tell you. Conjuring, when not known to be
conjuring, is very effective.

Much, no doubt, of Sir Timothy's power had come from
his praiseworthy industry. Though he cared nothing for the
making of laws, though he knew nothing of finance, though he
had abandoned his legal studies, still he worked hard. And because he had worked harder in a special direction than others
around him, therefore he was enabled to lead them. The
management of a party is a very great work in itself; and
when to that is added the management of the House of Commons, a man has enough upon his hands even though he
neglects altogether the ordinary pursuits of a Statesman.
Those around Sir Timothy were fond of their party; but they
were for the most part men who had not condescended to put
their shoulders to the wheel as he had done. Had there been
any very great light among them, had there been a Pitt or a
Peel,* Sir Timothy would have probably become Attorney-
General and have made his way to the bench;—but there had
been no Pitt and no Peel, and he had seen his opening. He
had studied the ways of Members. Parliamentary practice had
become familiar to him. He had shown himself to be ready at
all hours to fight the battle of the party he had joined. And no
man knew so well as did Sir Timothy how to elevate a simple
legislative attempt into a good faction fight. He had so
mastered his tricks of conjuring that no one could get to the
bottom of them, and had assumed a look of preternatural
gravity which made many young Members think that Sir
Timothy was born to be a king of men.

There were no doubt some among his older supporters who
felt their thraldom grievously. There were some lords in the
Upper House and some sons of the lords in the Lower,—with

pedigrees going back far enough for pride,—who found it irksome to recognise Sir Timothy as a master. No doubt he had worked very hard, and had worked for them. No doubt he knew how to do the work, and they did not. There was no other man among them to whom the lead could be conveniently transferred. But yet they were uncomfortable,—and perhaps a little ashamed.

It had arisen partly from this cause, that there had been something of a counter-reaction at the last general election. When the Houses met, the Ministers had indeed a majority, but a much lessened majority. The old Liberal constituencies had returned to an expression of their real feeling. This reassertion of the progress of the tide, this recovery from the partial ebb which checks the violence of every flow, is common enough in politics; but at the present moment there were many who said that all this had been accelerated by a feeling in the country that Sir Timothy was hardly all that the country required as the leader of the country party.

CHAPTER XXII

The Duke in His Study

IT was natural that at such a time, when success greater than had been expected had attended the efforts of the Liberals, when some dozen unexpected votes had been acquired, the leading politicians of that party should have found themselves compelled to look about them and see how these good things might be utilised. In February they certainly had not expected to be called to power in the course of the existing session. Perhaps they did not expect it yet. There was still a Conservative majority,—though but a small majority. But the strength of the minority consisted, not in the fact that the majority against them was small, but that it was decreasing. How quickly does the snowball grow into hugeness as it is rolled on,—but when the change comes in the weather how quickly does it melt, and before it is gone become a thing ugly, weak, and formless! Where is the individual who does not assert to himself that he would be more loyal to a falling than to a rising friend? Such is perhaps the nature of each one of us. But when any large number of men act together, the falling friend is apt to be deserted. There was a general feeling among politicians that Lord Drummond's ministry,—or Sir Timothy's—was failing, and the Liberals, though they could not yet count the votes by which they might hope to be supported in power, nevertheless felt that they ought to be looking to their arms.

There had been a coalition.*They who are well read in the political literature of their country will remember all about that. It had perhaps succeeded in doing that for which it had been intended. The Queen's government had been carried on for two or three years. The Duke of Omnium had been the head of that Ministry; but during those years had suffered so much as to have become utterly ashamed of the coalition,—so much as to have said often to himself that under no circumstances would he again join any Ministry. At this time there was no idea of another coalition. That is a state of things which cannot come about frequently,—which can only be reproduced by men who have never hitherto felt the mean insipidity of such a condition. But they who had served on the Liberal side in that coalition must again put their shoulders to the wheel. Of course it was in every man's mouth that the Duke must be induced to forget his miseries and once more to take upon himself the duties of an active servant of the State.

But they who were most anxious on the subject, such men as Lord Cantrip, Mr. Monk, our old friend Phineas Finn, and a few others, were almost afraid to approach him. At the moment when the coalition was broken up he had been very bitter in spirit, apparently almost arrogant, holding himself aloof from his late colleagues,—and since that, troubles had come to him, which had aggravated the soreness of his heart. His wife had died, and he had suffered much through his children. What Lord Silverbridge had done at Oxford was matter of general conversation, and also what he had not done.

That the heir of the family should have become a renegade in politics was supposed greatly to have affected the father. Now Lord Gerald had been expelled from Cambridge, and Silverbridge was on the turf in conjunction with Major Tifto! Something, too, had oozed out into general ears about Lady Mary,—something which should have been kept secret as the grave. It had therefore come to pass that it was difficult even to address the Duke.

There was one man, and but one, who could do this with ease to himself;—and that man was at last put into motion at the instance of the leaders of the party. The old Duke of St. Bungay*wrote the following letter to the Duke of Omnium. The letter purported to be an excuse for the writer's own defalcation. But the chief object of the writer was to induce the younger Duke once more to submit to harness.

'Longroyston, 3rd June, 187—.

'DEAR DUKE OF OMNIUM,

'How quickly the things come round! I had thought that I should never again have been called upon even to think of the formation of another Liberal Ministry; and now, though it was but yesterday that we were all telling ourselves that we were thoroughly manumitted from our labours by the altered opinions of the country, sundry of our old friends are again putting their heads together.

'Did they not do so they would neglect a manifest duty. Nothing is more essential to the political well-being of the country than that the leaders on both sides in politics should be prepared for their duties. But for myself, I am bound at last to put in the old plea with a determination that it shall be respected. "Solve senescentem."* It is now, if I calculate rightly, exactly fifty years since I first entered public life in obedience to the advice of Lord Grey.* I had then already sat five years in the House of Commons. I assisted humbly in the emancipation of the Roman Catholics,*and have learned by the legislative troubles of just half a century that those whom we then invited to sit with us in Parliament have been in all

169

things our worst enemies. But what then? Had we benefited only those who love us, would not the sinners also,—or even the Tories,—have done as much as that?

'But such memories are of no avail now. I write to say that after so much of active political life, I will at last retire. My friends when they see me inspecting a pigsty or picking a peach are apt to remind me that I can still stand on my legs, and with more of compliment than of kindness will argue therefore that I ought still to undertake active duties in Parliament. I can select my own hours for pigs and peaches, and should I, through the dotage of age, make mistakes as to the breeding of the one or the flavour of the other, the harm done will not go far. In politics I have done my work. What you and others in the arena do will interest me more than all other things of this world, I think and hope, to my dying day. But I will not trouble the workers with the querulousness of old age.

'So much for myself. And now let me, as I go, say a parting word to him with whom in politics I have been for many years more in accord than with any other leading man. As nothing but age or infirmity would to my own mind have justified me in retiring, so do I think that you, who can plead neither age nor infirmity, will find yourself at last to want self-justification, if you permit yourself to be driven from the task either by pride or by indifference.

'I should express my feelings better were I to say by pride and diffidence. I look to our old friendship, to the authority given to me by my age, and to the thorough goodness of your heart for pardon in thus accusing you. That little men should have ventured to ill-use you, has hurt your pride. That these little men should have been able to do so has created your diffidence. Put you to a piece of work that a man may do, you have less false pride as to the way in which you may do it than any man I have known; and, let the way be open to you, as little diffidence as any. But in this political mill of ours in England, a man cannot always find the way open to do things. It does not often happen that an English statesman can go in and make a great score off his own bat. But not the less is he bound to play the game and to go to the wicket when he finds that his time has come.

'There are, I think, two things for you to consider in this matter, and two only. The first is your capacity, and the other is your duty. A man may have found by experience that he is unfitted for public life. You and I have known men in regard to whom we have thoroughly wished that such experience had been reached. But this is a matter in which a man who doubts himself is bound to take the evidence of those around him. The whole party is most anxious for your co-operation. If this be so,—and I make you the assurance from most conclusive evidence,—you are bound to accept the common consent of your political friends on that matter. You perhaps think that at a certain period of your life you failed. They all agree with me that you did not fail. It is a matter on which you should be bound by our opinion rather than by your own.

'As to that matter of duty I shall have less difficulty in carrying you with me. Though this renewed task may be personally disagreeable to you, even though your tastes should lead you to some other life,—which I think is not the case,—still if your country wants you, you should serve your country. It is a work as to which such a one as you has no option. Of most of those who choose public life,—it may be said that were they not there, there would be others as serviceable. But when a man such as you has shown himself to be necessary, as long as health and age permits he cannot recede without breach of manifest duty. The work to be done is so important, the numbers to be benefited are so great, that he cannot be justified in even remembering that he has a self.

'As I have said before, I trust that my own age and your goodness will induce you to pardon this great interference. But whether pardoned or not I shall always be

'Your most affectionate friend,
'St. Bungay.'

171

The Duke,—our Duke,—on reading this letter was by no means pleased by its contents. He could ill bear to be reminded either of his pride or of his diffidence. And yet the accusations which others made against him were as nothing to those with which he charged himself. He would do this till at last he was forced to defend himself against himself by asking himself whether he could be other than as God had made him. It is the last and the poorest makeshift of a defence to which a man can be brought in his own court! Was it his fault that he was so thin-skinned that all things hurt him? When some coarse man said to him that which ought not to have been said, was it his fault that at every word a penknife had stabbed him? Other men had borne these buffets without shrinking, and had shown themselves thereby to be more useful, much more efficacious; but he could no more imitate them than he could procure for himself the skin of a rhinoceros or the tusk of an elephant. And this shrinking was what men called pride,—was the pride of which his old friend wrote! 'Have I ever been haughty, unless in my own defence?' he asked himself, remembering certain passages of humility in his life,—and certain passages of haughtiness also.

And the Duke told him also that he was diffident. Of course he was diffident. Was it not one and the same thing? The very pride of which he was accused was no more than that shrinking which comes from the want of trust in oneself. He was a shy man. All his friends and all his enemies knew that;—it was thus that he still discoursed with himself;—a shy, self-conscious, timid, shrinking, thin-skinned man! Of course he was diffident. Then why urge him on to tasks for which he was by nature unfitted?

And yet there was much in his old friend's letter which moved him. There were certain words which he kept on repeating to himself. 'He cannot be justified in even remembering that he has a self.' It was a hard thing to say of any man, but yet a true thing of such a man as his correspondent had described. His correspondent had spoken of a man who should know himself to be capable of serving the State. If a man were capable, and was sure within his own bosom of his own capacity, it would be his duty. But what if he were not so satisfied? What if he felt that any labours of his would be vain, and all self-abnegation useless? His friend had told him that on that matter he was bound to take the opinion of others. Perhaps so. But if so, had not that opinion been given to him very plainly when he was told that he was both proud and diffident? That he was called upon to serve his country by good service, if such were within his power, he did acknowledge freely; but not that he should allow himself to be stuck up as a ninepin only to be knocked down! There are politicians for whom such occupation seems to be proper;—and who like it too. A little office, a little power, a little rank, a little pay, a little niche in the ephemeral history of the year will reward many men adequately for being knocked down.

And yet he loved power, and even when thinking of all this allowed his mind from time to time to run away into a dreamland of prosperous political labours. He thought what it would be to be an all-beneficent Prime Minister, with a loyal majority, with a well-conditioned unanimous cabinet, with a grateful people, and an appreciative Sovereign. How well might a man spend himself night and day, even to death, in the midst of labours such as these.

Half an hour after receiving the Duke's letter he suddenly jumped up and sat himself down at his desk. He felt it to be necessary that he should at once write to his old friend;—and the more necessary that he should do so at once, because he had resolved that he would do so before he had made up his mind on the chief subject of that letter. It did not suit him to say either that he would or that he would not do as his friend advised him. The reply was made in a very few words. 'As to myself,' he said, after expressing his regret that the Duke should find it necessary to retire from public life—'as to myself, pray understand that whatever I may do I shall never cease to be grateful for your affectionate and high-spirited counsels.'

Then his mind recurred to a more immediate and, for the moment, a heavier trouble. He had as yet given no answer to that letter from Mrs. Finn, which the reader will perhaps remember. It might indeed be passed over without an answer; but to him that was impossible. She had accused him in the very strongest language of injustice, and had made him understand that if he were unjust to her, then would he be most ungrateful. He, looking at the matter with his own lights, had thought that he had been right, but had resolved to submit the question to another person. As judge in the matter he had chosen Lady Cantrip, and Lady Cantrip had given judgment against him.

He had pressed Lady Cantrip for a decided opinion, and she had told him that she, in the same position, would have done just as Mrs. Finn had done. He had constituted Lady Cantrip his judge, and had resolved that her judgment should be final. He declared to himself that he did not understand it. If a man's house be on fire, do you think of certain rules of etiquette before you bid him send for the engines? If a wild beast be loose, do you go through some ceremony before you caution the wanderers abroad? There should not have been a moment! But, nevertheless, it was now necessary that he should conform himself to the opinion of Lady Cantrip, and in doing so he must apologise for the bitter scorn with which he had allowed himself to treat his wife's most loyal and loving friend.

The few words to the Duke had not been difficult, but this letter seemed to be an Herculean task. It was made infinitely more difficult by the fact that Lady Cantrip had not seemed to think that this marriage was impossible. 'Young people when they have set their minds upon it do so generally prevail at last!' These had been her words, and they discomforted him greatly. She had thought the marriage to be possible. Had she not almost expressed an opinion that they ought to be allowed to marry? And if so, would it not be his duty to take his girl away from Lady Cantrip? As to the idea that young people, because they have declared themselves to be in love, were to have just what they wanted,—with that he did not agree at all. Lady Cantrip had told him that young people generally did prevail at last. He knew the story of one young person, whose position in her youth had been very much the same as that of his daughter now, and she had not prevailed. And in her case had not the opposition which had been made to her wishes been most fortunate? That young person had become his wife, his Glencora, his Duchess. Had she been allowed to have her own way when she was a child, what would have been her fate? Ah what! Then he had to think of it all. Might she not have been alive now, and perhaps happier than she had ever been with him? And had he remained always unmarried, devoted simply to politics, would not the troubles of the world have been lighter on him? But what had that to do with it? In these matters it was not the happiness of this or that individual which should be considered. There is a propriety in things;— and only by an adherence to that propriety on the part of individuals can the general welfare be maintained. A King in this country, or the heir or the possible heir to the throne, is debarred from what might possibly be a happy marriage by regard to the good of his subjects. To the Duke's thinking the maintenance of the aristocracy of the country was second only in importance to the maintenance of the Crown. How should the aristocracy be maintained if its wealth were allowed to fall into the hands of an adventurer!

Such were the opinions with regard to his own order of one who was as truly Liberal in his ideas as any man in England, and who had argued out these ideas to their consequences. As by the spread of education and increase of general well-being every proletaire was brought nearer to a Duke, so by such action would the Duke be brought nearer to a proletaire. Such drawing-nearer of the classes was the object to which all this man's political action tended. And yet it was a dreadful thing to him that his own daughter should desire to marry a man so much beneath her own rank and fortune as Frank Tregear.

He would not allow himself to believe that the young people

could ever prevail; but nevertheless, as the idea of the thing had not alarmed Lady Cantrip as it had him, it was necessary that he should make some apology to Mrs. Finn. Each moment of procrastination was a prick to his conscience. He now therefore dragged out from the secrecy of some close drawer Mrs. Finn's letter and read it through to himself once again. Yes—it was true that he had condemned her, and that he had punished her. Though he had done nothing to her, and said nothing, and written but very little, still he had punished her most severely.

She had written as though the matter was almost one of life and death to her. He could understand that too. His uncle's conduct to this woman, and his wife's, had created the intimacy which had existed. Through their efforts she had become almost as one of the family. And now to be dismissed, like a servant who had misbehaved herself! And then her arguments in her own defence were all so good,—if only that which Lady Cantrip had laid down as law was to be held as law. He was aware now that she had had no knowledge of the matter till his daughter had told her of the engagement at Matching. Then it was evident also that she had sent this Tregear to him immediately on her return to London. And at the end of the letter she accused him of what she had been pleased to call his usual tenacity in believing ill of her! He had been obstinate,—too obstinate in this respect, but he did not love her the better for having told him of it.

At last he did put his apology into words.

'MY DEAR MRS. FINN,

'I believe I had better acknowledge to you at once that I have been wrong in my judgment as to your conduct in a certain matter. You tell me that I owe it to you to make this acknowledgment,—and I make it. The subject is, as you may imagine, so painful that I will spare myself, if possible, any further allusion to it. I believe I did you a wrong, and therefore I write to ask your pardon.

'I should perhaps apologise also for delay in my reply. I

have had much to think of in this matter, and have many others also on my mind.

'Believe me to be,

'Yours faithfully,

'OMNIUM.'

It was very short, and as being short was infinitely less troublesome at the moment than a fuller epistle; but he was angry with himself, knowing that it was too short, feeling that it was ungracious. He should have expressed a hope that he might soon see her again,—only he had no such wish. There had been times at which he had liked her, but he knew that he did not like her now. And yet he was bound to be her friend! If he could only do some great thing for her, and thus satisfy his feeling of indebtedness towards her! But all the favours had been from her to him and his.

CHAPTER XXIII

Frank Tregear wants a Friend

SIX or seven weeks had passed since Tregear had made his communication to the Duke, and during that time he had heard not a word about the girl he loved. He knew, indeed, that she was at The Horns, and probably had reason to suppose that she was being guarded there, as it were, out of his reach. This did not surprise him; nor did he regard it as a hardship. It was to be expected that she should be kept out of his sight. But this was a state of things to which, as he thought, there should not be more than a moderate amount of submission. Six weeks was not a very long period, but it was perhaps long enough for evincing that respect which he owed to the young lady's father. Something must be done some day. How could he expect her to be true to him unless he took some means of showing himself to be true to her?

In these days he did not live very much with her brother. He not only disliked, but distrusted Major Tifto, and had so expressed himself as to give rise to angry words. Silverbridge had said that he knew how to take care of himself. Tregear had replied that he had his doubts on that matter. Then the Member of Parliament had declared that at any rate he did not intend to be taken care of by Frank Tregear! In such a state of things it was not possible that there should be any close confidence as to Lady Mary. Nor does it often come to pass that the brother is the confidant of the sister's lover. Brothers hardly like their sisters to have lovers, though they are often well satisfied that their sisters should find husbands. Tregear's want of rank and wealth added something to this feeling in the mind of this brother; so that Silverbridge, though he felt himself to be deterred by friendship from any open opposition, still was almost inimical. 'It won't do, you know,' he had said to his brother Gerald, shaking his head.

Tregear, however, was determined to be active in the matter, to make some effort, to speak to somebody. But how to make an effort,—and to whom should he speak? Thinking of all this he remembered that Mrs. Finn had sent for him and had told him to go with his love story to the Duke. She had been almost severe with him;—but after the interview was over, he had felt that she had acted well and wisely. He therefore determined that he would go to Mrs. Finn.

She had as yet received no answer from the Duke, though nearly a fortnight had elapsed since she had written her letter. During that time she had become very angry. She felt that he was not treating her as a gentleman should treat a lady, and certainly not as the husband of her late friend should have treated the friend of his late wife. She had a proud consciousness of having behaved well to the Pallisers, and now this head of the Pallisers was rewarding her by evil treatment. She had been generous; he was ungenerous. She had been honest; he was deficient even in that honesty for which she had given him credit. And she had been unable to obtain any of that consolation which could have come to her from talking of her wrongs. She could not complain to her husband, because there were reasons that made it essential that her husband should not quarrel with the Duke. She was hot with indignation at the very moment in which Tregear was announced.

He began by apologising for his intrusion, and she of course assured him that he was welcome. 'After the liberty which I took with you, Mr. Tregear, I am only too well pleased that you should come and see me.'

'I am afraid,' he said, 'that I was a little rough.'

'A little warm;—but that was to be expected. A gentleman never likes to be interfered with on such a matter.'

'The position was and is difficult, Mrs. Finn.'

'And I am bound to acknowledge the very ready way in which you did what I asked you to do.'

'And now, Mrs. Finn, what is to come next?'

'Ah!'

'Something must be done! You know of course that the Duke did not receive me with any great favour.'

'I did not suppose he would.'

'Nor did I. Of course he would object to such a marriage, But a man in these days cannot dictate to his daughter what husband she should marry.'

'Perhaps he can dictate to her what husband she shall not marry.'

'Hardly that. He may put impediments in the way; and the Duke will do so. But if I am happy enough to have won the affections of his daughter,—so as to make it essential to her happiness that she should become my wife,—he will give way.'

'What am I to say, Mr. Tregear?'

'Just what you think.'

'Why should I be made to say what I think on so delicate a matter? Or of what use would be my thoughts? Remember how far I am removed from her.'

'You are his friend.'

'Not at all! No one less so!' As she said this she could not hinder the colour from coming into her face. 'I was her friend, —Lady Glencora's; but with the death of my friend there was an end of all that.'

179

'You were staying with him,—at his request. You told me so yourself.'

'I shall never stay with him again. But all that, Mr. Tregear, is of no matter. I do not mean to say a word against him;—not a word. But if you wish to interest any one as being the Duke's friend, then I can assure you I am the last person in London to whom you should come. I know no one to whom the Duke is likely to entertain feelings so little kind as to-wards me.' This she said in a peculiarly solemn way that startled Tregear. But before he could answer her a servant entered the room with a letter. She recognised at once the Duke's handwriting. Here was the answer for which she had been so long waiting in silent expectation! She could not keep it unread till he was gone. 'Will you allow me a moment?' she whispered, and then she opened the envelope. As she read the few words her eyes became laden with tears. They quite sufficed to relieve the injured pride which had sat so heavy at her heart. 'I believe I did you a wrong, and therefore I ask your pardon!' It was so like what she had believed the man to be! She could not be longer angry with him. And yet the very last words she had spoken were words complaining of his conduct. 'This is from the Duke,' she said, putting the letter back into its envelope.

'Oh, indeed.'

'It is odd that it should have come while you were here.'

'Is it,—is it,—about Lady Mary?'

'No;—at least,—not directly. I perhaps spoke more harshly about him than I should have done. The truth is I had expected a line from him, and it had not come. Now it is here; but I do not suppose I shall ever see much of him. My intimacy was with her. But I would not wish you to remember what I said just now, if—if——'

'If what, Mrs. Finn? You mean, perhaps, if I should ever be allowed to call myself his son-in-law. It may seem to you to be arrogant, but it is an honour which I expect to win.'

'Faint heart,*—you know, Mr. Tregear.'

'Exactly. One has to tell oneself that very often. You will help me?'

'Certainly not,' she said, as though she were much startled. 'How can I help you?'

'By telling me what I should do. I suppose if I were to go down to Richmond I should not be admitted.'

'If you ask me, I think not;—not to see Lady Mary. Lady Cantrip would perhaps see you.'

'She is acting the part of—duenna.'

'As I should do also, if Lady Mary were staying with me. You don't suppose that if she were here I would let her see you in my house without her father's leave?'

'I suppose not.'

'Certainly not; and therefore I conceive that Lady Cantrip will not do so either.'

'I wish she were here.'

'It would be of no use. I should be a dragon in guarding her.'

'I wish you would let me feel that you were like a sister to me in this matter.'

'But I am not your sister, nor yet your aunt, nor yet your grandmother. What I mean is that I cannot be on your side.'

'Can you not?'

'No, Mr. Tregear. Think how long I have known these other people.'

'But just now you said that he was your enemy.'

'I did say so; but as I have unsaid it since, you as a gentleman will not remember my words. At any rate I cannot help you in this.'

'I shall write to her.'

'It can be nothing to me. If you write she will show your letter either to her father or to Lady Cantrip.'

'But she will read it first.'

'I cannot tell how that may be. In fact I am the very last person in the world to whom you should come for assistance in this matter. If I gave any assistance to anybody I should be bound to give it to the Duke.'

181

'I cannot understand that, Mrs. Finn.'

'Nor can I explain it, but it would be so. I shall always be very glad to see you, and I do feel that we ought to be friends, —because I took such a liberty with you. But in this matter I cannot help you.'

When she said this he had to take his leave. It was impossible that he should further press his case upon her, though he would have been very glad to extract from her some kindly word. It is such a help in a difficulty to have somebody who will express even a hope that the difficulty is perhaps not invincible! He had no one to comfort him in this matter. There was one dear friend,—as a friend dearer than any other, —to whom he might go, and who would after some fashion bid him prosper. Mabel would encourage him. She had said that she would do so. But in making that promise she had told him that Romeo would not have spoken of his love for Juliet to Rosalind, whom he had loved before he saw Juliet. No doubt she had gone on to tell him that he might come to her and talk freely of his love for Lady Mary,—but after what had been said before, he felt that he could not do so without leaving a sting behind. When a man's love goes well with him,—so well as to be in some degree oppressive to him even by its prosperity,—when the young lady has jumped into his arms and the father and mother have been quite willing, then he wants no confidant. He does not care to speak very much of the matter which among his friends is apt to become a subject for raillery. When you call a man Benedick he does not come to you with ecstatic descriptions of the beauty and the wit of his Beatrice.* But no one was likely to call him Benedick in reference to Lady Mary.

In spite of his manner, in spite of his apparent self-sufficiency, this man was very soft within. Less than two years back he had been willing to sacrifice all the world for his cousin Mabel, and his cousin Mabel had told him that he was wrong. 'It does not pay to sacrifice the world for love.' So cousin Mabel had said, and had added something as to its being necessary that she should marry a rich man, and expedient that he should marry a rich woman. He had thought much about it, and had declared to himself that on no account would he marry a woman for her money. Then he had encountered Lady Mary Palliser. There had been no doubt, no resolution after that, no thinking about it;—but downright love. There was nothing left of real regret for his cousin in his bosom. She had been right. That love had been impossible. But this would be possible,—ah, so deliciously possible,—if only her father and mother would assist! The mother, imprudent in this as in all things, had assented. The reader knows the rest.

It was in every way possible. 'She will have money enough,' the Duchess had said, 'if only her father can be brought to give it you.' So Tregear had set his heart upon it, and had said to himself that the thing was to be done. Then his friend the Duchess had died, and the real difficulties had commenced. From that day he had not seen his love, or heard from her. How was he to know whether she would be true to him? And where was he to seek for that sympathy which he felt to be so necessary to him? A wild idea had come into his head that Mrs. Finn would be his friend;—but she had repudiated him.

He went straight home and at once wrote to the girl. The letter was a simple love-letter, and as such need not be given here. In what sweetest language he could find he assured her that even though he should never be allowed to see her or to hear from her, that still he should cling to her. And then he added this passage: 'If your love for me be what I think it to be, no one can have a right to keep us apart. Pray be sure that I shall not change. If you change let me know it;—but I shall as soon expect the heavens to fall.'

CHAPTER XXIV

'She must be made to obey'

LADY MARY PALLISER down at The Horns had as much liberty allowed to her as is usually given to young ladies in these very free days. There was indeed no restriction placed upon her at all. Had Tregear gone down to Richmond and asked for the young lady, and had Lady Cantrip at the time been out and the young lady at home, it would have depended altogether upon the young lady whether she would have seen her lover or not. Nevertheless Lady Cantrip kept her eyes open, and when the letter came from Tregear she was aware that the letter had come. But the letter found its way into Lady Mary's hands and was read in the seclusion of her own bedroom. 'I wonder whether you would mind reading that,' she said very shortly afterwards to Lady Cantrip. 'What answer ought I to make?'

'Do you think any answer ought to be made, my dear?'

'Oh yes; I must answer him.'

'Would your papa wish it?'

'I told papa that I would not promise not to write to him. I think I told him that he should see any letters that there were. But if I show them to you, I suppose that will do as well.'

'You had better keep your word to him absolutely.'

'I am not afraid of doing so, if you mean that. I cannot bear to give him pain, but this is a matter in which I mean to have my own way.'

'Mean to have your own way!' said Lady Cantrip, much surprised by the determined tone of the young lady.

'Certainly I do. I want you to understand so much! I suppose papa can keep us from marrying for ever and ever if he pleases, but he never will make me say that I will give up Mr. Tregear. And if he does not yield I shall think him cruel. Why should he wish to make me unhappy all my life?'

'He certainly does not wish that, my dear.'

'But he will do it.'

'I cannot go against your father, Mary.'

'No, I suppose not. I shall write to Mr. Tregear, and then I will show you what I have written. Papa shall see it too if he pleases. I will do nothing secret, but I will never give up Mr. Tregear.'

Lord Cantrip came down to Richmond that evening, and his wife told him that in her opinion it would be best that the Duke should allow the young people to marry, and should give them money enough to live upon. 'Is not that a strong order?' asked the Earl. The Countess acknowledged that it was a 'strong order,' but suggested that for the happiness of them all it might as well be done at first as at last.

The next morning Lady Mary showed her a copy of the reply which she had already sent to her lover.

'DEAR FRANK,

'You may be *quite sure* that I shall *never* give you up. I will not write more at present because papa does not wish me to do so. I shall show papa your letter and my answer.

'Your own most affectionate

'MARY.'

'Has it gone?' asked the Countess.

'I put it myself into the pillar letter-box.'*Then Lady Cantrip felt that she had to deal with a very self-willed young lady indeed.

That afternoon Lady Cantrip asked Lady Mary whether she might be allowed to take the two letters up to town with the express purpose of showing them to the Duke. 'Oh yes,' said Mary, 'I think it would be so much the best. Give papa my kindest love, and tell him from me that if he wants to make his poor little girl happy he will forgive her and be kind to her in all this.' Then the Countess made some attempt to argue the matter. There were proprieties! High rank might be a blessing or might be the reverse—as people thought of it;— but all men acknowledged that much was due to it. 'Noblesse oblige.' It was often the case in life that women were called upon by circumstances to sacrifice their inclinations! What right had a gentleman to talk of marriage who had no means? These things she said and very many more, but it was to no purpose. The young lady asserted that as the gentleman was a gentleman there need be no question as to rank, and that in regard to money there need be no difficulty if one of them had sufficient. 'But you have none but what your father may give you,' said Lady Cantrip. 'Papa can give it us without any trouble,' said Lady Mary. This child had a clear idea of what she thought to be her own rights. Being the child of rich parents she had the right to money. Being a woman she had a right to a husband. Having been born free she had a right to choose one for herself. Having had a man's love given to her she had a right to keep it. 'One doesn't know which she is most like, her father or her mother,' Lady Cantrip said afterwards to her husband. 'She has his cool determination, and her hot-headed obstinacy.'

She did show the letters to the Duke, and in answer to a word or two from him explained that she could not take upon herself to debar her guest from the use of the post. 'But she will write nothing without letting you know it.'

'She ought to write nothing at all.'

'What she feels is much worse than what she writes.'

'If there were no intercourse she would forget him.'

'Ah; I don't know,' said the Countess sorrowfully; 'I thought so once.'

'All children are determined as long as they are allowed to have their own way.'

'I mean to say that it is the nature of her character to be obstinate. Most girls are prone to yield. They have not character enough to stand against opposition. I am not speaking now only of affairs like this. It would be the same with her in any thing. Have you not always found it so?'

Then he had to acknowledge to himself that he had never found out anything in reference to his daughter's character. She had been properly educated;—at least he hoped so. He had seen her grow up, pretty, sweet, affectionate, always obedient to him;—the most charming plaything in the world on the few occasions in which he had allowed himself to play. But as to her actual disposition, he had never taken any trouble to inform himself. She had been left to her mother,—as other girls are left. And his sons had been left to their tutors. And now he had no control over any of them. 'She must be made to obey like others,' he said at last, speaking through his teeth.

There was something in this which almost frightened Lady Cantrip. She could not bear to hear him say that the girl must be made to yield, with that spirit of despotic power under which women were restrained in years now passed. If she could have spoken her own mind it would have been to this effect: 'Let us do what we can to lead her away from this desire of hers; and in order that we may do so, let us tell her that her marriage with Mr. Tregear is out of the question. But if we do not succeed,—say in the course of the next twelve months,—let us give way. Let us make it a matter of joy that the young man himself is so acceptable and well-behaved.' That was her idea, and with that she would have indoctrined the Duke had she been able. But his was different. 'She must be made to obey,' he said. And, as he said it, he seemed to be indifferent as to the sorrow which such enforced obedience might bring upon his child. In answer to this she could only shake her head. 'What do you mean?' he asked. 'Do you think we ought to yield?'

'Not at once, certainly.'

'But at last?'

'What can you do, Duke? If she be as firm as you, can you bear to see her pine away in her misery?'

'Girls do not do like that,' he said.

'Girls, like men, are very different. They generally will yield to external influences. English girls, though they be-come the most loving wives in the world, do not generally become so riven by an attachment as to become deep sufferers when it is disallowed. But here, I fear, we have to deal with one who will suffer after this fashion.'

'Why should she not be like others?'

'It may be so. We will try. But you see what she says in

her letter to him. She writes as though your authority were to be nothing in that matter of giving up. In all that she says to me there is the same spirit. If she is firm, Duke, you must yield.'

'Never! She shall never marry him with my sanction.'

There was nothing more to be said, and Lady Cantrip went her way. But the Duke, though he could say nothing more, continued to think of it hour after hour. He went down to the House of Lords to listen to a debate in which it was intended to cover the ministers with heavy disgrace. But the Duke could not listen even to his own friends. He could listen to nothing as he thought of the condition of his children.

He had been asked whether he could bear to see his girl suffer, as though he were indifferent to the sufferings of his child. Did he not know of himself that there was no father who would do more for the welfare of his daughter? Was he not sure of the tenderness of his own heart? In all that he was doing was he governed by anything but a sense of duty? Was it personal pride or love of personal aggrandisement? He thought that he could assure himself that he was open to no such charge. Would he not die for her,—or for them,—if he could so serve them? Surely this woman had accused him most wrongfully when she had intimated that he could see his girl suffer without caring for it. In his indignation he determined —for awhile,—that he would remove her from the custody of Lady Cantrip. But then, where should he place her? He was aware that his own house would be like a grave to a girl just fit to come out into the world. In this coming autumn she must go somewhere,—with someone. He himself, in his present frame of mind, would be but a sorry travelling companion.

Lady Cantrip had said that the best hope of escape would lie in the prospect of another lover. The prescription was disagreeable, but it had availed in the case of his own wife. Before he had ever seen her as Lady Glencora McCloskie she had been desirous of giving herself and all her wealth to one Burgo Fitzgerald, who had been altogether unworthy. The Duke could remember well how a certain old Lady Midlothian had first hinted to him that Lady Glencora's property was very large, and had then added that the young lady herself was very beautiful. And he could remember how his uncle, the late Duke, who had seldom taken much trouble in merely human affairs, had said a word or two—'I have heard a whisper about you and Lady Glencora McCloskie, nothing could be better.' The result had been undoubtedly good. His Cora and all her money had been saved from a worthless spendthrift. He had found a wife who he now thought had made him happy. And she had found at any rate a respectable husband. The idea when picked to pieces is not a nice idea. 'Let us look out for a husband for this girl, so that we may get her married,—out of the way of her lover.' It is not nice. But it had succeeded in one case, and why should it not succeed in another?

But how was it to be done? Who should do it? Whom should he select to play the part which he had undertaken in that other arrangement? No worse person could be found than himself for managing such an affair. When the idea had first been raised he had thought that Lady Cantrip would do it all; but now he was angry with Lady Cantrip.

How was it to be done? How should it be commenced? How had it been commenced in his own case? He did not in the least know how he had been chosen. Was it possible that his uncle, who was the proudest man in England, should have condescended to make a bargain with an old dowager whom everybody had despised? And in what way had he been selected? No doubt he had been known to be the heir-apparent to a dukedom and to ducal revenues. In his case old Lady Midlothian had begun the matter with him. It occurred to him that in royal marriages such beginnings are quite common.

But who should be the happy man? Then he began to count up the requisite attributes. He must be of high rank, and an eldest son, and the possessor of, or the heir to, a good estate. He did despise himself when he found that he put these things first,—as a matter of course. Nevertheless he did put them first. He was ejecting this other man because he possessed none of these attributes. He hurried himself on to add that the man must be of good character, and such as a young girl might learn to love. But yet he was aware that he added these things for his conscience's sake. Tregear's character was good, and certainly the girl loved him. But was it not clear to all who knew anything of such matters that Mr. Francis Tregear should not have dared even to think of marrying the daughter of the Duke of Omnium?

Who should be the happy man? There were so many who evidently were unfit. Young Lord Percival was heir to a ruined estate and a beggared peerage. Lord Glasslough was odious to all men. There were three or four others of whom he thought that he knew some fatal objection. But when he remembered Lord Popplecourt there seemed to be no objection which need be fatal.

Lord Popplecourt was a young peer whose father had died two years since and whose estates were large and unembarrassed. The late lord, who had been a Whig of the old fashion, had been the Duke's friend. They had been at Oxford and in the House of Commons together, and Lord Popplecourt had always been true to his party. As to the son, the Duke remembered to have heard lately that he was not given to waste his money. He drove a coach about London a good deal, but had as yet not done anything very foolish. He had taken his degree at Oxford, thereby showing himself to be better than Silverbridge. He had also taken his seat in the House of Lords and had once opened his mouth. He had not indeed appeared often again; but at Lord Popplecourt's age much legislation is not to be expected from a young peer. Then he thought of the man's appearance. Popplecourt was not specially attractive, whereas Tregear was a very handsome man. But so also had been Burgo Fitzgerald,—almost abnormally beautiful, while he, Plantagenet Palliser, as he was then, had been quite as insignificant in appearance as Lord Popplecourt.

Lord Popplecourt might possibly do. But then how should the matter be spoken of to the young man? After all, would it not be best that he should trust Lady Cantrip?

CHAPTER XXV

A Family Breakfast-table

LORD SILVERBRIDGE had paid all his Derby losses without any difficulty. They had not been very heavy for a man in his position, and the money had come without remonstrance. When asking for it he was half ashamed of himself, but could still find consolation by remembering how much worse had befallen many young men whom he knew. He had never 'plunged.'*In fact he had made the most prudent book*in the world; and had so managed affairs that even now the horse which had been beaten was worth more than all he had lost and paid. 'This is getting serious,' he had said to his partner when, on making out a rough account, he had brought the Major in a debtor to him of more than a thousand pounds. The Major had remarked that as he was half-owner of the horses his partner had good security for the money. Then something of an unwritten arrangement was made. The 'Prime Minister' was now one of the favourites for the Leger. If the horse won that race there would be money enough for everything. If that race were lost, then there should be a settlement by the transfer of the stud*to the younger partner. 'He's safe to pull it off,' said the Major.

At this time both his sons were living with the Duke in London. It had been found impracticable to send Lord Gerald back to Cambridge. The doors of Trinity were closed against him. But some interest had been made in his favour, and he was to be transferred to Oxford. All the truth had been told, and there had been a feeling that the lad should be allowed another chance. He could not however go to his new Alma Mater*till after the long vacation. In the meantime he was to be taken by a tutor down to a cottage on Dartmoor and there be made to read;*—with such amusement in the meantime as might be got from fishing, and playing cricket with the West Devon county club. 'It isn't a very bright look-out for the summer,' his brother had said to him, 'but it's better than breaking out on the loose altogether. You be a credit to the family and all that sort of thing. Then I'll give up the borough to you. But mind you stick to the Liberals. I've made an ass of myself.' However in these early days of June Lord Gerald had not yet got his tutor.

Though the father and the two young men were living together they did not see very much of each other. The Duke breakfasted at nine and the repast was a very simple one. When they failed to appear, he did not scold,—but would simply be disappointed. At dinner they never met. It was supposed that Lord Gerald passed his mornings in reading, and some little attempts were made in that direction. It is to be feared they did not come to much. Silverbridge was very kind to Gerald, feeling an increased tenderness for him on account of that Cambridge mishap. Now they were much together, and occasionally, by a strong effort, would grace their father's breakfast-table with their company.

It was not often that he either reproached them or preached to them. Though he could not live with them on almost equal terms, as some fathers can live with their sons, though he could not laugh at their fun or make them laugh at his wit, he knew that it would have been better both for him and them if he had possessed this capacity. Though the life which they lived was distasteful to him,—though racehorses were an abomination to him, and the driving of coaches a folly, and club-life a manifest waste of time, still he recognised these things as being, if not necessary, yet unavoidable evils. To Gerald he would talk about Oxford, avoiding all allusions to past Cambridge misfortunes; but in the presence of Silverbridge, whose Oxford career had been so peculiarly unfortunate, he would make no allusion to either of the universities. To his eldest son he would talk of Parliament, which of all subjects would have been the most congenial had they agreed in politics. As it was he could speak more freely to him on that than any other matter.

One Thursday night as the two brothers went to bed on returning from the Beargarden, at a not very late hour, they agreed that they would 'give the governor a turn' the next morning,—by which they meant that they would drag themselves out of bed in time to breakfast with him. 'The worst of it is that he never will let them get anything to eat,' said Gerald. But Silverbridge explained that he had taken that matter into his own hands, and had specially ordered broiled salmon and stewed kidneys. 'He won't like it, you know,' said Gerald. 'I'm sure he thinks it wicked to eat anything but toasted bacon before lunch.'

At a very little after nine Silverbridge was in the breakfast-room, and there found his father. 'I suppose Gerald is not up yet,' said the Duke almost crossly.

'Oh yes he is, sir. He'll be here directly.'

'Have you seen him this morning?'

'No; I haven't seen him. But I know he'll be here. He said he would, last night.'

'You speak of it as if it were an undertaking.'

'No, not that, sir. But we are not always quite up to time.'

'No; indeed you are not. Perhaps you sit late at the House.'

'Sometimes I do,' said the young member, with a feeling almost akin to shame as he remembered all the hours spent at the Beargarden. 'I have had Gerald there in the Gallery sometimes. It is just as well he should know what is being done.'

'Quite as well.'

'I shouldn't wonder if he gets a seat some day.'

'I don't know how that may be.'

'He won't change as I have done. He'll stick to your side. Indeed I think he'd do better in the House than I shall. He has more gift of the gab.'

'That is not the first thing requisite.'

'I know all that, sir. I've read your letter more than once, and I showed it to him.'

There was something sweet and pleasant in the young man's manner by which the father could hardly not be captivated. They had now sat down, and the servant had brought in the unusual accessories for a morning feast. 'What is all that?' asked the Duke.

'Gerald and I are so awfully hungry of a morning,' said the son apologising.

'Well;—it's a very good thing to be hungry;—that is if you can get plenty to eat. Salmon, is it? I don't think I'll have any myself. Kidneys! Not for me. I think I'll take a bit of fried bacon. I also am hungry, but not awfully hungry.'

'You never seem to me to eat anything, sir.'

'Eating is an occupation from which I think a man takes the more pleasure the less he considers it. A rural labourer who sits on the ditch-side with his bread and cheese and an onion has more enjoyment out of it than any Lucullus.'

'But he likes a good deal of it.'

'I do not think he ever over-eats himself,—which Lucullus does. I have envied a ploughman his power,—his dura ilia,*— but never an epicure the appreciative skill of his palate. If Gerald does not make haste he will have to exercise neither the one nor the other upon that fish.'

'I will leave a bit for him, sir,—and here he is. You are twenty minutes late, Gerald. My father says that bread and cheese and onions would be better for you than salmon and stewed kidneys.'

'No, Silverbridge;—I said no such thing; but that if he were a hedger and ditcher the bread and cheese and onions would be as good.'

'I should not mind trying them at all,' said Gerald. 'Only one never does have such things for breakfast. Last winter a lot of us skated to Ely, and we ate two or three loaves of bread and a whole cheese at a pot-house!*And as for beer, we drank the public dry.'

'It was because for the time you had been a hedger and ditcher.'

'Proby was a ditcher I know, when he went right through into one of the dykes. Just push on that dish, Silverbridge. It's no good you having the trouble of helping me half-a-dozen times. I don't think things are a bit the nicer because they cost a lot of money. I suppose that is what you mean, sir.'

194

'Something of that kind, Gerald. Not to have money for your wants;—that must be troublesome.'

'Very bad indeed,' said Silverbridge, shaking his head wisely, as a Member of Parliament might do who felt that something should be done to put down such a lamentable state of things.

'I don't complain,' said Gerald. 'No fellow ever had less right to complain. But I never felt that I had quite enough. Of course it was my own fault.'

'I should say so, my boy. But then there are a great many like you. Let their means be what they may, they never have quite enough. To be in any difficulty with regard to money,—to owe what you cannot pay, or even to have to abstain from things which you have told yourself are necessary to yourself or to those who depend on you,—creates a feeling of meanness.'

'That is what I have always felt,' said Silverbridge. 'I cannot bear to think that I should like to have a thing and that I cannot afford it.'

'You do not quite understand me, I fear. The only case in which you can be justified in desiring that which you cannot afford is when the thing is necessary;—as bread may be, or clothes.'

'As when a fellow wants a lot of new breeches before he has paid his tailor's bill.'

'As when a poor man,' said the Duke impressively, 'may long to give his wife a new gown, or his children boots to keep their feet from the mud and snow.' Then he paused a moment, but the serious tone of his voice and the energy of his words had sent Gerald headlong among his kidneys. 'I say that in such cases money must be regarded as a blessing.'

'A ten-pound note will do so much,' said Silverbridge.

'But beyond that it ought to have no power of conferring happiness, and certainly cannot drive away sorrow. Not though you build palaces out into the deep, can that help you. You read your Horace, I hope. "Scandunt eodum quo dominus minæ."'*

'I recollect that,' said Gerald. 'Black care sits behind the horseman.'

'Even though he have a groom riding after him beautiful with exquisite boots. As far as I have been able to look out into the world——'

'I suppose you know it as well as anybody,' said Silverbridge,—who was simply desirous of making himself pleasant to the 'dear old governor.'

'As far as my experience goes, the happiest man is he who, being above the troubles which money brings, has his hands the fullest of work. If I were to name the class of men whose lives are spent with the most thorough enjoyment, I think I should name that of barristers who are in large practice and also in Parliament.'

'Isn't it a great grind, sir?' asked Silverbridge.

'A very great grind, as you call it. And there may be the grind and not the success. But——' He had now got up from his seat at the table and was standing with his back against the chimney-piece, and as he went on with his lecture,—as the word 'But' came from his lips—he struck the fingers of one hand lightly on the palm of the other as he had been known to do at some happy flight of oratory in the House of Commons. 'But it is the grind that makes the happiness. To feel that your hours are filled to overflowing, that you can barely steal minutes enough for sleep, that the welfare of many is entrusted to you, that the world looks on and approves, that some good is always being done to others,—above all things some good to your country;—that is happiness. For myself I can conceive none other.'

'Books,' suggested Gerald, as he put the last morsel of the last kidney into his mouth.

'Yes, books! Cicero and Ovid have told us that to literature only could they look for consolation in their banishment. But then they speak of a remedy for sorrow, not of a source of joy. No young man should dare to neglect literature. At some period of his life he will surely need consolation. And he may be certain that should he live to be an old man, there will be none other,—except religion. But for that feeling of self-contentment, which creates happiness—hard work, and hard work alone, can give it to you.'

'Books are hard work themselves sometimes,' said Gerald.

'As for money,' continued the father, not caring to notice this interruption, 'if it be regarded in any other light than as a shield against want, as a rampart under the protection of which you may carry on your battle, it will fail you. I was born a rich man.'

'Few people have cared so little about it as you,' said the elder son.

'And you, both of you, have been born to be rich.' This assertion did not take the elder brother by surprise. It was a matter of course. But Lord Gerald, who had never as yet heard anything as to his future destiny from his father, was interested by the statement. 'When I think of all this,—of what constitutes happiness,—I am almost tempted to grieve that it should be so.'

'If a large fortune were really a bad thing,' said Gerald, 'a man could I suppose get rid of it.'

'No;—it is a thing of which a man cannot get rid,—unless by shameful means. It is a burden which he must carry to the end.'

'Does anybody wish to get rid of it, as Sindbad*did of the Old Man?' asked Gerald pertinaciously. 'At any rate I have enjoyed the kidneys.'

'You assured us just now that the bread and cheese at Ely were just as good.' The Duke as he said this looked as though he knew that he had taken all the wind out of his adversary's sails. 'Though you add carriage to carriage, you will not be carried more comfortably.'

'A second horse out hunting is a comfort,' said Silverbridge.

'Then at any rate don't desire a third for show. But such comforts will cease to be joys when they become matters of course. That a boy who does not see a pudding once a year should enjoy a pudding when it comes I can understand; but the daily pudding, or the pudding twice a day, is soon no more

197

than simple daily bread,—which will or will not be sweet as it shall or shall not have been earned.' Then he went slowly to the door, but, as he stood with the handle of it in his hand, he turned round and spoke another word. 'When, hereafter, Gerald, you may chance to think of that bread and cheese at Ely, always remember that you had skated from Cambridge.'

The two brothers then took themselves to some remote part of the house where arrangements had been made for smoking, and there they finished the conversation. 'I was very glad to hear what he said about you, old boy.' This of course came from Silverbridge.

'I didn't quite understand him.'

'He meant you to understand that you wouldn't be like other younger brothers.'

'Then what I have will be taken from you.'

'There is lots for three or four of us. I do agree that if a fellow has as much as he can spend he ought not to want anything more. Morton was telling me the other day something about the settled estates. I sat in that office with him all one morning. I could not understand it all, but I observed that he said nothing about the Scotch property.* You'll be a laird, and I wish you joy with all my heart. The governor will tell you all about it before long. He's going to have two eldest sons.'

'What an unnatural piece of cruelty to me;—and so unnecessary!'

'Why?'

'He says that a property is no better than a burden. But I'll try and bear it.'

198

CHAPTER XXVI

Dinner at the Beargarden

THE Duke was in the gallery of the House of Commons which is devoted to the use of peers, and Silverbridge, having heard that his father was there, had come up to him. It was then about half-past five, and the House had settled down to business. Prayers had been read, petitions had been presented, and Ministers had gone through their course of baiting with that equanimity and air of superiority which always belongs to a well-trained occupant of the Treasury bench.

The Duke was very anxious that his son should attend to his parliamentary duties, but he was too proud a man and too generous to come to the House as a spy. It was his present habit always to be in his own place when the Lords were sitting, and to remain there while the Lords sat. It was not, for many reasons, an altogether satisfactory occupation, but it was the best which his life afforded him. He would never,

199

however, come across into the other House, without letting
his son know of his coming, and Lord Silverbridge had on this
occasion been on the look-out, and had come up to his father
at once. 'Don't let me take you away,' said the Duke, 'if you
are particularly interested in your Chief's defence,' for Sir
Timothy Beeswax was defending some measure of legal reform*in which he was said to have fallen into trouble.

'I can hear it up here, you know, sir.'

'Hardly if you are talking to me.'

'To tell the truth it's a matter I don't care much about.
They've got into some mess as to the number of Judges and
what they ought to do. Finn was saying that they had so
arranged that there was one Judge who never could possibly
do anything.'

'If Mr. Finn said so it would probably be so, with some
little allowance for Irish exaggeration. He is a clever man,
with less of his country's hyperbole than others;—but still
not without his share.'

'You know him well, I suppose.'

'Yes;—as one man does know another in the political world.'

'But he is a friend of yours? I don't mean an "honourable
friend," which is great bosh; but you know him at home.'

'Oh yes;—certainly. He has been staying with me at
Matching. In public life such intimacies come from politics.'

'You don't care very much about him then.'

The Duke paused a moment before he answered. 'Yes I
do;—and in what I said just now perhaps I wronged him. I
have been under obligations to Mr. Finn,*—in a matter as to
which he behaved very well. I have found him to be a gentleman. If you come across him in the House I would wish you
to be courteous to him. I have not seen him since we came
from abroad. I have been able to see nobody. But if ever again
I should entertain my friends at my table, Mr. Finn would
be one who would always be welcome there.' This he said
with a sadly serious air as though wishing that his words
should be noted. At the present moment he was remembering
that he owed recompense to Mrs. Finn, and was making an

effort to pay the debt. 'But your leader is striking out into unwonted eloquence. Surely we ought to listen to him.'

Sir Timothy was a fluent speaker, and when there was nothing to be said was possessed of great plenty of words. And he was gifted with that peculiar power which enables a man to have the last word in every encounter,—a power which we are apt to call repartee, which is in truth the readiness which comes from continual practice. You shall meet two men of whom you shall know the one to be endowed with the brilliancy of true genius, and the other to be possessed of but moderate parts, and shall find the former never able to hold his own against the latter. In a debate, the man of moderate parts will seem to be greater than the man of genius. But this skill of tongue, this glibness of speech is hardly an affair of intellect at all. It is,—as is style to the writer,—not the wares which he has to take to market, but the vehicle in which they may be carried. Of what avail to you is it to have filled granaries with corn if you cannot get your corn to the consumer? Now Sir Timothy was a great vehicle, but he had not in truth much corn to send. He could turn a laugh against an adversary;—no man better. He could seize, at the moment, every advantage which the opportunity might give him. The Treasury Bench on which he sat and the big box on the table before him were to him fortifications of which he knew how to use every stone. The cheers and the jeers of the House had been so measured by him that he knew the value and force of every sound. Politics had never been to him a study; but to parliamentary strategy he had devoted all his faculties. No one knew so well as Sir Timothy how to make arrangements for business, so that every detail should be troublesome to his opponents. He could foresee a month beforehand that on a certain day a Royal concert*would make the house empty, and would generously give that day to a less observant adversary. He knew how to blind the eyes of members to the truth. Those on the opposite side of the House would find themselves checkmated by his astuteness,—when, with all their pieces on the board, there should be none which they could move. And this to him was Government! It was to these purposes that he conceived that a great Statesman should devote himself! Parliamentary management! That, in his mind, was under this Constitution of ours the one act essential for Government.

In all this he was very great; but when it might fall to his duty either to suggest or to defend any real piece of proposed legislation he was less happy. On this occasion he had been driven to take the matter in hand because he had previously been concerned in it as a lawyer. He had allowed himself to wax angry as he endeavoured to answer certain personal criticisms. Now Sir Timothy was never stronger than when he simulated anger. His mock indignation was perhaps his most powerful weapon. But real anger is a passion which few men can use with judgment. And now Sir Timothy was really angry, and condescended to speak of our old friend Phineas who had made the onslaught as a bellicose Irishman. There was an over-true story as to our friend having once been seduced into fighting a duel,* and those who wished to decry him sometimes alluded to the adventure. Sir Timothy had been called to order, but the Speaker had ruled that 'bellicose Irishman' was not beyond the latitude of parliamentary animadversion. Then Sir Timothy had repeated the phrase with emphasis, and the Duke hearing it in the gallery had made his remark as to the unwonted eloquence of his son's parliamentary chief.

'Surely we ought to listen to him,' said the Duke. And for a short time they did listen. 'Sir Timothy is not a man I like, you know,' said the son, feeling himself obliged to apologise for his subjection to such a chief.

'I never particularly loved him myself.'

'They say that he is a sort of necessity.'

'A Conservative Fate,' said the Duke.

'Well, yes; he is so,—so awfully clever! We all feel that we could not get on without him. When you were in, he was one of your party.'

'Oh yes;—he was one of us. I have no right to complain of you for using him. But when you say you could not get on without him, does it not occur to you that should he,—let us say be taken up to heaven,—you would have to get on without him.'

'Then he would be,—out of the way, sir.'

'What you mean perhaps is that you do not know how to get rid of him.'

'Of course I don't pretend to understand much about it; but they all think that he does know how to keep the party together. I don't think we are proud of him.'

'Hardly that.'

'He is awfully useful. A man has to look out so sharp to be always ready for those other fellows! I beg your pardon, sir, but I mean your side.'

'I understand who the other fellows are.'

'And it isn't everybody who will go through such a grind. A man to do it must be always ready. He has so many little things to think of. As far as I can see we all feel that we could not get along very well without him.' Upon the whole the Duke was pleased with what he heard from his son. The young man's ideas about politics were boyish, but they were the ideas of a clear-headed boy. Silverbridge had picked up some of the ways of the place, though he had not yet formed any sound political opinions.

Then Sir Timothy finished a long speech with a flowery peroration, in which he declared that if Parliament were desirous of keeping the realms of Her Majesty free from the invasions of foreigners it must be done by maintaining the dignity of the Judicial bench. There were some clamours at this; and although it was now dinner-time Phineas Finn, who had been called a bellicose Irishman, was able to say a word or two. 'The Right Honorable gentleman no doubt means,' said Phineas, 'that we must carry ourselves with some increased external dignity. The world is bewigging*itself, and we must buy a bigger wig than any we have got, in order to confront the world with proper self-respect. Turveydrop*and deportment will suffice for us against any odds.'

About half-past seven the House became very empty.

'Where are you going to dine, sir?' asked Silverbridge. The Duke, with something like a sigh, said he supposed he should dine at home.

'You never were at the Beargarden;—were you, sir?' asked Silverbridge suddenly.

'Never,' said the Duke.

'Come and dine with me.'

'I am not a member of the club.'

'We don't care at all about that. Anybody can take in anybody.'

'Does not that make it promiscuous?'

'Well;—no; I don't know that it does. It seems to go on very well. I daresay there are some cads there sometimes. But I don't know where one doesn't meet cads. There are plenty in the House of Commons.'

'There is something in that, Silverbridge, which makes me think that you have not realised the difference between private and public life. In the former you choose your own associates and are responsible for your choice. In the latter you are concerned with others for the good of the State; and though, even for the State's sake, you would not willingly be closely allied with those whom you think dishonest, the outward manners and fashions of life need create no barriers. I should not turn up my nose at the House of Commons because some constituency might send them an illiterate shoemaker; but I might probably find the illiterate shoemaker an unprofitable companion for my private hours.'

'I don't think there will be any shoemakers at the Beargarden.'

'Even if there were I would go and dine with you. I shall be glad to see the place where you, I suppose, pass many hours.'

'I find it a very good shop to dine at. The place at the House is so stuffy and nasty. Besides, one likes to get away for a little time.'

'Certainly. I never was an advocate for living in the House. One should always change the atmosphere.' Then they got into a cab and went to the club. Silverbridge was a little afraid of what he was doing. The invitation had come from him on the spur of the moment, and he hardly ventured to think that his father would accept it. And now he did not quite know how the Duke would go through the ceremony. 'The other fellows' would all come and stare at a man whom they had all been taught to regard as the most un-Beargardenish of men. But he was especially anxious to make things pleasant for his father.

'What shall I order?' said the son as he took the Duke into a dressing-room to wash his hands. The Duke suggested that anything sufficient for his son would certainly be sufficient for him.

Nothing especial occurred during the dinner, which the Duke appeared to enjoy very much. 'Yes; I think it is very good soup,' he said. 'I don't think they ever give me any soup at home.' Then the son expressed his opinion that unless his father looked about rather more sharply, 'they' very soon would provide no dinner at all, remarking that experience had taught him that the less people demanded the more they were 'sat upon.' The Duke did like his dinner,—or rather he liked the feeling that he was dining with his son. A report that the Duke of Omnium was with Lord Silverbridge soon went round the room, and they who were justified by some previous acquaintance came up to greet him. To all who did so he was very gracious, and was specially so to Lord Popplecourt, who happened to pass close by the table.

'I think he is a fool,' whispered Silverbridge as soon as Popplecourt had passed.

'What makes you think so?'

'We thought him an ass at Eton.'

'He has done pretty well, however.'

'Oh yes, in a way.'

'Somebody has told me that he is a careful man about his property.'

'I believe he is all that,' said Silverbridge.

'Then I don't see why you should think him a fool.'

To this Silverbridge made no reply; partly perhaps because

he had nothing to say,—but hindered also by the coming in of Tregear. This was an accident, the possibility of which had not crossed him. Unfortunately too the Duke's back was turned, so that Tregear, as he walked up the room, could not see who was sitting at his friend's table. Tregear coming up stood close to the Duke's elbow before he recognised the man, and spoke some word or two to Silverbridge. 'How do you do, Mr. Tregear,' said the Duke, turning round.

'Oh, my Lord, I did not know that it was you.'

'You hardly would. I am quite a stranger here. Silverbridge and I came up from the House together, and he has been hospitable enough to give me a dinner. I will tell you an odd thing for a London man, Mr. Tregear. I have not dined at a London club for fifteen years before this.'

'I hope you like it, sir,' said Silverbridge.

'Very much indeed. Good-evening, Mr. Tregear. I suppose you have to go to your dinner now.'

Then they went into one of the rooms upstairs to have coffee, the son declining to go into the smoking-room, and assuring his father that he did not in the least care about a cigar after dinner. 'You would be smothered, sir.' The Duke did as he was bidden and went upstairs. There was in truth a strong reason for avoiding the publicity of the smoking-room. When bringing his father to the club he had thought nothing about Tregear but he had thought about Tifto. As he entered he had seen Tifto at a table dining alone, and had bobbed his head at him. Then he had taken the Duke to the further end of the room, and had trusted that fear would keep the Major in his place. Fear had kept the Major in his place. When the Major learned who the stranger was, he had become silent and reserved. Before the father and son had finished their dinner, Tifto had gone to his cigar; and so that danger was over.

'By George, there's Silverbridge has got his governor to dinner,' said Tifto, standing in the middle of the room, and looking round as though he were announcing some confusion of the heavens and earth.

'Why shouldn't Lord Silverbridge have his father to dine with him?' asked Mr. Lupton.

'I believe I know Silverbridge as well as any man, and by George it is the very last thing of the kind that I should have expected. There have been no end of quarrels.'

'There has been no quarrel at all,' said Tregear, who had then just entered the room. 'Nothing on earth would make Silverbridge quarrel with his father, and I think it would break the Duke's heart to quarrel with his son.' Tifto endeavoured to argue the matter out; but Tregear having made the assertion on behalf of his friend would not allow himself to be enticed into further speech. Nevertheless there was a good deal said by others, during which the Major drank two glasses of whisky-and-water. In the dining-room he had been struck with awe by the Duke's presence, and had certainly no idea of presenting himself personally to the great man. But Bacchus lent him aid, and when the discussion was over and the whisky had been swallowed, it occurred to him that he would go upstairs and ask to be introduced.

In the meantime the Duke and his son were seated in close conversation on one of the upstairs sofas. It was a rule at the Beargarden that men might smoke all over the house except in the dining-room;—but there was one small chamber called the library, in which the practice was not often followed. The room was generally deserted, and at this moment the father and son were the only occupants. 'A club,' said the Duke, as he sipped his coffee, 'is a comfortable and economical residence. A man gets what he wants well-served, and gets it cheap. But it has its drawbacks.'

'You always see the same fellows,' said Silverbridge.

'A man who lives much at a club is apt to fall into a selfish mode of life. He is taught to think that his own comfort should always be the first object. A man can never be happy unless his first objects are outside himself. Personal self-indulgence begets a sense of meanness which sticks to a man even when he has got beyond all hope of rescue. It is for that reason,—among others,—that marriage is so desirable.'

'A man should marry, I suppose.'

'Unless a man has on his shoulders the burden of a wife and children he should, I think, feel that he has shirked out of school. He is not doing his share of the work of the Commonwealth.'

'Pitt was not married, sir.'

'No;—and a great many other good men have remained unmarried. Do you mean to be another Pitt?'

'I don't intend to be a Prime Minister.'

'I would not recommend you to entertain that ambition. Pitt perhaps hardly had time for marriage. You may be more lucky.'

'I suppose I shall marry some day.'

'I should be glad to see you marry early,' said the Duke, speaking in a low voice, almost solemnly, but in his quietest, sweetest tone of voice. 'You are peculiarly situated. Though as yet you are only the heir to the property and honours of our family, still, were you married, almost everything would be at your disposal. There is so much which I should only be too ready to give up to you!'

'I can't bear to hear you talking of giving up anything,' said Silverbridge energetically.

Then the father looked round the room furtively, and seeing that the door was shut, and that they were assuredly alone, he put out his hand and gently stroked the young man's hair. It was almost a caress,—as though he would have said to himself, 'Were he my daughter, I would kiss him.' 'There is much I would fain give up,' he said. 'If you were a married man the house in Carlton Terrace would be fitter for you than for me. I have disqualified myself for taking that part in society which should be filled by the head of our family. You who have inherited so much from your mother would, if you married pleasantly, do all that right well.' He paused for a moment and then asked a straightforward question, very quickly—'You have never thought of anyone yet, I suppose?'

Silverbridge had thought very much of somebody. He was quite aware that he had almost made an offer to Lady Mabel.

She certainly had not given him any encouragement; but the very fact that she had not done so allured him the more. He did believe that he was thoroughly in love with Lady Mabel. She had told him that he was too young,—but he was older than Lady Mab herself by a week. She was beautiful;—that was certain. It was acknowledged by all that she was clever. As for blood, of which he believed his father thought much, there was perhaps none better in England. He had heard it said of her,—as he now well remembered, in his father's presence,—that she had behaved remarkably well in trying circumstances. She had no fortune;—everybody knew that; but then he did not want fortune. Would not this be a good opportunity for breaking the matter to his father? 'You have never thought of any one?' said the Duke,—again very sweetly, very softly.

'But I have!' Lord Silverbridge as he made the announcement blushed up to the eyes.

Then there came over the father something almost of fear. If he was to be told, how would it be if he could not approve?

'Yes I have,' said Silverbridge, recovering himself. 'If you wish it, I will tell you who it is.'

'Nay, my boy;—as to that consult your own feelings. Are you sure of yourself?'

'Oh yes.'

'Have you spoken to her?'

'Well;—yes, in part. She has not accepted me, if you mean that. Rather the contrary.' Now the Duke would have been very unwilling to say that his son would certainly be accepted by any girl in England to whom he might choose to offer his hand. But when the idea of a doubt was suggested to him, it did seem odd that his son should ask in vain. What other young man was there who could offer so much, and who was at the same time so likely to be loved for his own sake? He smiled however and was silent. 'I suppose I may as well out with it,' continued Silverbridge. 'You know Lady Mabel Grex?'

'Lady Mabel Grex? Yes;—I know her.'

'Is there any objection?'

'Is she not your senior?'

'No, sir; no; she is younger than I am.'

'Her father is not a man I esteem.'

'But she has always been so good!' Then the Duke was again silent. 'Have you not heard that, sir?'

'I think I have.'

'Is not that a great deal?'

'A very great deal. To be good must of all qualities be the best. She is very beautiful.'

'I think so, sir. Of course she has no money.'

'It is not needed. It is not needed. I have no objection to make. If you are sure of your own mind——'

'I am quite sure of that, sir.'

'Then I will raise no objection. Lady Mabel Grex! Her father, I fear, is not a worthy man. I hear that he is a gambler.'

'He is so poor!'

'That makes it worse, Silverbridge. A man who gambles because he has money that he can afford to lose is, to my thinking, a fool. But he who gambles because he has none, is—well, let us hope the best of him. You may give her my love.'

'She has not accepted me.'

'But should she do so, you may.'

'She almost rejected me. But I am not sure that she was in earnest, and I mean to try again.' Just at that moment the door was opened and Major Tifto walked into the room.

CHAPTER XXVII

Major Tifto and the Duke

'I BEG your pardon, Silverbridge,' said the Major, entering the room, 'but I was looking for Longstaff.'

'He isn't here,' said Silverbridge, who did not wish to be interrupted by his racing friend.

'Your father, I believe?' said Tifto. He was red in the face but was in other respects perhaps improved in appearance by his liquor. In his more sober moments he was not always able to assume that appearance of equality with his companions which it was the ambition of his soul to achieve. But a second glass of whisky-and-water would always enable him to cock his tail and bark before the company with all the courage of my lady's pug. 'Would you do me the great honour to introduce me to his Grace?'

Silverbridge was not prone to turn his back upon a friend because he was low in the world. He had begun to understand that he had made a mistake by connecting himself with the Major, but at the club he always defended his partner. Though he not unfrequently found himself obliged to snub the Major himself, he always countenanced the little Master of Hounds, and was true to his own idea of 'standing to a fellow.' Nevertheless he did not wish to introduce his friend to his father. The Duke saw it all at a glance, and felt that the introduction should be made. 'Perhaps,' said he, getting up from his chair, 'this is Major Tifto.'

'Yes;—my Lord Duke. I am Major Tifto.'

The Duke bowed graciously.

'My father and I were engaged about private matters,' said Silverbridge.

'I beg ten thousand pardons,' exclaimed the Major. 'I did not intend to intrude.'

'I think we had done,' said the Duke. 'Pray sit down, Major Tifto.' The Major sat down. 'Though now I bethink myself, I have to beg your pardon;—that I a stranger should ask you to sit down in your own club.'

'Don't mention it, my Lord Duke.'

'I am so unused to clubs, that I forgot where I was.'

'Quite so, my Lord Duke. I hope you think that Silverbridge is looking well?'

'Yes;—yes. I think so.'

Silverbridge bit his lips and turned his face away to the door.

'We didn't make a very good thing of our Derby nag the other day. Perhaps your Grace has heard all that?'

'I did hear that the horse in which you are both interested had failed to win the race.'

'Yes, he did. The Prime Minister, we call him, your Grace,—out of compliment to a certain Ministry which I wish it was going on to-day instead of the seedy lot we've got in. I think, my Lord Duke, that any one you may ask will tell you that I know what running is. Well;—I can assure you,—your Grace, that is,—that since I've seen 'orses I've never seen a 'orse fitter than him. When he got his canter that morning, it was nearly even betting. Not that I or Silverbridge were fools enough to put on anything at that rate. But I never saw a 'orse so bad ridden. I don't mean to say anything, my Lord Duke, against the man. But if that fellow hadn't been squared, or else wasn't drunk, or else wasn't off his head, that 'orse must have won,—my Lord Duke.'

'I do not know anything about racing, Major Tifto.'

'I suppose not, your Grace. But as I and Silverbridge are together in this matter I thought I'd just let your Grace know that we ought to have had a very good thing. I thought that perhaps your Grace might like to know that.'

'Tifto, you are making an ass of yourself,' said Silverbridge.

'Making an ass of myself!' exclaimed the Major.

'Yes;—considerably.'

'I think you are a little hard upon your friend,' said the Duke, with an attempt at a laugh. 'It is not to be supposed that he should know how utterly indifferent I am to everything connected with the turf.'

'I thought, my Lord Duke, you might care about learning how Silverbridge was going on.' This the poor little man said almost with a whine. His partner's roughness had knocked out of him nearly all the courage which Bacchus had given him.

'So I do; anything that interests him, interests me. But perhaps of all his pursuits racing is the one to which I am least able to lend an attentive ear. That every horse has a head, and that all did have tails till they were ill-used, is the extent of my stable knowledge.'

212

'Very good indeed, my Lord Duke; very good indeed! Ha, ha, ha!—all horses have heads, and all have tails! Heads and tails. Upon my word that is the best thing I have heard for a long time. I will do myself the honour of wishing your Grace goodnight. By-bye, Silverbridge.' Then he left the room, having been made supremely happy by what he considered to have been the Duke's joke. Nevertheless he would remember the snubbing and would be even with Silverbridge some day. Did Lord Silverbridge think that he was going to look after his Lordship's 'orses, and do this always on the square, and then be snubbed for doing it!

'I am very sorry that he should have come in to trouble you,' said the son.

'He has not troubled me much. I do not know whether he has troubled you. If you are coming down to the House again I will walk with you.' Silverbridge of course had to go down to the House again, and they started together. 'That man did not trouble me, Silverbridge; but the question is whether such an acquaintance must not be troublesome to you.'

'I'm not very proud of him, sir.'

'But I think one ought to be proud of one's friends.'

'He isn't my friend in that way at all.'

'In what way then?'

'He understands racing.'

'He is the partner of your pleasure then;—the man in whose society you love to enjoy the recreation of the race-course.'

'It is, sir, because he understands it.'

'I thought that a gentleman on the turf would have a trainer for that purpose;—not a companion. You mean to imply that you can save money by leaguing yourself with Major Tifto?'

'No, sir,—indeed.'

'If you associate with him, not for pleasure, then it surely must be for profit. That you should do the former would be to me so surprising that I must regard it as impossible. That you should do the latter—is, I think, a reproach.' This he said with no tone of anger in his voice,—so gently that Silverbridge at first hardly understood it. But gradually all that was meant came in upon him, and he felt himself to be ashamed of himself.

'He is bad,' he said at last.

'Whether he be bad I will not say; but I am sure that you can gain nothing by his companionship.'

'I will get rid of him,' said Silverbridge, after a considerable pause. 'I cannot do so at once, but I will do it.'

'It will be better, I think.'

'Tregear has been telling me the same thing.'

'Is he objectionable to Mr. Tregear?' asked the Duke.

'Oh yes. Tregear cannot bear him. You treated him a great deal better than Tregear ever does.'

'I do not deny that he is entitled to be treated well;—but so also is your groom. Let us say no more about him. And so it is to be Mabel Grex?'

'I did not say so, sir. How can I answer for her? Only it was so pleasant for me to know that you would approve if it should come off.'

'Yes;—I will approve. When she has accepted you——'

'But I don't think she will.'

'If she should, tell her that I will go to her at once. It will be much to have a new daughter;—very much that you should have a wife. Where would she like to live?'

'Oh, sir, we haven't got as far as that yet.'

'I dare say not; I dare say not,' said the Duke. 'Gatherum is always thought to be dull.'

'She wouldn't like Gatherum, I'm sure.'

'Have you asked her?'

'No, sir. But nobody ever did like Gatherum.'

'I suppose not. And yet, Silverbridge, what a sum of money it cost!'

'I believe it did.'

'All vanity; and vexation of spirit!'

The Duke no doubt was thinking of certain scenes*passed

at the great house in question, which scenes had not been delightful to him. 'No, I don't suppose she would wish to live at Gatherum. The Horns was given expressly by my uncle to your dear mother, and I should like Mary to have the place.'

'Certainly.'

'You should live among your tenantry. I don't care so very much for Matching.'

'It is the one place you do like, sir.'

'However, we can manage all that. Carlton Terrace I do not particularly like; but it is a good house, and there you should hang up your hat when in London. When it is settled, let me know at once.'

'But if it should never be settled?'

'I will ask no questions; but if it be settled, tell me.' Then in Palace Yard he was turning to go, but before he did so, he said another word leaning on his son's shoulder. 'I do not think that Mabel Grex and Major Tifto would do well together at all.'

'There shall be an end to that, sir.'

'God bless you, my boy!' said the Duke.

Lord Silverbridge sat in the House—or, to speak more accurately, in the smoking-room of the House—for about an hour thinking over all that had passed between himself and his father. He certainly had not intended to say anything about Lady Mab, but on the spur of the moment it had all come out. Now at any rate it was decided for him that he must, in set terms, ask her to be his wife. The scene which had just occurred had made him thoroughly sick of Major Tifto. He must get rid of the Major, and there could be no way of doing this at once so easy and so little open to observation as marriage. If he were but once engaged to Mabel Grex the dismissal of Tifto would be quite a matter of course. He would see Lady Mabel again on the morrow and ask her in direct language to be his wife.

CHAPTER XXVIII

Mrs. Montacute Jones's Garden-party

IT was known to all the world that Mrs. Montacute Jones's
first great garden-party was to come off on Wednesday,
16th June, at Roehampton. Mrs. Montacute Jones, who lived
in Grosvenor Place and had a country house in Gloucestershire, and a place for young men to shoot at in Scotland, also
kept a suburban elysium at Roehampton, in order that she
might give two garden-parties every year. When it is said
that all these costly luxuries appertained to Mrs. Montacute
Jones, it is to be understood that they did in truth belong to
Mr. Jones, of whom nobody heard much. But of Mrs. Jones,
—that is, Mrs. Montacute Jones,—everybody heard a great
deal. She was an old lady who devoted her life to the amusement of—not only her friends, but very many who were not
her friends. No doubt she was fond of Lords and Countesses,
and worked very hard to get round her all the rank and

fashion of the day. It must be acknowledged that she was a worldly old woman. But no more good-natured old woman lived in London, and everybody liked to be asked to her garden-parties. On this occasion there was to be a considerable infusion of royal blood,—German, Belgian, French, Spanish, and of native growth. Everybody who was asked would go, and everybody had been asked,—who was anybody. Lord Silverbridge had been asked, and Lord Silverbridge intended to be there. Lady Mary, his sister, could not even be asked, because her mother was hardly more than three months dead; but it is understood in the world that women mourn longer than men.

Silverbridge had mounted a private hansom cab in which he could be taken about rapidly,—and, as he said himself, without being shut up in a coffin. In this vehicle he had himself taken to Roehampton, purporting to kill two birds with one stone. He had not as yet seen his sister since she had been with Lady Cantrip. He would on this day come back by The Horns.

He was well aware that Lady Mab would be at the garden-party. What place could be better for putting the question he had to ask? He was by no means so confident as the heir to so many good things might perhaps have been without overdue self-confidence.

Entering through the house into the lawn he encountered Mrs. Montacute Jones, who, with a seat behind her on the terrace, surrounded by flowers, was going through the immense labour of receiving her guests.

'How very good of you to come all this way, Lord Silverbridge, to eat my strawberries.'

'How very good of you to ask me! I did not come to eat your strawberries but to see your friends.'

'You ought to have said you came to see me, you know. Have you met Miss Boncassen yet?'

'The American beauty? No. Is she here?'

'Yes; and she particularly wants to be introduced to you; you won't betray me, will you?'

'Certainly not; I am as true as steel.'

'She wanted, she said, to see if the eldest son of the Duke of Omnium really did look like any other man.'

'Then I don't want to see her,' said Silverbridge with a look of vexation.

'There you are wrong, for there was real downright fun in the way she said it. There they are, and I shall introduce you.' Then Mrs. Montacute Jones absolutely left her post for a minute or two, and taking the young lord down the steps of the terrace did introduce him to Mr. Boncassen, who was standing there amidst a crowd, and to Miss Boncassen the daughter.

Mr. Boncassen was an American who had lately arrived in England with the object of carrying out certain literary pursuits in which he was engaged within the British Museum. He was an American who had nothing to do with politics and nothing to do with trade. He was a man of wealth and a man of letters. And he had a daughter who was said to be the prettiest young woman either in Europe or in America at the present time.

Isabel Boncassen*was certainly a very pretty girl. I wish that my reader would believe my simple assurance. But no such simple assurance was ever believed, and I doubt even whether any description will procure for me from the reader that amount of faith which I desire to achieve. But I must make the attempt. General opinion generally considered Miss Boncassen to be small, but she was in truth something above the average height of English women. She was slight, without that look of slimness which is common to girls, and especially to American girls. That her figure was perfect the reader must believe on my word, as any detailed description of her arms, feet, bust, and waist, would be altogether ineffective. Her hair was dark brown and plentiful; but it added but little to her charms, which depended on other matters. Perhaps what struck the beholder first was the excessive brilliancy of her complexion. No pink was ever pinker, no alabaster whiteness was ever more like alabaster; but under

218

and around and through it all there was a constantly changing hue which gave a vitality to her countenance which no fixed colours can produce. Her eyes, too, were full of life and brilliancy, and even when she was silent her mouth would speak. Nor was there a fault within the oval of her face upon which the hypercritics of mature age could set a finger. Her teeth were excellent both in form and colour, but were seen but seldom. Who does not know that look of ubiquitous ivory produced by teeth which are too perfect in a face which is otherwise poor? Her nose at the base spread a little,—so that it was not purely Grecian. But who has ever seen a nose to be eloquent and expressive, which did not so spread? It was, I think, the vitality of her countenance,—the way in which she could speak with every feature, the command which she had of pathos, of humour, of sympathy, of satire, the assurance which she gave by every glance of her eye, every elevation of her brow, every curl of her lip, that she was alive to all that was going on,—it was all this rather than those feminine charms which can be catalogued and labelled that made all acknowledge that she was beautiful.

'Lord Silverbridge,' said Mr. Boncassen, speaking a little through his nose, 'I am proud to make your acquaintance, sir. Your father is a man for whom we in our country have a great respect. I think, sir, you must be proud of such a father.'

'Oh yes,—no doubt,' said Silverbridge awkwardly. Then Mr. Boncassen continued his discourse with the gentlemen around him. Upon this our friend turned to the young lady. 'Have you been long in England, Miss Boncassen?'

'Long enough to have heard about you and your father,' she said, speaking with no slightest twang.

'I hope you have not heard any evil of me.'

'Well!'

'I'm sure you can't have heard much good.'

'I know you didn't win the Derby.'

'You've been long enough to hear that?'

'Do you suppose we don't interest ourselves about the Derby in New York? Why, when we arrived at Queenstown* I was leaning over the taffrail so that I might ask the first man on board the tender*whether the Prime Minister had won.'

'And he said he hadn't.'

'I can't conceive why you of all men should call your horse by such a name. If my father had been President of the United States, I don't think I'd call a horse President.'

'I didn't name the horse.'

'I'd have changed it. But is it not very impudent in me to be finding fault with you the first time I have ever seen you? Shall you have a horse at Ascot?'*

'There will be something going, I suppose. Nothing that I care about.' Lord Silverbridge had made up his mind that he would go to no races with Tifto before the Leger. The Leger would be an affair of such moment as to demand his presence. After that should come the complete rupture between him and Tifto.

Then there was a movement among the elders, and Lord Silverbridge soon found himself walking alone with Miss Boncassen. It seemed to her to be quite natural to do so, and there certainly was no reason why he should decline anything so pleasant. It was thus that he had intended to walk with Mabel Grex;—only as yet he had not found her. 'Oh yes,' said Miss Boncassen, when they had been together about twenty minutes; 'we shall be here all the summer, and all the fall, and all the winter. Indeed father means to read every book in the British Museum before he goes back.'

'He'll have something to do.'

'He reads by steam, and he has two or three young men with him to take it all down and make other books out of it; —just as you'll see a lady take a lace shawl and turn it all about till she has trimmed a petticoat with it. It is the same lace all through,—and so I tell father it's the same knowledge.'

'But he puts it where more people will find it.'

'The lady endeavours to do the same with the lace. That depends on whether people look up or down. Father however is a very learned man. You mustn't suppose that I am laughing at him. He is going to write a very learned book. Only everybody will be dead before it can be half finished.' They still went on together, and then he gave her his arm and took her into the place where the strawberries and cream were prepared. As he was going in he saw Mabel Grex walking with Tregear, and she bowed to him pleasantly and playfully. 'Is that lady a great friend of yours?' asked Miss Boncassen.

'A very great friend indeed.'

'She is very beautiful.'

'And clever as well,—and good as gold.'

'Dear me! Do tell me who it is that owns all these qualities.'

'Lady Mabel Grex. She is daughter of Lord Grex. That man with her is my particular friend. His name is Frank Tregear, and they are cousins.'

'I am so glad they are cousins.'

'Why glad?'

'Because his being with her won't make you unhappy.'

'Supposing I was in love with her,—which I am not,—do you suppose it would make me jealous to see her with another man?'

'In our country*it would not. A young lady may walk about with a young gentleman just as she might with another young lady; but I thought it was different here. Do you know, judging by English ways, I believe I am behaving very improperly in walking about with you so long. Ought I not to tell you to go away?'

'Pray do not.'

'As I am going to stay here so long I wish to behave well to English eyes.'

'People know who you are, and discount all that.'

'If the difference be very marked they do. For instance, I needn't wear a hideous long bit of cloth over my face in

Constantinople because I am a woman. But when the discrepancies are small, then they have to be attended to. So I shan't walk about with you any more.'

'Oh yes, you will,' said Silverbridge, who began to think that he liked walking about with Miss Boncassen.

'Certainly not. There is Mr. Sprottle. He is father's secretary. He will take me back.'

'Cannot I take you back as well as Mr. Sprottle?'

'Indeed no;—I am not going to monopolise such a man as you. Do you think that I don't understand that everybody will be making remarks upon the American girl who won't leave the son of the Duke of Omnium alone? There is your particular friend Lady Mabel, and here is my particular friend Mr. Sprottle.'

'May I come and call?'

'Certainly. Father will only be too proud,—and I shall be prouder. Mother will be the proudest of all. Mother very seldom goes out. Till we get a house we are at The Langham. Thank you, Mr. Sprottle. I think we'll go and find father.'

Lord Silverbridge found himself close to Lady Mabel and Tregear, and also to Miss Cassewary, who had now joined Lady Mabel. He had been much struck with the American beauty, but was not on that account the less anxious to carry out his great plan. It was essentially necessary that he should do so at once, because the matter had been settled between him and his father. He was anxious to assure her that if she would consent, then the Duke would be ready to pour out all kinds of paternal blessings on their heads. 'Come and take a turn among the haycocks,' he said.

'Frank declares,' said Lady Mabel, 'that the hay is hired for the occasion. I wonder whether that is true.'

'Anybody can see,' said Tregear, 'that it has not been cut off the grass it stands upon.'

'If I could find Mrs. Montacute Jones I'd ask her where she got it,' said Lady Mabel.

'Are you coming?' asked Silverbridge impatiently.

'I don't think I am. I have been walking round the hay-cocks till I am tired of them.'

'Anywhere else then?'

'There isn't anywhere else. What have you done with your American beauty? The truth is, Lord Silverbridge, you ask me for my company when she won't give you hers any longer. Doesn't it look like it, Miss Cassewary?'

'I don't think Lord Silverbridge is the man to forget an old friend for a new one.'

'Not though the new friend be as lovely as Miss Boncassen?'

'I don't know that I ever saw a prettier girl,' said Tregear.

'I quite admit it,' said Lady Mabel. 'But that is no salve for my injured feelings. I have heard so much about Miss Boncassen's beauty for the last week, that I mean to get up a company of British females, limited, for the express purpose of putting her down. Who is Miss Boncassen that we are all to be put on one side for her?'

Of course he knew that she was joking, but he hardly knew how to take her joke. There is a manner of joking which carries with it much serious intention. He did feel that Lady Mabel was not gracious to him because he had spent half an hour with this new beauty, and he was half inclined to be angry with her. Was it fitting that she should be cross with him, seeing that he was resolved to throw at her feet all the good things that he had in the world? 'Bother Miss Boncassen,' he said; 'you might as well come and take a turn with a fellow.'

'Come along, Miss Cassewary,' said she. 'We will go round the haycocks yet once again.' So they turned and the two ladies accompanied Lord Silverbridge.

But this was not what he wanted. He could not say what he had to say in the presence of Miss Cassewary,—nor could he ask her to take herself off in another direction. Nor could he take himself off. Now that he had joined himself to these two ladies he must make with them the tour of the gardens. All this made him cross. 'These kind of things are a great bore,' he said.

'I dare say you would rather be in the House of Commons; —or, better still, at the Beargarden.'

'You mean to be ill-natured when you say that, Lady Mab.'

'You ask us to come and walk with you, and then you tell us that we are bores!'

'I did nothing of the kind.'

'I should have thought that you would be particularly pleased with yourself for coming here to-day, seeing that you have made Miss Boncassen's acquaintance. To be allowed to walk half an hour alone with the acknowledged beauty of the two hemispheres ought to be enough even for Lord Silverbridge.'

'That is nonsense, Lady Mab.'

'Nothing gives so much zest to admiration as novelty. A republican charmer must be exciting after all the blasées habituées of the London drawing-rooms.'

'How can you talk such nonsense, Mabel?' said Miss Casseway.

'But it is so. I feel that people must be sick of seeing me. I know I am very often sick of seeing them. Here is something fresh,—and not only unlike, but so much more lovely. I quite acknowledge that. I may be jealous, but no one can say that I am spiteful. I wish that some republican Adonis or Apollo would crop up,—so that we might have our turn. But I don't think the republican gentlemen are equal to the republican ladies. Do you, Lord Silverbridge?'

'I haven't thought about it.'

'Mr. Sprottle for instance.'

'I have not the pleasure of knowing Mr. Sprottle.'

'Now we've been round the haycocks, and really, Lord Silverbridge, I don't think we have gained much by it. Those forced marches never do any good.' And so they parted.

He was thinking with a bitter spirit of the ill-result of his morning's work when he again found himself close to Miss Boncassen in the crowd of departing people on the terrace. 'Mind you keep your word,' she said. And then she turned to her father. 'Lord Silverbridge has promised to call.'

'Mrs. Boncassen will be delighted to make his acquaintance.'

He got into his cab and was driven off towards Richmond. As went he began to think of the two young women with whom he had passed his morning. Mabel had certainly behaved badly to him. Even if she suspected nothing of his object, did she not owe it to their friendship to be more courteous to him than she had been? And if she suspected that object, should she not at any rate have given him the opportunity?

Or could it be that she was really jealous of the American girl? No;—that idea he rejected instantly. It was not compatible with the innate modesty of his disposition. But no doubt the American girl was very lovely. Merely as a thing to be looked at she was superior to Mabel. He did feel that as to mere personal beauty she was in truth superior to anything he had ever seen before. And she was clever too;—and good-humoured;—whereas Mabel had been both ill-natured and unpleasant.

CHAPTER XXIX

The Lovers meet

LORD SILVERBRIDGE found his sister alone. 'I particularly want you,' said he, 'to come and call on Mabel Grex. She wishes to know you, and I am sure you would like her.'

'But I haven't been out anywhere yet,' she said. 'I don't feel as though I wanted to go anywhere.'

Nevertheless she was very anxious to know Lady Mabel Grex, of whom she had heard much. A girl if she has had a former love passage says nothing of it to her new lover; but a man is not so reticent. Frank Tregear had perhaps not told her everything but he had told her something. 'I was very fond of her;—very fond of her,' he had said. 'And so I am still,' he had added. 'As you are my love of loves, she is my friend of friends.' Lady Mary had been satisfied by the assurance, but had become anxious to see the friend of friends. She resisted at first her brother's entreaties. She felt that her father in delivering her over to the seclusion of The Horns had intended to preclude her from showing herself in London. She was conscious that she was being treated with cruelty, and had a certain pride in her martyrdom. She would obey her father to the letter; she would give him no right to call her conduct in question; but he and any other to whom he might entrust the care of her, should be made to know that she thought him cruel. He had his power to which she must submit. But she also had hers,—to which it was possible he might be made to submit. 'I do not know that papa would wish me to go,' she said.

'But it is just what he would wish. He thinks a good deal about Mabel.'

'Why should he think about her at all?'

'I can't exactly explain,' said Silverbridge, 'but he does.'

'If you mean to tell me that Mabel Grex is anything particular to you, and that papa approves of it, I will go all round the world to see her.' But he had not meant to tell her this. The request had been made at Lady Mabel's instance. When his sister had spoken of her father's possible objection, then he had become eager in explaining the Duke's feeling, not remembering that such anxiety might betray himself. At that moment Lady Cantrip came in, and the question was referred to her. She did not see any objection to such a visit, and expressed her opinion that it would be a good thing that Mary should be taken out. 'She should begin to go somewhere,' said Lady Cantrip. And so it was decided. On the next Friday he would come down early in his hansom and drive her up to Belgrave Square. Then he would take her to Carlton Terrace, and Lady Cantrip's carriage should pick her up there and bring her home. He would arrange it all.

'What did you think of the American beauty?' asked Lady Cantrip when that was settled.

'I thought she was a beauty.'

'So I perceived. You had eyes for nobody else,' said Lady Cantrip, who had been at the garden-party.

'Somebody introduced her to me, and then I had to walk about the grounds with her. That's the kind of thing one always does in those places.'

'Just so. That is what "those places" are meant for, I suppose. But it was not apparently a great infliction.' Lord Silverbridge had to explain that it was not an infliction;— that it was a privilege, seeing that Miss Boncassen was both clever and lovely; but that it did not mean anything in particular.

When he took his leave he asked his sister to go out into the grounds with him for a moment. This she did almost unwillingly, fearing that he was about to speak to her of Tregear. But he had no such purpose on his mind. 'Of course you know,' he began, 'all that was nonsense you were saying about Mabel.'

'I did not know.'

'I was afraid you might blurt out something before her.'

'I should not be so imprudent.'

'Girls do make such fools of themselves sometimes. They are always thinking about people being in love. But it is the truth that my father said to me the other day how very much he liked what he had heard of her, and that he would like you to know her.'

On that same evening Silverbridge wrote from the Beargarden the shortest possible note to Lady Mabel, telling her what he had arranged. 'I and Mary propose to call in B. Square on Friday at two. I must be early because of the House. You will give us lunch. S.' There was no word of endearment,—none even of those ordinary words which people who hate each other use to one another. But he received the next day at home a much more kindly-written note from her:

227

'Dear Lord Silverbridge,

'You are so good! You always do just what you think people will like best. Nothing could please me so much as seeing your sister, of whom of course I have heard *very very* much. There shall be nobody here but Miss Cass.

'Yours most sincerely,

'M. G.'

'How I do wish I were a man!' his sister said to him when they were in the hansom together.

'You'd have a great deal more trouble.'

'But I'd have a hansom of my own, and go where I pleased. How would you like to be shut up at a place like The Horns?'

'You can go out if you like it.'

'Not like you. Papa thinks it's the proper place for me to live in, and so I must live there. I don't think a woman ever chooses how or where she shall live herself.'

'You are not going to take up woman's rights,* I hope.'

'I think I shall if I stay at The Horns much longer. What would papa say if he heard that I was going to give a lecture at an Institute?'

'The governor has had so many things to bear that a trifle such as that would make but little difference.'

'Poor papa!'

'He was dreadfully cut up about Gerald. And then he is so good! He said more to me about Gerald than he ever did about my own little misfortune at Oxford; but to Gerald himself he said almost nothing. Now he has forgiven me because he thinks I am constant at the House.'

'And are you?'

'Not so much as he thinks. I do go there,—for his sake. He has been so good about my changing sides.'

'I think you were quite right there.'

'I am beginning to think I was quite wrong. What did it matter to me?'

'I suppose it did make papa unhappy.'

'Of course it did;—and then this affair of yours.' As soon

as this was said Lady Mary at once hardened her heart against her father. Whether Silverbridge was or was not entitled to his own political opinions,—seeing that the Pallisers had for ages been known as staunch Whigs and Liberals,—might be a matter for question. But that she had a right to her own lover she thought that there could be no question. As they were sitting in the cab he could hardly see her face, but he was aware that she was in some fashion arming herself against opposition. 'I am sure that this makes him very unhappy,' continued Silverbridge.

'It cannot be altered,' she said.

'It will have to be altered.'

'Nothing can alter it. He might die, indeed;—or so might I.'

'Or he might see that it is no good,—and change his mind,' suggested Silverbridge.

'Of course that is possible,' said Lady Mary very curtly,—showing plainly by her manner that the subject was one which she did not choose to discuss any further.

'It is very good of you to come to me,' said Lady Mabel, kissing her new acquaintance. 'I have heard so much about you.'

'And I also of you.'

'I, you know, am one of your brother's stern Mentors. There are three or four of us determined to make him a pattern young legislator. Miss Cassewary is another. Only she is not quite so stern as I am.'

'He ought to be very much obliged.'

'But he is not;—not a bit. Are you, Lord Silverbridge?'

'Not so much as I ought to be, perhaps.'

'Of course there is an opposing force. There are the race-horses, and the drag, and Major Tifto. No doubt you have heard of Major Tifto. The Major is the Mr. Worldly-Wiseman*who won't let Christian go to the Strait Gate. I am afraid he hasn't read his Pilgrim's Progress. But we shall prevail, Lady Mary, and he will get to the beautiful city at last.'

'What is the beautiful city?' he asked.

'A seat in the Cabinet, I suppose;—or that general respect

which a young nobleman achieves when he has shown himself able to sit on a bench for six consecutive hours without appearing to go to sleep.'

Then they went to lunch, and Lady Mary did find herself to be happy with her new acquaintance. Her life since her mother's death had been so sad, that this short escape from it was a relief to her. Now for awhile she found herself almost gay. There was an easy liveliness about Lady Mabel,—a grain of humour and playfulness conjoined,—which made her feel at home at once. And it seemed to her as though her brother was at home. He called the girl Lady Mab, and Queen Mab, and once plain Mabel, and the old woman he called Miss Cass. It surely, she thought, must be the case that Lady Mabel and her brother were engaged.

'Come upstairs into my own room,—it is nicer than this,' said Lady Mabel, and they went from the dining-room into a pretty little sitting-room with which Silverbridge was very well acquainted. 'Have you heard of Miss Boncassen?' Mary said she had heard something of Miss Boncassen's great beauty. 'Everybody is talking about her. Your brother met her at Mrs. Montacute Jones's garden-party, and was made a conquest of instantly.'

'I wasn't made a conquest of at all,' said Silverbridge.

'Then he ought to have been made a conquest of. I should be if I were a man. I think she is the loveliest person to look at and the nicest person to listen to that I ever came across. We all feel that, as far as this season is concerned, we are cut out. But we don't mind it so much because she is a foreigner.' Then just as she said this the door was opened and Frank Tregear was announced.

Everybody there present knew as well as does the reader, what was the connexion between Tregear and Lady Mary Palliser. And each knew that the other knew it. It was therefore impossible for them not to feel themselves guilty among themselves. The two lovers had not seen each other since they had been together in Italy. Now they were brought face to face in this unexpected manner! And nobody except Tregear was at first quite sure whether somebody had not done something to arrange the meeting. Mary might naturally suspect that Lady Mabel had done this in the interest of her friend Tregear, and Silverbridge could not but suspect that it was so. Lady Mabel, who had never before met the other girl, could hardly refrain from thinking that there had been some underhand communication,—and Miss Casseway was clearly of opinion that there had been some understanding.

Silverbridge was the first to speak. 'Halloo, Tregear, I didn't know that we were to see you.'

'Nor I, that I should see you,' said he. Then of course there was a shaking of hands all round, in the course of which ceremony he came to Mary the last. She gave him her hand, but had not a word to say to him. 'If I had known that you were here,' he said, 'I should not have come; but I need hardly say how glad I am to see you,—even in this way.' Then the two girls were convinced that the meeting was accidental; but Miss Cass still had her doubts.

Conversation became at once very difficult. Tregear seated himself near, but not very near, to Lady Mary, and made some attempt to talk to both the girls at once. Lady Mabel plainly showed that she was not at her ease;—whereas Mary seemed to be stricken dumb by the presence of her lover. Silverbridge was so much annoyed by a feeling that this interview was a treason to his father, that he sat cudgelling his brain to think how he should bring it to an end. Miss Casseway was dumbfounded by the occasion. She was the one elder in the company who ought to see that no wrong was committed. She was not directly responsible to the Duke of Omnium, but she was thoroughly permeated by a feeling that it was her duty to take care that there should be no clandestine love meetings in Lord Grex's house. At last Silverbridge jumped up from his chair. 'Upon my word, Tregear, I think you had better go,' said he.

'So do I,' said Miss Cassewary. 'If it is an accident——'

'Of course it is an accident,' said Tregear angrily,—looking round at Mary, who blushed up to her eyes.

'I did not mean to doubt it,' said the old lady. 'But as it has occurred, Mabel, don't you think that he had better go?'

'He won't bite anybody, Miss Cass.'

'She would not have come if she had expected it,' said Silverbridge.

'Certainly not,' said Mary, speaking for the first time. 'But now he is here——' Then she stopped herself, rose from the sofa, sat down, and then rising again, stepped up to her lover, who rose at the same moment,—and threw herself into his arms and put up her lips to be kissed.

'This won't do at all,' said Silverbridge. Miss Cassewary clasped her hands together and looked up to heaven. She probably had never seen such a thing done before. Lady Mabel's eyes were filled with tears, and though in all this there was much to cause her anguish, still in her heart of hearts she admired the brave girl who could thus show her truth to her lover.

'Now go,' said Mary through her sobs.

'My own one,' ejaculated Tregear.

'Yes, yes, yes; always your own. Go,—go; go.' She was weeping and sobbing as she said this, and hiding her face with her handkerchief. He stood for a moment irresolute, and then left the room without a word of adieu to any one.

'You have behaved very badly,' said the brother.

'She has behaved like an angel,' said Mabel, throwing her arms round Mary as she spoke, 'like an angel. If there had been a girl whom you loved and who loved you, would you not have wished it? Would you not have worshipped her for showing that she was not ashamed of her love?'

'I am not a bit ashamed,' said Mary.

'And I say that you have no cause. No one knows him as I do. How good he is, and how worthy!' Immediately after that Silverbridge took his sister away, and Lady Mabel, escaping from Miss Cass, was alone. 'She loves him almost as I have loved him,' she said to herself. 'I wonder whether he can love her as he did me?'

CHAPTER XXX

What came of the Meeting

Not a word was said in the cab as Lord Silverbridge took his sister to Carlton Terrace, and he was leaving her without any reference to the scene which had taken place, when an idea struck him that this would be cruel. 'Mary,' he said, 'I was very sorry for all that.'

'It was not my doing.'

'I suppose it was nobody's doing. But I am very sorry that it occurred. I think that you should have controlled yourself.'

'No!' she almost shouted.

'I think so.'

'No;—if you mean by controlling myself, holding my tongue. He is the man I love,—whom I have promised to marry.'

'But, Mary,—do ladies generally embrace their lovers in public?'

'No;—nor should I. I never did such a thing in my life before. But as he was there I had to show that I was not ashamed of him! Do you think I should have done it if you all had not been there?' Then again she burst into tears.

He did not quite know what to make of it. Mabel Grex had declared that she had behaved like an angel. But yet, as he thought of what he had seen, he shuddered with vexation. 'I was thinking of the governor,' he said.

'He shall be told everything.'

'That you met Tregear?'

'Certainly; and that I—kissed him. I will do nothing that I am ashamed to tell everybody.'

'He will be very angry.'

'I cannot help it. He should not treat me as he is doing. Mr. Tregear is a gentleman. Why did he let him come? Why did you bring him? But it is of no use. The thing is settled. Papa can break my heart, but he cannot make me say that I am not engaged to Mr. Tregear.'

On that night Mary told the whole of her story to Lady

Cantrip. There was nothing that she tried to conceal. 'I got up,' she said, 'and threw my arms round him. Is he not all the world to me?'

'Had it been planned?' asked Lady Cantrip.

'No;—no! Nothing had been planned. They are cousins and very intimate, and he goes there constantly. Now I want you to tell papa all about it.'

Lady Cantrip began to think that it had been an evil day for her when she had agreed to take charge of this very determined young lady; but she consented at once to write to the Duke. As the girl was in her hands she must take care not to lay herself open to reproaches. As this objectionable lover had either contrived a meeting, or had met her without contriving, it was necessary that the Duke should be informed. 'I would rather you wrote the letter,' said Lady Mary. 'But pray tell him that all along I have meant him to know all about it.'

Till Lady Cantrip seated herself at her writing-table she did not know how great the difficulty would be. It cannot in any circumstances be easy to write to a father as to his daughter's love for an objectionable lover; but the Duke's character added much to the severity of the task. And then that embrace! She knew that the Duke would be struck with horror as he read of such a tale, and she found herself almost struck with horror as she attempted to write it. When she came to the point she found she could not write it. 'I fear there was a good deal of warmth shown on both sides,' she said, feeling that she was calumniating the man, as to whose warmth she had heard nothing. 'It is quite clear,' she added, 'tnat this is not a passing fancy on her part.'

It was impossible that the Duke should be made to understand exactly what had occurred. That Silverbridge had taken Mary he did understand, and that they had together gone to Lord Grex's house. He understood also that the meeting had taken place in the presence of Silverbridge and of Lady Mabel. 'No doubt it was all an accident,' Lady Cantrip wrote. How could it be an accident?

234

'You had Mary up in town on Friday,' he said to his son on the following Sunday morning.

'Yes, sir.'

'And that friend of yours came in?'

'Yes, sir.'

'Do you not know what my wishes are?'

'Certainly I do;—but I could not help his coming. You do not suppose that anybody had planned it?'

'I hope not.'

'It was simply an accident. Such an accident as must occur over and over again,—unless Mary is to be locked up.'

'Who talks of locking anybody up? What right have you to speak in that way?'

'I only meant that of course they will stumble across each other in London.'

'I think I will go abroad,' said the Duke. He was silent for awhile, and then repeated his words. 'I think I will go abroad.'

'Not for long, I hope, sir.'

'Yes;—to live there. Why should I stay here? What good can I do here? Everything I see and everything I hear is a pain to me.' The young man of course could not but go back in his mind to the last interview which he had had with his father, when the Duke had been so gracious and apparently so well pleased.

'Is there anything else wrong,—except about Mary?' Silverbridge asked.

'I am told that Gerald owes about fifteen hundred pounds at Cambridge.'

'So much as that! I knew he had a few horses there.'

'It is not the money, but the absence of principle,—that a young man should have no feeling that he ought to live within certain prescribed means! Do you know what you have had from Mr. Morton?'

'Not exactly, sir.'

'It is different with you. But a man, let him be who he may, should live within certain means. As for your sister, I think she will break my heart.' Silverbridge found it to be quite impossible to say anything in answer to this. 'Are you going to church?' asked the Duke.

'I was not thinking of doing so particularly.'

'Do you not ever go?'

'Yes;—sometimes. I will go with you now, if you like it, sir.'

'I had thought of going, but my mind is too much harassed. I do not see why you should not go.'

But Silverbridge, though he had been willing to sacrifice his morning to his father,—for it was, I fear, in that way that he had looked at it,—did not see any reason for performing a duty which his father himself omitted. And there were various matters also which harassed him. On the previous evening, after dinner, he had allowed himself to back the Prime Minister for the Leger to a very serious amount. In fact he had plunged, and now stood to lose some twenty thousand pounds on the doings of the last night. And he had made these bets under the influence of Major Tifto. It was the remembrance of this, after the promise made to his father, that annoyed him the most. He was imbued with a feeling that it behoved him as a man to 'pull himself together', as he would have said himself, and to live in accordance with certain rules. He could make the rules easily enough, but he had never yet succeeded in keeping any one of them. He had determined to sever himself from Tifto; and, in doing that, had intended to sever himself from affairs of the turf generally. This resolution was not yet a week old. It was on that evening that he had resolved that Tifto should no longer be his companion; and now he had to confess to himself that because he had drunk three or four glasses of champagne he had been induced by Tifto to make those wretched bets.

And he had told his father that he intended to ask Mabel Grex to be his wife. He had so committed himself that the offer must now be made. He did not specially regret that, though he wished that he had been more reticent. 'What a fool a man is to blurt out everything!' he said to himself. A wife would be a good thing for him; and where could he possibly find a better wife than Mabel Grex? In beauty she was no doubt inferior to Miss Boncassen. There was something about Miss Boncassen which made it impossible to forget her. But Miss Boncassen was an American, and on many accounts out of the question. It did not occur to him that he would fall in love with Miss Boncassen; but still it seemed hard to him that this intention of marriage should stand in his way of having a good time with Miss Boncassen for a few weeks. No doubt there were objections to marriage. It clipped a fellow's wings. But then, if he were married, he might be sure that Tifto would be laid aside. It was such a great thing to have got his father's assured consent to a marriage. It meant complete independence in money matters.

Then his mind ran away to a review of his father's affairs. It was a genuine trouble to him that his father should be so unhappy. Of all the griefs which weighed upon the Duke's mind, that in reference to his sister was the heaviest. The money which Gerald owed at Cambridge would be nothing if that other sorrow could be conquered. Nor had Tifto and his own extravagance caused the Duke any incurable wounds. If Tregear could be got out of the way, his father, he thought, might be reconciled to other things. He felt very tender-hearted about his father; but he had no remorse in regard to his sister as he made up his mind that he would speak very seriously to Tregear.

He had wandered into St. James's Park, and had lighted by this time half-a-dozen cigarettes one after another, as he sat on one of the benches. He was a handsome youth, all but six feet high, with light hair, with round blue eyes, and with all that aristocratic look, which had belonged so peculiarly to the late Duke but which was less conspicuous in the present head of the family. He was a young man whom you would hardly pass in a crowd without observing,—but of whom you would say, after due observation, that he had not as yet put off all his childish ways. He now sat with his legs stretched out, with his cane in his hands, looking down upon the water. He was trying to think. He worked hard at thinking. But the bench was hard and, upon the whole, he was not satisfied with his position. He had just made up his mind that he would look up Tregear, when Tregear himself appeared on the path before him.

'Tregear!' exclaimed Silverbridge.

'Silverbridge!' exclaimed Tregear.

'What on earth makes you walk about here on a Sunday morning?'

'What on earth makes you sit there? That I should walk here, which I often do, does not seem to me odd. But that I should find you is marvellous. Do you often come?'

'Never was here in my life before. I strolled in because I had things to think of.'

'Questions to be asked in Parliament? Notices of motions, Amendments in Committee, and that kind of thing?'

'Go on, old fellow.'

'Or perhaps Major Tifto has made important revelations.'

'D—— Major Tifto.'

'With all my heart,' said Tregear.

'Sit down here,' said Silverbridge. 'As it happened, at the moment when you came up I was thinking of you.'

'That was kind.'

'And I was determined to go to you. All this about my sister must be given up.'

'Must be given up?'

'It can never lead to any good. I mean that there never can be a marriage.' Then he paused, but Tregear was determined to hear him out. 'It is making my father so miserable that you would pity him if you could see him.'

'I dare say I should. When I see people unhappy I always pity them. What I would ask you to think of is this. If I were to commission you to tell your sister that everything between us should be given up, would not she be so unhappy that you would have to pity her?'

'She would get over it.'

'And so will your father.'

'He has a right to have his own opinion on such a matter.'

238

'And so have I. And so has she. His rights in this matter are very clear and very potential.* I am quite ready to admit that we cannot marry for many years to come, unless he will provide the money. You are quite at liberty to tell him that I say so. I have no right to ask your father for a penny, and I will never do so. The power is all in his hands. As far as I know my own purposes, I shall not make any immediate attempt even to see her. We did meet, as you saw, the other day, by the merest chance. After that, do you think that your sister wishes me to give her up?'

'As for supposing that girls are to have what they wish, that is nonsense.'

'For young men I suppose equally so. Life ought to be a life of self-denial, no doubt. Perhaps it might be my duty to retire from this affair, if by doing so I should sacrifice only myself. The one person of whom I am bound to think in this matter is the girl I love.'

'That is just what she would say about you.'

'I hope so.'

'In that way you support each other. If it were any other man circumstanced just like you are, and any other girl placed like Mary, you would be the first to say that the man was behaving badly. I don't like to use hard language to you, but in such a case you would be the first to say of another man —that he was looking after the girl's money.'

Silverbridge as he said this looked forward steadfastly on to the water, regretting much that cause for quarrel should have arisen, but thinking that Tregear would find himself obliged to quarrel. But Tregear, after a few moments' silence, having thought it out, determined that he would not quarrel. 'I think I probably might,' he said, laying his hand on Silverbridge's arm. 'I think I perhaps might express such an opinion.'

'Well then!'

'I have to examine myself, and find out whether I am guilty of the meanness which I might perhaps be too ready to impute to another. I have done so, and I am quite sure that I am not drawn to your sister by any desire for her money. I did not seek her because she was a rich man's daughter, nor,—because she is a rich man's daughter,—will I give her up. She shall be mistress of the occasion. Nothing but a word from her shall induce me to leave her;—but a word from her, if it comes from her own lips,—shall do so.' Then he took his friend's hand in his, and, having grasped it, walked away without saying another word.

CHAPTER XXXI

Miss Boncassen's River-party. No. 1

THRICE within the next three weeks did Lord Silverbridge go forth to ask Mabel to be his wife, but thrice in vain. On one occasion she would talk on other things. On the second Miss Cassewary would not leave her. On the third the conversation turned in a very disagreeable way on Miss Boncassen, as to whom Lord Silverbridge could not but think that Lady Mabel said some very ill-natured things. It was no doubt true that he, during the last three weeks, had often been in Miss Boncassen's company, that he had danced with her, ridden with her, taken her to the House of Lords and to the House of Commons, and was now engaged to attend upon her at a river-party up above Maidenhead. But Mabel had certainly no right to complain. Had he not thrice during the same period come there to lay his coronet at her feet;—and now, at this very moment, was it not her fault that he was not going through the ceremony?

'I suppose,' she said, laughing, 'that it is all settled.'

'What is all settled?'

'About you and the American beauty.'

'I am not aware that anything particular has been settled.'

'Then it ought to be,—oughtn't it? For her sake, I mean.'

'That is so like an English woman,' said Lord Silverbridge. 'Because you cannot understand a manner of life a little different from your own you will impute evil.'

'I have imputed no evil, Lord Silverbridge, and you have no right to say so.'

'If you mean to assert,' said Miss Cass, 'that the manners of American young ladies are freer than those of English young ladies, it is you that are taking away their characters.'

'I don't say it would be at all bad,' continued Lady Mabel. 'She is a beautiful girl, and very clever, and would make a charming Duchess. And then it would be such a delicious change to have an American Duchess.'

'She wouldn't be a Duchess.'

'Well, Countess, with Duchessship before her in the re-mote future. Wouldn't it be a change, Miss Cass?'

'Oh decidedly!' said Miss Cass.

'And very much for the better. Quite a case of new blood, you know. Pray don't suppose that I mean to object. Everybody who talks about it approves. I haven't heard a dissentient voice. Only as it has gone so far, and as English people are too stupid, you know, to understand all these new ways,—don't you think perhaps——?'

'No, I don't think. I don't think anything except that you are very ill-natured.' Then he got up and, after making formal adieux to both the ladies, left the house.

As soon as he was gone Lady Mabel began to laugh, but the least apprehensive*ears would have perceived that the laughter was affected. Miss Casseway did not laugh at all, but sat bolt upright and looked very serious. 'Upon my honour,' said the younger lady, 'he is the most beautifully simple-minded human being I ever knew in my life.'

'Then I wouldn't laugh at him.'

'How can one help it? But of course I do it with a purpose.'

'What purpose?'

'I think he is making a fool of himself. If somebody does not interfere he will go so far that he will not be able to draw back without misbehaving.'

'I thought,' said Miss Cassewary, in a very low voice, almost whispering, 'I thought that he was looking for a wife elsewhere.'

'You need not think of that again,' said Lady Mab, jumping up from her seat. 'I had thought of it too. But as I told you before, I spared him. He did not really mean it with me; —nor does he mean it with this American girl. Such young men seldom mean. They drift into matrimony. But she will not spare him. It would be a national triumph. All the States would sing a pæan of glory. Fancy a New York belle having compassed a Duke!'

'I don't think it possible. It would be too horrid.'

'I think it quite possible. As for me, I could teach myself to think it best as it is, were I not so sure that I should be better for him than so many others. But I shouldn't love him.'

'Why not love him?'

'He is such a boy. I should always treat him like a boy,—spoiling him and petting him, but never respecting him. Don't run away with any idea that I should refuse him from conscientious motives, if he were really to ask me. I too should like to be a Duchess. I should like to bring all this misery at home to an end.'

'But you did refuse him.'

'Not exactly;—because he never asked me. For the moment I was weak, and so I let him have another chance. I shall not have been a good friend to him if it ends in his marrying this Yankee.'

Lord Silverbridge went out of the house in a very ill humour,—which however left him when in the course of the afternoon he found himself up at Maidenhead with Miss Boncassen. Miss Boncassen at any rate did not laugh at him. And then she was so pleasant, so full of common sense, and so completely intelligent! 'I like you,' she had said, 'because I feel that you will not think that you ought to make love to me. There is nothing I hate so much as the idea that a young man and a young woman can't be acquainted with each other without some such tomfoolery as that.' This had exactly expressed his own feeling. Nothing could be so pleasant as his intimacy with Isabel Boncassen.

Mrs. Boncassen seemed to be a homely person, with no

desire either to speak, or to be spoken to. She went out but seldom, and on those rare occasions did not in any way interfere with her daughter. Mr. Boncassen filled a prouder situation. Everybody knew that Miss Boncassen was in England, because it suited Mr. Boncassen to spend many hours in the British Museum. But still the daughter hardly seemed to be under control from the father. She went alone where she liked; talked to those she liked; and did what she liked. Some of the young ladies of the day thought that there was a good deal to be said in favour of the freedom which she enjoyed.

There is however a good deal to be said against it. All young ladies cannot be Miss Boncassens, with such an assurance of admirers as to be free from all fear of loneliness. There is a comfort for a young lady in having a pied-à-terre to which she may retreat in case of need. In American circles, where girls congregate without their mothers, there is a danger felt by young men that if a lady be once taken in hand, there will be no possibility of getting rid of her,—no mamma to whom she may be taken and under whose wings she may be dropped. 'My dear,' said an old gentleman the other day walking through an American ball-room, and addressing himself to a girl whom he knew well,—'My dear——' But the girl bowed and passed on, still clinging to the arm of the young man who accompanied her. But the old gentleman was cruel, and possessed of a determined purpose. 'My dear,' said he again, catching the young man tight by the collar and holding him fast. 'Don't be afraid; I've got him; he shan't desert you; I'll hold him here till you have told me how your father does.' The young lady looked as if she didn't like it, and the sight of her misery gave rise to a feeling that, after all, mammas perhaps may be a comfort.

But in her present phase of life Miss Boncassen suffered no misfortune of this kind. It had become a privilege to be allowed to attend upon Miss Boncassen, and the feeling of this privilege had been enhanced by the manner in which Lord Silverbridge had devoted himself to her. Fashion of course makes fashion. Had not Lord Silverbridge been so very much struck by the charm of the young lady, Lords Glasslough and Popplecourt would not perhaps have found it necessary to run after her. As it was, even that most unenergetic of young men, Dolly Longstaff, was moved to profound admiration.

On this occasion they were all up the river at Maidenhead. Mr. Boncassen had looked about for some means of returning the civilities offered to him, and had been instigated by Mrs.

Montacute Jones to do it after this fashion. There was a magnificent banquet spread in a summer-house on the river bank. There were boats, and there was a band, and there was a sward for dancing. There was lawn-tennis, and fishing-rods, —which nobody used,—and better still, long shady secluded walks in which gentlemen might stroll,—and ladies too, if they were kind enough. The whole thing had been arranged by Mrs. Montacute Jones. As the day was fine, as many of the old people had abstained from coming, as there were plenty of young men of the best sort, and as nothing had been spared in reference to external comforts, the party promised to be a success. Every most lovely girl in London of course was there,—except Lady Mabel Grex. Lady Mabel was in the habit of going everywhere, but on this occasion she had refused Mrs. Boncassen's invitation. 'I don't want to see her triumphs,' she had said to Miss Cass.

Everybody went down by railway of course, and innumerable flies and carriages had been provided to take them to the scene of action. Some immediately got into boats and rowed themselves up from the bridge,—which, as the thermometer was standing at eighty in the shade, was an inconsiderate proceeding. 'I don't think I am quite up to that,' said Dolly Longstaff, when it was proposed to him to take an oar. 'Miss Amazon will do it. She rows so well, and is so strong.' Whereupon Miss Amazon, not at all abashed, did take the oar; and as Lord Silverbridge was on the seat behind her with the other oar she probably enjoyed her task.

'What a very nice sort of person Lady Cantrip is.' This was said to Silverbridge by that generally silent young nobleman Lord Popplecourt. The remark was the more singular because Lady Cantrip was not at the party,—and the more so again because, as Silverbridge thought, there could be but little in common between the Countess who had his sister in charge and the young lord beside him, who was not fast only because he did not like to risk his money.

'Well,—yes; I dare say she is.'

'I thought so, peculiarly. I was at that place at Richmond yesterday.'

'The devil you were! What were you doing at The Horns?'

'Lady Cantrip's grandmother was,—I don't quite know what she was, but something to us. I know I've got a picture of her at Popplecourt. Lady Cantrip wanted to ask me something about it, and so I went down. I was so glad to make acquaintance with your sister.'

'You saw Mary, did you?'

'Oh yes; I lunched there. I'm to go down and meet the Duke some day.'

'Meet the Duke!'

'Why not?'

245

'No reason on earth,—only I can't imagine the governor going to Richmond for his dinner. Well! I am very glad to hear it. I hope you'll get on well with him.'

'I was so much struck with your sister.'

'Yes; I dare say,' said Silverbridge, turning away into the path where he saw Miss Boncassen standing with some other ladies. It certainly did not occur to him that Popplecourt was to be brought forward as a suitor for his sister's hand.

'I believe this is the most lovely place in the world,' Miss Boncassen said to him.

'We are so much the more obliged to you for bringing us here.'

'We don't bring you. You allow us to come with you and see all that is pretty and lovely.'

'Is it not your party?'

'Father will pay the bill, I suppose,—as far as that goes. And mother's name was put on the cards. But of course we know what that means. It is because you and a few others like you have been so kind to us, that we are able to be here at all.'

'Everybody, I should think, must be kind to you.'

'I do have a good time pretty much; but nowhere so good as here. I fear that when I get back I shall not like New York.'

'I have heard you say, Miss Boncassen, that Americans were more likeable than the English.'

'Have you? Well, yes; I think I have said so. And I think it is so. I'd sooner have to dance with a bank clerk in New York, than with a bank clerk here.'

'Do you ever dance with bank clerks?'

'Oh dear yes. At least I suppose so. I dance with whoever comes up. We haven't got lords in America, you know!'

'You have got gentlemen?'

'Plenty of them;—but they are not so easily defined as lords. I do like lords.'

'Do you?'

'Oh yes,—and ladies;—Countesses I mean and women of

that sort. Your Lady Mabel Grex is not here. Why wouldn't she come?'

'Perhaps you didn't ask her.'

'Oh yes I did;—especially for your sake.'

'She is not my Lady Mabel Grex,' said Lord Silverbridge with unnecessary energy.

'But she will be.'

'What makes you think that?'

'You are devoted to her.'

'Much more to you, Miss Boncassen.'

'That is nonsense, Lord Silverbridge.'

'Not at all.'

'It is also—untrue.'

'Surely I must be the best judge of that myself?'

'Not a doubt; a judge not only whether it be true, but if true whether expedient,—or even possible. What did I say to you when we first began to know each other?'

'What did you say?'

'That I liked knowing you;—that was frank enough;— that I liked knowing you because I knew that there would be no tomfoolery of love-making.' Then she paused; but he did not quite know how to go on with the conversation at once, and she continued her speech. 'When you condescend to tell me that you are devoted to me, as though that were the kind of thing that I expect to have said when I take a walk with a young man in a wood, is not that the tomfoolery of love-making?' She stopped and looked at him, so that he was obliged to answer.

'Then why do you ask me if I am devoted to Lady Mabel? Would not that be tomfoolery too?'

'No. If I thought so, I would not have asked the question. I did specially invite her to come here because I thought you would like it. You have got to marry somebody.'

'Some day, perhaps.'

'And why not her?'

'If you come to that, why not you?' He felt himself to be getting into deep waters as he said this,—but he had a meaning to express if only he could find the words to express it. 'I don't say whether it is tomfoolery, as you call it, or not; but whatever it is, you began it.'

'Yes;—yes. I see. You punish me for my unpremeditated impertinence in suggesting that you are devoted to Lady Mabel by the premeditated impertinence of pretending to be devoted to me.'

'Stop a moment. I cannot follow that.' Then she laughed. 'I will swear that I did not intend to be impertinent.'

'I hope not.'

'I am devoted to you.'

'Lord Silverbridge!'

'I think you are——'

'Stop, stop. Do not say it.'

'Well I won't;—not now. But there has been no tom-foolery.'

'May I ask a question, Lord Silverbridge? You will not be angry? I would not have you angry with me.'

'I will not be angry,' he said.

'Are you not engaged to marry Lady Mabel Grex?'

'No.'

'Then I beg your pardon. I was told that you were engaged to her. And I thought your choice was so fortunate, so happy! I have seen no girl here that I admire half so much. She almost comes up to my idea of what a young woman should be.'

'Almost!'

'Now I am sure that if not engaged to her you must be in love with her, or my praise would have sufficed.'

'Though one knows a Lady Mabel Grex, one may become acquainted with a Miss Boncassen.'

There are moments in which stupid people say clever things, obtuse people say sharp things, and good-natured people say ill-natured things. 'Lord Silverbridge,' she said, 'I did not expect that from you.'

'Expect what? I meant it simply.'

'I have no doubt you meant it simply. We Americans think ourselves sharp, but I have long since found out that we may meet more than our matches over here. I think we will go back. Mother means to try to get up a quadrille.'

'You will dance with me?'

'I think not. I have been walking with you, and I had better dance with someone else.'

'You can let me have one dance.'

'I think not. There will not be many.'

'Are you angry with me?'

'Yes, I am; there.' But as she said this she smiled. 'The truth is, I thought I was getting the better of you, and you turned round and gave me a pat on the head to show me that you could be master when it pleased you. You have defended your intelligence at the expense of your good-nature.'

'I'll be shot if I know what it all means,' he said, just as he was parting with her.

CHAPTER XXXII

Miss Boncassen's River-party. No. 2

LORD SILVERBRIDGE made up his mind that as he could not dance with Miss Boncassen he would not dance at all. He was not angry at being rejected, and when he saw her stand up with Dolly Longstaff he felt no jealousy. She had refused to dance with him not because she did not like him, but because she did not wish to show that she liked him. He could understand that, though he had not quite followed all the ins and outs of her little accusations against him. She had flattered him—without any intention of flattery on her part. She had spoken of his intelligence and had complained that he had been too sharp to her. Mabel Grex when most sweet to him, when most loving, always made him feel that he was her inferior. She took no trouble to hide her conviction of his youthfulness. This was anything but flattering. Miss Boncassen, on the other hand, professed herself to be almost afraid of him.

'There shall be no tomfoolery of love-making,' she had said. But what if it were not tomfoolery at all? What if it were good, genuine, earnest love-making? He certainly was not pledged to Lady Mabel. As regarded his father there would be a difficulty. In the first place he had been fool enough to tell his father that he was going to make an offer to Mabel Grex. And then his father would surely refuse his consent to a marriage with an American stranger. In such case there would be no unlimited income, no immediate pleasantness of magnificent life such as he knew would be poured out upon him if he were to marry Mabel Grex. As he thought of this, however, he told himself that he would not sell himself for money and magnificence. He could afford to be independent, and gratify his own taste. Just at this moment he was of opinion that Isabel Boncassen would be the sweeter companion of the two.

He had sauntered down to the place where they were

dancing and stood by, saying a few words to Mrs. Boncassen. 'Why are you not dancing, my Lord?' she asked.

'There are enough without me.'

'I guess you young aristocrats are never over-fond of doing much with your own arms and legs.'

'I don't know about that; polo, you know, for the legs, and lawn-tennis for the arms, is hard work enough.'

'But it must always be something new-fangled; and after all it isn't of much account. Our young men like to have quite a time at dancing.'

It all came through her nose! And she looked so common! What would the Duke say to her, or Mary, or even Gerald? The father was by no means so objectionable. He was a tall, straight, ungainly man, who always wore black clothes. He had dark, stiff, short hair, a long nose, and a forehead that was both high and broad. Ezekiel Boncassen*was the very man,—from his appearance,—for a President of the United States; and there were men who talked of him for that high office. That he had never attended to politics was supposed to be in his favour. He had the reputation of being the most learned man in the States, and reputation itself often suffices to give a man dignity of manner. He, too, spoke through his nose, but the peculiar twang coming from a man would be supposed to be virile and incisive. From a woman, Lord Silverbridge thought it to be unbearable. But as to Isabel, had she been born within the confines of some lordly park in Hertfordshire, she could not have been more completely free from the abomination.

'I am sorry that you should not be enjoying yourself,' said Mr. Boncassen, coming to his wife's relief.

'Nothing could have been nicer. To tell the truth, I am standing idle by way of showing my anger against your daughter, who would not dance with me.'

'I am sure she would have felt herself honoured,' said Mr. Boncassen.

'Who is the gentleman with her?' asked the mother.

'A particular friend of mine—Dolly Longstaff.'

'Dolly!' ejaculated Mrs. Boncassen.

'Everybody calls him so. His real name I believe to be Adolphus.'

'Is he,—is he—just anybody?' asked the anxious mother.

'He is a very great deal,—as people go here. Everybody knows him. He is asked everywhere, but he goes nowhere. The greatest compliment paid to you here is his presence.'

'Nay, my Lord, there are the Countess Montague, and the Marchioness of Capulet, and Lord Tybalt, and——'

'They go everywhere. They are nobodies. It is a charity to even invite them. But to have had Dolly Longstaff once is a triumph for life.'

'Laws!' said Mrs. Boncassen, looking hard at the young man who was dancing. 'What has he done?'

'He never did anything in his life.'

'I suppose he's very rich.'

'I don't know. I should think not. I don't know anything about his riches, but I can assure you that having had him down here will quite give a character to the day.'

In the meantime Dolly Longstaff was in a state of great excitement. Some part of the character assigned to him by Lord Silverbridge was true. He very rarely did go anywhere, and yet was asked to a great many places. He was a young man,—though not a very young man,—with a fortune of his own and the expectation of a future fortune. Few men living could have done less for the world than Dolly Longstaff,— and yet he had a position of his own. Now he had taken it into his head to fall in love with Miss Boncassen. This was an accident which had probably never happened to him before, and which had disturbed him much. He had known Miss Boncassen a week or two before Lord Silverbridge had seen her, having by some chance dined out and sat next to her. From that moment he had become changed, and had gone hither and thither in pursuit of the American beauty. His passion having become suspected by his companions had excited their ridicule. Nevertheless he had persevered;—and now he was absolutely dancing with the lady out in the open air. 'If this goes on, your friends will have to look after you and put you somewhere,' Mr. Lupton had said to him in one of the intervals of the dance. Dolly had turned round and scowled, and suggested that if Mr. Lupton would mind his own affairs it would be as well for the world at large.

At the present crisis Dolly was very much excited. When the dance was over, as a matter of course, he offered the lady his arm, and as a matter of course she accepted it. 'You'll take a turn; won't you?' he said.

'It must be a very short turn,' she said,—'as I am expected to make myself busy.'

'Oh, bother that.'

'It bothers me; but it has to be done.'

'You have set everything going now. They'll begin dancing again without your telling them.'

'I hope so.'

'And I've got something I want to say.'

'Dear me; what is it?'

They were now on a path close to the riverside, in which there were many loungers. 'Would you mind coming up to the temple?' he said.

'What temple?'

'Oh such a beautiful place. The Temple of the Winds, I think they call it, or Venus;—or—or—Mrs. Arthur de Bever.'

'Was she a goddess?'

'It is something built to her memory. Such a view of the river! I was here once before and they took me up there. Everybody who comes here goes and sees Mrs. Arthur de Bever. They ought to have told you.'

'Let us go then,' said Miss Boncassen. 'Only it must not be long.'

'Five minutes will do it all.' Then he walked rather quickly up a flight of rural steps. 'Lovely spot; isn't it?'

'Yes, indeed.'

'That's Maidenhead Bridge;—that's—somebody's place; —and now I've got something to say to you.'

'You're not going to murder me now you've got me up here alone?' said Miss Boncassen laughing.

'Murder you!' said Dolly, throwing himself into an attitude that was intended to express devoted affection. 'Oh no!'

'I am glad of that.'

'Miss Boncassen!'

'Mr. Longstaff! If you sigh like that you'll burst yourself.'

'I'll—what?'

'Burst yourself!' and she nodded her head at him.

Then he clapped his hands together, and turned his head away from her towards the little temple. 'I wonder whether she knows what love is,' he said, as though he were addressing himself to Mrs. Arthur de Bever.

'No, she don't,' said Miss Boncassen.

'But I do,' he shouted, turning back towards her. 'I do. If any man were ever absolutely, actually, really in love, I am the man.'

'Are you indeed, Mr. Longstaff? Isn't it pleasant?'

'Pleasant;—pleasant? Oh, it could be so pleasant.'

'But who is the lady? Perhaps you don't mean to tell me that.'

'You mean to say you don't know?'

'Haven't the least idea in life.'

'Let me tell you then that it could only be one person. It never was but one person. It never could have been but one person. It is you.' Then he put his hand well on his heart.

'Me!' said Miss Boncassen, choosing to be ungrammatical in order that he might be more absurd.

'Of course it is you. Do you think that I should have brought you all the way up here to tell you that I was in love with anybody else?'

'I thought I was brought to see Mrs. de Somebody, and the view.'

'Not at all,' said Dolly emphatically.

'Then you have deceived me.'

'I will never deceive you. Only say that you will love me, and I will be as true to you as the North Pole.'

'Is that true to me?'

'You know what I mean.'

'But if I don't love you?'

'Yes, you do!'

'Do I?'

'I beg your pardon,' said Dolly. 'I didn't mean to say that. Of course a man shouldn't make sure of a thing.'

'Not in this case, Mr. Longstaff; because really I entertain no such feeling.'

'But you can if you please. Just let me tell you who I am.'

'That will do no good whatever, Mr. Longstaff.'

'Let me tell you at any rate. I have a very good income of my own as it is.'

'Money can have nothing to do with it.'

'But I want you to know that I can afford it. You might perhaps have thought that I wanted your money.'

'I will attribute nothing evil to you, Mr. Longstaff. Only it is quite out of the question that I should—respond as I suppose you wish me to; and therefore, pray, do not say anything further.'

She went to the head of the little steps but he interrupted her. 'You ought to hear me,' he said.

'I have heard you.'

'I can give you as good a position as any man without a title in England.'

'Mr. Longstaff, I rather fancy that wherever I may be I can make a position for myself. At any rate I shall not marry with the view of getting one. If my husband were an English Duke I should think myself nothing, unless I was something as Isabel Boncassen.'

When she said this she did not bethink herself that Lord Silverbridge would in the course of nature become an English Duke. But the allusion to an English Duke told intensely on Dolly, who had suspected that he had a noble rival. 'English Dukes aren't so easily got,' he said.

'Very likely not. I might have expressed my meaning better had I said an English Prince.'

'That's quite out of the question,' said Dolly. 'They can't do it,—by Act of Parliament,—except in a hugger-mugger* left-handed way, that wouldn't suit you at all.'

'Mr. Longstaff,—you must forgive me—if I say—that of all the gentlemen—I have ever met in this country or in any other—you are the—most obtuse.' This she brought out in little disjointed sentences, not with any hesitation, but in a way to make every word she uttered more clear to an intelligence which she did not believe to be bright. But in this belief she did some injustice to Dolly. He was quite alive to the disgrace of being called obtuse, and quick enough to avenge himself at the moment.

'Am I?' said he. 'How humble-minded you must be when you think me a fool because I have fallen in love with such a one as yourself.'

'I like you for that,' she replied laughing, 'and withdraw the epithet as not being applicable. Now we are quits and can forget and forgive;—only let there be the forgetting.'

'Never!' said Dolly, with his hand again on his heart.

'Then let it be a little dream of your youth,—that you once met a pretty American girl who was foolish enough to refuse all that you would have given her.'

'So pretty! So awfully pretty!' Thereupon she curtsied. 'I have seen all the handsome women in England going for the last ten years, and there has not been one who has made me think that it would be worth my while to get off my perch for her.'

'And now you would desert your perch for me!'

'I have already.'

'But you can get up again. Let it be all a dream. I know men like to have had such dreams. And in order that the dream may be pleasant the last word between us shall be kind. Such admiration from such a one as you is an honour,—and I will reckon it among my honours. But it can be no more than a dream.' Then she gave him her hand. 'It shall be so;—shall it not?' Then she paused. 'It must be so, Mr. Longstaff.'

'Must it?'

'That and no more. Now I wish to go down. Will you come with me? It will be better. Don't you think it is going to rain?'

Dolly looked up at the clouds. 'I wish it would with all my heart.'

'I know you are not so ill-natured. It would spoil all.'

'You have spoiled all.'

'No, no. I have spoiled nothing. It will only be a little dream about "that strange American girl, who really did make me feel queer for half an hour." Look at that. A great big drop —and the cloud has come over us as black as Erebus. Do hurry down.' He was leading the way. 'What shall we do for carriages to get us to the inn?'

'There's the summer-house.'

'It will hold about half of us. And think what it will be to be in there waiting till the rain shall be over! Everybody has been so good-humoured and now they will be so cross!'

The rain was falling in big heavy drops, slow and far between, but almost black with their size. And the heaviness of the cloud which had gathered over them made everything black.

'Will you have my arm?' said Silverbridge, who saw Miss Boncassen scudding along, with Dolly Longstaff following as fast as he could.

'Oh dear no. I have got to mind my dress. There;—I have gone right into a puddle. Oh dear!' So she ran on, and Silverbridge followed close behind her, leaving Dolly Longstaff in the distance.

It was not only Miss Boncassen who got her feet into a puddle and splashed her stockings. Many did so who were not obliged by their position to maintain good-humour under their misfortunes. The storm had come on with such un-expected quickness that there had been a general stampede to the summer-house. As Isabel had said, there was comfortable room for not more than half of them. In a few minutes people were crushed who never ought to be crushed. A Countess for whom treble-piled sofas were hardly good enough was seated

257

on the corner of a table till some younger and less gorgeous lady could be made to give way. And the Marchioness was declaring she was as wet through as though she had been dragged in a river. Mrs. Boncassen was so absolutely quelled as to have retired into the kitchen attached to the summer-house. Mr. Boncassen, with all his country's pluck and pride, was proving to a knot of gentlemen round him on the verandah, that such treachery in the weather was a thing unknown in his happier country. Miss Boncassen had to do her best to console the splashed ladies. 'Oh Mrs. Jones, is it not a pity! What can I do for you?'

'We must bear it, my dear. It often does rain, but why on this special day should it come down out of buckets?'

'I never was so wet in all my life,' said Dolly Longstaff, poking in his head.

'There's somebody smoking,' said the Countess angrily. There was a crowd of men smoking out on the verandah. 'I never knew anything so nasty,' the Countess continued, leaving it in doubt whether she spoke of the rain, or the smoke, or the party generally.

Damp gauzes, splashed stockings, trampled muslins, and features which have perhaps known something of rouge and certainly encountered something of rain may be made, but can only, by supreme high breeding, be made compatible with good-humour. To be moist, muddy, rumpled and smeared, when by the very nature of your position it is your duty to be clear-starched up to the pellucidity of crystal, to be spotless as the lily, to be crisp as the ivy-leaf, and as clear in complexion as a rose,—is it not, O gentle readers, felt to be a disgrace? It came to pass, therefore, that many were now very cross. Carriages were ordered under the idea that some improvement might be made at the inn which was nearly a mile distant. Very few, however, had their own carriages, and there was jockeying for the vehicles. In the midst of all this Silverbridge remained as near to Miss Boncassen as circumstances would admit. 'You are not waiting for me,' she said.

'Yes, I am. We might as well go up to town together.'

'Leave me with father and mother. Like the captain of a ship, I must be the last to leave the wreck.'

'But I'll be the gallant sailor of the day who always at the risk of his life sticks to the skipper to the last moment.'

'Not at all;—just because there will be no gallantry. But come and see us to-morrow and find out whether we have got through it alive.'

CHAPTER XXXIII

The Langham Hotel

'WHAT an abominable climate,' Mrs. Boncassen had said when they were quite alone at Maidenhead.

'My dear, you didn't think you were to bring New York along with you when you came here,' replied her husband.

'I wish I was going back to-morrow.'

'That's a foolish thing to say. People here are very kind, and you are seeing a great deal more of the world than you would ever see at home. I am having a very good time. What do you say, Bell?'

'I wish I could have kept my stockings clean.'

'But what about the young men?'

'Young men are pretty much the same everywhere, I guess. They never have their wits about them. They never mean what they say, because they don't understand the use of words. They are generally half impudent and half timid. When in love they do not at all understand what has befallen them. What they want they try to compass as a cow does when it stands stretching out its head towards a stack of hay which it cannot reach. Indeed there is no such thing as a young man, for a man is not really a man till he is middle-aged. But take them at their worst they are a deal too good for us, for they become men some day, whereas we must only be women to the end.'

'My word, Bella!' exclaimed the mother.

'You have managed to be tolerably heavy upon God's creatures, taking them in a lump,' said the father. 'Boys, girls, and cows! Something has gone wrong with you besides the rain.'

'Nothing on earth, sir,—except the boredom.'

'Some young man has been talking to you, Bella.'

'One or two, mother; and I got to be thinking if any one of them should ask me to marry him, and if moved by some evil destiny I were to take him, whether I should murder him, or myself, or run away with one of the others.'

'Couldn't you bear with him till, according to your own theory, he would grow out of his folly?' said the father.

'Being a woman,—no. The present moment is always everything to me. When that horrid old harridan halloaed out that somebody was smoking, I thought I should have died. It was very bad just then.'

'Awful!' said Mrs. Boncassen, shaking her head.

'I didn't seem to feel it much,' said the father. 'One doesn't look to have everything just what one wants always. If I did I should go nowhere;—but my total life would be less enjoyable. If ever you do get married, Bell, you should remember that.'

'I mean to get married some day, so that I shouldn't be made love to any longer.'

'I hope it will have that effect,' said the father.

'Mr. Boncassen!' ejaculated the mother.

'What I say is true. I hope it will have that effect. It had with you, my dear.'

'I don't know that people didn't think of me as much as of anybody else, even though I was married.'

'Then, my dear, I never knew it.'

Miss Boncassen, though she had behaved serenely and with good temper during the process of Dolly's proposal, had not liked it. She had a very high opinion of herself, and was certainly entitled to have it by the undisguised admiration of all that came near her. She was not more indifferent to the admiration of young men than are other young ladies. But she was not proud of the admiration of Dolly Longstaff. She was here among strangers whose ways were unknown to her, whose rank and standing in the world were vague to her, and wonderful in their dimness. She knew that she was associating with men very different from those at home where young men were supposed to be under the necessity of earning their bread. At New York she would dance, as she had said, with bank clerks. She was not prepared to admit that a young London lord was better than a New York bank clerk. Judging the men on their own individual merits she might find the bank clerk to be the better of the two. But a certain sweetness of the aroma of rank was beginning to permeate her republican senses. The softness of a life in which no occupation was compulsory had its charms for her. Though she had complained of the insufficient intelligence of young men she was alive to the delight of having nothings said to her pleasantly. All this had affected her so strongly that she had almost felt that a life among these English luxuries would be a pleasant life. Like most Americans who do not as yet know the country, she had come with an inward feeling that as an American and a republican she might probably be despised.

There is not uncommonly a savageness of self-assertion about Americans which arises from a too great anxiety to be admitted to fellowship with Britons. She had felt this, and conscious of reputation already made by herself in the social life of New York, she had half trusted that she would be well received in London, and had half convinced herself that she would be rejected. She had not been rejected. She must have become quite aware of that. She had dropped very quickly the idea that she would be scorned. Ignorant as she had been of English life, she perceived that she had at once become popular. And this had been so in spite of her mother's homeliness and her father's awkwardness. By herself and by her own gifts she had done it. She had found out concerning herself that she had that which would commend her to other society than that of the Fifth Avenue. Those lords of whom she had heard were as plenty with her as blackberries. Young Lord Silverbridge, of whom she was told that of all the young lords of the day he stood first in rank and wealth, was peculiarly her friend. Her brain was firmer than that of most girls, but even her brain was a little turned. She never told herself that it would be well for her to become the wife of such a one. In her more thoughtful moments she told herself that it would not be well. But still the allurement was strong upon her. Park Lane was sweeter than the Fifth Avenue. Lord Silverbridge was nicer than the bank clerk.

But Dolly Longstaff was not. She would certainly prefer

the bank clerk to Dolly Longstaff. And yet Dolly Longstaff was the one among her English admirers who had come forward and spoken out. She did not desire that any one should come forward and speak out. But it was an annoyance to her that this special man should have done so.

The waiter at the Langham understood American ways perfectly, and when a young man called between three and four o'clock, asking for Mrs. Boncassen, said that Miss Boncassen was at home. The young man took off his hat, brushed up his hair, and followed the waiter up to the sitting-room. The door was opened and the young man was announced. 'Mr. Longstaff.'

Miss Boncassen was rather disgusted. She had had enough of this English lover. Why should he have come after what had occurred yesterday? He ought to have felt that he was absolved from the necessity of making personal inquiries. 'I am glad to see that you got home safe,' she said as she gave him her hand.

'And you too, I hope?'

'Well;—so, so; with my clothes a good deal damaged and my temper rather worse.'

'I am so sorry.'

'It should not rain on such days. Mother has gone to church.'

'Oh;—indeed. I like going to church myself sometimes.'

'Do you now?'

'I know what would make me like to go to church.'

'And father is at the Athenæum. He goes there to do a little light reading in the library on Sunday afternoon.'

'I shall never forget yesterday, Miss Boncassen.'

'You wouldn't if your clothes had been spoilt as mine were.'

'Money will repair that.'

'Well; yes; but when I've had a petticoat flounced particularly to order I don't like to see it ill-treated. There are emotions of the heart which money can't touch.'

'Just so;—emotions of the heart! That's the very phrase.'

She was determined if possible to prevent a repetition of the scene which had taken place up at Mrs. de Bever's temple. 'All my emotions are about my dress.'

'All?'

'Well; yes; all. I guess I don't care much for eating and drinking.' In saying this she actually contrived to produce something of a nasal twang.

'Eating and drinking!' said Dolly. 'Of course they are necessities;—and so are clothes.'

'But new things are such ducks!'*

'Trowsers may be,' said Dolly.

Then she took a prolonged gaze at him, wondering whether he was or was not such a fool as he looked. 'How funny you are,' she said.

'A man does not generally feel funny after going through what I suffered yesterday, Miss Boncassen.'

'Would you mind ringing the bell?'

'Must it be done quite at once?'

'Quite,—quite,' she said. 'I can do it myself for the matter of that.' And she rang the bell somewhat violently. Dolly sank back again into his seat, remarking in his usual apathetic way that he had intended to obey her behest but had not understood that she was in so great a hurry. 'I am always in a hurry,' she said. 'I like things to be done—sharp.' And she hit the table a crack. 'Please bring me some iced water,' this of course was addressed to the waiter. 'And a glass for Mr. Longstaff.'

'None for me, thank you.'

'Perhaps you'd like soda and brandy?'

'Oh dear no;—nothing of the kind. But I am so much obliged to you all the same.' As the water-bottle was in fact standing in the room, and as the waiter had only to hand the glass, all this created but little obstacle. Still it had its effect, and Dolly, when the man had retired, felt that there was a difficulty in proceeding. 'I have called to-day——' he began.

'That has been so kind of you. But mother has gone to church.'

'I am very glad that she has gone to church, because I wish to——'

'Oh laws! There's a horse has tumbled down in the street. I heard it.'

'He has got up again,' said Dolly, looking leisurely out of the window. 'But as I was saying——'

'I don't think that the water we Americans drink can be good. It makes the women become ugly so young.'

'You will never become ugly.'

She got up and curtsied to him, and then, still standing, made him a speech. 'Mr. Longstaff, it would be absurd of me to pretend not to understand what you mean. But I won't have any more of it. Whether you are making fun of me, or whether you are in earnest, it is just the same.'

'Making fun of you!'

'It does not signify. I don't care which it is. But I won't have it. There!'

'A gentleman should be allowed to express his feelings and to explain his position.'

'You have expressed and explained more than enough, and I won't have any more. If you will sit down and talk about something else, or else go away, there shall be an end of it;— but if you go on, I will ring the bell again. What can a man gain by going on when a girl has spoken as I have done?' They were both at this time standing up, and he was now as angry as she was.

'I've paid you the greatest compliment a man can pay a woman,' he began.

'Very well. If I remember rightly I thanked you for it yesterday. If you wish it, I will thank you again to-day. But it is a compliment which becomes very much the reverse if it be repeated too often. You are sharp enough to understand that I have done everything in my power to save us both from this trouble.'

'What makes you so fierce, Miss Boncassen?'

'What makes you so foolish?'

'I suppose it must be something peculiar to American ladies.'

'Just that;—something peculiar to American ladies. They don't like—well; I don't want to say anything more that can be called fierce.'

At this moment the door was again opened and Lord Silverbridge was announced. 'Halloa, Dolly, are you here?'

'It seems that I am.'

'And I am here too,' said Miss Boncassen, smiling her prettiest.

'None the worse for yesterday's troubles, I hope?'

'A good deal the worse. I have been explaining all that to Mr. Longstaff, who has been quite sympathetic with me about my things.'

'A terrible pity that shower,' said Dolly.

'For you,' said Silverbridge, 'because, if I remember right, Miss Boncassen was walking with you;—but I was rather glad of it.'

'Lord Silverbridge!'

'I regarded it as a direct interposition of Providence, because you would not dance with me.'

'Any news to-day, Silverbridge?' asked Dolly.

'Nothing particular. They say that Coalheaver can't run for the Leger.'

'What's the matter?' asked Dolly vigorously.

'Broke down at Ascot. But I daresay it's a lie.'

'Sure to be a lie,' said Dolly. 'What do you think of Madame Scholzdam,*Miss Boncassen?'

'I am not a good judge.'

'Never heard anything equal to it yet in this world,' said Dolly. 'I wonder whether that's true about Coalheaver?'

'Tifto says so.'

'Which at the present moment,' asked Miss Boncassen, 'is the greater favourite with the public, Madame Scholzdam or Coalheaver?'

'Coalheaver is a horse, Miss Boncassen.'

'Oh,—a horse!'

'Perhaps I ought to say a colt.'

'Oh,—a colt.'

'Do you suppose, Dolly, that Miss Boncassen doesn't know all that?' asked Silverbridge.

'He supposes that my American ferocity has never been sufficiently softened for the reception of polite erudition.'

'You two have been quarrelling, I fear.'

'I never quarrel with a woman,' said Dolly.

'Nor with a man in my presence, I hope,' said Miss Boncassen.

'Somebody does seem to have got out of bed at the wrong side,' said Silverbridge.

'I did,' said Miss Boncassen. 'I got out of bed at the wrong side. I am cross. I can't get over the spoiling of my flounces. I think you had better both go away and leave me. If I could walk about the room for half an hour and stamp my feet, I should get better.' Silverbridge thought that as he had come last, he certainly ought to be left last. Miss Boncassen felt that, at any rate, Mr. Longstaff should go. Dolly felt that his manhood required him to remain. After what had taken place he was not going to leave the field vacant for another. Therefore he made no effort to move.

'That seems rather hard upon me,' said Silverbridge. 'You told me to come.'

'I told you to come and ask after us all. You have come and asked after us, and have been informed that we are very bad. What more can I say? You accuse me of getting out of bed the wrong side, and I own that I did.'

'I meant to say that Dolly Longstaff had done so.'

'And I say it was Silverbridge,' said Dolly.

'We aren't very agreeable together, are we? Upon my word I think you'd better both go.' Silverbridge immediately got up from his chair; upon which Dolly also moved.

'What the mischief is up?' asked Silverbridge, when they were under the porch together.

'The truth is, you never can tell what you are to do with those American girls.'

'I suppose you have been making up to her.'

'Nothing in earnest. She seemed to me to like admiration; so I told her I admired her.'

'What did she say then?'

'Upon my word, you seem to be very great at cross-examining. Perhaps you had better go back and ask her.'

'I will, next time I see her.' Then he stepped into his cab, and in a loud voice ordered the man to drive him to the Zoo. But when he had gone a little way up Portland Place, he stopped the driver and desired he might be taken back again to the hotel. As he left the vehicle he looked round for Dolly, but Dolly had certainly gone. Then he told the waiter to take his card to Miss Boncassen, and explain that he had something to say which he had forgotten.

'So you have come back again?' said Miss Boncassen, laughing.

'Of course I have. You didn't suppose I was going to let that fellow get the better of me. Why should I be turned out because he had made an ass of himself!'

'Who said he made an ass of himself?'

'But he had; hadn't he?'

'No;—by no means,' said she after a little pause.

'Tell me what he had been saying.'

'Indeed I shall do nothing of the kind. If I told you all he said, then I should have to tell the next man all that you may say. Would that be fair?'

'I should not mind,' said Silverbridge.

'I dare say not, because you have nothing particular to say. But the principle is the same. Lawyers and doctors and parsons talk of privileged communications. Why should not a young lady have her privileged communications?'

'But I have something particular to say.'

'I hope not.'

'Why should you hope not?'

'I hate having things said particularly. Nobody likes conversation so well as I do; but it should never be particular.'

'I was going to tell you that I came back to London yesterday in the same carriage with old Lady Clanfiddle, and that she swore that no consideration on earth would ever induce her to go to Maidenhead again.'

'That isn't particular.'

'She went on to say;—you won't tell of me; will you?'

'It shall all be privileged.'

'She went on to say that Americans couldn't be expected to understand English manners.'

'Perhaps they may be all the better for that.'

'Then I spoke up. I swore I was awfully in love with you.'

'You didn't.'

'I did;—that you were, out and away, the finest girl I ever saw in my life. Of course you understand that her two daughters were there. And that as for manners,—unless the rain could be attributed to American manners,—I did not think anything had gone wrong.'

'What about the smoking?'

'I told her they were all Englishmen, and that if she had been giving the party herself they would have smoked just as much. You must understand that she never does give any parties.'

'How could you be so ill-natured?'

'There was ever so much more of it. And it ended in her telling me that I was a schoolboy. I found out the cause of it all. A great spout of rain had come upon her daughter's hat, and that had produced a most melancholy catastrophe.'

'I would have given her mine willingly.'

'An American hat;—to be worn by Lady Violet Clanfiddle!'

'It came from Paris last week, sir.'

'But must have been contaminated by American contact.'

'Now, Lord Silverbridge,' said she, getting up, 'if I had a stick I'd whip you.'

'It was such fun.'

'And you come here and tell it all to me?'

'Of course I do. It was a deal too good to keep it to myself. "American manners!"' As he said this he almost succeeded in looking like Lady Clanfiddle.

At that moment Mr. Boncassen entered the room, and was

immediately appealed to by his daughter. 'Father, you must turn Lord Silverbridge out of the room.'

'Dear me! If I must,—of course I must. But why?'

'He is saying everything horrid he can about Americans.'

After this they settled down for a few minutes to general conversation, and then Lord Silverbridge again took his leave. When he was gone Isabel Boncassen almost regretted that the 'something particular' which he had threatened to say had not been less comic in its nature.

CHAPTER XXXIV

Lord Popplecourt

WHEN the reader was told that Lord Popplecourt had found Lady Cantrip very agreeable it is to be hoped that the reader was disgusted. Lord Popplecourt would certainly not have given a second thought to Lady Cantrip unless he had been specially flattered. And why should such a man have been flattered by a woman who was in all respects his superior? The reader will understand. It had been settled by the wisdom of the elders that it would be a good thing that Lord Popplecourt should marry Lady Mary Palliser.

The mutual assent which leads to marriage should no doubt be spontaneous. Who does not feel that? Young love should speak from its first doubtful unconscious spark,—a spark which any breath of air may quench or cherish,—till it becomes a flame which nothing can satisfy but the union of the two lovers. No one should be told to love, or bidden to marry, this man or that woman. The theory of this is plain to us all, and till we have sons or daughters whom we feel imperatively obliged to control, the theory is unassailable. But the duty is so imperative! The Duke had taught himself to believe that as his wife would have been thrown away on the world had she been allowed to marry Burgo Fitzgerald, so would his daughter be thrown away were she allowed to marry Mr. Tregear. Therefore the theory of spontaneous love must in this case be set aside. Therefore the spark,—would that it had been no more!—must be quenched. Therefore there could be no union of two lovers;—but simply a prudent and perhaps splendid marriage.

Lord Popplecourt was a man in possession of a large estate which was unencumbered. His rank in the peerage was not high; but his barony was of an old date,—and, if things went well with him, something higher in rank might be open to him. He had good looks of that sort which recommend themselves to pastors and masters, to elders and betters. He had regular features. He looked as though he were steady. He was not impatient nor rollicking. Silverbridge was also good-looking;—but his good looks were such as would give a pang to the hearts of anxious mothers of daughters. Tregear was the handsomest man of the three;—but then he looked as though he had no betters and did not care for his elders. Lord Popplecourt, though a very young man, had once stammered through half-a-dozen words in the House of Lords, and had been known to dine with the 'Benevolent Funds.' Lord Silverbridge had declared him to be a fool. No one thought him to be bright. But in the eyes of the Duke,—and of Lady Cantrip, —he had his good qualities.

But the work was very disagreeable. It was the more hard upon Lady Cantrip because she did not believe in it. If it could be done, it would be expedient. But she felt very strongly that it could not be done. No doubt that Lady Glencora had been turned from her evil destiny; but Lady Glencora had been younger than her daughter was now, and possessed of less character. Nor was Lady Cantrip blind to the difference between a poor man with a bad character, such as that Burgo had been, and a poor man with a good character, such as was Tregear. Nevertheless she undertook to aid the work, and condescended to pretend to be so interested in the portrait of some common ancestor as to persuade the young man to have it photographed, in order that the bringing down of the photograph might lead to something.

He took the photograph, and Lady Cantrip said very much to him about his grandmother, who was the old lady in question. 'She could,' she said, 'just remember the features of the dear old woman.' She was not habitually a hypocrite, and she hated herself for what she was doing, and yet her object was simply good,—to bring together two young people who might advantageously marry each other. The mere talking about the old woman would be of no service. She longed to bring out the offer plainly, and say, 'There is Lady Mary Palliser. Don't you think she'd make a good wife for you?' But she could not, as yet, bring herself to be so indelicately plain. 'You haven't seen the Duke since?' she asked.

'He spoke to me only yesterday in the House. I like the Duke.'

'If I may be allowed to say so, it would be for your advantage that he should like you;—that is, if you mean to take a part in politics.'

'I suppose I shall,' said Popplecourt. 'There isn't much else to do.'

'You don't go to races?' He shook his head. 'I am glad of that,' said Lady Cantrip. 'Nothing is so bad as the turf. I fear Lord Silverbridge is devoting himself to the turf.'

'I don't think it can be good for any man to have much to do with Major Tifto. I suppose Silverbridge knows what he's about.'

Here was an opportunity which might have been used. It would have been so easy for her to glide from the imperfections of the brother to the perfections of the sister. But she could not bring herself to do it quite at once. She approached the matter however as nearly as she could without making her grand proposition. She shook her head sadly in reference to Silverbridge, and then spoke of the Duke. 'His father is so anxious about him.'

'I dare say.'

'I don't know any man who is more painfully anxious about his children. He feels the responsibility so much since his wife's death. There is Lady Mary.'

'She's all right, I should say.'

'All right! oh yes. But when a girl is possessed of so many things,—rank, beauty, intelligence, large fortune,——'

'Will Lady Mary have much?'

'A large portion of her mother's money, I should say. When all these things are joined together, a father of course feels most anxious as to their disposal.'

'I suppose she is clever.'

'Very clever,' said Lady Cantrip.

'I think a girl may be too clever you know,' said Lord Popplecourt.

'Perhaps she may. But I know more who are too foolish. I am so much obliged to you for the photograph.'

'Don't mention it.'

'I really did not mean that you should send a man down.'

On that occasion the two young people did not see each other. Lady Mary did not come down, and Lady Cantrip lacked the courage to send for her. As it was, might it not be possible that the young man should be induced to make himself agreeable to the young lady without any further explanation? But love-making between young people cannot well take place unless they be brought together. There was a difficulty in bringing them together at Richmond. The Duke had indeed spoken of meeting Lord Popplecourt at dinner there;— but this was to have followed the proposition which Lady Cantrip should make to him. She could not yet make the proposition, and therefore she hardly knew how to arrange the dinner. She was obliged at last to let the wished-for lover go away without arranging anything. When the Duke should have settled his autumn plans, then an attempt must be made to induce Lord Popplecourt to travel in the same direction.

That evening Lady Cantrip said a few words to Mary respecting the proposed suitor. 'There is nothing I have such a horror of as gambling,' she said.

'It is dreadful.'

'I am very glad to think that Nidderdale does not do anything of that sort.' It was perhaps on the cards that Nidderdale should do things of which she knew nothing. 'I hope Silverbridge does not bet.'

'I don't think he does.'

'There's Lord Popplecourt,—quite a young man,—with everything at his own disposal, and a very large estate. Think of the evil he might do if he were given that way.'

'Does he gamble?'

'Not at all. It must be such a comfort to his mother!'

'He looks to me as though he never would do anything,' said Lady Mary. Then the subject was dropped.

It was a week after this, towards the end of July, that the Duke wrote a line to Lady Cantrip, apologizing for what he had done, but explaining that he had asked Lord Popplecourt to dine at The Horns on a certain Sunday. He had, he said, been assured by Lord Cantrip that such an arrangement would be quite convenient. It was clear from his letter that he was much in earnest. Of course there was no reason why the dinner should not be eaten. Only the speciality of the invitation to Lord Popplecourt must not be so glaring that he himself should be struck by the strangeness of it. There must be a little party made up. Lord Nidderdale and his wife were therefore bidden to come down, and Silverbridge, who at first consented rather unwillingly,—and Lady Mabel Grex, as to whom the Duke made a special request that she might be asked. This last invitation was sent express from Lady Mary, and included Miss Cass. So the party was made up. The careful reader will perceive that there were to be ten of them.

'Isn't it odd papa wanting to have Lady Mabel?' Mary said to Lady Cantrip.

'Does he not know her, my dear?'

'He hardly ever spoke to her. I'll tell you what; I expect Silverbridge is going to marry her.'

'Why shouldn't he?'

'I don't know why he shouldn't. She is very beautiful, and very clever. But if so, papa must know all about it. It does seem so odd that papa of all people should turn match-maker, or even that he should think of it.'

'So much is thrown upon him now,' said Lady Cantrip

'Poor papa!' Then she remembered herself, and spoke with a little start. 'Of course I am not thinking of myself. Arranging a marriage is very different from preventing any one from marrying.'

'Whatever he may think to be his duty he will be sure to do it,' said the elder lady very solemnly.

Lady Mabel was surprised by the invitation, but she was

not slow to accept it. 'Papa will be here and will be so glad to meet you,' Lady Mary had said. Why should the Duke of Omnium wish to meet her? 'Silverbridge will be here too,' Mary had gone on to say. 'It is just a family party. Papa, you know, is not going anywhere; nor am I.' By all this Lady Mabel's thoughts were much stirred, and her bosom somewhat moved. And Silverbridge also was moved by it. Of course he could not but remember that he had pledged himself to his father to ask Lady Mabel to be his wife. He had faltered since. She had been, he thought, unkind to him, or at any rate indifferent. He had surely said enough to her to make her know what he meant; and yet she had taken no trouble to meet him half way. And then Isabel Boncassen had intervened. Now he was asked to dinner in a most unusual manner!

Of all the guests invited Lord Popplecourt was perhaps the least disturbed. He was quite alive to the honour of being noticed by the Duke of Omnium, and alive also to the flattering courtesy shown to him by Lady Cantrip. But justice would not be done him unless it were acknowledged that he had as yet flattered himself with no hopes in regard to Lady Mary Palliser. He, when he prepared himself for his journey down to Richmond, thought much more of the Duke than of the Duke's daughter.

'Oh yes, I can drive you down if you like that kind of thing,' Silverbridge said to him on the Saturday evening.

'And bring me back?'

'If you will come when I am coming. I hate waiting for a fellow.'

'Suppose we leave at half-past ten.'

'I won't fix any time; but if we can't make it suit there'll be the governor's carriage.'

'Will the Duke go down in his carriage?'

'I suppose so. It's quicker and less trouble than the railway.' Then Lord Popplecourt reflected that he would certainly come back with the Duke if he could so manage it, and there floated before his eyes visions of under-secretaryships, all of which might owe their origin to this proposed drive up from Richmond.

At six o'clock on the Sunday evening Silverbridge called for Lord Popplecourt. 'Upon my word,' said he, 'I didn't ever expect to see you in my cab.'

'Why not me especially?'

'Because you're not one of our lot.'

'You'd sooner have Tifto, I dare say.'

'No, I wouldn't. Tifto is not at all a pleasant companion, though he understands horses. You're going in for heavy politics, I suppose.'

'Not particularly heavy.'

'If not, why on earth does my governor take you up? You won't mind my smoking, I dare say.' After this there was no conversation between them.

CHAPTER XXXV

'*Don't you think——?*'

IT was pretty to see the Duke's reception of Lady Mabel. 'I knew your mother many years ago,' he said, 'when I was young myself. Her mother and my mother were first cousins and dear friends.' He held her hand as he spoke and looked at her as though he meant to love her. Lady Mabel saw that it was so. Could it be possible that the Duke had heard anything;—that he should wish to receive her? She had told herself and had told Miss Casseway that though she had spared Silverbridge, yet she knew that she would make him a good wife. If the Duke thought so also, then surely she need not doubt.

'I knew we were cousins,' she said, 'and have been so proud of the connection! Lord Silverbridge does come and see us sometimes.'

Soon after that Silverbridge and Popplecourt came in. If the story of the old woman in the portrait may be taken as evidence of a family connexion between Lady Cantrip and

Lord Popplecourt, everybody there was more or less connected with everybody else. Nidderdale had been a first cousin of Lady Glencora, and he had married a daughter of Lady Cantrip. They were manifestly a family party,—thanks to the old woman in the picture.

It is a point of conscience among the—perhaps not ten thousand,* but say one thousand of bluest blood,—that everybody should know who everybody is. Our Duke, though he had not given his mind much to the pursuit, had nevertheless learned his lesson. It is a knowledge which the possession of the blue blood itself produces. There are countries with bluer blood than our own in which to be without such knowledge is a crime.

When the old lady in the portrait had been discussed, Popplecourt was close to Lady Mary. They two had no idea why such vicinity had been planned. The Duke knew, of course, and Lady Cantrip. Lady Cantrip had whispered to her daughter that such a marriage would be suitable, and the daughter had hinted it to her husband. Lord Cantrip of course was not in the dark. Lady Mabel had expressed a hint on the matter to Miss Cass, who had not repudiated it. Even Silverbridge had suggested to himself that something of the kind might be in the wind, thinking that, if so, none of them knew much about his sister Mary. But Popplecourt himself was divinely innocent. His ideas of marriage had as yet gone no farther than a conviction that girls generally were things which would be pressed on him, and against which he must arm himself with some shield. Marriage would have to come, no doubt; but not the less was it his duty to live as though it were a pit towards which he would be tempted by female allurements. But that a net should be spread over him here he was much too humble-minded to imagine.

'Very hot,' he said to Lady Mary.

'We found it warm in church to-day.'

'I dare say. I came down here with your brother in his hansom cab. What a very odd thing to have a hansom cab!'

'I should like one.'

278

'Should you indeed?'

'Particularly if I could drive it myself. Silverbridge does, at night, when he thinks people won't see him.'

'Drive the cab in the streets! What does he do with his man?'

'Puts him inside. He was out once without the man and took up a fare,—an old woman, he said. And when she was going to pay him he touched his hat and said he never took money from ladies.'

'Do you believe that?'

'Oh yes. I call that good fun, because it did no harm. He had his lark. The lady was taken where she wanted to go, and she saved her money.'

'Suppose he had upset her,' said Lord Popplecourt, looking as an old philosopher might have looked when he had found some clenching answer to another philosopher's argument.

'The real cabman might have upset her worse,' said Lady Mary.

'Don't you feel it odd that we should meet here?' said Lord Silverbridge to his neighbour, Lady Mabel.

'Anything unexpected is odd,' said Lady Mabel. It seemed to her to be very odd,—unless certain people had made up their minds as to the expediency of a certain event.

'That is what you call logic;—isn't it? Anything unexpected is odd!'

'Lord Silverbridge, I won't be laughed at. You have been at Oxford and ought to know what logic is.'

'That at any rate is ill-natured,' he replied, turning very red in the face.

'You don't think I meant it. Oh, Lord Silverbridge, say that you don't think I meant it. You cannot think I would willingly wound you. Indeed, indeed, I was not thinking.' It had in truth been an accident. She could not speak aloud because they were closely surrounded by others, but she looked up in his face to see whether he were angry with her. 'Say that you do not think I meant it.'

'I do not think you meant it.'

'I would not say a word to hurt you,—oh, for more than I can tell you.'

'It is all bosh, of course,' he said laughing; 'but I do not like to hear the old place named. I have always made a fool of myself. Some men do it and don't care about it. But I do it, and yet it makes me miserable.'

'If that be so you will soon give over making—what you call a fool of yourself. For myself I like the idea of wild oats. I look upon them like measles. Only you should have a doctor ready when the disease shows itself.'

'What sort of a doctor ought I to have?'

'Ah;—you must find out that yourself. That sort of feeling which makes you feel miserable;—that is a doctor itself.'

'Or a wife?'

'Or a wife,—if you can find a good one. There are wives, you know, who aggravate the disease. If I had a fast husband I should make him faster by being fast myself. There is nothing I envy so much as the power of doing half-mad things.'

'Women can do that too.'

'But they go to the dogs. We are dreadfully restricted. If you like champagne you can have a bucketful. I am obliged to pretend that I only want a very little. You can bet thousands. I must confine myself to gloves. You can flirt with any woman you please. I must wait till somebody comes,—and put up with it if nobody does come.'

'Plenty come, no doubt.'

'But I want to pick and choose. A man turns the girls over one after another as one does the papers when one is fitting up a room, or rolls them out as one rolls out the carpets. A very careful young man like Lord Popplecourt might reject a young woman because her hair didn't suit the colour of his furniture.'

'I don't think that I shall choose my wife as I would papers and carpets.'

The Duke, who sat between Lady Cantrip and her daughter did his best to make himself agreeable. The conversation ha~

been semi-political,—political to the usual feminine extent, and had consisted chiefly of sarcasms from Lady Cantrip against Sir Timothy Beeswax. 'That England should put up with such a man,' Lady Cantrip had said, 'is to me shocking! There used to be a feeling in favour of gentlemen.' To this the Duke had responded by asserting that Sir Timothy had displayed great aptitude for parliamentary life, and knew the House of Commons better than most men. He said nothing against his foe, and very much in his foe's praise. But Lady Cantrip perceived that she had succeeded in pleasing him.

When the ladies were gone the politics became more serious. 'That unfortunate quarrel*is to go on the same as ever, I suppose,' said the Duke, addressing himself to the two young men who had seats in the House of Commons. They were both on the Conservative side in politics. The three peers present were all Liberals.

'Till next session, I think, sir,' said Silverbridge.

'Sir Timothy, though he did lose his temper, has managed it well,' said Lord Cantrip.

'Phineas Finn lost his temper worse than Sir Timothy,' said Lord Nidderdale.

'But yet I think he had the feeling of the House with him,' said the Duke. 'I happened to be present in the gallery at the time.'

'Yes,' said Nidderdale, 'because he "owned up." The fact is if you "own up" in a genial sort of way the House will forgive anything. If I were to murder my grandmother, and when questioned about it were to acknowledge that I had done it——' Then Lord Nidderdale stood up and made his speech as he might have made it in the House of Commons. ' "I regret to say, sir, that the old woman did get in my way when I was in a passion. Unfortunately I had a heavy stick in my hand and I did strike her over the head. Nobody can regret it so much as I do! Nobody can feel so acutely the position in which I am placed! I have sat in this House for many years, and many gentlemen know me well. I think, Sir, that they will acknowledge that I am a man not deficient in filial piety or general humanity. Sir, I am sorry for what I did in a moment of heat. I have now spoken the truth, and I shall leave myself in the hands of the House." My belief is I should get such a round of applause as I certainly shall never achieve in any other way. It is not only that a popular man may do it, —like Phineas Finn,—but the most unpopular man in the House may make himself liked by owning freely that he has done something that he ought to be ashamed of.' Nidderdale's unwonted eloquence was received in good part by the assembled legislators.

'Taking it altogether,' said the Duke, 'I know of no assembly in any country in which good-humour prevails so generally, in which the members behave to each other so well, in which rules are so universally followed, or in which the president is so thoroughly sustained by the feeling of the members.'

'I hear men say that it isn't quite what it used to be,' said Silverbridge.

'Nothing will ever be quite what it used to be.'

'Changes for the worse, I mean. Men are doing all kinds of things, just because the rules of the House allow them.'

'If they be within rule,' said the Duke, 'I don't know who is to blame them. In my time, if any man stretched a rule too far the House would not put up with it.'

'That's just it,' said Nidderdale. 'The House puts up with anything now. There is a great deal of good feeling no doubt, but there's no earnestness about anything. I think you are more earnest than we; but then you are such horrid bores. And each earnest man is in earnest about something that nobody else cares for.'

When they were again in the drawing-room, Lord Popplecourt was seated next to Lady Mary. 'Where are you going this autumn?' he asked.

'I don't know in the least. Papa said something about going abroad.'

'You won't be at Custins?' Custins was Lord Cantrip's country seat in Dorsetshire.

282

'I know nothing about myself as yet. But I don't think I shall go anywhere unless papa goes too.'

'Lady Cantrip has asked me to be at Custins in the middle of October. They say it is about the best pheasant-shooting in England.'

'Do you shoot much?'

'A great deal. I shall be in Scotland on the Twelfth.* I and Reginald Dobbs have a place together. I shall get to my own partridges on the 1st of September. I always manage that. Popplecourt is in Suffolk, and I don't think any man in England can beat me for partridges.'

'What do you do with all you slay?'

'Leadenhall Market.* I make it pay,—or very nearly. Then I shall run back to Scotland for the end of the stalking, and I can easily manage to be at Custins by the middle of October. I never touch my own pheasants till November.'

'Why are you so abstemious?'

'The birds are heavier and it answers better. But if I thought you would be at Custins it would be much nicer.' Lady Mary again told him that as yet she knew nothing of her father's autumn movements.

But at the same time the Duke was arranging his autumn movements, or at any rate those of his daughter. Lady Cantrip had told him that the desirable son-in-law had promised to go to Custins, and suggested that he and Mary should also be there. In his daughter's name he promised, but he would not bind himself. Would it not be better that he should be absent? Now that the doing of this thing was brought nearer to him so that he could see and feel its details, he was disgusted by it. And yet it had answered so well with his wife!

'Is Lord Popplecourt intimate here?' Lady Mabel asked her friend, Lord Silverbridge.

'I don't know. I am not.'

'Lady Cantrip seems to think a great deal about him.'

'I dare say. I don't.'

'Your father seems to like him.'

'That's possible too. They're going back to London together in the governor's carriage. My father will talk high politics all the way, and Popplecourt will agree with everything.'

'He isn't intended to—to——? You know what I mean.'

'I can't say that I do.'

'To cut out poor Frank.'

'It's quite possible.'

'Poor Frank!'

'You had a great deal better say poor Popplecourt!—or poor governor, or poor Lady Cantrip.'

'But a hundred countesses can't make your sister marry a man she doesn't like.'

'Just that. They don't go the right way about it.'

'What would you do?'

'Leave her alone. Let her find out gradually that what she wants can't be done.'

'And so linger on for years,' said Lady Mabel reproachfully.

'I say nothing about that. The man is my friend.'

'And you ought to be proud of him.'

'I never knew anybody yet that was proud of his friends. I like him well enough, but I can quite understand that the governor should object.'

'Yes, we all know that,' said she sadly.

'What would your father say if you wanted to marry someone who hadn't a shilling?'

'I should object myself,—without waiting for my father. But then,—neither have I a shilling. If I had money, do you think I wouldn't like to give it to the man I loved?'

'But this is a case of giving somebody else's money. They won't make her give it up by bringing such a young ass as that down here. If my father has persistency enough to let her cry her eyes out, he'll succeed.'

'And break her heart. Could you do that?'

'Certainly not. But then I'm soft. I can't refuse.'

'Can't you?'

'Not if the person who asks me is in my good books. You try me.'

'What shall I ask for?'

'Anything.'

'Give me that ring off your finger,' she said. He at once took it off his hand. 'Of course you know I am in joke. You don't imagine that I would take it from you?' He still held it towards her. 'Lord Silverbridge, I expect that with you I may say a foolish word without being brought to sorrow by it. I know that that ring belonged to your great-uncle,—and to fifty Pallisers before.'

'What would it matter?'

'And it would be wholly useless to me, as I could not wear it.'

'Of course it would be too big,' said he, replacing the ring on his own finger. 'But when I talk of anyone being in my good books, I don't mean a thing like that. Don't you know there is nobody on earth I——' there he paused and blushed, and she sat motionless, looking at him expecting, with her colour too somewhat raised,—'whom I like so well as I do you?' It was a lame conclusion. She felt it to be lame. But as regarded him, the lameness at the moment had come from a timidity which forbade him to say the word 'love' even though he had meant to say it.

She recovered herself instantly. 'I do believe it,' she said. 'I do think that we are real friends.'

'Would you not take a ring from a—real friend?'

'Not that ring;—nor a ring at all after I had asked for it in joke. You understand it all. But to go back to what we were talking about,—if you can do anything for Frank, pray do. You know it will break her heart. A man of course bears it better, but he does not perhaps suffer the less. It is all his life to him. He can do nothing while this is going on. Are you not true enough to your friendship to exert yourself for him?' Silverbridge put his hand up and rubbed his head as though he were vexed. 'Your aid would turn everything in his favour.'

285

'You do not know my father.'

'Is he so inexorable?'

'It is not that, Mabel. But he is so unhappy. I cannot add to his unhappiness by taking part against him.'

In another part of the room Lady Cantrip was busy with Lord Popplecourt. She had talked about pheasants, and had talked about grouse, had talked about moving the address in the House of Lords in some coming Session, and the great value of political alliances early in life, till the young peer began to think that Lady Cantrip was the nicest of women. Then after a short pause she changed the subject.

'Don't you think Lady Mary very beautiful?'

'Uncommon,' said his Lordship.

'And her manners so perfect. She has all her mother's ease without any of that—— You know what I mean.'

'Quite so,' said his Lordship.

'And then she has got so much in her.'

'Has she though?'

'I don't know any girl of her age so thoroughly well educated. The Duke seems to take to you.'

'Well, yes;—the Duke is very kind.'

'Don't you think——?'

'Eh!'

'You have heard of her mother's fortune?'

'Tremendous!'

'She will have, I take it, quite a third of it. Whatever I say I'm sure you will take in confidence; but she is a dear dear girl; and I am anxious for her happiness almost as though she belonged to me.'

Lord Popplecourt went back to town in the Duke's carriage, but was unable to say a word about politics. His mind was altogether filled with the wonderful words that had been spoken to him. Could it be that Lady Mary had fallen violently in love with him? He would not at once give himself up to the pleasing idea, having so thoroughly grounded himself in the belief that female nets were to be avoided. But when he got home he did think favourably of it. The daughter of a Duke,—

and such a Duke! So lovely a girl, and with such gifts! And then a fortune which would make a material addition to his own large property!

CHAPTER XXXVI

Tally-ho Lodge

WE all know that very clever distich* concerning the great fleas and the little fleas which tells us that no animal is too humble to have its parasite. Even Major Tifto had his inferior friend. This was a certain Captain Green,—for the friend also affected military honours. He was a man somewhat older than Tifto, of whose antecedents no one was supposed to know anything. It was presumed of him that he lived by betting, and it was boasted by those who wished to defend his character that when he lost he paid his money like a gentleman. Tifto during the last year or two had been anxious to support Captain Green, and had always made use of this argument: 'Where the d—— he gets his money I don't know;—but when he loses, there it is.'

Major Tifto had a little 'box' of his own in the neighbourhood of Egham, at which he had a set of stables a little bigger than his house, and a set of kennels a little bigger than his stables. It was here he kept his horses and hounds, and himself too when business connected with his sporting life did not take him to town. It was now the middle of August and he had come to Tally-ho Lodge, there to look after his establishments, to make arrangements for cub-hunting, and to prepare for the autumn racing campaign. On this occasion Captain Green was enjoying his hospitality and assisting him by sage counsels. Behind the little box was a little garden,—a garden that was very little; but, still, thus close to the parlour window, there was room for a small table to be put on the grass-plat, and for a couple of armchairs. Here the Major and the Captain were seated about eight o'clock one evening, with convivial good things within their reach. The good things were gin-and-water and pipes. The two gentlemen had not dressed strictly for dinner. They had spent a great part of the day handling the hounds and the horses, dressing wounds, curing sores, and ministering to canine ailments, and had been detained over their work too long to think of their toilet. As it was they had an eye to business. The stables at one corner and the kennels at the other were close to the little garden, and the doings of a man and a boy who were still at work among the animals could be directed from the armchairs on which the two sportsmen were sitting.

It must be explained that ever since the Silverbridge election there had been a growing feeling in Tifto's mind that he had been ill-treated by his partner. The feeling was strengthened by the admirable condition of Prime Minister. Surely more consideration had been due to a man who had produced such a state of things!

'I wouldn't quarrel with him, but I'd make him pay his way,' said the prudent Captain.

'As for that, of course he does pay—his share.'

'Who does all the work?'

'That's true.'

'The fact is, Tifto, you don't make enough out of it. When a small man like you has to deal with a big man like that, he may take it out of him in one of two ways. But he must be deuced clever if he can get it both ways.'

'What are you driving at?' asked Tifto, who did not like being called a small man, feeling himself to be every inch a master of foxhounds.

'Why, this!—Look at that d—— fellow fretting that 'orse with a switch. If you can't strap a 'orse without a stick in your hand, don't you strap him at all, you——' Then there came a volley of abuse out of the Captain's mouth, in the middle of which the man threw down the rubber he was using and walked away.

'You come back,' halloed Tifto, jumping up from his seat with his pipe in his mouth. Then there was a general quarrel between the man and his two masters, in which the man at last was victorious. And the horse was taken into the stable in an unfinished condition. 'It's all very well to say "Get rid of him," but where am I to get anybody better? It has come to such a pass that now if you speak to a fellow he walks out of the yard.'

They then returned to the state of affairs, as it was between Tifto and Lord Silverbridge. 'What I was saying is this,' continued the Captain. 'If you choose to put yourself up to live with a fellow like that on equal terms——'

'One gentleman with another, you mean?'

'Put it so. It don't quite hit it off, but put it so. Why then you get your wages when you take his arm and call him Silverbridge.'

'I don't want wages from any man,' said the indignant Major.

'That comes from not knowing what wages is. I do want wages. If I do a thing I like to be paid for it. You are paid for it after one fashion, I prefer the other.'

'Do you mean he should give me——a salary?'

'I'd have it out of him some way. What's the good of young chaps of that sort if they aren't made to pay? You've got this young swell in tow. He's going to be about the richest man in England;—and what the deuce better are you for it?' Tifto sat meditating, thinking of the wisdom which was being spoken. The same ideas had occurred to him. The happy chance which had made him intimate with Lord Silverbridge had not yet enriched him. 'What is the good of chaps of that sort if they are not made to pay?' The words were wise words. But yet how glorious he had been when he was elected at the Beargarden, and had entered the club as the special friend of the heir of the Duke of Omnium.

After a short pause, Captain Green pursued his discourse. 'You said salary.'

'I did mention the word.'

'Salary and wages is one. A salary is a nice thing if it's paid regular. I had a salary once myself for looking after a stud of 'orses at Newmarket, only the gentleman broke up and it never went very far.'

'Was that Marley Bullock?'

'Yes; that was Marley Bullock. He's abroad somewhere now with nothing a year paid quarterly to live on. I think he does a little at cards. He'd had a good bit of money once, but most of it was gone when he came my way.'

'You didn't make by him?'

'I didn't lose nothing. I didn't have a lot of 'orses under me without getting something out of it.'

'What am I to do?' asked Tifto. 'I can sell him a horse now and again. But if I give him anything good there isn't much to come out of that.'

'Very little I should say. Don't he put his money on his 'orses?'

'Not very free. I think he's coming out freer now.'

'What did he stand to win on the Derby?'

'A thousand or two perhaps.'

'There may be something got handsome out of that,' said the Captain, not venturing to allow his voice to rise above a whisper. Major Tifto looked hard at him but said nothing. 'Of course you must see your way.'

'I don't quite understand.'

'Race 'orses are expensive animals,—and races generally is expensive.'

'That's true.'

'When so much is dropped, somebody has to pick it up. That's what I've always said to myself. I'm as honest as another man.'

'That's of course,' said the Major civilly.

'But if I don't keep my mouth shut, somebody 'll have my teeth out of my head. Every one for himself and God for us all. I suppose there's a deal of money flying about. He'll put a lot of money on this 'orse of yours for the Leger if he's managed right. There's more to be got out of that than calling him Silverbridge and walking arm-in-arm. Business is business. I don't know whether I make myself understood.'

The gentleman did not quite make himself understood; but Tifto endeavoured to read the riddle. He must in some way make money out of his friend Lord Silverbridge. Hitherto he had contented himself with the brilliancy of the connection; but now his brilliant friend had taken to snubbing him, and had on more than one occasion made himself disagreeable. It seemed to him that Captain Green counselled him to put up with that, but counselled him at the same time to—pick up some of his friend's money. He didn't think that he could ask Lord Silverbridge for a salary—he who was a Master of Foxhounds, and a member of the Beargarden. Then his friend had suggested something about the young lord's bets. He was endeavouring to unriddle all this with a brain that was already somewhat muddled with alcohol, when Captain Green got up from his chair and standing over the Major spoke his last words for that night as from an oracle. 'Square is all very well, as long as others are square to you;—but when they aren't, then I say square be d——. Square! what comes of it? Work your heart out, and then it's no good.'

The Major thought about it much that night, and was thinking about it still when he awoke on the next morning. He would like to make Lord Silverbridge pay for his late insolence. It would answer his purpose to make a little money, —as he told himself,—in any honest way. At the present moment he was in want of money, and on looking into his affairs declared to himself that he had certainly impoverished himself by his devotion to Lord Silverbridge's interests. At breakfast on the following morning he endeavoured to bring his friend back to the subject. But the Captain was cross, rather than oracular. 'Everybody,' he said, 'ought to know his own business. He wasn't going to meddle or make. What he had said had been taken amiss.' This was hard upon Tifto, who had taken nothing amiss.

'Square be d——!' There was a great deal in the lesson there enunciated which demanded consideration. Hitherto the Major had fought his battles with a certain adherence to squareness. If his angles had not all been perfect angles, still there had always been an attempt at geometrical accuracy. He might now and again have told a lie about a horse—but who that deals in horses has not done that? He had been alive to the value of underhand information from racing-stables, but who won't use a tip if he can get it? He had lied about the expense of his hounds, in order to enhance the subscription of his members. Those were things which everybody did in his line. But Green had meant something beyond this.

As far as he could see out in the world at large, nobody was square. You had to keep your mouth shut, or your teeth would be stolen out of it. He didn't look into a paper without seeing that on all sides of him men had abandoned the idea of squareness. Chairmen, directors, members of Parliament, ambassadors,—all the world, as he told himself,—were trying to get on by their wits. He didn't see why he should be more square than anybody else. Why hadn't Silverbridge taken him down to Scotland for the grouse?

CHAPTER XXXVII

Grex

FAR away*from all known places, in the northern limit of the Craven district, on the borders of Westmorland but in Yorkshire, there stands a large, rambling, most picturesque old house called Grex. The people around call it the Castle, but it is not a castle. It is an old brick building supposed to have been erected in the days of James the First, having oriel windows, twisted chimneys, long galleries, gàble ends, a quadrangle of which the house surrounds three sides, terraces, sun-dials, and fishponds. But it is so sadly out of repair as to be altogether unfit for the residence of a gentleman and his family. It stands not in a park, for the land about it is divided into paddocks by low stone walls, but in the midst of lovely scenery, the ground rising all round it in low irregular hills or fells, and close to it, a quarter of a mile from the back of the house, there is a small dark lake, not serenely lovely as are some of the lakes in Westmorland, but attractive by the darkness of its waters and the gloom of the woods around it.

This is the country seat of Earl Grex,—which however he had not visited for some years. Gradually the place had got into such a condition that his absence is not surprising. An owner of Grex, with large means at his disposal and with a taste for the picturesque to gratify,—one who could afford to pay for memories and who was willing to pay dearly for such luxuries, might no doubt restore Grex. But the Earl had neither the money nor the taste.

Lord Grex had latterly never gone near the place, nor was his son Lord Percival fond of looking upon the ruin of his property. But Lady Mabel loved it with a fond love. With all her lightness of spirit she was prone to memories, prone to melancholy, prone at times almost to seek the gratification of sorrow. Year after year when the London season was over she would come down to Grex and spend a week or two amidst its desolation. She was now going on to a seat in Scotland belonging to Mrs. Montacute Jones called Killancodlem; but she was in the meanwhile passing a desolate fortnight at Grex in company with Miss Cassewary. The gardens were let,— and being let of course were not kept in further order than as profit might require. The man who rented them lived in the big house with his wife, and they on such occasions as this would cook and wait upon Lady Mabel.

Lady Mabel was at the home of her ancestors, and the faithful Miss Cass was with her. But at the moment and at the spot at which the reader shall see her, Miss Cass was not with her. She was sitting on a rock about twelve feet above the lake looking upon the black water; and on another rock a few feet from her was seated Frank Tregear. 'No,' she said, 'you should not have come. Nothing can justify it. Of course as you are here I could not refuse to come out with you. To make a fuss about it would be the worst of all. But you should not have come.'

'Why not? Whom does it hurt? It is a pleasure to me. If it be the reverse to you, I will go.'

'Men are so unmanly. They take such mean advantages. You know it is a pleasure to me to see you.'

'I had hoped so.'

'But it is a pleasure I ought not to have,—at least not here.'

'That is what I do not understand,' said he. 'In London, where the Earl could bark at me if he happened to find me, I could see the inconvenience of it. But here, where there is nobody but Miss Cass——'

'There are a great many others. There are the rooks, and stones, and old women;—all of which have ears.'

'But of what is there to be ashamed? There is nothing in the world to me so pleasant as the companionship of my friends.'

'Then go after Silverbridge.'

'I mean to do so;—but I am taking you by the way.'

'It is all unmanly,' she said, rising from her stone; 'you know that it is so. Friends! Do you mean to say that it would make no difference whether you were here with me or with Miss Cass?'

'The greatest difference in the world.'

'Because she is an old woman and I am a young one, and because in intercourse between young men and young women there is something dangerous to the women and therefore pleasant to the men.'

'I never heard anything more unjust. You cannot think I desire anything injurious to you.'

'I do think so.' She was still standing and spoke now with great vehemence. 'I do think so. You force me to throw aside the reticence I ought to keep. Would it help me in my prospects if your friend Lord Silverbridge knew that I was here?'

'How should he know?'

'But if he did? Do you suppose that I want to have visits paid to me of which I am afraid to speak? Would you dare to tell Lady Mary that you had been sitting alone with me on the rocks at Grex?'

'Certainly I would.'

'Then it would be because you have not dared to tell her certain other things which have gone before. You have sworn to her no doubt that you love her better than all the world.'

'I have.'

'And you have taken the trouble to come here to tell me that,—to wound me to the core by saying so; to show me that, though I may still be sick, you have recovered,—that is if you ever suffered! Go your way and let me go mine. I do not want you.'

'Mabel!'

'I do not want you. I know you will not help me, but you need not destroy me.'

'You know that you are wronging me.'

'No! You understand it all though you look so calm. I hate your Lady Mary Palliser. There! But if by anything I could do I could secure her to you I would do it,—because you want it.'

'She will be your sister-in-law,—probably.'

'Never. It will never be so.'

'Why do you hate her?'

'There again! You are so little of a man that you can ask me why!' Then she turned away as though she intended to go down to the marge of the lake.

But he rose up and stopped her. 'Let us have this out, Mabel, before we go,' he said. 'Unmanly is a heavy word to hear from you, and you have used it a dozen times.'

'It is because I have thought it a thousand times. Go and get her if you can;—but why tell me about it?'

'You said you would help me.'

'So I would, as I would help you do anything you might want; but you can hardly think that after what has passed I can wish to hear about her.'

'It was you spoke of her.'

'I told you you should not be here,—because of her and because of me. And I tell you again, I hate her. Do you think I can hear you speak of her as though she were the only woman you had ever seen without feeling it? Did you ever swear that you loved any one else?'

'Certainly, I have so sworn.'

'Have you ever said that nothing could alter that love?'

'Indeed I have.'

'But it is altered. It has all gone. It has been transferred to one who has more advantages of beauty, youth, wealth, and position.'

'Oh Mabel, Mabel!'

'But it is so.'

'When you say this do you not think of yourself?'

'Yes. But I have never been false to any one. You are false to me.'

'Have I not offered to face all the world with you?'

'You would not offer it now?'

'No,' he said, after a pause,—'not now. Were I to do so, I should be false. You bade me take my love elsewhere, and I did so.'

'With the greatest ease.'

'We agreed it should be so; and you have done the same.'

'That is false. Look me in the face and tell me whether you do not know it to be false!'

'And yet I am told that I am injuring you with Silverbridge.'

'Oh,—so unmanly again! Of course I have to marry. Who does not know it? Do you want to see me begging my bread about the streets? You have bread; or if not, you might earn it. If you marry for money——'

'The accusation is altogether unjustifiable.'

'Allow me to finish what I have to say. If you marry for money you will do that which is in itself bad, and which is also unnecessary. What other course would you recommend me to take? No one goes into the gutter while there is a clean path open. If there be no escape but through the gutter, one has to take it.'

'You mean that my duty to you should have kept me from marrying all my life.'

'Not that;—but a little while, Frank; just a little while. Your bloom is not fading; your charms are not running from you. Have you not a strength which I cannot have? Do you not feel that you are a tree, standing firm in the ground, while I am a bit of ivy that will be trodden in the dirt unless it can be made to cling to something? You should not liken yourself to me, Frank.'

'If I could do you any good!'

'Good! What is the meaning of good? If you love, it is good to be loved again. It is good not to have your heart torn in pieces. You know that I love you.' He was standing close to her, and put out his hand as though he would twine his arm round her waist. 'Not for worlds,' she said. 'It belongs to that Palliser girl. And as I have taught myself to think that what there is left of me may perhaps belong to some other one, worthless as it is, I will keep it for him. I love you,—but there can be none of that softness of love between us.' Then there was a pause, but as he did not speak she went on. 'But remember, Frank,—our position is not equal. You have got over your little complaint. It probably did not go deep with you, and you have found a cure. Perhaps there is a satisfaction in finding that two young women love you.'

'You are trying to be cruel to me.'

'Why else should you be here? You know I love you,—

with all my heart, with all my strength, and that I would give the world to cure myself. Knowing this, you come and talk to me of your passion for this other girl.'

'I had hoped we might both talk rationally as friends.'

'Friends! Frank Tregear, I have been bold enough to tell you I love you; but you are not my friend, and cannot be my friend. If I have before asked you to help me in this mean catastrophe of mine, in my attack upon that poor boy, I withdraw my request. I think I will go back to the house now.'

'I will walk back to Ledburgh if you wish it without going to the house again.'

'No; I will have nothing that looks like being ashamed. You ought not to have come, but you need not run away.' Then they walked back to the house together and found Miss Casseway on the terrace. 'We have been to the lake,' said Mabel, 'and have been talking of old days. I have but one ambition now in the world.' Of course Miss Casseway asked what the remaining ambition was. 'To get money enough to purchase this place from the ruins of the Grex property. If I could own the house and the lake, and the paddocks about, and had enough income to keep one servant and bread for us to eat—of course including you, Miss Cass——'

'Thank'ee, my dear; but I am not sure I should like it.'

'Yes; you would. Frank would come and see us perhaps once a year. I don't suppose anybody else cares about the place, but to me it is the dearest spot in the world.' So she went on in almost high spirits, though alluding to the general decadence of the Grex family, till Tregear took his leave.

'I wish he had not come,' said Miss Casseway when he was gone.

'Why should you wish that? There is not so much here to amuse me that you should begrudge me a stray visitor.'

'I don't think that I grudge you anything in the way of pleasure, my dear; but still he should not have come. My lord, if he knew it, would be angry.'

'Then let him be angry. Papa does not do so much for me that I am bound to think of him at every turn.'

'But I am,—or rather I am bound to think of myself, if I take his bread.'

'Bread!'

'Well;—I do take his bread, and I take it on the understanding that I will be to you what a mother might be,—or an aunt.'

'Well,—and if so! Had I a mother living would not Frank Tregear have come to visit her, and in visiting her, would he not have seen me,—and should we not have walked out together?'

'Not after all that has come and gone.'

'But you are not a mother nor yet an aunt, and you have to do just what I tell you. And don't I know that you trust me in all things? And am I not trustworthy?'

'I think you are trustworthy.'

'I know what my duty is and I mean to do it. No one shall ever have to say of me that I have given way to self-indulgence. I couldn't help his coming, you know.'

That same night, after Miss Cassewary had gone to bed, when the moon was high in the heavens and the world around her was all asleep, Lady Mabel again wandered out to the lake, and again seated herself on the same rock, and there she sat thinking of her past life and trying to think of that before her. It is so much easier to think of the past than of the futu' —to remember what has been than to resolve what shall be! She had reminded him of the offer which he had made and repeated to her more than once,—to share with her all his chances in life. There would have been almost no income for them. All the world would have been against her. She would have caused his ruin. Her light on the matter had been so clear that it had not taken her very long to decide that such a thing must not be thought of. She had at last been quite stern in her decision.

Now she was broken-hearted because she found that he had left her in very truth. Oh yes;—she would marry the boy, if she could so arrange. Since that meeting at Richmond he had sent her the ring reset. She was to meet him down in Scotland within a week or two from the present time. Mrs. Montacute Jones had managed that. He had all but offered to her a second time at Richmond. But all that would not serve to make her happy. She declared to herself that she did not wish to see Frank Tregear again; but still it was a misery to her that his heart should in truth be given to another woman.

CHAPTER XXXVIII

Crummie-Toddie

ALMOST at the last moment Silverbridge and his brother Gerald were induced to join Lord Popplecourt's shooting-party in Scotland. The party perhaps might more properly be called the party of Reginald Dobbes, who was a man knowing in such matters. It was he who made the party up. Popplecourt and Silverbridge were to share the expense between them, each bringing three guns. Silverbridge brought his brother and Frank Tregear,—having refused a most piteous petition on the subject from Major Tifto. With Popplecourt of course came Reginald Dobbes, who was, in truth, to manage everything, and Lord Nidderdale, whose wife had generously permitted him this recreation. The shooting was in the west of Perthshire, known as Crummie-Toddie, and comprised an enormous acreage of so-called forest and moor. Mr. Dobbes declared that nothing like it had as yet been produced in Scotland. Everything had been made to give way to deer and grouse. The thing had been managed so well that the tourist nuisance had been considerably abated. There was hardly a potato patch left in the district, nor a head of cattle to be seen. There were no inhabitants remaining, or so few that they could be absorbed in game-preserving or cognate duties. Reginald Dobbes, who was very great at grouse, and supposed to be capable of outwitting a deer by venatical*wiles more perfectly than any other sportsman in Great Britain, regarded Crummie-Toddie as the nearest thing there was to a Paradise on earth. Could he have been allowed to pass one or two special laws for his own protection, there might still have been improvement. He would like the right to have all intruders thrashed by the gillies*within an inch of their lives; and he would have had a clause in his lease against the making of any new roads, opening of footpaths, or building of bridges. He had seen somewhere in print a plan for running a railway from Callender to Fort Augustus right through Crummie-Toddie! If this were done in his time the beauty of the world would be over. Reginald Dobbes was a man of about forty, strong, active, well-made, about five feet ten in height, with broad shoulders and greatly-developed legs. He was not a handsome man, having a protrusive nose, high cheek-bones, and long upper lip; but there was a manliness about his face which redeemed it. Sport was the business of his life, and he thoroughly despised all who were not sportsmen. He fished and shot and hunted during nine or ten months of the year, filling up his time as best he might with coaching, polo, and pigeon-shooting. He regarded it as a great duty to keep his body in the firmest possible condition. All his eating and all his drinking was done upon a system, and he would consider himself to be guilty of weak self-indulgence were he to allow himself to break through sanitary rules. But it never occurred to him that his whole life was one of self-indulgence. He could walk his thirty miles with his gun on his shoulder as well now as he could ten years ago; and being sure of this, was thoroughly contented with himself. He had a patrimony amounting to perhaps £1000 a year, which he husbanded so as to enjoy all his amusements to perfection. No one had ever heard of his sponging on his friends. Of money he rarely spoke, sport being in his estimation the only subject worthy of a man's words. Such was Reginald Dobbes, who was now to be the master of the shooting at Crummie-Toddie.

Crummie-Toddie was but twelve miles from Killancodlem, Mrs. Montacute Jones's highland seat; and it was this vicinity which first induced Lord Silverbridge to join the party. Mabel Grex was to be at Killancodlem, and, determined as he still was to ask her to be his wife, he would make this his opportunity. Of real opportunity there had been none at Richmond. Since he had had his ring altered and had sent it to her there had come but a word or two of answer. 'What am I to say? You unkindest of men! To keep it or to send it back would make me equally miserable. I shall keep it till you are married, and then give it to your wife.' This affair of the ring had made him more intent than ever. After that he heard that Isabel Boncassen would also be at Killancodlem, having been induced to join Mrs. Montacute Jones's swarm of visitors. Though he was dangerously devoid of experience, still he felt that this was unfortunate. He intended to marry Mabel Grex. And he could assure himself that he thoroughly loved her. Nevertheless he liked making love to Isabel Boncassen. He was quite willing to marry and settle down, and looked forward with satisfaction to having Mabel Grex for his wife. But it would be pleasant to have a six-months run of flirting and love-making before this settlement, and he had certainly never seen anyone with whom this would be so delightful as with Miss

Boncassen. But that the two ladies should be at the same house was unfortunate.

He and Gerald reached Crummie-Toddie late on the evening of August 11th, and found Reginald Dobbes alone. That was on Wednesday. Popplecourt and Nidderdale ought to have made their appearance on that morning, but had telegraphed to say that they would be detained two days on their route. Tregear, whom hitherto Dobbes had never seen, had left his arrival uncertain. This carelessness on such matters was very offensive to Mr. Dobbes, who loved discipline and exactitude. He ought to have received the two young men with open arms because they were punctual; but he had been somewhat angered by what he considered the extreme youth of Lord Gerald. Boys who could not shoot were, he thought, putting themselves forward before their time. And Silverbridge himself was by no means a first-rate shot. Such a one as Silverbridge had to be endured because from his position and wealth he could facilitate such arrangements as these. It was much to have to do with a man who would not complain if an extra fifty pounds were wanted. But he ought to have understood that he was bound in honour to bring down competent friends. Of Tregear's shooting Dobbes had been able to learn nothing. Lord Gerald was a lad from the Universities; and Dobbes hated University lads. Popplecourt and Nidderdale were known to be efficient. They were men who could work hard and do their part of the required slaughter. Dobbes proudly knew that he could make up for some deficiency by his own prowess; but he could not struggle against three bad guns. What was the use of so perfecting Crummie-Toddie as to make it the best bit of ground for grouse and deer in Scotland, if the men who came there failed by their own incapacity to bring up the grand total of killed to a figure which would render Dobbes and Crummie-Toddie famous through the whole shooting world? He had been hard at work on other matters. Dogs had gone amiss,—or guns, and he had been made angry by the champagne which Popplecourt caused to be sent down. He knew what champagne meant. Whisky-and-water, and not much of it, was the liquor which Reginald Dobbes loved in the mountains.

'Don't you call this a very ugly country?' Silverbridge asked as soon as he arrived. Now it is the case that the traveller who travels into Argyllshire, Perthshire, and Inverness, expects to find lovely scenery; and it was also true that the country through which they had passed for the last twenty miles had been not only bleak and barren, but uninteresting and ugly. It was all rough open moorland, never rising into mountains, and graced by no running streams, by no forest scenery, almost by no foliage. The lodge itself did indeed stand close upon a little river, and was reached by a bridge that crossed it; but there was nothing pretty either in the river or the bridge. It was a placid black little streamlet, which in that portion of its course was hurried by no steepness, had no broken rocks in its bed, no trees on its low banks, and played none of those gambols which make running water beautiful. The bridge was a simple low construction with a low parapet, carrying an ordinary roadway up to the hall door. The lodge itself was as ugly as a house could be, white, of two stories, with the door in the middle and windows on each side, with a slate roof, and without a tree near it. It was in the middle of the shooting, and did not create a town around itself as do sumptuous mansions, to the great detriment of that seclusion which is favourable to game. 'Look at Killancodlem,' Dobbes had been heard to say—'a very fine house for ladies to flirt in; but if you find a deer within six miles of it I will eat him first and shoot him afterwards.' There was a Spartan simplicity about Crummie-Toddie which pleased the Spartan mind of Reginald Dobbes.

'Ugly, do you call it?'

'Infernally ugly,' said Lord Gerald.

'What did you expect to find? A big hotel, and a lot of cockneys? If you come after grouse, you must come to what the grouse thinks pretty.'

'Nevertheless, it is ugly,' said Silverbridge, who did not choose to be 'sat upon.' 'I have been at shootings in Scotland

before, and sometimes they are not ugly. This I call beastly.'
Whereupon Reginald Dobbes turned upon his heel and walked
away.

'Can you shoot?' he said afterwards to Lord Gerald.

'I can fire off a gun, if you mean that,' said Gerald.

'You have never shot much?'

'Not what you call very much. I'm not so old as you are,
you know. Everything must have a beginning.' Mr. Dobbes
wished 'the beginning' might have taken place elsewhere; but
there had been some truth in the remark.

'What on earth made you tell him crammers*like that?'
asked Silverbridge, as the brothers sat together afterwards
smoking on the wall of the bridge.

'Because he made an ass of himself; asking me whether I
could shoot.'

On the next morning they started at seven. Dobbes had
determined to be cross, because, as he thought, the young
men would certainly keep him waiting; and was cross because
by their punctuality they robbed him of any just cause for
offence. During the morning on the moor they were hardly
ever near enough each other for much conversation, and very
little was said. According to arrangement made they returned
to the house for lunch, it being their purpose not to go far
from home till their numbers were complete. As they came
over the bridge and put down their guns near the door, Mr.
Dobbes spoke the first good-humoured word they had heard
from his lips. 'Why did you tell me such an infernal ——, I
would say lie, only perhaps you mightn't like it?'

'I told you no lie,' said Gerald.

'You've only missed two birds all the morning, and you
have shot forty-two. That's uncommonly good sport.'

'What have you done?'

'Only forty,' and Mr. Dobbes seemed for the moment to
be gratified by his own inferiority. 'You are a deuced sight
better than your brother.'

'Gerald's about the best shot I know,' said Silverbridge.

'Why didn't he tell?'

'Because you were angry when we said the place was ugly.'

'I see all about it,' said Dobbes. 'Nevertheless when a fellow comes to shoot he shouldn't complain because a place isn't pretty. What you want is a decent house as near as you can have it to your ground. If there is anything in Scotland to beat Crummie-Toddie I don't know where to find it. Shooting is shooting you know, and touring is touring.'

Upon that he took very kindly to Lord Gerald, who, even after the arrival of the other men, was second only in skill to Dobbes himself. With Nidderdale, who was an old companion, he got on very well. Nidderdale ate and drank too much, and refused to be driven beyond a certain amount of labour, but was in other respects obedient and knew what he was about. Popplecourt was disagreeable, but he was a fairly good shot and understood what was expected of him. Silverbridge was so good-humoured, that even his manifest faults, —shooting carelessly, lying in bed and wanting his dinner,— were, if not forgiven, at least endured. But Tregear was an abomination. He could shoot well enough and was active, and when he was at the work seemed to like it;—but he would stay away whole days by himself, and when spoken to would answer in a manner which seemed to Dobbes to be flat mutiny. 'We are not doing it for our bread,' said Tregear.

'I don't know what you mean.'

'There's no duty in killing a certain number of these animals.' They had been driving deer on the day before and were to continue the work on the day in question. 'I'm not paid fifteen shillings a week for doing it.'

'I suppose if you undertake to do a thing you mean to do it. Of course you're not wanted. We can make the double party without you.'

'Then why the mischief should you growl at me?'

'Because I think a man should do what he undertakes to do. A man who gets tired after three days' work of this kind would become tired if he were earning his bread.'

'Who says I am tired? I came here to amuse myself.'

'Amuse yourself!'

306

'And as long as it amuses me I shall shoot, and when it does not I shall give it up.'

This vexed the governor of Crummie-Toddie much. He had learned to regard himself as the arbiter of the fate of men while they were sojourning under the same autumnal roof as himself. But a defalcation which occurred immediately afterwards was worse. Silverbridge declared his intention of going over one morning to Killancodlem. Reginald Dobbes muttered a curse between his teeth, which was visible by the anger on his brow to all the party. 'I shall be back to-night, you know,' said Silverbridge.

'A lot of men and women who pretend to come there for shooting,' said Dobbes angrily, 'but do all the mischief they can.'

'One must go and see one's friends, you know.'

'Some girl!' said Dobbes.

But worse happened than the evil so lightly mentioned. Silverbridge did go over to Killancodlem; and presently there came back a man with a cart, who was to return with a certain not small proportion of his luggage.

'It's hardly honest, you know,' said Reginald Dobbes.

CHAPTER XXXIX

Killancodlem

MR. DOBBES was probably right in his opinion that hotels, tourists, and congregations of men are detrimental to shooting. Crummie-Toddie was in all respects suited for sport. Killancodlem, though it had the name of a shooting-place, certainly was not so. Men going there took their guns. Gamekeepers were provided and gillies,—and, in a moderate quantity, game. On certain grand days a deer or two might be shot,—and would be very much talked about afterwards. But a glance at the place would suffice to show that Killancodlem was not intended for sport. It was a fine castellated mansion, with beautiful though narrow grounds, standing in the valley of the Archay River, with a mountain behind and the river in front. Between the gates and the river there was a public road on which a stage-coach ran, with loud-blown horns and the noise of many tourists. A mile beyond the Castle was the famous Killancodlem hotel which made up a hundred and twenty beds, and at which half as many more guests would sleep on occasions under the tables. And there was the Killancodlem post-office halfway between the two. At Crummie-Toddie they had to send nine miles for their letters and newspapers. At Killancodlem there was lawn-tennis*and a billiard-room and dancing every night. The costumes of the ladies were lovely, and those of the gentlemen, who were wonderful in knickerbockers, picturesque hats and variegated stockings, hardly less so. And then there were carriages and saddle-horses, and paths had been made hither and thither through the rocks and hills for the sake of the scenery. Scenery! To hear Mr. Dobbes utter the single word was as good as a play. Was it for such cockney purposes as those that Scotland had been created, fit mother for grouse and deer?

Silverbridge arrived just before lunch, and was soon made to understand that it was impossible that he should go back that day. Mrs. Jones was very great on that occasion. 'You are afraid of Reginald Dobbes,' she said severely.

'I think I am rather.'

'Of course you are. How came it to pass that you of all men should submit yourself to such a tyrant?'

'Good shooting, you know,' said Silverbridge.

'But you dare not call an hour your own—or your soul. Mr. Dobbes and I are sworn enemies. We both like Scotland, and unfortunately we have fallen into the same neighbour-hood. He looks upon me as the genius of sloth. I regard him as the incarnation of tyranny. He once said there should be no women in Scotland,—just an old one here and there, who would know how to cook grouse. I offered to go and cook his grouse!'

'Any friend of mine,' continued Mrs. Jones, 'who comes down to Crummie-Toddie without staying a day or two with me,—will never be my friend any more. I do not hesitate to tell you, Lord Silverbridge, that I call for your surrender, in

308

order that I may show my power over Reginald Dobbes. Are you a Dobbite?'

'Not thorough-going,' said Silverbridge.

'Then be a Montacute Jones-ite; or a Boncassenite, if, as is possible, you prefer a young woman to an old one.' At this moment Isabel Boncassen was standing close to them.

'Killancodlem against Crummie-Toddie for ever!' said Miss Boncassen, waving her handkerchief. As a matter of course a messenger was sent back to Crummie-Toddie for the young lord's wearing apparel.

The whole of that afternoon he spent playing lawn-tennis with Miss Boncassen. Lady Mabel was asked to join the party, but she refused, having promised to take a walk to a distant waterfall where the Codlem falls into the Archay. A gentleman in knickerbockers was to have gone with her, and two other young ladies; but when the time came she was weary, she said,—and she sat almost the entire afternoon looking at the game from a distance. Silverbridge played well, but not so well as the pretty American. With them were joined two others somewhat inferior, so that Silverbridge and Miss Boncassen were on different sides. They played game after game, and Miss Boncassen's side always won.

Very little was said between Silverbridge and Miss Boncassen which did not refer to the game. But Lady Mabel, looking on, told herself that they were making love to each other before her eyes. And why shouldn't they? She asked herself that question in perfect good faith. Why should they not be lovers? Was ever anything prettier than the girl in her country dress, active as a fawn and as graceful? Or could anything be more handsome, more attractive to a girl, more good-humoured, or better bred in his playful emulation than Silverbridge?

'When youth and pleasure meet, To chase the glowing hours with flying feet!'*she said to herself over and over again.

But why had he sent her the ring? She would certainly give him back the ring and bid him bestow it at once upon Miss Boncassen. Inconstant boy! Then she would get up and wander away for a time and rebuke herself. What right had she even to think of inconstancy? Could she be so irrational, so unjust, as to be sick for his love, as to be angry with him because he seemed to prefer another? Was she not well aware that she herself did not love him;—but that she did love another man? She had made up her mind to marry him in order that she might be a duchess, and because she could give herself to him without any of that horror which would be her fate in submitting to matrimony with one or another of the young men around her. There might be disappointment. If he escaped her there would be bitter disappointment. But seeing how it was, had she any further ground for hope? She certainly had no ground for anger!

It was thus, within her own bosom, she put questions to herself. And yet all this before her was simply a game of play in which the girl and the young man were as eager for victory as though they were children. They were thinking neither of love nor love-making. That the girl should be so lovely was no doubt a pleasure to him;—and perhaps to her also that he should be joyous to look at and sweet of voice. But he, could he have been made to tell all the truth within him, would have still owned that it was his purpose to make Mabel his wife.

When the game was over and the propositions made for further matches and the like,—Miss Boncassen said that she would betake herself to her own room. 'I never worked so hard in my life before,' she said. 'And I feel like a navvie. I could drink beer out of a jug and eat bread and cheese. I won't play with you any more, Lord Silverbridge, because I am beginning to think it is unladylike to exert myself.'

'Are you not glad you came over?' said Lady Mabel to him as he was going off the ground almost without seeing her.

'Pretty well,' he said.

'Is not that better than stalking?'

'Lawn-tennis?'

'Yes;—lawn-tennis,—with Miss Boncassen.'

'She plays uncommonly well.'

'And so do you.'

310

'Ah, she has such an eye for distances.'

'And you,—what have you an eye for? Will you answer me a question?'

'Well;—yes; I think so.'

'Truly.'

'Certainly; if I do answer it.'

'Do you not think her the most beautiful creature you ever saw in your life?' He pushed back his cap and looked at her without making any immediate answer. 'I do. Now tell me what you think.'

'I think that perhaps she is.'

'I knew you would say so. You are so honest that you could not bring yourself to tell a fib,—even to me about that. Come here and sit down for a moment.' Of course he sat down by her. 'You know that Frank came to see me at Grex?'

'He never mentioned it.'

'Dear me;—how odd!'

'It was odd,' said he in a voice which showed that he was angry. She could hardly explain to herself why she told him this at the present moment. It came partly from jealousy, as though she had said to herself, 'Though he may neglect me, he shall know that there is someone who does not;'—and partly from an eager half-angry feeling that she would have nothing concealed. There were moments with her in which she thought that she could arrange her future life in accordance with certain wise rules over which her heart should have no influence. There were others, many others, in which her feelings completely got the better of her. And now she told herself that she would be afraid of nothing. There should be no deceit, no lies!

'He went to see you at Grex!' said Silverbridge.

'Why should he not have come to me at Grex?'

'Only it is so odd that he did not mention it. It seems to me that he is always having secrets with you of some kind.'

'Poor Frank! There is no one else who would come to see me at that tumbledown old place. But I have another thing to say to you. You have behaved badly to me.'

'Have I?'

'Yes, sir. After my folly about that ring you should have known better than to send it to me. You must take it back again.'

'You shall do exactly what you said you would. You shall give it to my wife,—when I have one.'

'That did very well for me to say in a note. I did not want to send my anger to you over a distance of two or three hundred miles by the postman. But now that we are together you must take it back.'

'I will do no such thing,' said he sturdily.

'You speak as though this were a matter in which you can have your own way.'

'I mean to have mine about that.'

'Any lady then must be forced to take any present that a gentleman may send her! Allow me to assure you that the usages of society do not run in that direction. Here is the ring. I knew that you would come over to see—well, to see some-one here, and I have kept it ready in my pocket.'

'I came over to see you.'

'Lord Silverbridge! But we know that in certain employments all things are fair.' He looked at her not knowing what were the employments to which she alluded. 'At any rate you will oblige me by—by—by not being troublesome, and putting this little trinket into your pocket.'

'Never! Nothing on earth shall make me do it.'

At Killancodlem they did not dine till half-past eight. Twilight was now stealing on these two, who were still out in the garden, all the others having gone in to dress. She looked round to see that no other eyes were watching them as she still held the ring. 'It is there,' she said, putting it on the bench between them. Then she prepared to rise from the seat so that she might leave it with him.

But he was too quick for her, and was away at a distance before she had collected her dress. And from a distance he spoke again, 'If you choose that it shall be lost, so be it.'

'You had better take it,' said she, following him slowly. he would not turn back;—nor would she. They met again

312

in the hall for a moment. 'I should be sorry it should be lost,' said he, 'because it belonged to my great-uncle. And I had hoped that I might live to see it very often.'

'You can fetch it,' she said, as she went to her room. He however would not fetch it. She had accepted it, and he would not take it back again, let the fate of the gem be what it might.

But to the feminine and more cautious mind the very value of the trinket made its position out there on the bench, within the grasp of any dishonest gardener, a burden to her. She could not reconcile it to her conscience that it should be so left. The diamond was a large one, and she had heard it spoken of as a stone of great value,—so much so, that Silver-bridge had been blamed for wearing it ordinarily. She had asked for it in joke, regarding it as a thing which could not be given away. She could not go down herself and take it up again; but neither could she allow it to remain. As she went to her room she met Mrs. Jones already coming from hers. 'You will keep us all waiting,' said the hostess.

'Oh no;—nobody ever dressed so quickly. But, Mrs. Jones, will you do me a favour?'

'Certainly.'

'And will you let me explain something?'

'Anything you like,—from a hopeless engagement down to a broken garter.'

'I am suffering neither from one or the other. But there is a most valuable ring lying out in the garden. Will you send for it?' Then of course the story had to be told. 'You will, I hope, understand how I came to ask for it foolishly. It was because it was the one thing which I was sure he would not give away.'

'Why not take it?'

'Can't you understand? I wouldn't for the world. But you will be good enough,—won't you, to see that there is nothing else in it?'

'Nothing of love?'

'Nothing in the least. He and I are excellent friends. We are cousins, and intimate, and all that. I thought I might have

313

had my joke, and now I am punished for it. As for love, don't you see he is over head and ears in love with Miss Boncassen?'

This was very imprudent on the part of Lady Mabel, who, had she been capable of clinging fast to her policy, would not now in a moment of strong feeling have done so much to raise obstacles in her own way. 'But you will send for it, won't you, and have it put on his dressing-table to-night?' When he went to bed Lord Silverbridge found it on his table.

But before that time came he had twice danced with Miss Boncassen, Lady Mabel having refused to dance with him. 'No,' she said, 'I am angry with you. You ought to have felt that it did not become you as a gentleman to subject me to inconvenience by throwing upon me the charge of that diamond. You may be foolish enough to be indifferent about its value, but as you have mixed me up with it I cannot afford to have it lost.'

'It is yours.'

'No, sir; it is not mine, nor will it ever be mine. But I wish you to understand that you have offended me.'

This made him so unhappy for the time that he almost told the story to Miss Boncassen. 'If I were to give you a ring,' he said, 'would not you accept it?'

'What a question!'

'What I mean is, don't you think all those conventional rules about men and women are absurd?'

'As a progressive American, of course I am bound to think all conventional rules are an abomination.'

'If you had a brother and I gave him a stick he'd take it.'

'Not across his back, I hope.'

'Or if I gave your father a book?'

'He'd take books to any extent, I should say.'

'And why not you a ring?'

'Who said I wouldn't? But after all this you mustn't try me.'

'I was not thinking of it.'

'I'm so glad of that! Well;—if you'll promise that you'll never offer me one, I'll promise that I'll take it when it comes. But what does all this mean?'

314

'It is not worth talking about.'

'You have offered somebody a ring, and somebody hasn't taken it. May I guess?'

'I had rather you did not.'

'I could, you know.'

'Never mind about that. Now come and have a turn. I am bound not to give you a ring; but you are bound to accept anything else I may offer.'

'No, Lord Silverbridge;—not at all. Nevertheless we'll have a turn.'

That night before he went up to his room he had told Isabel Boncassen that he loved her. And when he spoke he was telling her the truth. It had seemed to him that Mabel had become hard to him, and had over and over again rejected the approaches to tenderness which he had attempted to make in his intercourse with her. Even though she were to accept him, what would that be worth to him if she did not love him? So many things had been added together! Why had Tregear gone to Grex, and having gone there why had he kept his journey a secret? Tregear he knew was engaged to his sister; —but for all that, there was a closer intimacy between Mabel and Tregear than between Mabel and himself. And surely she might have taken his ring!

And then Isabel Boncassen was so perfect! Since he had first met her he had heard her loveliness talked of on all sides. It seemed to be admitted everywhere that so beautiful a creature had never before been seen in London. There is even a certain dignity attached to that which is praised by all lips. Miss Boncassen as an American girl, had she been judged to be beautiful only by his own eyes, might perhaps have seemed to him to be beneath his serious notice. In such a case he might have felt himself unable to justify so extraordinary a choice. But there was an acclamation of assent as to this girl! Then came the dancing,—the one dance after another; the pressure of the hand, the entreaty that she would not, just on this occasion, dance with any other man, the attendance on her when she took her glass of wine, the whispered encouragement of Mrs. Montacute Jones, the half-resisting and yet half-yielding conduct of the girl. 'I shall not dance at all again,' she said when he asked her to stand up for another. 'Think of all that lawn-tennis this morning.'

'But you will play to-morrow?'

'I thought you were going.'

'Of course I shall stay now,' he said, and as he said it he put his hand on her hand, which was on his arm. She drew it away at once. 'I love you so dearly,' he whispered to her; 'so dearly.'

'Lord Silverbridge!'

'I do. I do. Can you say that you will love me in return?'

'I cannot,' she said slowly. 'I have never dreamed of such a thing. I hardly know now whether you are in earnest.'

'Indeed, indeed I am.'

'Then I will say good-night, and think about it. Everybody is going. We will have our game to-morrow at any rate.'

When he went to his room he found the ring on his dressing-table.

CHAPTER XL

'And then!'

ON the next morning Miss Boncassen did not appear at breakfast. Word came that she had been so fatigued by the lawn-tennis as not to be able to leave her bed. 'I have been to her,' said Mrs. Montacute Jones, whispering to Lord Silverbridge, as though he were particularly interested. 'There's nothing really the matter. She will be down to lunch.'

'I was afraid she might be ill,' said Silverbridge, who was now hardly anxious to hide his admiration.

'Oh no;—nothing of that sort; but she will not be able to play again to-day. It was your fault. You should not have made her dance last night.' After that Mrs. Jones said a word about it all to Lady Mabel. 'I hope the Duke will not be angry with me.'

'Why should he be angry with you?'

'I don't suppose he will approve of it, and perhaps he'll say I brought them together on purpose.'

Soon afterwards Mabel asked Silverbridge to walk with her

317

to the waterfall. She had worked herself into such a state of mind that she hardly knew what to do, what to wish, or how to act. At one moment she would tell herself that it was better in every respect that she should cease to think of being Duchess of Omnium. It was not fit that she should think of it. She herself cared but little for the young man, and he—she would tell herself—now appeared to care as little for her. And yet to be Duchess of Omnium! But was it not clear that he was absolutely in love with this other girl? She had played her cards so badly that the game was now beyond her powers. Then other thoughts would come. Was it beyond her powers? Had he not told her in London that he loved her? Had he not given her the ring which she well knew he valued? Ah;—if she could but have been aware of all that had passed between Silverbridge and the Duke, how different would have been her feelings! And then would it not be so much better for him that he should marry her, one of his own class, than this American girl, of whom nobody knew anything? And then,—to be the daughter of the Duke of Omnium, to be the future Duchess, to escape from all the cares which her father's vices and follies had brought upon her, to have come to an end of all her troubles! Would it not be sweet?

She had made her mind up to nothing when she asked him to walk up to the waterfall. There was present to her only the glimmer of an idea that she ought to caution him not to play with the American girl's feelings. She knew herself to be aware that, when the time for her own action came, her feminine feelings would get the better of her purpose. She could not craftily bring him to the necessity of bestowing himself upon her. Had that been within the compass of her powers, opportunities had not been lacking to her. On such occasions she had always 'spared him.' And should the opportunity come again, again she would spare him. But she might perhaps do some good,—not to herself, that was now out of the question,—but to him, by showing him how wrong he was in trifling with this girl's feelings.

And so they started for their walk. He of course would

have avoided it had it been possible. When men in such matters have two strings to their bow, much inconvenience is felt when the two become entangled. Silverbridge no doubt had come over to Killancodlem for the sake of making love to Mabel Grex, and instead of doing so he had made love to Isabel Boncassen. And during the watches of the night, and as he had dressed himself in the morning, and while Mrs. Jones had been whispering to him her little bulletin as to the state of the young lady's health, he had not repented himself of the change. Mabel had been, he thought, so little gracious to him that he would have given up that notion earlier, but for his indiscreet declaration to his father. On the other hand, making love to Isabel Boncassen seemed to him to possess some divine afflatus of joy which made it of all imaginable occupations the sweetest and most charming. She had admitted of no embrace. Indeed he had attempted none, unless that touch of the hand might be so called, from which she had immediately withdrawn. Her conduct had been such that he had felt it to be incumbent on him, at the very moment, to justify the touch by a declaration of love. Then she had told him that she would not promise to love him in return. And yet it had been so sweet, so heavenly sweet!

During the morning he had almost forgotten Mabel. When Mrs. Jones told him that Isabel would keep her room, he longed to ask for leave to go and make some inquiry at the door. She would not play lawn-tennis with him. Well;—he did not now care much for that. After what he had said to her she must at any rate give him some answer. She had been so gracious to him that his hopes ran very high. It never occurred to him to fancy that she might be gracious to him because he was heir to the Dukedom of Omnium. She herself was so infinitely superior to all wealth, to all rank, to all sublunary arrangements, conventions, and considerations, that there was no room for confidence of that nature. But he was confident because her smile had been sweet, and her eyes bright, —and because he was conscious, though unconsciously conscious, of something of the sympathy of love.

But he had to go to the waterfall with Mabel. Lady Mabel was always dressed perfectly,—having great gifts of her own in that direction. There was a freshness about her which made her morning costume more charming than that of the evening, and never did she look so well as when arrayed for a walk. On this occasion she had certainly done her best. But he, poor blind idiot, saw nothing of this. The white gauzy fabric which had covered Isabel's satin petticoat on the previous evening still filled his eyes. Those perfect boots, the little glimpses of party-coloured stockings above them, the looped-up skirt, the jacket fitting but never binding that lovely body and waist, the jaunty hat with its small fresh feathers, all were nothing to him. Nor was the bright honest face beneath the hat anything to him now;—for it was an honest face, though misfortunes which had come had somewhat marred the honesty of the heart.

At first the conversation was about indifferent things,—Killancodlem and Mrs. Jones, Crummie-Toddie and Reginald Dobbes. They had gone along the high-road as far as the post-office, and had turned up through the wood and reached a seat whence there was a beautiful view down upon the Archay, before a word was said affecting either Miss Boncassen or the ring. 'You got the ring safe?' she said.

'Oh yes.'

'How could you be so foolish as to risk it?'

'I did not regard it as mine. You had accepted it,—I thought.'

'But if I had, and then repented of my fault in doing so, should you not have been willing to help me in setting myself right with myself? Of course, after what had passed, it was a trouble to me when it came. What was I to do? For a day or two I thought I would take it, not as liking to take it, but as getting rid of the trouble in that way. Then I remembered its value, its history, the fact that all who knew you would want to know what had become of it,—and I felt that it should be given back. There is only one person to whom you must give it.'

'Who is that?' he said quickly.

'Your wife;—or to her who is to become your wife. No other woman can be justified in accepting such a present.'

'There has been a great deal more said about it than it's worth,' said he, not anxious at the present moment to discuss any matrimonial projects with her. 'Shall we go on to the Fall?' Then she got up and led the way till they came to the little bridge from which they could see the Falls of the Codlem below them. 'I call that very pretty,' he said.

'I thought you would like it.'

'I never saw anything of that kind more jolly. Do you care for scenery, Mabel?'

'Very much. I know no pleasure equal to it. You have never seen Grex?'

'Is it like this?'

'Not in the least. It is wilder than this, and there are not so many trees; but to my eyes it is very beautiful. I wish you had seen it.'

'Perhaps I may some day.'

'That is not likely now,' she said. 'The house is in ruins. If I had just money enough to keep it for myself, I think I could live alone there and be happy.'

'You;—alone! Of course you mean to marry?'

'Mean to marry! Do persons marry because they mean it? With nineteen men out of twenty the idea of marrying them would convey the idea of hating them. You can mean to marry. No doubt you do mean it.'

'I suppose I shall,—some day. How very well the house looks from here.' It was incumbent upon him at the present moment to turn the conversation.

But when she had a project in her head it was not so easy to turn her away. 'Yes, indeed,' she said, 'very well. But as I was saying,—you can mean to marry.'

'Anybody can mean it.'

'But you can carry out a purpose. What are you thinking of doing now?'

'Upon my honour, Mabel, that is unfair.'

'Are we not friends?'

'I think so.'

'Dear friends?'

'I hope so.'

'Then may I not tell you what I think? If you do not mean to marry that American young lady you should not raise false hopes.'

'False—hopes!' He had hopes, but he had never thought that Isabel could have any.

'False hopes;—certainly. Do you not know that everyone was looking at you last night?'

'Certainly not.'

'And that that old woman is going about talking of it as her doing, pretending to be afraid of your father, whereas nothing would please her better than to humble a family so high as yours.'

'Humble!' exclaimed Lord Silverbridge.

'Do you think your father would like it? Would you think that another man would be doing well for himself by marrying Miss Boncassen?'

'I do,' said he energetically.

'Then you must be very much in love with her.'

'I say nothing about that.'

'If you are so much in love with her that you mean to face the displeasure of all your friends——'

'I do not say what I mean. I could talk more freely to you than to anyone else, but I won't talk about that even to you. As regards Miss Boncassen, I think that any man might marry her, without discredit. I won't have it said that she can be inferior to me,—or to anybody.'

There was a steady manliness in this which took Lady Mabel by surprise. She was convinced that he intended to offer his hand to the girl, and now was actuated chiefly by a feeling that his doing so would be an outrage to all English propriety. If a word might have an effect it would be her duty to speak that word. 'I think you are wrong there, Lord Silverbridge.'

'I am sure I am right.'

'What have you yourself felt about your sister and Mr. Tregear?'

'It is altogether different;—altogether. Frank's wife will be simply his wife. Mine, should I outlive my father, will be Duchess of Omnium.'

'But your father? I have heard you speak with bitter regret of this affair of Lady Mary's, because it vexes him. Would your marriage with an American lady vex him less?'

'Why should it vex him at all? Is she vulgar, or ill to look at, or stupid?'

'Think of her mother.'

'I am not going to marry her mother. Nor for the matter of that am I going to marry her. You are taking all that for granted in a most unfair way.'

'How can I help it after what I saw yesterday?'

'I will not talk any more about it. We had better go down or we shall get no lunch.' Lady Mabel, as she followed him, tried to make herself believe that all her sorrow came from regret that so fine a scion of the British nobility should throw himself away upon an American adventuress.

The guests were still at lunch when they entered the dining-room, and Isabel was seated close to Mrs. Jones. Silverbridge at once went up to her,—and place was made for him as though he had almost a right to be next to her. Miss Boncassen herself bore her honours well, seeming to regard the little change at table as though it was of no moment. 'I became so eager about that game,' she said, 'that I went on too long.'

'I hope you are now none the worse.'

'At six o'clock this morning I thought I should never use my legs again.'

'Were you awake at six?' said Silverbridge, with pitying voice.

'That was it. I could not sleep. Now I begin to hope that sooner or later I shall unstiffen.'

During every moment, at every word that he uttered, he

was thinking of the declaration of love which he had made to her. But it seemed to him as though the matter had not dwelt on her mind. When they drew their chairs away from the table he thought that not a moment was to be lost before some further explanation of their feelings for each other should be made. Was not the matter which had been so far discussed of vital importance for both of them? And, glorious as she was above all other women, the offer which he had made must have some weight with her. He did not think that he proposed to give more than she deserved, but still, that which he was so willing to give was not a little. Or was it possible that she had not understood his meaning? If so, he would not willingly lose a moment before he made it plain to her. But she seemed content to hang about with the other women, and when she sauntered about the grounds seated herself on a garden-chair with Lady Mabel, and discussed with great eloquence the general beauty of Scotch scenery. An hour went on in this way. Could it be that she knew that he had offered to make her his wife? During this time he went and returned more than once, but still she was there, on the same garden-seat, talking to those who came in her way.

Then on a sudden she got up and put her hand on his arm. 'Come and take a turn with me,' she said. 'Lord Silverbridge, do you remember anything of last night?'

'Remember!'

'I thought for a while this morning that I would let it pass as though it had been mere trifling.'

'It would have wanted two to let it pass in that way,' he said, almost indignantly.

On hearing this she looked up at him, and there came over her face that brilliant smile, which to him was perhaps the most potent of her spells. 'What do you mean by—wanting two?'

'I must have a voice in that as well as you.'

'And what is your voice?'

'My voice is this. I told you last night that I loved you. This morning I ask you to be my wife.'

'It is a very clear voice,' she said,—almost in a whisper; but in a tone so serious that it startled him.

'It ought to be clear,' he said doggedly.

'Do you think I don't know that? Do you think that if I liked you well last night I don't like you better now?'

'But do you—like me?'

'That is just the thing I am going to say nothing about.'

'Isabel!'

'Just the one thing I will not allude to. Now you must listen to me.'

'Certainly.'

'I know a great deal about you. We Americans are an inquiring people, and I have found out pretty much everything.' His mind misgave him as he felt she had ascertained his former purpose respecting Mabel. 'You,' she said, 'among young men in England are about the foremost, and therefore, —as I think,—about the foremost in the world. And you have all personal gifts;—youth and spirits—— Well, I will not go on and name the others. You are, no doubt, supposed to be entitled to the best and sweetest of God's feminine creatures.'

'You are she.'

'Whether you be entitled to me or not I cannot yet say. Now I will tell you something of myself. My father's father* came to New York as a labourer from Holland, and worked upon the quays in that city. Then he built houses, and became rich, and was almost a miser;—with the good sense, however, to educate his only son. What my father is you see. To me he is sterling gold, but he is not like your people. My dear mother is not at all like your ladies. She is not a lady in your sense,—though with her unselfish devotion to others she is something infinitely better. For myself I am,—well, meaning to speak honestly, I will call myself pretty and smart. I think I know how to be true.'

'I am sure you do.'

'But what right have you to suppose I shall know how to be a Duchess?'

'I am sure you will.'

'Now listen to me. Go to your friends and ask them. Ask that Lady Mabel;—ask your father;—ask that Lady Cantrip. And above all, ask yourself. And allow me to require you to take three months to do this. Do not come to see me for three months.'

'And then?'

'What may happen then I cannot tell, for I want three months also to think of it myself. Till then, good-bye.' She gave him her hand and left it in his for a few seconds. He tried to draw her to him; but she resisted him, still smiling. Then she left him.

CHAPTER XLI

Ischl*

IT was a custom with Mrs. Finn almost every autumn to go off to Vienna, where she possessed considerable property, and there to inspect the circumstances of her estate. Sometimes her husband would accompany her, and he did so in this year of which we are now speaking. One morning in September they were together at an hotel at Ischl, whither they had come from Vienna, when as they went through the hall into the courtyard, they came, in the very doorway, upon the Duke of Omnium and his daughter. The Duke and Lady Mary had just arrived, having passed through the mountains from the salt-mine district, and were about to take up their residence in the hotel for a few days. They had travelled very slowly, for Lady Mary had been ill, and the Duke had expressed his determination to see a doctor at Ischl.

There is no greater mistake than in supposing that only the young blush. But the blushes of middle life are luckily not seen through the tan which has come from the sun and the gas and the work and the wiles of the world. Both the Duke and Phineas blushed; and though their blushes were hidden, that peculiar glance of the eye which always accompanies a blush was visible enough from one to the other. The elder lady kept her countenance admirably, and the younger one had no occasion for blushing. She at once ran forward and kissed her friend. The Duke stood with his hat off waiting to give his hand to the lady, and then took that of his late colleague. 'How odd that we should meet here,' he said, turning to Mrs. Finn.

'Odd enough to us that your Grace should be here,' she said, 'because we had heard nothing of your intended coming.'

'It is so nice to find you,' said Lady Mary. 'We are this moment come. Don't say that you are this moment going.'

'At this moment we are only going as far as Halstadt.'*

'And are coming back to dinner? Of course they will dine with us. Will they not, papa?' The Duke said that he hoped they would. To declare that you are engaged at an hotel, unless there be some real engagement, is almost an impossibility. There was no escape, and before they were allowed to get into their carriage they had promised they would dine with the Duke and his daughter.

'I don't know that it is especially a bore,' Mrs. Finn said to her husband in the carriage. 'You may be quite sure that of whatever trouble there may be in it, he has much more than his share.'

'His share should be the whole,' said her husband. 'No one else has done anything wrong.'

When the Duke's apology had reached her, so that there was no longer any ground for absolute hostility, then she had told the whole story to her husband. He at first was very indignant. What right had the Duke to expect that any ordinary friend should act duenna over his daughter in accordance with his caprices? This was said and much more of the kind. But any humour towards quarrelling which Phineas Finn might have felt for a day or two was quieted by his wife's prudence. 'A man,' she said, 'can do no more than apologise. After that there is no room for reproach.'

At dinner the conversation turned at first on British politics, in which Mrs. Finn was quite able to take her part. Phineas was decidedly of opinion that Sir Timothy Beeswax and Lord Drummond could not live another session. And on this subject a good deal was said. Later in the evening the Duke found himself sitting with Mrs. Finn in the broad verandah over the hotel garden, while Lady Mary was playing to Phineas within. 'How do you think she is looking?' asked the father.

'Of course I see that she has been ill. She tells me that she was far from well at Salzburg.'

'Yes;—indeed for three or four days she frightened me much. She suffered terribly from headaches.'

'Nervous headaches?'

'So they said there. I feel quite angry with myself because I did not bring a doctor with us. The trouble and ceremony of such an accompaniment is no doubt disagreeable.'

'And I suppose seemed when you started to be unnecessary?'

'Quite unnecessary.'

'Does she complain again now?'

'She did to-day—a little.'

The next day Lady Mary could not leave her bed; and the Duke in his sorrow was obliged to apply to Mrs. Finn. After what had passed on the previous day Mrs. Finn of course called, and was shown at once up to her young friend's room. There she found the girl in great pain, lying with her two thin hands up to her head, and hardly able to utter more than a word. Shortly after that Mrs. Finn was alone with the Duke, and then there took place a conversation between them which the lady thought to be very remarkable.

'Had I better send for a doctor from England?' he asked. In answer to this Mrs. Finn expressed her opinion that such a measure was hardly necessary, that the gentleman from the town who had been called in seemed to know what he was about, and that the illness, lamentable as it was, did not seem to be in any way dangerous. 'One cannot tell what it comes from,' said the Duke dubiously.

'Young people, I fancy, are often subject to such maladies.'

'It must come from something wrong.'

'That may be said of all sickness.'

'And therefore one tries to find out the cause. She says that she is unhappy.' These last words he spoke slowly and in a low voice. To this Mrs. Finn could make no reply. She did not doubt but that the girl was unhappy, and she knew well why; but the source of Lady Mary's misery was one to which she could not very well allude. 'You know all the misery about that young man.'

'That is a trouble that requires time to cure it,' she said,— not meaning to imply that time would cure it by enabling the girl to forget her lover; but because in truth she had not known what else to say.

'If time will cure it.'

'Time, they say, cures all sorrows.'

'But what should I do to help time? There is no sacrifice I would not make,—no sacrifice! Of myself I mean. I would devote myself to her,—leave everything else on one side. We purpose being back in England in October; but I would remain here if I thought it better for her comfort.'

'I cannot tell, Duke.'

'Neither can I. But you are a woman and might know better than I do. It is so hard that a man should be left with a charge of which from its very nature he cannot understand the duties.' Then he paused, but she could find no words which would suit at the moment. It was almost incredible to her that after what had passed he should speak to her at all as to the condition of his daughter. 'I cannot, you know,' he said very seriously, 'encourage a hope that she should be allowed to marry that man.'

'I do not know.'

'You yourself, Mrs. Finn, felt that when she told you about it at Matching.'

'I felt that you would disapprove of it.'

'Disapprove of it! How could it be otherwise? Of course you felt that. There are ranks in life in which the first comer that suits a maiden's eye may be accepted as a fitting lover. I will not say but that they who are born to such a life may be the happier. They are, I am sure, free from troubles to which they are incident whom fate has called to a different sphere. But duty is—duty;—and whatever pang it may cost, duty should be performed.'

'Certainly.'

'Certainly;—certainly; certainly,' he said, re-echoing her word.

'But then, Duke, one has to be so sure what duty requires. In many matters this is easy enough, and the only difficulty comes from temptation. There are cases in which it is so hard to know.'

'Is this one of them?'

'I think so.'

'Then the maiden should—in any class of life—be allowed to take the man—that just suits her eye?' As he said this his mind was intent on his Glencora and on Burgo Fitzgerald.

'I have not said so. A man may be bad, vicious, a spend-thrift,—eaten up by bad habits.' Then he frowned, thinking that she also had her mind intent on his Glencora and on that Burgo Fitzgerald, and being most unwilling to have the difference between Burgo and Frank Tregear pointed out to him. 'Nor have I said,' she continued, 'that even were none of these faults apparent in the character of a suitor, the lady should in all cases be advised to accept a young man because he has made himself agreeable to her. There may be dis-crepancies.'

'There are,' said he, still with a low voice but with infinite energy,—'insurmountable discrepancies.'

'I only said that this was a case in which it might be diffi-cult for you to see your duty plainly.'

'Why should it be?'

'You would not have her—break her heart?' Then he was silent for awhile, turning over in his mind the proposition which now seemed to have been made to him. If the question came to that,—should she be allowed to break her heart and die, or should he save her from that fate by sanctioning her marriage with Tregear? If the choice could be put to him plainly by some supernal power, what then would he choose? If duty required him to prevent this marriage, his duty could not be altered by the fact that his girl would avenge herself upon him by dying! If such a marriage were in itself wrong, that wrong could not be made right by the fear of such a catastrophe. Was it not often the case that duty required that someone should die? And yet as he thought of it,—thought that the someone whom his mind had suggested was the one female creature now left belonging to him,—he put his hand up to his brow and trembled with agony. If he knew, if in truth he believed that such would be the result of firmness on his part,—then he would be infirm, then he must yield. Sooner than that, he must welcome this Tregear to his house. But why should he think that she would die? This woman had now asked him whether he would be willing to break his girl's heart. It was a frightful question; but he could see that it had come naturally in the sequence of the conversation which he had forced upon her. Did girls break their hearts in such emergencies? Was it not all romance? 'Men have died and worms have eaten them,—but not for love.'*He remembered it all and carried on the argument in his mind, though the pause was but for a minute. There might be suffering, no doubt. The higher the duties the keener the pangs! But would it become him to be deterred from doing right because she for a time might find that she had made the world bitter to herself? And were there not feminine wiles,—tricks by which women learn to have their way in opposition to the judgment of their lords and masters? He did not think that his Mary was wilfully guilty of any scheme. The suffering he knew was true suffering. But not the less did it become him to be on his guard against attacks of this nature.

'No,' he said at last; 'I would not have her break her heart,—if I understand what such words mean. They are generally, I think, used fantastically.'

'You would not wish to see her overwhelmed by sorrow?'

'Wish it! What a question to ask a father!'

'I must be more plain in my language, Duke. Though such

a marriage be distasteful to you, it might perhaps be preferable to seeing her sorrowing always.'

'Why should it? I have to sorrow always. We are told that man is born to sorrow as surely as the sparks fly upwards.'*

'Then I can say nothing further.'

'You think I am cruel.'

'If I am to say what I really think I shall offend you.'

'No;—not unless you mean offence.'

'I shall never do that to you, Duke. When you talk as you do now you hardly know yourself. You think you could see her suffering, and not be moved by it. But were it to be continued long you would give way. Though we know that there is an infinity of grief in this life, still we struggle to save those we love from grieving. If she be steadfast enough to cling to her affection for this man, then at last you will have to yield.' He looked at her frowning, but did not say a word. 'Then it will perhaps be a comfort for you to know that the man himself is trustworthy and honest.'

There was a terrible rebuke in this; but still, as he had called it down upon himself, he would not resent it, even in his heart. 'Thank you,' he said, rising from his chair. 'Perhaps you will see her again this afternoon.' Of course she assented, and, as the interview had taken place in his rooms, she took her leave.

This which Mrs. Finn had said to him was all to the same effect as that which had come from Lady Cantrip; only it was said with a higher spirit. Both the women saw the matter in the same light. There must be a fight between him and his girl; but she, if she could hold out for a certain time, would be the conqueror. He might take her away and try what absence would do, or he might have recourse to that specific which had answered so well in reference to his own wife; but if she continued to sorrow during absence, and if she would have nothing to do with the other lover,—then he must at last give way! He had declared that he was willing to sacrifice himself,—meaning thereby that if a lengthened visit to the cities of China, or a prolonged sojourn in the Western States of

America would wean her from her love, he would go to China or to the Western States. At present his self-banishment had been carried no farther than Vienna. During their travels hitherto Tregear's name had not once been mentioned. The Duke had come away from home resolved not to mention it, —and she was minded to keep it in reserve till some seeming catastrophe should justify a declaration of her purpose. But from first to last she had been sad, and latterly she had been ill. When asked as to her complaint she would simply say that she was not happy. To go on with this through the Chinese cities could hardly be good for either of them. She would not wake herself to any enthusiasm in regard to scenery, costume, pictures, or even discomforts. Wherever she was taken it was all barren to her.

As their plans stood at present, they were to return to England so as to enable her to be at Custins by the middle of October. Had he taught himself to hope that any good could be done by prolonged travelling he would readily have thrown over Custins and Lord Popplecourt. He could not bring himself to trust much to the Popplecourt scheme. But the same contrivance had answered on that former occasion. When he spoke to her about their plans, she expressed herself quite ready to go back to England. When he suggested those Chinese cities, her face became very long and she was immediately attacked by paroxysms of headaches.

'I think I should take her to some place on the seashore in England,' said Mrs. Finn.

'Custins is close to the sea,' he replied. 'It is Lord Cantrip's place in Dorsetshire. It was partly settled that she was to go there.'

'I suppose she likes Lady Cantrip.'

'Why should she not?'

'She has not said a word to me to the contrary. I only fear she would feel that she was being sent there,—as to a convent.'

'What ought I to do then?'

'How can I venture to answer that? What she would like best, I think, would be to return to Matching with you, and

to settle down in a quiet way for the winter.' The Duke shook
his head. That would be worse than travelling. She would
still have headaches and still tell him that she was unhappy.
'Of course I do not know what your plans are, and pray believe me that I should not obtrude my advice if you did not
ask me.'

'I know it,' he said. 'I know how good you are and how
reasonable. I know how much you have to forgive.'

'Oh, no.'

'And, if I have not said so as I should have done, it has not
been from want of feeling. I do believe you did what you thought
best when Mary told you that story at Matching.'

'Why should your Grace go back to that?'

'Only that I may acknowledge my indebtedness to you,
and say to you somewhat fuller than I could do in my letter
that I am sorry for the pain which I gave you.'

'All that is over now,—and shall be forgotten.'

Then he spoke of his immediate plans. He would at once
go back to England by slow stages,—by very slow stages,—
staying a day or two at Salzburg, at Ratisbon, at Nuremberg,
at Frankfort, and so on. In this way he would reach England
about the 10th of October, and Mary would then be ready to
go to Custins by the time appointed.

In a day or two Lady Mary was better. 'It is terrible while
it lasts,' she said, speaking to Mrs. Finn of her headache,
'but when it has gone then I am quite well. Only'—she added
after a pause—'only I can never be happy again while papa
thinks as he does now.' Then there was a party made up before they separated for an excursion to the Hintersee*and the
Obersee. On this occasion Lady Mary seemed to enjoy herself,
as she liked the companionship of Mrs. Finn. Against Lady
Cantrip she never said a word. But Lady Cantrip was always a
duenna to her, whereas Mrs. Finn was a friend. While the Duke
and Phineas were discussing politics together—thoroughly enjoying the weakness of Lord Drummond and the iniquity of
Sir Timothy—which they did with augmented vehemence from
their ponies' backs, the two women in lower voices talked

over their own affairs. 'I dare say you will be happy at Custins',
said Mrs. Finn.

'No; I shall not. There will be people there whom I don't
know, and I don't want to know. Have you heard anything
about him, Mrs. Finn?'

Mrs. Finn turned round and looked at her,—for a moment
almost angrily. Then her heart relented. 'Do you mean—
Mr. Tregear?'

'Yes, Mr. Tregear.'

'I think I heard that he was shooting with Lord Silverbridge.'

'I am glad of that,' said Mary.

'It will be pleasant for both of them.'

'I am very glad they should be together. While I know
that, I feel that we are not altogether separated. I will never
give it up, Mrs. Finn,—never; never. It is no use taking me
to China.' In that Mrs. Finn quite agreed with her.

CHAPTER XLII

Again at Killancodlem

SILVERBRIDGE remained at Crummie-Toddie under the
dominion of Reginald Dobbes till the second week in
September. Popplecourt, Nidderdale, and Gerald Palliser were
there also, very obedient, and upon the whole efficient. Tregear was intractable, occasional, and untrustworthy. He was
the cause of much trouble to Mr. Dobbes. He would entertain
a most heterodox and injurious idea that, as he had come
to Crummie-Toddie for amusement, he was not bound to do
anything that did not amuse him. He would not understand
that in sport as in other matters there was an ambition,
driving a man on to excel always and be ahead of others. In
spite of this Mr. Dobbes had cause for much triumph. It was
going to be the greatest thing ever done by six guns in
Scotland. As for Gerald, whom he had regarded as a boy, and
who had offended him by saying that Crummie-Toddie was

ugly,—he was ready to go round the world for him. He had indoctrinated Gerald with all his ideas of a sportsman,—even to a contempt for champagne and a conviction that tobacco should be moderated. The three lords too had proved themselves efficient, and the thing was going to be a success. But just when a day was of vital importance, when it was essential that there should be a strong party for a drive, Silverbridge found it absolutely necessary that he should go over to Killancodlem.

'She has gone,' said Nidderdale.

'Who the —— is she?' asked Silverbridge, almost angrily.

'Everybody knows who she is,' said Popplecourt.

'It will be a good thing when some She has got hold of you, my boy, so as to keep you in your proper place.'

'If you cannot withstand that sort of attraction you ought not to go in for shooting at all,' said Dobbes.

'I shouldn't wonder at his going,' continued Nidderdale, 'if we didn't all know that the American is no longer there. She has gone to—Bath I think they say.'

'I suppose it's Mrs. Jones herself,' said Popplecourt.

'My dear boys,' said Silverbridge, 'you may be quite sure that when I say that I am going to Killancodlem I mean to go to Killancodlem, and that no chaff about young ladies,—which I think very disgusting,—will stop me. I shall be sorry if Dobbes's roll of the killed should be lessened by a single hand, seeing that his ambition sets that way. Considering the amount of slaughter we have perpetrated, I really think that we need not be over anxious.' After this nothing further was said. Tregear, who knew that Mabel Grex was still at Killancodlem, had not spoken.

In truth Mabel had sent for Lord Silverbridge, and this had been her letter:

'DEAR LORD SILVERBRIDGE,

'Mrs. Montacute Jones is cut to the heart because you have not been over to see her again, and she says that it is lamentable to think that such a man as Reginald Dobbes should have so much power over you. "Only twelve miles," she says, "and he knows that we are here!" I told her that you knew Miss Boncassen was gone.

'But though Miss Boncassen has left us we are a very pleasant party, and surely you must be tired of such a place as Crummie-Toddie. If only for the sake of getting a good dinner once in a way do come over again. I shall be here yet for ten days. As they will not let me go back to Grex I don't know where I could be more happy. I have been asked to go to Custins, and suppose I shall turn up there some time in the autumn.

'And now shall I tell you what I expect? I do expect that you will come over to—see me. "I did see her the other day," you will say, "and she did not make herself pleasant." I know that. How was I to make myself pleasant when I found myself so completely snuffed out by your American beauty? Now she is away, and Richard will be himself.* Do come, because in truth I want to see you.

'Yours always sincerely,

'MABEL GREX.'

On receiving this he at once made up his mind to go to Killancodlem, but he could not make up his mind why it was that she had asked him. He was sure of two things; sure in the first place that she had intended to let him know that she did not care about him; and then sure that she was aware of his intention in regard to Miss Boncassen. Everybody at Killancodlem had seen it,—to his disgust; but still that it was so had been manifest. And he had consoled himself, feeling that it would matter nothing should he be accepted. She had made an attempt to talk him out of his purpose. Could it be that she thought it possible a second attempt might be successful? If so, she did not know him.

She had in truth thought not only that this, but that something further than this, might be possible. Of course the prize loomed larger before her eyes as the prospects of obtaining it became less. She could not doubt that he had intended to offer

337

her his hand when he had spoken to her of his love in London. Then she had stopped him;—had 'spared him,' as she had told her friend. Certainly she had then been swayed by some feeling that it would be ungenerous in her to seize greedily the first opportunity he had given her. But he had again made an effort. He surely would not have sent her the ring had he not intended her to regard him as her lover. When she received the ring her heart had beat very high. Then she had sent that little note, saying that she would keep it till she could give it to his wife. When she wrote that she had intended the ring should be her own. And other things pressed upon her mind. Why had she been asked to the dinner at Richmond? Why was she invited to Custins? Little hints had reached her of the Duke's goodwill towards her. If on that side the marriage were approved, why should she destroy her own hopes?

Then she had seen him with Miss Boncassen, and in her pique had forced the ring back upon him. During that long game on the lawn her feelings had been very bitter. Of course the girl was the lovelier of the two. All the world was raving of her beauty. And there was no doubt as to the charm of her wit and manner. And then she had no touch of that blasé used-up way of life of which Lady Mabel was conscious herself. It was natural that it should be so. And was she, Mabel Grex, the girl to stand in his way and to force herself upon him, if he loved another? Certainly not,—though there might be a triple ducal coronet to be had.

But were there not other considerations? Could it be well that the heir of the house of Omnium should marry an American girl, as to whose humble birth whispers were already afloat? As his friend, would it not be right that she should tell him what the world would say? As his friend, therefore, she had given him her counsel.

When he was gone the whole thing weighed heavily upon her mind. Why should she lose the prize if it might still be her own? To be Duchess of Omnium! She had read of many of the other sex, and of one or two of her own, who by settled resolution had achieved greatness* in opposition to all obstacles. Was this thing beyond her reach? To hunt him, and catch him, and marry him to his own injury,—that would be impossible to her. She was sure of herself there. But how infinitely better would this be for him! Would she not have all his family with her,—and all the world of England? In how short a time would he not repent his marriage with Miss Boncassen! Whereas, were she his wife, she would so stir herself for his joys, for his good, for his honour, that there should be no possibility of repentance. And he certainly had loved her. Why else had he followed her, and spoken such words to her? Of course he had loved her! But then there had come this blaze of beauty and had carried off,—not his heart but his imagination. Because he had yielded to such fascination, was she to desert him, and also to desert herself? From day to day she thought of it, and then she wrote that letter. She hardly knew what she would do, what she might say; but she would trust to the opportunity to do and say something.

'If you have no room for me,' he said to Mrs. Jones, 'you must scold Lady Mab. She has told me that you told her to invite me.'

'Of course I did. Do you think I would not sleep in the stables, and give you up my own bed if there were no other? It is so good of you to come!'

'So good of you, Mrs. Jones, to ask me.'

'So very kind to come when all the attraction has gone!' Then he blushed and stammered, and was just able to say that his only object in life was to pour out his adoration at the feet of Mrs. Montacute Jones herself.

There was a certain Lady Fawn,*—a pretty mincing married woman of about twenty-five, with a husband much older, who liked mild flirtations with mild young men. 'I am afraid we've lost your great attraction,' she whispered to him.

'Certainly not as long as Lady Fawn is here,' he said, seating himself close to her on a garden bench, and seizing suddenly hold of her hand. She gave a little scream and a jerk, and so relieved herself from him. 'You see,' said he, 'people do make such mistakes about a man's feelings.'

'Lord Silverbridge!'

'It's quite true, but I'll tell you all about it another time,' and so he left her. All these little troubles, his experience in the 'House,' the necessity of snubbing Tifto, the choice of a wife, and his battle with Reginald Dobbes, were giving him by degrees age and flavour.

Lady Mabel had fluttered about him on his first coming, and had been very gracious, doing the part of an old friend. 'There is to be a big shooting to-morrow,' she said, in presence of Mrs. Jones.

'If it is to come to that,' he said, 'I might as well go back to Dobbydom.'

'You may shoot if you like,' said Lady Mabel.

'I haven't even brought a gun with me.'

'Then we'll have a walk,—a whole lot of us,' she said.

In the evening, about an hour before dinner, Silverbridge and Lady Mabel were seated together on the bank of a little stream which ran on the other side of the road, but on a spot not more than a furlong from the hall-door. She had brought him there, but she had done so without any definite scheme. She had made no plan of campaign for the evening, having felt relieved when she found herself able to postpone the project of her attack till the morrow. Of course there must be an attack, but how it should be made she had never had the courage to tell herself. The great women of the world,* the Semiramises, the Pocahontas, the Ida Pfeiffers, and the Charlotte Cordays, had never been wanting to themselves when the moment for action came. Now she was pleased to have this opportunity added to her; this pleasant minute in which some soft preparatory word might be spoken; but the great effort should be made on the morrow.

'Is not this nicer than shooting with Mr. Dobbes?' she asked.

'A great deal nicer. Of course I am bound to say so.'

'But in truth. I want to find out what you really like. Men are so different. You need not pay me any compliment; you know that well enough.'

'I like you better than Dobbes,—if you mean that.'

'Even so much is something.'

'But I am fond of shooting.'

'Only a man may have enough of it.'

'Too much, if he is subject to Dobbes, as Dobbes likes them to be. Gerald likes it.'

'Did you think it odd,' she said after a pause, 'that I should ask you to come over again?'

'Was it odd?' he replied.

'That is as you may take it. There is certainly no other man in the world to whom I would have done it.'

'Not to Tregear?'

'Yes,' she said; 'yes,—to Tregear, could I have been as sure of a welcome for him as I am for you. Frank is in all respects the same as a brother to me. That would not have seemed odd;—I mean to myself.'

'And has this been—odd,—to yourself?'

341

'Yes. Not that anybody else has felt it so. Only I,—and perhaps you. You felt it so?'

'Not especially. I thought you were a very good fellow. I have always thought that;—except when you made me take back the ring.'

'Does that still fret you?'

'No man likes to take back a thing. It makes him seem to have been awkward and stupid in giving it.'

'It was the value——'

'You should have left me to judge of that.'

'If I have offended you I will beg your pardon. Give me anything else, anything but that, and I will take it.'

'But why not that?' said he.

'Now that you have fitted it for a lady's finger it should go to your wife. No one else should have it.'

Upon this he brought the ring once more out of his pocket and again offered it to her. 'No; anything but that. That your wife must have.' Then he put the ring back again. 'It would have been nicer for you had Miss Boncassen been here.' In saying this she followed no plan. It came rather from pique. It was almost as though she had asked him whether Miss Boncassen was to have the ring.

'What makes you say that?'

'But it would.'

'Yes, it would,' he replied stoutly, turning round as he lay on the ground and facing her.

'Has it come to that?'

'Come to what? You ask me a question and I answer you truly.'

'You cannot be happy without her?'

'I did not say so. You ask me whether I should like to have her here,—and I say Yes. What would you think of me if I said No?'

'My being here is not enough?' This should not have been said, of course, but the little speech came from the exquisite pain of the moment. She had meant to have said hardly anything. She had intended to be happy with him, just touching

342

lightly on things which might lead to that attack which must be made on the morrow. But words will often lead whither the speaker has not intended. So it was now, and in the soreness of her heart she spoke. 'My being here is not enough?'

'It would be enough,' he said, jumping on his feet, 'if you understood all, and would be kind to me.'

'I will at any rate be kind to you,' she replied, as she sat upon the bank looking at the running water.

'I have asked Miss Boncassen to be my wife.'

'And she has accepted?'

'No; not as yet. She is to take three months to think of it. Of course I love her best of all. If you will sympathise with me in that, then I will be as happy with you as the day is long.'

'No,' said she, 'I cannot. I will not.'

'Very well.'

'There should be no such marriage. If you have told me in confidence——'

'Of course I have told you in confidence.'

'It will go no farther; but there can be no sympathy between us. It—it—it is not,—is not——' Then she burst into tears.

'Mabel!'

'No, sir, no; no! What did you mean? But never mind. I have no questions to ask, not a word to say. Why should I? Only this,—that such a marriage will disgrace your family. To me it is no more than to anybody else. But it will disgrace your family.'

How she got back to the house she hardly knew; nor did he. That evening they did not again speak to each other, and on the following morning there was no walk to the mountains. Before dinner he drove himself back to Crummie-Toddie, and when he was taking his leave she shook hands with him with her usual pleasant smile.

CHAPTER XLIII

What happened at Doncaster

THE Leger this year was to be run on the 14th September, and while Lord Silverbridge was amusing himself with the deer at Crummie-Toddie and at Killancodlem with the more easily pursued young ladies, the indefatigable Major was hard at work in the stables. This came a little hard on him. There was the cub-hunting to be looked after, which made his presence at Runnymede necessary, and then that 'pig-headed fellow, Silverbridge' would not have the horses trained anywhere but at Newmarket. How was he to be in two places at once? Yet he was in two places almost at once: cub-hunting in the morning at Egham and Bagshot, and sitting on the same evening at the stable-door at Newmarket, with his eyes fixed upon Prime Minister.

Gradually had he and Captain Green come to understand each other, and though they did at last understand each other, Tifto would talk as though there were no such correct intelligence;—when for instance he would abuse Lord Silverbridge for being pig-headed. On such occasions the Captain's remark would generally be short. 'That be blowed!' he would say, implying that that state of things between the two partners, in which such complaints might be natural, had now been brought to an end. But on one occasion, about a week before the race, he spoke out a little plainer. 'What's the use of your going on with all that before me? It's settled what you've got to do.'

'I don't know that anything is settled,' said the Major.

'Ain't it? I thought it was. If it ain't you'll find yourself in the wrong box. You've as straight a tip as a man need wish for, but if you back out you'll come to grief. Your money's all on the other way already.'

On the Friday before the race Silverbridge dined with Tifto at the Beargarden. On the next morning they went down to Newmarket to see the horse get a gallop, and came back the same evening. During all this time, Tifto was more than ordinarily pleasant to his patron. The horse and the certainty of the horse's success were the only subjects mooted. 'It isn't what I say,' repeated Tifto, 'but look at the betting. You can't get five to four against him. They tell me that if you want to do anything on the Sunday the pull*will be the other way.'

'I stand to lose over £20,000 already,' said Silverbridge, almost frightened by the amount.

'But how much are you on to win?' said Tifto. 'I suppose you could sell your bets for £5,000 down.'

'I wish I knew how to do it,' said Silverbridge. But this was an arrangement, which, if made just now, would not suit the Major's views.

They went to Newmarket, and there they met Captain Green. 'Tifto,' said the young Lord, 'I won't have that fellow with us when the horse is galloping.'

'There isn't an honester man, or a man who understands a horse's paces better in all England,' said Tifto.

'I won't have him standing alongside of me on the Heath,' said his Lordship.

'I don't know how I'm to help it.'

'If he's there I'll send the horse in;—that's all.' Then Tifto found it best to say a few words to Captain Green. But the Captain also said a few words to himself. 'D—— young fool; he don't know what he's dropping into.' Which assertion, if you lay aside the unnecessary expletive, was true to the letter. Lord Silverbridge was a young fool, and did not at all know into what a mess he was being dropped by the united experience, perspicuity, and energy of the man whose company on the Heath he had declined.

The horse was quite a 'picture to look at.' Mr. Pook the trainer assured his Lordship that for health and condition he had never seen anything better. 'Stout all over,' said Mr. Pook, 'and not an ounce of what you may call flesh. And bright! just feel his coat, my Lord! That's 'ealth,—that is; not dressing, nor yet macassar!'*

And then there were various evidences produced of his pace,—how he had beaten that horse, giving him two pounds; how he had been beaten by that, but only on a mile course; the Leger distance*was just the thing for Prime Minister; how by a lucky chance that marvellous quick rat of a thing that had won the Derby had not been entered for the autumn race; how Coalheaver was known to have had bad feet. 'He's a stout 'orse, no doubt,—is the 'Eaver,' said Mr. Pook, 'and that's why the betting-men have stuck to him. But he'll be nowhere on Wednesday. They're beginning to see it now, my Lord. I wish they wasn't so sharp-sighted.'

In the course of the day, however, they met a gentleman who was of a different opinion. He said loudly that he looked on the Heaver as the best three-year-old in England. Of course as matters stood he wasn't going to back the Heaver at even money;—but he'd take twenty-five to thirty in hundreds between the two. All this ended in the bet being accepted and duly booked by Lord Silverbridge. And in this way Silverbridge added two thousand four hundred pounds to his responsibilities.

But there was worse than this coming. On the Sunday

afternoon he went down to Doncaster, of course in company
with the Major. He was alive to the necessity of ridding himself of the Major; but it had been acknowledged that that
duty could not be performed till after this race had been run.
As he sat opposite to his friend on their journey to Doncaster,
he thought of this in the train. It should be done immediately
on their return to London after the race. But the horse, his
Prime Minister, was by this time so dear to him that he intended if possible to keep possession of the animal.

When they reached Doncaster the racing-men were all
occupied with Prime Minister. The horse and Mr. Pook had
arrived that day from Newmarket, viâ Cambridge and Peterborough. Tifto, Silverbridge, and Mr. Pook visited him together three times that afternoon and evening;—and the
Captain also visited the horse, though not in company with
Lord Silverbridge. To do Mr. Pook justice, no one could be
more careful. When the Captain came round with the Major,
Mr. Pook was there. But Captain Green did not enter the
box,—had no wish to do so, was of opinion that on such
occasions no one whose business did not carry him there
should go near a horse. His only object seemed to be to compliment Mr. Pook as to his care, skill, and good fortune.

It was on the Tuesday evening that the chief mischief was
done. There was a club at which many of the racing-men
dined, and there Lord Silverbridge spent his evening. He was
the hero of the hour, and everybody flattered him. It must be
acknowledged that his head was turned. They dined at eight
and much wine was drunk. No one was tipsy, but many were
elated; and much confidence in their favourite animals was
imparted to men who had been sufficiently cautious before
dinner. Then cigars and soda-and-brandy became common
and our young friend was not more abstemious than others.
Large sums were named, and at last in three successive bets
Lord Silverbridge backed his horse for more than forty thousand pounds. As he was making the second bet Mr.
Lupton came across to him and begged him to hold his hand.
'It will be a nasty sum for you to lose, and winning it will be

nothing to you,' he said. Silverbridge took it good-humoured-ly, but said that he knew what he was about. 'These men will pay,' whispered Lupton; 'but you can't be quite sure what they're at.' The young man's brow was covered with perspiration. He was smoking quick and had already smoked more than was good for him. 'All right,' he said. 'I'll mind what I'm about.' Mr. Lupton could do no more, and retired.

Before the night was over bets had been booked to the amount stated, and the Duke's son, who had promised that he would never plunge, stood to lose about seventy thousand pounds*upon the race.

While this was going on Tifto sat not far from his patron, but completely silent. During the day and early in the evening a few sparks of the glory which scintillated from the favourite horse flew in his direction. But he was on this occasion unlike himself, and though the horse was to be run in his name had very little to say in the matter. Not a boast came out of his mouth during dinner or after dinner. He was so moody that his partner, who was generally anxious to keep him quiet, more than once endeavoured to encourage him.

But he was unable to rouse himself. It was still within his power to run straight; to be on the square, if not with Captain Green, at any rate with Lord Silverbridge. But to do so he must make a clean breast with his Lordship and confess the intended sin. As he heard all that was being done, his conscience troubled him sorely. With pitch*of this sort he had never soiled himself before. He was to have three thousand pounds from Green, and then there would be the bets he himself had laid against the horse,—by Green's assistance! It would be the making of him. Of what use had been all his 'square' work to him? And then Silverbridge had behaved so badly to him! But still, as he sat there during the evening, he would have given a hand to have been free from the attempt. He had had no conception before that he could become subject to such misery from such a cause. He would make it straight with Silverbridge this very night,—but that Silverbridge was ever lighting fresh cigars and ever having his glass refilled. It was clear to him that on this night Silverbridge could not be made to understand anything about it. And the deed in which he himself was to be the chief actor was to be done very early in the following morning. At last he slunk away to bed.

On the following morning, the morning of the day on which the race was to be run, the Major tapped at his patron's door about seven o'clock. Of course there was no answer, though the knock was repeated. When young men overnight drink as much brandy-and-water as Silverbridge had done, and smoke as many cigars, they are apt not to hear knocks at their door made at seven o'clock. Nor was his Lordship's servant up,—so that Tifto had no means of getting at him except by personal invasion of the sanctity of his bedroom. But there was no time, not a minute, to be lost. Now, within this minute that was pressing on him, Tifto must choose his course. He opened the door and was standing at the young man's head.

'What the d—— does this mean?' said his Lordship angrily, as soon as his visitor had succeeded in waking him.

Tifto muttered something about the horse which Silverbridge failed to understand. The young man's condition was by no means pleasant. His mouth was furred by the fumes of tobacco. His head was aching. He was heavy with sleep, and this intrusion seemed to him to be a final indignity offered to him by the man whom he now hated. 'What business have you to come in here?' he said, leaning on his elbow. 'I don't care a

straw for the horse. If you have anything to say send my servant. Get out!'

'Oh;—very well,' said Tifto;—and Tifto got out.

It was about an hour afterwards that Tifto returned, and on this occasion a groom from the stables, and the young Lord's own servant, and two or three other men were with him. Tifto had been made to understand that the news now to be communicated, must be communicated by himself, whether his Lordship were angry or not. Indeed, after what had been done his Lordship's anger was not of much moment. In his present visit he was only carrying out the pleasant little plan which had been arranged for him by Captain Green. 'What the mischief is up?' said Silverbridge, rising in his bed.

Then Tifto told his story, sullenly, doggedly, but still in a perspicuous*manner, and with words which admitted of no doubt. But before he told the story he had excluded all but himself and the groom. He and the groom had taken the horse out of the stable, it being the animal's nature to eat his corn better after slight exercise, and while doing so a nail had been picked up.

'Is it much?' asked Silverbridge, jumping still higher in his bed. Then he was told that it was very much,—that the iron had driven itself into the horse's frog, and that there was actually no possibility that the horse should run on that day.

'He can't walk, my Lord,' said the groom, in that authoritative voice which grooms use when they desire to have their own way, and to make their masters understand that they at any rate are not to have theirs.

'Where is Pook?' asked Silverbridge. But Mr. Pook was also still in bed.

It was soon known to Lord Silverbridge as a fact that in very truth the horse could not run. Then sick with headache, with a stomach suffering unutterable things, he had, as he dressed himself, to think of his seventy thousand pounds. Of course the money would be forthcoming. But how would his father look at him? How would it be between him and his father now? After such a misfortune how would he be able to break that other matter to the Duke, and say that he had changed his mind about his marriage,—that he was going to abandon Lady Mabel Grex, and give his hand and a future Duchess's coronet to an American girl whose grandfather had been a porter?

A nail in his foot! Well! He had heard of such things before. He knew that such accidents had happened. What an ass must he have been to risk such a sum on the well-being and safety of an animal who might any day pick up a nail in his foot? Then he thought of the caution which Lupton had given him. What good would the money have done him had he won it? What more could he have than he now enjoyed? But to lose such a sum of money! With all his advantages of wealth he felt himself to be as forlorn and wretched as though he had nothing left in the world before him.

CHAPTER XLIV

How it was done

THE story was soon about the town, and was the one matter for discussion in all racing quarters. About the town! It was about England, about all Europe. It had travelled to America and the Indies, to Australia and the Chinese cities before two hours were over. Before the race was run the accident was discussed and something like the truth surmised in Cairo, Calcutta, Melbourne, and San Francisco. But at Doncaster it was so all-pervading a matter that down to the tradesmen's daughters and the boys at the free-school*the town was divided into two parties, one party believing it to have been a 'plant,' and the other holding that the cause had been natural. It is hardly necessary to say that the ring,*as a rule, belonged to the former party. The ring always suspects. It did not behove even those who would win by the transaction to stand up for its honesty.

The intention had been to take the horse round a portion of the outside of the course near to which his stable stood. A boy rode him and the groom and Tifto went with him. At a certain spot on their return Tifto had exclaimed that the horse was going lame in his off fore-foot. As to this exclamation the boy and the two men were agreed. The boy was then made to dismount and run for Mr. Pook; and as he started Tifto commenced to examine the horse's foot. The boy saw him raise the off fore-leg. He himself had not found the horse lame under him, but had been so hustled and hurried out of the saddle by Tifto and the groom that he had not thought on that matter till he was questioned. So far the story told by Tifto and the groom was corroborated by the boy,—except as to the horse's actual lameness. So far the story was believed by all men,—except in regard to the actual lameness. And so far it was true. Then, according to Tifto and the groom, the other foot was looked at, but nothing was seen. This other foot, the near fore-foot, was examined by the groom, who declared himself to be so flurried by the lameness of such a horse at such a time, that he hardly knew what he saw or what he did not see. At any rate then in his confusion he found no cause of lameness, but the horse was led into the stable as lame as a tree. Here Tifto found the nail inserted into the very cleft of the frog*of the near fore-foot, and so inserted that he could not extract it till the farrier came. That the farrier had extracted the nail from the part of the foot indicated was certainly a fact.

Then there was the nail. Only those who were most peculiarly privileged were allowed to see the nail. But it was buzzed about the racing quarters that the head of the nail,— an old rusty, straight, and well-pointed nail,—bore on it the mark of a recent hammer. In answer to this it was alleged that the blacksmith in extracting the nail with his pincers, had of course operated on its head, had removed certain particles of rust, and might easily have given it the appearance of having been struck. But in answer to this the farrier, who was a sharp fellow, and quite beyond suspicion in the matter, declared that he had very particularly looked at the nail before he extracted it,—had looked at it with the feeling on his mind that something base might too probably have been done,— and that he was ready to swear that the clear mark on the head of the nail was there before he touched it. And then not in the stable, but lying under the little dungheap away from the stable-door, there was found a small piece of broken iron bar, about a foot long, which might have answered for a hammer,—a rusty bit of iron; and amidst the rust of this was found such traces as might have been left had it been used in striking such a nail. There were some who declared that neither on the nail nor on the iron could they see anything. And among these was the Major. But Mr. Lupton brought a strong magnifying-glass to bear, and the world of examiners was satisfied that the marks were there.

It seemed however to be agreed that nothing could be done. Silverbridge would not lend himself at all to those who suspected mischief. He was miserable enough, but in this great trouble he would not separate himself from Tifto. 'I don't believe a word of all that,' he said to Mr. Lupton.

'It ought to be investigated at any rate,' said Lupton.

'Mr. Pook may do as he likes, but I will have nothing to do with it.'

Then Tifto came to him swaggering. Tifto had to go through a considerable amount of acting, for which he was not very well adapted. The Captain would have done it better. He would have endeavoured to put himself altogether into the same boat with his partner, and would have imagined neither suspicion or enmity on his partner's part till suspicion or enmity had been shown. But Tifto, who had not expected that the matter would be allowed to pass over without some inquiry, began by assuming that Silverbridge would think evil of him. Tifto, who at this moment would have given all that he had in the world not to have done the deed, who now hated the instigator of the deed, and felt something almost akin to love for Silverbridge, found himself to be forced by circumstances to defend himself by swaggering. 'I don't understand all this that's going on, my Lord,' he said.

'Neither do I,' replied Silverbridge.

'Any horse is subject to an accident. I am, I suppose, as great a sufferer as you are, and a deuced sight less able to bear it.'

'Who has said anything to the contrary? As for bearing it, we must take it as it comes,—both of us. You may as well know now as later that I have done with racing—for ever.'

'What do you tell me that for? You can do as you like and I can do as I like about that. If I had had my way about the horse this never would have happened. Taking a horse out at that time in the morning,—before a race!'

'Why, you went with him yourself.'

'Yes;—by Pook's orders. You allowed Pook to do just as he pleased. I should like to know what money Pook has got on it, and which way he laid it.' This disgusted Silverbridge so much that he turned away and would have no more to say to Tifto.

Before one o'clock, at which hour it was stated nominally

that the races would commence, general opinion had formed itself,—and general opinion had nearly hit the truth. General opinion declared that the nail had been driven in wilfully,—that it had been done by Tifto himself, and that Tifto had been instigated by Captain Green. Captain Green perhaps overacted his part a little. His intimacy with the Major was well known, and yet, in all this turmoil, he kept himself apart as though he had no interest in the matter. 'I have got my little money on, and what little I have I lose,' he said in answer to inquiries. But everyone knew that he could not but have a great interest in a race, as to which the half owner of the favourite was a peculiarly intimate friend of his own. Had he come down to the stables and been seen about the place with Tifto it might have been better. As it was, though he was very quiet, his name was soon mixed up in the matter. There was one man who asserted it as a fact known to himself that Green and Villiers,—one Gilbert Villiers,—were in partnership together. It was very well known that Gilbert Villiers would win two thousand five hundred pounds from Lord Silverbridge.

Then minute investigation was made into the betting of certain individuals. Of course there would be great plunder, and where would the plunder go? Who would get the money which poor Silverbridge would lose? It was said that one at least of the large bets made on that Tuesday evening could be traced to the same Villiers though not actually made by him. More would be learned when the settling-day should come. But there was quite enough already to show that there were many men determined to get to the bottom of it all if possible.

There came upon Silverbridge in his trouble a keen sense of his position and a feeling of the dignity which he ought to support. He clung during great part of the morning to Mr. Lupton. Mr. Lupton was much his senior and they had never been intimate; but now there was comfort in his society. 'I am afraid you are hit heavily,' said Mr. Lupton.

'Something over seventy thousand pounds!'

'Looking at what will be your property it is of course nothing. But if ——'

'If what?'

'If you go to the Jews*for it then it will become a great deal.'

'I shall certainly not do that.'

'Then you may regard it as a trifle,' said Lupton.

'No, I can't. It is not a trifle. I must tell my father. He'll find the money.'

'There is no doubt about that.'

'He will. But I feel at present that I would rather change places with the poorest gentleman I know than have to tell him. I have done with races, Lupton.'

'If so, this will have been a happy day for you. A man in your position can hardly make money by it, but he may lose so much! If a man really likes the amusement,—as I do,—and risks no more than what he has in his pocket, that may be very well.'

'At any rate I have done with it.'

Nevertheless he went to see the race run, and everybody seemed to be touched with pity for him. He carried himself well, saying as little as he could of his own horse, and taking, or affecting to take, great interest in the race. After the race he managed to see all those to whom he had lost heavy stakes, —having to own to himself, as he did so, that not one of them was a gentleman to whom he should like to give his hand. To them he explained that his father was abroad,—that probably his liabilities could not be settled till after his father's return. He however would consult his father's agent and would then appear on settling-day. They were all full of the blandest courtesies. There was not one of them who had any doubt as to getting his money,—unless the whole thing might be disputed on the score of Tifto's villany. Even then payment could not be disputed, unless it was proved that he who demanded the money had been one of the actual conspirators. After having seen his creditors he went away up alone to London.

When in London he went to Carlton Terrace and spent the night in absolute solitude. It had been his plan to join Gerald for some partridge-shooting at Matching, and then to go yachting till such time as he should be enabled to renew his suit to Miss Boncassen. Early in November he would again ask her to be his wife. These had been his plans. But now it seemed that everything was changed. Partridge-shooting and yachting must be out of the question till this terrible load was taken off his shoulders. Soon after his arrival at the house two telegrams followed him from Doncaster. One was from Gerald. 'What is all this about Prime Minister? Is it a sell? I am so unhappy.' The other was from Lady Mabel,—for among other luxuries Mrs. Montacute Jones had her own telegraph-wire*at Killancodlem. 'Can this be true? We are all so miserable. I do hope it is not much.' From which he learned that his misfortune was already known to all his friends.

And now what was he to do? He ate his supper, and then without hesitating for a moment,—feeling that if he did hesitate the task would not be done on that night,—he sat down and wrote the following letter:

'Carlton Terrace, Sept. 14, 18—.

'My dear Mr. Moreton,

'I have just come up from Doncaster. You have probably heard what has been Prime Minister's fate. I don't know whether any horse has ever been such a favourite for the Leger. Early in the morning he was taken out and picked up a nail. The consequence was he could not run.

'Now I must come to the bad part of my story. I have lost seventy thousand pounds! It is no use beating about the bush. The sum is something over that. What am I to do? If I tell you that I shall give up racing altogether I dare say you will not believe me. It is a sort of thing a man always says when he wants money; but I feel now I cannot help saying it.

'But what shall I do? Perhaps, if it be not too much trouble, you will come up to town and see me. You can send me a word by the wires.

'You may be sure of this, I shall make no attempt to raise the money elsewhere, unless I find that my father will not help me. You will understand that of course it must be paid. You

357

will understand also what I must feel about telling my father, but I shall do so at once. I only wait till I can hear from you.

'Yours faithfully,

'SILVERBRIDGE.'

During the next day two despatches reached Lord Silverbridge, both of them coming as he sat down to his solitary dinner. The first consisted of a short but very civil note.

'Messrs. Comfort and Criball present their compliments to the Earl of Silverbridge.

'Messrs. C. and C. beg to offer their apologies for interfering, but desire to inform his Lordship that should cash be wanting to any amount in consequence of the late races, they will be happy to accommodate his Lordship on most reasonable terms at a moment's notice, upon his Lordship's single bond.

'Lord Silverbridge may be sure of absolute secrecy.

'Crasham Court, Crutched Friars, Sept. 15, 18—.'

The other despatch was a telegram from Mr. Moreton saying that he would be in Carlton Terrace by noon on the following day.

CHAPTER XLV

'There shall not be Another Word about It'

EARLY in October the Duke was at Matching with his daughter, and Phineas Finn and his wife were both with them. On the day after they parted at Ischl the first news respecting Prime Minister had reached him,—namely, that his son's horse had lost the race. This would not have annoyed him at all, but that the papers which he read contained some vague charge of swindling against somebody, and hinted that Lord Silverbridge had been a victim. Even this would not have troubled him,—might in some sort have comforted him, —were it not made evident to him that his son had been closely associated with swindlers in these transactions. If it were a mere question of money, that might be settled without difficulty. Even though the sum lost might have grown out of what he might have expected into some few thousands, still he would bear it without a word, if only he could separate his boy from bad companions. Then came Mr. Moreton's letter telling the whole.

At the meeting which took place between Silverbridge and his father's agent at Carlton Terrace it was settled that Mr. Moreton should write the letter. Silverbridge tried and found that he could not do it. He did not know how to humiliate himself sufficiently, and yet could not keep himself from making attempts to prove that according to all recognised chances his bets had been good bets.

Mr. Moreton was better able to accomplish the task. He knew the Duke's mind. A very large discretion had been left in Mr. Moreton's hands in regard to moneys which might be needed on behalf of that dangerous heir!—so large that he had been able to tell Lord Silverbridge that if the money was in truth lost according to Jockey Club rules, it should all be forthcoming on the settling-day,—certainly without assistance from Messrs. Comfort and Criball. The Duke had been nervously afraid of such men of business as Comfort and Criball, and from the earliest days of his son's semi-manhood had been on his guard against them. Let any sacrifice be made so that his son might be kept clear from Comforts and Criballs. To Mr. Moreton he had been very explicit. His own pecuniary resources were so great that they could bear some ravaging without serious detriment. It was for his son's character and standing in the world, for his future respectability and dignity, that his fears were so keen, and not for his own money. By one so excitable, so fond of pleasure as Lord Silverbridge, some ravaging would probably be made. Let it be met by ready money. Such had been the Duke's instructions to his own trusted man of business, and, acting on these instructions, Mr. Moreton was able to tell the heir that the money should be forthcoming.

Mr. Moreton, after detailing the extent and the nature of the loss, and the steps which he had decided upon taking, went on to explain the circumstances as best he could. He had made some inquiry, and felt no doubt that a gigantic swindle had been perpetrated by Major Tifto and others. The swindle had been successful. Mr. Moreton had consulted certain gentlemen of high character versed in affairs of the turf. He mentioned Mr. Lupton among others,—and had been assured that though the swindle was undoubted, the money had better be paid. It was thought to be impossible to connect the men who had made the bets with the perpetrators of the fraud;— and if Lord Silverbridge were to abstain from paying his bets because his own partner had ruined the animal which belonged to them jointly, the feeling would be against him rather than in his favour. In fact the Jockey Club could not sustain him in such refusal. Therefore the money would be paid. Mr. Moreton, with some expressions of doubt, trusted that he might be thought to have exercised a wise discretion. Then he went on to express his own opinion in regard to the lasting effect which the matter would have upon the young man. 'I think,' said he, 'that his Lordship is heartily sickened of racing, and that he will never return to it.'

The Duke was of course very wretched when these tidings

first reached him. Though he was a rich man, and of all men the least careful of his riches, still he felt that seventy thousand pounds was a large sum of money to throw away among a nest of swindlers. And then it was excessively grievous to him that his son should have been mixed up with such men. Wishing to screen his son, even from his own anger, he was careful to remember that the promise made that Tifto should be dismissed, was not to take effect 'till after this race had been run. There had been no deceit in that. But then Silverbridge had promised that he would not 'plunge.' There are, however, promises which from their very nature may be broken without falsehood. Plunging is a doubtful word, and the path down to it, like all doubtful paths,—is slippery and easy! If that assurance with which Mr. Moreton ended his letter could only be made true, he could bring himself to forgive even this offence. The boy must be made to settle himself in life. The Duke resolved that his only revenge should be to press on that marriage with Mabel Grex.

At Coblenz, on their way home, the Duke and his daughter were caught up by Mr. and Mrs. Finn, and the matter of the young man's losses was discussed. Phineas had heard all about it, and was loud in denunciations against Tifto, Captain Green, Gilbert Villiers, and others whose names had reached him. The money, he thought, should never have been paid. The Duke however declared that the money would not cause a moment's regret, if only the whole thing could be got rid of at that cost. It had reached Finn's ears that Tifto was already at loggerheads with his associates. There was some hope that the whole thing might be brought to light by this means. For all that the Duke cared nothing. If only Silverbridge and Tifto could for the future be kept apart, as far as he and his were concerned, good would have been done rather than harm. While they were in this way together on the Rhine it was decided that very soon after their return to England Phineas and Mrs. Finn should go down to Matching.

When the Duke arrived in London his sons were not there. Gerald had gone back to Oxford, and Silverbridge had merely left an address. Then his sister wrote him a very short letter. 'Papa will be so glad if you will come to Matching. Do come.' Of course he came, and presented himself some few days after the Duke's arrival.

But he dreaded this meeting with his father which, however, let it be postponed for ever so long, must come at last. In reference to this he made a great resolution,—that he would go instantly as soon as he might be sent for. When the summons came he started; but, though he was by courtesy an Earl, and by fact was not only a man but a Member of Parliament, though he was half engaged to marry one young lady and ought to have been engaged to marry another, though he had come to an age at which Pitt was a great minister and Pope a great poet, still his heart was in his boots, as a schoolboy's might be, when he was driven up to the house at Matching.

In two minutes, before he had washed the dust from his face and hands, he was with his father. 'I am glad to see you, Silverbridge,' said the Duke, putting out his hand.

'I hope I see you well, sir.'

'Fairly well. Thank you. Travelling I think agrees with me. I miss, not my comforts, but a certain knowledge of how things are going on, which comes to us I think through our skins when we are at home. A feeling of absence pervades me. Otherwise I like it. And you;—what have you been doing?'

'Shooting a little,' said Silverbridge, in a mooncalf*tone.

'Shooting a great deal, if what I see in the newspapers be true about Mr. Reginald Dobbes and his party. I presume it is a religion to offer up hecatombs*to the autumnal gods,— who must surely take a keener delight in blood and slaughter than those bloodthirsty gods of old.'

'You should talk to Gerald about that, sir.'

'Has Gerald been so great at his sacrifices? How will that suit with Plato? What does Mr. Simcox say?'

'Of course they were all to have a holiday just at that time. But Gerald is reading. I fancy that Gerald is clever.'

'And he is a great Nimrod?'

'As to hunting.'

'Nimrod I fancy got his game in any way that he could compass it. I do not doubt but that he trapped foxes.'

'With a rifle at deer, say for four hundred yards, I would back Gerald against any man of his age in England or Scotland.'

'As for backing, Silverbridge, do not you think that we had better have done with that?' This was said hardly in a tone of reproach, with something even of banter in it; and as the question was asked the Duke was smiling. But in a moment all that sense of joyousness which the young man had felt in singing his brother's praises was expelled. His face fell, and he stood before his father almost like a culprit. 'We might as well have it out about this racing,' continued the Duke. 'Something has to be said about it. You have lost an enormous sum of money.' The Duke's tone in saying this became terribly severe. Such at least was its sound in his son's ears. He did not mean to be severe.

But when he did speak of that which displeased him his voice naturally assumed that tone of indignation with which in days of yore he had been wont to denounce the public extravagance of his opponents in the House of Commons. The father paused, but the son could not speak at the moment.

'And worse than that,' continued the Duke; 'you have lost it in as bad company as you could have found had you picked all England through.'

'Mr. Lupton, and Sir Henry Playfair, and Lord Stirling were in the room when the bets were made.'

'Were the gentlemen you name concerned with Major Tifto?'

'No, sir.'

'Who can tell with whom he may be in a room? Though rooms of that kind are, I think, best avoided.' Then the Duke paused again, but Silverbridge was now sobbing so that he could hardly speak. 'I am sorry that you should be so grieved,' continued the father, 'but such delights cannot, I think, lead to much real joy.'

'It is for you, sir,' said the son, rubbing his eyes with the hand which supported his head.

'My grief in the matter might soon be cured.'

'How shall I cure it? I will do anything to cure it.'

'Let Major Tifto and the horses go.'

'They are gone,' said Silverbridge energetically, jumping from his chair as he spoke. 'I will never own a horse again, or a part of a horse. I will have nothing more to do with races. You will believe me?'

'I will believe anything that you tell me.'

'I won't say I will not go to another race, because——'

'No; no. I would not have you hamper yourself. Nor shall you bind yourself by any further promises. You have done with racing.'

'Indeed, indeed I have, sir.'

Then the father came up to the son and put his arms round the young man's shoulders and embraced him. 'Of course it made me unhappy.'

'I knew it would.'

'But if you are cured of this evil, the money is nothing. What is it all for but for you and your brother and sister? It was a large sum, but that shall not grieve me. The thing itself is so dangerous that, if with that much of loss we can escape, I will think that we have made not a bad market. Who owns the horse now?'

'The horses shall be sold.'

'For anything they may fetch so that we may get clear of this dirt. And the Major?'

'I know nothing of him. I have not seen him since that day.'

'Has he claims on you?'

'Not a shilling. It is all the other way.'

'Let it go then. Be quit of him, however it may be. Send a messenger so that he may understand that you have abandoned racing altogether. Mr. Moreton might perhaps see him.'

That his father should forgive so readily and yet himself suffer so deeply, affected the son's feelings so strongly that for a time he could hardly repress his sobs. 'And now there shall not be a word more said about it,' said the Duke suddenly.

Silverbridge in his confusion could make no answer.

'There shall not be another word said about it,' said the

Duke again. 'And now what do you mean to do with yourself immediately?'

'I'll stay here, sir, as long as you do. Finn, and Warburton, and I have still a few coverts to shoot.'

'That's a good reason for staying anywhere.'

'I meant that I would remain while you remained, sir.'

'That at any rate is a good reason, as far as I am concerned. But we go to Custins next week.'

'There's a deal of shooting to be done at Gatherum,' said the heir.

'You speak of it as if it were the business of your life,—on which your bread depended.'

'One can't expect game to be kept up if nobody goes to shoot it.'

'Can't one? I didn't know.*I should have thought that the less was shot the more there would be to shoot; but I am ignorant in such matters.' Silverbridge then broke forth into a long explanation as to coverts, gamekeepers, poachers, breeding, and the expectations of the neighbourhood at large, in the middle of which he was interrupted by the Duke. 'I am afraid, my dear boy, that I am too old to learn. But as it is so manifestly a duty, go and perform it like a man. Who will go with you?'

'I will ask Mr. Finn to be one.'

'He will be very hard upon you in the way of politics.'

'I can answer him better than I can you, sir. Mr. Lupton said he would come for a day or two. He'll stand to me.'

After that his father stopped him as he was about to leave the room. 'One more word, Silverbridge. Do you remember what you were saying when you walked down to the House with me from your club that night?' Silverbridge remembered very well what he had said. He had undertaken to ask Mabel Grex to be his wife, and had received his father's ready approval to the proposition. But at this moment he was unwilling to refer to that matter. 'I have thought about it very much since that,' said the Duke. 'I may say that I have been thinking of it every day. If there were anything to tell me, you would let me know;—would you not?'

'Yes, sir.'

'Then there is nothing to be told? I hope you have not changed your mind.'

Silverbridge paused a moment, trusting that he might be able to escape the making of any answer;—but the Duke evidently intended to have an answer. 'It appeared to me, sir, that it did not seem to suit her,' said the hardly-driven young man. He could not now say that Mabel had shown a disposition to reject his offer, because as they had been sitting by the brookside at Killancodlem, even he, with all his self-diffidence, had been forced to see what were her wishes. Her confusion, and too evident despair when she heard of the offer to the American girl, had plainly told her tale. He could not now plead to his father that Mabel Grex would refuse his offer. But his self-defence, when first he found that he had lost himself in love for the American, had been based on that idea. He had done his best to make Mabel understand him. If he had not actually offered to her, he had done the next thing to it. And he had run after her, till he was ashamed of such running. She had given him no encouragement;—and therefore he had been justified. No doubt he must have been mistaken; that he now perceived; but still he felt himself to be justified. It was impossible that he should explain all this to his father. One thing he certainly could not say,—just at present. After his folly in regard to those heavy debts he could not at once risk his father's renewed anger by proposing to him an American daughter-in-law. That must stand over, at any rate till the girl had accepted him positively. 'I am afraid it won't come off, sir,' he said at last.

'Then I am to presume that you have changed your mind?'

'I told you when we were speaking of it that I was not confident.'

'She has not——'

'I can't explain it all, sir,—but I fear it won't come off.'

Then the Duke, who had been sitting, got up from his chair and with his back to the fire made a final little speech. 'We decided just now, Silverbridge, that nothing more should be said about that unpleasant racing business, and nothing more shall be said by me. But you must not be surprised if I am anxious to see you settled in life. No young man could be more bound by duty to marry early than you are. In the first place you have to repair the injury done by my inaptitude for society. You have explained to me that it is your duty to have the Barsetshire coverts properly shot, and I have acceded to your views. Surely it must be equally your duty to see your Barsetshire neighbours. And you are a young man every feature of whose character would be improved by matrimony. As far as means are concerned you are almost as free to make arrangements as though you were already the head of the family.'

'No, sir.'

'I could never bring myself to dictate to a son in regard to his choice of a wife. But I will own that when you told me that you had chosen I was much gratified. Try and think again when you are pausing amidst your sacrifices at Gatherum, whether that be possible. If it be not, still I would wish you to bear in mind what is my idea as to your duty.' Silverbridge said that he would bear this in mind, and then escaped from the room.

CHAPTER XLVI

Lady Mary's Dream

WHEN the Duke and his daughter reached Custins they found a large party assembled, and were somewhat surprised at the crowd. Lord and Lady Nidderdale were there, which might have been expected as they were part of the family. With Lord Popplecourt had come his recent friend Adolphus Longstaff. That too might have been natural. Mr. and Miss Boncassen were there also, who at this moment were quite strangers to the Duke; and Mr. Lupton. The Duke also found Lady Chiltern,*whose father-in-law had more than once sat in the same Cabinet with himself, and Mr. Monk, who was generally spoken of as the head of the coming Liberal Government, and the Ladies Adelaide and Flora FitzHoward, the still unmarried but not very juvenile daughters of the Duke of St. Bungay. These with a few others made a large party, and rather confused the Duke, who had hardly reflected that discreet and profitable love-making was more likely to go on among numbers, than if the two young people were thrown together with no other companions.

Lord Popplecourt had been made to understand what was expected of him, and after some hesitation had submitted himself to the conspiracy. There would not be less at any rate than two hundred thousand pounds;—and the connexion would be made with one of the highest families in Great Britain. Though Lady Cantrip had said very few words, those words had been expressive; and the young bachelor peer had given in his adhesion. Some vague half-defined tale had been told him,—not about Tregear, as Tregear's name had not been mentioned,—but respecting some dream of a young man who had flitted across the girl's path during her mother's lifetime. 'All girls have such dreams,' Lady Cantrip had suggested. Whereupon Lord Popplecourt said that he supposed it was so. 'But a softer, purer, more unsullied flower never waited on its stalk till the proper fingers should come to pluck it,' said Lady Cantrip, rising to unaccustomed poetry on behalf of her friend the Duke. Lord Popplecourt accepted the poetry and was ready to do his best to pluck the flower.

Soon after the Duke's arrival Lord Popplecourt found himself in one of the drawing-rooms with Lady Cantrip and his proposed father-in-law. A hint had been given him that he might as well be home early from shooting, so as to be in the way. As the hour in which he was to make himself specially agreeable, both to the father and to the daughter, had drawn nigh, he became somewhat nervous, and now, at this moment, was not altogether comfortable. Though he had been concerned in no such matter before, he had an idea that love was a soft kind of thing which ought to steal on one unawares and come and go without trouble. In his case it came upon him with a rough demand for immediate hard work. He had not previously thought that he was to be subjected to such labours, and at this moment almost resented the interference with his ease. He was already a little angry with Lady Cantrip, but at the same time felt himself to be so much in subjection to her that he could not rebel.

The Duke himself when he saw the young man was hardly more comfortable. He had brought his daughter to Custins, feeling that it was his duty to be with her; but he would have preferred to leave the whole operation to the care of Lady Cantrip. He hardly liked to look at the fish whom he wished to catch for his daughter. Whenever this aspect of affairs presented itself to him, he would endeavour to console himself by remembering the past success of a similar transaction. He thought of his own first interview with his wife. 'You have heard,' he had said, 'what our friends wish.' She had pouted her lips, and when gently pressed had at last muttered, with her shoulder turned to him, that she supposed it was to be so. Very much more coercion had been used to her then than either himself or Lady Cantrip had dared to apply to his daughter. He did not think that his girl in her present condition of mind would signify to Lord Popplecourt that 'she supposed it was to be so.' Now that the time for the transaction was present he felt almost sure it would never be transacted. But still he must go on with it. Were he now to abandon his scheme, would it not be tantamount to abandoning everything? So he wreathed his face in smiles,—or made some attempt at it,—as he greeted the young man.

'I hope you and Lady Mary had a pleasant journey abroad,' said Lord Popplecourt. Lord Popplecourt, being aware that he had been chosen as a son-in-law, felt himself called upon to be familiar as well as pleasant. 'I often thought of you and Lady Mary, and wondered what you were about.'

'We were visiting lakes and mountains, churches and picture galleries, cities and salt-mines,' said the Duke.

'Does Lady Mary like that sort of thing?'

'I think she was pleased with what she saw.'

'She has been abroad a great deal before, I believe. It depends so much on whom you meet when abroad.'

This was unfortunate, because it recalled Tregear to the Duke's mind. 'We saw very few people whom we knew,' he said.

'I've been shooting in Scotland with Silverbridge, and Gerald, and Reginald Dobbes, and Nidderdale,—and that fellow Tregear, who is so thick with Silverbridge.'

'Indeed!'

'I'm told that Lord Gerald is going to be the great shot of his day,' said Lady Cantrip.

'It is a distinction,' said the Duke bitterly.

'He did not beat me by so much,' continued Popplecourt. 'I think Tregear did the best with his rifle. One morning he potted three. Dobbes was disgusted. He hated Tregear.'

'Isn't it stupid,—half-a-dozen men getting together in that way?' asked Lady Cantrip.

'Nidderdale is always jolly.'

'I am glad to hear that,' said the mother-in-law.

'And Gerald is a regular brick.' The Duke bowed. 'Silverbridge used always to be going off to Killancodlem, where there were a lot of ladies. He is very sweet, you know, on this American girl whom you have here.' Again the Duke winced.

'Dobbes is awfully good as to making out the shooting, but then he is a tyrant. Nevertheless I agree with him, if you mean to do a thing you should do it.'

'Certainly,' said the Duke. 'But you should make up your mind first whether the thing is worth doing.'

'Just so,' said Popplecourt. 'And as grouse and deer together are about the best things out, most of us made up our minds that it was worth doing. But that fellow Tregear would argue it out. He said a gentleman oughtn't to play billiards as well as a marker.'*

'I think he was right,' said the Duke.

'Do you know Mr. Tregear, Duke?'

'I have met him—with my son.'

'Do you like him?'

'I have seen very little of him.'

'I cannot say I do. He thinks so much of himself. Of course he is very intimate with Silverbridge, and that is all that any one knows of him.' The Duke bowed almost haughtily, though why he bowed he could hardly have explained to himself. Lady Cantrip bit her lips in disgust. 'He's just the fellow,' continued Popplecourt, 'to think that some princess has fallen in love with him.' Then the Duke left the room.

'You had better not talk to him about Mr. Tregear,' said Lady Cantrip.

'Why not?'

'I don't know whether he approves of the intimacy between him and Lord Silverbridge.'

'I should think not;—a man without any position or a shilling in the world.'

'The Duke is peculiar. If a subject is distasteful to him he does not like it to be mentioned. You had better not mention Mr. Tregear.' Lady Cantrip, as she said this, blushed inwardly at her own hypocrisy.

It was of course contrived at dinner that Lord Popplecourt should take out Lady Mary. It is impossible to discover how such things get wind, but there was already an idea prevalent at Custins that Lord Popplecourt had matrimonial views, and that these views were looked upon favourably. 'You may be quite sure of it, Mr. Lupton,' Lady Adelaide FitzHoward had said. 'I'll make a bet they're married before this time next year.'

'It will be a terrible case of Beauty and the Beast,' said Lupton.

Lady Chiltern had whispered a suspicion of the same kind, and had expressed a hope that the lover would be worthy of the girl. And Dolly Longstaff had chaffed his friend Popplecourt on the subject, Popplecourt having laid himself open by indiscreet allusions to Dolly's love for Miss Boncassen. 'Everybody can't have it as easily arranged for him as you,— a Duke's daughter and a pot of money without so much as the trouble of asking for it!'

'What do you know about the Duke's children?'

'That's what it is to be a lord and not to have a father.' Popplecourt tried to show that he was disgusted; but he felt himself all the more strongly bound to go on with his project.

It was therefore a matter of course that these should-be lovers would be sent out of the room together. 'You'll give your arm to Mary,' Lady Cantrip said, dropping the ceremonial prefix. Lady Mary of course went out as she was bidden. Though everybody else knew it, no idea of what was intended had yet come across her mind.

The should-be lover immediately reverted to the Austrian tour, expressing a hope that his neighbour had enjoyed herself. 'There's nothing I like so much myself,' said he, remembering some of the Duke's words, 'as mountains, cities, salt-mines, and all that kind of thing. There's such a lot of interest about it.'

'Did you ever see a salt-mine?'

'Well,—not exactly a salt-mine; but I have coalmines on my property in Staffordshire. I'm very fond of coal. I hope you like coal.'

'I like salt a great deal better—to look at.'

'But which do you think pays best? I don't mind telling you,—though it's a kind of thing I never talk about to

372

strangers,—the royalties from the Blogownie and Toodlem mines go up regularly two thousand pounds every year.'

'I thought we were talking about what was pretty to look at.'

'So we were. I'm as fond of pretty things as anybody. Do you know Reginald Dobbes?'

'No, I don't. Is he pretty?'

'He used to be so angry with Silverbridge, because Silverbridge would say Crummie-Toddie was ugly.'

'Was Crummie-Toddie ugly?'

'Just a plain house on a moor.'

'That sounds ugly.'

'I suppose your family like pretty things?'

'I hope so.'

'I do, I know.' Lord Popplecourt endeavoured to look as though he intended her to understand that she was the pretty thing which he most particularly liked. She partly conceived his meaning, and was disgusted accordingly. On the other side of her sat Mr. Boncassen, to whom she had been introduced in the drawing-room,—and who had said a few words to her about some Norwegian poet. She turned round to him, and asked him some questions about the Skald, and so, getting into conversation with him, managed to turn her shoulder to her suitor. On the other side of him sat Lady Rosina de Courcy,*to whom, as being an old woman and an old maid, he felt very little inclined to be courteous. She said a word, asking him whether he did not think the weather was treacherous. He answered her very curtly, and sat bolt upright, looking forward on the table, and taking his dinner as it came to him. He had been put there in order that Lady Mary Palliser might talk to him, and he regarded interference on the part of that old American as being ungentlemanlike. But the old American disregarded him, and went on with his quotations from the Scandinavian bard.

But Mr. Boncassen sat next to Lady Cantrip, and when at last he was called upon to give his ear to the Countess, Lady Mary was again vacant for Popplecourt's attentions.

'Are you very fond of poetry?' he asked.

'Very fond.'

'So am I. Which do you like best, Tennyson or Shake-speare?'

'They are very unlike.'

'Yes;—they are unlike. Or Moore's Melodies.* I am very fond of "When in death I shall calm recline." I think this equal to anything. Reginald Dobbes would have it that poetry is all bosh.'

'Then I think that Mr. Reginald Dobbes must be all bosh himself.'

'There was a man there named Tregear who had brought some books.' Then there was a pause. Lady Mary had not a word to say. 'Dobbes used to declare that he was always pretending to read poetry.'

'Mr. Tregear never pretends anything.'

'Do you know him?' asked the rival.

'He is my brother's most particular friend.'

'Ah! yes. I dare say Silverbridge has talked to you about him. I think he's a stuck-up sort of fellow.' To this there was not a word of reply. 'Where did your brother pick him up?'

'They were at Oxford together.'

'I must say I think he gives himself airs;—because, you know, he's nobody.'

'I don't know anything of the kind,' said Lady Mary, becoming very red. 'And as he is my brother's most particular friend,—his very friend of friends,—I think you had better not abuse him to me.'

'I don't think the Duke is very fond of him.'

'I don't care who is fond of him. I am very fond of Silverbridge, and I won't hear his friend ill-spoken of. I dare say he had some books with him. He is not at all the sort of a man to go to a place and satisfy himself with doing nothing but killing animals.'

'Do you know him, Lady Mary?'

'I have seen him, and of course I have heard a great deal of him from Silverbridge. I would rather not talk any more about him.'

'You seem to be very fond of Mr. Tregear,' he said angrily.

'It is no business of yours, Lord Popplecourt, whether I am fond of anybody or not. I have told you that Mr. Tregear is my brother's friend, and that ought to be enough.'

Lord Popplecourt was a young man possessed of a certain amount of ingenuity. It was said of him that he knew on which side his bread was buttered, and that if you wished to take him in you must get up early. After dinner and during the night he pondered a good deal on what he had heard. Lady Cantrip had told him there had been a—dream. What was he to believe about that dream? Had he not better avoid the error of putting too fine a point upon it, and tell himself at once that a dream in this instance meant a—lover? Lady Mary had already been troubled by a lover! He was disposed to believe that young ladies often do have objectionable lovers, and that things get themselves right afterwards. Young ladies can be made to understand the beauty of coal-mines almost as readily as young gentlemen. There would be the two hundred thousand pounds; and there was the girl, beautiful, well-born, and thoroughly well-mannered. But what if this Tregear and the dream were one and the same? If so, had he not received plenty of evidence that the dream had not yet passed away? A remnant of affection for the dream would not have been a fatal barrier, had not the girl been so fierce with him in defence of her dream. He remembered, too, what the Duke had said about Tregear, and Lady Cantrip's advice to him to be silent in respect to this man. And then do girls generally defend their brothers' friends as she had defended Tregear? He thought not. Putting all these things together on the following morning he came to an uncomfortable belief that Tregear was the dream.

Soon after that he found himself near to Dolly Longstaff as they were shooting. 'You know that fellow Tregear, don't you?'

'Oh Lord, yes. He is Silverbridge's pal.'

'Did you ever hear anything about him?'

'What sort of thing?'

'Was he ever—ever in love with anyone?'

'I fancy he used to be awfully spooney on Mab Grex. I remember hearing that they were to have been married, only that neither of them had sixpence.'

'Oh—Lady Mabel Grex! That's a horse of another colour.'*

'And which is the horse of your colour?'

'I haven't got a horse,' said Lord Popplecourt, going away to his own corner.

CHAPTER XLVII

Miss Boncassen's Idea of Heaven

IT was generally known that Dolly Longstaff had been heavily smitten by the charms of Miss Boncassen; but the world hardly gave him credit for the earnestness of his affection. Dolly had never been known to be in earnest in anything;—but now he was in very truth in love. He had agreed to be Popplecourt's companion at Custins because he had heard that Miss Boncassen would be there. He had thought over the matter with more consideration than he had ever before given to any subject. He had gone so far as to see his own man of business, with a view of ascertaining what settlements he could make and what income he might be able to spend. He had told himself over and over again that he was not the 'sort of fellow' that ought to marry; but it was all of no avail. He confessed to himself that he was completely 'bowled over,'—'knocked off his pins!'

'Is a fellow to have no chance?' he said to Miss Boncassen at Custins.

'If I understand what a fellow means, I am afraid not.'

'No man alive was ever more in earnest than I am.'

'Well, Mr. Longstaff, I do not suppose that you have been trying to take me in all this time.'

'I hope you do not think ill of me.'

'I may think well of a great many gentlemen without wishing to marry them.'

376

'But does love go for nothing?' said Dolly, putting his hand upon his heart. 'Perhaps there are so many that love you.'

'Not above half-a-dozen or so.'

'You can make a joke of it, when I———. But I don't think, Miss Boncassen, you at all realise what I feel. As to settlements and all that, your father could do what he likes with me.'

'My father has nothing to do with it, and I don't know what settlements mean. We never think anything of settlements in our country. If two young people love each other they go and get married.'

'Let us do the same here.'

'But the two young people don't love each other. Look here, Mr. Longstaff; it's my opinion that a young woman ought not to be pestered.'

'Pestered!'

'You force me to speak in that way. I've given you an answer ever so many times. I will not be made to do it over and over again.'

'It's that d—— fellow, Silverbridge,' he exclaimed almost angrily. On hearing this Miss Boncassen left the room without speaking another word, and Dolly Longstaff found himself alone. He saw what he had done as soon as she was gone. After that he could hardly venture to persevere again—here at Custins. He weighed it over in his mind for a long time, almost coming to a resolution in favour of hard drink. He had never felt anything like this before. He was so uncomfortable that he couldn't eat his luncheon, though in accordance with his usual habit he had breakfasted off soda-and-brandy and a morsel of devilled toast. He did not know himself in his changed character. 'I wonder whether she understands that I have four thousand pounds a year of my own, and shall have twelve thousand pounds more when my governor goes! She was so headstrong that it was impossible to explain anything to her.'

'I'm off to London,' he said to Popplecourt that afternoon. 'Nonsense! you said you'd stay for ten days.'

'All the same, I'm going at once. I've sent to Bridport for a trap, and I shall sleep to-night at Dorchester.'

'What's the meaning of it all?'

'I've had some words with somebody. Don't mind asking any more.'

'Not with the Duke?'

'The Duke! No; I haven't spoken to him.'

'Or Lord Cantrip?'

'I wish you wouldn't ask questions.'

'If you've quarrelled with anybody you ought to consult a friend.'

'It's nothing of that kind.'

'Then it's a lady. It's the American girl!'

'Don't I tell you I don't want to talk about it? I'm going. I've told Lady Cantrip that my mother wasn't well and wants to see me. You'll stop your time out, I suppose?'

'I don't know.'

'You've got it all square, no doubt. I wish I'd a handle to my name. I never cared for it before.'

'I'm sorry you're so down in the mouth. Why don't you try again? The thing is to stick to 'em like wax. If ten times of asking won't do, go in twenty times.'

Dolly shook his head despondently. 'What can you do when a girl walks out of the room and slams the door in your face? She'll get it hot and heavy before she has done. I know what she's after. She might as well cry for the moon.' And so Dolly got into the trap and went to Bridport, and slept that night at the hotel at Dorchester.

Lord Popplecourt, though he could give such excellent advice to his friend, had been able as yet to do very little in his own case. He had been a week at Custins, and had said not a word to denote his passion. Day after day he had prepared himself for the encounter, but the lady had never given him the opportunity. When he sat next to her at dinner she would be very silent. If he stayed at home on a morning she was not visible. During the short evenings he could never get her attention. And he made no progress with the Duke. The

Duke had been very courteous to him at Richmond, but here he was monosyllabic and almost sullen.

Once or twice Lord Popplecourt had a little conversation with Lady Cantrip. 'Dear girl!' said her ladyship. 'She is so little given to seeking admiration.'

'I dare say.'

'Girls are so different, Lord Popplecourt. With some of them it seems that a gentleman need have no trouble in explaining what it is that he wishes.'

'I don't think Lady Mary is like that at all.'

'Not in the least. Any one who addresses her must be prepared to explain himself fully. Nor ought he to hope to get much encouragement at first. I do not think that Lady Mary will bestow her heart till she is sure she can give it with safety.' There was an amount of falsehood in this which was proof at any rate of very strong friendship on the part of Lady Cantrip.

After a few days Lady Mary became more intimate with the American and his daughter than with any others of the party. Perhaps she liked to talk about the Scandinavian poets, of whom Mr. Boncassen was so fond. Perhaps she felt sure that her transatlantic friend would not make love to her. Perhaps it was that she yielded to the various allurements of Miss Boncassen. Miss Boncassen saw the Duke of Omnium for the first time at Custins, and there had the first opportunity of asking herself how such a man as that would receive from his son and heir such an announcement as Lord Silverbridge would have to make him should she at the end of three months accept his offer. She was quite aware that Lord Silverbridge need not repeat the offer unless he were so pleased. But she thought that he would come again. He had so spoken that she was sure of his love; and had so spoken as to obtain hers. Yes;—she was sure that she loved him. She had never seen anything like him before;—so glorious in his beauty, so gentle in his manhood, so powerful and yet so little imperious, so great in condition, and yet so little confident in his own greatness, so bolstered up with external advantages, and so little apt to trust anything but his own heart and his own voice. In asking for her love he had put forward no claim but his own love. She was glad he was what he was. She counted at their full value all his natural advantages. To be an English Duchess! Oh—yes; her ambition understood it all! But she loved him, because in the expression of his love no hint had fallen from him of the greatness of the benefits which he could confer upon her. Yes, she would like to be a Duchess; but not to be a Duchess would she become the wife of a man who should begin his courtship by assuming a superiority.

Now the chances of society had brought her into the company of his nearest friends. She was in the house with his father and with his sister. Now and again the Duke spoke a few words to her, and always did so with a peculiar courtesy. But she was sure that the Duke had heard nothing of his son's courtship. And she was equally sure that the matter had not reached Lady Mary's ears. She perceived that the Duke and her father would often converse together. Mr. Boncassen would discuss republicanism generally, and the Duke would explain that theory of monarchy as it prevails in England, which but very few Americans have ever been made to understand. All this Miss Boncassen watched with pleasure. She was still of opinion that it would not become her to force her way into a family which would endeavour to repudiate her. She would not become this young man's wife if all connected with the young man were resolved to reject the contact. But if she could conquer them,—then,—then she thought that she could put her little hand into that young man's grasp with a happy heart.

It was in this frame of mind that she laid herself out not unsuccessfully to win the esteem of Lady Mary Palliser. 'I do not know whether you approve it,' Lady Cantrip said to the Duke; 'but Mary has become very intimate with our new American friend.' At this time Lady Cantrip had become very nervous,—so as almost to wish that Lady Mary's difficulties might be unravelled elsewhere than at Custins.

'They seem to be sensible people,' said the Duke. 'I don't know when I have met a man with higher ideas on politics than Mr. Boncassen.'

'His daughter is popular with everybody.'

'A nice ladylike girl,' said the Duke, 'and appears to have been well educated.'

It was now near the end of October, and the weather was peculiarly fine. Perhaps in our climate, October would of all months be the most delightful if something of its charms were not detracted from by the feeling that with it will depart the last relics of the delights of summer. The leaves are still there with their gorgeous colouring, but they are going. The last rose still lingers on the bush, but it is the last. The woodland walks are still pleasant to the feet, but caution is heard on every side as to the coming winter.

The park at Custins, which was spacious, had many woodland walks attached to it, from which, through vistas of the timber, distant glimpses of the sea were caught. Within half a mile of the house the woods were reached, and within a mile the open sea was in sight,—and yet the wanderers might walk for miles without going over the same ground. Here, without other companions, Lady Mary and Miss Boncassen found themselves one afternoon, and here the latter told her story to her lover's sister. 'I so long to tell you something,' she said.

'Is it a secret?' asked Lady Mary.

'Well; yes; it is,—if you will keep it so. I would rather you should keep it a secret. But I will tell you.' Then she stood still, looking into the other's face. 'I wonder how you will take it.'

'What can it be?'

'Your brother has asked me to be his wife.'

'Silverbridge!'

'Yes;—Lord Silverbridge. You are astonished.'

Lady Mary was very much astonished,—so much astonished that words escaped from her, which she regretted afterwards. 'I thought there was someone else.'

'Who else?'

'Lady Mabel Grex. But I know nothing.'

'I think not,' said Miss Boncassen slowly. 'I have seen them together and I think not. There might be somebody, though I think not her. But why do I say that? Why do I malign him, and make so little of myself? There is no one else, Lady Mary. Is he not true?'

'I think he is true.'

'I am sure he is true. And he has asked me to be his wife.'

'What did you say?'

'Well;—what do you think? What is it probable that such a girl as I would say when such a man as your brother asks her to be his wife? Is he not such a man as a girl would love?'

'Oh yes.'

'Is he not handsome as a god?' Mary stared at her with all her eyes. 'And sweeter than any god those pagan races knew? And is he not good-tempered, and loving; and has he not that perfection of manly dash without which I do not think I could give my heart to any man?'

'Then you have accepted him?'

'And his rank and his wealth! The highest position in all the world in my eyes.'

'I do not think you should take him for that.'

'Does it not all help? Can you put yourself in my place? Why should I refuse him? No, not for that. I would not take him for that. But if I love him,—because he is all that my imagination tells me that a man ought to be;—if to be his wife seems to me to be the greatest bliss that could happen to a woman; if I feel that I could die to serve him, that I could live to worship him, that his touch would be sweet to me, his voice music, his strength the only support in the world on which I would care to lean,—what then?'

'Is it so?'

'Yes, it is so. It is after that fashion that I love him. He is my hero;—and not the less so because there is none higher than he among the nobles of the greatest land under the sun. Would you have me for a sister?' Lady Mary could not answer all at once. She had to think of her father;—and then she thought of her own lover. Why should not Silverbridge be as well entitled to his choice as she considered herself to be? And yet how would it be with her father? Silverbridge would in process of time be the head of the family. Would it be proper that he should marry an American?

'You would not like me for a sister?'

'I was thinking of my father. For myself I like you.'

'Shall I tell you what I said to him?'

'If you will.'

'I told him that he must ask his friends;—that I would not be his wife to be rejected by them all. Nor will I. Though it be heaven I will not creep there through a hole. If I cannot go in with my head upright, I will not go even there.' Then she turned round as though she were prepared in her emotion to walk back to the house alone. But Lady Mary ran after her, and having caught her, put her arm round her waist and kissed her.

'I at any rate will love you,' said Lady Mary.

'I will do as I have said,' continued Miss Boncassen. 'I will do as I have said. Though I love your brother down to the ground he shall not marry me without his father's consent.' Then they returned arm-in-arm close together; but very little more was said between them.

When Lady Mary entered the house she was told that Lady Cantrip wished to see her in her own room.

MISS BONCASSEN'S IDEA OF HEAVEN

CHAPTER XLVIII

The Party at Custins is broken up

THE message was given to Lady Mary after so solemn a fashion that she was sure some important communication was to be made to her. Her mind at that moment had been filled with her new friend's story. She felt that she required some time to meditate before she could determine what she herself would wish; but when she was going to her own room, in order that she might think it over, she was summoned to Lady Cantrip. 'My dear,' said the Countess, 'I wish you to do something to oblige me.'

'Of course I will.'

'Lord Popplecourt wants to speak to you.'

'Who?'

'Lord Popplecourt.'

'What can Lord Popplecourt have to say to me?'

'Can you not guess? Lord Popplecourt is a young nobleman, standing very high in the world, possessed of ample means, just in that position in which it behoves such a man to look about for a wife.' Lady Mary pressed her lips together, and clenched her two hands. 'Can you not imagine what such a gentleman may have to say?' Then there was a pause, but she made no immediate answer. 'I am to tell you, my dear, that your father would approve of it.'

'Approve of what?'

'He approves of Lord Popplecourt as a suitor for your hand.'

'How can he?'

'Why not, Mary? Of course he has made it his business to ascertain all particulars as to Lord Popplecourt's character and property.'

'Papa knows that I love somebody else.'

'My dear Mary, that is all vanity.'

'I don't think that papa can want to see me married to a man when he knows that with all my heart and soul——'

'Oh Mary!'

'When he knows,' continued Mary, who would not be put down, 'that I love another man with all my heart. What will Lord Popplecourt say if I tell him that? If he says anything to me, I shall tell him. Lord Popplecourt! He cares for nothing but his coal-mines. Of course, if you bid me see him I will; but it can do no good. I despise him, and if he troubles me I shall hate him. As for marrying him,—I would sooner die this minute.'

After this Lady Cantrip did not insist on the interview. She expressed her regret that things should be as they were,— explained in sweetly innocent phrases that in a certain rank of life young ladies could not always marry the gentlemen to whom their fancies might attach them, but must, not unfrequently, postpone their youthful inclinations to the will of their elders,—or in less delicate language, that though they might love in one direction they must marry in another; and then expressed a hope that her dear Mary would think over these things and try to please her father. 'Why does he not try to please me?' said Mary. Then Lady Cantrip was obliged to see Lord Popplecourt, a necessity which was a great nuisance to her. 'Yes;—she understands what you mean. But she is not prepared for it yet. You must wait awhile.'

'I don't see why I am to wait.'

'She is very young,—and so are you, indeed. There is plenty of time.'

'There is somebody else I suppose.'

'I told you,' said Lady Cantrip, in her softest voice, 'that there has been a dream across her path.'

'It's that Tregear!'

'I am not prepared to mention names,' said Lady Cantrip, astonished that he should know so much. 'But indeed you must wait.'

'I don't see it, Lady Cantrip.'

'What can I say more? If you think that such a girl as Lady Mary Palliser, the daughter of the Duke of Omnium, possessed of fortune, beauty, and every good gift, is to come like a bird to your call, you will find yourself mistaken. All that her friends can do for you will be done. The rest must remain with yourself.' During that evening Lord Popplecourt endeavoured to make himself pleasant to one of the FitzHoward young ladies, and on the next morning he took his leave of Custins.

'I will never interfere again in reference to anybody else's child as long as I live,' Lady Cantrip said to her husband that night.

Lady Mary was very much tempted to open her heart to Miss Boncassen. It would be delightful to her to have a friend; but were she to engage Miss Boncassen's sympathies on her behalf, she must of course sympathise with Miss Boncassen in return. And what if, after all, Silverbridge were not devoted to the American beauty! What if it should turn out that he was going to marry Lady Mabel Grex! 'I wish you would call me Isabel,' her friend said to her. 'It is so odd,—since I have left New York I have never heard my name from any lips except father's and mother's.'

'Has not Silverbridge ever called you by your Christian name?'

'I think not. I am sure he never has.' But he had, though it had passed by her at the moment without attention. 'It all came from him so suddenly. And yet I expected it. But it was too sudden for Christian names and pretty talk. I do not even know what his name is.'

'Plantagenet;—but we always call him Silverbridge.'

'Plantagenet is very much prettier. I shall always call him Plantagenet. But I recall that. You will not remember that against me?'

'I will remember nothing that you do not wish.'

'I mean that if,—if all the grandeurs of all the Pallisers could consent to put up with poor me, if heaven were opened to me with a straight gate, so that I could walk out of our republic into your aristocracy with my head erect, with the stars and stripes waving proudly round me till I had been accepted into the shelter of the Omnium griffins,—then I would call him——'

'There's one Palliser would welcome you.'

'Would you, dear? Then I will love you so dearly. May I call you Mary?'

387

'Of course you may.'

'Mary is the prettiest name under the sun. But Plantagenet is so grand! Which of the kings did you branch off from?'

'I know nothing about it. From none of them, I should think. There is some story about a Sir Guy who was a king's friend. I never trouble myself about it. I hate aristocracy.'

'Do you, dear?'

'Yes,' said Mary, full of her own grievances. 'It is an abominable bondage, and I do not see that it does any good at all.'

'I think it is so glorious,' said the American. 'There is no such mischievous nonsense in all the world as equality. That is what father says. What men ought to want is liberty.'

'It is terrible to be tied up in a small circle,' said the Duke's daughter.

'What do you mean, Lady Mary?'

'I thought you were to call me Mary. What I mean is this. Suppose that Silverbridge loves you better than all the world.'

'I hope he does. I think he does.'

'And suppose he cannot marry you, because of his— aristocracy?'

'But he can.'

'I thought you were saying yourself——'

'Saying what? That he could not marry me! No, indeed! But that under certain circumstances I would not marry him. You don't suppose that I think he would be disgraced? If so I would go away at once, and he should never again see my face or hear my voice. I think myself good enough for the best man God ever made. But if others think differently, and those others are so closely concerned with him, and would be so closely concerned with me, as to trouble our joint lives,—then will I neither subject him to such sorrow nor will I encounter it myself.'

'It all comes from what you call aristocracy.'

'No, dear;—but from the prejudices of an aristocracy. To tell the truth, Mary, the more difficult a place is to get into, the more the right of going in is valued. If everybody could be a Duchess and a Palliser, I should not perhaps think so much about it.'

'I thought it was because you loved him.'

'So I do. I love him entirely. I have said not a word of that to him;—but I do, if I know at all what love is. But if you love a star, the pride you have in your star will enhance your love. Though you know that you must die of your love, still you must love your star.'

And yet Mary could not tell her tale in return. She could not show the reverse picture;—that she being a star was anxious to dispose of herself after the fashion of poor human rushlights. It was not that she was ashamed of her love, but that she could not bring herself to yield altogether in reference to the great descent which Silverbridge would have to make.

On the day after this,—the last day of the Duke's sojourn at Custins, the last also of the Boncassens' visit,—it came to pass that the Duke and Mr. Boncassen, with Lady Mary and Isabel, were all walking in the woods together. And it so happened when they were at a little distance from the house, each of the girls was walking with the other girl's father. Isabel had calculated what she would say to the Duke should a time for speaking come to her. She could not tell him of his son's love. She could not ask his permission. She could not explain to him all her feelings, or tell him what she thought of her proper way of getting into heaven. That must come afterwards if it should ever come at all. But there was something that she could tell. 'We are so different from you,' she said, speaking of her own country.

'And yet so like,' said the Duke smiling;—'your language, your laws, your habits!'

'But still there is such a difference! I do not think there is a man in the whole Union more respected than father.'

'I dare say not.'

'Many people think that if he would only allow himself to be put in nomination, he might be the next president.'

'The choice, I am sure, would do your country honour.'

389

'And yet his father was a poor labourer who earned his bread among the shipping at New York. That kind of thing would be impossible here.'

'My dear young lady, there you wrong us.'

'Do I?'

'Certainly! A Prime Minister with us might as easily come from the same class.'

'Here you think so much of rank. You are—a Duke.'

'But a Prime Minister can make a Duke; and if a man can raise himself by his own intellect to that position, no one will think of his father or his grandfather. The sons of merchants have with us been Prime Ministers more than once, and no Englishmen ever were more honoured among their countrymen. Our peerage is being continually recruited from the ranks of the people, and hence it gets its strength.'

'Is it so?'

'There is no greater mistake than to suppose that inferiority of birth is a barrier to success in this country.'

She listened to this and to much more on the same subject with attentive ears,—not shaken in her ideas as to the English aristocracy in general, but thinking that she was perhaps learning something of his own individual opinions. If he were more liberal than others, on that liberality might perhaps be based her own happiness and fortune.

He, in all this, was quite unconscious of the working of her mind. Nor in discussing such matters generally did he ever mingle his own private feelings, his own pride of race and name, his own ideas of what was due to his ancient rank with the political creed by which his conduct in public life was governed. The peer who sat next to him in the House of Lords, whose grandmother had been a washerwoman and whose father an innkeeper, was to him every whit as good a peer as himself. And he would as soon sit in counsel with Mr. Monk, whose father had risen from a mechanic to be a merchant, as with any nobleman who could count ancestors against himself. But there was an inner feeling in his bosom as to his own family, his own name, his own children, and his own personal self, which was kept altogether apart from his grand political theories. It was a subject on which he never spoke; but the feeling had come to him as a part of his birthright. And he conceived that it would pass·through him to his children after the same fashion. It was this which made the idea of a marriage between his daughter and Tregear intolerable to him, and which would operate as strongly in regard to any marriage which his son might contemplate. Lord Grex was not a man with whom he would wish to form any intimacy. He was, we may say, a wretched unprincipled old man, bad all round; and such the Duke knew him to be. But the blue blood and the rank were there; and as the girl was good herself, he would have been quite contented that his son should marry the daughter of Lord Grex. That one and the same man should have been in one part of himself so unlike the other part,—that he should have one set of opinions so contrary to another set,—poor Isabel Boncassen did not understand.

CHAPTER XLIX

The Major's Fate

THE affair of Prime Minister and the nail was not allowed to fade away into obscurity. Through September and October it was made matter for pungent inquiry. The Jockey Club was alive. Mr. Pook was very instant,—with many Pookites anxious to free themselves from suspicion. Sporting men declared that the honour of the turf required that every detail of the case should be laid open. But by the end of October, though every detail had been surmised, nothing had in truth been discovered. Nobody doubted but that Tifto had driven the nail into the horse's foot, and that Green and Gilbert Villiers had shared the bulk of the plunder. They had gone off on their travels together, and the fact that each of them had been in possession of about twenty thousand pounds was proved. But then there is no law against two gentlemen having such a sum of money. It was notorious that Captain Green and Mr. Gilbert Villiers had enriched themselves to this extent by the failure of Prime Minister. But yet nothing was proved!

That the Major had either himself driven in the nail or seen it done, all racing men were agreed. He had been out with the horse in the morning and had been the first to declare that the animal was lame. And he had been with the horse till the farrier had come. But he had concocted a story for himself. He did not dispute that the horse had been lamed by the machinations of Green and Villiers,—with the assistance of the groom. No doubt, he said, these men, who had been afraid to face an inquiry, had contrived and had carried out the iniquity. How the lameness had been caused he could not pretend to say. The groom who was at the horse's head, and who evidently knew how these things were done, might have struck a nerve in the horse's foot with his boot. But when the horse was got into the stable he, Tifto,—so he declared,—at once ran out to send for the farrier. During the minutes so occupied the operation must have been made with the nail. That was Tifto's story,—and as he kept his ground, there were some few who believed it.

But though the story was so far good, he had at moments been imprudent, and had talked when he should have been silent. The whole matter had been a torment to him. In the first place his conscience made him miserable. As long as it had been possible to prevent the evil he had hoped to make a clean breast of it to Lord Silverbridge. Up to this period of his life everything had been 'square' with him. He had betted 'square,' and had ridden 'square,' and had run horses 'square.' He had taken a pride in this, as though it had been a great virtue. It was not without great inward grief that he had deprived himself of the consolations of these reflections! But when he had approached his noble partner, his noble partner snubbed him at every turn,—and he did the deed.

His reward was to be three thousand pounds,—and he got his money. The money was very much to him,—would perhaps have been almost enough to comfort him in his misery, had not those other rascals got so much more. When he heard that the groom's fee was higher than his own, it almost broke his heart. Green and Villiers, men of infinitely lower standing, —men at whom the Beargarden would not have looked,—had absolutely netted fortunes on which they could live in comfort. No doubt they had run away while Tifto still stood his ground;—but he soon began to doubt whether to have run away with twenty thousand pounds was not better than to remain with such small plunder as had fallen to his lot, among such faces as those which now looked upon him! Then when he had drunk a few glasses of whisky-and-water, he said something very foolish as to his power of punishing that swindler Green.

An attempt had been made to induce Silverbridge to delay the payment of his bets;—but he had been very eager that they should be paid. Under the joint auspices of Mr. Lupton and Mr. Moreton the horses were sold, and the establishment was annihilated,—with considerable loss, but with great despatch. The Duke had been urgent. The Jockey Club, and the racing world, and the horsey fraternity generally, might do what seemed to them good,—so that Silverbridge was extricated from the matter. Silverbridge was extricated,—and the Duke cared nothing for the rest.

But Silverbridge could not get out of the mess quite so easily as his father wished. Two questions arose about Major Tifto, outside the racing world, but within the domain of the world of sport and pleasure generally, as to one of which it was impossible that Silverbridge should not express an opinion. The first question had reference to the Mastership of the Runnymede hounds. In this our young friend was not bound to concern himself. The other affected the Beargarden Club; and, as Lord Silverbridge had introduced the Major, he could hardly forbear from the expression of an opinion.

There was a meeting of the subscribers to the hunt in the last week of October. At that meeting Major Tifto told his story. There he was, to answer any charge which might be brought against him. If he had made money by losing the race,—where was it and whence had it come? Was it not clear that a conspiracy might have been made without his knowledge;—and clear also that the real conspirators had levanted?* He had not levanted! The hounds were his own. He had undertaken to hunt the country for this season, and they had undertaken to pay him a certain sum of money. He should expect and demand that sum of money. If they chose to make any other arrangement for the year following they could do so. Then he sat down and the meeting was adjourned,—the secretary having declared that he would not act in that capacity any longer, nor collect the funds. A farmer had also asserted that he and his friends had resolved that Major Tifto should not ride over their fields. On the next day the Major had his hounds out, and some of the London men, with a few of the neighbours, joined him. Gates were locked; but the hounds ran, and those who chose to ride managed to follow them. There are men who will stick to their sport though Apollyon* himself should carry the horn. Who cares whether the lady who fills a theatre be or be not a moral young woman, or whether the bandmaster who keeps such excellent time in a ball has or has not paid his debts? There were men of this sort who supported Major Tifto;—but then there was a general opinion that the Runnymede hunt would come to an end unless a new master could be found.

Then in the first week in November a special meeting was called at the Beargarden, at which Lord Silverbridge was asked to attend. 'It is impossible that he should be allowed to remain in the club.' This was said to Lord Silverbridge by Mr. Lupton. 'Either he must go or the club must be broken up.'

Silverbridge was very unhappy on the occasion. He had at last been reasoned into believing that the horse had been made the victim of foul play; but he persisted in saying that there was no conclusive evidence against Tifto. The matter was argued with him. Tifto had laid bets against the horse; Tifto had been hand-and-glove with Green; Tifto could not have been absent from the horse above two minutes; the thing could not have been arranged without Tifto. As he had brought Tifto into the club, and had been his partner on the turf, it was his business to look into the matter. 'But for all that,' said he, 'I'm not going to jump on a man when he's down, unless I feel sure that he's guilty.'

Then the meeting was held, and Tifto himself appeared. When the accusation was made by Mr. Lupton, who proposed that he should be expelled, he burst into tears. The whole story was repeated,—the nail, and the hammer, and the lameness; and the moments were counted up, and poor Tifto's bets and friendship with Green were made apparent,—and the case was submitted to the club. An old gentleman who had been connected with the turf all his life, and who would not have scrupled, by square betting, to rob his dearest friend of his last shilling, seconded the proposition,—telling all the story over again. Then Major Tifto was asked whether he wished to say anything.

'I've got to say that I'm here,' said Tifto, still crying, 'and if I'd done anything of that kind, of course I'd have gone with the rest of 'em. I put it to Lord Silverbridge to say whether I'm that sort of fellow.' Then he sat down.

Upon this there was a pause, and the club was manifestly of opinion that Lord Silverbridge ought to say something. 'I think that Major Tifto should not have betted against the horse,' said Silverbridge.

'I can explain that,' said the Major. 'Let me explain that. Everybody knows that I'm a man of small means. I wanted to 'edge;* I only wanted to 'edge.'

Mr. Lupton shook his head. 'Why have you not shown me your book?'

'I told you before that it was stolen. Green got hold of it. I did win a little. I never said I didn't. But what has that to do with hammering a nail into a horse's foot? I have always been true to you, Lord Silverbridge, and you ought to stick up for me now.'

'I will have nothing further to do with the matter,' said Silverbridge, 'one way or the other,' and he walked out of the room,—and out of the club. The affair was ended by a magnanimous declaration on the part of Major Tifto that he would not remain in a club in which he was suspected, and by a consent on the part of the meeting to receive the Major's instant resignation.

CHAPTER L

The Duke's Arguments

THE Duke before he left Custins had an interview with Lady Cantrip, at which that lady found herself called upon to speak her mind freely. 'I don't think she cares about Lord Popplecourt,' Lady Cantrip said.

'I am sure I don't know why she should,' said the Duke, who was often very aggravating even to his friend.

'But as we had thought——'

'She ought to do as she is told,' said the Duke, remembering how obedient his Glencora had been. 'Has he spoken to her?'

'I think not.'

'Then how can we tell?'

'I asked her to see him, but she expressed so much dislike that I could not press it. I am afraid, Duke, that you will find it difficult to deal with her.'

'I have found it very difficult!'

'As you have trusted me so much——'

'Yes;—I have trusted you, and do trust you. I hope you understand that I appreciate your kindness.'

'Perhaps then you will let me say what I think.'

'Certainly, Lady Cantrip.'

'Mary is a very peculiar girl,—with great gifts,—but——'

'But what?'

'She is obstinate. Perhaps it would be fairer to say that she has great firmness of character. It is within your power to separate her from Mr. Tregear. It would be foreign to her character to—to—leave you, except with your approbation.'

'You mean, she will not run away.'

'She will do nothing without your permission. But she will remain unmarried unless she be allowed to marry Mr. Tregear.'

'What do you advise then?'

'That you should yield. As regards money, you could give them what they want. Let him go into public life. You could manage that for him.'

'He is Conservative!'

'What does that matter when the question is one of your daughter's happiness? Everybody tells me that he is clever and well conducted.'

He betrayed nothing by his face as this was said to him. But as he got into the carriage he was a miserable man. It is very well to tell a man that he should yield, but there is nothing so wretched to a man as yielding. Young people and women have to yield,—but for such a man as this, to yield is in itself a misery. In this matter the Duke was quite certain of the propriety of his judgment. To yield would be not only to mortify himself, but to do wrong at the same time. He had convinced himself that the Popplecourt arrangement would

397

come to nothing. Nor had he and Lady Cantrip combined been able to exercise over her the sort of power to which Lady Glencora had been subjected. If he persevered,—and he still was sure, almost sure, that he would persevere,—his object must be achieved after a different fashion. There must be infinite suffering,—suffering both to him and to her. Could she have been made to consent to marry someone else, terrible as the rupture might have been, she would have reconciled herself at last to her new life. So it had been with his Glencora, after a time. Now the misery must go on from day to day beneath his eyes, with the knowledge on his part that he was crushing all joy out of her young life, and the conviction on her part that she was being treated with continued cruelty by her father! It was a terrible prospect! But if it was manifestly his duty to act after this fashion, must he not do his duty?

If he were to find that by persevering in this course he would doom her to death, or perchance to madness,—what then? If it were right, he must still do it. He must still do it, if the weakness incident to his human nature did not rob him of the necessary firmness. If every foolish girl were indulged, all restraint would be lost, and there would be an end to those rules as to birth and position by which he thought his world was kept straight. And then, mixed with all this, was his feeling of the young man's arrogance in looking for such a match. Here was a man without a shilling, whose manifest duty it was to go to work so that he might earn his bread, who instead of doing so, had hoped to raise himself to wealth and position by entrapping the heart of an unwary girl! There was something to the Duke's thinking base in this, and much more base because the unwary girl was his own daughter. That such a man as Tregear should make an attack upon him and select his rank, his wealth, and his child as the stepping-stones by which he intended to rise! What could be so mean as that a man should seek to live by looking out for a wife with money? But what so impudent, so arrogant, so unblushingly disregardful of propriety, as that he should endeavour to select his victim from such a family as that of the Pallisers,

and that he should lay his impious hand on the very daughter
of the Duke of Omnium?

But together with all this there came upon him moments
of ineffable tenderness. He felt as though he longed to take
her in his arms and tell her, that if she were unhappy, so would
he be unhappy too,—to make her understand that a hard
necessity had made this sorrow common to them both. He
thought that, if she would only allow it, he could speak of her
love as a calamity which had befallen them, as from the hand
of fate, and not as a fault. If he could make a partnership in
misery with her, so that each might believe that each was
acting for the best, then he could endure all that might come.
But, as he was well aware, she regarded him as being simply
cruel to her. She did not understand that he was performing
an imperative duty. She had set her heart upon a certain object,
and having taught herself that in that way happiness might
be reached, had no conception that there should be something
in the world, some idea of personal dignity, more valuable to
her than the fruition of her own desires! And yet every word
he spoke to her was affectionate. He knew that she was
bruised, and if it might be possible he would pour oil into her
wounds,—even though she would not recognise the hand
which relieved her.

They slept one night in town,—where they encountered
Silverbridge soon after his retreat from the Beargarden. 'I
cannot quite make up my mind, sir, about that fellow Tifto,'
he said to his father.

'I hope you have made up your mind that he is no fit companion for yourself.'

'That's over. Everybody understands that, sir.'

'Is anything more necessary?'

'I don't like feeling that he has been ill-used. They have
made him resign the club, and I fancy they won't have him
at the hunt.'

'He has lost no money by you?'

'Oh no.'

'Then I think you may be indifferent. From all that I hear

I think he must have won money,—which will probably be a consolation to him.'

'I think they have been hard upon him,' continued Silver-bridge. 'Of course he is not a good man, nor a gentleman, nor possessed of very high feelings. But a man is not to be sacrificed altogether for that. There are so many men who are not gentlemen, and so many gentlemen who are bad fellows.'

'I have no doubt Mr. Lupton knew what he was about,' replied the Duke.

On the next morning the Duke and Lady Mary went down to Matching, and as they sat together in the carriage after leaving the railway the father endeavoured to make himself pleasant to his daughter. 'I suppose we shall stay at Matching now till Christmas,' he said.

'I hope so.'

'Whom would you like to have here?'

'I don't want any one, papa.'

'You will be very sad without somebody. Would you like the Finns?'

'If you please, papa. I like her. He never talks anything but politics.'

'He is none the worse for that, Mary. I wonder whether Lady Mabel Grex would come.'

'Lady Mabel Grex!'

'Do you not like her?'

'Oh yes, I like her;—but what made you think of her, papa?'

'Perhaps Silverbridge would come to us then.'

Lady Mary thought that she knew a great deal more about that than her father did. 'Is he fond of Lady Mabel, papa?'

'Well,—I don't know. There are secrets which should not be told. I think they are very good friends. I would not have her asked unless it would please you.'

'I like her very much, papa.'

'And perhaps we might get the Boncassens to come to us. I did say a word to him about it.' Now, as Mary felt, difficulty was heaping itself upon difficulty. 'I have seldom met a man in whose company I could take more pleasure than in that of

Mr. Boncassen; and the young lady seems to be worthy of her father.' Mary was silent, feeling the complication of the difficulties. 'Do you not like her?' asked the Duke.

'Very much indeed,' said Mary.

'Then let us fix a day and ask them. If you will come to me after dinner with an almanac we will arrange it. Of course you will invite that Miss Casseway too?'

The complication seemed to be very bad indeed. In the first place was it not clear that she, Lady Mary, ought not to be a party to asking Miss Boncassen to meet her brother at Matching? Would it not be imperative on her part to tell her father the whole story? And yet how could she do that? It had been told her in confidence, and she remembered what her own feelings had been when Mrs. Finn had suggested the propriety of telling the story which had been told to her! And how would it be possible to ask Lady Mabel to come to Matching to meet Miss Boncassen in the presence of Silverbridge? If the party could be made up without Silverbridge things might run smoothly.

As she was thinking of this in her own room, thinking also how happy she could be if one other name might be added to the list of guests, the Duke had gone alone into his library. There a pile of letters reached him, among which he found one marked 'Private,' and addressed in a hand which he did not recognise. This he opened suddenly,—with a conviction that it would contain a thorn,—and, turning over the page, found the signature to it was 'Francis Tregear.' The man's name was wormwood to him. He at once felt that he would wish to have his dinner, his fragment of a dinner, brought to him in that solitary room, and that he might remain secluded for the rest of the evening. But still he must read the letter;—and he read it.

'MY DEAR LORD DUKE,

'If my mode of addressing your Grace be too familiar I hope you will excuse it. It seems to me that if I were to use one more distant, I should myself be detracting something from my right to make the claim which I intend to put forward. You know what my feelings are in reference to your daughter. I do not pretend to suppose that they should have the least weight with you. But you know also what her feelings are for me. A man seems to be vain when he expresses his conviction of a woman's love for himself. But this matter is so important to her as well as to me that I am compelled to lay aside all pretence. If she do not love me as I love her, then the whole thing drops to the ground. Then it will be for me to take myself off from out of your notice,—and from hers, and to keep to myself whatever heart-breaking I may have to undergo. But if she be as steadfast in this matter as I am,—if her happiness be fixed on marrying me as mine is on marrying her,—then, I think, I am entitled to ask you whether you are justified in keeping us apart.

'I know well what are the discrepancies. Speaking from my own feeling I regard very little those of rank. I believe myself to be as good a gentleman as though my father's forefathers had sat for centuries past in the House of Lords. I believe that you would have thought so also, had you and I been brought in contact on any other subject. The discrepancy in regard to money is, I own, a great trouble to me. Having no wealth of my own I wish that your daughter were so circumstanced that I could go out into the world and earn bread for her. I know myself so well that I dare say positively that her money, —if it be that she will have money,—had no attractions for me when I first became acquainted with her, and adds nothing now to the persistency with which I claim her hand.

'But I venture to ask whether you can dare to keep us apart if her happiness depends on her love for me? It is now more than six months since I called upon you in London and explained my wishes. You will understand me when I say that I cannot be contented to sit idle, trusting simply to the assurance which I have of her affection. Did I doubt it, my way would be more clear. I should feel in that case that she would yield to your wishes, and I should then, as I have said before, just take myself out of the way. But if it be not so, then I am bound to do something,—on her behalf as well as my own. What am I to do? Any endeavour to meet her clandestinely is against my instincts, and would certainly be rejected by her. A secret correspondence would be equally distasteful to both of us. Whatever I do in this matter, I wish you to know that I do it.

> 'Yours always,
> 'Most faithfully, and with the greatest respect,
> 'FRANCIS TREGEAR.'

He read the letter very carefully, and at first was simply astonished by what he considered to be the unparalleled arrogance of the young man. In regard to rank this young gentleman thought himself to be as good as anybody else! In regard to money he did acknowledge some inferiority. But that was a misfortune, and could not be helped! Not only was the letter arrogant;—but the fact that he should dare to write any letter on such a subject was proof of most unpardonable arrogance. The Duke walked about the room thinking of it till he was almost in a passion. Then he read the letter again and was gradually pervaded by a feeling of its manliness. Its arrogance remained, but with its arrogance there was a certain boldness which induced respect. Whether I am such a son-in-law as you would like or not, it is your duty to accept me, if by refusing to do so you will render your daughter miserable. That was Mr. Tregear's argument. He himself might be prepared to argue in answer that it was his duty to reject such a son-in-law, even though by rejecting him he might make his daughter miserable. He was not shaken; but with his condemnation of the young man there was mingled something of respect.

He continued to digest the letter before the hour of dinner, and when the almanac was brought to him he fixed on certain days. The Boncassens he knew would be free from engagements in ten days' time. As to Lady Mabel, he seemed to think it almost certain that she would come. 'I believe she is always going about from one house to another at this time of the year,' said Mary.

'I think she will come to us if it be possible,' said the Duke. 'And you must write to Silverbridge.'

'And what about Mr. and Mrs. Finn?'

'She promised she would come again, you know. They are at their own place in Surrey. They will come unless they have friends with them. They have no shooting, and nothing brings people together now except shooting. I suppose there are things here to be shot. And be sure you write to Silverbridge.'

CHAPTER LI
The Duke's Guests

'THE DUKE OF OMNIUM presents his compliments to Mr. Francis Tregear, and begs to acknowledge the receipt of Mr. Tregear's letter of ———. The Duke has no other communication to make to Mr. Tregear, and must beg to decline any further correspondence.' This was the reply which the Duke wrote to the applicant for his daughter's hand. And he wrote it at once. He had acknowledged to himself that Tregear had shown a certain manliness in his appeal; but not on that account was such a man to have all that he demanded! It seemed to the Duke that there was no alternative between such a note as that given above and a total surrender.

But the post did not go out during the night, and the note lay hidden in the Duke's private drawer till the morning. There was still that 'locus pœnitentiæ'* which should be accorded to all letters written in anger. During the day he thought over it all constantly, not in any spirit of yielding, not descending a single step from that altitude of conviction which made him feel that it might be his duty absolutely to sacrifice his daughter,—but asking himself whether it might not be well that he should explain the whole matter at length to the young man. He thought he could put the matter strongly. It was not by his own doing that he belonged to an aristocracy which, if all exclusiveness were banished from it, must cease to exist. But being what he was, having been born to such privileges and such limitations, was he not bound in duty to maintain a certain exclusiveness? He would appeal to the young man himself to say whether marriage ought to be free between all classes of the community. And if not between all, who was to maintain the limits but they to whom authority in such matters is given? So much in regard to rank! And then he would ask this young man whether he thought it fitting that a young man whose duty, according to all known principles, it must be to earn his bread, should avoid that manifest duty by taking a wife who could maintain him. As he roamed about his park alone he felt that he could write such a letter as would make an impression even upon a lover. But when he had come back to his study, other reflections came to his aid. Though he might write the most appropriate letter in the world, would there not certainly be a reply? As to conviction, had he ever known an instance of a man who had been convinced by an adversary? Of course there would be a reply,—and replies. And to such a correspondence there would be no visible end. Words when once written remain, or may remain, in testimony for ever. So at last when the moment came he sent off those three lines, with his uncourteous compliments and his demand that there should be no further correspondence.

At dinner he endeavoured to make up for this harshness by increased tenderness to his daughter, who was altogether ignorant of the correspondence. 'Have you written your letters, dear?' She said she had written them.

'I hope the people will come.'

'If it will make you comfortable, papa!'

'It is for your sake I wish them to be here. I think that Lady Mabel and Miss Boncassen are just such girls as you would like.'

'I do like them; only ——'

'Only what?'

'Miss Boncassen is an American.'

'Is that an objection? According to my ideas it is desirable to become acquainted with persons of various nations. I have heard, no doubt, many stories of the awkward manners displayed by American ladies. If you look for them you may probably find American women who are not polished. I do not think I shall calumniate my own country if I say the same of English women. It should be our object to select for our own acquaintances the best we can find of all countries. It seems to me that Miss Boncassen is a young lady with whom any other young lady might be glad to form an acquaintance.'

This was a little sermon which Mary was quite contented to endure in silence. She was, in truth, fond of the young American beauty, and had felt a pleasure in the intimacy which the girl had proposed to her. But she thought it inexpedient that Miss Boncassen, Lady Mabel, and Silverbridge should be at Matching together. Therefore she made a reply to her father's sermon which hardly seemed to go to the point at issue. 'She is so beautiful!' she said.

'Very beautiful,' said the Duke. 'But what has that to do with it? My girl need not be jealous of any girl's beauty.' Mary laughed and shook her head. 'What is it, then?'

'Perhaps Silverbridge might admire her.'

'I have no doubt he would,—or does, for I am aware that they have met. But why should he not admire her?'

'I don't know,' said Lady Mary sheepishly.

'I fancy that there is no danger in that direction. I think Silverbridge understands what is expected from him.' Had not Silverbridge plainly shown that he understood what was expected from him when he selected Lady Mabel? Nothing could have been more proper, and the Duke had been altogether satisfied. That in such a matter there should have been a change in so short a time did not occur to him. Poor Mary was now completely silenced. She had been told that Silverbridge understood what was expected from him; and of course could not fail to carry home to herself an accusation that she failed to understand what was expected from her.

She had written her letters, but had not as yet sent them. Those to Mrs. Finn and to the two young ladies had been easy enough. Could Mr. and Mrs. Finn come to Matching on the 20th of November? 'Papa says that you promised to return, and thinks this time will perhaps suit you.' And then to Lady

Mabel: 'Do come if you can; and papa particularly says that he hopes Miss Cassewary will come also.' To Miss Boncassen she had written a long letter, but that too had been written very easily. 'I write to you instead of your mamma, because I know you. You must tell her that, and then she will not be angry. I am only papa's messenger, and I am to say how much he hopes that you will come on the 20th. Mr. Boncassen is to bring the whole British Museum if he wishes.' Then there was a little postscript which showed that there was already considerable intimacy between the two young ladies. 'We won't have either Mr. L. or Lord P.' Not a word was said about Lord Silverbridge. There was not even an initial to indicate his name.

But the letter to her brother was more difficult. In her epistles to those others she had so framed her words as if possible to bring them to Matching. But in writing to her brother, she was anxious so to write as to deter him from coming. She was bound to obey her father's commands. He had desired that Silverbridge should be asked to come,—and he was asked to come. But she craftily endeavoured so to word the invitation that he should be induced to remain away. 'It is all papa's doing,' she said; 'and I am glad that he should like to have people here. I have asked the Finns, with whom papa seems to have made up everything. Mr. Warburton*will be here of course, and I think Mr. Moreton is coming. He seems to think that a certain amount of shooting ought to be done. Then I have invited Lady Mabel Grex and Miss Cassewary, —all of papa's choosing, and the Boncassens. Now you will know whether the set will suit you. Papa has particularly begged that you will come,—apparently because of Lady Mabel. I don't at all know what that means. Perhaps you do. As I like Lady Mabel, I hope she will come.' Surely Silverbridge would not run himself into the jaws of the lion. When he heard that he was specially expected by his father to come to Matching in order that he might make himself agreeable to one young lady, he would hardly venture to come, seeing that he would be bound to make love to another young lady!

To Mary's great horror, all the invitations were accepted. Mr. and Mrs. Finn were quite at the Duke's disposal. That she had expected. The Boncassens would all come. This was signified in a note from Isabel, which covered four sides of the paper and was full of fun. But under her signature had been written a few words,—not in fun,—words which Lady Mary perfectly understood. 'I wonder, I wonder, I wonder!' Did the Duke when inviting her know of anything of his son's inclinations? Would he be made to know them now, during this visit? And what would he say when he did know them?

That the Boncassens would come was a matter of course; but Mary had thought that Lady Mabel would refuse. She had told Lady Mabel that the Boncassens had been asked, and to her thinking it had not been improbable that the young lady would be unwilling to meet her rival at Matching. But the invitation was accepted.

But it was her brother's ready acquiescence which troubled Mary chiefly. He wrote as though there were no doubt about the matter. 'Of course there is a deal of shooting to be done,' he said, 'and I consider myself bound to look after it. There ought not to be less than four guns,—particularly if Warburton is to be one of them. I like Warburton very much, and I think he shoots badly to ingratiate himself with the governor. I wonder whether the governor would get leave for Gerald for a week. He has been sticking to his work like a brick. If not, would he mind my bringing someone? You ask the governor and let me know. I'll be there on the 20th. I wonder whether they'll let me hear what goes on among them about politics. I'm sure there is not one of them hates Sir Timothy worse than I do. Lady Mab is a brick, and I'm glad you have asked her. I don't think she'll come, as she likes shutting herself up at Grex. Miss Boncassen is another brick. And if you can manage about Gerald I will say that you are a third.'

This would have been all very well had she not known that secret. Could it be that Miss Boncassen had been mistaken? She was forced to write again to say that her father did not think it right that Gerald should be brought away from his studies for the sake of shooting, and that the necessary fourth gun would be there in the person of one Barrington Erle.* Then she added: 'Lady Mabel Grex is coming, and so is Miss Boncassen.' But to this she received no reply.

Though Silverbridge had written to his sister in his usual careless style, he had considered the matter much. The three months were over. He had no idea of any hesitation on his part. He had asked her to be his wife, and he was determined to go on with his suit. Had he ever been enabled to make the same request to Mabel Grex, or had she answered him when he did half make it in a serious manner, he would have been true to her. He had not told his father, or his sister, or his friends, as Isabel had suggested. He would not do so till he should have received some more certain answer from her. But in respect to his love he was prepared to be quite as obstinate as his sister. It was a matter for his own consideration, and he would choose for himself. The three months were over, and it was now his business to present himself to the lady again.

That Lady Mabel should also be at Matching, would certainly be a misfortune. He thought it probable that she, knowing that Isabel Boncassen and he would be there together, would refuse the invitation. Surely she ought to do so. That was his opinion when he wrote to his sister. When he heard afterwards that she intended to be there, he could only suppose that she was prepared to accept the circumstances as they stood

CHAPTER LII

Miss Boncassen tells the Truth

ON the 20th of the month all the guests came rattling in at Matching one after another. The Boncassens were the first, but Lady Mabel with Miss Cassewary followed them quickly. Then came the Finns, and with them Barrington Erle. Lord Silverbridge was the last. He arrived by a train which reached the station at 7 P.M., and only entered the house as his father was taking Mrs. Boncassen into the dining-room. He dressed himself in ten minutes, and joined the party as they had finished their fish. 'I am awfully sorry,' he said, rushing up to his father, 'but I thought that I should just hit it.'

'There is no occasion for awe,' said the Duke, 'as a sufficiency of dinner is left. But how you should have hit it, as you say,—seeing that the train is not due at Bridstock till 7.5, I do not know.'

'I've done it often, sir,' said Silverbridge, taking the seat left vacant for him next to Lady Mabel. 'We've had a political caucus of the party,—all the members who could be got together in London,—at Sir Timothy's, and I was bound to attend.'

'We've all heard of that,' said Phineas Finn.

'And we pretty well know all the points of Sir Timothy's eloquence,' said Barrington Erle.

'I am not going to tell any of the secrets. I have no doubt that there were reporters present, and you will see the whole of it in the papers to-morrow.' Then Silverbridge turned to his neighbour. 'Well, Lady Mab, and how are you this long time?'

'But how are you? Think what you have gone through since we were at Killancodlem!'

'Don't talk of it.'

'I suppose it is not to be talked of.'

'Though upon the whole it has happened very luckily. I have got rid of the accursed horses, and my governor has shown what a brick he can be. I don't think there is another man in England who would have done as he did.'

'There are not many who could.'

'There are fewer who would. When they came into my bedroom that morning and told me that the horse could not run, I thought I should have broken my heart. Seventy thousand pounds gone!'

'Seventy thousand pounds!'

'And the honour and glory of winning the race! And then the feeling that one had been so awfully swindled! Of course I had to look as though I did not care a straw about it, and to go and see the race, with a jaunty air and a cigar in my mouth. That is what I call hard work.'

'But you did it!'

'I tried. I wish I could explain to you my state of mind that day. In the first place the money had to be got. Though it was to go into the hands of swindlers, still it had to be paid. I don't know how your father and Percival get on together;— but I felt very like the prodigal son.'

'It is very different with papa.'

'I suppose so. I felt very like hanging myself when I was alone that evening. And now everything is right again.'

'I am glad that everything is right,' she said, with a strong emphasis on the 'everything'.

'I have done with racing, at any rate. The feeling of being in the power of a lot of low blackguards is so terrible! I did love the poor brute so dearly. And now what have you been doing?'

'Just nothing;—and have seen nobody. I went back to Grex after leaving Killancodlem, and shut myself up in my misery.'

'Why misery?'

'Why misery! What a question for you to ask! Though I love Grex, I am not altogether fond of living alone; and though Grex has its charms, they are of a melancholy kind. And when I think of the state of our family affairs, that is not reassuring. Your father has just paid seventy thousand pounds for you. My father has been good enough to take something less than a quarter of that sum from me;—but still it was all that I was ever to have.'

'Girls don't want money.'

'Don't they? When I look forward it seems to me that a time will come when I shall want it very much.'

'You will marry,' he said. She turned round for a moment and looked at him, full in the face, after such a fashion that he did not dare to promise her further comfort in that direction. 'Things always do come right, somehow.'

'Let us hope so. Only nothing has ever come right with me yet. What is Frank doing?'

'I haven't seen him since he left Crummie-Toddie.'

'And your sister?' she whispered.

'I know nothing about it at all.'

'And you? I have told you everything about myself.'

'As for me, I think of nothing but politics now. I have told you about my racing experiences. Just at present shooting is up. Before Christmas I shall go into Chiltern's country for a little hunting.'

'You can hunt here?'

'I shan't stay long enough to make it worth while to have my horses down. If Tregear will go with me to the Brake,* I can mount him for a day or two. But I dare say you know more of his plans than I do. He went to see you at Grex.'

'And you did not.'

'I was not asked.'

'Nor was he.'

'Then all I can say is,' replied Silverbridge, speaking in a low voice, but with considerable energy, 'that he can use a freedom with Lady Mabel Grex upon which I cannot venture.'

'I believe you begrudge me his friendship. If you had no one else belonging to you with whom you could have any sympathy, would not you find comfort in a relation who could be almost as near to you as a brother?'

'I do not grudge him to you.'

'Yes; you do. And what business have you to interfere?'

'None at all;—certainly. I will never do it again.'

'Don't say that, Lord Silverbridge. You ought to have more mercy on me. You ought to put up with anything from me, —knowing how much I suffer.'

'I will put up with anything,' said he.

'Do, do. And now I will try to talk to Mr. Erle.'

Miss Boncassen was sitting on the other side of the table, between Mr. Monk and Phineas Finn, and throughout the dinner talked mock politics with the greatest liveliness. Silverbridge when he entered the room had gone round the table and had shaken hands with everyone. But there had been no other greeting between him and Isabel, nor had any sign passed from one to the other. No such greeting or sign had been possible. Nothing had been left undone which she had expected, or hoped. But, though she was lively, nevertheless she kept her eye upon her lover and Lady Mabel. Lady Mary had said that she thought her brother was in love with Lady Mabel. Could it be possible? In her own land she had heard absurd stories—stories which seemed to her to be absurd, of the treachery of lords and countesses, of the baseness of aristocrats, of the iniquities of high life in London. But her father had told her that, go where she might, she would find people in the main to be very like each other. It had seemed to her that nothing could be more ingenuous than this young man had been in the declaration of his love. No simplest republican could have spoken more plainly. But now, at this moment, she could not doubt but that her lover was very intimate with this other girl. Of course he was free. When she had refused to say a word to him of her own love or want of love, she had necessarily left him his liberty. When she had put him off for three months, of course he was to be his own master. But what must she think of him if it were so? And how could he have the courage to face her in his father's house if he intended to treat her in such a fashion? But of all this she showed nothing, nor was there a tone in her voice which betrayed her. She said her last word to Mr. Monk with so sweet a smile that that old bachelor wished he were younger for her sake.

In the evening after dinner there was music. It was discovered that Miss Boncassen sang divinely, and both Lady Mabel and Lady Mary accompanied her. Mr. Erle, and Mr. Warburton, and Mr. Monk, all of whom were unmarried, stood by enraptured. But Lord Silverbridge kept himself apart, and interested himself in a description which Mrs. Boncassen gave him of their young men and their young ladies in the States. He had hardly spoken to Miss Boncassen,—till he offered her sherry or soda-water before she retired for the night. She refused his courtesy with her usual smile, but showed no more emotion than though they two had now met for the first time in their lives.

He had quite made up his mind as to what he would do. When the opportunity should come in his way he would simply remind her that the three months were passed. But he was shy of talking to her in the presence of Lady Mabel and his father. He was quite determined that the thing should be done at once, but he certainly wished that Lady Mabel had not been there. In what she had said to him at the dinner-table she had made him understand that she would be a trouble to him. He remembered her look when he told her she would marry. It was as though she had declared to him that it was he who ought to be her husband. It referred back to that proffer of love which he had once made to her. Of course all this was disagreeable. Of course it made things difficult for

414

him. But not the less was it a thing quite assured that he would press his suit to Miss Boncassen. When he was talking to Mrs. Boncassen he was thinking of nothing else. When he was offering Isabel the glass of sherry he was telling himself that he would find his opportunity on the morrow,—though now, at that moment, it was impossible that he should make a sign. She, as she went to bed, asked herself whether it were possible that there should be such treachery;—whether it were possible that he should pass it all by as though he had never said a word to her!

During the whole of the next day, which was Sunday, he was equally silent. Immediately after breakfast, on the Monday, shooting commenced, and he could not find a moment in which to speak. It seemed to him that she purposely kept out of his way. With Mabel he did find himself for a few minutes alone, and was then interrupted by his sister and Isabel. 'I hope you have killed a lot of things,' said Miss Boncassen.

'Pretty well, among us all.'

'What an odd amusement it seems, going out to commit wholesale slaughter. However it is the proper thing, no doubt.'

'Quite the proper thing,' said Lord Silverbridge, and that was all.

On the next morning he dressed himself for shooting,—and then sent out the party without him. He had heard, he said, of a young horse for sale in the neighbourhood, and had sent to desire that it might be brought to him. And now he found his occasion.

'Come and play a game of billiards,' he said to Isabel, as the three girls with the other ladies were together in the drawing-room. She got up very slowly from her seat, and very slowly crept away to the door. Then she looked round as though expecting the others to follow her. None of them did follow her. Mary felt that she ought to do so; but, knowing all that she knew, did not dare. And what good could she have done by one such interruption? Lady Mabel would fain have gone too;—but neither did she quite dare. Had there been no special reason why she should or should not have gone with them, the thing would have been easy enough. When two people go to play billiards, a third may surely accompany them. But now, Lady Mabel found that she could not stir. Mrs. Finn, Mrs. Boncassen, and Miss Cassewary were all in the room, but none of them moved. Silverbridge led the way quickly across the hall, and Isabel Boncassen followed him very slowly. When she entered the room she found him standing with a cue in his hand. He at once shut the door, and walking up to her dropped the butt of the cue on the floor and spoke one word. 'Well!' he said.

'What does "well" mean?'

'The three months are over.'

'Certainly they are "over."'

'And I have been a model of patience.'

'Perhaps your patience is more remarkable than your constancy. Is not Lady Mabel Grex in the ascendant just now?'

'What do you mean by that? Why do you ask that? You told me to wait for three months. I have waited, and here I am.'

'How very—very—downright you are.'

'Is not that the proper thing?'

'I thought I was downright,—but you beat me hollow. Yes, the three months are over. And now what have you got to say?' He put down his cue, and stretched out his arms as though he were going to take her and hold her to his heart. 'No;—no; not that,' she said laughing. 'But if you will speak, I will hear you.'

'You know what I said before. Will you love me, Isabel?'

'And you know what I said before. Do they know that you love me? Does your father know it, and your sister? Why did they ask me to come here?'

'Nobody knows it. But say that you love me, and everyone shall know it at once. Yes; one person knows it. Why did you mention Lady Mabel's name? She knows it.'

'Did you tell her?'

'Yes. I went again to Killancodlem after you were gone, and then I told her.'

'But why her? Come, Lord Silverbridge. You are straightforward with me, and I will be the same with you. You have told Lady Mabel; I have told Lady Mary.'

'My sister!'

'Yes;—your sister. And I am sure she disapproves it. She did not say so; but I am sure it is so. And then she told me something.'

'What did she tell you?'

'Has there never been reason to think that you intended to offer your hand to Lady Mabel Grex?'

'Did she tell you so?'

'You should answer my question, Lord Silverbridge. It is surely one which I have a right to ask.' Then she stood waiting for his reply, keeping herself at some little distance from him as though she were afraid that he would fly upon her. And indeed there seemed to be cause for such fear from the frequent gestures of his hands. 'Why do you not answer me? Has there been reason for such expectations?'

'Yes;—there has.'

'There has!'

'I thought of it,—not knowing myself; before I had seen you. You shall know it all if you will only say that you love me.'

'I should like to know it all first.'

'You do know it all;—almost. I have told you that she knows what I said to you at Killancodlem. Is not that enough?'

'And she approves!'

'What has that to do with it? Lady Mabel is my friend, but not my guardian.'

'Has she a right to expect that she should be your wife?'

'No;—certainly not. Why should you ask all this? Do you love me? Come, Isabel; say that you love me. Will you call me vain if I say that I almost think you do? You cannot doubt about my love;—not now.'

'No;—not now.'

'You needn't. Why won't you be as honest to me? If you hate me, say so;—but if you love me——!'

417

'I do not hate you, Lord Silverbridge.'

'And is that all?'

'You asked me the question.'

'But you do love me? By George, I thought you would be more honest and straightforward.'

Then she dropped her badinage and answered him seriously. 'I thought I had been honest and straightforward. When found that you were in earnest at Killancodlem——'

'Why did you ever doubt me?'

'When I felt that you were in earnest, then I had to be in earnest too. And I thought so much about it that I lay awake nearly all that night. Shall I tell you what I thought?'

'Tell me something that I should like to hear.'

'I will tell you the truth. "Is it possible," I said to myself, "that such a man as that can want me to be his wife; he an Englishman, of the highest rank and the greatest wealth, and one that any girl in the world would love?"'

'Psha!' he exclaimed.

'That is what I said to myself.' Then she paused, and looking into her face he saw that there was a glimmer of a tear in each eye. 'One that any girl must love when asked for her love;—because he is so sweet, so good, and so pleasant.'

'I know that you are chaffing.'

'Then I went on asking myself questions. And is it possible that I, who by all his friends will be regarded as a nobody, who am an American,—with merely human workaday blood in my veins,—that such a one as I should become his wife? Then I told myself that it was not possible. It was not in accordance with the fitness of things. All the dukes in England would rise up against it, and especially that duke whose good-will would be imperative.'

'Why should he rise up against it?'

'You know he will. But I will go on with my story of myself. When I had settled that in my mind, I just cried myself to sleep. It had been a dream. I had come across one who in his own self seemed to combine all that I had ever thought of as being lovable in man——'

'Isabel!'

'And in his outward circumstances soared as much above my thoughts as the heaven is above the earth. And he had whispered to me soft, loving, heavenly words. No;—no, you shall not touch me. But you shall listen to me. In my sleep I could be happy again and not see the barriers. But when I woke I made up my mind. "If he comes to me again," I said —"if it should be that he should come to me again, I will tell him that he shall be my heaven on earth,—if,—if,—if the ill-will of his friends would not make that heaven a hell to both of us." I did not tell you quite all that.'

'You told me nothing but that I was to come again in three months.'

'I said more than that. I bade you ask your father. Now you have come again. You cannot understand a girl's fears and doubts. How should you? I thought perhaps you would not come. When I saw you whispering to that highly-born well-bred beauty, and remembered what I was myself, I thought that—you would not come.'

'Then you must love me.'

'Love you! Oh, my darling!—No, no, no,' she said, as she retreated from him round the corner of the billiard-table, and stood guarding herself from him with her little hands. 'You ask if I love you. You are entitled to know the truth. From the sole of your foot to the crown of your head I love you as I think a man would wish to be loved by the girl he loves. You have come across my life, and have swallowed me up, and made me all your own. But I will not marry you to be rejected by your people. No; nor shall there be a kiss between us till I know that it will not be so.'

'May I speak to your father?'

'For what good? I have not spoken to father or mother because I have known that it must depend upon your father. Lord Silverbridge, if he will tell me that I shall be his daughter I will become your wife,—oh, with such perfect joy, with such perfect truth! If it can never be so, then let us be torn apart,— with whatever struggle, still at once. In that case I will get myself back to my own country as best I may, and will pray to God that all this may be forgotten.' Then she made her way round to the door, leaving him fixed to the spot in which she had been standing. But as she went she made a little prayer to him. 'Do not delay my fate. It is all in all to me.' And so he was left alone in the billiard-room.

CHAPTER LIII
'Then I am as proud as a Queen'

DURING the next day or two the shooting went on without much interruption from love-making. The love-making was not prosperous all round. Poor Lady Mary had nothing to comfort her. Could she have been allowed to see the letter which her lover had written to her father, the comfort would have been, if not ample, still very great. Mary told herself again and again that she was quite sure of Tregear;—but it was hard upon her that she could not be made certain that her certainty was well grounded. Had she known that Tregear had written, though she had not seen a word of his letter, it would have comforted her. But she had heard nothing of the letter. In June last she had seen him, by chance, for a few minutes, in Lady Mabel's drawing-room. Since that she had not heard from him or of him. That was now more than five months since. How could her love serve her,—how could her very life serve her, if things were to go on like that? How was she to bear it? Thinking of this she resolved—she almost resolved—that she would go boldly to her father and desire that she might be given up to her lover.

Her brother, though more triumphant,—for how could he fail to triumph after such words as Isabel had spoken to him? —still felt his difficulties very seriously. She had imbued him with a strong sense of her own firmness, and she had declared that she would go away and leave him altogether if the Duke should be unwilling to receive her. He knew that the Duke would be unwilling. The Duke, who certainly was not handy

in those duties of match-making which seemed to have fallen
upon him at the death of his wife, showed by a hundred
little signs his anxiety that his son and heir should arrange
his affairs with Lady Mabel. These signs were manifest
to Mary,—were disagreeably manifest to Silverbridge,—
were unfortunately manifest to Lady Mabel herself. They
were manifest to Mrs. Finn, who was clever enough to perceive that the inclinations of the young heir were turned in
another direction. And gradually they became manifest to
Isabel Boncassen. The host himself, as host, was courteous
to all his guests. They had been of his own selection, and he
did his best to make himself pleasant to them all. But he
selected two for his peculiar notice,—and those two were
Miss Boncassen and Lady Mabel. While he would himself
walk, and talk, and argue after his own peculiar fashion with
the American beauty,—explaining to her matters political
and social, till he persuaded her to promise to read his pamphlet upon decimal coinage,—he was always making awkward
efforts to throw Silverbridge and Lady Mabel together. The
two girls saw it all and knew well how the matter was,—knew
that they were rivals, and knew each the ground on which she
herself and on which the other stood. But neither was satisfied
with her advantage, or nearly satisfied. Isabel would not take
the prize without the Duke's consent;—and Mabel could not
have it without that other consent. 'If you want to marry an
English Duke,' she once said to Isabel in that anger which she
was unable to restrain, 'there is the Duke himself. I never saw
a man more absolutely in love.' 'But I do not want to marry
an English Duke,' said Isabel, 'and I pity any girl who has any
idea of marriage except that which comes from a wish to give
back love for love.'

Through it all the father never suspected the real state of
his son's mind. He was too simple to think it possible that
the purpose which Silverbridge had declared to him as they
walked together from the Beargarden had already been thrown
to the winds. He did not like to ask why the thing was not
settled. Young men, he thought, were sometimes shy, and

young ladies not always ready to give immediate encouragement. But, when he saw them together, he concluded that
matters were going in the right direction. It was, however,
an opinion which he had all to himself.

During the three or four days which followed the scene in
the billiard-room Isabel kept herself out of her lover's way.
She had explained to him that which she wished him to do,
and she left him to do it. Day by day she watched the circumstances of the life around her, and knew that it had not been
done. She was sure that it could not have been done while the
Duke was explaining to her the beauty of quints,* and expa-
tiating on the horrors of twelve pennies, and twelve inches,
and twelve ounces,—variegated in some matters by sixteen
and fourteen! He could not know that she was ambitious of
becoming his daughter-in-law, while he was opening out to
her the mysteries of the House of Lords, and explaining how
it came to pass that while he was a member of one House of
Parliament, his son should be sitting as a member of another;
—how it was that a nobleman could be a commoner, and how
a peer of one part of the Empire could sit as the representative
of a borough in another part. She was an apt scholar. Had
there been a question of any other young man marrying her,
he would probably have thought that no other young man
could have done better.

Silverbridge was discontented with himself. The greatest
misfortune was that Lady Mabel should be there. While she
was present to his father's eyes he did not know how to declare
his altered wishes. Every now and then she would say to him
some little word indicating her feelings of the absurdity of his
passion. 'I declare I don't know whether it is you or your
father that Miss Boncassen most affects,' she said. But to this
and to other similar speeches he would make no answer. She
had extracted his secret from him at Killancodlem, and might
use it against him if she pleased. In his present frame of mind
he was not disposed to joke with her upon the subject.

On that second Sunday,—the Boncassens were to return to
London on the following Tuesday,—he found himself alone

with Isabel's father. The American had been brought out at his own request to see the stables, and had been accompanied round the premises by Silverbridge and by Mr. Warburton, by Isabel and by Lady Mary. As they got out into the park the party were divided, and Silverbridge found himself with Mr. Boncassen. Then it occurred to him that the proper thing for a young man in love was to go, not to his own father, but to the lady's father. Why should not he do as others always did? Isabel no doubt had suggested a different course. But that which Isabel had suggested was at the present moment impossible to him. Now, at this instant, without a moment's forethought, he determined to tell his story to Isabel's father, —as any other lover might tell it to any other father.

'I am very glad to find ourselves alone, Mr. Boncassen,' he said. Mr. Boncassen bowed and showed himself prepared to listen. Though so many at Matching had seen the whole play, Mr. Boncassen had seen nothing of it.

'I don't know whether you are aware of what I have got to say.'

'I cannot quite say that I am, my lord. But whatever it is, I am sure I shall be delighted to hear it.'

'I want to marry your daughter,' said Silverbridge. Isabel had told him that he was downright, and in such a matter he had hardly as yet learned how to express himself with those paraphrases in which the world delights. Mr. Boncassen stood stock still, and in the excitement of the moment pulled off his hat. 'The proper thing is to ask your permission to go on with it.'

'You want to marry my daughter!'

'Yes. That is what I have got to say.'

'Is she aware of your——intention?'

'Quite aware. I believe I may say that if other things go straight, she will consent.'

'And your father—the Duke?'

'He knows nothing about it,—as yet.'

'Really this takes me quite by surprise. I am afraid you have not given enough thought to the matter.'

'I have been thinking about it for the last three months,' said Lord Silverbridge.

'Marriage is a very serious thing.'

'Of course it is.'

'And men generally like to marry their equals.'

'I don't know about that. I don't think that counts for much. People don't always know who are their equals.'

'That is quite true. If I were speaking to you or to your father theoretically I should perhaps be unwilling to admit superiority on your side because of your rank and wealth. I could make an argument in favour of any equality with the best Briton that ever lived,—as would become a true-born Republican.'

'That is just what I mean.'

'But when the question becomes one of practising,—a question for our lives, for our happiness, for our own conduct, then, knowing what must be the feelings of an aristocracy in such a country as this, I am prepared to admit that your father would be as well justified in objecting to a marriage between a child of his and a child of mine, as I should be in objecting to one between my child and the son of some mechanic in our native city.'

'He wouldn't be a gentleman,' said Silverbridge.

'That is a word of which I don't quite know the meaning.'

'I do,' said Silverbridge confidently.

'But you could not define it. If a man be well educated, and can keep a good house over his head, perhaps you may call him a gentleman. But there are many such with whom your father would not wish to be so closely connected as you propose.'

'But I may have your sanction?' Mr. Boncassen again took off his hat and walked along thoughtfully. 'I hope you don't object to me personally.'

'My dear young lord, your father has gone out of his way to be civil to me. Am I to return his courtesy by bringing a great trouble upon him?'

'He seems to be very fond of Miss Boncassen.'

'Will he continue to be fond of her when he has heard this? What does Isabel say?'

'She says the same as you, of course.'

'Why of course;—except that it is evident to you as it is to me that she could not with propriety say anything else?'

'I think she would,—would like it, you know.'

'She would like to be your wife!'

'Well;—yes. If it were all serene, I think she would consent.'

'I dare say she would consent,—if it were all serene. Why should she not? Do not try her too hard, Lord Silverbridge. You say you love her.'

'I do, indeed.'

'Then think of the position in which you are placing her. You are struggling to win her heart.' Silverbridge as he heard this assured himself that there was no need for any further struggling in that direction. 'Perhaps you have won it. Yet she may feel that she cannot become your wife. She may well say to herself that this which is offered to her is so great, that she does not know how to refuse it; and may yet have to say, at the same time, that she cannot accept it without disgrace. You would not put one that you love into such a position?'

'As for disgrace,—that is nonsense. I beg your pardon, Mr. Boncassen.'

'Would it be no disgrace that she should be known here, in England, to be your wife, and that none of those of your rank,—of what would then be her own rank,—should welcome her into her new world?'

'That would be out of the question.'

'If your own father refused to welcome her, would not others follow suit?'

'You don't know my father.'

'You seem to know him well enough to fear that he would object.'

'Yes;—that is true.'

'What more do I want to know?'

425

'If she were once my wife he would not reject her. Of all human beings he is in truth the kindest and most affectionate.'

'And therefore you would try him after this fashion? No, my lord; I cannot see my way through these difficulties. You can say what you please to him as to your own wishes. But you must not tell him that you have any sanction from me.'

That evening the story was told to Mrs. Boncassen, and the matter was discussed among the family. Isabel in talking to them made no scruple of declaring her own feelings; and though in speaking to Lord Silverbridge she had spoken very much as her father had done afterwards, yet in this family conclave she took her lover's part. 'That is all very well, father,' she said; 'I told him the same thing myself. But if he is man enough to be firm I shall not throw him over,—not for all the dukes in Europe. I shall not stay here to be pointed at. I will go back home. If he follows me then I shall choose to forget all about his rank. If he loves me well enough to show that he is in earnest, I shall not disappoint him for the sake of pleasing his father.' To this neither Mr. nor Mrs. Boncassen was able to make any efficient answer. Mrs. Boncassen, dear good woman, could see no reason why two young people who loved each other should not be married at once. Dukes and duchesses were nothing to her. If they couldn't be happy in England, then let them come and live in New York. She didn't understand that anybody could be too good for her daughter. Was there not an idea that Mr. Boncassen would be the next President? And was not the President of the United States as good as the Queen of England?

Lord Silverbridge, when he left Mr. Boncassen, wandered about the park by himself. King Cophetua married the beggar's daughter. He was sure of that. King Cophetua probably had not a father; and the beggar, probably, was not high-minded. But the discrepancy in that case was much greater. He intended to persevere, trusting much to a belief that when once he was married his father would 'come round.' His father always did come round. But the more he thought of it the more impossible it seemed to him that he should ask his father's consent at the present moment. Lady Mabel's presence in the house was an insuperable obstacle. He thought that he could do it if he and his father were alone together, or comparatively alone. He must be prepared for an opposition, at any rate of some days, which opposition would make his father quite unable to entertain his guests while it lasted.

But as he could not declare his wishes to his father, and was thus disobeying Isabel's behests, he must explain the difficulty to her. He felt already that she would despise him for his cowardice,—that she would not perceive the difficulties in his way, or understand that he might injure his cause by precipitation. Then he considered whether he might not possibly make some bargain with his father. How would it be if he should consent to go back to the Liberal party on being allowed to marry the girl he loved? As far as his political feelings were concerned he did not think that he would much object to make the change. There was only one thing certain,—that he must explain his condition to Miss Boncassen before she went.

He found no difficulty now in getting the opportunity. She was equally anxious, and as well disposed to acknowledge her anxiety. After what had passed between them she was not desirous of pretending that the matter was one of small moment to herself. She had told him that it was all the world to her, and had begged him to let her know her fate as quickly as possible. On that last Monday morning they were in the grounds together, and Lady Mabel, who was walking with Mrs. Finn, saw them pass through a little gate which led from the gardens into the Priory ruins. 'It all means nothing,' Mabel said with a little laugh to her companion.

'If so, I am sorry for the young lady,' said Mrs. Finn.

'Don't you think that one always has to be sorry for the young ladies? Young ladies generally have a bad time of it. Did you ever hear of a gentleman who had always to roll a stone*to the top of a hill, but it would always come back upon him?'

'That gentleman I believe never succeeded,' said Mrs. Finn.

'The young ladies I suppose do sometimes.'

In the meantime Isabel and Silverbridge were among the ruins together. 'This is where the old Pallisers used to be buried,' he said.

'Oh, indeed. And married, I suppose.'

'I dare say. They had a priest of their own, no doubt, which must have been convenient. This block of a fellow without any legs left is supposed to represent Sir Guy.* He ran away with half-a-dozen heiresses, they say. I wish things were as easily done now.'

'Nobody should have run away with me. I have no idea of going on such a journey except on terms of equality,—just step and step alike.' Then she took hold of his arm and put out one foot. 'Are you ready?'

'I am very willing.'

'But are you ready,—for a straightforward walk off to church before all the world? None of your private chaplains, such as Sir Guy had at his command. Just the registrar, if there is nothing better,—so that it be public, before all the world.'

'I wish we could start this instant.'

'But we can't,—can we?'

'No, dear. So many things have to be settled.'

'And what have you settled on since you last spoke to me?'

'I have told your father everything.'

'Yes;—I know that. What good does that do? Father is not a Duke of Omnium. No one supposed that he would object.'

'But he did,' said Silverbridge.

'Yes;—as I do,—for the same reason; because he would not have his daughter creep in at a hole. But to your own father you have not ventured to speak.' Then he told his story, as best he knew how. It was not that he feared his father, but that he felt that the present moment was not fit. 'He wishes you to marry that Lady Mabel Grex,' she said. He nodded his head. 'And you will marry her?'

'Never! I might have done so, had I not seen you. I should have done so, if she had been willing. But now I never can,—never, never.' Her hand had dropped from his arm, but now

she put it up again for a moment, so that he might feel the
pressure of her fingers. 'Say that you believe me.'

'I think I do.'

'You know I love you.'

'I think you do. I am sure I hope you do. If you don't, then
I am—a miserable wretch.'

'With all my heart I do.'

'Then I am as proud as a queen. You will tell him soon?'

'As soon as you are gone. As soon as we are alone together.
I will;—and then I will follow you to London. Now shall we
not say, Good-bye?'

'Good-bye, my own,' she whispered.

'You will let me have one kiss?'

Her hand was in his, and she looked about as though to see
that no eyes were watching them. But then, as the thoughts
came rushing to her mind, she changed her purpose. 'No,'
she said. 'What is it but a trifle! It is nothing in itself. But
I have bound myself to myself by certain promises, and you
must not ask me to break them. You are as sweet to me as
I can be to you, but there shall be no kissing till I know that
I shall be your wife. Now take me back.'

CHAPTER LIV

'I don't think she is a snake'

On the following day, Tuesday, the Boncassens went, and then there were none of the guests left but Mrs. Finn and Lady Mabel Grex,—with of course Miss Cassewary. The Duke had especially asked both Mrs. Finn and Lady Mabel to remain, the former, through his anxiety to show his repentance for the injustice he had formerly done her, and the latter in the hope that something might be settled as soon as the crowd of visitors should have gone. He had never spoken quite distinctly to Mabel. He had felt that the manner in which he had learned his son's purpose,—that which once had been his son's purpose,—forbade him to do so. But he had so spoken as to make Lady Mabel quite aware of his wish. He would not have told her how sure he was that Silverbridge would keep no more racehorses, how he trusted that Silverbridge had done with betting, how he believed that the young member would take a real interest in the House of Commons, had he not intended that she should take a special interest in the young man. And then he had spoken about the house in London. It was to be made over to Silverbridge as soon as Silverbridge should marry. And there was Gatherum Castle. Gatherum was rather a trouble than otherwise. He had ever felt it to be so, but had nevertheless always kept it open perhaps for a month in the year. His uncle had always resided there for a fortnight at Christmas. When Silverbridge was married it would become the young man's duty to do something of the same kind. Gatherum was the White Elephant of the family, and Silverbridge must enter in upon his share of the trouble. He did not know that in saying all this he was offering his son as a husband to Lady Mabel, but she understood it as thoroughly as though he had spoken the words.

But she knew the son's mind also. He had indeed himself told her all his mind. 'Of course I love her best of all,' he had said. When he told her of it she had been so overcome that she had wept in her despair;—had wept in his presence. She had declared to him her secret,—that it had been her intention to become his wife, and then he had rejected her! It had all been shame, and sorrow, and disappointment to her. And she could not but remember that there had been a moment when she might have secured him by a word. A look would have done it; a touch of her finger on that morning. She had known then that he had intended to be in earnest,—that he only waited for encouragement. She had not given it because she had not wished to grasp too eagerly at the prize,—and now the prize was gone! She had said that she had spared him;—but then she could afford to joke, thinking that he would surely come back to her.

She had begun her world with so fatal a mistake! When she was quite young, when she was little more than a child but still not a child, she had given all her love to a man whom she soon found that it would be impossible she should ever marry. He had offered to face the world with her, promising to do the best to smooth the rough places, and to soften the stones for her feet. But she, young as she was, had felt that both he and she belonged to a class which could hardly endure poverty with contentment. The grinding need for money, the absolute necessity of luxurious living, had been pressed upon her from her childhood. She had seen it and acknowledged it, and had told him, with precocious wisdom, that that which he offered to do for her sake would be a folly for them both. She had not stinted the assurance of her love, but had told him that they must both turn aside and learn to love elsewhere. He had done so, with too complete readiness! She had dreamed of a second love, which should obliterate the first,—which might still leave to her the memory of the romance of her early passion. Then this boy had come in her way! With him all her ambition might have been satisfied. She desired high rank and great wealth. With him she might have had it all. And then, too, though there would always be the memory of that early passion, yet she could in another fashion love this youth. He was pleasant to her, and gracious;

431

—and she had told herself that if it should be so that this great
fortune might be hers, she would atone to him fully for that
past romance by the wife-like devotion of her life. The cup
had come within the reach of her fingers, but she had not
grasped it. Her happiness, her triumphs, her great success
had been there, present to her, and she had dallied with her
fortune. There had been a day on which he had been all but
at her feet, and on the next he had been prostrate at the feet of
another. He had even dared to tell her so,—saying of that
American that 'of course he loved her the best!'

Over and over again since that, she had asked herself
whether there was no chance. Though he had loved that
other one best she would take him if it were possible. When
the invitation came from the Duke she would not lose a chance.
She had told him that it was impossible that he, the heir to the
Duke of Omnium, should marry an American. All his family,
all his friends, all his world would be against him. And then
he was so young,—and, as she thought, so easily led. He was
lovable and prone to love;—but surely his love could not be
very strong, or he would not have changed so easily.

She did not hesitate to own to herself that this American
was very lovely. She too, herself, was beautiful. She too had
a reputation for grace, loveliness, and feminine high-bred
charm. She knew all that, but she knew also that her attractions were not so bright as those of her rival. She could not
smile or laugh and throw sparks of brilliance around her as
did the American girl. Miss Boncassen could be graceful as
a nymph in doing the awkwardest thing! When she had pretended to walk stiffly along, to some imaginary marriage
ceremony, with her foot stuck out before her, with her chin
in the air, and one arm akimbo, Silverbridge had been all afire
with admiration. Lady Mabel understood it all. The American girl must be taken away,—from out of the reach of the
young man's senses,—and then the struggle must be made.

Lady Mabel had not been long at Matching before she
learned that she had much in her favour. She perceived that
the Duke himself had no suspicion of what was going on, and

that he was strongly disposed in her favour. She unravelled it all in her own mind. There must have been some agreement, between the father and the son, when the son had all but made his offer to her. More than once she was half-minded to speak openly to the Duke, to tell him all that Silverbridge had said to her and all that he had not said, and to ask the father's help in scheming against that rival. But she could not find the words with which to begin. And then, might he not despise her, and, despising her, reject her, were she to declare her desire to marry a man who had given his heart to another woman? And so, when the Duke asked her to remain after the departure of the other guests, she decided that it would be best to bide her time. The Duke, as she assented, kissed her hand, and she knew that this sign of grace was given to his intended daughter-in-law.

In all this she half confided her thoughts and her prospects to her old friend, Miss Casseway. 'That girl has gone at last,' she said to Miss Cass.

'I fear she has left her spells behind her, my dear.'

'Of course she has. The venom out of the snake's tooth will poison all the blood; but still the poor bitten wretch does not always die.'

'I don't think she is a snake.'

'Don't be moral, Cass. She is a snake in my sense. She has got her weapons, and of course it is natural enough that she should use them. If I want to be Duchess of Omnium, why shouldn't she?'

'I hate to hear you talk of yourself in that way.'

'Because you have enough of the old school about you to like conventional falsehood. This young man did in fact ask me to be his wife. Of course I meant to accept him,—but I didn't. Then comes this convict's granddaughter.'

'Not a convict's!'

'You know what I mean. Had he been a convict it would have been all the same. I take upon myself to say that, had the world been informed that an alliance had been arranged between the eldest son of the Duke of Omnium and the daughter of Earl Grex,—the world would have been satisfied. Every unmarried daughter of every peer in England would have envied me,—but it would have been comme il faut.'

'Certainly, my dear.'

'But what would be the feeling as to the convict's grand-daughter?'

'You don't suppose that I would approve it;—but it seems to me that in these days young men do just what they please.'

'He shall do what he pleases, but he must be made to be pleased with me.' So much she said to Miss Casseway; but she did not divulge any plan. The Boncassens had just gone off to the station, and Silverbridge was out shooting. If anything could be done here at Matching, it must be done quickly, as Silverbridge would soon take his departure. She did not know it, but, in truth, he was remaining in order that he might, as he said, 'have all this out with the governor.'

She tried to realise for herself some plan, but when the evening came nothing was fixed. For a quarter of an hour, just as the sun was setting, the Duke joined her in the gardens, —and spoke to her more plainly than he had ever spoken before. 'Has Silverbridge come home?' he asked.

'I have not seen him.'

'I hope you and Mary get on well together.'

'I think so, Duke. I am sure we should if we saw more of each other.'

'I sincerely hope you may. There is nothing I wish for Mary so much as that she should have a sister. And there is no one whom I would be so glad to hear her call by that name as yourself.' How could he have spoken plainer?

The ladies were all together in the drawing-room when Silverbridge came bursting in rather late. 'Where's the governor?' he asked, turning to his sister.

'Dressing, I should think; but what is the matter?'

'I want to see him. I must be off to Cornwall to-morrow morning.'

'To Cornwall!' said Miss Casseway. 'Why to Cornwall?'

asked Lady Mabel. But Mary, connecting Cornwall with Frank Tregear, held her peace.

'I can't explain it all now, but I must start very early to-morrow.' Then he went off to his father's study, and finding the Duke still there explained the cause of his intended journey. The member for Polpenno had died, and Frank Tregear had been invited to stand for the borough. He had written to his friend to ask him to come and assist in the struggle. 'Years ago there used to be always a Tregear in for Polpenno,' said Silverbridge.

'But he is a younger son.'*

'I don't know anything about it,' said Silverbridge, 'but as he has asked me to go I think I ought to do it.' The Duke, who was by no means the man to make light of the political obligations of friendship, raised no objection.

'I wish,' said he, 'that something could have been arranged between you and Mabel before you went.' The young man stood in the gloom of the dark room aghast. This was certainly not the moment for explaining everything to his father. 'I have set my heart very much upon it, and you ought to be gratified by knowing that I quite approve your choice.'

All that had been years ago,—in last June;—before Mrs. Montacute Jones's garden-party, before that day in the rain at Maidenhead, before the brightness of Killancodlem, before the glories of Miss Boncassen had been revealed to him. 'There is no time for that kind of thing now,' he said weakly.

'I thought that when you were here together——'

'I must dress now, sir; but I will tell you all about it when I get back from Cornwall. I will come back direct to Matching, and will explain everything.' So he escaped.

It was clear to Lady Mabel that there was no opportunity now for any scheme. Whatever might be possible must be postponed till after this Cornish business had been completed. Perhaps it might be better so. She had thought that she would appeal to himself, that she would tell him of his father's wishes, of her love for him,—of the authority which he had once given her for loving him,—and of the absolute impossibility

435

of his marriage with the American. She thought that she could do it, if not efficiently at any rate effectively. But it could not be done on the very day on which the American had gone.

It came out in the course of the evening that he was going to assist Frank Tregear in his canvass. The matter was not spoken of openly, as Tregear's name could hardly be mentioned. But everybody knew it, and it gave occasion to Mabel for a few words apart with Silverbridge. 'I am so glad you are going to him,' she said in a little whisper.

'Of course I go when he wishes me. I don't know that I can do him any good.'

'The greatest good in the world. Your name will go so far! It will be everything to him to be in Parliament. And when are we to meet again?' she said.

'I shall turn up somewhere,' he replied as he gave her his hand to wish her good-bye.

On the following morning the Duke proposed to Lady Mabel that she should stay at Matching for yet another fortnight,—or even for a month if it might be possible. Lady Mabel, whose father was still abroad, was not sorry to accept the invitation.

CHAPTER LV
*Polpenno**

POLWENNING, the seat of Mr. Tregear, Frank's father, was close to the borough of Polpenno,—so close that the gates of the grounds opened into the town. As Silverbridge had told his father, many of the Tregear family had sat for the borough. Then there had come changes, and strangers had made themselves welcome by their money. When the vacancy now occurred a deputation waited upon Squire Tregear and asked him to stand. The deputation would guarantee that the expense should not exceed—a certain limited sum. Mr. Tregear for himself had no such ambition. His eldest son was abroad and was not at all such a man as one would choose to

make into a Member of Parliament. After much consideration in the family, Frank was invited to present himself to the
constituency. Frank's aspirations in regard to Lady Mary
Palliser were known at Polwenning, and it was thought that
they would have a better chance of success if he could write
the letters M.P. after his name. Frank acceded, and as he was
starting wrote to ask the assistance of his friend Lord Silverbridge. At that time there were only nine days more before
the election, and Mr. Carbottle, the Liberal candidate, was
already living in great style at the Camborne Arms.

Mr. and Mrs. Tregear and an elder sister of Frank's, who
quite acknowledged herself to be an old maid, were very glad
to welcome Frank's friend. On the first morning of course
they discussed the candidates' prospects. 'My best chance of
success,' said Frank, 'arises from the fact that Mr. Carbottle
is fatter than the people here seem to approve.'

'If his purse be fat,' said old Mr. Tregear, 'that will carry
off any personal defect.' Lord Silverbridge asked whether the
candidate was not too fat to make speeches. Miss Tregear
declared that he had made three speeches daily for the last
week, and that Mr. Williams the rector, who had heard him,
declared him to be a godless dissenter. Mrs. Tregear thought
that it would be much better that the place should be dis-
franchised altogether than that such a horrid man should be
brought into the neighbourhood. 'A godless dissenter!' she
said, holding up her hands in dismay. Frank thought that they
had better abstain from allusion to their opponent's religion.
Then Mr. Tregear made a little speech. 'We used,' he said,
'to endeavour to get someone to represent us in Parliament,
who would agree with us on vital subjects,*such as the Church
of England and the necessity of religion. Now it seems to be
considered ill-mannered to make any allusion to such subjects!' From which it may be seen that this old Tregear was
very conservative indeed.

When the old people were gone to bed the two young men
discussed the matter. 'I hope you'll get in,' said Silverbridge.
'And if I can do anything for you of course I will.'

'It is always good to have a real member along with one,' said Tregear.

'But I begin to think I am a very shaky Conservative myself.'

'I am sorry for that.'

'Sir Timothy is such a beast,' said Silverbridge.

'Is that your notion of a political opinion? Are you to be this or that in accordance with your own liking or disliking for some particular man? One is supposed to have opinions of one's own.'

'Your father would be down on a man because he is a dissenter.'

'Of course my father is old-fashioned.'

'It does seem so hard to me,' said Silverbridge, 'to find any difference between the two sets. You who are a true Conservative are much more like to my father, who is a Liberal, than to your own, who is on the same side as yourself.'

'It may be so, and still I may be a good Conservative.'

'It seems to me in the House to mean nothing more than choosing one set of companions or choosing another. There are some awful cads who sit along with Mr. Monk;—fellows that make you sick to hear them, and whom I couldn't be civil to. But I don't think there is anybody I hate so much as old Beeswax. He has a contemptuous way with his nose which makes me long to pull it.'

'And you mean to go over in order that you may be justified in doing so. I think I soar a little higher,' said Tregear.

'Oh, of course. You're a clever fellow,' said Silverbridge, not without a touch of sarcasm.

'A man may soar higher than that without being very clever. If the party that calls itself Liberal were to have all its own way who is there that doesn't believe that the church would go at once, then all distinction between boroughs, the House of Lords immediately afterwards, and after that the Crown?'

'Those are not my governor's ideas.'*

'Your governor couldn't help himself. A Liberal party, with

plenipotentiary power, must go on right away to the logical conclusion of its arguments. It is only the conservative feeling of the country which saves such men as your father from being carried headlong to ruin by their own machinery. You have read Carlyle's French Revolution.'

'Yes, I have read that.'

'Wasn't it so there? There were a lot of honest men who thought they could do a deal of good by making everybody equal. A good many were made equal by having their heads cut off. That's why I mean to be member for Polpenno and to send Mr. Carbottle back to London. Carbottle probably doesn't want to cut anybody's head off.'

'I dare say he's as conservative as anybody.'

'But he wants to be a member of Parliament; and, as he hasn't thought much about anything, he is quite willing to lend a hand to communism, radicalism, socialism, chopping people's heads off, or anything else.'

'That's all very well,' said Silverbridge, 'but where should we have been if there had been no Liberals? Robespierre and his pals cut off a lot of heads, but Louis XIV and Louis XV locked up more in prison.' And so he had the last word in the argument.

The whole of the next morning was spent in canvassing, and the whole of the afternoon. In the evening there was a great meeting at the Polwenning Assembly Room, which at the present moment was in the hands of the Conservative party. Here Frank Tregear made an oration, in which he declared his political convictions. The whole speech was said at the time to be very good; but the portion of it which was apparently esteemed the most, had direct reference to Mr. Carbottle. Who was Mr. Carbottle? Why had he come to Polpenno? Who had sent for him? Why Mr. Carbottle rather than anybody else? Did not the people of Polpenno think that it might be as well to send Mr. Carbottle back to the place from whence he had come? These questions, which seemed to Silverbridge to be as easy as they were attractive, almost made him desirous of making a speech himself.

Then Mr. Williams, the rector, followed, a gentleman who had many staunch friends and many bitter enemies in the town. He addressed himself chiefly to that bane of the whole country,—as he conceived them,—the godless dissenters; and was felt by Tregear to be injuring the cause by every word he spoke. It was necessary that Mr. Williams should liberate his own mind, and therefore he persevered with the godless dissenters at great length,—not explaining, however, how a

man who thought enough about his religion to be a dissenter could be godless, or how a godless man should care enough about religion to be a dissenter.

Mr. Williams was heard with impatience, and then there was a clamour for the young lord. He was the son of an ex-Prime Minister, and therefore of course he could speak. He was himself a member of Parliament, and therefore could speak. He had boldly severed himself from the faulty political tenets of his family, and therefore on such an occasion as this was peculiarly entitled to speak. When a man goes electioneering, he must speak. At a dinner-table to refuse is possible:—or in any assembly convened for a semi-private purpose, a gentleman may declare that he is not prepared for the occasion. But in such an emergency as this, a man,—and a member of Parliament,—cannot plead that he is not prepared. A son of a former Prime Minister who had already taken so strong a part in politics as to have severed himself from his father, not prepared to address the voters of a borough whom he had come to canvass! The plea was so absurd, that he was thrust on to his feet before he knew what he was about.

It was in truth his first public speech. At Silverbridge he had attempted to repeat a few words, and in his failure had been covered by the Sprugeons and the Sprouts. But now he was on his legs in a great room, in an unknown town, with all the aristocracy of the place before him! His eyes at first swam a little, and there was a moment in which he thought he would run away. But, on that morning, as he was dressing, there had come to his mind the idea of the possibility of such a moment as this, and a few words had occurred to him. 'My friend Frank Tregear,' he began, rushing at once at his subject, 'is a very good fellow, and I hope you'll elect him.' Then he paused, not remembering what was to come next; but the sentiment which he had uttered appeared to his auditors to be so good in itself and so well-delivered, that they filled up a long pause with continued clappings and exclamations. 'Yes,' continued the young member of Parliament, encouraged by the kindness of the crowd, 'I have known Frank Tregear ever so long, and I don't think you could find a better member of Parliament anywhere.' There were many ladies present and they thought that the Duke's son was just the person who ought to come electioneering among them. His voice was much pleasanter to their ears than that of old Mr. Williams. The women waved their handkerchiefs and the men stamped their feet. Here was an orator come among them! 'You all know all about it just as well as I do,' continued the orator, 'and I am sure you feel that he ought to be member for Polpenno.' There could be no doubt about that as far as the opinion of the audience went. 'There can't be a better fellow than Frank Tregear, and I ask you all to give three cheers for the new member.' Ten times three cheers were given, and the Carbottleites outside the door who had come to report what was going on at the Tregear meeting were quite of opinion that this eldest son of the former Prime Minister was a tower of strength. 'I don't know anything about Mr. Carbottle,' continued Silverbridge, who was almost growing to like the sound of his own voice. 'Perhaps he's a good fellow too.' 'No; no, no. A very bad fellow indeed,' was heard from different parts of the room. 'I don't know anything about him. I wasn't at school with Carbottle.' This was taken as a stroke of the keenest wit, and was received with infinite cheering. Silverbridge was in the pride of his youth, and Carbottle was sixty at the least. Nothing could have been funnier. 'He seems to be a stout old party, but I don't think he's the man for Polpenno. I think you'll return Frank Tregear. I was at school with him;—and I tell you, that you can't find a better fellow anywhere than Frank Tregear.' Then he sat down, and I am afraid he felt that he had made the speech of the evening. 'We are so much obliged to you, Lord Silverbridge,' Miss Tregear said as they were walking home together. 'That's just the sort of thing that the people like. So reassuring, you know. What Mr. Williams says about the dissenters is of course true; but it isn't reassuring.'

'I hope I didn't make a fool of myself to-night,' Silverbridge said when he was alone with Tregear,—probably with some little pride in his heart.

'I ought to say that you did, seeing that you praised me so violently. But, whatever it was, it was well taken. I don't know whether they will elect me; but had you come down as a candidate, I am quite sure they would have elected you.' Silverbridge was hardly satisfied with this. He wished to have been told that he had spoken well. He did not, however, resent his friend's coldness. 'Perhaps, after all, I did make a fool of myself,' he said to himself as he went to bed.

On the next day, after breakfast, it was found to be raining heavily. Canvassing was of course the business of the hour, and canvassing is a business which cannot be done indoors. It was soon decided that the rain should go for nothing. Could an agreement have been come to with the Carbottleites it might have been decided that both parties should abstain, but as that was impossible the Tregear party could not afford to lose the day. As Mr. Carbottle, by reason of his fatness and natural slowness, would perhaps be specially averse to walking about in the slush and mud, it might be that they would gain something; so after breakfast they started with umbrellas,—Tregear, Silverbridge, Mr. Newcomb the curate, Mr. Pinebott the conservative attorney, with four or five followers who were armed with books and pencils, and who ticked off on the list of the voters the names of the friendly, the doubtful, and the inimical.

Parliamentary canvassing*is not a pleasant occupation. Perhaps nothing more disagreeable, more squalid, more revolting to the senses, more opposed to personal dignity, can be conceived. The same words have to be repeated over and over again in the cottages, hovels, and lodgings of poor men and women who only understand that the time has come round in which they are to be flattered instead of being the flatterers. 'I think I am right in supposing that your husband's principles are Conservative, Mrs. Bubbs.' 'I don't know nothing about it. You'd better call again and see Bubbs hissel.' 'Certainly I will do so. I shouldn't at all like to leave the borough without seeing Mr. Bubbs. I hope we shall have your influence, Mrs. Bubbs.' 'I don't know nothing about it. My folk at home allays vote buff,*and I think Bubbs ought to go buff too. Only mind this; Bubbs don't never come home to his dinner. You must come arter six, and I hope he's to have some'at for his trouble. He won't have my word to vote unless he have some'at.' Such is the conversation in which the candidate takes a part, while his cortège at the door is criticising his very imperfect mode of securing Mrs. Bubbs' good wishes. Then he goes on to the next house, and the same thing with some variation is endured again. Some guide, philosopher, and friend, who accompanies him, and who is the chief of the

443

cortège, has calculated on his behalf that he ought to make twenty such visitations an hour, and to call on two hundred constituents in the course of the day. As he is always falling behind in his number, he is always being driven on by his philosopher, till he comes to hate the poor creatures to whom he is forced to address himself, with a most cordial hatred.

It is a nuisance to which no man should subject himself in any weather. But when it rains there is superadded a squalor and an ill humour to all the party which makes it almost impossible for them not to quarrel before the day is over. To talk politics to Mrs. Bubbs under any circumstances is bad, but to do so with the conviction that the moisture is penetrating from your greatcoat through your shirt to your bones, and that while so employed you are breathing the steam from those seven other wet men at the door, is abominable. To have to go through this is enough to take away all the pride which a man might otherwise take from becoming a member of Parliament. But to go through it and then not to become a member is base indeed! To go through it and to feel that you are probably paying at the rate of a hundred pounds a day for the privilege is most disheartening. Silverbridge, as he backed up Tregear in the uncomfortable work, congratulated himself on the comfort of having a Mr. Sprugeon and a Mr. Sprout*who could manage his borough for him without a contest.

They worked on that day all the morning till one, when they took luncheon, all reeking with wet, at the King's Head, —so that a little money might be legitimately spent in the cause. Then, at two, they sallied out again, vainly endeavouring to make their twenty calls within the hour. About four, when it was beginning to be dusk, they were very tired, and Silverbridge had ventured to suggest that as they were all wet through, and as there was to be another meeting in the Assembly Room that night, and as nobody in that part of the town seemed to be at home, they might perhaps be allowed to adjourn for the present. He was thinking how nice it would be to have a glass of hot brandy-and-water and then lounge till dinner-time. But the philosophers received the proposition with stern disdain. Was his Lordship aware that Mr. Carbottle had been out all day from eight in the morning, and was still at work; that the Carbottleites had already sent for lanterns and were determined to go on till eight o'clock among the artisans who would then have returned from their work? When a man had put his hand to the plough, the philosophers thought that that man should complete the furrow!

The philosophers' view had just carried the day, the discussion having been held under seven or eight wet umbrellas at the corner of a dirty little lane leading into the High Street; when suddenly, on the other side of the way, Mr. Carbottle's cortège made its appearance. The philosophers at once informed them that on such occasions it was customary that the rival candidates should be introduced. 'It will take ten minutes,' said the philosophers; 'but then it will take them ten minutes too.' Upon this Tregear, as being the younger of the two, crossed over the road, and the introduction was made.

There was something comfortable in it to the Tregear party, as no imagination could conceive anything more wretched than the appearance of Mr. Carbottle. He was a very stout man of sixty, and seemed to be almost carried along by his companions. He had pulled his coat-collar up and his hat down till very little of his face was visible, and in attempting to look at Tregear and Silverbridge he had to lift up his chin till the rain ran off his hat on to his nose. He had an umbrella in one hand and a stick in the other, and was wet through to his very skin. What were his own feelings cannot be told, but his philosophers, guides, and friends would allow him no rest. 'Very hard work, Mr. Tregear,' he said, shaking his head.

'Very hard indeed, Mr. Carbottle.' Then the two parties went on, each their own way, without another word.

CHAPTER LVI
The news is sent to Matching

THERE were nine days of this work, during which Lord Silverbridge became very popular and made many speeches. Tregear did not win half so many hearts, or recommend himself so thoroughly to the political predilections of the borough;—but nevertheless he was returned. It would probably be unjust to attribute this success chiefly to the young Lord's eloquence. It certainly was not due to the strong religious feelings of the rector. It is to be feared that even the thoughtful political convictions of the candidate did not altogether produce the result. It was that chief man among the candidate's guides and friends, that leading philosopher who would not allow anybody to go home from the rain, and who kept his eyes so sharply open to the pecuniary doings of the Carbottleites, that Mr. Carbottle's guides and friends had hardly dared to spend a shilling;—it was he who had in truth been efficacious. In every attempt they had made to spend their money they had been looked into and circumvented. As

Mr. Carbottle had been brought down to Polpenno on purpose that he might spend money,—as he had nothing but his
money to recommend him, and as he had not spent it,—the
free and independent electors of the borough had not seen
their way to vote for him. Therefore the Conservatives were
very elate with their triumph. There was a great Conservative reaction. But the electioneering guide, philosopher, and
friend, in the humble retirement of his own home,—he was a
tailor in the town, whose assistance at such periods had long
been in requisition,—he knew very well how the seat had been
secured. Ten shillings a head would have sent three hundred
true Liberals to the ballot-boxes!*The mode of distributing
the money had been arranged; but the Conservative tailor had
been too acute, and not half-a-sovereign could be passed. The
tailor got twenty-five pounds for his work, and that was
smuggled in among the bills for printing.

Mr. Williams, however, was sure that he had so opened
out the iniquities of the dissenters as to have convinced the
borough. Yes; every Salem and Zion and Ebenezer*in his
large parish would be closed. 'It is a great thing for the
country,' said Mr. Williams.

'He'll make a capital member,' said Silverbridge, clapping
his friend on the back.

'I hope he'll never forget,' said Mr. Williams, 'that he
owes his seat to the Protestant and Church-of-England principles which have sunk so deeply into the minds of the thoughtful portion of the inhabitants of this borough.'

'Whom should they elect but a Tregear?' said the mother,
feeling that her rector took too much of the praise to himself.

'I think you have done more for us than any one else,'
whispered Miss Tregear to the young Lord. 'What you said
was so reassuring!' The father before he went to bed expressed to his son, with some trepidation, a hope that all this
would lead to no great permanent increase of expenditure.

That evening before he went to bed Lord Silverbridge
wrote to his father an account of what had taken place at
Polpenno.

447

'Polwenning, 15th December.

My dear Father,

'Among us all we have managed to return Tregear. I am afraid you will not be quite pleased because it will be a vote lost to your party. But I really think that he is just the fellow to be in Parliament. If he were on your side I'm sure he's the kind of man you'd like to bring into office. He is always thinking about those sort of things. He says that, if there were no Conservatives, such Liberals as you and Mr. Monk would be destroyed by the Jacobins.*There is something in that. Whether a man is a Conservative or not himself, I suppose there ought to be Conservatives.' The Duke as he read this made a memorandum in his own mind that he would explain to his son that every carriage should have a drag to its wheels, but that an ambitious soul would choose to be the coachman rather than the drag.

'It was beastly work!' The Duke made another memorandum to instruct his son that no gentleman above the age of a schoolboy should allow himself so use such a word in such a sense. 'We had to go about in the rain up to our knees in mud for eight or nine days, always saying the same thing. And of course all that we said was bosh.' Another memorandum—or rather two, one as to the slang, and another as to the expediency of teaching something to the poor voters on such occasions. 'Our only comfort was that the Carbottle people were quite as badly off as us.' Another memorandum as to the grammar. The absence of Christian charity did not at the moment affect the Duke. 'I made ever so many speeches, till at last it seemed to be quite easy.' Here there was a very grave memorandum. Speeches easy to young speakers are generally very difficult to old listeners. 'But of course it was all bosh.' This required no separate memorandum.

'I have promised to go up to town with Tregear for a day or two. After that I will stick to my purpose of going to Matching again. I will be there about the 22nd, and will then stay over Christmas. After that I am going into the Brake country for some hunting. It is such a shame to have a lot of horses and never to ride them!

'Your most affectionate Son,

'SILVERBRIDGE.'

The last sentence gave rise in the Duke's mind to the necessity of a very elaborate memorandum on the subject of amusements generally.

By the same post another letter went from Polpenno to Matching which also gave rise to some mental memoranda. It was as follows:

'MY DEAR MABEL,

'I am a Member of the British House of Commons! I have sometimes regarded myself as being one of the most peculiarly unfortunate men in the world, and yet now I have achieved that which all commoners in England think to be the greatest honour within their reach, and have done so at an age at which very few achieve it but the sons of the wealthy and the powerful.

'I now come to my misfortunes. I know that as a poor man I ought not to be a member of Parliament. I ought to be earning my bread as a lawyer or a doctor. I have no business to be what I am, and when I am forty I shall find that I have eaten up all my good things instead of having them to eat.

'I have one chance before me. You know very well what that is. Tell her that my pride in being a member of Parliament is much more on her behalf than on my own. The man who dares to love her ought at any rate to be something in the world. If it might be,—if ever it may be,—I should wish to be something for her sake. I am sure you will be glad of my success yourself, for my own sake.

'Your affectionate Friend and Cousin,

'FRANCIS TREGEAR.'

The first mental memorandum in regard to this came from the writer's assertion that he at forty would have eaten up all his good things. No! He being a man might make his way to good things though he was not born to them. He surely would win his good things for himself. But what good things were in store for her? What chance of success was there for her? But the reflection which was the most bitter to her of all came from her assurance that his love for that other girl was so genuine. Even when he was writing to her there was no spark left of the old romance! Some hint of a recollection of past feelings, some half-concealed reference to the former passion might have been allowed to him! She as a woman,— as a woman all whose fortune must depend on marriage,— could indulge in no such allusions; but surely he need not have been so hard!

But still there was another memorandum. At the present moment she would do all that he desired as far as it was in her power. She was anxious that he should marry Lady Mary Palliser, though so anxious also that something of his love should remain with herself! She was quite willing to convey that message,—if it might be done without offence to the Duke. She was there with the object of ingratiating herself with the Duke. She must not impede her favour with the Duke by making herself the medium of any secret communications between Mary and her lover.

But how should she serve Tregear without risk of offending the Duke? She read the letter again and again, and thinking it to be a good letter she determined to show it to the Duke.

'Mr. Tregear has got in at Polpenno,' she said on the day on which she and the Duke had received their letters.

'So I hear from Silverbridge.'

'It will be a good thing for him, I suppose.'

'I do not know,' said the Duke coldly.

'He is my cousin, and I have always been interested in his welfare.'

'That is natural.'

'And a seat in Parliament will give him something to do.'

'Certainly it ought,' said the Duke.

'I do not think that he is an idle man.' To this the Duke made no answer. He did not wish to be made to talk about Tregear. 'May I tell you why I say all this?' she asked softly,

450

pressing her hand on the Duke's arm ever so gently. To this the Duke assented, but still coldly. 'Because I want to know what I ought to do. Would you mind reading that letter? Of course you will remember that Frank and I have been brought up almost as brother and sister.'

The Duke took the letter in his hand and did read it, very slowly. 'What he says about young men without means going into Parliament is true enough.' This was not encouraging, but as the Duke went on reading, Mabel did not think it necessary to argue the matter. He had to read the last paragraph twice before he understood it. He did read it twice, and then folding the letter very slowly gave it back to his companion.

'What ought I to do?' asked Lady Mabel.

'As you and I, my dear, are friends, I think that any carrying of a message to Mary would be breaking confidence. I think that you should not speak to Mary about Mr. Tregear.' Then he changed the subject. Lady Mabel of course understood that after that she could not say a word to Mary about the election at Polpenno.

CHAPTER LVII

The meeting at 'The Bobtailed Fox'

IT was now the middle of December, and matters were not comfortable in the Runnymede country. The Major with much pluck had carried on his operations in opposition to the wishes of the resident members of the hunt. The owners of coverts had protested, and farmers had sworn that he should not ride over their lands. There had even been some talk among the younger men of thrashing him if he persevered. But he did persevere, and had managed to have one or two good runs. Now it was the fortune of the Runnymede hunt that many of those who rode with the hounds were strangers to the country,—men who came down by train from London, gentlemen of perhaps no great distinction, who could ride hard, but as to whom it was thought that as they did not provide the land to ride over, or the fences to be destroyed, or the coverts for the foxes, or the greater part of the subscription, they ought not to oppose those by whom all these things were supplied. But the Major, knowing where his strength lay, had managed to get a party to support him. The contract to hunt the country had been made with him in last March, and was good for one year. Having the kennels and the hounds under his command he did hunt the country; but he did so amidst a storm of contumely and ill will.

At last it was decided that a general meeting of the members of the hunt should be called together with the express object of getting rid of the Major. The gentlemen of the neighbourhood felt that the Major was not to be borne, and the farmers were very much stronger against him than the gentlemen. It had now become a settled belief among sporting men in England that the Major had with his own hands driven the nail into the horse's foot. Was it to be endured that the Runnymede farmers should ride to hounds under a master who had been guilty of such an iniquity as that? 'The Staines and Egham Gazette,' which had always supported the Runnymede hunt, declared in very plain terms that all who rode with the Major were enjoying their sport out of the plunder which had been extracted from Lord Silverbridge. Then a meeting was called for Saturday, the 18th December, to be held at that well-known sporting little inn The Bobtailed Fox. The members of the hunt were earnestly called upon to attend. It was,—so said the printed document which was issued,—the only means by which the hunt could be preserved. If gentlemen who were interested did not put their shoulders to the wheel, the Runnymede hunt must be regarded as a thing of the past. One of the documents was sent to the Major with an intimation that if he wished to attend no objection would be made to his presence. The chair would be taken at half-past twelve punctually by that popular and well-known old sportsman Mr. Mahogany Topps.

Was ever the master of a hunt treated in such a way! His

452

presence not objected to! As a rule the master of a hunt does not attend hunt meetings, because the matter to be discussed is generally that of the money to be subscribed for him, as to which it is as well he should not hear the pros and cons. But it is presumed that he is to be the hero of the hour, and that he is to be treated to his face, and spoken of behind his back, with love, admiration, and respect. But now this master was told his presence would be allowed! And then this fox-hunting meeting was summoned for half-past twelve on a hunting-day; —when, as all the world knew, the hounds were to meet at eleven, twelve miles off! Was ever anything so base? said the Major to himself. But he resolved that he would be equal to the occasion. He immediately issued cards to all the members, stating that on that day the meet had been changed from Croppingham Bushes, which was ever so much on the other side of Bagshot, to The Bobtailed Fox,—for the benefit of the hunt at large, said the card,—and that the hounds would be there at half-past one.

Whatever might happen, he must show a spirit. In all this there were one or two of the London brigade who stood fast to him. 'Cock your tail, Tifto,' said one hard-riding supporter, 'and show 'em you aren't afraid of nothing.' So Tifto cocked his tail and went to the meeting in his best new scarlet coat, with his whitest breeches, his pinkest boots, and his neatest little bows at his knees. He entered the room with his horn in his hand, as a symbol of authority, and took off his hunting-cap to salute the assembly with a jaunty air. He had taken two glasses of cherry brandy, and as long as the stimulant lasted would no doubt be able to support himself with audacity.

Old Mr. Topps, in rising from his chair, did not say very much. He had been hunting in the Runnymede country for nearly fifty years, and had never seen anything so sad as this before. It made him, he knew, very unhappy. As for foxes, there were always plenty of foxes in his coverts. His friend Mr. Jawstock, on the right, would explain what all this was about. All he wanted was to see the Runnymede hunt properly kept up. Then he sat down, and Mr. Jawstock rose to his legs.

Mr. Jawstock was a gentleman well known in the Runnymede country, who had himself been instrumental in bringing Major Tifto into these parts. There is often someone in a hunting country who never becomes a master of hounds himself, but who has almost as much to say about the business as the master himself. Sometimes at hunt meetings he is rather unpopular, as he is always inclined to talk. But there are occasions on which his services are felt to be valuable,—as were Mr. Jawstock's at present. He was about forty-five years of age, was not much given to riding, owned no coverts himself, and was not a man of wealth; but he understood the nature of hunting, knew all its laws, and was a judge of horses, of hounds, —and of men; and could say a thing when he had to say it.

Mr. Jawstock sat on the right hand of Mr. Topps, and a place was left for the master opposite. The task to be performed was neither easy nor pleasant. It was necessary that the orator should accuse the gentleman opposite to him,— a man with whom he himself had been very intimate,—of iniquity so gross and so mean, that nothing worse can be conceived. 'You are a swindler, a cheat, a rascal of the very deepest dye;—a rogue so mean that it is revolting to be in the same room with you!' That was what Mr. Jawstock had to say. And he said it. Looking round the room, occasionally appealing to Mr. Topps, who on these occasions would lift up his hands in horror, but never letting his eye fall for a moment on the Major, Mr. Jawstock told his story. 'I did not see it done,' said he. 'I know nothing about it. I never was at Doncaster in my life. But you have evidence of what the Jockey Club thinks. The Master of our Hunt has been banished from racecourses.' Here there was considerable opposition, and a few short but excited little dialogues were maintained;—throughout all which Tifto restrained himself like a Spartan. 'At any rate he has been thoroughly disgraced,' continued Mr. Jawstock, 'as a sporting man. He has been driven out of the Beargarden Club.' 'He resigned in disgust at their treatment,' said a friend of the Major's. 'Then let him resign in disgust at ours,' said Mr. Jawstock, 'for we won't have him here. Cæsar wouldn't keep a wife who was suspected of infidelity, nor will the Runnymede country endure a Master of Hounds who is supposed to have driven a nail into a horse's foot.'

Two or three other gentlemen had something to say before the Major was allowed to speak,—the upshot of the discourse of all of them being the same. The Major must go.

Then the Major got up, and certainly as far as attention went he had full justice done him. However clamorous they might intend to be afterwards that amount of fair play they were all determined to afford him. The Major was not excellent at speaking, but he did perhaps better than might have been expected. 'This is a very disagreeable position,' he said, 'very disagreeable indeed. As for the nail in the horse's foot I know no more about it than the babe unborn. But I've got two things to say, and I'll say what aren't the most consequence first. These hounds belong to me.' Here he paused, and a loud contradiction came from many parts of the room. Mr. Jawstock, however, proposed that the Major should be heard to the end. 'I say they belong to me,' repeated the Major. 'If anybody tries his hand at anything else the law will soon set that to rights. But that aren't of much consequence. What I've got to say is this. Let the matter be referred. If that 'orse had a nail run into his foot,—and I don't say he hadn't,—who was the man most injured? Why, Lord Silverbridge. Everybody knows that. I suppose he dropped well on to eighty thousand pounds! I propose to leave it to him. Let him say. He ought to know more about it than any one. He and I were partners in the horse. His Lordship aren't very sweet upon me just at present. Nobody need fear that he'll do me a good turn. I say leave it to him.'

In this matter the Major had certainly been well advised. A rumour had become prevalent among sporting circles that Silverbridge had refused to condemn the Major. It was known that he had paid his bets without delay, and that he had, to some extent, declined to take advice from the leaders of the Jockey Club. The Major's friends were informed that the young lord had refused to vote against him at the club. Was it not more than probable that if this matter were referred to him he would refuse to give a verdict against his late partner?

The Major sat down, put on his cap, and folded his arms akimbo, with his horn sticking out from his left hand. For a time there was general silence, broken, however, by murmurs in different parts of the room. Then Mr. Jawstock whispered something into the ear of the Chairman, and Mr. Topps, rising from his seat, suggested to Tifto that he should retire. 'I think so,' said Mr. Jawstock. 'The proposition you have made can be discussed only in your absence.' Then the Major held a consultation with one of his friends, and after that did retire.

When he was gone the real hubbub of the meeting commenced. There were some there who understood the nature of Lord Silverbridge's feelings in the matter. 'He would be the last man in England to declare him guilty,' said Mr. Jawstock. 'Whatever my lord says, he shan't ride across my land,' said a farmer in the background. 'I don't think any gentleman ever made a fairer proposition,—since anything was anything,' said a friend of the Major's, a gentleman who kept livery stables in Long Acre. 'We won't have him here,' said another farmer,—whereupon Mr. Topps shook his head sadly. 'I don't think any gentleman ought to be condemned without a 'earing,' said one of Tifto's admirers, 'and where you're to get anyone to hunt the country like him, I don't know as any body is prepared to say.' 'We'll manage that,' said a young gentleman from the neighbourhood of Bagshot, who thought that he could hunt the country himself quite as well as Major Tifto. 'He must go from here; that's the long and the short of it,' said Mr. Jawstock. 'Put it to the vote, Mr. Jawstock,' said the livery-stable keeper. Mr. Topps, who had had great experience in public meetings, hereupon expressed an opinion that they might as well go to a vote. No doubt he was right if the matter was one which must sooner or later be decided in that manner.

Mr. Jawstock looked round the room trying to calculate

what might be the effect of a show of hands. The majority was with him; but he was well aware that of this majority some few would be drawn away by the apparent justice of Tifto's proposition. And what was the use of voting? Let them vote as they might, it was out of the question that Tifto should remain master of the hunt. But the chairman had acceded, and on such occasions it is difficult to go against the chairman.

Then there came a show of hands,—first for those who desired to refer the matter to Lord Silverbridge, and afterwards for Tifto's direct enemies,—for those who were anxious to banish Tifto out of hand, without reference to any one. At last the matter was settled. To the great annoyance of Mr. Jawstock and the farmers, the meeting voted that Lord Silverbridge should be invited to give his opinion as to the innocence or guilt of his late partner.

The Major's friends carried the discussion out to him as he sat on horseback, as though he had altogether gained the battle and was secure in his position as Master of the Runnymede Hunt for the next dozen years. But at the same time there came a message from Mr. Mahogany Topps. It was now half-past two, and Mr. Topps expressed a hope that Major Tifto would not draw the country on the present occasion. The Major, thinking that it might be as well to conciliate his enemies, rode solemnly and slowly home to Tallyho Lodge in the middle of his hounds.

CHAPTER LVIII
The Major is deposed

WHEN Silverbridge undertook to return with Tregear to London instead of going off direct to Matching, it is to be feared that he was simply actuated by a desire to postpone his further visit to his father's house. He had thought that Lady Mabel would surely be gone before his task at Polpenno was completed. As soon as he should again find himself in his father's presence he would at once declare his intention of marrying Isabel Boncassen. But he could not see his way to doing it while Lady Mabel should be in the house.

'I think you will find Mabel still at Matching,' said Tregear on their way up. 'She will wait for you, I fancy.'

'I don't know why she should wait for me,' said Silver-bridge almost angrily.

'I thought that you and she were fast friends.'

'I suppose we are—after a fashion. She might wait for you perhaps.'

'I think she would,—if I could go there.'

'You are much thicker with her than I ever was. You went to see her at Grex,—when nobody else was there.'

'Is Miss Cassewary nobody?'

'Next door to it,' said Silverbridge, half jealous of the favours shown to Tregear.

'I thought,' said Tregear, 'that there would be a closer intimacy between you and her.'

'I don't know why you should think so.'

'Had you never any such idea yourself?'

'I haven't any now,—so there may be an end of it. I don't think a fellow ought to be cross-questioned on such a subject.'

'Then I am very sorry for Mabel,' said Tregear. This was uttered solemnly, so that Silverbridge found himself debarred from making any flippant answer. He could not altogether defend himself. He had been quite justified, he thought, in changing his mind, but he did not like to own that he had changed it so quickly.

'I think we had better not talk any more about it,' he said, after pausing for a few moments. After that nothing more was said between them on the subject.

Up in town Silverbridge spent two or three days pleasantly enough, while a thunderbolt was being prepared for him, or rather, in truth, two thunderbolts. During these days he was much with Tregear; and though he could not speak freely of his own matrimonial projects, still he was brought round to give some sort of assent to the engagement between Tregear and his sister. This new position which his friend had won for himself did in some degree operate on his judgment. It was not perhaps that he himself imagined that Tregear as a member of Parliament would be worthier, but that he fancied that such would be the Duke's feelings. The Duke had declared that Tregear was nobody. That could hardly be said of a man who had a seat in the House of Commons;—certainly could not be said by so staunch a politician as the Duke.

But had he known of those two thunderbolts he would not have enjoyed his time at the Beargarden. The thunderbolts fell upon him in the shape of two letters which reached his hands at the same time, and were as follows:

'The Bobtailed Fox. Egham. 18th December.
'My Lord,

'At a meeting held in this house to-day in reference to the hunting of the Runnymede country, it was proposed that the management of the hounds should be taken out of the hands of Major Tifto, in consequence of certain conduct of which it is alleged that he was guilty at the last Doncaster races.

'Major Tifto was present, and requested that your Lordship's opinion should be asked as to his guilt. I do not know myself that we are warranted in troubling your Lordship on the subject. I am, however, commissioned by the majority of the gentlemen who were present to ask you whether you think that Major Tifto's conduct on that occasion was of such a nature as to make him unfit to be the depositary of that influence, authority, and intimacy which ought to be at the command of a Master of Hounds.

'I feel myself bound to inform your Lordship that the hunt generally will be inclined to place great weight upon your opinion; but that it does not undertake to reinstate Major Tifto, even should your opinion be in his favour.

'I have the honour to be,
'My Lord,
'Your Lordship's most obedient Servant,
'JEREMIAH JAWSTOCK.
'Juniper Lodge, Staines.'

459

Mr. Jawstock, when he had written this letter, was proud of his own language, but still felt that the application was a very lame one. Why ask any man for an opinion, and tell him at the same time that his opinion might probably not be taken? And yet no other alternative had been left to him. The meeting had decided that the application should be made; but Mr. Jawstock was well aware that let the young Lord's answer be what it might, the Major would not be endured as master in the Runnymede country. Mr. Jawstock felt that the passage in which he explained that a Master of Hounds should be a depositary of influence and intimacy, was good;— but yet the application was lame, very lame.

Lord Silverbridge as he read it thought that it was very unfair. It was a most disagreeable thunderbolt. Then he opened the second letter, of which he well knew the hand-writing. It was from the Major. Tifto's letters were very legible, but the writing was cramped, showing that the opera-tion had been performed with difficulty. Silverbridge had hoped that he might never receive another epistle from his late partner. The letter, as follows, had been drawn out for Tifto in rough by the livery-stable keeper in Long Acre.

'My dear Lord Silverbridge,

'I venture respectfully to appeal to your Lordship for an act of justice. Nobody has more of a true-born Englishman's feeling of fair play between man and man than your Lordship; and as you and me have been a good deal together, and your Lordship ought to know me pretty well, I venture to appeal to your Lordship for a good word.

'All that story from Doncaster has got down into the country where I am M.F.H. Nobody could have been more sorry than me that your Lordship dropped your money. Would not I have been prouder than anything to have a horse in my name win the race! Was it likely I should lame him? Anyways I didn't, and I don't think your Lordship thinks it was me. Of course your Lordship and me is two now;—but that don't alter the facts.

'What I want is your Lordship to send me a line, just stating your Lordship's opinion that I didn't do it, and didn't have nothing to do with it;—which I didn't. There was a meeting at The Bobtailed Fox yesterday, and the gentlemen was all of one mind to go by what your Lordship would say. I couldn't desire nothing fairer. So I hope your Lordship will stand to me now, and write something that will pull me through.

'With all respects I beg to remain,
'Your Lordship's most dutiful Servant,
'T. TIFTO.'

There was something in this letter which the Major himself did not quite approve. There was an absence of familiarity about it which annoyed him. He would have liked to call upon his late partner to declare that a more honourable man than Major Tifto had never been known on the turf. But he felt himself to be so far down in the world that it was not safe for him to hold an opinion of his own, even against the livery-stable keeper!

Silverbridge was for a time in doubt whether he should answer the letters at all, and if so how he should answer them. In regard to Mr. Jawstock and the meeting at large, he regarded the application as an impertinence. But as to Tifto himself he vacillated much between pity, contempt, and absolute condemnation. Everybody had assured him that the man had certainly been guilty. The fact that he had made bets against their joint horse,—bets as to which he had said nothing till after the race was over,—had been admitted by himself. And yet it was possible that the man might not be such a rascal as to be unfit to manage the Runnymede hounds. Having himself got rid of Tifto, he would have been glad that the poor wretch should have been left with his hunting honours. But he did not think that he could write to his late partner any letter that would preserve those honours to him.

At Tregear's advice he referred the matter to Mr. Lupton. Mr. Lupton was of opinion that both the letters should be answered, but that the answer to each should be very short. 'There is a prejudice about the world just at present,' said Mr. Lupton, 'in favour of answering letters. I don't see why I am to be subjected to an annoyance because another man has taken a liberty. But it is better to submit to public opinion. Public opinion thinks that letters should be answered.' Then Mr. Lupton dictated the answers.

'Lord Silverbridge presents his compliments to Mr. Jawstock, and begs to say that he does not feel himself called upon to express any opinion as to Major Tifto's conduct at Doncaster.' That was the first. The second was rather less simple, but not much longer.

'SIR,

'I do not feel myself called upon to express any opinion either to you or to others as to your conduct at Doncaster. Having received a letter on the subject from Mr. Jawstock I have written to him to this effect.

'Your obedient Servant,
'SILVERBRIDGE.

'To T. Tifto, Esq.,
'Tallyho Lodge.'

Poor Tifto, when he got this very curt epistle, was broken-hearted. He did not dare to show it. Day after day he told the livery-stable keeper that he had received no reply, and at last asserted that his appeal had remained altogether unanswered. Even this he thought was better than acknowledging the rebuff which had reached him. As regarded the meeting which had been held,—and any further meetings which might be held,—at The Bobtailed Fox, he did not see the necessity, as he explained to the livery-stable keeper, of acknowledging that he had written any letter to Lord Silverbridge.

The letter to Mr. Jawstock was of course brought forward. Another meeting at The Bobtailed Fox was convened. But in the meantime hunting had been discontinued in the Runnymede country. The Major with all his pluck, with infinite cherry brandy, could not do it. Men who had a few weeks since been on very friendly terms, and who had called each other Dick and Harry when the squabble first began, were now talking of 'punching' each other's heads. Special whips had been procured by men who intended to ride, and special bludgeons by the young farmers who intended that nobody should ride as long as Major Tifto kept the hounds. It was said that the police would interfere. It was whispered that the hounds would be shot,—though Mr. Topps, Mr. Jawstock, and others declared that no crime so heinous as that had ever been contemplated in the Runnymede country.

The difficulties were too many for poor Tifto, and the hounds were not brought out again under his influence.

A second meeting was summoned, and an invitation was sent to the Major similar to that which he had before received;—but on this occasion he did not appear. Nor were there many of the gentlemen down from London. This second meeting might almost have been called select. Mr. Mahogany Topps was there of course, in the chair, and Mr. Jawstock took the place of honour and of difficulty on his right hand. There was the young gentleman from Bagshot, who considered himself quite fit to take Tifto's place if somebody else would pay the bills and settle the money, and there was the sporting old parson from Croppingham. Three or four other members of the hunt were present, and perhaps half-a-dozen farmers, ready to declare that Major Tifto should never be allowed to cross their fields again.

But there was no opposition. Mr. Jawstock read the young lord's note, and declared that it was quite as much as he expected. He considered that the note, short as it was, must be decisive. Major Tifto, in appealing to Lord Silverbridge, had agreed to abide by his Lordship's answer, and that answer was now before them. Mr. Jawstock ventured to propose that Major Tifto should be declared to be no longer Master of the Runnymede Hounds. The parson from Croppingham seconded the proposition, and Major Tifto was formally deposed.

CHAPTER LIX

No one can tell what may come to pass

THEN Lord Silverbridge necessarily went down to Matching, knowing that he must meet Mabel Grex. Why should she have prolonged her visit? No doubt it might be very pleasant for her to be his father's guest at Matching, but she had been there above a month! He could understand that his father should ask her to remain. His father was still brooding over that foolish communication which had been made to him on the night of the dinner at the Beargarden. His father was still intending to take Mabel to his arms as a daughter-in-law. But Lady Mabel herself knew that it could not be so! The whole truth had been told to her. Why should she remain at Matching for the sake of being mixed up in a scene the acting of which could not fail to be disagreeable to her?

He found the house very quiet and nearly empty. Mrs. Finn was there with the two girls, and Mr. Warburton had come back. Miss Casseway had gone to a brother's house. Other guests to make Christmas merry there were none. As he looked round at the large rooms he reflected that he himself was there only for a special purpose. It was his duty to break the news of his intended marriage to his father. As he stood before the fire, thinking how best he might do this, it occurred to him that a letter from a distance would have been the ready and simple way. But then it had occurred to him also, when at a distance, that a declaration of his purpose face to face was the simplest and readiest way. If you have to go headlong into the water you should take your plunge without hesitating. So he told himself, making up his mind that he would have it all out that evening.

At dinner Lady Mabel sat next to his father, and he could watch the special courtesy with which the Duke treated the girl whom he was so desirous of introducing to his house. Silverbridge could not talk about the election at Polpenno because all conversation about Tregear was interdicted in the

presence of his sister. He could say nothing as to the Runnymede hunt and the two thunderbolts which had fallen on him,
as Major Tifto was not a subject on which he could expatiate
in the presence of his father. He asked a few questions about
the shooting, and referred with great regret to his absence
from the Brake country.

'I am sure Mr. Cassewary could spare you for another fortnight,' the Duke said to his neighbour, alluding to a visit
which she now intended to make.

'If so he would have to spare me altogether,' said Mabel,
'for I must meet my father in London in the middle of January.'

'Could you not put it off to another year?'

'You would think I had taken root and was growing at
Matching.'

'Of all our products you would be the most delightful, and
the most charming,—and we would hope the most permanent,'
said the courteous Duke.

'After being here so long I need hardly say that I like
Matching better than any place in the world. I suppose it is
the contrast to Grex.'

'Grex was a palace,' said the Duke, 'before a wall of this
house had been built.'

'Grex is very old, and very wild,—and very uncomfortable.
But I love it dearly. Matching is the very reverse of Grex.'

'Not I hope in your affections.'

'I did not mean that. I think one likes a contrast. But I must
go, say on the first of January, to pick up Miss Cassewary.'

It was certain, therefore, that she was going on the first of
January. How would it be if he put off the telling of his story
for yet another week, till she should be gone? Then he looked
around and bethought himself that the time would hang
very heavy with him. And his father would daily expect from
him a declaration exactly opposed to that which he had to
make. He had no horses to ride. As he went on listening he
almost convinced himself that the proper thing to do would
be to go back to London and thence write to his father. He
made no confession to his father on that night.

On the next morning there was a heavy fall of snow, but nevertheless everybody managed to go to church. The Duke, as he looked at Lady Mabel tripping along over the swept paths in her furs and short petticoats and well-made boots, thought that his son was a lucky fellow to have the chance of winning the love of such a girl. No remembrance of Miss Boncassen came across his mind as he saw them close together. It was so important that Silverbridge should marry and thus be kept from further follies! And it was so momentous to the fortunes of the Palliser family generally that he should marry well! In thinking so it did not occur to him that the grand-daughter of an American labourer might be offered to him. A young lady fit to be Duchess of Omnium was not to be found everywhere. But this girl, he thought as he saw her walking briskly and strongly through the snow, with every mark of health about her, with every sign of high breeding, very beautiful, exquisite in manner, gracious as a goddess, was fit to be a Duchess! Silverbridge at this moment was walking close to her side,—in good looks, in gracious manner, in high breeding her equal,—in worldly gifts infinitely her superior. Surely she would not despise him! Silverbridge at the moment was expressing a hope that the sermon would not be very long.

After lunch Mabel came suddenly behind the chair on which Silverbridge was sitting and asked him to take a walk with her. Was she not afraid of the snow? 'Perhaps you are,' she said laughing. 'I do not mind it in the least.' When they were but a few yards from the front door, she put her hand upon his arm, and spoke to him as though she had arranged the walk with reference to that special question, 'And now tell me all about Frank.'

She had arranged everything. She had a plan before her now, and had determined in accordance with that plan that she would say nothing to disturb him on this occasion. If she could succeed in bringing him into good humour with herself, that should be sufficient for to-day. 'Now tell me everything about Frank.'

'Frank is member of Parliament for Polpenno. That is all.'

'That is so like a man and so unlike a woman. What did he say? What did he do? How did he look? What did you say? What did you do? How did you look?'

'We looked very miserable, when we got wet through, walking about all day in the rain.'

'Was that necessary?'

'Quite necessary. We looked so mean and draggled that nobody would have voted for us, only that poor Mr. Carbottle looked meaner and more draggled.'

'The Duke says you made ever so many speeches.'

'I should think I did. It is very easy to make speeches down at a place like that. Tregear spoke like a book.'

'He spoke well?'

'Awfully well. He told them that all the good things that had ever been done in Parliament had been carried by the Tories. He went back to Pitt's time, and had it all at his fingers' ends.'

'And quite true.'

'That's just what it was not. It was all a crammer. But it did as well.'

'I am glad he is a member. Don't you think the Duke will come round a little now?'

When Tregear and the election had been sufficiently discussed, they came by degrees to Major Tifto and the two thunderbolts. Silverbridge, when he perceived that nothing was to be said about Isabel Boncassen, or his own freedom in the matter of love-making, was not sorry to have a friend from whom he could find sympathy for himself in his own troubles. With some encouragement from Mabel the whole story was told. 'Was it not a great impertinence?' she asked.

'It was an awful bore. What could I say? I was not going to pronounce judgment against the poor devil. I daresay he was good enough for Mr. Jawstock.'

'But I suppose he did cheat horribly.'

'I daresay he did. A great many of them do cheat. But what of that? I was not bound to give him a character, bad or good.'

'Certainly not.'

'He had not been my servant. It was such a letter. I'll show it you when we get in!—asking whether Tifto was fit to be the depositary of the intimacy of the Runnymede hunt! And then Tif's letter;—I almost wept over that.'

'How could he have had the audacity to write at all?'

'He said that "him and me had been a good deal together." Unfortunately that was true. Even now I am not quite sure that he lamed the horse himself.'

'Everybody thinks he did. Percival says there is no doubt about it.'

'Percival knows nothing about it. Three of the gang ran away, and he stood his ground. That's about all we do know.'

'What did you say to him?'

'I had to address him as Sir, and beg him not to write to me any more. Of course they mean to get rid of him, and I couldn't do him any good. Poor Tifto! Upon the whole I think I hate Jawstock worse than Tifto.'

Lady Mabel was content with her afternoon's work. When they had been at Matching before the Polpenno election, there had apparently been no friendship between them,—at any rate no confidential friendship. Miss Boncassen had been there, and he had had neither ears nor eyes for any one else. But now something like the feeling of old days had been restored. She had not done much towards her great object;—but then she had known that nothing could be done till he should again be in a good humour with her.

On the Sunday, the Monday, and the Tuesday they were again together. In some of these interviews Silverbridge described the Polpenno people, and told her how Miss Tregear had been reassured by his eloquence. He also read to her the Jawstock and Tifto correspondence, and was complimented by her as to his prudence and foresight. 'To tell the truth I consulted Mr. Lupton,' he said, not liking to take credit for wisdom which had not been his own. Then they talked about Grex, and Killancodlem, about Gerald and the shooting, about Mary's love for Tregear, and about the work of the coming Session. On all these subjects they were comfortable and confidential,—Miss Boncassen's name never having been as yet so much as mentioned.

But still the real work was before her. She had not hoped to bring him round to kneel once more at her feet by such gentle measures as these. She had not dared to dream that he could in this way be taught to forget the past autumn and all its charms. She knew well that there was something very difficult before her. But, if that difficult thing might be done at all, these were the preparations which must be made for the doing of it.

It was arranged that she should leave Matching on Saturday, the first day of the new year. Things had gone on in the manner described till the Thursday had come. The Duke had been impatient but had restrained himself. He had seen that they were much together and that they were apparently friends. He too told himself that there were two more days, and that before the end of those days everything might be pleasantly settled!

It had become a matter of course that Silverbridge and Mabel should walk together in the afternoon. He himself had felt that there was danger in this,—not danger that he should be untrue to Isabel, but that he should make others think that he was true to Mabel. But he excused himself on the plea that he and Mabel had been intimate friends,—were still intimate friends, and that she was going away in a day or two. Mary, who watched it all, was sure that misery was being prepared for someone. She was aware that by this time her father was anxious to welcome Mabel as his daughter-in-law. She strongly suspected that something had been said between her father and her brother on the subject. But then she had Isabel Boncassen's direct assurance that Silverbridge was engaged to her! Now when Isabel's back was turned, Silverbridge and Mabel were always together.

On the Thursday after lunch they were again out together. It had become so much a habit that the walk repeated itself without an effort. It had been part of Mabel's scheme that it should be so. During all this morning she had been thinking of her scheme. It was all but hopeless. So much she had declared to herself. But forlorn hopes do sometimes end in splendid triumphs. That which she might gain was so much! And what could she lose? The sweet bloom of her maiden shame? That, she told herself, with bitterest inward tears, was already gone from her. Frank Tregear at any rate knew where her heart had been given. Frank Tregear knew that having lost her heart to one man she was anxious to marry another. He knew that she was willing to accept the coronet of a duchess as her consolation. That bloom of her maiden shame, of which she quite understood the sweetness, the charm, the value—was gone when she had brought herself to such a state that any human being should know that, loving one man, she should be willing to marry another. The sweet treasure was gone from her. Its aroma was fled. It behoved her now to be ambitious, cautious,—and if possible successful.

When first she had so resolved, success seemed to be easily within her reach. Of all the golden youths that crossed her path no one was so pleasant to her eye, to her ear, to her feelings generally as this Duke's young heir. There was a coming manliness about him which she liked,—and she liked even the slight want of present manliness. Putting aside Frank Tregear she could go nearer to loving him than any other man she had ever seen. With him she would not be turned from her duties by disgust, by dislike, or dismay. She could even think that the time would come when she might really love him. Then she had all but succeeded, and she might have succeeded altogether had she been but a little more prudent. But she had allowed her great prize to escape from her fingers.

But the prize was not yet utterly beyond her grasp. To recover it,—to recover even the smallest chance of recovering it, there would be need of great exertion. She must be bold, sudden, unwomanlike,—and yet with such display of woman's charm that he at least should discover no want. She must be false, but false with such perfect deceit, that he must regard her as a pearl of truth. If anything could lure him back it must be his conviction of her passionate love. And she must be strong;—so strong as to overcome not only his weakness, but all that was strong in him. She knew that he did love that other girl,—and she must overcome even that. And to do this she must prostrate herself at his feet,—as, since the world began, it has been man's province to prostrate himself at the feet of the woman he loves.

To do this she must indeed bid adieu to the sweet bloom of her maiden shame! But had she not done so already when, by the side of the brook at Killancodlem, she had declared to him plainly enough her despair at hearing that he loved that other girl? Though she were to grovel at his feet she could not speak more plainly than she had spoken then. She could not tell her story now more plainly than she had done then; but,—though the chances were small,—perchance she might tell it more effectually.

'Perhaps this will be our last walk,' she said. 'Come down to the seat over the river.'

'Why should it be the last? You'll be here to-morrow.'

'There are so many slips in such things,' she said laughing. 'You may get a letter from your constituents that will want all the day to answer. Or your father may have a political communication to make to me. But at any rate come.' So they went to the seat.

It was a spot in the park from whence there was a distant view over many lands, and low beneath the bench, which stood on the edge of a steep bank, ran a stream which made a sweeping bend in this place, so that a reach of the little river might be seen both to the right and to the left. Though the sun was shining, the snow under their feet was hard with frost. It was an air such as one sometimes finds in England, and often in America. Though the cold was very perceptible, though water in the shade was freezing at this moment, there was no feeling of damp, no sense of bitter wind. It was a sweet and jocund air, such as would make young people prone to run and skip. 'You are not going to sit down with all the snow on the bench,' said Silverbridge.

On their way thither she had not said a word that would disturb him. She had spoken to him of the coming Session, and had managed to display to him the interest which she took in his parliamentary career. In doing this she had flattered him to the top of his bent.*If he would return to his father's politics, then would she too become a renegade. Would he speak in the next Session? She hoped he would speak. And if he did, might she be there to hear him? She was cautious not to say a word of Frank Tregear, understanding something of that strange jealousy which could exist even when he who was jealous did not love the woman who caused it.

'No,' she said, 'I do not think we can sit. But still I like to be here with you. All that some day will be your own.' Then she stretched her hands out to the far view.

'Some of it, I suppose. I don't think it is all ours. As for that, if we cared for extent of acres, one ought to go to Barsetshire.'

'Is that larger?'

'Twice as large, I believe, and yet none of the family like being there. The rental*is very well.'

'And the borough,' she said, leaning on his arm and looking up into his face. 'What a happy fellow you ought to be.'

'Bar Tifto,—and Mr. Jawstock.'

'You have got rid of Tifto and all those troubles very easily.'

'Thanks to the governor.'

'Yes, indeed. I do love your father so dearly.'

'So do I—rather.'

'May I tell you something about him?' As she asked the question she was standing very close to him, leaning upon his arm, with her left hand crossed upon her right. Had others been there, of course she would not have stood in such a guise. She knew that,—and he knew it too. Of course there was something in it of declared affection,—of that kind of love which most of us have been happy enough to give and receive, without intending to show more than true friendship will allow at special moments.

'Don't tell me anything about him I shan't like to hear.'

'Ah;—that is so hard to know. I wish you would like to hear it.'

'What can it be?'

'I cannot tell you now.'

'Why not? And why did you offer?'

'Because—— Oh, Silverbridge.'

He certainly as yet did not understand it. It had never occurred to him that she would know what were his father's wishes. Perhaps he was slow of comprehension as he urged her to tell him what this was about his father. 'What can you tell me about him, that I should not like to hear?'

'You do not know? Oh, Silverbridge, I think you know.' Then there came upon him a glimmering of the truth. 'You do know.' And she stood apart looking him full in the face.

'I do not know what you can have to tell me.'

'No;—no. It is not I that should tell you. But yet it is so. Silverbridge, what did you say to me when you came to me that morning in the Square?'

'What did I say?'

'Was I not entitled to think that you—loved me?' To this he had nothing to reply, but stood before her silent and frowning. 'Think of it, Silverbridge. Was it not so? And because I did not at once tell you all the truth, because I did not there say that my heart was all yours, were you right to leave me?'

'You only laughed at me.'

'No;—no; no; I never laughed at you. How could I laugh when you were all the world to me? Ask Frank;—he knew. Ask Miss Cass;—she knew. And can you say you did not know; you, you, you yourself? Can any girl suppose that such words as these are to mean nothing when they have been spoken? You knew I loved you.'

'No;—no.'

'You must have known it. I will never believe but that you knew it. Why should your father be so sure of it?'

'He never was sure of it.'

'Yes, Silverbridge; yes. There is not one in the house who

does not see that he treats me as though he expected me to be his son's wife. Do you not know that he wishes it?' He fain would not have answered this; but she paused for his answer and then repeated her question. 'Do you not know that he wishes it?'

'I think he does,' said Silverbridge; 'but it can never be so.'

'Oh, Silverbridge;—oh, my loved one! Do not say that to me! Do not kill me at once!' Now she placed her hands one on each arm as she stood opposite to him and looked up into his face. 'You said you loved me once. Why do you desert me now? Have you a right to treat me like that;—when I tell you that you have all my heart?' The tears were now streaming down her face, and they were not counterfeit tears.

'You know,' he said, submitting to her hands, but not lifting his arm to embrace her.

'What do I know?'

'That I have given all I have to give to another.' As he said this he looked away sternly, over her shoulder, to the distance.

'That American girl!' she exclaimed, starting back, with some show of sternness also on her brow.

'Yes;—that American girl,' said Silverbridge.

Then she recovered herself immediately. Indignation, natural indignation, would not serve her turn in the present emergency. 'You know that cannot be. You ought to know it. What will your father say? You have not dared to tell him. That is so natural,' she added, trying to appease his frown. 'How possibly can it be told to him? I will not say a word against her.'

'No; do not do that.'

'But there are fitnesses of things which such a one as you cannot disregard without preparing for yourself a whole life of repentance.'

'Look here, Mabel.'

'Well?'

'I will tell you the truth.'

'Well?'

474

'I would sooner lose all;—the rank I have; the rank that I am to have; all these lands that you have been looking on; my father's wealth, my seat in Parliament,—everything that fortune has done for me,—I would give them all up, sooner than lose her.' Now at any rate he was a man. She was sure of that now. This was more, very much more, not only than she had expected from him, but more than she had thought it possible that his character should have produced.

His strength reduced her to weakness. 'And I am nothing,' she said.

'Yes, indeed; you are Lady Mabel Grex,—whom all women envy, and whom all men honour.'

'The poorest wretch this day under the sun.'

'Do not say that. You should take shame to say that.'

'I do take shame;—and I do say it. Sir, do you not feel what you owe me? Do you not know that you have made me the wretch I am? How did you dare to talk to me as you did talk when you were in London? You tell me that I am Lady Mabel Grex;—and yet you come to me with a lie on your lips,—with such a lie as that! You must have taken me for some nursemaid on whom you had condescended to cast your eye! It cannot be that even you should have dared to treat Lady Mabel Grex after such a fashion as that! And now you have cast your eye on this other girl. You can never marry her!'

'I shall endeavour to do so.'

'You can never marry her,' she said, stamping her foot. She had now lost all the caution which she had taught herself for the prosecution of her scheme,—all the care with which she had burdened herself. Now she was natural enough. 'No,—you can never marry her. You could not show yourself after it in your clubs, or in Parliament, or in the world. Come home, do you say? No, I will not go to your home. It is not my home. Cold;—of course I am cold;—cold through to the heart.'

'I cannot leave you alone here,' he said, for she had now turned from him, and was walking with hurried steps and short turns on the edge of the bank, which at this place was almost a precipice.

'You have left me,—utterly in the cold—more desolate than I am here even though I should spend the night among the trees. But I will go back, and will tell your father everything. If my father were other than he is,—if my brother were better to me, you would not have done this.'

'If you had a legion of brothers it would have been the same,' he said, turning sharp upon her.

They walked on together, but without a word till the house was in sight. Then she looked round at him, and stopped him on the path as she caught his eye. 'Silverbridge!' she said.

'Lady Mabel.'

'Call me Mabel. At any rate call me Mabel. If I have said anything to offend you—I beg your pardon.'

'I am not offended—but unhappy.'

'If you are unhappy, what must I be? What have I to look forward to? Give me your hand, and say that we are friends.'

'Certainly we are friends,' he said, as he gave her his hand.

'Who can tell what may come to pass?' To this he would make no answer, as it seemed to imply that some division between himself and Isabel Boncassen might possibly come to pass. 'You will not tell any one that I love you?'

'I tell such a thing as that!'

'But never forget it yourself. No one can tell what may come to pass.'

Lady Mabel at once went up to her room. She had played her scene, but was well aware that she had played it altogether unsuccessfully.

CHAPTER LX

Lord Gerald in further trouble

WHEN Silverbridge got back to the house he was by no means well pleased with himself. In the first place he was unhappy to think that Mabel was unhappy, and that he had made her so. And then she had told him that he would not have dared to have acted as he had done, but that her father and her brother were careless to defend her. He had replied fiercely that a legion of brothers, ready to act on her behalf, would not have altered his conduct; but not the less did he feel that he had behaved badly to her. It could not now be altered. He could not now be untrue to Isabel. But certainly he had said a word or two to Mabel which he could not remember without regret. He had not thought that a word from him could have been so powerful. Now, when that word was recalled to his memory by the girl to whom it had been spoken, he could not quite acquit himself.

And Mabel had declared to him that she would at once appeal to his father. There was an absurdity in this at which he could not but smile,—that the girl should complain to his father because he would not marry her! But even in doing this she might cause him great vexation. He could not bring himself to ask her not to tell her story to the Duke. He must take all that as it might come.

While he was thinking of all this in his own room a servant brought him two letters. From the first which he opened he soon perceived that it contained an account of more troubles. It was from his brother Gerald, and was written from Auld Reikie, the name of a house in Scotland belonging to Lord Nidderdale's people.

'DEAR SILVER,

'I have got into a most awful scrape. That fellow Percival is here, and Dolly Longstaff, and Nidderdale, and Popplecourt, and Jack Hindes, and Perry who is in the Coldstreams, and one or two more, and there has been a lot of cards, and I have lost ever so much money. I wouldn't mind it so much but Percival has won it all,—a fellow I hate; and now I owe him—three thousand four hundred pounds! He has just told me he is hard up and that he wants the money before the week is over. He can't be hard up because he has won from everybody;—but of course I had to tell him that I would pay him.

'Can you help me? Of course I know that I have been a fool.

477

Percival knows what he is about and plays regularly for money. When I began I didn't think that I could lose above twenty or thirty pounds. But it got on from one thing to another, and when I woke this morning I felt I didn't know what to do with myself. You can't think how the luck went against me. Everybody says that they never saw such cards.

'And now do tell me how I am to get out of it. Could you manage it with Mr. Moreton? Of course I will make it all right with you some day. Moreton always lets you have whatever you want. But perhaps you couldn't do this without letting the governor know. I would rather anything than that. There is some money owing at Oxford also, which of course he must know.

'I was thinking that perhaps I might get it from some of those fellows in London. There are people called Comfort and Criball, who let men have money constantly. I know two or three up at Oxford who have had it from them. Of course I couldn't go to them as you could do, for, in spite of what the governor said to us up in London one day, there is nothing that must come to me. But you could do anything in that way, and of course I would stand to it.

'I know you won't throw me over, because you always have been such a brick. But above all things don't tell the governor. Percival is such a nasty fellow, otherwise I shouldn't mind it. He spoke this morning as though I was treating him badly,—though the money was only lost last night; and he looked at me in a way that made me long to kick him. I told him not to flurry himself, and that he should have his money. If he speaks to me like that again I will kick him.

'I will be at Matching as soon as possible, but I cannot go till this is settled. Nid'—meaning Lord Nidderdale,—'is a brick.

'Your affectionate Brother,
'GERALD.'

The other was from Nidderdale, and referred to the same subject.

'DEAR SILVERBRIDGE,

'Here has been a terrible nuisance. Last night some of the men got to playing cards, and Gerald lost a terribly large sum to Percival. I did all that I could to stop it, because I saw that Percival was going in for a big thing. I fancy that he got as much from Dolly Longstaff as he did from Gerald;—but it won't matter much to Dolly; or if it does, nobody cares. Gerald told me he was writing to you about it, so I am not betraying him.

'What is to be done? Of course Percival is behaving badly. He always does. I can't turn him out of the house, and he seems to intend to stick to Gerald till he has got the money. He has taken a cheque from Dolly dated two months hence. I am in an awful funk for fear Gerald should pitch into him. He will, in a minute, if anything rough is said to him. I suppose the straightest thing would be to go to the Duke at once, but Gerald won't hear of it. I hope you won't think me wrong to tell you. If I could help him I would. You know what a bad doctor I am for that sort of complaint.

'Yours always,
'NIDDERDALE.'

The dinner-bell had rung before Silverbridge had come to an end of thinking of this new vexation, and he had not as yet made up his mind what he had better do for his brother. There was one thing as to which he was determined,—that it should not be done by him, nor, if he could prevent it, by Gerald. There should be no dealings with Comfort and Criball. The Duke had succeeded, at any rate, in filling his son's mind with a horror of aid of that sort. Nidderdale had suggested that the 'straightest' thing would be to go direct to the Duke. That no doubt would be straight,—and efficacious. The Duke would not have allowed a boy of his to be a debtor to Lord Percival for a day, let the debt have been contracted how it might. But Gerald had declared against this course,—and Silverbridge himself would have been most unwilling to adopt it. How could he have told that story to the Duke, while there was that other infinitely more important story of his own, which must be told at once?

In the midst of all these troubles he went down to dinner. 'Lady Mabel,' said the Duke, 'tells me that you two have been to see Sir Guy's look-out.'

She was standing close to the Duke and whispered a word into his ear. 'You said you would call me Mabel.'

'Yes, sir,' said Silverbridge, 'and I have made up my mind that Sir Guy never stayed there very long in winter. It was awfully cold.'

'I had furs on,' said Mabel. 'What a lovely spot it is, even in this weather.' Then dinner was announced. She had not been cold. She could still feel the tingling heat of her blood as she had implored him to love her.

Silverbridge felt that he must write to his brother by the first post. The communication was of a nature that would bear no delay. If his hands had been free he would himself have gone off to Auld Reikie. At last he made up his mind. The first letter he wrote was neither to Nidderdale nor to Gerald, but to Lord Percival himself.

'DEAR PERCIVAL,

'Gerald writes me word that he has lost to you at cards £3,400, and he wants me to get him the money. It is a terrible nuisance, and he has been an ass. But of course I shall stand to him for anything he wants. I haven't got £3,400 in my pocket, and I don't know any one who has;—that is among our set. But I send you my I. O. U. for the amount, and will promise to get you the money in two months. I suppose that will be sufficient, and that you will not bother Gerald any more about it.

'Yours truly,
'SILVERBRIDGE.'

Then he copied this letter and enclosed the copy in another which he wrote to his brother.

480

'Dear Gerald,

'What an ass you have been! But I don't suppose you are worse than I was at Doncaster. I will have nothing to do with such people as Comfort and Criball. That is the sure way to the D——! As for telling Moreton,*that is only a polite and roundabout way of telling the governor. He would immediately ask the governor what was to be done. You will see what I have done. Of course I must tell the governor before the end of February, as I cannot get the money in any other way. But that I will do. It does seem hard upon him. Not that the money will hurt him much; but that he would so like to have a steady-going son.

'I suppose Percival won't make any bother about the I. O. U. He'll be a fool if he does. I wouldn't kick him if I were you,— unless he says anything very bad. You would be sure to come to grief somehow. He is a beast.

'Your affectionate Brother,
'Silverbridge.'

With these letters that special grief was removed from his mind for awhile. Looking over the dark river of possible trouble which seemed to run between the present moment and the time at which the money must be procured, he thought that he had driven off this calamity of Gerald's to infinite distance. But into that dark river he must now plunge almost at once. On the next day, he managed so that there should be no walk with Mabel. In the evening he could see that the Duke was uneasy;—but not a word was said to him. On the following morning Lady Mabel took her departure. When she went from the door, both the Duke and Silverbridge were there to bid her farewell. She smiled and was as gracious as though everything had gone according to her heart's delight. 'Dear Duke, I am so obliged to you for your kindness,' she said, as she put up her cheek for him to kiss. Then she gave her hand to Silverbridge. 'Of course you will come and see me in town.' And she smiled upon them all;—having courage enough to keep down all her sufferings.

'Come in here a moment, Silverbridge,' said the father as they returned into the house together. 'How is it now between you and her?'

CHAPTER LXI
'Bone of my bone'

'How is it now between you and her?' That was the question which the Duke put to his son as soon as he had closed the door of the study. Lady Mabel had just been dismissed from the front door on her journey, and there could be no doubt as to the 'her' intended. No such question would have been asked had not Silverbridge himself declared to his father his purpose of making Lady Mabel his wife. On that subject the Duke, without such authority, would not have interfered. But he had been consulted, had acceded, and had encouraged the idea by excessive liberality on his part. He had never dropped it out of his mind for a moment. But when he found that the girl was leaving his house without any explanation, then he became restless and inquisitive.

They say that perfect love casteth out fear.* If it be so the love of children to their parents is seldom altogether perfect,—and perhaps had better not be quite perfect. With this young man it was not that he feared anything which his father could do to him, that he believed that in consequence of the declaration which he had to make his comforts and pleasures would be curtailed, or his independence diminished. He knew his father too well to dread such punishment. But he feared that he would make his father unhappy, and he was conscious that he had so often sinned in that way. He had stumbled so frequently! Though in action he would so often be thoughtless,—yet he understood perfectly the effect which had been produced on his father's mind by his conduct. He had it at heart 'to be good to the governor,' to gratify that most loving of all possible friends, who, as he knew well, was always thinking of his welfare. And yet he never had been 'good to the governor';—nor had Gerald;—and to all this was added his sister's determined perversity. It was thus he feared his father.

He paused for a moment, while the Duke stood with his back to the fire looking at him. 'I'm afraid that it is all over, sir,' he said.

'All over!'

'I am afraid so.'

'Why is it all over? Has she refused you?'

'Well, sir;—it isn't quite that.' Then he paused again. It was so difficult to begin about Isabel Boncassen.

'I am sorry for that,' said the Duke, almost hesitating; 'very sorry. You will understand, I hope, that I should make no inquiry in such a matter, unless I had felt myself warranted in doing so by what you had yourself told me in London.'

'I understand all that.'

'I have been very anxious about it, and have even gone so far as to make some preparations for what I had hoped would be your early marriage.'

'Preparations!' exclaimed Silverbridge, thinking of church bells, bride cake, and wedding presents.

'As to the property. I am so anxious that you should enjoy all the settled independence which can belong to an English gentleman. I never plough or sow. I know no more of sheep and bulls than of the extinct animals of earlier ages. I would not have it so with you. I would fain see you surrounded by those things which ought to interest a nobleman in this country. Why is it all over with Lady Mabel Grex?'

The young man looked imploringly at his father, as though earnestly begging that nothing more might be said about Mabel. 'I had changed my mind before I found out that she was really in love with me!' He could not say that. He could not hint that he might still have Mabel if he would. The only thing for him was to tell everything about Isabel Boncassen. He felt that in doing this he must begin with himself. 'I have rather changed my mind, sir,' he said, 'since we were walking together in London that night.'

'Have you quarrelled with Lady Mabel?'

'Oh dear no. I am very fond of Mabel;—only not just like that.'

'Not just like what?'

'I had better tell the whole truth at once.'

'Certainly tell the truth, Silverbridge. I cannot say that you are bound in duty to tell the whole truth even to your father in such a matter.'

'But I mean to tell you everything. Mabel did not seem to care for me much—in London. And then I saw someone,—someone I liked better.' Then he stopped, but as the Duke did not ask any questions he plunged on. 'It was Miss Boncassen.'

'Miss Boncassen!'

'Yes, sir,' said Silverbridge, with a little access of decision.

'The American young lady?'

'Yes, sir.'

'Do you know anything of her family?'

'I think I know all about her family. It is not much in the way of—family.'

'You have not spoken to her about it?'

'Yes, sir;—I have settled it all with her, on condition——'

'Settled it with her that she is to be your wife!'

'Yes, sir,—on condition that you will approve.'

'Did you go to her, Silverbridge, with such a stipulation as that?'

'It was not like that.'

'How was it then?'

'She stipulated. She will marry me if you will consent.'

'It was she then who thought of my wishes and my feeling; —not you?'

'I knew that I loved her. What is a man to do when he feels like that? Of course I meant to tell you.' The Duke was now looking very black. 'I thought you liked her, sir.'

'Liked her! I did like her. I do like her. What has that to do with it? Do you think I like none but those with whom I should think it fitting to ally myself in marriage? Is there to be no duty in such matters, no restraint, no feeling of what is due to your own name, and to others who bear it? The lad out there who is sweeping the walks can marry the first girl that pleases his eye if she will take him. Perhaps his lot is the happier because he owns such liberty. Have you the same freedom?'

'I suppose I have,—by law.'

'Do you recognise no duty but what the laws impose upon you? Should you be disposed to eat and drink in bestial excess, because the laws would not hinder you? Should you lie and sleep all the day, the law would say nothing! Should you neglect every duty which your position imposes on you, the law could not interfere! To such a one as you the law can be no guide. You should so live as not to come near the law,— or to have the law to come near to you. From all evil against which the law bars you, you should be barred, at an infinite distance, by honour, by conscience, and nobility. Does the law require patriotism, philanthropy, self-abnegation, public service, purity of purpose, devotion to the needs of others who have been placed in the world below you? The law is a great thing,—because men are poor and weak, and bad. And it is great, because where it exists in its strength, no tyrant can be above it. But between you and me there should be no mention of law as the guide of conduct. Speak to me of honour, of duty, and of nobility; and tell me what they require of you.'

Silverbridge listened in silence and with something of true admiration in his heart. But he felt the strong necessity of declaring his own convictions on one special point here, at once, in this new crisis of the conversation. That accident in regard to the colour of the Dean's lodge had stood in the way of his logical studies,—so that he was unable to put his argument into proper shape; but there belonged to him a certain natural astuteness which told him that he must put in his rejoinder at this particular point. 'I think I am bound in honour and in duty to marry Miss Boncassen,' he said. 'And, if I understand what you mean, by nobility just as much.'

'Because you have promised.'

485

'Not only for that. I have promised and therefore I am bound. She has—well, she has said that she loves me, and therefore of course I am bound. But it is not only that.'

'What do you mean?'

'I suppose a man ought to marry the woman he loves,—if he can get her.'

'No; no; not so; not always so. Do you think that love is a passion that cannot be withstood?'

'But here we are both of one mind, sir. When I saw how you seemed to take to her——'

'Take to her! Can I not interest myself in human beings without wishing to make them flesh of my flesh, bone of my bone? What am I to think of you? It was but the other day that all that you are now telling me of Miss Boncassen, you were telling me of Lady Mabel Grex.' Here poor Silverbridge bit his lips and shook his head, and looked down upon the ground. This was the weak part of his case. He could not tell his father the whole story about Mabel,—that she had coyed his love, so that he had been justified in thinking himself free from any claim in that direction when he had encountered the infinitely sweeter charms of Isabel Boncassen. 'You are weak as water,' said the unhappy father.

'I am not weak in this.'

'Did you not say exactly the same about Lady Mabel?'

There was a pause, so that he was driven to reply. 'I found her as I thought indifferent, and then—I changed my mind.'

'Indifferent! What does she think about it now? Does she know of this? How does it stand between you two at the present moment?'

'She knows that I am engaged to—Miss Boncassen.'

'Does she approve of it?'

'Why should I ask her, sir? I have not asked her.'

'Then why did you tell her? She could not but have spoken her mind when you told her. There must have been much between you when this was talked of.'

The unfortunate young man was obliged to take some time before he could answer this appeal. He had to own that his

486

father had some justice on his side, but at the same time he could reveal nothing of Mabel's secret. 'I told her because we were friends. I did not ask her approval; but she did disapprove. She thought that your son should not marry an American girl without family.'

'Of course she would feel that.'

'Now I have told you what she said, and I hope you will ask me no further questions about her. I cannot make Lady Mabel my wife;—though, for the matter of that, I ought not to presume that she would take me if I wished it. I had intended to ask you to-day to consent to my marriage with Miss Boncassen.'

'I cannot give you my consent.'

'Then I am very unhappy.'

'How can I believe as to your unhappiness when you would have said the same about Lady Mabel Grex a few weeks ago?'

'Nearly eight months,' said Silverbridge.

'What is the difference? It is not the time, but the disposition of the man! I cannot give you my consent. The young lady sees it in the right light, and that will make your escape easy.'

'I do not want to escape.'

'She has indicated the cause which will separate you.'

'I will not be separated from her,' said Silverbridge, who was beginning to feel that he was subjugated to tyranny. If he chose to marry Isabel, no one could have a right to hinder him.

'I can only hope that you will think better of it, and that when next you speak to me on that or any other subject you will answer me with less arrogance.'

This rebuke was terrible to the son, whose mind at the present moment was filled with two ideas, that of constancy to Isabel Boncassen, and then of respect and affection for his father. 'Indeed, sir,' he said, 'I am not arrogant, and if I have answered improperly I beg your pardon. But my mind is made up about this, and I thought you had better know how it is.'

'I do not see that I can say anything else to you now.'

'I think of going to Harrington this afternoon.' Then the

Duke, with further very visible annoyance, asked where Harrington was. It was explained that Harrington was Lord Chiltern's seat, Lord Chiltern being the Master of the Brake hounds;—that it was his son's purpose to remain six weeks among the Brake hounds, but that he should stay only a day or two with Lord Chiltern. Then it appeared that Silverbridge intended to put himself up at a hunting inn in the neighbourhood, and the Duke did not at all like the plan. That his son should choose to live at an inn, when the comforts of an English country house were open to him, was distasteful and almost offensive to the Duke. And the matter was not improved when he was made to understand that all this was to be done for the sake of hunting. There had been the shooting in Scotland; then the racing,—ah, alas! yes,—the racing, and the betting at Doncaster! Then the shooting at Matching had been made to appear to be the chief reason why he himself had been living in his own house! And now his son was going away to live at an inn in order that more time might be devoted to hunting! 'Why can't you hunt here at home, if you must hunt?'

'It is all woodland,' said Silverbridge.

'I thought you wanted woods. Lord Chiltern is always troubling me about Trumpington Wood.'*

This breeze about the hunting enabled the son to escape without any further allusion to Miss Boncassen. He did escape, and proceeded to turn over in his mind all that had been said. His tale had been told. A great burden was thus taken off his shoulders. He could tell Isabel so much, and thus free himself from the suspicion of having been afraid to declare his purpose. She should know what he had done, and should be made to understand that he had been firm. He had, he thought, been very firm and gave himself some credit on that head. His father, no doubt, had been firm too, but that he had expected. His father had said much. All that about honour and duty had been very good; but this was certain,—that when a young man had promised a young woman he ought to keep his word. And he thought that there were certain changes going on in the management of the world which his father did not quite understand. Fathers never do quite understand the changes which are manifest to their sons. Some years ago it might have been improper that an American girl should be elevated to the rank of an English Duchess; but now all that was altered.

The Duke spent the rest of the day alone, and was not happy in his solitude. All that Silverbridge had told him was sad to him. He had taught himself to think that he could love Lady Mabel as an affectionate father wishes to love his son's wife. He had set himself to wish to like her, and had been successful. Being most anxious that his son should marry he had prepared himself to be more than ordinarily liberal,—to be in every way gracious. His children were now everything to him, and among his children his son and heir was the chief. From the moment in which he had heard from Silverbridge that Lady Mabel was chosen he had given himself up to considering how he might best promote their interests,—how he might best enable them to live, with that dignity and splendour which he himself had unwisely despised. That the son who was to come after him should be worthy of the place assigned to his name had been, of personal objects, the nearest to his heart. There had been failures, but still there had been left room for hope. The boy had been unfortunate at Eton;— but how many unfortunate boys had become great men! He had disgraced himself by his folly at college,—but, though some lads will be men at twenty, others are then little more than children. The fruit that ripens the soonest is seldom the best. Then had come Tifto and the racing mania. Nothing could be worse than Tifto and race-horses. But from that evil Silverbridge had seemed to be made free by the very disgust which the vileness of the circumstance had produced. Perhaps Tifto driving a nail into his horse's foot had on the whole been serviceable. That apostacy from the political creed of the Pallisers had been a blow,—much more felt than the loss of the seventy thousand pounds;—but even under that blow he had consoled himself by thinking that a Conservative patriotic nobleman may serve his country,—even as a Conservative. In the midst of this he had felt that the surest resource for his son against evil would be in an early marriage. If he would marry becomingly, then might everything still be made pleasant. If his son would marry becomingly nothing which a father could do should be wanting to add splendour and dignity to his son's life.

In thinking of all this he had by no means regarded his own mode of life with favour. He knew how jejune*his life had been,—how devoid of other interests than that of the public service to which he had devoted himself. He was thinking of this when he told his son that he had neither ploughed and sowed or been the owner of sheep or oxen. He often thought of this, when he heard those around him talking of the sports, which, though he condemned them as the employments of a life, he now regarded wistfully, hopelessly as far as he himself was concerned, as proper recreations for a man of wealth. Silverbridge should have it all, if he could arrange it. The one thing necessary was a fitting wife;—and the fitting wife had been absolutely chosen by Silverbridge himself.

It may be conceived, therefore, that he was again unhappy. He had already been driven to acknowledge that these children of his,—thoughtless, restless, though they seemed to be,— still had a will of their own. In all which how like they were to their mother! With her, however, his word, though it might be resisted, had never lost its authority. When he had declared that a thing should not be done, she had never persisted in saying that she would do it. But with his children it was otherwise. What power had he over Silverbridge,—or for the matter of that, even over his daughter? They had only to be firm and he knew that he must be conquered.

'I thought that you liked her,' Silverbridge had said to him. How utterly unconscious, thought the Duke, must the young man have been of all that his position required of him when he used such an argument! Liked her! He did like her. She was clever, accomplished, beautiful, well-mannered,—as far as he knew endowed with all good qualities! Would not many

490

an old Roman have said as much for some favourite Greek slave,—for some freedman whom he would admit to his very heart? But what old Roman ever dreamed of giving his daughter to the son of a Greek bondsman! Had he done so, what would have become of the name of a Roman citizen? And was it not his duty to fortify and maintain that higher, smaller, more precious pinnacle of rank on which Fortune had placed him and his children?

Like her! Yes! he liked her certainly. He had by no means always found that he best liked the companionship of his own order. He had liked to feel around him the free battle of the House of Commons. He liked the power of attack and defence in carrying on which an English politician cares nothing for rank. He liked to remember that the son of any tradesman might, by his own merits, become a peer of Parliament. He would have liked to think that his son should share all these tastes with him. Yes,—he liked Isabel Boncassen. But how different was that liking from a desire that she should be bone of his bone, and flesh of his flesh!

CHAPTER LXII
The Brake country

'WHAT does your father mean to do about Trumpington Wood?' That was the first word from Lord Chiltern after he had shaken hands with his guest.

'Isn't it all right yet?'

'All right? No! How can a wood like that be all right without a man about the place who knows anything of the nature of a fox? In your grandfather's time——'

'My great-uncle you mean.'

'Well;—your great-uncle!—they used to trap the foxes there. There was a fellow named Fothergill who used to come there for shooting. Now it is worse than ever. Nobody shoots there because there is nothing to shoot. There isn't a keeper. Every scamp is allowed to go where he pleases, and of course there isn't a fox in the whole place. My huntsman laughs at me when I ask him to draw it.' As the indignant Master of the Brake Hounds said this the very fire flashed from his eyes.

'My dear,' said Lady Chiltern expostulating, 'Lord Silverbridge hasn't been in the house above half an hour.'

'What does that matter? When a thing has to be said it had better be said at once.'

Phineas Finn was staying at Harrington with his intimate friends*the Chilterns, as were also a certain Mr. and Mrs. Maule, both of whom were addicted to hunting,—the lady, whose maiden name had been Palliser, being a cousin to Lord Silverbridge. On that day also a certain Mr. and Mrs. Spooner dined at Harrington. Mr. and Mrs. Spooner were both very much given to hunting, as seemed to be necessarily the case with everybody admitted to that house. Mr. Spooner was a gentleman who might be on the wrong side of fifty, with a red nose, very vigorous, and submissive in regard to all things but port-wine. His wife was perhaps something more than half his age, a stout, hard-riding, handsome woman. She had been the penniless daughter of a retired officer,—but yet had managed to ride on whatever animal any one would lend her. Then Mr. Spooner, who had for many years been part and parcel of the Brake hunt, and who was much in want of a wife, had, luckily for her, cast his eyes upon Miss Leatherside. It was thought that upon the whole she made him a good wife. She hunted four days a week, and he could afford to keep horses for her. She never flirted, and wanted no one to open gates. Tom Spooner himself was not always so forward as he used to be; but his wife was always there and would tell him all that he did not see himself. And she was a good housewife, taking care that nothing should be spent lavishly, except upon the stable. Of him, too, and of his health, she was careful, never scrupling to say a word in season when he was likely to hurt himself, either among the fences or among the decanters. 'You ain't so young as you were, Tom. Don't think of doing it.' This she would say to him with a loud voice when she would find him pausing at a fence. Then she would hop over herself and he would go round. She was 'quite a providence to him,' as her mother, old Mrs. Leatherside, would say.

She was hardly the woman that one would have expected to meet as a friend in the drawing-room of Lady Chiltern. Lord Chiltern was perhaps a little rough, but Lady Chiltern was all that a mother, a wife, and a lady ought to be. She probably felt that some little apology ought to be made for Mrs. Spooner. 'I hope you like hunting,' she said to Silverbridge.

'Best of all things,' said he enthusiastically.

'Because you know this is Castle Nimrod, in which nothing is allowed to interfere with the one great business of life.'

'It's like that; is it?'

'Quite like that. Lord Chiltern has taken up hunting as his duty in life, and he does it with his might and main. Not to have a good day is a misery to him;—not for himself but because he feels that he is responsible. We had one blank day last year, and I thought that he never would recover it. It was that unfortunate Trumpington Wood.'

'How he will hate me.'

'Not if you will praise the hounds judiciously. And then there is a Mr. Spooner coming here to-night. He is the first-lieutenant. He understands all about the foxes, and all about the farmers. He has got a wife.'

'Does she understand anything?'

'She understands him. She is coming too. They have not been married long, and he never goes anywhere without her.'

'Does she ride?'

'Well; yes. I never go out myself now because I have so much of it all at home. But I fancy she does ride a good deal. She will talk hunting too. If Chiltern were to leave the country I think they ought to make her master. Perhaps you'll think her rather odd; but really she is a very good woman.'

'I am sure I shall like her.'

'I hope you will. You know Mr. Finn. He is here. He and my husband are very old friends. And Adelaide Maule is your cousin. She hunts too. And so does Mr. Maule,—only not quite so energetically. I think that is all we shall have.'

Immediately after that all the guests came in at once, and a discussion was heard as they were passing through the hall. 'No;—that wasn't it,' said Mrs. Spooner loudly. 'I don't care what Dick said.' Dick Rabbit was the first whip, and seemed to have been much exercised with the matter now under dispute. 'The fox never went into Grobby Gorse at all. I was there and saw Sappho give him a line down the bank.'

'I think he must have gone into the gorse, my dear,' said her husband. 'The earth was open, you know.'

'I tell you she didn't. You weren't there, and you can't know. I'm sure it was a vixen by her running. We ought to have killed that fox, my Lord.' Then Mrs. Spooner made her obeisance to her hostess. Perhaps she was rather slow in doing this, but the greatness of the subject had been the cause. These are matters so important, that the ordinary civilities of the world should not stand in their way.

'What do you say, Chiltern?' asked the husband.

'I say that Mrs. Spooner isn't very often wrong, and that Dick Rabbit isn't very often right about a fox.'

'It was a pretty run,' said Phineas.

'Just thirty-four minutes,' said Mr. Spooner.

'Thirty-two up to Grobby Gorse,' asserted Mrs. Spooner. 'The hounds never hunted a yard after that. Dick hurried them into the gorse, and the old hound wouldn't stick to his line when she found that no one believed her.'

This was on a Monday evening, and the Brake hounds went out generally five days a week. 'You'll hunt to-morrow, I suppose?' Lady Chiltern said to Silverbridge.

'I hope so.'

'You must hunt to-morrow. Indeed there is nothing else to do. Chiltern has taken such a dislike to shooting-men, that he won't shoot pheasants himself. We don't hunt on Wednesdays or Sundays, and then everybody lies in bed. Here is Mr. Maule, he lies in bed on other mornings as well, and spends the rest of his day riding about the country looking for the hounds.'

'Does he ever find them?'

'What did become of you all to-day?' said Mr. Maule, as he took his place at the dinner-table. 'You can't have drawn any of the coverts regularly.'

'Then we found our foxes without drawing them,' said the master.

'We chopped one*at Bromleys,' said Mr. Spooner.

'I went there.'

'Then you ought to have known better,' said Mrs. Spooner. 'When a man loses the hounds in that country, he ought to go direct to Brackett's Wood. If you had come on to Brackett's, you'd have seen as good a thirty-two minutes as ever you wished to ride.' When the ladies went out of the room Mrs. Spooner gave a parting word of advice to her husband, and to the host. 'Now, Tom, don't you drink port-wine. Lord Chiltern, look after him, and don't let him have port-wine.'

Then there began an altogether different phase of hunting conversation. As long as the ladies were there it was all very well to talk of hunting as an amusement, good sport, a thirty minutes or so, the delight of having a friend in a ditch, or the glory of a stiff-built rail were fitting subjects for a lighter hour. But now the business of the night was to begin. The difficulties, the enmities, the precautions, the resolutions, the resources of the Brake hunt were to be discussed. And from thence the conversation of these devotees strayed away to the perils at large to which hunting in these modern days is subjected;—not the perils of broken necks and crushed ribs, which can be reduced to an average, and so an end made of that small matter; but the perils from outsiders, the perils from new-fangled prejudices, the perils from more modern sports, the perils from over-cultivation, the perils from extended population, the perils from increasing railroads, the perils from literary ignorances, the perils from intruding cads, the perils from indifferent magnates,—the Duke of Omnium, for instance;—and that peril of perils, the peril of decrease of funds and increase of expenditure! The jaunty gentleman who puts on his dainty breeches and his pair of boots, and on his single horse rides out on a pleasant morning to some neighbouring meet, thinking himself a sportsman, has but a faint idea of the troubles which a few staunch workmen endure in order that he may not be made to think that his boots, and his breeches, and his horse, have been in vain.

A word or two further was at first said about that unfortunate wood for which Silverbridge at the present felt himself responsible. Finn said that he was sure the Duke would look to it, if Silverbridge would mention it. Chiltern simply groaned. Silverbridge said nothing, remembering how many troubles he had on hand at this moment. Then by degrees their solicitude worked itself round to the cares of a neighbouring hunt. The A. R. U. had lost their master. One Captain Glomax*was going, and the county had been driven to the necessity of advertising for a successor. 'When hunting comes to that,' said Lord Chiltern, 'one begins to think that it is in a bad way.' It may always be observed that when hunting-men speak seriously of their sport, they speak despondingly. Everything is going wrong. Perhaps the same thing may be remarked in other pursuits. Farmers are generally on the verge of ruin. Trade is always bad. The Church is in danger. The House of Lords isn't worth a dozen years' purchase. The throne totters.

'An itinerant master with a carpet-bag*never can carry on a country,' said Mr. Spooner.

'You ought really to have a gentleman of property in the county,' said Lord Chiltern, in a self-deprecating tone. His father's acres lay elsewhere.

'It should be someone who has a real stake in the country,' replied Mr. Spooner,—'whom the farmers can respect. Glomax understood hunting no doubt, but the farmers didn't care for him. If you don't have the farmers with you you can't have hunting.' Then he filled a glass of port.

'If you don't approve of Glomax, what do you think of a man like Major Tifto?' asked Mr. Maule.

'That was in the Runnymede,' said Spooner contemptuously.

'Who is Major Tifto?' asked Lord Chiltern.

'He is the man,' said Silverbridge boldly, 'who owned Prime Minister with me, when he didn't win the Leger last September.'

'There was a deuce of a row,' said Maule. Then Mr. Spooner, who read his 'Bell's Life' and 'Field' very religiously, and who never missed an article in 'Bayley's,'*proceeded to give them an account of everything that had taken place in the Runnymede Hunt. It mattered but little that he was wrong in all his details. Narrations always are. The result to which he came was nearly right when he declared that the Major had been turned off, that a committee had been appointed, and that Messrs. Topps and Jawstock had been threatened with a lawsuit.

'That comes,' said Lord Chiltern solemnly, 'of employing men like Major Tifto in places for which they are radically unfit. I dare say Major Tifto knew how to handle a pack of hounds,—perhaps almost as well as my huntsman, Fowler. But I don't think a county would get on very well which appointed Fowler Master of Hounds. He is an honest man, and therefore would be better than Tifto. But—it would not do. It is a position in which a man should at any rate be a gentleman. If he be not, all those who should be concerned in maintaining the hunt will turn their backs upon him. When I take my hounds over this man's ground, and that man's ground, certainly without doing him any good, I have to think of a great many things. I have to understand that those whom I cannot compensate by money, I have to compensate by courtesy. When I shake hands with a farmer and express my obligation to him because he does not lock his gates, he is gratified. I don't think any decent farmer would care much for shaking hands with Major Tifto. If we fall into that kind of thing there must soon be an end of hunting. Major Tiftos are cheap no doubt; but in hunting, as in most other things, cheap and nasty go together. If men don't choose to put their hands in their pockets they had better say so, and give the thing up altogether. If you won't take any more wine, we'll go to the ladies. Silverbridge, the trap will start from the door to-morrow morning precisely at 9.30 A.M. Grantingham Cross is fourteen miles.' Then they all left their chairs,—but as they did so Mr. Spooner finished the bottle of port-wine.

'I never heard Chiltern speak so much like a book before,' said Spooner to his wife, as she drove him home that night.

The next morning everybody was ready for a start at half-past nine, except Mr. Maule,—as to whom his wife declared that she had left him in bed when she came down to breakfast. 'He can never get there if we don't take him,' said Lord Chiltern, who was in truth the most good-natured man in the world. Five minutes were allowed him, and then he came down with a large sandwich in one hand and a button-hook in the other, with which he was prepared to complete his toilet. 'What the deuce makes you always in such a hurry?' were the first words he spoke as Lord Chiltern got on the box. The Master knew him too well to argue the point. 'Well; —he always is in a hurry,' said the sinner, when his wife accused him of ingratitude.

'Where's Spooner?' asked the Master when he saw Mrs. Spooner without her husband at the meet.

'I knew how it would be when I saw the port-wine,' she said in a whisper that could be heard all round. 'He has got it this time sharp,—in his great toe. We shan't find at Grantingham. They were cutting wood there last week. If I were you, my Lord, I'd go away to the Spinnies at once.'

'I must draw the country regularly,'*muttered the Master.

The country was drawn regularly, but in vain till about two o'clock. Not only was there no fox at Grantingham Wood, but none even at the Spinnies. And at two, Fowler, with an anxious face, held a consultation with his more anxious master. Trumpington Wood lay on their right, and that no doubt would have been the proper draw. 'I suppose we must try it,' said Lord Chiltern.

Old Fowler looked very sour. 'You might as well look for a fox under my wife's bed, my Lord.'

'I dare say we should find one there,' said one of the wags of the hunt. Fowler shook his head, feeling that this was no time for joking.

'It ought to be drawn,' said Chiltern.

'Of course you know best, my Lord. I wouldn't touch it,— never no more. Let 'em all know what the Duke's Wood is.'

'This is Lord Silverbridge, the Duke's son,' said Chiltern laughing.

'I beg your Lordship's pardon,' said Fowler, taking off his cap. 'We shall have a good time coming, some day. Let me trot 'em off to Michaelmas Daisies, my Lord. I'll be there in thirty minutes.' In the neighbouring parish of St. Michael de Dezier there was a favourite little gorse which among hunting-men had acquired this unreasonable name. After a little consideration the Master yielded, and away they trotted.

'You'll cross the ford, Fowler?' asked Mrs. Spooner.

'Oh yes, ma'am; we couldn't draw the Daisies this afternoon if we didn't.'

'It'll be up to the horses' bellies.'

'Those who don't like it can go round.'

'They'd never be there in time, Fowler.'

'There's a many, ma'am, as don't mind that. You won't be one to stay behind.' The water was up to the horses' bellies, but, nevertheless, Mrs. Spooner was at the gorse side when the Daisies were drawn.

They found*and were away in a minute. It was all done so quickly that Fowler, who had alone gone into the gorse, had hardly time to get out with his hounds. The fox ran right back, as though he were making for the Duke's pernicious wood. In the first field or two there was a succession of gates, and there was not much to do in the way of jumping. Then the fox, keeping straight ahead, deviated from the line by which they had come, making for the brook by a more direct course. The ruck of the horsemen, understanding the matter very well, left the hounds, and went to the right, riding for the ford. The ford was of such a nature that but one horse could pass it at a time, and that one had to scramble through deep mud. 'There'll be the devil to pay there,' said Lord Chiltern, going straight with his hounds. Phineas Finn and Dick Rabbit were close after him. Old Fowler had craftily gone to the ford; but Mrs. Spooner, who did not intend to be shaken off, followed the Master, and close with her was Lord Silverbridge. 'Lord Chiltern hasn't got it right,' she said. 'He can't do it among these bushes.' As she spoke the Master put his horse at the bushes and then—disappeared. The lady had been right. There was no ground at that spot to take off from, and the bushes had impeded him. Lord Chiltern got over, but his horse was in the water. Dick Rabbit and poor Phineas Finn were stopped in their course by the necessity of helping the Master in his trouble.

But Mrs. Spooner, the judicious Mrs. Spooner, rode at the stream where it was, indeed, a little wider, but at a place in which the horse could see what he was about, and where he could jump from and to firm ground. Lord Silverbridge followed her gallantly. They both jumped the brook well, and then were together. 'You'll beat me in pace,' said the lady as he rode alongside of her. 'Take the fence ahead straight, and then turn sharp to your right.' With all her faults Mrs. Spooner was a thorough sportsman.

He did take the fence ahead,—or rather tried to do so. It was a bank and a double ditch,—not very great in itself, but requiring a horse to land on the top and go off with a second spring. Our young friend's nag, not quite understanding the nature of the impediment, endeavoured to 'swallow it whole,' as hard-riding men say, and came down in the further ditch. Silverbridge came down on his head, but the horse pursued his course,—across a heavily-ploughed field.

This was very disagreeable. He was not in the least hurt, but it became his duty to run after his horse. A very few furrows of that work suffice to make a man think that hunting altogether is a 'beastly sort of thing.' Mrs. Spooner's horse, who had shown himself to be a little less quick of foot than his own, had known all about the bank and the double ditch, and had, apparently of his own accord, turned down to the right, either seeing or hearing the hounds, and knowing that the ploughed ground was to be avoided. But his rider soon changed his course. She went straight after the riderless horse, and when Silverbridge had reduced himself to utter speechlessness by his exertions, brought him back his steed.

'I am,—I am, I am—so sorry,' he struggled to say,—and then as she held his horse for him he struggled up into the saddle.

'Keep down this furrow,' said Mrs. Spooner, 'and we shall be with them in the second field. There's nobody near them yet.'

CHAPTER LXIII
'I've seen 'em like that before'

On this occasion Silverbridge stayed only a few days at Harrington, having promised Tregear to entertain him at The Baldfaced Stag. It was here that his horses were standing, and he now intended, by limiting himself to one horse a day, to mount his friend for a couple of weeks. It was settled at last that Tregear should ride his friend's horse one day, hire the next, and so on. 'I wonder what you'll think of Mrs. Spooner?' he said.

'Why should I think anything of her?'

'Because I doubt whether you ever saw such a woman before. She does nothing but hunt.'

'Then I certainly shan't want to see her again.'

'And she talks as I never heard a lady talk before.'

'Then I don't care if I never see her at all.'

'But she is the most plucky and most good-natured human being I ever saw in my life. After all, hunting is very good fun.'

'Very; if you don't do it so often as to be sick of it.'

'Long as I have known you I don't think I ever saw you ride yet.'

'We used to have hunting down in Cornwall, and thought we did it pretty well. And I have ridden in South Wales, which I can assure you isn't an easy thing to do. But you mustn't expect much from me.'

They were both out the Monday and Tuesday in that week, and then again on the Thursday without anything special in the way of sport. Lord Chiltern, who had found Silverbridge to be a young man after his own heart, was anxious that he should come back to Harrington and bring Tregear with him. But to this Tregear would not assent, alleging that he should feel himself to be a burden both to Lord and Lady Chiltern. On the Friday Tregear did not go out, saying that he would avoid the expense, and on that day there was a good run. 'It is always the way,' said Silverbridge. 'If you miss a day, it is sure to be the best thing of the season. An hour and a quarter with hardly anything you could call a check! It is the only very good thing I have seen since I have been here. Mrs. Spooner was with them all through.'

'And I suppose you were with Mrs. Spooner.'

'I wasn't far off. I wish you had been there.'

On the next day the meet was at the kennels, close to Harrington, and Silverbridge drove his friend over in a gig,

The Master and Lady Chiltern, Spooner and Mrs. Spooner,
Maule and Mrs. Maule, Phineas Finn, and a host of others
condoled with the unfortunate young man because he had not
seen the good thing yesterday. 'We've had it a little faster
once or twice,' said Mrs. Spooner with deliberation, 'but
never for so long. Then it was straight as a line, and a real
open kill. No changing, you know. We did go through the
Daisies, but I'll swear to its being the same fox.' All of which
set Tregear wondering. How could she swear to her fox? And
if they had changed, what did it matter? And if it had been
a little crooked, why would it have been less enjoyable? And
was she really so exact a judge of pace as she pretended to
be? 'I'm afraid we shan't have anything like that to-day,'
she continued. 'The wind's in the west, and I never do like
a westerly wind.'

'A little to the north,' said her husband, looking round the
compass.

'My dear,' said the lady, 'you never know where the wind
comes from. Now don't you think of taking off your com-
forter. I won't have it.'

Tregear was riding his friend's favourite hunter, a thoroughbred bay horse, very much more than up to his rider's weight,
and supposed to be peculiarly good at timber, water, or any
well-defined kind of fence, however high or however broad.
They found at a covert near the kennels, and killed their fox
after a burst of a few minutes. They found again, and having
lost their fox, all declared that there was not a yard of scent.
'I always know what a west wind means,' said Mrs. Spooner.

Then they lunched, and smoked, and trotted about with an
apparent acknowledgement that there wasn't much to be done.
It was not right that they should expect much after so good
a thing as they had had yesterday. At half-past two Mr.
Spooner had been sent home by his Providence, and Mrs.
Spooner was calculating that she would be able to ride her
horse again on the Tuesday, when on a sudden the hounds
were on a fox. It turned out afterwards that Dick Rabbit had
absolutely ridden him up among the stubble, and that the

hounds had nearly killed him before he had gone a yard. But the astute animal, making the best use of his legs till he could get the advantage of the first ditch, ran, and crept, and jumped absolutely through the pack. Then there was shouting, and yelling, and riding. The men who were idly smoking threw away their cigars. Those who were loitering at a distance lost their chance. But the real sportsmen, always on the alert, always thinking of the business in hand, always mindful that there may be at any moment a fox just before the hounds, had a glorious opportunity of getting 'well away.' Among these no one was more intent, or, when the moment came, 'better away', than Mrs. Spooner.

Silverbridge had been talking to her and had the full advantage of her care. Tregear was riding behind with Lord Chiltern, who had been pressing him to come with his friend to Harrington. As soon as the shouting was heard Chiltern was off like a rocket. It was not only that he was anxious to 'get well away,' but that a sense of duty compelled him to see how the thing was being done. Old Fowler certainly was a little slow, and Dick Rabbit, with the true bloody-minded instinct of a whip,* was a little apt to bustle a fox back into covert. And then, when a run commences with a fast rush, riders are apt to over-ride the hounds, and then the hounds will over-run the fox. All of which has to be seen to by a Master who knows his business.

Tregear followed, and being mounted on a fast horse was soon as forward as a judicious rider would desire. 'Now, Runks, don't you press on and spoil it all,' said Mrs. Spooner to the hard-riding objectionable son of old Runks the vet from Rufford. But young Runks did press on till the Master spoke a word. The word shall not be repeated, but it was efficacious.

At that moment there had been a check,—as there is generally after a short spurt, when fox, hounds, and horsemen get off together, and not always in the order in which they have been placed here. There is too much bustle, and the pack becomes disconcerted. But it enabled Fowler to get up, and by dint of growling at the men and conciliating his hounds, he soon picked up the scent. 'If they'd all stand still for two minutes and be —— to them,' he muttered aloud to himself, 'they'd 'ave some'at to ride arter. They might go then, and there's some of 'em 'd soon be nowhere.'

But in spite of Fowler's denunciations there was, of course, another rush. Runks had slunk away, but by making a little distance was now again ahead of the hounds. And unfortunately there was half-a-dozen with him. Lord Chiltern was very wrath. 'When he's like that,' said Mrs. Spooner to Tregear, 'it's always well to give him a wide berth.' But as the hounds were now running fast it was necessary that even in taking this precaution due regard should be had to the fox's line. 'He's back for Harrington bushes,' said Mrs. Spooner. And as she said so, she rode at a bank, with a rail at the top of it perhaps a foot-and-a-half high, with a deep drop into the field beyond. It was not a very nice place, but it was apparently the only available spot in the fence. She seemed to know it well, for as she got close to it she brought her horse almost to a stand and so took it. The horse cleared the rail, seemed just to touch the bank on the other side, while she threw herself back almost on to his crupper, and so came down with perfect ease. But she, knowing that it would not be easy to all horses, paused a moment to see what would happen.

Tregear was next to her and was intending to 'fly' the fence. But when he saw Mrs. Spooner pull her horse and pause, he also had to pull his horse. This he did so as to enable her to take her leap without danger or encumbrance from him, but hardly so as to bring his horse to the bank in the same way. It may be doubted whether the animal he was riding would have known enough and been quiet enough to have performed the acrobatic manœuvre which had carried Mrs. Spooner so pleasantly over the peril. He had some idea of this, for the thought occurred to him that he would turn and ride fast at the jump. But before he could turn he saw that Silverbridge was pressing on him. It was thus his only resource to do as Mrs. Spooner had done. He was too close to the rail, but still he tried it. The horse attempted to jump, caught his foot against the bar, and of course went over head-foremost. This probably would have been nothing, had not Silverbridge with his rushing beast been immediately after them. When the young lord saw that his friend was down it was too late for him to stop his course. His horse was determined to have the fence,—and did have it. He touched nothing, and would have skimmed in glory over the next field had he not come right down on Tregear and Tregear's steed. There they were, four of them, two men and two horses in one confused heap.

The first person with them was Mrs. Spooner, who was off her horse in a minute. And Silverbridge too was very soon on his legs. He at any rate was unhurt, and the two horses were up before Mrs. Spooner was out of her saddle. But Tregear did not move. 'What are we to do?' said Lord Silverbridge, kneeling down over his friend. 'Oh, Mrs. Spooner, what are we to do?'

The hunt had passed on and no one else was immediately with them. But at this moment Dick Rabbit, who had been left behind to bring up his hounds, appeared above the bank. 'Leave your horse and come down,' said Mrs. Spooner. 'Here is a gentleman who has hurt himself.' Dick wouldn't leave his horse, but was soon on the scene, having found his way through another part of the fence.

'No; he ain't dead,' said Dick—'I've seen 'em like that before, and they wurn't dead. But he's had a hawful squeege.' Then he passed his hand over the man's neck and chest. 'There's a lot of 'em is broke,' said he. 'We must get him into farmer Tooby's.'

After awhile he was got into farmer Tooby's, when that surgeon came who is always in attendance on a hunting-field. The surgeon declared that he had broken his collar-bone, two of his ribs, and his left arm. And then one of the animals had struck him on the chest as he raised himself. A little brandy was poured down his throat, but even under that operation he gave no sign of life. 'No, missis, he aren't dead,' said Dick to Mrs. Tooby; 'no more he won't die this bout; but he's got it very nasty.'

That night Silverbridge was sitting by his friend's bedside at ten o'clock in Lord Chiltern's house. Tregear had spoken a few words, and the bones had been set. But the doctor had not felt himself justified in speaking with that assurance which Dick had expressed. The man's whole body had been bruised by the horse which had fallen on him. The agony of Silverbridge was extreme, for he knew that it had been his doing. 'You were a little too close,' Mrs. Spooner had said to him, 'but nobody saw it and we'll hold our tongues.' Silverbridge however would not hold his tongue. He told everybody how it had happened, how he had been unable to stop his horse, how he had jumped upon his friend, and perhaps killed him. 'I don't know what I am to do. I am so miserable,' he said to Lady Chiltern with the tears running down his face.

The two remained at Harrington and their luggage was brought over from The Baldfaced Stag. The accident had happened on a Saturday. On the Sunday there was no comfort. On the Monday the patient's recollection and mind were re-established, and the doctor thought that perhaps, with great care, his constitution would pull him through. On that day the consternation at Harrington was so great that Mrs. Spooner would not go to the meet. She came over from Spoon Hall, and spent a considerable part of the day in the sick man's room. 'It's sure to come right if it's above the vitals,' she said, expressing an opinion which had come from much experience. 'That is,' she added, 'unless the neck's broke. When poor old Jack Stubbs drove his head into his cap and dislocated his wertebury, of course it was all up with him.' The patient heard this and was seen to smile.

On the Tuesday there arose the question of family communication. As the accident would make its way into the papers a message had been sent to Polwenning to say that various bones had been broken, but that the patient was upon the whole doing well. Then there had been different messages backwards and forwards, in all of which there had been an

attempt to comfort old Mrs. Tregear. But on the Tuesday
letters were written. Silverbridge, sitting in his friend's room,
sent a long account of the accident to Mrs. Tregear, giving
a list of the injuries done.

'Your sister,' whispered the poor fellow from his pillow.

'Yes,—yes;—yes, I will.'

'And Mabel Grex.' Silverbridge nodded assent and again
went to the writing-table. He did write to his sister, and in
plain words told her everything. 'The doctor says he is not
now in danger.' Then he added a postscript. 'As long as I am
here I will let you know how he is.'

CHAPTER LXIV
'I believe him to be a worthy young man'

LADY MARY and Mrs. Finn were alone when the tidings
came from Silverbridge. The Duke had been absent, having gone to spend an unpleasant week in Barsetshire. Mary
had taken the opportunity of his absence to discuss her own
prospects at full length. 'My dear,' said Mrs. Finn, 'I will

not express an opinion. How can I after all that has passed? I have told the Duke the same. I cannot be heart and hand with either without being false to the other.' But still Lady Mary continued to talk about Tregear.

'I don't think papa has a right to treat me in this way,' she said. 'He wouldn't be allowed to kill me, and this is killing me.'

'While there is life there is hope,' said Mrs. Finn.

'Yes; while there is life there is hope. But one doesn't want to grow old first.'

'There is no danger of that yet, Mary.'

'I feel very old. What is the use of life without something to make it sweet? I am not even allowed to hear anything that he is doing. If he were to ask me, I think I would go away with him to-morrow.'

'He would not be foolish enough for that.'

'Because he does not suffer as I do. He has his borough, and his public life, and a hundred things to think of. I have got nothing but him. I know he is true;—quite as true as I am. But it is I that have the suffering in all this. A man can never be like a girl. Papa ought not to make me suffer like this.'

That took place on the Monday. On the Tuesday Mrs. Finn received a letter from her husband giving his account of the accident. 'As far as I can learn,' he said, 'Silverbridge will write about it to-morrow.' Then he went on to give a by no means good account of the state of the patient. The doctor had declared him to be out of immediate danger, and had set the broken bones. As tidings would be sent on the next day she had better say nothing about the accident to Lady Mary. This letter reached Matching on Tuesday and made the position of Mrs. Finn very disagreeable. She was bound to carry herself as though nothing was amiss, knowing, as she did so, the condition of Mary's lover.

On the evening of that day Lady Mary was more lively than usual, though her liveliness was hardly of a happy nature. 'I don't know what papa can expect. I've heard him say a hundred times that to be in Parliament is the highest place a gentleman can fill, and now Frank is in Parliament.' Mrs.

Finn looked at her with beseeching eyes, as though begging her not to speak of Tregear. 'And then to think of their having that Lord Popplecourt there! I shall always hate Lady Cantrip, for it was her place. That she should have thought it possible! Lord Popplecourt! Such a creature! Hyperion to a satyr.*Isn't it true? Oh, that papa should have thought it possible!' Then she got up, and walked about the room, beating her hands together. All this time Mrs. Finn knew that Tregear was lying at Harrington with half his bones broken, and in danger of his life!

On the next morning Lady Mary received her letters. There were two lying before her plate when she came into breakfast, one from her father and the other from Silverbridge. She read that from the Duke first while Mrs. Finn was watching her. 'Papa will be home on Saturday,' she said. 'He declares that the people in the borough are quite delighted with Silverbridge for a member. And he is quite jocose. "They used to be delighted with me once," he says, "but I suppose everybody changes."' Then she began to pour out the tea before she opened her brother's letter. Mrs. Finn's eyes were still on her anxiously. 'I wonder what Silverbridge has got to say about the Brake Hunt.' Then she opened her letter.

'Oh;—oh!' she exclaimed,—'Frank has killed himself.'

'Killed himself! Not that. It is not so bad as that.'

'You had heard it before?'

'How is he, Mary?'

'Oh, heavens! I cannot read it. Do you read it. Tell me all. Tell me the truth. What am I to do? Where shall I go?' Then she threw up her hands, and with a loud scream fell on her knees with her head upon the chair. In the next moment Mrs. Finn was down beside her on the floor. 'Read it; why do you not read it? If you will not read it, give it to me.'

Mrs. Finn did read the letter, which was very short, but still giving by no means an unfavourable account of the patient. 'I am sorry to say he has broken ever so many bones, and we were very much frightened about him.' Then the writer went into details, from which a reader who did not read the words carefully might well imagine that the man's life was still in danger.

Mrs. Finn did read it all, and did her best to comfort her friend. 'It has been a bad accident,' she said, 'but it is clear that he is getting better. Men do so often break their bones, and then seem to think nothing of it afterwards.'

'Silverbridge says it was his fault. What does he mean?'

'I suppose he was riding too close to Mr. Tregear, and that they came down together. Of course it is distressing, but I do not think you need make yourself positively unhappy about it.'

'Would you not be unhappy if it were Mr. Finn?' said Mary, jumping up from her knees. 'I shall go to him. I should go mad if I were to remain here and know nothing about it but what Silverbridge will tell me.'

'I will telegraph to Mr. Finn.'

'Mr. Finn won't care. Men are so heartless. They write about each other just as though it did not signify in the least whether anybody were dead or alive. I shall go to him.'

'You cannot do that.'

'I don't care now what anybody may think. I choose to be considered as belonging to him, and if papa were here I would say the same.' It was of course not difficult to make her understand that she could not go to Harrington, but it was by no means easy to keep her tranquil. She would send a telegram herself. This was debated for a long time, till at last Lady Mary insisted that she was not subject to Mrs. Finn's authority. 'If papa were here, even then I would send it.' And she did send it, in her own name, regardless of the fact pointed out to her by Mrs. Finn, that the people at the post-office would thus know her secret. 'It is no secret,' she said. 'I don't want it to be a secret.' The telegram went in the following words: 'I have heard it. I am so wretched. Send me one word to say how you are.' She got an answer back, with Tregear's own name to it, on that afternoon. 'Do not be unhappy. I am doing well. Silverbridge is with me.'

On the Thursday Gerald came home from Scotland. He had

arranged his little affair with Lord Percival, not however without some difficulty. Lord Percival had declared he did not understand I.O.U.'s in an affair of that kind. He had always thought that gentlemen did not play for stakes which they could not pay at once. This was not said to Gerald himself;—or the result would have been calamitous. Nidderdale was the go-between, and at last arranged it,—not however till he had pointed out that Percival, having won so large a sum of money from a lad under twenty-one years of age, was very lucky in receiving substantial security for its payment.

Gerald had chosen the period of his father's absence for his return. It was necessary that the story of the gambling debt should be told the Duke in February. Silverbridge had explained that to him, and he had quite understood it. He, indeed, would be up at Oxford in February, and, in that case, the first horror of the thing would be left to poor Silverbridge! Thinking of this, Gerald felt that he was bound to tell his father himself. He resolved that he would do so, but was anxious to postpone the evil day. He lingered therefore in Scotland till he knew that his father was in Barsetshire.

On his arrival he was told of Tregear's accident. 'Oh, Gerald; have you heard?' said his sister. He had not as yet heard, and then the history was repeated to him. Mary did not attempt to conceal her own feelings. She was as open with her brother as she had been with Mrs. Finn.

'I suppose he'll get over it,' said Gerald.

'Is that all you say?' she asked.

'What can I say better? I suppose he will. Fellows always do get over that kind of thing. Herbert de Burgh smashed both his thighs, and now he can move about again,—of course with crutches.'

'Gerald! How can you be so unfeeling!'

'I don't know what you mean. I always liked Tregear, and I am very sorry for him. If you would take it a little quieter, I think it would be better.'

'I could not take it quietly. How can I take it quietly when he is more than all the world to me?'

'You should keep that to yourself.'

'Yes,—and so let people think that I didn't care, till I broke my heart! I shall say just the same to papa when he comes home.' After that the brother and sister were not on very good terms with each other for the remainder of the day.

On the Saturday there was a letter from Silverbridge to Mrs. Finn. Tregear was better; but was unhappy because it had been decided that he could not be moved for the next month. This entailed two misfortunes on him;—first that of being the enforced guest of persons who were not,—or, hitherto had not been, his own friends,—and then his absence from the first meeting of Parliament. When a gentleman has been in Parliament some years he may be able to reconcile himself to an obligatory vacation with a calm mind. But when the honours and glory are new, and the tedium of the benches has not yet been experienced, then such an accident is felt to be a grievance. But the young member was out of danger, and was, as Silverbridge declared, in the very best quarters which could be provided for a man in such a position.

Phineas Finn told him all the politics; Mrs. Spooner related to him, on Sundays and Wednesdays, all the hunting details; while Lady Chiltern read to him light literature, because he was not allowed to hold a book in his hand. 'I wish it were me,' said Gerald. 'I wish I were there to read to him,' said Mary.

Then the Duke came home. 'Mary,' said he, 'I have been distressed to hear of this accident.' This seemed to her to be the kindest word she had heard from him for a long time. 'I believe him to be a worthy young man. I am sorry that he should be the cause of so much sorrow to you—and to me.'

'Of course I was sorry for his accident,' she replied, after pausing awhile; 'but now that he is better I will not call him a cause of sorrow—to me.' Then the Duke said nothing further about Tregear; nor did she.

'So you have come at last,' he said to Gerald. That was the first greeting,—to which the son responded by an awkward smile. But in the course of the evening he walked straight up to his father—'I have something to tell you, sir,' said he.

'Something to tell me?'

'Something that will make you very angry.'

CHAPTER LXV
'Do you ever think what money is?'

GERALD told his story, standing bolt upright, and looking his father full in the face as he told it. 'You lost three thousand four hundred pounds at one sitting to Lord Percival —at cards!'

'Yes, sir.'

'In Lord Nidderdale's house?'

'Yes, sir. Nidderdale wasn't playing. It wasn't his fault.'

'Who were playing?'

'Percival, and Dolly Longstaff, and Jack Hinde,—and I. Popplecourt was playing at first.'

'Lord Popplecourt!'

514

'Yes, sir. But he went away when he began to lose.'

'Three thousand four hundred pounds! How old are you?'

'I am just twenty-one.'

'You are beginning the world well, Gerald! What is the engagement which Silverbridge has made with Lord Percival?'

'To pay him the money at the end of next month.'

'What had Silverbridge to do with it?'

'Nothing, sir. I wrote to Silverbridge because I didn't know what to do. I knew he would stand to me.'

'Who is to stand to either of you if you go on thus I do not know.' To this Gerald of course made no reply, but an idea came across his mind that he knew who would stand both to himself and his brother. 'How did Silverbridge mean to get the money?'

'He said he would ask you. But I thought that I ought to tell you.'

'Is that all?'

'All what, sir?'

'Are there other debts?' To this Gerald made no reply. 'Other gambling debts.'

'No, sir;—not a shilling of that kind. I have never played before.'

'Does it ever occur to you that going on at that rate you may very soon lose all the fortune that will ever come to you? You were not yet of age and you lost three thousand four hundred pounds at cards to a man whom you probably knew to be a professed gambler!' The Duke seemed to wait for a reply, but poor Gerald had not a word to say. 'Can you explain to me what benefit you proposed to yourself when you played for such stakes as that?'

'I hoped to win back what I had lost.'

'Facilis descensus Averni!'*said the Duke, shaking his head. 'Noctes atque dies patet atri janua Ditis.' No doubt, he thought, that as his son was at Oxford, admonitions in Latin would serve him better than in his native tongue. But Gerald, when he heard the grand hexameter rolled out in his father's grandest tone, entertained a comfortable feeling that the

worst of the interview was over. 'Win back what you had
lost! Do you think that that is the common fortune of young
gamblers when they fall among those who are more experienced than themselves?'

'One goes on, sir, without reflecting.'

'Go on without reflecting! Yes; and where to? where to?
Oh Gerald, where to? Whither will such progress without
reflection take you?' 'He means—to the devil,' the lad said
inwardly to himself, without moving his lips. 'There is but
one goal for such going on as that. I can pay three thousand
four hundred pounds for you certainly. I think it hard that
I should have to do so; but I can do it,—and I will do it.'

'Thank you, sir,' murmured Gerald.

'But how can I wash your young mind clean from the foul
stain which has already defiled it? Why did you sit down to
play? Was it to win the money which these men had in their
pockets?'

'Not particularly.'

'It cannot be that a rational being should consent to risk the
money he has himself,—to risk even the money which he has
not himself,—without a desire to win that which as yet belongs to his opponents. You desired to win.'

'I suppose I did hope to win.'

'And why? Why did you want to extract their property
from their pockets, and to put it into your own? That the
footpad on the road should have such desire when, with his
pistol, he stops the traveller on his journey we all understand.
And we know what we think of the footpad,—and what we
do to him. He is a poor creature, who from his youth upwards
has had no good thing done for him, uneducated, an outcast,
whom we should pity more than we despise him. We take
him as a pest which we cannot endure, and lock him up where
he can harm us no more. On my word, Gerald, I think that the
so-called gentleman who sits down with the deliberate intention of extracting money from the pockets of his antagonists,
who lays out for himself that way of repairing the short-
comings of fortune, who looks to that resource as an aid to

his means,—is worse, much worse, than the public robber!
He is meaner, more cowardly, and has I think in his bosom
less of the feelings of an honest man. And he probably has
been educated,—as you have been. He calls himself a gentleman. He should know black from white. It is considered
terrible to cheat at cards.'

'There was nothing of that, sir.'

'The man who plays and cheats has fallen low indeed.'

'I understand that, sir.'

'He who plays that he may make an income, but does not
cheat, has fallen nearly as low. Do you ever think what
money is?'

The Duke paused so long, collecting his own thoughts and
thinking of his own words, that Gerald found himself obliged
to answer. 'Cheques, and sovereigns, and bank-notes,' he
replied with much hesitation.

'Money is the reward of labour,' said the Duke, 'or rather,
in the shape it reaches you, it is your representation of that
reward. You may earn it yourself, or, as is, I am afraid, more
likely to be the case with you, you may possess it honestly
as prepared for you by the labour of others who have stored it
up for you. But it is a commodity of which you are bound to
see that the source is not only clean but noble. You would
not let Lord Percival give you money.'

'He wouldn't do that, sir, I am sure.'

'Nor would you take it. There is nothing so comfortable as
money,—but nothing so defiling if it be come by unworthily;
nothing so comfortable, but nothing so noxious if the mind
be allowed to dwell upon it constantly. If a man have enough,
let him spend it freely. If he wants it, let him earn it honestly.
Let him do something for it, so that the man who pays it to
him may get its value. But to think that it may be got by
gambling, to hope to live after that fashion, to sit down with
your fingers almost in your neighbour's pockets, with your
eye on his purse, trusting that you may know better than he
some studied calculations as to the pips*concealed in your
hands, praying to the only god you worship that some special

card may be vouchsafed to you,—that I say is to have left far, far behind you, all nobility, all gentleness, all manhood! Write me down Lord Percival's address and I will send him the money.'

Then the Duke wrote a cheque for the money claimed and sent it with a note, as follows:—'The Duke of Omnium presents his compliments to Lord Percival. The Duke has been informed by Lord Gerald Palliser that Lord Percival has won at cards from him the sum of three thousand four hundred pounds. The Duke now encloses a cheque for that amount, and requests that the document which Lord Percival holds from Lord Silverbridge as security for the amount, may be returned to Lord Gerald.' Let the noble gambler have his prey. He was little solicitous about that. If he could only so operate on the mind of this son,—so operate on the minds of both his sons, as to make them see the foolishness of folly, the ugliness of what is mean, the squalor and dirt of ignoble pursuits, then he could easily pardon past faults. If it were half his wealth, what would it signify if he could teach his children to accept those lessons without which no man can live as a gentleman, let his rank be the highest known, let his wealth be as the sands, his fashion unrivalled?

The word or two which his daughter had said to him, declaring that she still took pride in her lover's love, and then this new misfortune on Gerald's part, upset him greatly. He almost sickened of politics when he thought of his domestic bereavement and his domestic misfortunes. How completely had he failed to indoctrinate his children with the ideas by which his own mind was fortified and controlled! Nothing was so base to him as a gambler, and they had both commenced their career by gambling. From their young boyhood nothing had seemed so desirable to him as that they should be accustomed by early training to devote themselves to the service of their country. He saw other young noblemen around him who at eighteen were known as debaters at their colleges, or at twenty-five were already deep in politics, social science, and educational projects. What good would all his wealth or all his position do for his children if their minds could rise to nothing beyond the shooting of deer and the hunting of foxes? There was young Lord Buttercup, the son of the Earl of Woolantallow, only a few months older than Silverbridge,— who was already a junior lord, and as constant at his office, or during the Session on the Treasury Bench, as though there were not a pack of hounds or a card-table in Great Britain! Lord Buttercup, too, had already written an article in 'The Fortnightly'*on the subject of Turkish finance. How long would it be before Silverbridge would write an article, or Gerald sign his name in the service of the public?

And then those proposed marriages,—as to which he was beginning to know that his children would be too strong for him! Anxious as he was that both his sons should be per-meated by Liberal politics, studious as he had ever been to teach them that the highest duty of those high in rank was to use their authority to elevate those beneath them, still he was hardly less anxious to make them understand that their second duty required them to maintain their own position. It was by feeling this second duty,—by feeling it and performing it,— that they would be enabled to perform the rest. And now both Silverbridge and his girl were bent upon marriages by which they would depart out of their own order! Let Silverbridge marry whom he might, he could not be other than heir to the honours of his family. But by his marriage he might either support or derogate from these honours. And now, having at first made a choice that was good, he had altered his mind from simple freak, captivated by a pair of bright eyes and an arch smile; and without a feeling in regard to his family, was anxious to take to his bosom the granddaughter of an Ameri-can day-labourer!

And then his girl,—of whose beauty he was so proud, from whose manners, and tastes, and modes of life he had expected to reap those good things, in a feminine degree, which his sons as young men seemed so little fitted to give him! By slow degrees he had been brought round to acknowledge that the young man was worthy. Tregear's conduct had been felt by the Duke to be manly. The letter he had written was a good letter. And then he had won for himself a seat in the House of Commons. When forced to speak of him to this girl he had been driven by justice to call him worthy. But how could he serve to support and strengthen that nobility, the endurance and perpetuation of which should be the peculiar care of every Palliser?

And yet as the Duke walked about his room he felt that his opposition either to the one marriage or to the other was vain. Of course they would marry according to their wills.

That same night Gerald wrote to his brother before he went to bed, as follows:

'DEAR SILVER,—I was awfully obliged to you for sending me the I.O.U. for that brute Percival. He only sneered when he took it, and would have said something disagreeable, but that he saw that I was in earnest. I know he did say something to Nid, only I can't find out what. Nid is an easy-going fellow, and, as I saw, didn't want to have a rumpus.

'But now what do you think I've done? Directly I got home I told the governor all about it! As I was in the train I made up my mind that I would. I went slap at it. If there is anything that never does any good, it's craning. I did it all at one rush, just as though I was swallowing a dose of physic. I wish I could tell you all that the governor said, because it was really tip-top. What is a fellow to get by playing high,—a fellow like you and me? I didn't want any of that beast's money. I don't suppose he had any. But one's dander gets up, and one doesn't like to be done, and so it goes on. I shall cut that kind of thing altogether. You should have heard the governor spouting Latin! And then the way he sat upon Percival, without mentioning the fellow's name! I do think it mean to set yourself to work to win money at cards,—and it is awfully mean to lose more than you have got to pay.

'Then at the end the governor said he'd send the beast a cheque for the amount. You know his way of finishing up, just like two fellows fighting;—when one has awfully punished the other he goes up and shakes hands with him. He did pitch into me,—not abusing me, nor even saying a word about the money, which he at once promised to pay, but laying it on to gambling with a regular cat-o'-nine-tails. And then there was an end of it. He just asked the fellow's address and said that he would send him the money. I will say this;—I don't think there's a greater brick than the governor out anywhere.

'I am awfully sorry about Tregear. I can't quite make out how it happened. I suppose you were too near him, and Melrose always does rush at his fences. One fellow shouldn't be too near another fellow,—only it so often happens that it can't be helped. It's just like anything else, if nothing comes of it then it's all right. But if anybody comes to grief then he has got to be pitched into. Do you remember when I nearly cut over old Sir Simon Slobody? Didn't I hear about it!

'I am awfully glad you didn't smash up Tregear altogether, because of Mary. I am quite sure it is no good anybody setting up his back against that. It's one of the things that have got to be. You always have said that he is a good fellow. If so, what's the harm? At any rate it has got to be.

'Your affectionate Brother,
'GERALD.

'I go up in about a week.'

CHAPTER LXVI

The three attacks

DURING the following week the communications between Harrington and Matching were very frequent. There were no further direct messages between Tregear and Lady Mary, but she heard daily of his progress. The Duke was conscious of the special interest which existed in his house as to the condition of the young man, but, after his arrival, not a word was spoken for some days between him and his daughter on the subject. Then Gerald went back to his college, and the Duke made his preparations for going up to town and making some attempt at parliamentary activity.

It was by no concert that an attack was made upon him from three quarters at once as he was preparing to leave Matching. On the Sunday morning during church time,—for on that day Lady Mary went to her devotions alone,—Mrs. Finn was closeted for an hour with the Duke in his study. 'I think you ought to be aware,' she said to the Duke, 'that though I trust Mary implicitly and know her to be thoroughly high principled, I cannot be responsible for her, if I remain with her here.'

'I do not quite follow your meaning.'

'Of course there is but one matter on which there can, probably, be any difference between us. If she should choose to write to Mr. Tregear, or to send him a message, or even to go to him, I could not prevent it.'

'Go to him!' exclaimed the horrified Duke.

'I merely suggest such a thing in order to make you understand that I have absolutely no control over her.'

'What control have I?'

'Nay; I cannot define that. You are her father, and she acknowledges your authority. She regards me as a friend— and as such treats me with the sweetest affection. Nothing can be more gratifying than her manner to me personally.'

'It ought to be so.'

'She has thoroughly won my heart. But still I know that if there were a difference between us she would not obey me. Why should she?'

'Because you hold my deputed authority.'

'Oh, Duke, that goes for very little anywhere. No one can depute authority. It comes too much from personal accidents, and too little from reason or law to be handed over to others. Besides, I fear, that on one matter concerning her you and I are not agreed.'

'I shall be sorry if it be so.'

'I feel that I am bound to tell you my opinion.'

'Oh yes.'

522

'You think that in the end Lady Mary will allow herself to be separated from Tregear. I think that in the end they will become man and wife.'

This seemed to the Duke to be not quite so bad as it might have been. Any speculation as to results were very different from an expressed opinion as to propriety. Were he to tell the truth as to his own mind, he might perhaps have said the same thing. But one is not to relax in one's endeavours to prevent that which is wrong, because one fears that the wrong may be ultimately perpetrated. 'Let that be as it may,' he said, 'it cannot alter my duty.'

'Nor mine, Duke, if I may presume to think that I have a duty in this matter.'

'That you should encounter the burden of the duty binds me to you for ever.'

'If it be that they will certainly be married one day——'

'Who has said that? Who has admitted that?'

'If it be so; if it seems to me that it must be so,—then how can I be anxious to prolong her sufferings? She does suffer terribly.' Upon this the Duke frowned, but there was more of tenderness in his frown than in the hard smile which he had hitherto worn. 'I do not know whether you see it all.' He well remembered all that he had seen when he and Mary were travelling together. 'I see it; and I do not pass half an hour with her without sorrowing for her.' On hearing this he sighed and turned his face away. 'Girls are so different! There are many who though they be genuinely in love, though their natures are sweet and affectionate, are not strong enough to support their own feelings in resistance to the will of those who have authority over them.' Had it been so with his wife? At this moment all the former history passed through his mind. 'They yield to that which seems to be inevitable, and allow themselves to be fashioned by the purposes of others. It is well for them often that they are so plastic. Whether it would be better for her that she should be so I will not say.'

'It would be better,' said the Duke doggedly.

'But such is not her nature. She is as determined as ever.'

'I may be determined too.'

'But if at last it will be of no use,—if it be her fate either to be married to this man or die of a broken heart——'

'What justifies you in saying that? How can you torture me by such a threat?'

'If I think so, Duke, I am justified. Of late I have been with her daily,—almost hourly. I do not say that this will kill her now,—in her youth. It is not often, I fancy, that women die after that fashion. But a broken heart may bring the sufferer to the grave after a lapse of many years. How will it be with you if she should live like a ghost beside you for the next twenty years, and you should then see her die, faded and withered before her time,—all her life gone without a joy,— because she had loved a man whose position in life was displeasing to you? Would the ground on which the sacrifice had been made then justify itself to you? In thus performing your duty to your order would you feel satisfied that you had performed that to your child?'

She had come there determined to say it all,—to liberate her own soul as it were,—but had much doubted the spirit in which the Duke would listen to her. That he would listen to her she was sure,—and then if he chose to cast her out, she would endure his wrath. It would not be to her now as it had been when he accused her of treachery. But, nevertheless, bold as she was and independent, he had imbued her, as he did all those around him, with so strong a sense of his personal dignity, that when she had finished she almost trembled as she looked in his face. Since he had asked her how she could justify to herself the threats which she was using he had sat still with his eyes fixed upon her. Now, when she had done, he was in no hurry to speak. He rose slowly and walking towards the fireplace stood with his back towards her, looking down upon the fire. She was the first to speak again. 'Shall I leave you now?' she said in a low voice.

'Perhaps it will be better,' he answered. His voice, too, was very low. In truth he was so moved that he hardly knew how to speak at all. Then she rose and was already on her way to the door when he followed her. 'One moment, if you please,' he said almost sternly. 'I am under a debt of gratitude to you of which I cannot express my sense in words. How far I may agree with you, and where I may disagree, I will not attempt to point out to you now.'

'Oh no.'

'But all that you have troubled yourself to think and to feel in this matter, and all that true friendship has compelled you to say to me, shall be written down in the tablets of my memory.'

'Duke!'

'My child has at any rate been fortunate in securing the friendship of such a friend.' Then he turned back to the fireplace, and she was constrained to leave the room without another word.

She had determined to make the best plea in her power for Mary; and while she was making the plea had been almost surprised by her own vehemence; but the greater had been her vehemence, the stronger, she thought, would have been the Duke's anger. And as she had watched the workings of his face she had felt for a moment that the vials of his wrath were about to be poured out upon her. Even when she left the room she almost believed that had he not taken those moments for consideration at the fireplace his parting words would have been different. But, as it was, there could be no question now of her departure. No power was left to her of separating herself from Lady Mary. Though the Duke had not as yet acknowledged himself to be conquered, there was no doubt to her now but that he would be conquered. And she, either here or in London, must be the girl's nearest friend up to the day when she should be given over to Mr. Tregear.

That was one of the three attacks which were made upon the Duke before he went up to his parliamentary duties.

The second was as follows: Among the letters on the following morning one was brought to him from Tregear. It is hoped that the reader will remember the lover's former letter and the very unsatisfactory answer which had been sent to it. Nothing could have been colder, less propitious, or more inveterately hostile than the reply. As he lay in bed with his broken bones at Harrington he had ample time for thinking over all this. He knew every word of the Duke's distressing note by heart, and had often lashed himself to rage as he had repeated it. But he could effect nothing by showing his anger. He must go on and still do something. Since the writing of that letter he had done something. He had got his seat in Parliament. And he had secured the interest of his friend Silverbridge. This had been partially done at Polwenning; but the accident in the Brake country had completed the work. The brother had at last declared himself in his friend's favour. 'Of course I should be glad to see it,' he had said while sitting by Tregear's bedside. 'The worst is that everything does seem to go against the poor governor.'

Then Tregear made up his mind that he would write another letter. Personally he was not in the best condition for doing this as he was lying in bed with his left arm tied up, and with straps and bandages all round his body. But he could sit up in bed, and his right hand and arm were free. So he declared to Lady Chiltern his purpose of writing a letter. She tried to dissuade him gently and offered to be his secretary. But when he assured her that no secretary could write this letter for him she understood pretty well what would be the subject of the letter. With considerable difficulty Tregear wrote his letter.

'MY LORD DUKE,'—On this occasion he left out the epithet which he had before used—

'Your Grace's reply to my last letter was not encouraging, but in spite of your prohibition I venture to write to you again. If I had the slightest reason for thinking that your daughter was estranged from me, I would not persecute either you or her. But if it be true that she is as devoted to me as I am to her, can I be wrong in pleading my cause? Is it not evident to you that she is made of such stuff that she will not be controlled in her choice,—even by your will?

'I have had an accident in the hunting-field and am now writing from Lord Chiltern's house, where I am confined to bed. But I think you will understand me when I say that even in this helpless condition I feel myself constrained to do something. Of course I ask for nothing from you on my own behalf, —but on her behalf may I not add my prayers to hers?

'I have the honour to be,

'Your Grace's very faithful Servant,
'FRANCIS TREGEAR.'

This coming alone would perhaps have had no effect. The Duke had desired the young man not to address him again; and the young man had disobeyed him. No mere courtesy would now have constrained him to send any reply to this further letter. But coming as it did while his heart was still throbbing with the effects of Mrs. Finn's words, it was allowed to have a certain force. The argument used was a true argument. His girl was devoted to the man who sought her hand. Mrs. Finn had told him that sooner or later he must yield,—unless he was prepared to see his child wither and fade at his side. He had once thought that he would be prepared even for that. He had endeavoured to strengthen his own will by arguing with himself that when he saw a duty plainly before him, he should cleave to that let the results be what they might. But that picture of her face withered and wan after twenty years of sorrowing had had its effect upon his heart. He even made excuses within his own breast in the young man's favour. He was in Parliament now, and what may not be done for a young man in Parliament? Altogether the young man appeared to him in a light different from that through which he had viewed the presumptuous, arrogant, utterly unjustifiable suitor who had come to him, now nearly a year since, in Carlton Terrace.

He went to breakfast with Tregear's letter in his pocket, and was then gracious to Mrs. Finn, and tender to his daughter. 'When do you go, papa?' Mary asked.

'I shall take the 11.45 train. I have ordered the carriage at a quarter before eleven.'

'May I go to the train with you, papa?'

'Certainly; I shall be delighted.'

'Papa!' Mary said as soon as she found herself seated beside her father in the carriage.

'My dear.'

'Oh, papa!' and she threw herself on to his breast. He put his arm round her and kissed her,—as he would have had so much delight in doing, as he would have done so often before, had there not been this ground of discord. She was very sweet to him. It had never seemed to him that she had disgraced herself by loving Tregear—but that a great misfortune had fallen upon her. Silverbridge when he had gone into a racing partnership with Tifto, and Gerald when he had played for money which he did not possess, had—degraded themselves in his estimation. He would not have used such a word; but it was his feeling. They were less noble, less pure than they might have been, had they kept themselves free from such stain. But this girl,—whether she should live and fade by his side, or whether she should give her hand to some fitting noble suitor,—or even though she might at last become the wife of this man who loved her, would always have been pure. It was sweet to him to have something to caress. Now in the solitude of his life, as years were coming on him, he felt how necessary it was that he should have someone who would love him. Since his wife had left him he had been debarred from these caresses by the necessity of showing his antagonism to her dearest wishes. It had been his duty to be stern. In all his words to his daughter he had been governed by a conviction that he never ought to allow the duty of separating her from her lover to be absent from his mind. He was not prepared to acknowledge that that duty had ceased;—but yet there had crept over him a feeling that as he was half conquered, why should he not seek some recompense in his daughter's love?

'Papa,' she said, 'you do not hate me?'

'Hate you, my darling?'

'Because I am disobedient. Oh, papa, I cannot help it. He should not have come. He should not have been let to come.'

He had not a word to say to her. He could not as yet bring

himself to tell her,—that it should be as she desired. Much less could he now argue with her as to the impossibility of such a marriage as he had done on former occasions when the matter had been discussed. He could only press his arm tightly round her waist, and be silent. 'It cannot be altered now, papa. Look at me. Tell me that you love me.'

'Have you doubted my love?'

'No, papa,—but I would do anything to make you happy; anything that I could do. Papa, you do not want me to marry Lord Popplecourt?'

'I would not have you marry any man without loving him.'

'I never can love anybody else. That is what I wanted you to know, papa.'

To this he made no reply, nor was there anything else said upon the subject before the carriage drove up to the railway station. 'Do not get out, dear,' he said, seeing that her eyes had been filled with tears. 'It is not worth while. God bless you, my child! You will be up in London I hope in a fortnight, and we must try to make the house a little less dull for you.'

And so he had encountered the third attack.

Lady Mary, as she was driven home, recovered her spirits wonderfully. Not a word had fallen from her father which she could use hereafter as a refuge from her embarrassments. He had made her no promise. He had assented to nothing. But there had been something in his manner, in his gait, in his eye, in the pressure of his arm, which made her feel that her troubles would soon be at an end.

'I do love you so much,' she said to Mrs. Finn late on that afternoon.

'I am glad of that, dear.'

'I shall always love you,—because you have been on my side all through.'

'No, Mary;—that is not so.'

'I know it is so. Of course you have to be wise because you are older. And papa would not have you here with me if you were not wise. But I know you are on my side,—and papa knows it too. And someone else shall know it some day.'

CHAPTER LXVII
'He is such a beast'

LORD SILVERBRIDGE remained hunting in the Brake country till a few days before the meeting of Parliament, and had he been left to himself he would have had another week in the country and might probably have overstayed the opening day; but he had not been left to himself. In the last week in January an important despatch reached his hands, from no less important a person than Sir Timothy Beeswax, suggesting to him that he should undertake the duty of seconding the address in the House of Commons. When the proposition first reached him it made his hair stand on end. He had never yet risen to his feet in the House. He had spoken at those election meetings in Cornwall, and had found it easy enough. After the first or second time he had thought it good fun. But he knew that standing up in the House of Commons would be different from that. Then there would be the dress! 'I should so hate to fig myself out and look like a guy,' he said to Tregear, to whom of course he confided the offer that was made to him. Tregear was very anxious that he should accept it. 'A man should never refuse anything of that kind which comes in his way,' Tregear said.

'It is only because I am the governor's son,' Silverbridge pleaded.

'Partly so perhaps. But if it be altogether so, what of that? Take the goods the gods provide you. Of course all these things which our ambition covets are easier to Duke's sons than to others. But not on that account should a Duke's son refuse them. A man when he sees a rung vacant on the ladder should always put his feet there.'

'I'll tell you what,' said Silverbridge. 'If I thought this was all fair sailing I'd do it. I should feel certain that I should come a cropper, but still I'd try it. As you say, a fellow should try. But it's all meant as a blow at the governor. Old Beeswax thinks that if he can get me up to swear that he and his crew are real first-chop hands, that will hit the governor hard. It's as much as saying to the governor,—"This chap belongs to me, not to you." That's a thing I won't go in for.' Then Tregear counselled him to write to his father for advice, and at the same time to ask Sir Timothy to allow him a day or two for consideration. This counsel he took. His letter reached his father two days before he left Matching. In answer to it there came first a telegram begging Silverbridge to be in London on the Monday, and then a letter, in which the Duke expressed himself as being anxious to see his son before giving a final answer to the question. Thus it was that Silverbridge had been taken away from his hunting.

Isbael Boncassen, however, was now in London, and from her it was possible that he might find consolation. He had written to her soon after reaching Harrington, telling her that he had had it all out with the governor. 'There is a good deal that I can only tell you when I see you,' he said. Then he assured her with many lover's protestations that he was and always would be till death altogether her own most loving S. To this he had received an answer by return of post. She would be delighted to see him up in town,—as would her father and mother. They had now got a comfortable house in Brook Street. And then she signed herself his sincere friend, Isabel. Silverbridge thought that it was cold, and remembered certain scraps in another feminine handwriting in which more passion was expressed. Perhaps this was the way with American young ladies when they were in love.

'Yes,' said the Duke, 'I am glad that you have come up at once, as Sir Timothy should have his answer without further delay.'

'But what shall I say?'

The Duke, though he had already considered the matter very seriously, nevertheless took a few minutes to consider it again. 'The offer,' said he, 'must be acknowledged as very flattering.'

'But the circumstances are not usual.'

'It cannot often be the case that a minister should ask the

son of his keenest political oponent to render him such a service. But, however, we will put that aside.'

'Not quite, sir.'

'For the present we will put that on one side. Not looking at the party which you may be called upon to support, having for the moment no regard to this or that line in politics, there is no opening to the real duties of parliamentary life which I would sooner see accorded to you than this.'

'But if I were to break down?' Talking to his father he could not quite venture to ask what might happen if he were to 'come a cropper.'

'None but the brave deserve the fair,' said the Duke slapping his hands upon the table. 'Why, if we fail, "We fail!* But screw your courage to the sticking place, And we'll not fail." What high point would ever be reached if caution such as that were allowed to prevail? What young men have done before cannot you do? I have no doubt of your capacity. None.'

'Haven't you, sir?' said Silverbridge, considerably gratified,—and also surprised.

'None in the least. But, perhaps, some of your diligence.'

'I could learn it by heart, sir,—if you mean that.'

'But I don't mean that; or rather I mean much more than that. You have first to realise in your mind the thing to be said, and then the words in which you should say it, before you come to learning by heart.'

'Some of them I suppose would tell me what to say.'

'No doubt with your inexperience it would be unfit that you should be left entirely to yourself. But I would wish you to know,—perhaps I should say to feel,—that the sentiments to be expressed by you were just.'

'I should have to praise Sir Timothy.'

'Not that necessarily. But you would have to advocate that course in Parliament which Sir Timothy and his friends have taken and propose to take.'

'But I hate him like poison.'

'There need be no personal feeling in the matter. I remember that when I moved the address in your house Mr. Mildmay was Prime Minister,—a man for whom my regard and esteem were unbounded,—who had been in political matters the preceptor of my youth, whom as a patriotic statesman I almost worshipped, whom I now remember as a man whose departure from the arena of politics left the country very destitute. No one has sprung up since like to him,—or hardly second to him. But in speaking on so large a subject as the policy of a party, I thought it beneath me to eulogise a man. The same policy reversed may keep you silent respecting Sir Timothy.'

'I needn't of course say what I think about him.'

'I suppose you do agree with Sir Timothy as to his general policy? On no other condition can you undertake such a duty.'

'Of course I have voted with him.'

'So I have observed,—not so regularly perhaps as Mr. Roby would have desired.' Mr. Roby*was the Conservative whip.

'And I suppose the people at Silverbridge expect me to support him.'

'I hardly know how that may be. They used to be contented with my poor services. No doubt they feel they have changed for the better.'

'You shouldn't say that, sir.'

'I am bound to suppose that they think so, because when the matter was left in their own hands they at once elected a Conservative. You need not fear that you will offend them by seconding the address. They will probably feel proud to see their young member brought forward on such an occasion; as I shall be proud to see my son.'

'You would if it were on the other side, sir.'

'Yes, Silverbridge, yes; I should be very proud if it were on the other side. But there is a useful old adage which bids us not cry for spilt milk. You have a right to your opinions, though perhaps I may think that in adopting what I must call new opinions you were a little precipitate. We cannot act together in politics. But not the less on that account do I wish to see you take an active and useful part on that side to which you have attached yourself.' As he said this he rose from his seat and spoke with emphasis, as though he were addressing some imaginary Speaker or a house of legislators around. 'I shall be proud to hear you second the address. If you do it as gracefully and as fitly as I am sure you may if you will give yourself the trouble, I shall hear you do it with infinite satisfaction, even though I shall feel at the same time anxious to answer all your arguments and to disprove all your assertions. I should be listening no doubt to my opponent;—but I should be proud to feel that I was listening to my son. My advice to you is to do as Sir Timothy has asked you.'

'He is such a beast, sir,' said Silverbridge.

'Pray do not speak in that way on matters so serious.'

'I do not think you quite understand it, sir.'

'Perhaps not. Can you enlighten me?'

'I believe he has done this only to annoy you.'

The Duke, who had again seated himself, and was leaning back in his chair, raised himself up, placed his hands on the table before him, and looked his son hard in the face. The idea which Silverbridge had just expressed had certainly occurred to himself. He remembered well all the circumstances of the time when he and Sir Timothy Beeswax had been members of the same government;—and he remembered how animosities had grown, and how treacherous he had thought the man. From the moment in which he had read the minister's letter to the young member, he had felt that the offer had too probably come from a desire to make the political separation between himself and his son complete. But he had thought that in counselling his son he was bound to ignore such a feeling; and it certainly had not occurred to him that Silverbridge would be astute enough to perceive the same thing.

'What makes you fancy that?' said the Duke, striving to conceal by his manner, but not altogether successful in concealing, the gratification which he certainly felt.

'Well, sir, I am not sure that I can explain it. Of course it is putting you in a different boat from me.'

'You have already chosen your boat.'

534

'Perhaps he thinks I may get out again. I dislike the skipper so much, that I am not sure that I shall not.'

'Oh, Silverbridge,—that is such a fault! So much is included in that which is unstatesmanlike, unpatriotic, almost dishonest! Do you mean to say that you would be this or that in politics according to your personal liking for an individual?'

'When you don't trust the leader, you can't believe very firmly in the followers,' said Silverbridge doggedly. 'I won't say, sir, what I may do. Though I dare say that what I think is not of much account, I do think a good deal about it.'

'I am glad of that.'

'And as I think it not at all improbable that I may go back again, if you don't mind it, I will refuse.' Of course after that the Duke had no further arguments to use in favour of Sir Timothy's proposition.

CHAPTER LXVIII

Brook Street

SILVERBRIDGE had now a week on his hands which he felt he might devote to the lady of his love. It was a comfort to him that he need have nothing to do with the address. To have to go, day after day, to the Treasury in order that he might learn his lesson, would have been disagreeable to him. He did not quite know how the lesson would have been communicated, but fancied it would have come from 'Old Roby,' whom he did not love much better than Sir Timothy. Then the speech must have been composed, and afterwards submitted to someone,—probably to old Roby again, by whom no doubt it would be cut and slashed, and made quite a different speech than he had intended. If he had not praised Sir Timothy himself, Roby,—or whatever other tutor might have been assigned to him,—would have put the praise in. And then how many hours it would have taken to learn 'the horrid thing' by heart. He proudly felt that he had not been prompted by idleness to decline the task; but not the less was he glad to have shuffled the burden from off his shoulders.

Early the next morning he was in Brook Street, having sent a note to say he would call, and having even named the hour. And yet when he knocked at the door, he was told with the utmost indifference by a London footman, that Miss Boncassen was not at home,—also that Mrs. Boncassen was not at home;—also that Mr. Boncassen was not at home. When he asked at what hour Miss Boncassen was expected home, the man answered him, just as though he had been anybody else, that he knew nothing about it. He turned away in disgust, and had himself driven to the Beargarden. In his misery he had recourse to game-pie and a pint of champagne for his lunch. 'Halloa, old fellow, what is this I hear about you?' said Nidderdale, coming in and sitting opposite to him.

'I don't know what you have heard.'

'You are going to second the address. What made them pick you out from the lot of us?'

'It is just what I am not going to do.'

'I saw it all in the papers.'

'I dare say;—and yet it isn't true. I shouldn't wonder if they ask you.' At this moment a waiter handed a large official letter to Lord Nidderdale, saying that the messenger who had brought it was waiting for an answer in the hall. The letter bore the important signature of T. Beeswax on the corner of the envelope, and so disturbed Lord Nidderdale that he called at once for a glass of soda-and-brandy. When opened it was found to be very nearly a counterpart of that which Silverbridge had received down in the country. There was, however, added a little prayer that Lord Nidderdale would at once come down to the Treasury Chambers.

'They must be very hard up,' said Lord Nidderdale. 'But I shall do it. Cantrip is always at me to do something, and you see if I don't butter them up properly.' Then having fortified himself with game-pie and a glass of brown sherry he went away at once to the Treasury Chambers.

Silverbridge felt himself a little better after his lunch,—

better still when he had smoked a couple of cigarettes walking about the empty smoking-room. And as he walked he collected his thoughts. She could hardly have meant to slight him. No doubt her letter down to him at Harrington had been very cold. No doubt he had been ill-treated in being sent away so unceremoniously from the door. But yet she could hardly intend that everything between them should be over. Even an American girl could not be so unreasonable as that. He remembered the passionate way in which she had assured him of her love. All that could not have been forgotten! He had done nothing by which he could have forfeited her esteem. She had desired him to tell the whole affair to her father, and he had done so. Mr. Boncassen might perhaps have objected. It might be that this American was so prejudiced against English aristocrats as to desire no commerce with them. There were not many Englishmen who would not have welcomed him as son-in-law, but Americans might be different. Still,—still Isabel would hardly have shown her obedience to her father in this way. She was too independent to obey her father in a matter concerning her own heart. And if he had not been the possessor of her heart at that last interview, then she must have been false indeed! So he got once more into his hansom and had himself taken back to Brook Street.

Mrs. Boncassen was in the drawing-room alone.

'I am so sorry,' said the lady, 'but Mr. Boncassen has, I think, just gone out.'

'Indeed! and where is Isabel?'

'Isabel is downstairs,—that is if she hasn't gone out too. She did talk of going with her father to the Museum. She is getting quite bookish. She has got a ticket, and goes there, and has all the things brought to her just like the other learned folks.'

'I am anxious to see her, Mrs. Boncassen.'

'My! If she has gone out it will be a pity. She was only saying yesterday she wouldn't wonder if you shouldn't turn up.'

'Of course I've turned up, Mrs. Boncassen. I was here an hour ago.'

'Was it you who called and asked all them questions? My!
We couldn't make out who it was. The man said it was a
flurried young gentleman who wouldn't leave a card,—but
who wanted to see Mr. Boncassen most especial.'

'It was Isabel I wanted to see. Didn't I leave a card? No;
I don't think I did. I felt so—almost at home, that I didn't
think of a card.'

'That's very kind of you, Lord Silverbridge.'

'I hope you are going to be my friend, Mrs. Boncassen.'

'I am sure I don't know, Lord Silverbridge. Isabel is most
used to having her own way, I guess. I think when hearts are
joined almost nothing ought to stand between them. But Mr.
Boncassen does have doubts. He don't wish as Isabel should
force herself anywhere. But here she is, and now she can speak
for herself.' Whereupon not only did Isabel enter the room,
but at the same time Mrs. Boncassen most discreetly left it.
It must be confessed that American mothers are not afraid of
their daughters.

Silverbridge, when the door was closed, stood looking at
the girl for a moment and thought that she was more lovely

than ever. She was dressed for walking. She still had on her fur jacket, but had taken off her hat. 'I was in the parlour downstairs,' she said, 'when you came in, with papa; and we were going out together; but when I heard who was here, I made him go alone. Was I not good?'

He had not thought of a word to say, or a thing to do;—but he felt as he looked at her that the only thing in the world worth living for, was to have her for his own. For a moment he was half abashed. Then in the next she was close in his arms with his lips pressed to hers. He had been so sudden that she had been unable, at any rate thought that she had been unable, to repress him. 'Lord Silverbridge,' she said, 'I told you I would not have it. You have offended me.'

'Isabel!'

'Yes; Isabel! Isabel is offended with you. Why did you do it?'

Why did he do it? It seemed to him to be the most unnecessary question. 'I want you to know how I love you.'

'Will that tell me? That only tells me how little you think of me.'

'Then it tells you a falsehood;—for I am thinking of you always. And I always think of you as being the best and dearest and sweetest thing in the world. And now I think you dearer and sweeter than ever.' Upon this she tried to frown; but her frown at once broke out into a smile. 'When I wrote to say that I was coming why did you not stay at home for me this morning?'

'I got no letter, Lord Silverbridge.'

'Why didn't you get it?'

'That I cannot say, Lord Silverbridge.'

'Isabel, if you are so formal, you will kill me.'

'Lord Silverbridge, if you are so forward, you will offend me.' Then it turned out that no letter from him had reached the house; and as the letter had been addressed to Bruton Street*instead of Brook Street, the failure on the part of the post-office was not surprising.

Whether or no she were offended or he killed he remained

with her the whole of that afternoon. 'Of course I love you,' she said. 'Do you suppose I should be here with you if I did not, or that you could have remained in the house after what you did just now? I am not given to run into rhapsodies quite so much as you are,—and being a woman perhaps it is as well that I don't. But I think I can be quite as true to you as you are to me.'

'I am so much obliged to you for that,' he said, grasping at her hand.

'But I am sure that rhapsodies won't do any good. Now I'll tell you my mind.'

'You know mine,' said Silverbridge.

'I will take it for granted that I do. Your mind is to marry me will ye nill ye, as the people say.' He answered this by merely nodding his head and getting a little nearer to her. 'That is all very well in its way, and I am not going to say but what I am gratified.' Then he did grasp her hand. 'If it pleases you to hear me say so, Lord Silverbridge——'

'Not Lord!'

'Then I shall call you Plantagenet;—only it sounds so horribly historical. Why are you not Thomas or Abraham? But if it will please you to hear me say so, I am ready to acknowledge that nothing in all my life ever came near to the delight I have in your love.' Hereupon he almost succeeded in getting his arm round her waist. But she was strong, and seized his hand and held it. 'And I speak no rhapsodies. I tell you a truth which I want you to know and to keep in your heart,—so that you may be always, always sure of it.'

'I never will doubt it.'

'But that marrying will ye nill ye, will not suit me. There is so much wanted for happiness in life.'

'I will do all that I can.'

'Yes. Even though it be hazardous, I am willing to trust you. If you were as other men are, if you could do as you please as lower men may do, I would leave father and mother and my own country,—that I might be your wife. I would do that because I love you. But what will my life be here, if they

540

who are your friends turn their backs upon me? What will your life be, if, through all that, you continue to love me?'

'That will all come right.'

'And what will your life be, or mine,' she said, going on with her own thoughts without seeming to have heard his last words, 'if in such a condition as that you did not continue to love me?'

'I should always love you.'

'It might be very hard:—and if once felt to be hard, then impossible. You have not looked at it as I have done. Why should you? Even with a wife that was a trouble to you——'

'Oh, Isabel!'

His arm was now round her waist, but she continued speaking as though she were not aware of the embrace. 'Yes, a trouble! I shall not be always just what I am now. Now I can be bright and pretty and hold my own with others because I am so. But are you sure,—I am not,—that I am such stuff as an English lady should be made of? If in ten years' time you found that others did not think so,—that, worse again, you did not think so yourself, would you be true to me then?'

'I will always be true to you.'

She gently extricated herself, as though she had done so that she might better turn round and look into his face. 'Oh, my own one, who can say of himself that it would be so? How could it be so, when you would have all the world against you? You would still be what you are,—with a clog round your leg while at home. In Parliament, among your friends, at your clubs, you would be just what you are. You would be that Lord Silverbridge who had all good things at his disposal,—except that he had been unfortunate in his marriage! But what should I be?' Though she paused he could not answer her,—not yet. There was a solemnity in her speech which made it necessary that he should hear her to the end. 'I, too, have my friends in my own country. It is no disgrace to me there that my grandfather worked on the quays. No one holds her head higher than I do, or is more sure of being able to hold it. I have there that assurance of esteem and honour which you have here. I would lose it all to do you a good. But I will not lose it to do you an injury.'

'I don't know about injuries,' he said, getting up and walking about the room. 'But I am sure of this. You will have to be my wife.'

'If your father will take me by the hand and say that I shall be his daughter, I will risk all the rest. Even then it might not be wise; but we love each other too well not to run some peril. Do you think that I want anything better than to preside in your home, to soften your cares, to welcome your joys, to be the mother perhaps of your children, and to know that you are proud that I should be so? No, my darling. I can see a Paradise;—only, only, I may not be fit to enter it. I must use some judgment better than my own, sounder, dear, than yours. Tell the Duke what I say;—tell him with what language a son may use to his father. And remember that all you ask for yourself you will ask doubly for me.'

'I will ask him so that he cannot refuse me.'

'If you do I shall be contented. And now go. I have said ever so much, and I am tired.'

'Isabel! Oh, my love!'

'Yes; Isabel;—your love! I am that at any rate for the present,—and proud to be so as a queen. Well, if it must be, this once,—as I have been so hard to you.' Then she gave him her cheek to kiss, but of course he took more than she gave.

When he got out into the street it was dark and there was still standing the faithful cab. But he felt that at the present moment it would be impossible to sit still, and he dismissed the equipage. He walked rapidly along Brook Street into Park Lane, and from thence to the park, hardly knowing whither he went in the enthusiasm of the moment. He walked back to the Marble Arch, and thence round by the drive to the Guard House and the bridge over the Serpentine, by the Knightsbridge Barracks to Hyde Park Corner. Though he should give up everything and go and live in her own country with her, he would marry her. His politics, his hunting, his address to the Queen, his horses, his guns, his father's wealth, and his own rank,—what were they all to Isabel Boncassen? In meeting her he had met the one human being in all the world who could really be anything to him either in friendship or in love. When she had told him what she would do for him to make his home happy, it had seemed to him that all other delights must fade away from him for ever. How odious were Tifto and his racehorses, how unmeaning the noise of his club, how terrible the tedium of those parliamentary benches! He could not tell his love as she had told hers! He acknowledged to himself that his words could not be as her words,—nor his intellect as hers. But his heart could be as true. She had spoken to him of his name, his rank, and all his outside world around him. He would make her understand at last that they were nothing to him in comparison with her. When he had got round to Hyde Park Corner, he felt that he was almost compelled to go back again to Brook Street. In no other place could there be anything to interest him;—nowhere else could there be light, or warmth, or joy! But what would she think of him? To go back hot, and soiled with mud, in order that he might say one more adieu,—that possibly he might ravish one more kiss,—would hardly be manly. He must postpone all that for the morrow. On the morrow of course he would be there.

But his work was all before him! That prayer had to be made to his father; or rather some wonderful effort of eloquence must be made by which his father might be convinced that this girl was so infinitely superior to anything of feminine creation that had ever hitherto been seen or heard of, that all ideas as to birth, country, rank, or name ought in this instance to count for nothing. He did believe himself that he had found such a pearl, that no question of setting need be taken into consideration. If the Duke would not see it the fault would be in the Duke's eyes, or perhaps in his own words,—but certainly not in the pearl.

Then he compared her to poor Lady Mabel, and in doing so did arrive at something near the truth in his inward delineation of the two characters. Lady Mabel with all her grace, with all her beauty, with all her talent, was a creature of efforts, or, as it might be called, a manufactured article. She strove to be graceful, to be lovely, to be agreeable and clever. Isabel was all this and infinitely more without any struggle. When he was most fond of Mabel, most anxious to make her his wife, there had always been present to him a feeling that she was old. Though he knew her age to a day,—and knew her to be younger than himself, yet she was old. Something had gone of her native bloom, something had been scratched and chipped from the first fair surface, and this had been repaired by varnish and veneering. Though he had loved her he had never been altogether satisfied with her. But Isabel was as young as Hebe. He knew nothing of her actual years, but he did know that to have seemed younger, or to have seemed older,—to have seemed in any way different from what she was,—would have been to be less perfect.

CHAPTER LXIX
'Pert Poppet!'

O N a Sunday morning,—while Lord Silverbridge was alone in a certain apartment in the house in Carlton Terrace which was called his own sitting-room, the name was brought him of a gentleman who was anxious to see him. He had seen his father and had used all the eloquence of which he was master,—but not quite with the effect which he had desired. His father had been very kind, but he, too, had been eloquent; —and had, as is often the case with orators, been apparently more moved by his own words than by those of his adversary. If he had not absolutely declared himself as irrevocably hostile to Miss Boncassen he had not said a word that might be supposed to give token of assent.

Silverbridge, therefore, was moody, contemplative, and desirous of solitude. Nothing that the Duke had said had shaken him. He was still sure of his pearl, and quite determined that he would wear it. Various thoughts were running through his brain. What if he were to abdicate the title and become a republican? He was inclined to think that he could not abdicate, but he was quite sure that no one could prevent him from going to America and calling himself Mr. Palliser. That his father would forgive him and accept the daughter-in-law brought to him, were he in the first place to marry without sanction, he felt quite sure. What was there that his father would not forgive? But then Isabel would not assent to this. He was turning it all in his head and ever and anon trying to relieve his mind by 'Clarissa,'*which he was reading in conformity with his father's advice, when the gentleman's card was put into his hand. 'Whatever does he want here?' he said to himself; and then he ordered that the gentleman might be shown up. The gentleman in question was our old friend Dolly Longstaff. Dolly Longstaff and Silverbridge had been intimate as young men are. But they were not friends, nor, as far as Silverbridge knew, had Dolly ever set his foot in that house before. 'Well, Dolly,' said he, 'what's the matter now?'

'I suppose you are surprised to see me?'

'I didn't think that you were ever up so early.' It was at this time almost noon.

'Oh, come now, that's nonsense. I can get up as early as anybody else. I have changed all that for the last four months. I was at breakfast this morning very soon after ten.'

'What a miracle! Is there anything I can do for you?'

'Well yes,—there is. Of course you are surprised to see me?'

'You never were here before; and therefore it is odd.'

'It is odd; I felt that myself. And when I tell you what I have come about you will think it more odd. I know I can trust you with a secret.'

'That depends, Dolly.'

'What I mean is, I know you are good-natured. There are ever so many fellows that are one's most intimate friends, that would say anything on earth they could that was ill-natured.'

'I hope they are not my friends.'

'Oh yes, they are. Think of Glasslough, or Popplecourt, or Hindes! If they knew anything about you that you didn't want

545

to have known,—about a young lady or anything of that kind,
—don't you think they'd tell everybody?'

'A man can't tell anything he doesn't know.'

'That's true. I had thought of that myself. But then there's
a particular reason for my telling you this. It is about a young
lady! You won't tell; will you?'

'No, I won't. But I can't see why on earth you should come
to me. You are ever so many years older than I am.'

'I had thought of that too. But you are just the person I
must tell. I want you to help me.'

These last words were said in a whisper, and Dolly as he
said them had drawn nearer to his friend. Silverbridge remained in suspense, saying nothing by way of encouragement.
Dolly, either in love with his own mystery or doubtful of his
own purpose, sat still, looking eagerly at his companion.
'What the mischief is it?' asked Silverbridge impatiently.

'I have quite made up my own mind.'

'That's a good thing at any rate.'

'I am not what you would have called a marrying sort of
man.'

'I should have said,—no. But I suppose most men do marry
sooner or later.'

'That's just what I said to myself. It has to be done, you
know. There are three different properties coming to me. At
least one has come already.'

'You're a lucky fellow.'

'I've made up my mind; and when I say a thing I mean to
do it.'

'But what can I do?'

'That's just what I'm coming to. If a man does marry I
think he ought to be attached to her.' To this, as a broad
proposition, Silverbridge was ready to accede. But, regarding
Dolly as a middle-aged sort of fellow, one of those men who
marry because it is convenient to have a house kept for them,
he simply nodded his head. 'I am awfully attached to her,'
Dolly went on to say.

'That's all right.'

'Of course there are fellows who marry girls for their money. I've known men who have married their grand-mothers.'

'Not really!'

'That kind of thing. When a woman is old it does not much matter who she is. But my one! She's not old!'

'Nor rich?'

'Well; I don't know about that. But I'm not after her money. Pray understand that. It's because I'm downright fond of her. She's an American.'

'A what!' said Silverbridge, startled.

'You know her. That's the reason I've come to you. It's Miss Boncassen.' A dark frown came across the young man's face. That all this should be said to him was disgusting. That an owl like that should dare to talk of loving Miss Boncassen was offensive to him.

'It's because you know her that I've come to you. She thinks that you're after her.' Dolly as he said this lifted himself quickly up in his seat, and nodded his head mysteriously as he looked into his companion's face. It was as much as though he should say, 'I see you are surprised, but so it is.' Then he went on. 'She does, the pert poppet!' This was almost too much for Silverbridge; but still he contained himself. 'She won't look at me because she has got it into her head that perhaps some day she may be Duchess of Omnium! That of course is out of the question.'

'Upon my word all this seems to me to be so very—very, —distasteful that I think you had better say nothing more about it.'

'It is distasteful,' said Dolly; 'but the truth is I am so downright,—what you may call enamoured——'

'Don't talk such stuff as that here,' said Silverbridge, jumping up. 'I won't have it.'

'But I am. There is nothing I wouldn't do to get her. Of course it's a good match for her. I've got three separate properties; and when the governor goes off I shall have a clear fifteen thousand a year.'

'Oh, bother!'

'Of course that's nothing to you, but it is a very tidy income for a commoner. And how is she to do better?'

'I don't know how she could do much worse,' said Silver-bridge in a transport of rage. Then he pulled his moustache in vexation, angry with himself that he should have allowed himself to say even a word on so preposterous a supposition. Isabel Boncassen and Dolly Longstaff! It was Titania and Bottom over again. It was absolutely necessary that he should get rid of this intruder, and he began to be afraid that he could not do this without using language which would be uncivil. 'Upon my word,' he said, 'I think you had better not talk about it any more. The young lady is one for whom I have a very great respect.'

'I mean to marry her,' said Dolly, thinking thus to vindicate himself.

'You might as well think of marrying one of the stars.'

'One of the stars!'

'Or a royal princess!'

'Well! Perhaps that is your opinion, but I can't say that I agree with you. I don't see why she shouldn't take me. I can give her a position which you may call A1 out of the Peerage. I can bring her into society. I can make an English lady of her.'

'You can't make anything of her,—except to insult her,— and me too by talking of her.'

'I don't quite understand this,' said the unfortunate lover, getting up from his seat. 'Very likely she won't have me. Perhaps she has told you so.'

'She never mentioned your name to me in her life. I don't suppose she remembers your existence.'

'But I say that there can be no insult in such a one as me asking such a one as her to be my wife. To say that she doesn't remember my existence is absurd.'

'Why should I be troubled with all this?'

'Because I think you're making a fool of her, and because I'm honest. That's why,' said Dolly with much energy. There

548

was something in this which partly reconciled Silverbridge to his despised rival. There was a touch of truth about the man, though he was so utterly mistaken in his ideas. 'I want you to give over in order that I may try again. I don't think you ought to keep a girl from her promotion, merely for the fun of a flirtation. Perhaps you're fond of her;—but you won't marry her. I am fond of her, and I shall.'

After a minute's pause Silverbridge resolved that he would be magnanimous. 'Miss Boncassen is going to be my wife,' he said.

'Your wife!'

'Yes;—my wife. And now I think you will see that nothing further can be said about this matter.'

'Duchess of Omnium!'

'She will be Lady Silverbridge.'

'Oh; of course she'll be that first. Then I've got nothing further to say. I'm not going to enter myself to run against you. Only I shouldn't have believed it if anybody else had told me.'

'Such is my good fortune.'

'Oh ah,—yes; of course. That is one way of looking at it. Well; Silverbridge, I'll tell you what I shall do; I shall hook it.'

'No; no, not you.'

'Yes, I shall. I dare say you won't believe me, but I've got such a feeling about me here'—as he said this he laid his hand upon his heart,—'that if I stayed I should go in for hard drinking. I shall take the great Asiatic tour.*I know a fellow that wants to go, but he hasn't got any money. I dare say I shall be off before the end of next month. You don't know any fellow that would buy half-a-dozen hunters; do you?' Silverbridge shook his head. 'Good-bye,' said Dolly in a melancholy tone; 'I am sure I am very much obliged to you for telling me. If I'd known you'd meant it, I shouldn't have meddled, of course. Duchess of Omnium!'

'Look here, Dolly, I have told you what I should not have told any one, but I wanted to screen the young lady's name.'

'It was so kind of you.'

'Do not repeat it. It is a kind of thing that ladies are particular about. They choose their own time for letting everybody know.' Then Dolly promised to be as mute as a fish, and took his departure.

Silverbridge had felt, towards the end of the interview, that he had been arrogant to the unfortunate man,—particularly in saying that the young lady would not remember the existence of such a suitor,—and had also recognised a certain honesty in the man's purpose, which had not been the less honest because it was so absurd. Actuated by the consciousness of this, he had swallowed his anger, and had told the whole truth. Nevertheless things had been said which were horrible to him. This buffoon of a man had called his Isabel a—pert poppet! How was he to get over the remembrance of such an offence? And then the wretch had declared that he was—enamoured! There was sacrilege in the term when applied by such a man to Isabel Boncassen. He had thoughts of days to come, when everything would be settled, when he might sit close to her, and call her pretty names,—when he might in sweet familiarity tell her that she was a little Yankee and a fierce republican, and 'chaff' her about the stars and stripes; and then, as he pictured the scene to himself in his imagination, she would lean upon him and would give him back his chaff, and would call him an aristocrat and would laugh at his titles. As he thought of all this he would be proud with the feeling that such privileges would be his own. And now this wretched man had called her a pert poppet!

There was a sanctity about her,—a divinity which made it almost a profanity to have talked about her at all to such a one as Dolly Longstaff. She was his Holy of Holies, at which vulgar eyes should not even be allowed to gaze. It had been a most unfortunate interview. But this was clear; that, as he had announced his engagement to such a one as Dolly Longstaff, the matter now would admit of no delay. He would explain to his father that as tidings of the engagement had got abroad, honour to the young lady would compel him to come forward

openly as her suitor at once. If this argument might serve
him, then perhaps this intrusion would not have been altogether a misfortune.

CHAPTER LXX
'Love may be a great misfortune'

SILVERBRIDGE when he reached Brook Street that day was
surprised to find that a large party was going to lunch
there. Isabel had asked him to come, and he had thought her
the dearest girl in the world for doing so. But now his gratitude for that favour was considerably abated. He did not care
just now for the honour of eating his lunch in the presence of
Mr. Gotobed,*the American minister, whom he found there
already in the drawing-room with Mrs. Gotobed, nor with
Ezekiel Sevenkings,*the great American poet from the far
West, who sat silent and stared at him in an unpleasant way.
When Sir Timothy Beeswax was announced, with Lady Beeswax and her daughter, his gratification certainly was not
increased. And the last comer,—who did not arrive indeed
till they were all seated at the table,—almost made him start
from his chair and take his departure suddenly. That last
comer was no other than Mr. Adolphus Longstaff. As it happened he was seated next to Dolly, with Lady Beeswax on
the other side of him. Whereas his Holy of Holies was on the
other side of Dolly! The arrangement made seemed to him
to have been monstrous. He had endeavoured to get next to
Isabel; but she had so manœuvred that there should be a
vacant chair between them. He had not much regarded this
because a vacant chair may be pushed on one side. But before
he had made all his calculations Dolly Longstaff was sitting
there! He almost thought that Dolly winked at him in triumph,
—that very Dolly who an hour ago had promised to take
himself off upon his Asiatic travels!

Sir Timothy and the minister kept up the conversation very
much between them, Sir Timothy flattering everything that
was American, and the minister finding fault with very many

things that were English. Now and then Mr. Boncassen would put in a word to soften the severe honesty of his countryman, or to correct the euphemistic falsehoods of Sir Timothy. The poet seemed always to be biding his time. Dolly ventured to whisper a word to his neighbour. It was but to say that the frost had broken up. But Silverbridge heard it and looked daggers at everyone. Then Lady Beeswax expressed to him a hope that he was going to do great things in Parliament this session. 'I don't mean to go near the place,' he said, not at all conveying any purpose to which he had really come, but driven by the stress of the moment to say something that should express his general hatred of everybody. Mr. Lupton was there, on the other side of Isabel, and was soon engaged with her in a pleasant familiar conversation. Then Silverbridge remembered that he had always thought Lupton to be a most conceited prig. Nobody gave himself so many airs, or was so careful as to the dyeing of his whiskers. It was astonishing that Isabel should allow herself to be amused by such an antiquated coxcomb. When they had finished eating they moved about and changed their places, Mr. Boncassen being rather anxious to stop the flood of American eloquence which came from his friend Mr. Gotobed. British viands had become subject to his criticism, and Mr. Gotobed had declared to Mr. Lupton that he didn't believe that London could produce a dish of squash or tomatoes. He was quite sure you couldn't have sweet corn. Then there had been a moving of seats in which the minister was shuffled off to Lady Beeswax, and the poet found himself by the side of Isabel. 'Do you not regret our mountains and our prairies,' said the poet; 'our great waters and our green savannahs?' 'I think more perhaps of Fifth Avenue,' said Miss Boncassen. Silverbridge, who at this moment was being interrogated by Sir Timothy, heard every word of it.

'I was so sorry, Lord Silverbridge,' said Sir Timothy, 'that you could not accede to our little request.'

'I did not quite see my way,' said Silverbridge, with his eye upon Isabel.

'So I understood, but I hope that things will make themselves clearer to you shortly. There is nothing that I desire so much as the support of young men such as yourself,—the very cream, I may say, of the whole country. It is to the young conservative thoughtfulness and the truly British spirit of our springing aristocracy that I look for that reaction which I am sure will at last carry us safely over the rocks and shoals of communistic propensities.'

'I shouldn't wonder if it did,' said Silverbridge. They didn't think that he was going to remain down there talking politics to an old humbug like Sir Timothy when the sun, and moon, and all the stars had gone up into the drawing-room! For at that moment Isabel was making her way to the door.

But Sir Timothy had buttonholed him. 'Of course it is late now to say anything further about the address. We have arranged that. Not quite as I would have wished, for I had set my heart upon initiating you into the rapturous pleasure of parliamentary debate. But I hope that a good time is coming. And pray remember this, Lord Silverbridge;—there is no member sitting on our side of the House, and I need hardly say on the other, whom I would go farther to oblige than your father's son.'

'I'm sure that's very kind,' said Silverbridge, absolutely using a little force as he disengaged himself. Then he at once followed the ladies upstairs, passing the poet on the stairs. 'You have hardly spoken to me,' he whispered to Isabel. He knew that to whisper to her now, with the eyes of many upon him, with the ears of many open, was an absurdity; but he could not refrain himself.

'There are so many to be,—entertained, as people say! I don't think I ought to have to entertain you,' she answered, laughing. No one heard her but Silverbridge, yet she did not seem to whisper. She left him, however, at once, and was soon engaged in conversation with Sir Timothy.

A convivial lunch I hold to be altogether bad, but the worst of its many evils is that vacillating mind which does not know when to take its owner off. Silverbridge was on this occasion quite determined not to take himself off at all. As it was only a lunch the people must go, and then he would be left with Isabel. But the vacillation of the others was distressing to him. Mr. Lupton went, and poor Dolly got away apparently without a word. But the Beeswaxes and the Gotobeds would not go, and the poet sat staring immovably. In the meanwhile Silverbridge endeavoured to make the time pass lightly by talking to Mrs. Boncassen. He had been so determined to accept Isabel with all her adjuncts that he had come almost to like Mrs. Boncassen, and would certainly have taken her part violently had any one spoken ill of her in his presence.

Then suddenly he found that the room was nearly empty. The Beeswaxes and the Gotobeds were gone; and at last the poet himself, with a final glare of admiration at Isabel, had taken his departure. When Silverbridge looked round, Isabel also was gone. Then too Mrs. Boncassen had left the room suddenly. At the same instant Mr. Boncassen entered by another door, and the two men were alone together. 'My dear Lord Silverbridge,' said the father, 'I want to have a few words with you.' Of course there was nothing for him but to submit. 'You remember what you said to me down at Matching?'

'Oh yes; I remember that.'

'You did me the great honour of expressing a wish to make my child your wife.'

'I was asking for a very great favour.'

'That also;—for there is no greater favour I could do to any man than to give him my daughter. Nevertheless, you were doing me a great honour,—and you did it, as you do everything, with an honest grace that went far to win my heart. I am not at all surprised, sir, that you should have won hers.' The young man as he heard this could only blush and look foolish. 'If I know my girl, neither your money nor your title would go for anything.'

'I think much more of her love, Mr. Boncassen, than I do of anything else in the world.'

'But love, my Lord, may be a great misfortune.' As he said this the tone of his voice was altered, and there was a melancholy solemnity not only in his words but in his countenance. 'I take it that young people when they love rarely think of more than the present moment. If they did so the bloom would be gone from their romance. But others have to do this for them. If Isabel had come to me saying that she loved a poor man, there would not have been much to disquiet me. A poor man may earn bread for himself and his wife, and if he failed I could have found them bread. Nor, had she loved somewhat below her own degree, should I have opposed her. So long as her husband had been an educated man, there might have been no future punishment to fear.'

'I don't think she could have done that,' said Silverbridge.

'At any rate she has not done so. But how am I to look upon this that she has done?'

'I'll do my best for her, Mr. Boncassen.'

'I believe you would. But even your love can't make her an Englishwoman. You can make her a Duchess.'

'Not that, sir.'

'But you can't give her a parentage fit for a Duchess;—not fit at least in the opinion of those with whom you will pass your life, with whom,—or perhaps without whom,—she will be destined to pass her life, if she becomes your wife! Unfortunately it does not suffice that you should think it fit. Though you loved each other as well as any man and woman that ever were brought into each other's arms by the beneficence of God, you cannot make her happy.—unless you can assure her the respect of those around her.'

'All the world will respect her.'

'Her conduct,—yes. I think the world, your world, would learn to do that. I do not think it could help itself. But that would not suffice. I may respect the man who cleans my boots. But he would be a wretched man if he were thrown on me for society. I would not give him my society. Will your Duchesses and your Countesses give her theirs?'

'Certainly they will.'

555

'I do not ask for it as thinking it to be of more value than that of others; but were she to become your wife she would be so abnormally placed as to require it for her comfort. She would have become a lady of high rank,—not because she loves rank, but because she loves you.'

'Yes, yes, yes,' said Silverbridge, hardly himself knowing why he became impetuous.

'But having removed herself into that position, being as she would be, a Countess, or a Duchess, or what not, how could she be happy if she were excluded from the community of Countesses and Duchesses?'

'They are not like that,' said Silverbridge.

'I will not say that they are, but I do not know. Having Anglican*tendencies, I have been wont to contradict my countrymen when they have told me of the narrow exclusiveness of your nobles. Having found your nobles and your commoners all alike in their courtesy,—which is a cold word; in their hospitable friendships,—I would now not only contradict, but would laugh to scorn any such charge,'—so far he spoke somewhat loudly, and then dropped his voice as he concluded,—'were it anything less than the happiness of my child that is in question.'

'What am I to say, sir? I only know this; I am not going to lose her.'

'You are a fine fellow. I was going to say that I wished you were an American, so that Isabel need not lose you. But, my boy, I have told you that I do not know how it might be. Of all whom you know, who could best tell me the truth on such a subject? Who is there whose age will have given him experience, whose rank will have made him familiar with this matter, who from friendship to you would be least likely to decide against your wishes, who from his own native honesty would be most sure to tell the truth?'

'You mean my father,' said Silverbridge.

'I do mean your father. Happily he has taken no dislike to the girl herself. I have seen enough of him to feel sure that he is devoted to his own children.'

556

'Indeed he is.'

'A just and a liberal man;—one I should say not carried away by prejudices! Well,—my girl and I have just put our heads together, and we have come to a conclusion. If the Duke of Omnium will tell us that she would be safe as your wife,—safe from the contempt of those around her,—you shall have her. And I shall rejoice to give her to you,—not because you are Lord Silverbridge, not because of your rank and wealth; but because you are—that individual human being whom I now hold by the hand.'

When the American had come to an end, Silverbridge was too much moved to make any immediate answer. He had an idea in his own mind that the appeal was not altogether fair. His father was a just man,—just, affectionate, and liberal. But then it will so often happen that fathers do not want their sons to marry those very girls on whom the sons have set their hearts. He could only say that he would speak to his father again on the subject. 'Let him tell me that he is contented,' said Mr. Boncassen, 'and I will tell him that I am contented. Now, my friend, good-bye.' Silverbridge begged that he might be allowed to see Isabel before he was turned out; but Isabel had left the house in company with her mother.

CHAPTER LXXI
'What am I to say, Sir?'

WHEN Silverbridge left Mr. Boncassen's house he was resolved to go to his father without an hour's delay, and represent to the Duke exactly how the case stood. He would be urgent, piteous, submissive, and eloquent. In any other matter he would promise to make whatever arrangements his father might desire. He would make his father understand that all his happiness depended on this marriage. When once married he would settle down, even at Gatherum Castle if the Duke should wish it. He would not think of race-horses, he would desert the Beargarden, he would learn blue-books by heart, and only do as much shooting and hunting as would become a young nobleman in his position. All this he would say as eagerly and as pleasantly as it might be said. But he would add to all this an assurance of his unchangeable intention. It was his purpose to marry Isabel Boncassen. If he could do this with his father's good will,—so best. But at any rate he would marry her!

The world at this time was altogether busy with political rumours; and it was supposed that Sir Timothy Beeswax would do something very clever. It was supposed also that he would sever himself from some of his present companions. On that point everybody was agreed,—and on that point only everybody was right. Lord Drummond, who was the titular Prime Minister, and Sir Timothy, had, during a considerable part of the last session, and through the whole vacation, so belarded each other with praise in all their public expressions that it was quite manifest that they had quarrelled. When any body of statesmen make public asseverations by one or various voices, that there is no discord among them, not a dissentient voice on any subject, people are apt to suppose that they cannot hang together much longer. It is the man who has no peace at home that declares abroad that his wife is an angel. He who lives on comfortable terms with the partner of his troubles can afford to acknowledge the ordinary rubs of life. Old Mr. Mildmay,* who was Prime Minister for so many years, and whom his party worshipped, used to say that he had never found a gentleman who had quite agreed with him all round; but Sir Timothy has always been in exact accord with all his colleagues,—till he has left them, or they him. Never had there been such concord as of late,—and men, clubs, and newspapers now protested that as a natural consequence there would soon be a break-up.

But not on that account would it perhaps be necessary that Sir Timothy should resign,—or not necessary that his resignation should be permanent. The Conservative majority had dwindled,—but still there was a majority. It certainly was the

case that Lord Drummond could not get on without Sir
Timothy. But might it not be possible that Sir Timothy should
get on without Lord Drummond? If so he must begin his
action in this direction by resigning. He would have to place
his resignation, no doubt with infinite regret, in the hands of
Lord Drummond. But if such a step were to be taken now,
just as Parliament was about to assemble, what would become
of the Queen's speech, of the address, and of the noble peers
and noble and other commoners who were to propose and
second it in the two Houses of Parliament? There were those
who said that such a trick played at the last moment would
be very shabby. But then again there were those who foresaw
that the shabbiness would be made to rest anywhere rather
than on the shoulders of Sir Timothy. If it should turn out
that he had striven manfully to make things run smoothly;—
that the Premier's incompetence, or the Chancellor's obstinacy, or this or that Secretary's peculiarity of temper had done
it all;—might not Sir Timothy then be able to emerge from
the confused flood, and swim along pleasantly with his head
higher than ever above the waters?

In these great matters parliamentary management goes for
so much! If a man be really clever and handy at his trade, if he
can work hard and knows what he is about, if he can give and
take and be not thin-skinned or sore-bored, if he can ask
pardon for a peccadillo and seem to be sorry with a good
grace, if above all things he be able to surround himself with
the prestige of success, then so much will be forgiven him!
Great gifts of eloquence are hardly wanted, or a deep-seated
patriotism which is capable of strong indignation. A party has
to be managed, and he who can manage it best, will probably
be its best leader. The subordinate task of legislation and of
executive government may well fall into the inferior hands
of less astute practitioners. It was admitted on both sides that
there was no man like Sir Timothy for managing the House
or coercing a party, and there was therefore a general feeling
that it would be a pity that Sir Timothy should be squeezed out.
He knew all the little secrets of the business;—could arrange,

let the cause be what it might, to get a full House for himself and his friends, and empty benches for his opponents,—could foresee a thousand little things to which even a Walpole would have been blind, which a Pitt would not have condescended to regard, but with which his familiarity made him a very comfortable leader of the House of Commons. There were various ideas prevalent as to the politics of the coming session; but the prevailing idea was in favour of Sir Timothy.

The Duke was at Longroyston, the seat of his old political ally the Duke of St. Bungay, and had been absent from Sunday the 6th till the morning of Friday the 11th, on which day Parliament was to meet. On that morning at about noon a letter came to the son saying that his father had returned and would be glad to see him. Silverbridge was going to the House on that day and was not without his own political anxieties. If Lord Drummond remained in, he thought that he must, for the present, stand by the party which he had adopted. If, however, Sir Timothy should become Prime Minister there would be a loophole for escape. There were some three or four besides himself who detested Sir Timothy, and in such case he might perhaps have company in his desertion. All this was on his mind; but through all this he was aware that there was a matter of much deeper moment which required his energies. When his father's message was brought to him he told himself at once that now was the time for his eloquence.

'Well, Silverbridge,' said the Duke, 'how are matters going on with you?' There seemed to be something in his father's manner more than ordinarily jocund and good-humoured.

'With me, sir?'

'I don't mean to ask any party secrets. If you and Sir Timothy understand each other, of course you will be discreet.'

'I can't be discreet, sir, because I don't know anything about him.'

'When I heard,' said the Duke smiling, 'of your being in close conference with Sir Timothy——'

'I, sir?'

'Yes, you. Mr. Boncassen told me that you and he were so deeply taken up with each other at his house, that nobody could get a word with either of you.'

'Have you seen Mr. Boncassen?' asked the son, whose attention was immediately diverted from his father's political badinage.

'Yes;—I have seen him. I happened to meet him where I was dining last Sunday, and he walked home with me. He was so intent upon what he was saying that I fear he allowed me to take him out of his way.'

'What was he talking about?' said Silverbridge. All his preparations, all his eloquence, all his method, now seemed to have departed from him.

'He was talking about you,' said the Duke.

'He had told me that he wanted to see you. What did he say, sir?'

'I suppose you can guess what he said. He wished to know what I thought of the offer you have made to his daughter.'

The great subject had come up so easily, so readily, that he was almost aghast when he found himself in the middle of it. And yet he must speak of the matter, and that at once.

'I hope you raised no objection, sir,' he said.

'The objection came mainly from him; and I am bound to say that every word that fell from him was spoken with wisdom.'

'But still he asked you to consent.'

'By no means. He told me his opinion,—and then he asked me a question.'

'I am sure he did not say that we ought not to be married.'

'He did say that he thought you ought not to be married, if——'

'If what, sir?'

'If there were probability that his daughter would not be well received as your wife. Then he asked me what would be my reception of her.' Silverbridge looked up into his father's face with beseeching imploring eyes as though everything now depended on the next few words that he might utter. 'I shall think it an unwise marriage,' continued the Duke. Silverbridge when he heard this at once knew that he had gained his cause. His father had spoken of the marriage as a thing that was to happen. A joyous light dawned in his eyes, and the look of pain went from his brow, all which the Duke was not slow to perceive. 'I shall think it an unwise marriage,' he continued, repeating his words; 'but I was bound to tell him that were Miss Boncassen to become your wife she would also become my daughter.'

'Oh, sir.'

'I told him why the marriage would be distasteful to me. Whether I may be wrong or right I think it to be for the good of our country, for the good of our order, for the good of our individual families, that we should support each other by marriage. It is not as though we were a narrow class, already too closely bound together by family alliances. The room for choice might be wide enough for you without going across the Atlantic to look for her who is to be the mother of your

562

children. To this Mr. Boncassen replied that he was to look solely to his daughter's happiness. He meant me to understand that he cared nothing for my feelings. Why should he? That which to me is deep wisdom is to him an empty prejudice. He asked me then how others would receive her.'

'I am sure that everybody would like her,' said Silverbridge. 'I like her. I like her very much.'

'I am so glad.'

'But still all this is a sorrow to me. When however he put that question to me about the world around her,—as to those among whom her lot would be cast, I could not say that I thought she would be rejected.'

'Oh no!' The idea of rejecting Isabel!

'She has a brightness and a grace all her own,' continued the Duke, 'which will ensure her acceptance in all societies.'

'Yes, yes;—it is just that, sir.'

'You will be a nine days' wonder,—the foolish young nobleman who chose to marry an American.'

'I think it will be just the other way up, sir,—among the men.'

'But her place will I think be secure to her. That is what I told Mr. Boncassen.'

'It is all right with him then,—now?'

'If you call it all right. You will understand of course that you are acting in opposition to my advice,—and my wishes.'

'What am I to say, sir?' exclaimed Silverbridge, almost in despair. 'When I love the girl better than my life, and when you tell me that she can be mine if I choose to take her; when I have asked her to be my wife, and have got her to say that she likes me; when her father has given way, and all the rest of it, would it be possible that I should say now that I will give her up?'

'My opinion is to go for nothing,—in anything!' The Duke as he said this knew that he was expressing aloud a feeling which should have been restrained within his own bosom. It was natural that there should have been such plaints. The same suffering must be encountered in regard to Tregear and his daughter. In every way he had been thwarted. In every direction he was driven to yield. And yet now he had to undergo rebuke from his own son, because one of those inward plaints would force itself from his lips! Of course this girl was to be taken in among the Pallisers and treated with an idolatrous love,—as perfect as though 'all the blood of all the Howards'*were running in her veins. What further inch of ground was there for a fight? And if the fight were over, why should he rob his boy of one sparkle from off the joy of his triumph? Silverbridge was now standing before him abashed by that plaint, inwardly sustained no doubt by the conviction of his great success, but subdued by his father's wailing. 'However, —perhaps we had better let that pass,' said the Duke, with a long sigh. Then Silverbridge took his father's hand, and looked up in his face. 'I most sincerely hope that she may make you a good and loving wife,' said the Duke, 'and that she may do her duty by you in that not easy sphere of life to which she will be called.'

'I am quite sure she will,' said Silverbridge, whose ideas as to Isabel's duties were confined at present to a feeling that she would now have to give him kisses without stint.

'What I have seen of her personally recommends her to me,' said the Duke. 'Some girls are fools——'

'That's quite true, sir.'

'Who think that the world is to be nothing but dancing, and going to parties.'

'Many have been doing it for so many years,' said Silverbridge, 'that they can't understand that there should be an end of it.'

'A wife ought to feel the great responsibility of her position. I hope she will.'

'And the sooner she begins the better,' said Silverbridge stoutly.

'And now,' said the Duke, looking at his watch, 'we might as well have lunch and go down to the House. I will walk with you if you please. It will be about time for each of us.' Then the son was forced to go down and witness the somewhat faded ceremony of seeing Parliament opened by three Lords sitting in commission before the throne. Whereas but for such stress as his father had laid upon him, he would have disregarded his parliamentary duties and have rushed at once up to Brook Street. As it was he was so handed over from one political pundit to another, was so buttonholed by Sir Timothy, so chaffed as to the address by Phineas Finn, and at last so occupied with the whole matter that he was compelled to sit in his place till he had heard Nidderdale make his speech. This the young Scotch Lord did so well, and received so much praise for the doing of it, and looked so well in his uniform, that Silverbridge almost regretted the opportunity he had lost. At seven the sitting was over, the speeches, though full of interest, having been shorter than usual. They had been full of interest, but nobody understood in the least what was going to happen. 'I don't know anything about the Prime Minister,' said Mr. Lupton as he left the House with our hero and another not very staunch supporter of the Government, 'but I'll back Sir Timothy to be the Leader of the House on the last day of the session, against all comers. I don't think it much matters who is Prime Minister nowadays.'

At half-past seven Silverbridge was at the door in Brook Street. Yes; Miss Boncassen was at home. The servant thought that she was upstairs dressing. Then Silverbridge made his way without further invitation into the drawing-room. There he remained alone for ten minutes. At last the door opened, and Mrs. Boncassen entered. 'Dear! Lord Silver-bridge, who ever dreamed of seeing you? I thought all you Parliament gentlemen were going through your ceremonies. Isabel had a ticket and went down, and saw your father.'

'Where is Isabel?'

'She's gone.'

'Gone! Where on earth has she gone to?' asked Silver-bridge, as though fearing lest she had been carried off to the other side of the Atlantic. Then Mrs. Boncassen explained. Within the last three minutes Mrs. Montacute Jones had called and carried Isabel off to the play. Mrs. Jones was up in town for a week, and this had been a very old engagement. 'I hope you did not want her very particularly,' said Mrs. Boncassen.

'But I did,—most particularly,' said Lord Silverbridge. The door was opened and Mr. Boncassen entered the room. 'I beg your pardon for coming at such a time,' said the lover, 'but I did so want to see Isabel.'

'I rather think she wants to see you,' said the father.

'I shall go to the theatre after her.'

'That might be awkward,—particularly as I doubt whether anybody knows what theatre they are gone to. Can I receive a message for her, my lord?' This was certainly not what Lord Silverbridge had intended. 'You know, perhaps, that I have seen the Duke.'

'Oh yes;—and I have seen him. Everything is settled.'

'That is the only message she will want to hear when she comes home. She is a happy girl and I am proud to think that I should live to call such a grand young Briton as you my son-in-law.' Then the American took the young man's two hands and shook them cordially, while Mrs. Boncassen bursting into tears insisted on kissing him.

'Indeed she is a happy girl,' said she; 'but I hope Isabel won't be carried away too high and mighty.'

CHAPTER LXXII
Carlton Terrace

THREE days after this it was arranged that Isabel should be taken to Carlton Terrace to be accepted there into the full good graces of her future father-in-law, and to go through the pleasant ceremony of seeing the house in which it was to be her destiny to live as mistress. What can be more interesting to a girl than this first visit to her future home? And now Isabel Boncassen was to make her first visit to the house in Carlton Terrace, which the Duke had already declared his purpose of surrendering to the young couple. She was going among very grand things,—so grand that those whose affairs in life are less magnificent may think that her mind should have soared altogether above chairs and tables, and reposed itself among diamonds, gold and silver ornaments, rich necklaces, the old masters, and alabaster statuary. But Dukes and Duchesses must sit upon chairs,—or at any rate on sofas,— as well as their poorer brethren, and probably have the same regard for their comfort. Isabel was not above her future furniture, or the rooms that were to be her rooms, or the stairs which she would have to tread, or the pillow on which her head must rest. She had never yet seen even the outside of the house in which she was to live, and was now prepared to make her visit with as much enthusiasm as though her future abode was to be prepared for her in a small house in a small street beyond Islington.*

But the Duke was no doubt more than the house, the father-in-law more than the tables. Isabel, in the ordinary way of society, he had already known almost with intimacy. She, the while, had been well aware that if all things could possibly be made to run smoothly with her, this lordly host, who was so pleasantly courteous to her, would become her father-in-law. But she had known also that he, in his courtesy, had been altogether unaware of any such intention on her part, and that she would now present herself to him in an aspect very different from that in which she had hitherto been regarded. She was well aware that the Duke had not wished to take her into his family,—would not himself have chosen her for his son's wife. She had seen enough to make her sure that he had even chosen another bride for his heir. She had been too clever not to perceive that Lady Mabel Grex had been not only selected,—but almost accepted as though the thing had been certain. She had learned nearly the whole truth from Silverbridge, who was not good at keeping a secret from one to whom his heart was open. That story had been all but read by her with exactness. 'I cannot lose you now,' she had said to him, leaning on his arm;—'I cannot afford to lose you now. But I fear that someone else is losing you.'

567

To this he answered nothing, but simply pressed her closer to his side. 'Someone else,' she continued, 'who perhaps may have reason to think that you have injured her.' 'No,' he said boldly; 'no; there is no such person.' For he had never ceased to assure himself that in all that matter with Mabel Grex he had been guilty of no treachery. There had been a moment, indeed, in which she might have taken him; but she had chosen to let it pass from her. All of which, or nearly all of which,—Isabel now saw, and had seen also that the Duke had been a consenting party to that other arrangement. She had reason therefore to doubt the manner of her acceptance.

But she had been accepted. She had made such acceptance by him a stipulation in her acceptance of his son. She was sure of the ground on which she trod and was determined to carry herself, if not with pride, yet with dignity. There might be difficulties before her, but it should not be her fault if she were not as good a Countess, and,—when time would have it so,—as good a Duchess as another.

The visit was made not quite in the fashion in which Silverbridge himself had wished. His idea had been to call for Isabel in his cab and take her down to Carlton Terrace. 'Mother must go with me,' she had said. Then he looked blank,—as he could look when he was disappointed, as he had looked when she would not talk to him at the lunch, when she told him that it was not her business to entertain him. 'Don't be selfish,' she added, laughing. 'Do you think that mother will not want to have seen the house that I am to live in?'

'She shall come afterwards as often as she likes.'

'What,—paying me morning visits from New York! She must come now, if you please. Love me, love my mother.'

'I am awfully fond of her,' said Silverbridge, who felt that he really had behaved well to the old lady.

'So am I,—and therefore she shall go and see the house now. You are as good as gold,—and do everything just as I tell you. But a good time is coming, when I shall have to do everything that you tell me.' Then it was arranged that Mrs. and Miss Boncassen were to be taken down to the house in their own carriage, and were to be received at the door by Lord Silverbridge.

Another arrangement had also been made. Isabel was to be taken to the Duke immediately upon her arrival and to be left for awhile with him, alone, so that he might express himself as he might find fit to do to this newly-adopted child. It was a matter to him of such importance that nothing remaining to him in his life could equal it. It was not simply that she was to be the wife of his son,—though that in itself was a consideration very sacred. Had it been Gerald who was bringing to him a bride, the occasion would have had less of awe. But this girl, this American girl, was to be the mother and grandmother of future Dukes of Omnium,—the ancestress, it was to be hoped, of all future Dukes of Omnium! By what she might be, by what she might have in her of mental fibre, of high or low quality, of true or untrue womanliness, were to be fashioned those who in days to come might be amongst the strongest and most faithful bulwarks of the constitution. An England without a Duke of Omnium,—or at any rate without any Duke,—what would it be? And yet he knew that with bad Dukes his country would be in worse stress than though she had none at all. An aristocracy;—yes; but an aristocracy that shall be of the very best! He believed himself thoroughly in his order; but if his order, or many of his order, should become as was now Lord Grex, then, he thought, that his order not only must go to the wall but that, in the cause of humanity, it had better do so. With all this daily, hourly, always in his mind, this matter of the choice of a wife for his heir was to him of solemn importance.

When they arrived Silverbridge was there and led them first of all into the dining-room. 'My!' said Mrs. Boncassen, as she looked around her. 'I thought that our Fifth Avenue parlours whipped everything in the way of city houses.'

'What a nice little room for Darby and Joan*to sit down to eat a mutton-chop in,' said Isabel.

'It's a beastly great barrack,' said Silverbridge;—'but the best of it is that we never use it. We'll have a cosy little place for Darby and Joan;—you'll see. Now come to the governor. I've got to leave you with him.'

'Oh me! I am in such a fright.'

'He can't eat you,' said Mrs. Boncassen.

'And he won't even bite,' said Silverbridge.

'I should not mind that because I could bite again. But if he looks as though he thought I shouldn't do, I shall drop.'

'My belief is that he's almost as much in love with you as I am,' said Silverbridge, as he took her to the door of the Duke's room. 'Here we are, sir.'

'My dear,' said the Duke, rising up and coming to her, 'I am very glad to see you. It is good of you to come to me.' Then he took her in both his hands and kissed her forehead and her lips. She, as she put her face up to him, stood quite still in his embrace, but her eyes were bright with pleasure.

'Shall I leave her?' said Silverbridge.

'For a few minutes.'

'Don't keep her too long, for I want to take her all over the house.'

'A few minutes,—and then I will bring her up to the drawing-room.' Upon this the door was closed, and Isabel was alone with her new father. 'And so, my dear, you are to be my child.'

'If you will have me.'

'Come here and sit down by me. Your father has already told you that;—has he not?'

'He has told me that you had consented.'

'And Silverbridge has said as much?'

'I would sooner hear it from you than from either of them.'

'Then hear it from me. You shall be my child. And if you will love me you shall be very dear to me. You shall be my own child,—as dear as my own. I must either love his wife very dearly, or else I must be an unhappy man. And she must love me dearly, or I must be unhappy.'

'I will love you,' she said, pressing his hand.

570

'And now let me say some few words to you, only let there be no bitterness in them to your young heart. When I say that I take you to my heart, you may be sure that I do so thoroughly. You shall be as dear to me and as near as though you had been all English.'

'Shall I?'

'There shall no difference be made. My boy's wife shall be my daughter in very deed. But I had not wished it to be so.'

'I knew that;—but could I have given him up?'

'He at any rate could not give you up. There were little prejudices;—you can understand that.'

'Oh yes.'

'We who wear black coats could not bring ourselves readily to put on scarlet garments; nor should we sit comfortably with our legs crossed like Turks.'

'I am your scarlet coat and your cross-legged Turk,' she said, with feigned self-reproach in her voice, but with a sparkle of mirth in her eye.

'But when I have once got into my scarlet coat I can be very proud of it, and when I am once seated in my divan I shall find it of all postures the easiest. Do you understand me?'

'I think so.'

'Not a shade of any prejudice shall be left to darken my mind. There shall be no feeling but that you are in truth his chosen wife. After all neither can country, nor race, nor rank, nor wealth, make a good woman. Education can do much. But nature must have done much also.'

'Do not expect too much of me.'

'I will so expect that all shall be taken for the best. You know, I think, that I have liked you since I first saw you.'

'I know that you have always been good to me.'

'I have liked you from the first. That you are lovely perhaps is no merit; though, to speak the truth, I am well pleased that Silverbridge should have found so much beauty.'

'That is all a matter of taste, I suppose,' she said, laughing.

'But there is much that a young woman may do for herself which I think you have done. A silly girl, though she had been a second Helen, would hardly have satisfied me.'

'Or perhaps him,' said Isabel.

'Or him; and it is in that feeling that I find my chief satisfaction,—that he should have had the sense to have liked such a one as you better than others. Now I have said it. As not being one of us I did at first object to his choice. As being what you are yourself, I am altogether reconciled to it. Do not keep him long waiting.'

'I do not think he likes to be kept waiting for anything.'

'I dare say not. I dare say not. And now there is one thing else.' Then the Duke unlocked a little drawer that was close to his hand, and taking out a ring put it on her finger. It was a bar of diamonds, perhaps a dozen of them, fixed in a little circlet of gold. 'This must never leave you,' he said.

'It never shall,—having come from you.'

'It was the first present that I gave to my wife, and it is the first that I give to you. You may imagine how sacred it is to me. On no other hand could it be worn without something which to me would be akin to sacrilege. Now I must not keep you longer or Silverbridge will be storming about the house. He of course will tell me when it is to be; but do not you keep him long waiting.' Then he kissed her and led her up into the drawing-room. When he had spoken a word of greeting to Mrs. Boncassen, he left them to their own devices.

After that they spent the best part of an hour in going over the house; but even that was done in a manner unsatisfactory to Silverbridge. Wherever Isabel went, there Mrs. Boncassen went also. There might have been some fun in showing even the back kitchens to his bride-elect, by herself;—but there was none in wandering about those vast underground regions with a stout lady who was really interested with the cooking apparatus and the wash-houses. The bedrooms one after another became tedious to him when Mrs. Boncassen would make communications respecting each of them to her daughter. 'That is Gerald's room,' said Silverbridge. 'You have never seen Gérald. He is such a brick.' Mrs. Boncassen was charmed with the whips and sticks and boxing-gloves in Gerald's room, and expressed an opinion that young men in the States mostly carried their knick-knacks about with them to the Universities. When she was told that he had another collection of 'knick-knacks' at Matching, and another at Oxford, she thought that he was a very extravagant young man. Isabel, who had heard all about the gambling in Scotland, looked round at her lover and smiled.

'Well, my dear,' said Mrs. Boncassen, as they took their leave, 'it is a very grand house, and I hope with all my heart you may have your health there and be happy. But I don't know that you'll be any happier because it's so big.'

'Wait till you see Gatherum,' said Silverbridge. 'That, I own, does make me unhappy. It has been calculated that three months at Gatherum Castle would drive a philosopher mad.'

In all this there had been a certain amount of disappointment for Silverbridge; but on that evening, before dinner in Brook Street, he received compensation. As the day was one somewhat peculiar in its nature he decided that it should be kept altogether as a holiday, and he did not therefore go down to the House. And not going to the House of course he spent the time with the Boncassens. 'You know you ought to go,' Isabel said to him when they found themselves alone together in the back drawing-room.

'Of course I ought.'

'Then go. Do you think I would keep a Briton from his duties?'

'Not though the constitution should fall in ruins. Do you suppose that a man wants no rest after inspecting all the pots and pans in that establishment? A woman, I believe, could go on doing that kind of thing all day long.'

'You should remember at least that the—woman was interesting herself about your pots and pans.'

'And now, Bella, tell me what the governor said to you.' Then she showed him the ring. 'Did he give you that?' She nodded her head in assent. 'I did not think he would ever have parted with that.'

'It was your mother's.'

'She wore it always. I almost think that I never saw her hand without it. He would not have given you that unless he had meant to be very good to you.'

'He was very good to me. Silverbridge, I have a great deal to do, to learn to be your wife.'

'I'll teach you.'

'Yes; you'll teach me. But will you teach me right? There is something almost awful in your father's serious dignity and solemn appreciation of the responsibilities of his position. Will you ever come to that?'

'I shall never be a great man as he is.'

'It seems to me that life to him is a load;—which he does not object to carry, but which he knows must be carried with a great struggle.'

'I suppose it ought to be so with everyone.'

'Yes,' she said, 'but the higher you put your foot on the ladder the more constant should be your thought that your stepping requires care. I fear that I am climbing too high.'

'You can't come down now, my young woman.'

'I have to go on now,—and do it as best I can. I will try to do my best. I will try to do my best. I told him so, and now I tell you so. I will try to do my best.'

'Perhaps after all I am only a "pert poppet",' she said half an hour afterwards, for Silverbridge had told her of that terrible mistake made by poor Dolly Longstaff.

'Brute!' he exclaimed.

'Not at all. And when we are settled down in the real Darby-and-Joan way I shall hope to see Mr. Longstaff very often. I daresay he won't call me a pert poppet, and I shall not remind him of the word. But I shall always think of it; and remembering the way in which my character struck an educated Englishman,—who was not altogether ill-disposed towards me,—I may hope to improve myself.'

CHAPTER LXXIII

'*I have never loved you*'

SILVERBRIDGE had now been in town three or four weeks, and Lady Mabel Grex had also been in London all that time, and yet he had not seen her. She had told him that she loved him and had asked him plainly to make her his wife. He had told her that he could not do so,—that he was altogether resolved to make another woman his wife. Then she had rebuked him, and had demanded from him how he had dared to treat her as he had done. His conscience was clear. He had his own code of morals as to such matters, and had, as he regarded it, kept within the law. But she thought that she was badly treated, and had declared that she was now left out in the cold for ever through his treachery. Then her last word had been almost the worst of all, 'Who can tell what may come to pass?'—showing too plainly that she would not even now give up her hope. Before the month was up she wrote to him as follows:

'DEAR LORD SILVERBRIDGE,

'Why do you not come and see me? Are friends so plentiful with you that one so staunch as I may be thrown over? But of course I know why you do not come. Put all that aside,— and come. I cannot hurt you. I have learned to feel that certain things which the world regards as too awful to be talked of,— except in the way of scandal, may be discussed and then laid aside just like other subjects. What though I wear a wig or a wooden leg, I may still be fairly comfortable among my companions unless I crucify myself by trying to hide my misfortune. It is not the presence of the skeleton that crushes us. Not even that will hurt us much if we let him go about the house as he lists. It is the everlasting effort which the horror makes to peep out of his cupboard that robs us of our ease. At any rate come and see me.

'Of course I know that you are to be married to Miss Boncassen. Who does not know it? The trumpeters have been at
work for the last week.

'Your very sincere friend,

'MABEL.'

He wished that she had not written. Of course he must go
to her. And though there was a word or two in her letter
which angered him, his feelings towards her were kindly.
Had not that American angel flown across the Atlantic to his
arms he could have been well content to make her his wife.
But the interview at the present moment could hardly be
other than painful. She could, she said, talk of her own misfortunes, but the subject would be very painful to him. It was
not to him a skeleton, to be locked out of sight; but it had been
a misfortune, and the sooner that such misfortunes could be
forgotten the better.

He knew what she meant about trumpeters. She had intended to signify that Isabel in her pride had boasted of her
matrimonial prospects. Of course there had been trumpets.
Are there not always trumpets when a marriage is contemplated, magnificent enough to be called an alliance? As for
that he himself had blown the trumpets. He had told everybody that he was going to be married to Miss Boncassen.
Isabel had blown no trumpets. In her own straightforward
way she had told the truth to whom it concerned. Of course
he would go and see Lady Mabel, but he trusted that for her
own sake nothing would be said about trumpets.

'So you have come at last,' Mabel said when he entered the
room. 'No;—Miss Cassewary is not here. As I wanted to see
you alone I got her to go out this morning. Why did you not
come before?'

'You said in your letter that you knew why.'

'But in saying so I was accusing you of cowardice;—was
I not?'

'It was not cowardice.'

'Why then did you not come?'

'I thought you would hardly wish to see me so soon,—after what passed.'

'That is honest at any rate. You felt that I must be too much ashamed of what I said to be able to look you in the face.'

'Not that exactly.'

'Any other man would have felt the same, but no other man would be honest enough to tell me so. I do not think that ever in your life you have constrained yourself to the civility of a lie.'

'I hope not.'

'To be civil and false is often better than to be harsh and true. I may be soothed by the courtesy and yet not deceived by the lie. But what I told you in my letter,—which I hope you have destroyed——'

'I will destroy it.'

'Do. It was not intended for the partner of your future joys. As I told you then, I can talk freely. Why not? We know it, —both of us. How your conscience may be I cannot tell; but mine is clear from that soil with which you think it should be smirched.'

'I think nothing of the sort.'

'Yes, Silverbridge, you do. You have said to yourself this; —That girl has determined to get me, and she has not scrupled as to how she would do it.'

'No such idea has ever crossed my mind.'

'But you have never told yourself of the encouragement which you gave me. Such condemnation as I have spoken of would have been just if my efforts had been sanctioned by no words, no looks, no deeds from you. Did you give me warrant for thinking that you were my lover?'

That theory by which he had justified himself to himself seemed to fall away from him under her questioning. He could not now remember his words to her in those old days before Miss Boncassen had crossed his path; but he did know that he had once intended to make her understand that he loved her. She had not understood him;—or, understanding, had not

accepted his words; and therefore he had thought himself free.
But it now seemed that he had not been entitled so to regard
himself. There she sat, looking at him, waiting for his answer;
and he who had been so sure that he had committed no sin
against her, had not a word to say to her.

'I want your answer to that, Lord Silverbridge. I have told
you that I would have no skeleton in the cupboard. Down at
Matching, and before that at Killancodlem, I appealed to you,
asking you to take me as your wife.'

'Hardly that.'

'Altogether that! I will have nothing denied that I have
done,—nor will I be ashamed of anything. I did do so,—even
after this infatuation. I thought then that one so volatile might
perhaps fly back again.'

'I shall not do that,' said he, frowning at her.

'You need trouble yourself with no assurance, my friend.
Let us understand each other now. I am not now supposing
that you can fly back again. You have found your perch, and
you must settle on it like a good domestic barn-door fowl.'
Again he scowled. If she were too hard upon him he would
certainly turn upon her. 'No; you will not fly back again
now;—but was I, or was I not, justified when you came to
Killancodlem in thinking that my lover had come there?'

'How can I tell? It is my own justification I am thinking of.'

'I see all that. But we cannot both be justified. Did you mean
me to suppose that you were speaking to me words in earnest
when there,—sitting in that very spot,—you spoke to me of
your love.'

'Did I speak of my love?'

'Did you speak of your love! And now, Silverbridge,—for
if there be an English gentleman on earth I think that you are
one,—as a gentleman tell me this. Did you not even tell your
father that I should be your wife? I know you did.'

'Did he tell you?'

'Men such as you and he, who cannot even lie with your
eyelids, who will not condescend to cover up a secret by a
moment of feigned inanimation, have many voices. He did

tell me; but he broke no confidence. He told me, but did not mean to tell me. Now you also have told me.'

'I did. I told him so. And then I changed my mind.'

'I know you changed your mind. Men often do. A pinker pink, a whiter white,—a finger that will press you just half an ounce the closer,—a cheek that will consent to let itself come just a little nearer——!'

'No; no; no!' It was because Isabel had not easily consented to such approaches!

'Trifles such as these will do it;—and some such trifles have done it with you. It would be beneath me to make comparisons where I might seem to be the gainer. I grant her beauty. She is very lovely. She has succeeded.'

'I have succeeded.'

'But—I am justified, and you are condemned. Is it not so? Tell me like a man.'

'You are justified.'

'And you are condemned? When you told me that I should be your wife, and then told your father the same story, was I to think it all meant nothing! Have you deceived me?'

'I did not mean it.'

'Have you deceived me? What; you cannot deny it, and yet have not the manliness to own it to a poor woman who can only save herself from humiliation by extorting the truth from you!'

'Oh, Mabel, I am so sorry it should be so.'

'I believe you are,—with a sorrow that will last till she is again sitting close to you. Nor, Silverbridge, do I wish it to be longer. No;—no;—no. Your fault after all has not been great. You deceived, but did not mean to deceive me?'

'Never; never.'

'And I fancy you have never known how much you bore about with you. Your modesty has been so perfect that you have not thought of yourself as more than other men. You have forgotten that you have had in your hand the disposal to some one woman of a throne in Paradise.'

'I don't suppose you thought of that.'

'But I did. Why should I tell falsehoods now? I have determined that you should know everything,—but I could better confess to you my own sins when I had shown that you too have not been innocent. Not think of it! Do not men think of high titles and great wealth and power and place? And if men, why should not women? Do not men try to get them;— and are they not even applauded for their energy? A woman has but one way to try. I tried.'

'I do not think it was all for that.'

'How shall I answer that without a confession which even I am not hardened enough to make? In truth, Silverbridge, I have never loved you.'

He drew himself up slowly before he answered her, and gradually assumed a look very different from that easy boyish smile which was customary to him. 'I am glad of that,' he said.

'Why are you glad?'

'Now I can have no regrets.'

'You need have none. It was necessary to me that I should have my little triumph;—that I should show you that I knew how far you had wronged me! But now I wish that you should know everything. I have never loved you.'

'There is an end of it then.'

'But I have liked you so well,—so much better than all others! A dozen men have asked me to marry them. And though they might be nothing till they made that request, then they became—things of horror to me. But you were not a thing of horror. I could have become your wife, and I think that I could have learned to love you.'

'It is best as it is.'

'I ought to say so too; but I have a doubt I should have liked to be Duchess of Omnium, and perhaps I might have fitted the place better than one who can as yet know but little of its duties or its privileges. I may, perhaps, think that that other arrangement would have been better even for you.'

'I can take care of myself in that.'

'I should have married you without loving you, but I should have done so determined to serve you with a devotion which a woman who does love hardly thinks necessary. I would have so done my duty that you should never have guessed that my heart had been in the keeping of another man.'

'Another man!'

'Yes; of course. If there had been no other man, why not you? Am I so hard, do you think that I can love no one? Are you not such a one that a girl would naturally love,—were she not preoccupied? That a woman should love seems as necessary as that a man should not.'

'A man can love too.'

'No;—hardly. He can admire, and he can like, and he can fondle and be fond. He can admire, and approve, and perhaps worship. He can know of a woman that she is part of himself, the most sacred part, and therefore will protect her from the very winds. But all that will not make love. It does not come to a man that to be separated from a woman is to be dislocated from his very self. A man has but one centre, and that is himself. A woman has two. Though the second may never be seen by her, may live in the arms of another, may do all for that other that man can do for woman,—still, still, though he be half the globe asunder from her, still he is to her the half of her existence. If she really love, there is, I fancy, no end of it. To the end of time I shall love Frank Tregear.'

'Tregear!'

'Who else?'

'He is engaged to Mary.'

'Of course he is. Why not;—to her or whomsoever else he might like best? He is as true I doubt not to your sister as you are to your American beauty,—or as you would have been to me had fancy held. He used to love me.'

'You were always friends.'

'Always;—dear friends. And he would have loved me if a man were capable of loving. But he could sever himself from me easily, just when he was told to do so. I thought that I could do the same. But I cannot. A jackal is born a jackal, and not a lion, and cannot help himself. So is a woman born— a woman. They are clinging, parasite things, which cannot but adhere; though they destroy themselves by adhering. Do not suppose that I take a pride in it. I would give one of my eyes to be able to disregard him.'

'Time will do it.'

'Yes; time,—that brings wrinkles and rouge-pots and rheumatism. Though I have so hated those men as to be unable to endure them, still I want some man's house, and his name,—some man's bread and wine,—some man's jewels and titles and woods and parks and gardens,—if I can get them. Time can help a man in his sorrow. If he begins at forty to make speeches, or to win races, or to breed oxen, he can yet live a prosperous life. Time is but a poor consoler for a young woman who has to be married.'

'Oh, Mabel.'

'And now let there be not a word more about it. I know—that I can trust you.'

'Indeed you may.'

'Though you will tell her everything else you will not tell her this.'

'No;—not this.'

'And surely you will not tell your sister!'

'I shall tell no one.'

'It is because you are so true that I have dared to trust you. I had to justify myself,—and then to confess. Had I at that one moment taken you at your word, you would never have known anything of all this. "There is a tide in the affairs of men——!"*But I let the flood go by! I shall not see you again now before you are married; but come to me afterwards.'

CHAPTER LXXIV
'Let us drink a glass of wine together'

SILVERBRIDGE pondered it all much as he went home. What a terrible story was that he had heard! The horror to him was chiefly in this,—that she should yet be driven to marry some man without even fancying that she could love him! And this was Lady Mabel Grex, who, on his own first entrance into London life, now not much more than twelve months ago, had seemed to him to stand above all other girls in beauty, charm, and popularity!

As he opened the door of the house with his latch-key, who should be coming out but Frank Tregear,—Frank Tregear with his arm in a sling, but still with an unmistakable look of general satisfaction. 'When on earth did you come up?' asked Silverbridge. Tregear told him that he had arrived on the previous evening from Harrington. 'And why? The doctor would not have let you come if he could have helped it.'

'When he found he could not help it, he did let me come. I am nearly all right. If I had been nearly all wrong I should have had to come.'

'And what are you doing here?'

'Well; if you'll allow me I'll go back with you for a moment. What do you think I have been doing?'

'Have you seen my sister?'

'Yes, I have seen your sister. And I have done better than that. I have seen your father. Lord Silverbridge,—behold your brother-in-law.'

'You don't mean to say that it is arranged?'

'I do.'

'What did he say?'

'He made me understand by most unanswerable arguments, that I had no business to think of such a thing. I did not fight the point with him,—but simply stood there, as conclusive evidence of my business. He told me that we should have nothing to live on unless he gave us an income. I assured him that I would never ask him for a shilling. "But I cannot allow her to marry a man without an income," he said.'

'I know his way so well.'

'I had just two facts to go upon,—that I would not give her up, and that she would not give me up. When I pointed that out he tore his hair,—in a mild way, and said that he did not understand that kind of thing at all.'

'And yet he gave way.'

'Of course he did. They say that when a king of old would consent to see a petitioner for his life, he was bound by his royalty to mercy. So it was with the Duke. Then, very early in the argument, he forgot himself, and called her—Mary. I knew he had thrown up the sponge then.'

'How did he give way at last?'

'He asked me what were my ideas about life in general. I said that I thought Parliament was a good sort of thing, that I was lucky enough to have a seat, and that I should take lodgings somewhere in Westminster till——. "Till what?" he asked. "Till something is settled," I replied. Then he turned away from me and remained silent. "May I see Lady Mary?" I asked. "Yes; you may see her," he replied, as he rang the bell. Then when the servant was gone he stopped me. "I love her too dearly to see her grieve," he said. "I hope you will show that you can be worthy of her." Then I made some sort of protestation and went upstairs. While I was with Mary there came a message to me, telling me to come to dinner.'

'The Boncassens are all dining here.'

'Then we shall be a family party. So far I suppose I may say it is settled. When he will let us marry heaven only knows. Mary declares that she will not press him. I certainly cannot do so. It is all a matter of money.'

'He won't care about that.'

'But he may perhaps think that a little patience will do us good. You will have to soften him.' Then Silverbridge told all that he knew about himself. He was to be married in May, was to go to Matching for a week or two after his wedding, was then to see the Session to an end, and after that to travel with his wife in the United States. 'I don't suppose we shall be allowed to run about the world together so soon as that,' said Tregear, 'but I am too well satisfied with my day's work to complain.'

'Did he say what he meant to give her?'

'Oh dear no;—nor even that he meant to give her anything. I should not dream of asking a question about it. Nor when

584

he makes any proposition shall I think of having any opinion of my own.'

'He'll make it all right;—for her sake, you know.'

'My chief object as regards him, is that he should not think that I have been looking after her money. Well; good-bye. I suppose we shall all meet at dinner?'

When Tregear left him, Silverbridge went to his father's room. He was anxious that they should understand each other as to Mary's engagement.

'I thought you were at the House,' said the Duke.

'I was going there, but I met Tregear at the door. He tells me you have accepted him for Mary.'

'I wish that he had never seen her. Do you think that a man can be thwarted in everything and not feel it?'

'I thought—you had reconciled yourself—to Isabel.'

'If it were that alone I could do so the more easily, because personally she wins upon me. And this man, too;—it is not that I find fault with himself.'

'He is in all respects a high-minded gentleman.'

'I hope so. But yet, had he a right to set his heart there, where he could make his fortune,—having none of his own?'

'He did not think of that.'

'He should have thought of it. A man does not allow himself to love without any consideration or purpose. You say that he is a gentleman. A gentleman should not look to live on means brought to him by a wife. You say that he did not.'

'He did not think of it.'

'A gentleman should do more than not think of it. He should think that it shall not be so. A man should own his means or should earn them.'

'How many men, sir, do neither?'

'Yes; I know,' said the Duke. 'Such a doctrine nowadays is caviare to the general.*One must live as others live around one, I suppose. I could not see her suffer. It was too much for me. When I became convinced that this was no temporary passion, no romantic love which time might banish, that she was of such a temperament that she could not change,—then

I had to give way. Gerald, I suppose, will bring me some kitchen-maid for his wife.'

'Oh, sir, you should not say that to me.'

'No;—I should not have said it to you. I beg your pardon, Silverbridge.' Then he paused a moment, turning over certain thoughts within his own bosom. 'Perhaps, after all, it is well that a pride of which I am conscious should be rebuked. And it may be that the rebuke has come in such a form that I should be thankful. I know that I can love Isabel.'

'That to me will be everything.'

'And this young man has nothing that should revolt me. I think he has been wrong. But now that I have said it I will let all that pass from me. He will dine with us to-day.'

Silverbridge then went up to see his sister. 'So you have settled your little business, Mary?'

'Oh, Silverbridge, you will wish me joy?'

'Certainly. Why not?'

'Papa is so stern with me. Of course he has given way, and of course I am grateful. But he looks at me as though I had done something to be forgiven.'

'Take the good the gods provide you, Mary. That will all come right.'

'But I have not done anything wrong. Have I?'

'That is a matter of opinion. How can I answer about you when I don't quite know whether I have done anything wrong or not myself? I am going to marry the girl I have chosen. That's enough for me.'

'But you did change.'

'We need not say anything about that.'

'But I have never changed. Papa just told me that he would consent, and that I might write to him. So I did write, and he came. But papa looks at me as though I had broken his heart.'

'I tell you what it is, Mary. You expect too much from him. He has not had his own way with either of us, and of course he feels it.'

As Tregear had said, there was quite a family party in

Carlton Terrace, though as yet the family was not bound together by family ties. All the Boncassens were there, the father, the mother, and the promised bride. Mr. Boncassen bore himself with more ease than any one in the company, having at his command a gift of manliness which enabled him to regard this marriage exactly as he would have done any other. America was not so far distant but what he would be able to see his girl occasionally. He liked the young man and he believed in the comfort of wealth. Therefore he was satisfied. But when the marriage was spoken of, or written of, as 'an alliance,' then he would say a hard word or two about dukes and lords in general. On such an occasion as this he was happy and at his ease.

So much could not be said for his wife, with whom the Duke attempted to place himself on terms of family equality. But in doing this he failed to hide the attempt even from her, and she broke down under it. Had he simply walked into the room with her as he would have done on any other occasion, and then remarked that the frost was keen or the thaw disagreeable, it would have been better for her. But when he told her that he hoped she would often make herself at home in that house, and looked, as he said it, as though he were asking her to take a place among the goddesses of Olympus, she was troubled as to her answer. 'Oh, my Lord Duke,' she said, 'when I think of Isabel living here and being called by such a name, it almost upsets me.'

Isabel had all her father's courage, but she was more sensitive; and though she would have borne her honours well, was oppressed by the feeling that the weight was too much for her mother. She could not keep her ear from listening to her mother's words, or her eye from watching her mother's motions. She was prepared to carry her mother everywhere. 'As other girls have to be taken with their belongings, so must I, if I be taken at all.' This she had said plainly enough. There should be no division between her and her mother. But still, knowing that her mother was not quite at ease, she was hardly at ease herself.

Silverbridge came in at the last moment, and of course occupied a chair next to Isabel. As the House was sitting, it was natural that he should come up in a flurry. 'I left Phineas,' he said, 'pounding away in his old style at Sir Timothy. By-the-bye, Isabel, you must come down some day and hear Sir Timothy badgered. I must be back again about ten. Well, Gerald, how are they all at Lazarus?' He made an effort to be free and easy, but even he soon found that it was an effort.

Gerald had come up from Oxford for the occasion that he might make acquaintance with the Boncassens. He had taken Isabel in to dinner, but had been turned out of his place when his brother came in. He had been a little confused by the first impression made upon him by Mrs. Boncassen, and had involuntarily watched his father. 'Silver is going to have an odd sort of a mother-in-law,' he said afterwards to Mary, who remarked in reply that this would not signify, as the mother-in-law would be in New York.

Tregear's part was very difficult to play. He could not but feel that though he had succeeded, still he was as yet looked upon askance. Silverbridge had told him that by degrees the Duke would be won round, but that it was not to be expected that he should swallow at once all his regrets. The truth of this could not but be accepted. The immediate inconvenience, however, was not the less felt. Each and everyone there knew the position of each and everyone;—but Tregear felt it difficult to act up to his. He could not play the well-pleased lover openly, as did Silverbridge. Mary herself was disposed to be very silent. The heart-breaking tedium of her dull life had been removed. Her determination had been rewarded. All that she had wanted had been granted to her, and she was happy. But she was not prepared to show off her happiness before others. And she was aware that she was thought to have done evil by introducing her lover into her august family.

But it was the Duke who made the greatest efforts, and with the least success. He had told himself again and again that he was bound by every sense of duty to swallow all regrets. He had taken himself to task on this matter. He had done so even out loud to his son. He had declared that he would 'let it all pass from him.' But who does not know how hard it is for a man in such matters to keep his word to himself? Who has not said to himself at the very moment of his own delinquency, 'Now,—it is now,—at this very instant of time, that I should crush, and quench, and kill the evil spirit within me; it is now that I should abate my greed, or smother my ill-humour, or abandon my hatred. It is now, and here, that I should drive out the fiend, as I have sworn to myself that I would do,'— and yet has failed?

That it would be done, would be done at last, by this man was very certain. When Silverbridge assured his sister that 'it would come all right very soon,' he had understood his father's character. But it could not be completed quite at once. Had he been required to take Isabel only to his heart, it would have been comparatively easy. There are men, who do not seem at first sight very susceptible to feminine attractions, who nevertheless are dominated by the grace of flounces, who succumb to petticoats unconsciously, and who are half in love with every woman merely for her womanhood. So it was with the Duke. He had given way in regard to Isabel with less than half the effort that Frank Tregear was likely to cost him.

'You were not at the House, sir,' said Silverbridge when he felt that there was a pause.

'No, not to-day.' Then there was a pause again.

'I think that we shall beat Cambridge this year to a moral,' said Gerald, who was sitting at the round table opposite to his father. Mr. Boncassen, who was next to him, asked, in irony probably rather than in ignorance, whether the victory was to be achieved by mathematical or classical proficiency. Gerald turned and looked at him. 'Do you mean to say that you have never heard of the University boat-races?'

'Papa, you have disgraced yourself for ever,' said Isabel.

'Have I, my dear? Yes, I have heard of them. But I thought Lord Gerald's protestation was too great for a mere aquatic triumph.'

'Now you are poking your fun at me,' said Gerald.

'Well he may,' said the Duke sententiously. 'We have laid ourselves very open to having fun poked at us in this matter.'

'I think, sir,' said Tregear, 'that they are learning to do the same sort of thing at the American Universities.'

'Oh, indeed,' said the Duke in a solemn, dry, funeral tone. And then all the little life which Gerald's remark about the boat-race had produced, was quenched at once. The Duke was not angry with Tregear for his little word of defence,—but he was not able to bring himself into harmony with this one guest, and was almost savage to him without meaning it. He was continually asking himself why Destiny had been so hard upon him as to force him to receive there at his table as his son-in-law a man who was distasteful to him. And he was endeavouring to answer the question, taking himself to task and telling himself that his destiny had done him no injury, and that the pride which had been wounded was a false pride. He was making a brave fight; but during the fight he was hardly fit to be the genial father and father-in-law of young people who were going to be married to one another. But before the dinner was over he made a great effort. 'Tregear,' he said,—and even that was an effort, for he had never hitherto mentioned the man's name without the formal Mister,— 'Tregear, as this is the first time you have sat at my table, let me be old-fashioned, and ask you to drink a glass of wine with me.'

The glass of wine was drunk and the ceremony afforded infinite satisfaction at least to one person there. Mary could not keep herself from some expression of joy by pressing her finger for a moment against her lover's arm. He, though not usually given to such manifestations, blushed up to his eyes. But the feeling produced on the company was solemn rather than jovial. Everyone there understood it all. Mr. Boncassen could read the Duke's mind down to the last line. Even Mrs. Boncassen was aware that an act of reconciliation had been intended. 'When the governor drank that glass of wine it seemed as though half the marriage ceremony had been performed' Gerald said to his brother that evening. When the

Duke's glass was replaced on the table, he himself was conscious of the solemnity of what he had done, and was half ashamed of it.

When the ladies had gone upstairs the conversation became political and lively. The Duke could talk freely about the state of things to Mr. Boncassen, and was able gradually to include Tregear in the badinage with which he attacked the Conservatism of his son. And so the half-hour passed well. Upstairs the two girls immediately came together, leaving Mrs. Boncassen to chew the cud of the grandeur around her in the sleepy comfort of an arm-chair. 'And so everything is settled for both of us,' said Isabel.

'Of course I knew it was to be settled for you. You told me so at Custins.'

'I did not know it myself then. I only told you that he had asked me. And you hardly believed me.'

'I certainly believed you.'

'But you knew about—Lady Mabel Grex.'

'I only suspected something, and now I know it was a mistake. It has never been more than a suspicion.'

'And why, when we were at Custins, did you not tell me about yourself?'

'I had nothing to tell.'

'I can understand that. But is it not joyful that it should all be settled? Only poor Lady Mabel! You have got no Lady Mabel to trouble your conscience.' From which it was evident that Silverbridge had not told all.

CHAPTER LXXV
The Major's story

By the end of March Isabel was in Paris, whither she had forbidden her lover to follow her. Silverbridge was therefore reduced to the shifts of a bachelor's life, in which his friends seemed to think that he ought now to take special delight. Perhaps he did not take much delight in them. He was no doubt impatient to commence that steady married life for which he had prepared himself. But nevertheless, just at present, he lived a good deal at the Beargarden. Where was he to live? The Boncassens were in Paris, his sister was at Matching with a houseful of other Pallisers, and his father was again deep in politics.

Of course he was much in the House of Commons, but that also was stupid. Indeed everything would be stupid till Isabel came back. Perhaps dinner was more comfortable at the club than at the House. And then, as everybody knew, it was a good thing to change the scene. Therefore he dined at the club, and though he would keep his hansom and go down to the House again in the course of the evening, he spent many long hours at the Beargarden. 'There'll very soon be an end of this as far as you are concerned,' said Mr. Lupton to him one evening as they were sitting in the smoking-room after dinner.

'The sooner the better as far as this place is concerned.'

'This place is as good as any other. For the matter of that I like the Beargarden since we got rid of two or three not very charming characters.'

'You mean my poor friend Tifto,' said Silverbridge.

'No;—I was not thinking of Tifto. There were one or two here who were quite as bad as Tifto. I wonder what has become of that poor devil?'

'I don't know in the least. You heard of that row about the hounds?'

'And his letter to you.'

'He wrote to me,—and I answered him, as you know. But whither he vanished, or what he is doing, or how he is living, I have not the least idea.'

'Gone to join those other fellows abroad, I should say. Among them they got a lot of money,—as the Duke ought to remember.'

'He is not with them,' said Silverbridge, as though he were in some degree mourning over the fate of his unfortunate friend.

'I suppose Captain Green was the leader in all that?'

'Now it is all done and gone I own to a certain regard for the Major. He was true to me till he thought I snubbed him. I would not let him go down to Silverbridge with me. I always thought that I drove the poor Major to his malpractices.'

At this moment Dolly Longstaff sauntered into the room and came up to them. It may be remembered that Dolly had declared his purpose of emigrating. As soon as he heard that the Duke's heir had serious thoughts of marrying the lady whom he loved he withdrew at once from the contest, but, as he did so, he acknowledged that there could be no longer a home for him in the country which Isabel was to inhabit as the wife of another man. Gradually, however, better thoughts returned to him. After all, what was she but a 'pert poppet'? He determined that marriage 'clips a fellow's wings confoundedly,' and so he set himself to enjoy life after his old fashion. There was perhaps a little swagger as he threw himself into a chair and addressed the happy lover. 'I'll be shot if I didn't meet Tifto at the corner of the street.'

'Tifto!'

'Yes, Tifto. He looked awfully seedy, with a greatcoat buttoned up to his chin, a shabby hat and old gloves.'

'Did he speak to you?' asked Silverbridge.

'No;—nor I to him. He hadn't time to think whether he would speak or not, and you may be sure I didn't.'

Nothing further was said about the man, but Silverbridge was uneasy and silent. When his cigar was finished he got up saying that he should go back to the House. As he left the club he looked about him as though expecting to see his old friend, and when he had passed through the first street and had got into the Haymarket there he was! The Major came up to him, touched his hat, asked to be allowed to say a few words. 'I don't think it can do any good,' said Silverbridge. The man had not attempted to shake hands with him, or affected familiarity; but seemed to be thoroughly humiliated. 'I don't think I can be of any service to you, and therefore I had rather decline.'

'I don't want you to be of any service, my Lord.'

'Then what's the good?'

'I have something to say. May I come to you to-morrow?'

Then Silverbridge allowed himself to make an appointment, and an hour was named at which Tifto might call in Carlton Terrace. He felt that he almost owed some reparation to the wretched man,—whom he had unfortunately admitted among his friends, whom he had used, and to whom he had been uncourteous. Exactly at the hour named the Major was shown into his room.

Dolly had said that he was shabby,—but the man was altered rather than shabby. He still had rings on his fingers and studs in his shirt, and a jewelled pin in his cravat;—but he had shaven off his moustache and the tuft from his chin, and his hair had been cut short, and in spite of his jewellery there was a hang-dog look about him. 'I've got something that I particularly want to say to you, my Lord.' Silverbridge would not shake hands with him, but could not refrain from offering him a chair.

'Well;—you can say it now.'

'Yes;—but it isn't so very easy to be said. There are some things, though you want to say them ever so, you don't quite know how to do it.'

'You have your choice, Major Tifto. You can speak or hold your tongue.'

Then there was a pause, during which Silverbridge sat with his hands in his pockets trying to look unconcerned. 'But if you've got it here, and feel it as I do,'—the poor man as he said this put his hand upon his heart,—'you can't sleep in your bed till it's out. I did that thing that they said I did.'

'What thing?'

'Why, the nail! It was I lamed the horse.'

'I am sorry for it. I can say nothing else.'

'You ain't so sorry for it as I am. Oh no; you can never be that, my Lord. After all, what does it matter to you?'

'Very little. I meant that I was sorry for your sake.'

'I believe you are, my Lord. For though you could be rough

594

you was always kind. Now I will tell you everything, and then you can do as you please.'

'I wish to do nothing. As far as I am concerned the matter is over. It made me sick of horses, and I do not wish to have to think of it again.'

'Nevertheless, my Lord, I've got to tell it. It was Green who put me up to it. He did it just for the plunder. As God is my judge it was not for the money I did it.'

'Then it was revenge.'

'It was the devil got hold of me, my Lord. Up to that I had always been square,—square as a die! I got to think that your Lordship was upsetting. I don't know whether your Lordship remembers, but you did put me down once or twice rather uncommon.'

'I hope I was not unjust.'

'I don't say you was, my Lord. But I got a feeling on me that you wanted to get rid of me, and I all the time doing the best I could for the 'orses. I did do the best I could up to that very morning at Doncaster. Well;—it was Green put me up to it. I don't say I was to get nothing; but it wasn't so much more than I could have got by the 'orse winning. And I've lost pretty nearly all that I did get. Do you remember, my Lord,'—and now the Major sank his voice to a whisper,— 'when I come up to your bedroom that morning?'

'I remember it.'

'The first time?'

'Yes; I remember it.'

'Because I came twice, my Lord. When I came first it hadn't been done. You turned me out.'

'That is true, Major Tifto.'

'You was very rough then. Wasn't you rough?'

'A man's bedroom is generally supposed to be private.'

'Yes, my Lord,—that's true. I ought to have sent your man in first. I came then to confess it all, before it was done.'

'Then why couldn't you let the horse alone?'

'I was in their hands. And then you was so rough with me! So I said to myself I might as well do it;—and I did it.'

'What do you want me to say? As far as my forgiveness goes, you have it!'

'That's saying a great deal, my Lord,—a great deal,' said Tifto, now in tears. 'But I ain't said it all yet. He's here; in London!'

'Who's here?'

'Green. He's here. He doesn't think that I know, but I could lay my hand on him to-morrow.'

'There is no human being alive, Major Tifto, whose presence or absence could be a matter of more indifference to me.'

'I'll tell you what I'll do, my Lord. I'll go before any judge, or magistrate, or police-officer in the country, and tell the truth. I won't ask even for a pardon. They shall punish me and him too. I'm in that state of mind that any change would be for the better. But he,—he ought to have it heavy.'

'It won't be done by me, Major Tifto. Look here, Major Tifto; you have come here to confess that you have done me a great injury?'

'Yes, I have.'

'And you say you are sorry for it.'

'Indeed I am.'

'And I have forgiven you. There is only one way in which you can show your gratitude. Hold your tongue about it. Let it be as a thing done and gone. The money has been paid. The horse has been sold. The whole thing has gone out of my mind, and I don't want to have it brought back again.

'And nothing is to be done to Green!'

'I should say nothing,—on that score.'

'And he has got they say five-and-twenty thousand pounds clear money.'

'It is a pity, but it cannot be helped. I will have nothing further to do with it. Of course I cannot bind you, but I have told you my wishes.' The poor wretch was silent, but still it seemed as though he did not wish to go quite yet. 'If you have said what you have got to say, Major Tifto, I may as well tell you that my time is engaged.'

'And must that be all?'

'What else?'

'I am in such a state of mind, Lord Silverbridge, that it would be a satisfaction to tell it all, even against myself.'

'I can't prevent you.'

Then Tifto got up from his chair, as though he were going. 'I wish I knew what I was going to do with myself.'

'I don't know that I can help you, Major Tifto.'

'I suppose not, my Lord. I haven't twenty pounds left in all the world. It's the only thing that wasn't square that ever I did in all my life. Your Lordship couldn't do anything for me? We was very much together at one time, my Lord.'

'Yes, Major Tifto, we were.'

'Of course I was a villain. But it was only once; and your Lordship was so rough to me! I am not saying but what I was a villain. Think of what I did for myself by that one piece of wickedness! Master of hounds! member of the club! And the horse would have run in my name and won the Leger! And everybody knew as your Lordship and me was together in him!' Then he burst out into a paroxysm of tears and sobbing.

The young Lord certainly could not take the man into partnership again, nor could he restore to him either the hounds or his club,—or his clean hands. Nor did he know in what way he could serve the man, except by putting his hand into his pocket,—which he did. Tifto accepted the gratuity, and ultimately became an annual pensioner on his former noble partner, living on the allowance made him in some obscure corner of South Wales.

CHAPTER LXXVI
On deportment

FRANK TREGEAR had come up to town at the end of February. He remained in London, with an understanding that he was not to see Lady Mary again till the Easter holidays. He was then to pay a visit to Matching, and to enter in, it may be presumed, on the full fruition of his advantages as accepted suitor. All this had been arranged with a good deal of precision,—as though there had still been a hope left that Lady Mary might change her mind. Of course there was no such hope. When the Duke asked the young man to dine with him, when he invited him to drink that memorable glass of wine, when the young man was allowed, in the presence of the Boncassens, to sit next Lady Mary, it was of course settled. But the father probably found some relief in yielding by slow degrees. 'I would rather that there should be no correspondence till then,' he had said both to Tregear and to his daughter. And they had promised there should be no correspondence. At Easter they would meet. After Easter Mary was to come up to London to be present at her brother's wedding, to which also Tregear had been formally invited; and it was hoped that then something might be settled as to their own marriage. Tregear, with the surgeon's permission, took his seat in Parliament. He was introduced by two leading Members on the Conservative side, but immediately afterwards found himself seated next to his friend Silverbridge on the top bench behind the ministers. The House was very full, as there was a feverish report abroad that Sir Timothy Beeswax intended to make a statement. No one quite knew what the statement was to be; but every politician in the House and out of it thought that he knew that the statement would be a bid for higher power on the part of Sir Timothy himself. If there had been dissensions in the Cabinet, the secret of them had been well kept. To Tregear who was not as yet familiar with the

House there was no special appearance of activity; but Silver-bridge could see that there was more than wonted animation. That the Treasury bench should be full at this time was a thing of custom. A whole broadside of questions would be fired off, one after another, like a rattle of musketry down the ranks, when as nearly as possible the report of each gun is made to follow close upon that of the gun before,—with this exception, that in such case each little sound is intended to be as like as possible to the preceding; whereas with the rattle of the questions and answers, each question and each answer becomes a little more authoritative and less courteous than the last. The Treasury bench was ready for its usual respon-sive firing, as the questioners were of course in their places. The opposition front bench was also crowded, and those behind were nearly equally full. There were many Peers in the gallery, and a general feeling of sensation prevailed. All this Silverbridge had been long enough in the House to appreciate;—but to Tregear the House was simply the House.

'It's odd enough we should have a row the very first day you come,' said Silverbridge.

'You think there will be a row?'

'Beeswax has something special to say. He's not here yet, you see. They've left about six inches for him there between Roper and Sir Orlando. You'll have the privilege of looking just down on the top of his head when he does come. I shan't stay much longer after that.'

'Where are you going?'

'I don't mean to-day. But I should not have been here now,—in this very place I mean,—but I want to stick to you just at first. I shall move down below the gangway; and not improb-ably creep over to the other side before long.'

'You don't mean it?'

'I think I shall. I begin to feel I've made a mistake.'

'In coming to this side at all?'

'I think I have. After all it is not very important.'

'What is not important? I think it very important.'

'Perhaps it may be to you, and perhaps you may be able

to keep it up. But the more I think of it the less excuse I seem to have for deserting the old ways of the family. What is there in those fellows down there to make a fellow feel that he ought to bind himself to them neck and heels?'

'Their principles.'

'Yes, their principles! I believe I have some vague idea as to supporting property and land and all that kind of thing. I don't know that anybody wants to attack anything.'

'Somebody soon would want to attack it if there were no defenders.'

'I suppose there is an outside power,—the people, or public opinion, or whatever they choose to call it. And the country will have to go very much as that outside power chooses. Here, in Parliament, everybody will be as Conservative as the outside will let them. I don't think it matters on which side you sit;—but it does matter that you shouldn't have to act with those who go against the grain with you.'

'I never heard a worse political argument in my life.'

'I dare say not. However, here's Sir Timothy. When he looks in that way, all buckram,*deportment, and solemnity, I know he's going to pitch into somebody.'

At this moment the Leader of the House came in from behind the Speaker's chair and took his place between Mr. Roper and Sir Orlando Drought. Silverbridge had been right in saying that Sir Timothy's air was solemn. When a man has to declare a solemn purpose on a solemn occasion in a solemn place, it is needful that he should be solemn himself. And though the solemnity which befits a man best will be that which the importance of the moment may produce, without thought given by himself to his own outward person, still, who is there can refrain himself from some attempt? Who can boast, who that has been versed in the ways and duties of high places, that he has kept himself free from all study of grace, of feature, of attitude, of gait—or even of dress? For most of our bishops, for most of our judges, of our statesmen, our orators, our generals, for many even of our doctors and our parsons, even our attorneys, our tax-gatherers, and certainly our butlers and our coachmen, Mr. Turveydrop, the great professor of deportment, has done much. But there should always be the art to underlie and protect the art;—the art that can hide the art. The really clever archbishop,—the really potent chief justice, the man who, as a politician, will succeed in becoming a king of men, should know how to carry his buckram without showing it. It was in this that Sir Timothy perhaps failed a little. There are men who look as though they were born to wear blue ribbons. It has come, probably, from study, but it seems to be natural. Sir Timothy did not impose on those who looked at him as do these men. You could see a little of the paint, you could hear the crumple of the starch and the padding; you could trace something of uneasiness in the would-be composed grandeur of the brow. 'Turveydrop!' the spectator would say to himself. But after all it may be a question whether a man be open to reproach for not doing that well which the greatest among us,—if we could find one great enough,—would not do at all.

For I think we must hold that true personal dignity should be achieved,—must, if it be quite true, have been achieved,—without any personal effort. Though it be evinced, in part, by the carriage of the body, that carriage should be the fruit of the operation of the mind. Even when it be assisted by external garniture such as special clothes, and wigs, and ornaments, such garniture should have been prescribed by the sovereign or by custom, and should not have been selected by the wearer. In regard to speech a man may study all that which may make him suasive,*but if he go beyond that he will trench on those histrionic efforts which he will know to be wrong because he will be ashamed to acknowledge them. It is good to be beautiful, but it should come of God and not of the hairdresser. And personal dignity is a great possession; but a man should struggle for it no more than he would for beauty. Many, however, do struggle for it, and with such success that, though they do not achieve quite the real thing, still they get something on which they can bolster themselves up and be mighty.

Others, older men than Silverbridge, saw as much as did our young friend, but they were more complaisant and more reasonable. They, too, heard the crackle of the buckram, and were aware that the last touch of awe had come upon that brow just as its owner was emerging from the shadow of the Speaker's chair;—but to them it was a thing of course. A real Cæsar is not to be found every day, nor can we always have a Pitt to control our debates. That kind of thing, that last touch has its effect. Of course it is all paint,—but how would the poor girl look before the gaslights if there were no paint? The House of Commons likes a little deportment on occasions. If a special man looks bigger than you, you can console yourself by reflecting that he also looks bigger than your fellows. Sir Timothy probably knew what he was about, and did himself on the whole more good than harm by his little tricks.

As soon as Sir Timothy had taken his seat, Mr. Rattler got up from the opposition bench to ask him some question on a matter of finance. The brewers were anxious about publican licences.*Could the Chancellor of the Exchequer say a word on the matter? Notice had of course been given, and the questioner had stated a quarter of an hour previously that he would postpone his query till the Chancellor of the Exchequer was in the House.

Sir Timothy rose from his seat, and in his blandest manner began by apologising for his late appearance. He was sorry that he had been prevented by public business from being in his place to answer the honourable gentleman's question in its proper turn. And even now, he feared that he must decline to give any answer which could be supposed to be satisfactory. It would probably be his duty to make a statement to the House on the following day,—a statement which he was not quite prepared to make at the present moment. But in the existing state of things he was unwilling to make any reply to any question by which he might seem to bind the government to any opinion. Then he sat down. And rising again not long afterwards, when the House had gone through certain formal duties, he moved that it should be adjourned till the next day. Then all the members trooped out, and with the others Tregear and Lord Silverbridge. 'So that is the end of your first day of Parliament,' said Silverbridge.

'What does it all mean?'

'Let us go to the Carlton and hear what the fellows are saying.'

On that evening both the young men dined at Mr. Boncassen's house. Though Tregear had been cautioned not to write to Lady Mary, and though he was not to see her before Easter, still it was so completely understood that he was about to become her husband, that he was entertained in that capacity by all those who were concerned in the family. 'And so they will all go out,' said Mr. Boncassen.

'That seems to be the general idea,' said the expectant son-in-law. 'When two men want to be first and neither will give way, they can't very well get on in the same boat together.' Then he expatiated angrily on the treachery of Sir Timothy, and Tregear in a more moderate way joined in the same opinion.

'Upon my word, young men, I doubt whether you are right,' said Mr. Boncassen. 'Whether it can be possible that a man should have risen to such a position with so little patriotism as you attribute to our friend, I will not pretend to say. I should think that in England it was impossible. But of this I am sure, that the facility which exists here for a minister or ministers to go out of office without disturbance of the Crown, is a great blessing. You say the other party will come in.'

'That is most probable,' said Silverbridge.

'With us the other party never comes in,—never has a chance of coming in,—except once in four years, when the President is elected. That one event binds us all for four years.'

'But you do change your ministers,' said Tregear.

'A secretary may quarrel with the President, or he may have the gout, or be convicted of peculation.'

'And yet you think yourselves more nearly free than we are.'

'I am not so sure of that. We have had a pretty difficult task, that of carrying on a government in a new country, which is nevertheless more populous than almost any old country. The influxions are so rapid, that every ten years the nature of the people is changed. It isn't easy; and though I think on the whole we've done pretty well, I am not going to boast that Washington is as yet the seat of a political Paradise.'

CHAPTER LXXVII
'Mabel, good-bye'

WHEN Tregear first came to town with his arm in a sling, and bandages all round him,—in order that he might be formally accepted by the Duke,—he had himself taken to one other house besides the house in Carlton Terrace. He went to Belgrave Square, to announce his fate to Lady Mabel Grex;—but Lady Mabel Grex was not there. The Earl was ill at Brighton, and Lady Mabel had gone down to nurse him. The old woman who came to him in the hall told him that the Earl was very ill;—he had been attacked by the gout, but in spite of the gout, and in spite of the doctors, he had insisted on being taken to his club. Then he had been removed to Brighton, under the doctor's advice, chiefly in order that he might be kept out of the way of temptation. Now he was supposed to be very ill indeed. 'My Lord is so imprudent!' said the old woman, shaking her old head in real unhappiness. For though the Earl had been a tyrant to everyone near him, yet when a poor woman becomes old it is something to have a tyrant to protect her. 'My Lord' always had been imprudent. Tregear knew that it had been the theory of my Lord's life that to eat and drink and die was better than to abstain and live. Then Tregear wrote to his friend as follows:

'MY DEAR MABEL,

'I am up in town again as you will perceive, although I am still in a helpless condition and hardly able to write even this letter. I called to-day and was very sorry to hear so bad an account of your father. Had I been able to travel I should have come down to you. When I am able I will do so if you would wish to see me. In the meantime pray tell me how he is, and how you are.

'My news is this. The Duke has accepted me. It is great news to me, and I hope will be acceptable to you. I do believe that if ever a friend has been anxious for a friend's welfare you have been anxious for mine,—as I have been and ever shall be for yours.

'Of course this thing will be very much to me. I will not speak now of my love for the girl who is to become my wife. You might again call me Romeo. Nor do I like to say much of what may now be pecuniary prospects. I did not ask Mary to become my wife because I supposed she would be rich. But I could not have married her or any one else who had not money. What are the Duke's intentions I have not the slightest idea, nor shall I ask him. I am to go down to Matching at Easter, and shall endeavour to have some time fixed. I suppose the Duke will say something about money. If he does not, I shall not.

'Pray write to me at once, and tell me when I shall see you.
'Your affectionate Cousin,
'F. O. TREGEAR.'

In answer to this there came a note in a very few words. She congratulated him,—not very warmly,—but expressed a hope that she might see him soon. But she told him not to come to Brighton. The Earl was better but very cross, and she would be up in town before long.

Towards the end of the month it became suddenly known in London that Lord Grex had died at Brighton. There was a Garter to be given away, and everybody was filled with regret that such an ornament to the Peerage should have departed from them. The Conservative papers remembered how excellent a politician he had been in his younger days, and the world was informed that the family of Grex of Grex was about the oldest in Great Britain of which authentic records were in existence. Then there came another note from Lady Mabel to Tregear. 'I shall be in town on the 31st in the old house, with Miss Cassewary, and will see you if you can come on the 1st. Come early, at eleven, if you can.'

On the day named and at the hour fixed he was in Belgrave Square. He had known this house since he was a boy, and could well remember how, when he first entered it, he had thought with some awe of the grandeur of the Earl. The Earl had then not paid much attention to him, but he had become very much taken by the grace and good-nature of the girl who had owned him as a cousin. 'You are my cousin Frank,' she had said; 'I am so glad to have a cousin.' He could remember the words now as though they had been spoken only yesterday. Then there had quickly grown to be friendship between him and this, as he thought, sweetest of all girls. At that time he had just gone to Eton; but before he left Eton they had sworn to love each other. And so it had been and the thing had grown, till at last, just when he had taken his degree, two matters had been settled between them; the first was that each loved the other irretrievably, irrevocably, passionately; the second, that it was altogether out of the question that they should ever marry each other.

It is but fair to Tregear to say that this last decision origi-nated with the lady. He had told her that he certainly would hold himself engaged to marry her at some future time; but she had thrown this aside at once. How was it possible, she said, that two such beings, brought up in luxury, and taught to enjoy all the good things of the world, should expect to live and be happy together without an income? He offered to go to the bar;—but she asked him whether he thought it well that such a one as she should wait say a dozen years for such a process. 'When the time comes, I should be an old woman and you would be a wretched man.' She released him,—declared her own purpose of marrying well; and then, though there had been a moment in which her own assurance of her own love had been passionate enough, she went so far as to tell him that she was heart-whole. 'We have been two foolish children but we cannot be children any longer,' she said. 'There must be an end of it.'

What had hitherto been the result of this the reader knows, —and Tregear knew also. He had taken the privilege given to him, and had made so complete a use of it that he had in truth transferred his heart as well as his allegiance. Where is the young man who cannot do so;—how few are there who do not do so when their first fit of passion has come on them at one-and-twenty? And he had thought that she would do the same. But gradually he found that she had not done so, did not do so, could not do so! When she first heard of Lady Mary she had not reprimanded him,—but she could not keep herself from showing the bitterness of her disappointment. Though she would still boast of her own strength and of her own purpose, yet it was too clear to him that she was wounded and very sore. She would have liked him to remain single at any rate till she herself were married. But the permission had been hardly given before he availed himself of it. And then he talked to her not only of the brilliancy of his prospects,— which she could have forgiven,—but of his love—his love!

Then she had refused one offer after another, and he had known it all. There was nothing in which she was concerned that she did not tell him. Then young Silverbridge had come across her, and she had determined that he should be her husband. She had been nearly successful,—so nearly that at moments she had felt sure of success. But the prize had slipped from her through her own fault. She knew well enough that it was her own fault. When a girl submits to play such a game as that, she should not stand on too nice scruples. She had told herself this many a time since;—but the prize was gone.

All this Tregear knew, and knowing it almost dreaded the coming interview. He could not without actual cruelty have avoided her. Had he done so before he could not have continued to do so now, when she was left alone in the world. Her father had not been much to her, but still his presence had enabled her to put herself before the world as being somebody. Now she would be almost nobody. And she had lost her rich prize, while he,—out of the same treasury as it were, —had won his!

The door was opened to him by the same old woman, and he was shown, at a funereal pace, up into the drawing-room which he had known so well. He was told that Lady Mabel would be down to him directly. As he looked about him he could see that already had been commenced that work of division of spoil which is sure to follow the death of most of us. Things were already gone which used to be familiar to his eyes, and the room, though not dismantled, had been deprived of many of its little prettinesses and was ugly.

In about ten minutes she came down to him,—with so soft a step that he would not have been aware of her entrance had he not seen her form in the mirror. Then, when he turned round to greet her, he was astonished by the blackness of her appearance. She looked as though she had become ten years older since he had last seen her. As she came up to him she was grave and almost solemn in her gait, but there was no sign of any tears. Why should there have been a tear? Women weep, and men too, not from grief, but from emotion. Indeed, grave and slow as was her step, and serious, almost solemn, as was her gait, there was something of a smile on her mouth as she gave him her hand. And yet her face was very sad, declaring to him too plainly something of the hopelessness of her heart. 'And so the Duke has consented,' she said. He had told her that in his letter, but, since that, her father had died, and she had been left, he did not as yet know how far impoverished, but, he feared, with no pleasant worldly prospects before her.

'Yes, Mabel;—that I suppose will be settled. I have been so shocked to hear all this.'

'It has been very sad;—has it not? Sit down, Frank. You and I have a good deal to say to each other now that we have met. It was no good your going down to Brighton. He would not have seen you, and at last I never left him.'

'Was Percival there?' She only shook her head. 'That was dreadful.'

'It was not Percival's fault. He would not see him; nor till the last hour or two would he believe in his own danger. Nor was he ever frightened for a moment,—not even then.'

'Was he good to you?'

'Good to me! Well;—he liked my being there. Poor papa! It had gone so far with him that he could not be good to any one. I think that he felt that it would be unmanly not to be the same to the end.'

'He would not see Percival.'

'When it was suggested he would only ask what good Percival could do him. I did send for him at last, in my terror, but he did not see his father alive. When he did come he only told me how badly his father had treated him! It was very dreadful!'

'I did so feel for you.'

'I am sure you did, and will. After all, Frank, I think that the pious godly people have the best of it in this world. Let them be ever so covetous, ever so false, ever so hard-hearted, the mere fact that they must keep up appearances, makes them comfortable to those around them. Poor papa was not comfortable to me. A little hypocrisy, a little sacrifice to the feelings of the world, may be such a blessing.'

'I am sorry that you should feel it so.'

'Yes; it is sad. But you;—everything is smiling with you! Let us talk about your plans.'

'Another time will do for that. I had come to hear about your own affairs.'

'There they are,' she said, pointing round the room. 'I have no other affairs. You see that I am going from here.'

'And where are you going?' She shook her head. 'With whom will you live?'

'With Miss Cass,—two old maids together! I know nothing further.'

'But about money? That is if I am justified in asking.'

'What would you not be justified in asking? Do you not know that I would tell you every secret of my heart,—if my heart had a secret? It seems that I have given up what was to have been my fortune. There was a claim of £12,000 on Grex. But I have abandoned it.'

'And there is nothing.'

'There will be scrapings they tell me,—unless Percival refuses to agree. This house is mortgaged, but not for its value. And there are some jewels. But all that is detestable,— a mere grovelling among mean hundreds; whereas you,—you will soar among——'

'Oh Mabel! do not say hard things to me.'

'No, indeed! why should I,—I who have been preaching that comfortable doctrine of hypocrisy? I will say nothing hard. But I would sooner talk of your good things than of my evil ones.'

'I would not.'

'Then you must talk about them for my sake. How was it that the Duke came round at last?'

'I hardly know. She sent for me.'

'A fine high-spirited girl. These Pallisers have more courage about them than one expects from their outward manner. Silverbridge has plenty of it.'

'I remember telling you he could be obstinate.'

'And I remember that I did not believe you. Now I know it. He has the sort of pluck which enables a man to break a girl's heart,—or to destroy a girl's hopes,—without wincing. He can tell a girl to her face that she can go to the—mischief for him. There are so many men who can't do that, from cowardice, though their hearts be ever so well inclined. "I have changed my mind." There is something great in the courage of a man who can say that to a woman in so many words. Most of them, when they escape, escape by lies and subterfuges. Or they run away and won't allow themselves to be heard of. They trust to a chapter of accidents, and leave things to arrange themselves. But when a man can look a girl in the face with those seemingly soft eyes, and say with that seemingly soft mouth,—"I have changed my mind,"—though she would look him dead in return if she could, still she must admire him.'

'Are you speaking of Silverbridge now?'

'Of course I am speaking of Silverbridge. I suppose I ought to hide it all and not to tell you. But as you are the only person I do tell, you must put up with me. Yes;—when I taxed him with his falsehood,—for he had been false,—he answered me with those very words! "I have changed my mind." He could not lie. To speak the truth was a necessity to him, even at the expense of his gallantry, almost of his humanity.'

'Has he been false to you, Mabel?'

'Of course he has. But there is nothing to quarrel about, if you mean that. People do not quarrel now about such things. A girl has to fight her own battle with her own pluck and her own wits. As with these weapons she is generally stronger than her enemy, she succeeds sometimes although everything else is against her. I think I am courageous, but his courage beat mine. I craned at the first fence. When he was willing to swallow my bait, my hand was not firm enough to strike the hook in his jaws. Had I not quailed then I think I should have—"had him".'

'It is horrid to hear you talk like this.' She was leaning over from her seat, looking, black as she was, so much older than her wont, with something about her of that unworldly serious thoughtfulness which a mourning garb always gives. And yet her words were so worldly, so unfeminine!

'I have got to tell the truth to somebody. It was so, just as I have said. Of course I did not love him. How could I love him after what has passed? But there need have been nothing much in that. I don't suppose that Dukes' eldest sons often get married for love.'

'Miss Boncassen loves him.'

'I dare say the beggar's daughter loved King Cophetua When you come to distances such as that, there can be love.

The very fact that a man should have descended so far in quest of beauty,—the flattery of it alone,—will produce love. When the angels came after the daughters of men of course the daughters of men loved them. The distance between him and me is not great enough to have produced that sort of worship. There was no reason why Lady Mabel Grex should not be good enough wife for the son of the Duke of Omnium.'

'Certainly not.'

'And therefore I was not struck, as by the shining of a light from heaven. I cannot say I loved him. Frank,—I am beyond worshipping even an angel from heaven!'

'Then I do not know that you could blame him,' he said very seriously.

'Just so;—and as I have chosen to be honest I have told him everything. But I had my revenge first.'

'I would have said nothing.'

'You would have recommended—delicacy! No doubt you think that women should be delicate, let them suffer what they may. A woman should not let it be known that she has any human nature in her. I had him on the hip, and for a moment I used my power. He had certainly done me a wrong. He had asked for my love,—and with the delicacy which you commend, I had not at once grasped at all that such a request conveyed. Then, as he told me so frankly, "he changed his mind!" Did he not wrong me?'

'He should not have raised false hopes.'

'He told me that—he had changed his mind. I think I loved him then as nearly as ever I did,—because he looked me full in the face. Then,—I told him I had never cared for him, and that he need have nothing on his conscience. But I doubt whether he was glad to hear it. Men are so vain! I have talked too much of myself. And so you are to be the Duke's son-in-law. And she will have hundreds of thousands.'

'Thousands perhaps, but I do not think very much about it. I feel that he will provide for her.'

'And that you, having secured her, can creep under his

wing like an additional ducal chick. It is very comfortable. The Duke will be quite a Providence to you. I wonder that all young gentlemen do not marry heiresses;—it is so easy. And you have got your seat in Parliament too! Oh, your luck! When I look back upon it all it seems so hard to me! It was for you,—for you that I used to be anxious. Now it is I who have not an inch of ground to stand upon.' Then he approached her and put out his hand to her. 'No,' she said, putting both her hands behind her back, 'for God's sake let there be no tenderness. But is it not cruel? Think of my advantages at that moment when you and I agreed that our paths should be separate. My fortune then had not been made quite shipwreck by my father and brother. I had before me all that society could offer. I was called handsome and clever. Where was there a girl more likely to make her way to the top?'

'You may do so still.'

'No;—no;—I cannot. And you at least should not tell me so. I did not know then the virulence of the malady which had fallen on me. I did not know then that, because of you, other men would be abhorrent to me. I thought that I was as easy-hearted as you have proved yourself.'

'How cruel you can be.'

'Have I done anything to interfere with you? Have I said a word even to that young lad, when I might have said a word? Yes; to him I did say something; but I waited, and would not say it, while a word could hurt you. Shall I tell you what I told him? Just everything that has ever happened between you and me.'

'You did?'

'Yes;—because I saw that I could trust him. I told him because I wanted him to be quite sure that I had never loved him. But, Frank, I have put no spoke in your wheel. There has not been a moment since you told me of your love for this rich young lady in which I would not have helped you had help been in my power. Whomever I may have harmed, I have never harmed you.'

'Am I not as clear from blame towards you?'

613

'No, Frank. You have done me the terrible evil of ceasing to love me.'

'It was at your own bidding.'

'Certainly! but if I were to bid you to cut my throat, would you do it?'

'Was it not you who decided that we could not wait for each other?'

'And should it not have been for you to decide that you would wait?'

'You also would have married.'

'It almost angers me that you should not see the difference. A girl unless she marries becomes nothing, as I have become nothing now. A man does not want a pillar on which to lean. A man, when he has done as you had done with me, and made a girl's heart all his own, even though his own heart had been flexible and plastic as yours is, should have been true to her, at least for a while. Did it never occur to you that you owed something to me?'

'I have always owed you very much.'

'There should have been some touch of chivalry if not of love to make you feel that a second passion should have been postponed for a year or two. You could wait without growing old. You might have allowed yourself a little space to dwell —I was going to say on the sweetness of your memories. But they were not sweet, Frank; they were not sweet to you.'

'These rebukes, Mabel, will rob them of their sweetness,— for a time.'

'It is gone; all gone,' she said, shaking her head,—'gone from me because I have been so easily deserted; gone from you because the change has been so easy to you. How long was it, Frank, after you had left me before you were basking happily in the smiles of Lady Mary Palliser?'

'It was not very long, as months go.'

'Say days, Frank.'

'I have to defend myself, and I will do so with truth. It was not very long,—as months go; but why should it have been

614

less long, whether for months or days? I had to cure myself of a wound.'

'To put a plaster on a scratch, Frank.'

'And the sooner a man can do that the more manly he is. Is it a sign of strength to wail under a sorrow that cannot be cured,—or of truth to perpetuate the appearance of a woe?'

'Has it been an appearance with me?'

'I am speaking of myself now. I am driven to speak of myself by the bitterness of your words. It was you who decided.'

'You accepted my decision easily.'

'Because it was based not only on my unfitness for such a marriage, but on yours. When I saw that there would be perhaps some years of misery for you, of course I accepted your decision. The sweetness had been very sweet to me.'

'Oh Frank, was it ever sweet to you?'

'And the triumph of it had been very great. I had been assured of the love of her who among all the high ones of the world seemed to me to be the highest. Then came your decision. Do you really believe that I could abandon the sweetness, that I could be robbed of my triumph, that I could think I could never again be allowed to put my arm round your waist, never again to feel your cheek close to mine, that I should lose all that had seemed left to me among the gods, without feeling it?'

'Frank, Frank!' she said, rising to her feet, and stretching out her hands as though she were going to give him back all these joys.

'Of course I felt it. I did not then know what was before me.' When he said this she sank back immediately upon her seat. 'I was wretched enough. I had lost a limb and could not walk; my eyes, and must always hereafter be blind; my fitness to be among men, and must always hereafter be secluded. It is so that a man is stricken down when some terrible trouble comes upon him. But it is given to him to retrick his beams.'

'You have retricked yours.'

'Yes;—and the strong man will show his strength by doing

it quickly. Mabel, I sorrowed for myself greatly when that word was spoken, partly because I thought that your love could so easily be taken from me. And, since I have found that it has not been so, I have sorrowed for you also. But I do not blame myself, and—and I will not submit to have blame even from you.' She stared him in the face as he said this. 'A man should never submit to blame.'

'But if he has deserved it?'

'Who is to be the judge? But why should we contest this? You do not really wish to trample on me!'

'No;—not that.'

'Nor to disgrace me; nor to make me feel myself disgraced in my own judgment?' Then there was a pause for some moments as though he had left her without another word to say. 'Shall I go now?' he asked.

'Oh Frank!'

'I fear that my presence only makes you unhappy.'

'Then what will your absence do? When shall I see you again? But, no; I will not see you again. Not for many days,—not for years. Why should I? Frank, is it wicked that I should love you?' He could only shake his head in answer to this. 'If it be so wicked that I must be punished for it eternally, still I love you. I can never, never, never love another. You cannot understand it. Oh God,—that I had never understood it myself! I think, I think, that I would go with you now anywhere, facing all misery, all judgments, all disgrace. You know, do you not, that if it were possible, I should not say so. But as I know that you would not stir a step with me, I do say so.'

'I know it is not meant.'

'It is meant, though it could not be done. Frank, I must not see her, not for awhile;' not for years. I do not wish to hate her, but how can I help it? Do you remember when she flew into your arms in this room?'

'I remember it.'

'Of course you do. It is your great joy now to remember that, and such like. She must be very good! Though I hate her!'

'Do not say that you hate her, Mabel.'

'Though I hate her she must be good. It was a fine and a brave thing to do. I have done it; but never before the world like that; have I, Frank? Oh Frank, I shall never do it again. Go now, and do not touch me. Let us both pray that in ten years we may meet as passionless friends.' He came to her hardly knowing what he meant, but purposing, as though by instinct, to take her hand as he parted from her. But she, putting both her hands before her face, and throwing herself on to the sofa, buried her head among the cushions.

'Is there not to be another word?' he said. Lying as she did, she still was able to make a movement of dissent, and he left her, muttering just one word between his teeth, 'Mabel, good-bye.'

CHAPTER LXXVIII
The Duke returns to office

THAT farewell took place on the Friday morning. Tregear as he walked out of the Square knew now that he had been the cause of a great shipwreck. At first when that passionate love had been declared,—he could hardly remember whether with the fullest passion by him or by her,—he had been as a god walking upon air. That she who seemed to be so much above him should have owned that she was all his own seemed then to be world enough for him. For a few weeks he lived a hero to himself, and was able to tell himself that for him the glory of a passion was sufficient. In those halcyon moments no common human care is allowed to intrude itself. To one who has thus entered in upon the heroism of romance his own daily work, his dinners, clothes, income, father and mother, sisters and brothers, his own street and house are nothing. Hunting, shooting, rowing, Alpine-climbing, even speeches in Parliament,—if they perchance have been attained to,—all become leather or prunella.*The heavens have been opened to him, and he walks among them like a god. So it had been with Tregear. Then had come the second phase of his passion, —which is also not uncommon to young men who soar high in their first assaults. He was told that it would not do; and was not so told by a hard-hearted parent, but by the young lady herself. And she had spoken so reasonably, that he had yielded, and had walked away with that sudden feeling of a vile return to his own mean belongings, to his lodgings, and his income, which not a few ambitious young men have experienced. But she had convinced him. Then had come the journey to Italy, and the reader knows all the rest. He certainly had not derogated in transferring his affections,—but it may be doubted whether in his second love he had walked among the stars as in the first. A man can hardly mount twice among the stars. But he had been as eager,—and as true. And he had succeeded, without any flaw on his conscience. It had been agreed, when that first disruption took place, that he and Mabel should be friends; and, as to a friend, he had told her of his hopes. When first she had mingled something of sarcasm with her congratulations, though it had annoyed him, it had hardly made him unhappy. When she called him Romeo and spoke of herself as Rosaline, he took her remark as indicating some petulance rather than an enduring love. That had been womanly and he

618

could forgive it. He had his other great and solid happiness to support him. Then he had believed that she would soon marry, if not Silverbridge, then some other fitting young nobleman, and that all would be well. But now things were very far from well. The storm which was now howling round her afflicted him much.

Perhaps the bitterest feeling of all was that her love should have been so much stronger, so much more enduring than his own. He could not but remember how in his first agony he had blamed her because she had declared that they should be severed. He had then told himself that such severing would be to him impossible, and that had her nature been as high as his, it would have been as impossible to her. Which nature must he now regard as the higher? She had done her best to rid herself of the load of her passion and had failed. But he had freed himself with convenient haste. All that he had said as to the manliness of conquering grief had been wise enough. But still he could not quit himself of some feeling of disgrace in that he had changed and she had not. He tried to comfort himself with reflecting that Mary was all his own,—that in that matter he had been victorious and happy;—but for an hour or two he thought more of Mabel than of Mary.

When the time came in which he could employ himself he called for Silverbridge, and they walked together across the park to Westminster. Silverbridge was gay and full of eagerness as to the coming ministerial statement, but Tregear could not turn his mind from the work of the morning. 'I don't seem to care very much about it,' he said at last.

'I do care very much,' said Silverbridge.

'What difference will it make?'

'I breakfasted with the governor this morning, and I have not seen him in such good spirits since——, well, for a long time.' The date to which Silverbridge would have referred, had he not checked himself, was that of the evening on which it had been agreed between him and his father that Mabel Grex should be promoted to the seat of highest honour in the house of Palliser,—but that was a matter which must

619

henceforward be buried in silence. 'He did not say as much, but I feel perfectly sure that he and Mr. Monk have arranged a new government.'

'I don't see any matter for joy in that to Conservatives like you and me.'

'He is my father,—and as he is going to be your father-in-law I should have thought that you might have been pleased.'

'Oh, yes;—if he likes it. But I have heard so often of the crushing cares of office, and I had thought that of all living men he had been the most crushed by them.'

All that had to be done in the House of Commons on that afternoon was finished before five o'clock. By half-past five the House, and all the purlieus of the House, were deserted. And yet at four, immediately after prayers, there had been such a crowd that members had been unable to find seats! Tregear and Silverbridge having been early had succeeded, but those who had been less careful were obliged to listen as best they could in the galleries. The stretching out of necks and the holding of hands behind the ears did not last long. Sir Timothy had not had much to say, but what he did say was spoken with a dignity which seemed to anticipate future exaltation rather than present downfall. There had arisen a question in regard to revenue,—he need hardly tell them that it was that question in reference to brewers' licences to which the honourable gentleman opposite had alluded on the previous day,—as to which unfortunately he was not in accord with his noble friend the Prime Minister. Under the circumstances it was hardly possible that they should at once proceed to business, and he therefore moved that the House should stand adjourned till Tuesday next. That was the whole statement.

Not very long afterwards the Prime Minister made another statement in the House of Lords. As the Chancellor of the Exchequer had very suddenly resigned and had thereby broken up the Ministry, he had found himself compelled to place his resignation in the hands of her Majesty. Then that Housd was also adjourned. On that afternoon all the clubs were alive with admiration at the great cleverness displayed by Sir Timothy in this transaction. It was not only that he had succeeded in breaking up the Ministry,* and that he had done this without incurring violent disgrace; but he had so done it as to throw all the reproach upon his late unfortunate colleague. It was thus that Mr. Lupton explained it. Sir Timothy had been at the pains to ascertain on what matters connected with the Revenue, Lord Drummond,—or Lord Drummond's closest advisers,—had opinions of their own, opinions strong enough not to be abandoned; and having discovered that, he also discovered arguments on which to found an exactly contrary opinion. But as the Revenue had been entrusted specially to his unworthy hands, he was entitled to his own opinion on this matter. 'The majority of the House,' said Mr. Lupton, 'and the entire public, will no doubt give him credit for great self-abnegation.'

All this happened on the Friday. During the Saturday it was considered probable that the Cabinet would come to terms with itself, and that internal wounds would be healed. The general opinion was that Lord Drummond would give way. But on the Sunday morning it was understood that Lord Drummond would not yield. It was reported that Lord Drummond was willing to purchase his separation from Sir Timothy even at the expense of his office. That Sir Timothy should give way seemed to be impossible. Had he done so it would have been impossible for him to recover the respect of the House. Then it was rumoured that two or three others had gone with Sir Timothy. And on Monday morning it was proclaimed that the Prime Minister was not in a condition to withdraw his resignation. On the Tuesday the House met and Mr. Monk announced, still from the Opposition benches, that he had that morning been with the Queen. Then there was another adjournment, and all the Liberals knew that the gates of Paradise were again about to be opened to them.

This is only interesting to us as affecting the happiness and character of our Duke. He had consented to assist Mr. Monk in forming a government, and to take office under Mr. Monk's leadership. He had had many contests with himself before he could bring himself to this submission. He knew that if anything could once again make him contented it would be work; he knew that if he could serve his country it was his duty to serve it; and he knew also that it was only by the adhesion of such men as himself that the traditions of his party could be maintained. But he had been Prime Minister,—and he was sure he could never be Prime Minister again. There are in all matters certain little, almost hidden, signs, by which we can measure within our own bosoms the extent of our successes and our failures. Our Duke's friends had told him that his Ministry had been serviceable to the country; but no one had ever suggested to him that he would again be asked to fill the place which he had filled. He had stopped a gap. He would beforehand have declared himself willing to serve his country even in this way; but having done so,—having done that and no more than that,—he felt that he had failed. He had in his soreness declared to himself that he would never more take office. He had much to do to overcome this promise to himself;—but when he had brought himself to submit, he was certainly a happier man.

There was no going to see the Queen. That on the present occasion was done simply by Mr. Monk. But on the Wednesday morning his name appeared in the list of the new Cabinet as President of the Council. He was perhaps a little fidgety, a little too anxious to employ himself and to be employed, a little too desirous of immediate work;—but still he was happy and gracious to those around him. 'I suppose you like that particular office,' Silverbridge said to him.

'Well; yes;—not best of all, you know,' and he smiled as he made this admission.

'You mean Prime Minister?'

'No, indeed I don't. I am inclined to think that the Premier should always sit in your House. No, Silverbridge. If I could have my way,—which is of course impossible, for I cannot put off my honours,—I would return to my old place. I would return to the Exchequer where the work is hard and certain, where a man can do, or at any rate attempt to do, some special thing. A man there if he sticks to that and does not travel beyond it, need not be popular, need not be a partisan, need not be eloquent, need not be a courtier. He should understand his profession, as should a lawyer or a doctor. If he does that thoroughly he can serve his country without recourse to that parliamentary strategy for which I know that I am unfit.

'You can't do that in the House of Lords, sir.'

'No; no. I wish the title could have passed over my head, Silverbridge, and gone to you at once. I think we both should have been suited better. But there are things which one should not consider. Even in this place I may perhaps do something. Shall you attack us very bitterly?'

'I am the only man who does not mean to make any change.'

'How so?'

'I shall stay where I am,—on the Government side of the House.'

'Are you clear about that, my boy?'

'Quite clear.'

'Such changes should not be made without very much consideration.'

'I have already written to them at Silverbridge and have had three or four answers. Mr. De Boung says that the borough is more than grateful. Mr. Sprott regrets it much, and suggests a few months' consideration. Mr. Sprugeon seems to think it does not signify.'

'That is hardly complimentary.'

'No,—not to me. But he is very civil to the family. As long as a Palliser represents the borough, Mr. Sprugeon thinks that it does not matter much on which side he may sit. I have had my little vagary, and I don't think that I shall change again.'

'I suppose it is your republican bride-elect that has done that,' said the Duke, laughing.

CHAPTER LXXIX

The first wedding

As Easter Sunday fell on the 17th April, and as the arrangement of the new Cabinet, with its inferior offices, was not completed till the 6th of that month, there was only just time for the new elections before the holidays. Mr. Monk sat on his bench so comfortably that he hardly seemed ever to have been off it. And Phineas Finn resumed the peculiar ministerial tone of voice just as though he had never allowed himself to use the free and indignant strains of opposition. As to a majority,—nothing as yet was known about that. Some few besides Silverbridge might probably transfer themselves to the Government. None of the ministers lost their seats at the new elections. The opposite party seemed for a while to have been paralysed by the defection of Sir Timothy, and men who liked a quiet life were able to comfort themselves with the reflection that nothing could be done this session.

For our lovers this was convenient. Neither of them would have allowed their parliamentary energies to have interfered at such a crisis with his domestic affairs; but still it was well to have time at command. The day for the marriage of Isabel and Silverbridge had been now fixed. That was to take place on the Wednesday after Easter, and was to be celebrated by special royal favour in the chapel at Whitehall. All the Pallisers would be there, and all the relations of all the Pallisers, all the ambassadors, and of course all the Americans in London. It would be a 'wretched grind,' as Silverbridge said, but it had to be done. In the meantime the whole party, including the new President of the Council, were down at Matching. Even Isabel, though it must be presumed that she had much to do in looking after her bridal garments, was able to be there for a day or two. But Tregear was the person to whom this visit was of the greatest importance.

He had been allowed to see Lady Mary in London, but hardly to do more than see her. With her he had been alone for about five minutes, and then cruel circumstances,—circumstances, however, which were not permanently cruel,—had separated them. All their great difficulties had been settled, and no doubt they were happy. Tregear, though he had been as it were received into grace by that glass of wine, still had not entered into the intimacies of the house. This he felt himself. He had been told that he had better restrain himself from writing to Mary, and he had restrained himself. He had therefore no immediate opportunity of creeping into that perfect intimacy with the house and household which is generally accorded to a promised son-in-law.

On this occasion he travelled down alone, and as he approached the house he, who was not by nature timid, felt himself to be somewhat cowed. That the Duke should not be cold to him was almost impossible. Of course he was there in opposition to the Duke's wishes. Even Silverbridge had never quite liked the match. Of course he was to have all that he desired. Of course he was the most fortunate of men. Of course no man had ever stronger reason to be contented with the girl he loved. But still his heart was a little low as he was driven up to the door.

The first person whom he saw was the Duke himself, who, as the fly from the station arrived, was returning from his walk. 'You are welcome to Matching,' he said, taking off his hat with something of ceremony. This was said before the servants, but Tregear was then led into the study and the door was closed. 'I never do anything by halves, Mr. Tregear,' he said. 'Since it is to be so you shall be the same to me as though you had come under other auspices. Of yourself personally I hear all that is good. Consider yourself at home here, and in all things use me as your friend.' Tregear endeavoured to make some reply, but could not find words that were fitting. 'I think that the young people are out,' continued the Duke. 'Mr. Warburton will help you to find them if you like to go upon the search.' The words had been very gracious, but still there was something in the manner of the man which made Tregear find it almost impossible to regard him as he might have regarded another father-in-law. He had often heard the Duke spoken of as a man who could become awful if he pleased, almost without an effort. He had been told of the man's mingled simplicity, courtesy, and self-assertion against which no impudence or raillery could prevail. And now he seemed to understand it.

He was not driven to go under the private secretary's escort in quest of the young people. Mary had understood her business much better than that. 'If you please, sir, Lady Mary is in the little drawing-room,' said a well-arrayed young girl to him as soon as the Duke's door was closed. This was Lady Mary's own maid who had been on the look-out for the fly. Lady Mary had known all details, as to the arrival of the trains and the length of the journey from the station, and had not been walking with the other young people when the Duke had intercepted her lover. Even that delay she had thought was hard. The discreet maid opened the door of the little drawing-room,—and discreetly closed it instantly. 'At last!' she said, throwing herself into his arms.

'Yes,—at last.'

On this occasion time did not envy them. The long afternoons of spring had come, and as Tregear had reached the house between four and five they were able to go out together before the sun set. 'No,' she said when he came to inquire as to her life during the last twelve months; 'you had not much to be afraid of as to my forgetting.'

'But when everything was against me?'

'One thing was not against you. You ought to have been sure of that.'

'And so I was. And yet I felt that I ought not to have been sure. Sometimes, in my solitude, I used to think that I myself had been wrong. I began to doubt whether under any circumstances I could have been justified in asking your father's daughter to be my wife.'

'Because of his rank?'

'Not so much his rank as his money.'

'Ought that to be considered?'

'A poor man who marries a rich woman will always be suspected.'

'Because people are so mean and poor-spirited; and because they think that money is more than anything else. It should be nothing at all in such matters. I don't know how it can be anything. They have been saying that to me all along,—as though one were to stop to think whether one was rich or poor.' Tregear, when this was said, could not but remember that at a time not very much prior to that at which Mary had not stopped to think, neither for a while had he and Mabel. 'I suppose it was worse for me than for you,' she added.

'I hope not.'

'But it was, Frank; and therefore I ought to have it made up to me now. It was very bad to be alone here, particularly when I felt that papa always looked at me as though I were a sinner. He did not mean it, but he could not help looking at me like that. And there was nobody to whom I could say a word.'

'It was pretty much the same with me.'

'Yes; but you were not offending a father who could not keep himself from looking reproaches at you. I was like a boy at school who had been put into Coventry. And then they sent me to Lady Cantrip!'

'Was that very bad?'

'I do believe that if I were a young woman with a well-ordered mind, I should feel myself very much indebted to Lady Cantrip. She had a terrible task of it. But I could not teach myself to like her. I believe she knew all through that I should get my way at last.'

'That ought to have made you friends.'

'But yet she tried everything she could. And when I told her about that meeting up at Lord Grex's, she was so shocked! Do you remember that?'

'Do I remember it!'

'Were not you shocked?' This question was not to be answered by any word. 'I was,' she continued. 'It was an awful thing to do; but I was determined to show them all that I was in earnest. Do you remember how Miss Cassewary looked?'

'Miss Cassewary knew all about it.'

'I daresay she did. And so I suppose did Mabel Grex. I had thought that perhaps I might make Mabel a confidante, but——' Then she looked up into his face.

'But what?'

'You like Mabel, do you not? I do.'

'I like her very, very much.'

'Perhaps you have liked her too well for that, eh, Frank?'

'Too well for what?'

'That she should have heard all that I had to say about you with sympathy. If so, I am so sorry.'

'You need not fear that I have ever for a moment been untrue either to her or you.'

'I am sure you have not to me. Poor Mabel! Then they took me to Custins. That was worst of all. I cannot quite tell you what happened there.' Of course he asked her,—but, as she had said, she could not quite tell him about Lord Popplecourt.

The next morning the Duke asked his guest in a playful tone what was his Christian name. It could hardly be that he should not have known, but yet he asked the question. 'Francis Oliphant,' said Tregear. 'Those are two Christian names I suppose, but what do they call you at home?'

'Frank,' whispered Mary, who was with them.

'Then I will call you Frank, if you will allow me. The use of Christian names is, I think, pleasant and hardly common enough among us. I almost forget my own boy's name because the practice has grown up of calling him by a title.'

'I am going to call him Abraham,' said Isabel.

'Abraham is a good name, only I do not think he got it from his godfathers and godmothers.'

'Who can call a man Plantagenet? I should as soon think of calling my father-in-law Cœur de Lion.'

'So he is,' said Mary. Whereupon the Duke kissed the two girls and went his way,—showing that by this time he had adopted the one and the proposed husband of the other into his heart.

The day before the Duke started for London to be present at the grand marriage he sent for Frank. 'I suppose,' said he, 'that you would wish that some time should be fixed for your own marriage.' To this the accepted suitor of course assented. 'But before we can do that something must be settled about—money.' Tregear when he heard this became hot all over, and felt that he could not restrain his blushes. Such must be the feeling of a man when he finds himself compelled to own to a girl's father that he intends to live upon her money and not upon his own. 'I do not like to be troublesome,' continued the Duke, 'or to ask questions which might seem to be impertinent.'

'Oh no! Of course I feel my position. I can only say that it was not because your daughter might probably have money that I first sought her love.'

'It shall be so received. And now—— But perhaps it will be best that you should arrange all this with my man of business. Mr. Moreton shall be instructed. Mr. Moreton lives near my place in Barsetshire, but is now in London. If you will call on him he shall tell you what I would suggest. I hope you will find that your affairs will be comfortable. And now as to the time.'

Isabel's wedding was declared by the newspapers to have been one of the most brilliant remembered in the metropolis. There were six bridesmaids, of whom of course Mary was one,—and of whom poor Lady Mabel Grex was equally of course not another. Poor Lady Mabel was at this time with Miss Cassewary at Grex, paying what she believed would be a last visit to the old family home. Among the others were two American girls, brought into that august society for the sake of courtesy rather than of personal love. And there were two other Palliser girls and a Scotch McCloskie cousin. The breakfast was of course given by Mr. Boncassen at his house

in Brook Street, where the bridal presents were displayed.
And not only were they displayed; but a list of them, with an
approximating statement as to their value, appeared in one or
two of the next day's newspapers;—as to which terrible sin
against good taste neither was Mr. or Mrs. Boncassen guilty.
But in these days, in which such splendid things were done on
so very splendid a scale, a young lady cannot herself lay out
her friends' gifts so as to be properly seen by her friends. Some
well-skilled, well-paid hand is needed even for that, and hence
comes this public information on affairs which should surely
be private. In our grandmothers' time the happy bride's happy
mother herself compounded the cake;—or at any rate the
trusted housekeeper. But we all know that terrible tower of
silver which now stands niddle-noddling with its appendages
of flags and spears on the modern wedding breakfast-table.
It will come to pass with some of us soon that we must deny
ourselves the pleasure of having young friends, because their
marriage presents are so costly.

Poor Mrs. Boncassen had not perhaps a happy time with
her august guests on that morning; but when she retired to
give Isabel her last kiss in privacy she did feel proud to think
that her daughter would some day be an English Duchess.

CHAPTER LXXX
The second wedding

NOVEMBER is not altogether an hymeneal month, but it was
not till November that Lady Mary Palliser became the
wife of Frank Tregear. It was postponed a little, perhaps, in
order that the Silverbridges,—as they were now called,—
might be present. The Silverbridges, who were now quite
Darby and Joan, had gone to the States when the Session had
been brought to a close early in August, and had remained
there nearly three months. Isabel had taken infinite pleasure
in showing her English husband to her American friends, and
the American friends had no doubt taken a pride in seeing so
glorious a British husband in the hands of an American wife.

Everything was new to Silverbridge, and he was happy in his new possession. She too enjoyed it infinitely, and so it happened that they had been unwilling to curtail their sojourn. But in November they had to return, because Mary had declared that her marriage should be postponed till it could be graced by the presence of her elder brother.

The marriage of Silverbridge had been august. There had been a manifest intention that it should be so. Nobody knew with whom this originated. Mrs. Boncassen had probably been told that it ought to be so, and Mr. Boncassen had been willing to pay the bill. External forces had perhaps operated. The Duke had simply been passive and obedient. There had however been a general feeling that the bride of the heir of the house of Omnium should be produced to the world amidst a blare of trumpets and a glare of torches. So it had been. But both the Duke and Mary were determined that this other wedding should be different. It was to take place at Matching, and none would be present but they who were staying in the house, or who lived around,—such as tenants and dependants. Four clergymen united their forces to tie Isabel to her husband, one of whom was a bishop, one a canon, and the two others royal chaplains; but there was only to be the Vicar of the parish at Matching. And indeed there were no guests in the house except the two bridesmaids and Mr. and Mrs. Finn. As to Mrs. Finn, Mary had made a request, and then the Duke had suggested that the husband should be asked to accompany his wife.

It was very pretty. The church itself is pretty, standing in the park, close to the ruins of the old Priory, not above three hundred yards from the house. And they all walked, taking the broad pathway through the ruins, going under that figure of Sir Guy which Silverbridge had pointed out to Isabel when they had been whispering there together. The Duke led the way with his girl upon his arm. The two bridesmaids followed. Then Silverbridge and his wife, with Phineas and his wife. Gerald and the bridegroom accompanied them, belonging as it were to the same party! It was very rustic;—almost improper! 'This is altogether wrong, you know,' said Gerald. 'You should appear coming from some other part of the world, as if you were almost unexpected. You ought not to have been in the house at all, and certainly should have gone under some disguise.'

There had been rich presents too on this occasion, but they were shown to none except to Mrs. Finn and the bridesmaids, —and perhaps to the favoured servants in the house. At any rate there was nothing said of them in the newspapers. One present there was,—given not to the bride but to the bride-groom,—which he showed to no one except to her. This came to him only on the morning of his marriage, and the envelope containing it bore the postmark of Sedbergh. He knew the handwriting well before he opened the parcel. It contained a small signet-ring with his crest, and with it there were but a few words written on a scrap of paper. 'I pray that you may be happy. This was to have been given to you long ago, but I kept it back because of that decision.' He showed the ring to Mary and told her it had come from Lady Mabel;—but the scrap of paper no one saw but himself.

Perhaps the matter most remarkable in the wedding was the

hilarity of the Duke. One who did not know him well might have said that he was a man with few cares, and who now took special joy in the happiness of his children,—who was thoroughly contented to see them marry after their own hearts. And yet, as he stood there on the altar-steps giving his daughter to that new son and looking first at his girl, and then at his married son, he was reminding himself of all that he had suffered.

After the breakfast,—which was by no means a grand repast and at which the cake did not look so like an ill-soldered silver castle as that other construction had done,—the happy couple were sent away in a modest chariot to the railway station, and not above half-a-dozen slippers were thrown after them. There were enough for luck,—or perhaps there might have been luck even without them, for the wife thoroughly respected her husband, as did the husband his wife. Mrs. Finn, when she was alone with Phineas, said a word or two about Frank Tregear. 'When she first told me of her engagement I did not think it possible that she should marry him. But after he had been with me I felt sure that he would succeed.'

'Well, sir,' said Silverbridge to the Duke when they were out together in the park that afternoon, 'what do you think about him?'

'I think he is a manly young man.'

'He is certainly that. And then he knows things and understands them. It was never a surprise to me that Mary should have been so fond of him.'

'I do not know that one ought to be surprised at anything. Perhaps what surprised me most was that he should have looked so high. There seemed to be so little to justify it. But now I will accept that as courage which I before regarded as arrogance.'

EXPLANATORY NOTES

CHAPTER I

Page 1. (1) *our old friend*: the life story of Plantagenet Palliser, Duke of Omnium, unfolds, beginning with *The Small House at Allington* (serialized 1862–4) through *Can You Forgive Her?* (1864–5), *Phineas Finn* (1867–9), *The Eustace Diamonds* (1871–3), *Phineas Redux* (1873–4) and *The Prime Minister* (1875–6). Trollope 'lived with' the characters of Palliser and Glencora for sixteen years, and said in the *Autobiography* (written 1875–6) that 'Plantagenet Palliser stands more firmly on the ground than any other personage I have created'. It is apparent from the first sentence of *D.C.* that it is closely related to the other 'Palliser' novels, in particular to *Can You Forgive Her?*

(2) *Lady Mary, the only daughter*: in *The Prime Minister*, the Pallisers had 'two little girls' (Ch. XIX), one of whom is referred to as 'little Lady Glencora, the Duchess's eldest daughter' (Ch. LXVIII). Trollope seems to have forgotten about Lady Mary's sister.

(3) *the Italian lakes*: the Duke's attempt to enjoy his holiday is reminiscent of his efforts in *Can You Forgive Her?* to make the best of Switzerland ('He did not care for scenery', Ch. LXX). It was a complaint of many hardworking Victorians (such as Darwin and J. S. Mill) that pressures of work and thought had robbed them of the enjoyment of poetry, landscape, and other aesthetic pleasures.

(4) *banished*: see *Phineas Redux*, Ch. XXVI, and *The Prime Minister*, Ch. VI, for the history of Palliser's political career. Inheriting the Dukedom from his uncle meant that 'he could never sit again in the House of Commons'. The course of Palliser's Prime Ministership and of Glencora's 'troubles' as a leader of fashion is told in *The Prime Minister*.

Page 2. (1) *187–*: *D.C.* was composed between 2 May 1876 and 29 October 1876. It was serialized between 1879 and 1880 and published in 1880. The minister in power in *D.C.*, Sir Timothy Beeswax, bears some resemblance to Disraeli, who was Prime Minister from 1874 to 1880. *D.C.*, then, is set in the mid-1870s. But see notes to pp. 162 and 165 (1).

(2) *Matching Priory*: the Pallisers' country seat. See *Can You Forgive Her?*, Ch. XXII, for a description.

Page 4. (1) *guardians*: this recapitulation of the Pallisers' marital history is the first of many references back to *Can You Forgive Her?*. Ch. XVIII of *Can You Forgive Her?* describes the pressure placed on Glencora by her elderly relatives to marry Palliser.

(2) *Mrs. Finn*: the course of the friendship between Glencora and Madame Max Goesler, later Mrs. Finn, is described in *Phineas Finn*, *The Eustace Diamonds*, *Phineas Redux* and *The Prime Minister*. Madame Max is first seen in *Phineas Finn*, Ch. XL.

Page 5. (1) *ruins of the old Priory*: the reference will remind the reader of *Can You Forgive Her?* of a rash walk taken by Glencora among those ruins in the early days of her marriage (Ch. XXVII). See, also, p. 632 below.

(2) *M'Closkies*: in *Can You Forgive Her?* Glencora's maiden name is spelt 'M'Cluskie'.

Page 7. (1) *Lady Cantrip*: the Countess of Cantrip, of Custins in Dorset, wife of a Liberal Cabinet Minister, mother of two daughters (one of whom is married to Lord Nidderdale) appears first at a 'semi-political' dinner given by Glencora (*Phineas Finn*, Ch. XL) and again in *Phineas Finn*, *Phineas Redux* and *The Prime Minister* as a friend to the Finns and the Pallisers.

(2) *Mrs. Jeffrey Palliser*: he is a cousin of Palliser's, whose father had been the old Duke of Omnium's favourite son. He stood to inherit the dukedom if Glencora had had no children. See *Can You Forgive Her?*, Ch. XXV.

Page 8. *The Greys*: Alice Vavasor's reluctance to marry John Grey is the 'main' plot of *Can You Forgive Her?*. After that novel, the Greys play a much diminished part in the Palliser novels.

CHAPTER II

Page 9. *about fifteen hundred a year*: Tregear is later referred to as 'a commoner without an income' (p. 16). Dudley Baxter's *National Income* (1868) describes a 'large income' as over £5,000 a year.

Page 10. (1) *her own early days*: Glencora's renunciation of Burgo Fitzgerald, whom she loved at the time she was persuaded to marry Palliser (see *Can You Forgive Her?*) is constantly referred to in *D.C.*

(2) *the great wealth*: Glencora was 'a great heiress' and brought her husband an enormous fortune. See *Can You Forgive Her?*, Ch. XVIII, etc.

Page 13. (1) *Lady Midlothian*: Lady Mary, unlike her mother, refuses to be bullied by older women. Lady Midlothian was Glencora's aunt, who, though she had herself made an unfortunate marriage, took it upon herself to give advice to Alice Vavasor and to Glencora in *Can You Forgive Her?* (Ch. XXVI).

(2) *the reader may possibly know*: Trollope refers us to the history of Madame Max's 'disinterested' friendship with the Duke of Omnium and his family (found in *Phineas Finn* and *Phineas Redux*).

Page 15. *He is a gentleman*: the difficulty of defining the word is a constant theme of *D.C.* For a discussion of Trollope's idea of a gentleman, see *The Gentleman in Trollope* by Shirley Robin Letwin, Macmillan, 1982.

CHAPTER III

Page 19. *gone out in honours*: Tregear took a second-class degree, but gained special distinction for proficiency in scholarship beyond that required to pass the exam.

Page 20. *another man*: Burgo Fitzgerald, first described in Ch. XXIX of *Can You Forgive Her?*.

Page 21. *Crim Tartary*: Frank Tregear's brother's travels to Asia may also be a euphemistic way of saying that he is going to the devil, Tartary being associated with the nether regions as well as with the far Eastern lands of Ghenghis Khan and Tamburlaine.

Page 22. *to bell the cat*: to undertake something dangerous.

Page 23. *as one of the Conservative party*: 'There has never been a Tory Palliser known, you know', Jeffrey Palliser tells Alice in Ch. XXIII of *Can You Forgive Her?* Silverbridge's defection to the Conservatives is, to his father, a betrayal of his family's whole history.

Page 24. *my grandfather*: Silverbridge is in fact referring to his great-uncle, the old Duke of Omnium.

CHAPTER IV

Page 26. (1) *None but the brave*: Dryden, 'Alexander's Feast', 1. 15: 'None but the brave deserves the fair'. See also p. 532.

(2) *de l'audace*: Danton, Speech, 2 September 1792.

EXPLANATORY NOTES

Page 28. *an enormous legacy*: Madame Max refused to accept the legacy left her by the old Duke of Omnium (*Phineas Redux*, Ch. XXX) and Glencora arranged that the sum (of £25,000) should be transferred to Adelaide Palliser, Palliser's first cousin, so that she could marry the penniless Gerard Maule (*Phineas Redux*, Ch. LXIX).

Page 33. (1) *the county*: the county is West Barsetshire and 'the borough' is Silverbridge. Glencora explains in *Can You Forgive Her?*, Ch. XXII, that the old Duke of Omnium chose to keep Silverbridge as his 'pocket borough' after the 1832 Reform Bill. Palliser represented it in *The Small House at Allington* (hence the reference on p. 36: 'You used to sit for Silverbridge, papa') and 'gave' it to John Grey in *Can You Forgive Her?*. But when Palliser inherits the Dukedom and becomes Prime Minister, he is anxious not to be 'a borough-mongering lord' (*The Prime Minister*, Ch. XXVII) and resists Glencora's plot to bring in a Liberal candidate, Lopez. Arthur Fletcher, a Conservative, holds the seat in *The Prime Minister*. But, in spite of the Reform Bills of 1832 and 1867, and of the Ballot Act of 1872, the tenantry of the Duke of Omnium might still be expected to return a member of the family: in many agricultural counties and smaller boroughs the old oligarchical spirit continued strong as late as the 1880 elections.

The Duke wants his son to stand as a Liberal for West Barset, as the old Duke wanted Palliser to 'come in for the county' (*Can You Forgive Her?*, Ch. LXXIX), since it would be appropriate for the heir: county members were elected on a narrower franchise than those elected by boroughs, and were regarded as representing the aristocratic landed interest. Also, as he says (p. 36), 'There is hardly another agricultural county in England that will return a Liberal.' After the 1867 Reform Bill, most of the new county voters came from the middle class, and the general result was in favour of the Conservatives. The 1874 election showed that it was the Whigs, not the Tories, whose power had been challenged by the extension of the franchise. For the election, see further, p. 105.

(2) *the Radicals*: used from the early nineteenth century for supporters of radical reform and so for the extreme branch of the Liberal party.

CHAPTER V

Page 40. *Croesus*: last king of Lydia, legendary for his wealth.

638

Page 43. *Pandarus*: any go-between; character from Chaucer's *Troilus and Criseyde* or Shakespeare's *Troilus and Cressida*.

CHAPTER VI

Page 45. (1) *Beargarden Club*: see *The Way We Live Now* (1875).

(2) *Carlist army*: the main Carlist wars were waged between 1834–9 (for the claim of Don Carlos (1788–1855) to the Spanish throne) and between 1872–6. These dates would be too early or too late for Major Tifto; Trollope may have been thinking of the Carlist campaign of 1846–8 on behalf of Don Carlos's son.

Page 46. (1) *M.F.H.*: Master of Fox Hounds. Runnymede is on the South Bank of the Thames near Windsor (hence 'quasi-suburban'). The financial problems for Tifto are made clear by Trollope's accounts of 'The Master of Hounds' in *Hunting Sketches* (1865) and his essay 'On Hunting' in *British Sports and Pastimes* (1868) (a collection of essays first published in *St. Paul's Magazine*, edited by Trollope). In the latter, Trollope describes the change from the old 'grand phase' of hunting with a 'great lord' such as the Duke of Beaufort, to 'subscription packs'. 'It is too often the case that the amount subscribed is altogether inadequate for the purpose' ('On Hunting'). He estimates the Master's cost of maintaining a pack of foxhounds at £2,700 a year. Trollope lays down the rules for the Master in *Hunting Sketches*: 'The master of hounds shall be a country gentleman who takes a subscription, and who therefore, on becoming autocratic, makes himself answerable to certain general rules for the management of his autocracy. He shall hunt not less, let us say, than three days a week' (Tifto hunts five days a fortnight); 'He will draw fairly through the day, and indulge no caprices as to coverts . . . In the hunting-field, as in all other communities, republics, and governments, the power of the purse is everything . . . He should be a rich man. Whatever the subscription paid to him, he must go beyond it—very much beyond it—or there will grow up against him a feeling that he is mean.' No wonder Tifto needs to sell, and bet on racehorses, if he is to run his pack on £800 a year. (For the ideal M.F.H., see *Phineas Redux*, Ch. VII.)

(2) *blackballs*: votes to exclude a person from a club.

Page 47. (1) *steeple chases*: Trollope has the original meaning in mind, of a cross-country race in which men matched their hunters against each other by following the pointer of a steeple over any obstacles. Later, made-up steeplechase courses came into use.

(2) *Egham*: on the Thames near Windsor.

(3) *the great Leamington handicap:* run at Warwick on the steeplechase course laid out there in the mid-1840s.

Page 48. (1) *'straight tip'*: name of the winning horse.

(2) *Newmarket*: Trollope calls it 'the headquarters of the racing community' in *British Sports and Pastimes*.

Page 49. (1) *a dash at loo*: 'to have a dash on' meant to bet (used from *c.* 1865); 'loo' was a round card game played by a varying number of players.

(2) *blind hookey*: a card game (said in *The Century Dictionary* of 1911 to be 'frequently played on transatlantic steamers') in which the dealer offers the pack to the players and they divide it into several piles, face down. One of these, chosen at random, is the dealer's. Bets are placed on the remaining piles and all are turned face up. The bottom cards of each pile that are higher than that of the dealer's, win; those lower, lose. Also called 'dutch bank'.

Page 50. *at the Craven . . . and . . . at Chester*: the Craven Stakes were run in April, and the Chester Cup (first run in 1824) in early May. The Chester Cup was notorious for the heavy gambling associated with it and for the roughness of the course.

Page 51. (1) *Solomon*: a professional tipster.

(2) *Adolphus Longstaff*: son of the hard-up squire of Cavesham. He and his family become involved with the swindler Melmotte in *The Way We Live Now*, where his name is spelt 'Longestaffe'.

(3) *Lord Nidderdale*: eldest son of the Marquis of Auld Reekie and cousin of Glencora. In *The Way We Live Now* he offered to marry Marie Melmotte, but later marries Lord Cantrip's daughter. See further, p. 93.

Page 52. *Mdlle* [*Mlle.*] *Stuffa*: opera singers such as Adelina Patti and Christine Nilsson were the talk of the town.

CHAPTER VII

Page 53. *a conservative member*: Arthur Fletcher. See *The Prime Minister*; and p. 33, note (1) (above).

EXPLANATORY NOTES

Page 56. *Racing was an amusement*: Palliser's attitude to horse-racing as a pastime for aristocratic gentlemen is that of Trollope's contributor to *British Sports and Pastimes*, the Hon. Francis Lawley, who wrote the essay on 'Horse-Racing'. The sport has deteriorated due to the increase in heavy betting and money-lending: 'The racehorse, it would seem, is a more democratic leveller than Mr. Beales or Mr. Odger [President of the Reform League and working-class trades unionist]; a greater disintegrator of aristocratic society than the railroad, or the penny press, or the electric cable, or the Reform Bill itself . . . Since the death of Lord Palmerston, and the secession of Lord Derby and General Peel from active participation in Turf pursuits, we seem to have fallen upon times which forbid any politician who writes Right Honourable before his name to own a Derby favourite. The impure atmosphere which has long pervaded the Turf, and which led the Queen, influenced by her husband, to withdraw her countenance and interest from her people's favourite national pastime, warns all aspiring men in public life that the ownership of racehorses is now-a-days a *diminutio capitis*.' (1868).

Page 57. (1) *Communists*: first began to be used in the 1840s of those who supported the equal distribution of property.

(2) *the greatest benefit . . . greatest number*: Palliser's echo of Bentham ('The greatest happiness of the greatest number is the foundation of morals and legislation', *Works*, x. 142) suggests not so much that he is a wholehearted utilitarian as that, like Trollope, he believes that 'the peculiar excellencies of the English social system attempted to reconcile self-help and social order' (Asa Briggs, 'Trollope, Bagehot, and the English Constitution', *Victorian People*, 1955). Trollope calls himself an 'advanced Conservative Liberal' (*Autobiography*, Ch. XVI) and his views are often expressed through Palliser.

Page 59. *to endeavour to be just . . . study of his life*: here, as often, Trollope's account of Palliser resembles his account of Cicero, who 'had learned to feel that a man's final duty here on earth is his duty to other men' (*Cicero*, Vol. 2, Ch. 8; 1880) and whose *De Officiis*, like Palliser's 'code' in *D.C.*, is addressed to his son. (See Ruth Ap Roberts, *Trollope: Artist and Moralist*, Athens, Ohio, 1971, for a full account of Trollope's relation to Cicero.) Palliser mentions Cicero on p. 196.

CHAPTER VIII

Page 61. *Gatherum Castle*: the 'vast palace' which the old Duke of Omnium, Palliser's uncle, had built 'at the cost of nearly a quarter of a million' (*Can You Forgive Her?*, Ch. XVIII. It is first described in *Doctor Thorne*, Ch. XIX).

Page 63. *Lucullus*: a Roman (110–57 BC) whose luxurious banquets became proverbial.

CHAPTER IX

Page 69. *'in medias res'*: in the middle of things. From Horace, *Ars Poetica*, 148.

Page 71. *the Seven Dials*: 'one of the most remarkable localities in London, inhabited by bird-fanciers, keepers of stores of old clothes and old shoes, coster-mongers, patterers, and a motley assemblage of others, chiefly of the lower classes' (Mayhew, *London Labour and the London Poor*, 1862). It is just round the corner from the livery stables of Major Tifto's friend (p. 456)—and, obviously, not a 'gentleman's' area.

Page 72. *a government which contained many Conservatives*: Miss Cassewary refers to the coalition headed by Palliser in *The Prime Minister*.

Page 73. *the Beaufort*: a betting club, with a stiff entrance fee and an election for members. In *The Small House at Allington*, Bernard Dale and Adolphus Crosbie are members.

Page 75. (1) *the Duke's borough*: Silverbridge.
(2) *ratting himself*: deserting his own party.

Page 76. *brougham*: one-horse closed carriage.

CHAPTER X

Page 80. *like a Romeo . . . of his love for Juliet*: see *Romeo and Juliet*, I. ii and II. iii, for Romeo's earlier love for Rosaline. Mabel Grex's nickname, Lady Mab, is a reminder of Mercutio's 'Queen Mab' speech, *Romeo and Juliet*, I. iv. Further references to this play are made on pp. 182, 230, 252.

CHAPTER XI

Page 86. *The Horns*: a pretty riverside Richmond villa, given to Glencora by the old Duke. See *The Prime Minister*, Ch. XXXVII.

CHAPTER XII

Page 92. *The pity of it*: *Othello*, IV. i. Not a very apposite reference here, but one much liked by Trollope. See *He Knew He was Right*, Ch. XLV.

CHAPTER XIII

Page 103. *privity*: secrecy.

CHAPTER XIV

Page 105. *sundry politicians,—Mr. Sprugeon and Mr. Sprout and Mr. Du Boung*: Mr. Sprugeon, the Silverbridge ironmonger who proposed Lopez as a candidate for Silverbridge in *The Prime Minister*, but then threw him over (Ch. XXXIV); Mr. Sprout, a Silverbridge manufacturer of cork soles (those recommended by Lady Rosina de Courcy to Palliser in *The Prime Minister*, Ch. XXVII), who supported Mr. Du Boung (a Coalition candidate) against Lopez and Fletcher in the last Silverbridge election; Mr. Du Boung, the local brewer, who lost to Fletcher in that election. 'Du Boung used to be plain English as Bung before he got rich and made his name beautiful' (*The Prime Minister*, Ch. XXXIV). Du Boung has agreed not to stand at this election: see further, pp. 110–11.

Page 111. (1) *Dr. Tempest*: the old rector of Silverbridge, who chaired the commission to examine Mr. Crawley in *The Last Chronicle of Barset*.

(2) *Mr. Walker*: the town's leading attorney, of the firm of Walker and Winthrop, who deals with the Duke's local business.

CHAPTER XV

Page 121. *one or two things*: cf. Palliser's speech to Phineas Finn (*The Prime Minister*, Ch. LXVIII) on his parliamentary beliefs; Trollope's own idea of parliament in *Autobiography*, Ch. XVI and Trollope's *Life of Palmerston* (1882): 'To do the best he could for English interests, and to do that best in an honest and manly manner, was his object' (Ch. V).

CHAPTER XVI

Page 123. *Mr. Monk*: Joshua Monk, a Radical Liberal, MP for Pottery Hamlets, successively President of the Board of Trade,

Chancellor of the Exchequer and Prime Minister. Befriends Phineas Finn and is described as 'of all members of the Cabinet the most advanced Liberal'. (See *Phineas Finn*, Ch. XIV.)

Page 124. Sir Timothy Beeswax: Solicitor-General under Daubeny and in Palliser's Coalition government, from which he retired. Leader of the House of Commons in the Gresham and Drummond Governments. A Conservative enemy of Palliser, and an antithesis to him in every way, more fully described in Ch. XXI.

Page 126. When I was a child: 'I spake as a child, I understood as a child', 1 Cor. 13: 11.

Page 127. full of chaff: a great tease.

CHAPTER XVII

Page 129. Newmarket Second Spring Meeting: in May. (Presumably the Newmarket Handicap.)

Page 130. two pounds more: the value of horses is estimated on the turf by their ability to carry weight. In handicaps, horses carry weights according to their presumed capacity, as calculated by handicappers who are licensed by the Jockey Club and employed by the directors of different race-meetings. The handicap weight-for-age scale was devised by Admiral Rous, the Jockey Club steward, in the 1850s, and revised in 1873. The system was new enough to allow for mistakes: Lord Silverbridge had allowed an unfair handicap on Coalition.

Page 131. (1) *Prime Minister*: a horse called The Prime Minister was strongly backed at 7–1 for the 1851 Derby but came nowhere. A famous horse called Plenipotentiary (known as 'Plenipo') won in 1834, beating a fine horse called Glencoe. (Could there be an echo of these names in 'Planty Pall' and 'Glencora'?)

(2) *four to one*: the odds on Prime Minister are narrow (i.e. he is heavily fancied to win). By the end of the evening Silverbridge is prepared to wager even money (i.e. a bet that wins an identical sum if it succeeds) on his horse.

Page 132. money-lenders: Trollope was in trouble with a money-lender in his youth. See *Autobiography*, Ch. III.

Page 133. (1) *University pundits*: scholars or men of authority.

(2) *Member of Parliament*: 'To adjourn over Derby Day is part of

the unwritten law of parliament.' Palmerston, 1860, quoted in *British Sports and Pastimes*.

Page 134. (1) *three-year-old*: the first Derby was run in 1780 for three-year-old colts and fillies over the distance of a mile. It was extended to 1½ miles in 1784. The present Derby course was first used in 1872. The race was run on the Wednesday of the week of the 31 May. The winner needs both speed and staying power, as this discussion shows.

(2) *the Downs*: Epsom.

(3) *the Leger*: the St. Leger Stakes at Doncaster for three-year-old colts and fillies was run (over 1 mile, 6 furlongs and 127 yards) in the second week in September. The race was first run in 1776 and first named in 1778. At the time of *D.C.* it was, like the Derby, a great annual event (in 1892, 173 special trains conveyed huge crowds to the course). Betting on the Leger might be done months before the race.

Page 135. (1) *the Jockey Club*: the authority of the Jockey Club grew up during the 1780s and '90s; by the mid-nineteenth century its power as the governing body that regulates and controls horse-racing was firmly established.

(2) *crack shire pack*: top class county pack of hounds.

(3) *a drag*: a four-horse coach with seats inside and on top. Also called a 'four-in-hand'.

Page 137. *a hansom cab*: a two-wheeled one-horse carriage with a roof, the driver sat outside.

CHAPTER XVIII

Page 140. (1) *gated*: confined to college bounds.

(2) *the Oaks*: like the Derby, run at Epsom, over 1½ miles, in June. First run in 1779, and named after the house where in 1778 the Earl of Derby decided to start these two great races. For three-year-old fillies.

Page 145. *attaché*: junior member of the staff of an embassy or legation.

CHAPTER XIX

Page 153. (1) *Sir Orlando Drought*: a Conservative minister and enemy of Palliser, from whose Coalition government (as First Lord of the Admiralty) he resigned. See *The Prime Minister*, Ch. XXXVIII; also *Phineas Redux*, Chs. XXXV, LXIII, and *The Way We Live Now*, Chs. LXIX, LXXXIII.

(2) *sugar*: in 1874, the general duty on sugar was repealed in Northcote's budget. (In 1887 there was to be an International Conference to discuss the flooding of British markets with sugar sold at depressed prices by the protectionist countries of Europe.)

CHAPTER XX

Page 158. *Mrs. Montacute Jones*: an old lady lavish with her hospitality. She is the friend and champion of Mary Germain in *Is He Popenjoy?* (1878).

CHAPTER XXI

Page 162. *a great Conservative reaction*: Disraeli had come into office in 1874. John Halperin argues that Sir Timothy, as described here and in Ch. LXXVI, resembles Daubeny (in *Phineas Finn* and *Phineas Redux*) and that both are modelled on Disraeli (whom Trollope refers to in similar terms in *Autobiography* (Ch. VIII). (See *Trollope and Politics*, Macmillan, 1977.) P. D. Edwards, however, says of *D.C.* that Trollope carefully avoids 'allusions that would roughly date its action'. Since 'the great Conservative reaction' of 'no more than two years ago' there has already been a subsequent election at which a Liberal recovery began. At the end of the novel, the Conservatives are supplanted after less than three years in power. Trollope cannot have thought in 1876 that Disraeli's government would be so short-lived. (See *Anthony Trollope: His Art and Scope*, Harvester, 1978, esp. pp. 228–9.)

Page 165. (1) *lick the Russians*: public feeling was running extremely high in 1876 over the Russian conflict with Turkey. Later that year Trollope appeared on the same public platform as Gladstone to speak in favour of the Russians (*Times*, 9 Dec. 1876, 7–8). In 1877 the British cabinet decided to declare war with Russia if she were to invade Constantinople. In 1878, Jingoist war fever was at its height, and Queen Victoria wrote in her letters that 'war with Russia was inevitable now or later'.

(2) *get the better of the Americans*: the Treaty of Washington of 8 May 1871 gave to American subjects the liberty of fishing off

Eastern Canadian shores in return for liberty to British subjects to fish off the East Coast of the USA north of latitude 39. But this exchange of fishing privileges continued to be contentious until the treaty lapsed in 1885. Both these areas of public concern were of long standing, as P. D. Edwards points out, and do not date the novel exactly.

Page 166. *a Pitt or a Peel*: William Pitt the younger, great Conservative reformer and statesman, Prime Minister 1783–1801 and 1804–6; Robert Peel, the great Conservative Prime Minister who repealed the Corn Laws in 1846, thereby splitting the Tory party.

CHAPTER XXII

Page 168. *There had been a coalition*: the fortunes of the coalition under Palliser are given in *The Prime Minister*.

Page 169. (1) *the old Duke of St. Bungay*: first described in *Phineas Finn*, Ch. XXIX, as 'the very front and head of the aristocratic old Whigs of the country'; prominent in *Phineas Finn*, *Phineas Redux* and *The Prime Minister* as mentor, friend and adviser to Palliser and to Glencora.

(2) *Solve senescentem*: 'the ageing horse should be put out to grass' (Horace, *Epistles*, I. i. 8).

(3) *Lord Grey*: Whig prime minister from 1830–4, who described himself as 'aristocratic both by position and by nature'. The Duke's letter places him firmly in that old aristocratic Whig tradition.

(4) *the emancipation of the Roman Catholics*: the Roman Catholic Relief Bill was passed in April 1829.

CHAPTER XXIII

Page 180. *faint heart*: 'Faint heart ne'er wan/A lady fair': Burns, 'To Dr. Blacklock'.

Page 182. *Benedick . . . Beatrice*: see *Much Ado About Nothing*.

CHAPTER XXIV

Page 185. *the pillar letter-box*: Trollope himself claimed to have introduced the iron pillar box into England during his long career in the Post Office from 1834–67. See *Autobiography*, Ch. XV.

EXPLANATORY NOTES

CHAPTER XXV

Page 191. (1) *plunged*: bet recklessly.

(2) *book*: a betting book, or record of the number of bets made with different people.

(3) *the stud*: after his season as a three-year-old, Prime Minister would be retired to stud.

(4) *Alma Mater*: one's university.

(5) *to read*: reading parties of undergraduates and their tutors were commonly made up during the long summer vacations. See, for instance, Clough's *The Bothie of Tober-na-Vuolich* (1848).

Page 194. (1) *dura ilia*: Horace, *Epodes*, iii. Meaning 'his guts'.

(2) *pot-house*: an ale-house.

Page 195. *Scandunt eodem* . . . : Horace, *Odes*, III. i. 'Sed timor et minae/Scandunt eodem, quo dominus, . . . /Post equitem sedet atra cura.' 'Yet none may mount beyond the grip/Of fright and fear, that climb beside;/Black care can board the brazen ship/And ride with them that ride.' (Marris). Gerald replies with a schoolboy translation of the last line.

Page 197. *Sinbad*: 'The Old Man of the Sea' in the Arabian Nights story clings to Sinbad's shoulders and can only be got rid of by being made drunk.

Page 198. *the Scotch property*: part of Glencora's dowry.

CHAPTER XXVI

Page 200. (1) *some measure of legal reform*: in 1873, the Chancellor carried a measure which removed the old divisions between Courts of Law and substituted a Supreme Court. The constitution of the Supreme Court (numbers of judges, etc.) was being legislated between 1873 and 1887, when it was established.

(2) *under obligations to Mr. Finn*: see *The Prime Minister*, Ch. LVII, where Phineas Finn defends Palliser in the House of Commons against the charge of having corruptly paid Lopez's election expenses at Silverbridge.

Page 201. *a Royal concert*: the musical enthusiasm of Prince Albert, who started the concerts at Windsor Castle and Buckingham Palace in 1840, and arranged many of the programmes for the Philharmonic Society, was continued after his death in 1861. In

648

1876 there was a season of summer concerts at Buckingham Palace, known as 'State Concerts' or 'Her Majesty's Concerts'. The first, on 21 June 1876, was attended by most of the leading parliamentarians (Disraeli, Northcote, Bentinck, Gladstone, etc.) as well as by visiting heads of state and diplomats. These concerts, which would certainly 'empty' the House, were announced in advance in *The Times*.

Page 202. *a duel*: see *Phineas Finn*, Ch. XXXVIII.

Page 203. (1) *bewigging*: echoes of Dickens ('wiglomeration', or the activities of Chancery in *Bleak House*) and of Carlyle ('such mountains of wiggeries and folly', *Past and Present*).

(2) *Turveydrop*: old Mr. Turveydrop, 'a model of Deportment' and Master of a Dancing Academy, a Regency buck who has outlived his era, in *Bleak House* (esp. Ch. XIV). The comparison is meant to evoke Dickens's (and Carlyle's) attacks on dilettantism in public life. See further, p. 601.

CHAPTER XXVII

Page 214. *certain scenes*: see *The Prime Minister* (esp. Chs. XVIII, XIX, XXVII and XXVIII) for Glencora's lavish but misjudged house parties at Gatherum.

CHAPTER XXVIII

Page 218. *Isabel Boncassen*: cf. other American girls in Trollope, e.g. Ophelia Gledd ('that face was ever bright with motion, and her clear, deep, grey eyes, full of life and light, were always ready for some combat or some enterprise': 'Miss Ophelia Gledd' (1873) in *Lotta Schmidt* (1876)) and Caroline Spalding ('he thought he had never met any lady who talked better') in *He Knew He Was Right* (1869). Ophelia also has 'a certain nasal twang in speaking'. See also Introduction, pp. xix–xxv above.

Page 220. (1) *Queenstown*: from 1849 to 1922 this was the name of Cobh, a port of call for Atlantic liners in S.E. County Cork.

(2) *tender*: small boat used to take passengers off the liner.

(3) *Ascot*: probably a reference to the Ascot Gold Cup, first run in 1807, which had been growing in importance since the 1830s.

Page 221. *in our country*: the relative freedom of nineteenth-century American girls (see further, p. 243) is a frequent subject with both

American and English writers: see Fanny Trollope, *Domestic Manners of the Americans* (1832), Henry James, *Daisy Miller* (1878), 'An International Episode' (1878–9) and *The Portrait of a Lady* (1880–81), and Trollope, *North America* (1862) and works mentioned in note to p. 218 above. See also Introduction.

CHAPTER XXIX

Page 228. *woman's rights*: for Trollope's hostility to active feminism and feminists, see *North America* ('the best right a woman has is a right to a husband'), his lecture on 'The Higher Education of Women' (1868) ('I should deplore a system of education which would create competition between the sexes') and the characters of Wallachia Petrie in *He Knew He Was Right* and of Olivia Q. Fleabody in *Is He Popenjoy?* (1878). However, the American feminist Kate Field was his dear friend, and his sympathy for the nineteenth-century woman's sense of restriction was strong, as this novel demonstrates.

Page 229. *Mr. Worldly-Wiseman*: he persuades Christian not to go through 'the little Wicket-Gate'; 'he said he would show me a better way, and short, not so attended with difficulties' (*Pilgrim's Progress*).

CHAPTER XXX

Page 239. *potential*: powerful.

CHAPTER XXXI

Page 241. *apprehensive*: perceptive, sensitive.

CHAPTER XXXII

Page 251. *Ezekiel Boncassen*: Trollope's middle-aged American men are usually less sympathetic; cf. Jonas Spalding in *He Knew He Was Right* and Elias Gotobed in *The American Senator* (1877), who makes a brief appearance in Ch. LXX.

Page 252. *Nay, my Lord*: the pattern of references to *Romeo and Juliet* is continued, but the remark seems to come oddly from Mrs. Boncassen (it cannot be spoken by Isabel as she is dancing).

Page 256. *hugger-mugger*: secretly. An heir to the throne could not marry a commoner.

CHAPTER XXXIII

Page 260. *I got to be thinking*: Henry James commented that these words 'have much more the note of English American than of American English'. See Introduction, p. xix above.

Page 264. *Ducks*: the joke depends, of course, on the use of 'ducks' to mean trousers made of light-coloured linen.

Page 266. *Madame Scholzdam*: rival to Mdlle Stuffa (p. 52), presumably. Longstaff's small talk, true to Beargarden form, is all of horses and opera singers.

CHAPTER XXXV

Page 278. *ten thousand*: cf. *Can You Forgive Her?* Ch. I, where Trollope refers in the first sentence to 'the Upper Ten Thousand of this our English world.' Stephen Wall notes: 'The phrase seems to have been originated by the American writer N. P. Willis (1806–67). To judge by an article in *Punch*, 2 May 1863, it was in current use.' (*Can You Forgive Her?*, Penguin edition). There were an estimated 4,000 families in 'Society' at the end of the nineteenth century, often connected by family links or by association at school or University. See *Phineas Redux*, Ch. XXII.

Page 281. *that unfortunate quarrel*: presumably between Phineas Finn and Sir Timothy over the reform of the judiciary; but we are not given the details.

Page 283. (1) *the Twelfth*: grouse shooting began on 12 August.

(2) *Leadenhall Market*: London poultry market.

CHAPTER XXXVI

Page 287. *clever distich*: 'So, naturalists observe, a flea/Hath smaller fleas that on him prey/And these have smaller fleas to bite 'em,/And so proceed *ad infinitum*.' Swift, 'On Poetry', 1733.

CHAPTER XXXVII

Page 292. *Far away*: Trollope is responsive to the charm of northern fell scenery; cf. Vavasor Hall in *Can You Forgive Her?* and Humblethwaite Hall in *Sir Harry Hotspur* (1871).

CHAPTER XXXVIII

Page 301. (1) *venatical*: related to hunting.
    (2) *gillies*: hunting guides or attendants.

Page 305. *crammers*: lies (in use from mid-nineteenth century). Also p. 467.

CHAPTER XXXIX

Page 308. *lawn-tennis*: tennis played on grass was the latest thing in the 1870s. Se *Army and Navy Gazette*, XV, 151, 1874: 'A new game has just been patented by Major Wingfield. "Lawn Tennis"—for that is the name . . . is a clever adaptation of Tennis to the exigencies of an ordinary lawn' (OED).

Page 309. *'When youth . . . with flying feet'*: Byron, *Childe Harold's Pilgrimage*, st. 12: 'On with the dance! let joy be unconfined;/No sleep till morn, when Youth and Pleasure meet/To chase the glowing Hours with flying feet.'

CHAPTER XL

Page 320. *party-coloured*: variegated in colour.

Page 325. *My father's father*: cf. Ophelia Gledd, who is not ashamed of her grandfather 'because he stood in a store and sold leather with his bare hands', and the account of 'American ladies' in *North America*, Ch. XIV: 'They belong to the aristocracy of the land, by whatever means they may have become aristocrats. In America one does not enquire as to their birth, their training, or their old names.'

CHAPTER XLI

Page 326. *Ischl*: Baedeker's *Austria* (1929) describes Bad-Ischl as 'a well-known summer resort of imperial Austria, frequented as a watering-place for brine-baths since 1822. The brine (24% pure salt) and the sulphur spring, which are used externally, and the Klebelsberg salt spring, used exclusively for drinking, come from the salt-mine.' The salt-mine is a popular tourist attraction.

Page 327. *Halstadt*: or Hallstatt, 13 miles from Ischl, a picturesque market village on a lake in mountain scenery, with its own salt-mine.

Page 331. *Men have died . . . but not for love*: 'Men have died from time to time, and worms have eaten them, but not for love' (*As You Like It*, IV. i).

Page 332. *Man is born . . . sparks fly upwards*: 'Yet man is born unto trouble, as the sparks fly upward' (Job, 5: 7).

Page 334. *Hintersee*: a mountain near Salzburg, described in Baedeker as 'the fine Hintersee, 2247 ft.'

CHAPTER XLII

Page 337. *Richard will be himself*: Colley Cibber, *Richard III, altered*, V. iii: 'Conscience avaunt, Richard's himself again.'

Page 339. (1) achieved greatness: 'Some are born great, some achieve greatness, and some have greatness thrust upon them' (*Twelfth Night*, II. v).

(2) *Lady Fawn*: having tried to marry Violet Effingham and Madame Goesler, and then extricated himself from an engagement to Lizzie Eustace (*The Eustace Diamonds*), Lord Fawn develops, after his eventual marriage, 'very strict notions as to the bonds of matrimony' (*Phineas Redux*, Ch. XXXII).

Page 341. *great women of the world*: they are, respectively, the legendary Assyrian Queen, founder of Babylon; the American Indian who saved the life of Captain John Smith; the famous nineteenth-century Austrian world-traveller; and Marat's assassin.

CHAPTER XLIII

Page 345. *the pull*: the collective bets of a number of people who each stake a sum of money on a horse. The proceeds are divided by the backer.

Page 346. (1) *macassar*: oil.

(2) *the Leger distance*: see p. 134, note (3).

Page 348. *seventy thousand pounds*: almost the same sum which Trollope says he has earned (£68,959. 17s. 5d, in fact) in the *Autobiography*, Ch. XX. The 1870s were notorious for the feckless and spend-thrift behaviour of some aristocratic youth. It was said in 1874 that the Prince of Wales had incurred debts to £60,000 and that the Queen paid them herself.

Page 349. *pitch*: 'He that toucheth pitch shall be defiled therewith' (Eccles. 13:1).

Page 351. *perspicuous*: lucid.

CHAPTER XLIV

Page 352. (1) *free-school*: the grammar school, founded in 1553 and reorganized in 1862.

(2) *the ring*: the bookmakers.

Page 353. *frog*: an elastic, horny substance growing in the middle of the sole of a horse's hoof; the tenderest part of the hoof.

Page 356. *the Jews*: i.e. the money-lenders.

Page 357. *her own telegraph-wire*: the 1870s saw an enormous spread in telegraph offices all over the country, after the post office took over the telegraph system in 1870. To have one's own wire, though, was a luxury.

CHAPTER XLV

Page 362. (1) *mooncalf*: born fool.

(2) *hecatombs*: sacrifices.

Page 365. *I didn't know*: Palliser's lack of knowledge and interest in hunting outrages some of his hunting neighbours: see the 'Trumpeton Feud' in *Phineas Redux*.

CHAPTER XLVI

Page 368. *Lady Chiltern*: Violet Effingham, who married Oswald Chiltern after being pursued by Phineas: see *Phineas Finn*. Her father-in-law is Lord Brentford.

Page 371. *a marker*: a professional score-keeper in a competitive game such as billiards.

Page 373. *Lady Rosina de Courcy*: the ageing unmarried daughter of the Earl de Courcy; a friend to Palliser in *The Prime Minister*.

Page 374. *Moore's Melodies*: Popplecourt's light taste for Tom Moore's *Irish Melodies* does not recommend him to Lady Mary.

Page 376. *a horse of another colour*: 'My purpose is, indeed, a horse of that colour' (*Twelfth Night*, I. iii).

CHAPTER XLIX

Page 394. (1) *levanted*: bolted without paying his debts.
  (2) *Apollyon*: *Pilgrim's Progress*.

Page 395. *to 'edge*: to hedge, or make a covering bet for safety.

CHAPTER L

Page 404. *'locus poenitentiae'*: place of repentance (after Heb. 12: 17). In law, an opportunity to recede from some commitment or engagement.

CHAPTER LI

Page 407. *Mr. Warburton*: the Duke's private secretary.

Page 409. *Barrington Erle*: prominent Liberal and friend of Phineas in *Phineas Finn*, etc.

CHAPTER LII

Page 412. *the Brake*: Lord Chiltern is Master of the Brake Hounds. See further, Ch. LXII.

CHAPTER LIII

Page 422. *quints*: in talking to Isabel, the Duke reverts to the great passion of his political career, his attempt as Chancellor of the Exchequer to bring in decimal coinage. (See *The Eustace Diamonds*.)

Page 427. *a gentleman . . . roll a stone*: Sisyphus, condemned by

Hermes to this eternal punishment for refusing to return to the Underworld.

Page 428. Sir Guy: the family history of the Pallisers is told by Glencora in *Can You Forgive Her?*, Ch. XXII: 'I dare say Sir Guy was no better than he should be.' Sir Guy presides over the last scene of *D.C.*, p. 632. See Introduction, pp. xxiv–xxv.

CHAPTER LIV

Page 435. younger son: the elder would usually stand for Parliament but in this case, as we know, he is 'busy investigating the mountains of Crim Tartary' (p. 21).

CHAPTER LV

Page 436. Polpenno: Trollope's own unsuccessful attempt to stand for parliament in 1868 for the notoriously corrupt borough of Beverley is described in the *Autobiography*, Ch. XVI. The election at Polpenno shares some of the features of Beverley. Cf. the elections in *Ralph the Heir* (1870–71), *The Way We Live Now*, and the earlier Palliser novels.

Page 437. vital subjects: Trollope fought his own election partly on the Disestablishment of the Irish Church.

Page 438. my governor's ideas: this important conversation not only shows Silverbridge realizing that his father's influence has made him a Liberal after all; it also reflects the political climate of the 1870s and displays Trollope's political theory. In the *Autobiography* (Ch. XVI) he describes a Liberal as one who has in his mind 'I will not say equality, for the word is offensive, and presents to the imaginations of men ideas of communism, of ruin, and insane democracy,—but of a tendency towards equality. In following that, however, he knows that he must be hemmed in by safeguards, lest he be tempted to travel too quickly; and therefore he is glad to be accompanied on his way by the repressive action of a Conservative opponent.' This moderate 'Conservative Liberal-ism' echoes Gladstone ('Trust in the people qualified by prudence') and John Morley, editor of the *Fortnightly*, whose book *On Compromise* came out in 1876. The Liberal party in the 1874–80 House of Commons was a coalition of old Whigs and Radicals, the latter making up one third of the Liberal total. Radical Liberals were much more eager for positive state and municipal intervention than Gladstonian Liberals. Joseph Chamberlain (elected MP for Birmingham in 1876) campaigned through the '70s and '80s for a programme of social reform. Tregear's idea that radicalism might lead to the excesses of the French Revolution would have been fired by the 1871 Paris Commune, which alarmed British Conservatives. 'Socialism', though, was increasingly used in the '70s and '80s in a diluted sense by Liberals to mean interventionist policies designed to benefit the masses. The observation 'We are all socialists now' is attributed to Sir William Harcourt, Liberal, in 1887.

Page 443. (1) *parliamentary canvassing*: Trollope is eloquent about the miseries of canvassing at Beverley. *Autobiography*, Ch. XVI.

(2) *buff*: buff and blue were the Whig colours.

Page 444. a Mr. Sprugeon and a Mr. Sprout: see note to p. 105 above.

CHAPTER LVI

Page 447. (1) *ballot boxes*: Trollope had opposed the secret ballot in the 1868 Beverley campaign (when it was supported by most Liberals), feeling that it would lead to increased intimidation and corruption. The Ballot Act was passed in 1872. This dry account of the Polpenno election displays the kind of corruption Trollope had anticipated: Carbottle's attempt to 'buy' the Liberal vote at 10s a head is thwarted by a Conservative tailor who is himself 'bought' for £25.

(2) *Salem . . . Zion . . . Ebenezer*: usual names for Nonconformist chapels. Hostility between the establishment and the Dissenters was widespread: see Revd John Clifford, *Baptist Handbook*, 1877, speaking on 'Religious Life in the Rural Districts of England': 'It is intolerable that landowner and squire, justice of the peace and priest of the Church, should form a confederacy to close the chapel doors' (*Nonconformity in the 19th Century*, ed. D. M. Thompson, Routledge, 1972). Edward Miall, a leading Congregationalist, said in the House on 9 May 1871: 'Every town has its exclusive circles of social intercourse—the one appropriated to Churchmen, the other to Dissenters.' Mr. Williams, and Tregear's parents, regard his election as a victory for the Church over the Nonconformists (who in the West Country would very likely be Baptists or

Wesleyans). The use of the word 'dissenter' rather than 'noncon-formist' was rather old-fashioned by 1876.

Page 448. *Jacobins*: extreme political radicals (derived from the French Revolution).

CHAPTER LIX

Page 472. (1) *the top of his bent*: *Hamlet*, II. i.
(2) *the rental*: from the Gatherum lands and estates.

CHAPTER LX

Page 481. *Moreton*: earlier, Morton.

CHAPTER LXI

Page 482. *Perfect love casteth out fear*: 1 John 4: 18.

Page 488. *Trumpington Wood*: Trumpeton in *Phineas Redux*, *The Prime Minister*. See p. 365, note (1).

Page 490. *jejune*: deficient, thin, unsatisfying.

CHAPTER LXII

Page 492. *his intimate friends*: for the story of Phineas's relations with Violet and Oswald Chiltern, see *Phineas Finn* and *Phineas Redux*. For Gerard Maule's marriage to Adelaide Palliser, and for Mr. Spooner's courtship of Adelaide, see *Phineas Redux* (and see p. 28, note (1)). These two chapters allow Trollope to indulge in his favourite subject, which, he says in the *Autobiography*, Ch. IV, 'I have dragged into many novels.'

Page 495. *chopped one*: came suddenly on, or started one.

Page 496. (1) *Captain Glomax*: Master of the A.R.U. or U.R.U., the Ufford and Rufford United Hunt Club, in *The American Senator*.
(2) *carpet-bag*: adjective derived from the American Civil War for any opportunist looking to take over a district not his own.

Page 497. *Bell's Life* . . . *Field* . . . *Bayley's*: hunting and sporting journals.

Page 499. *draw the country regularly*: 'The M.F.H. . . . will draw fairly through the day, and indulge no caprices as to coverts.' *Hunting Sketches*, 1865. See p. 46, note (1).

Page 500. they found: 'With a gorse covert, the fox must be driven out quickly, so the rider must remain with the crowd.' ibid.

CHAPTER LXIII

Page 504. whip: whipper-in of the hounds.

CHAPTER LXIV

Page 510. Hyperion to a satyr: 'So excellent a king that was to this/Hyperion to a satyr' (*Hamlet*, I. ii).

CHAPTER LXV

Page 515. Facilis descensus Averni: 'Easy is the way down to the Underworld: by night and day dark Dis's door stands open' (Virgil, *Aeneid*, vi. 126).

Page 517. pips: marks on a playing card.

Page 519. 'The Fortnightly': Trollope was one of the founders of the *Fortnightly Review*, in 1865, a Liberal periodical edited by John Morley.

CHAPTER LXVII

Page 532. We fail!: *Macbeth*, I. vii.

Page 533. Mr. Roby: Thomas Roby, Secretary of the Admiralty, Secretary of the Treasury, and Chief Whip: see also *Phineas Finn*, *Phineas Redux* and *The Prime Minister*, where he works as a pair with Mr. Rattler (mentioned on p. 602).

CHAPTER LXVIII

Page 539. Bruton Street: in *The Eustace Diamonds*, Trollope inconsistently moved Lady Linlithgow from Brook Street to Bruton Street. Naturally, Trollope takes every opportunity to champion the reliability of the Post Office.

CHAPTER LXIX

Page 545. *Clarissa*: Samuel Richardson's long epistolary eighteenth-century novel (1747–8).

Page 549. *the great Asiatic tour*: to Crim Tartary, presumably, like Tregear's brother.

CHAPTER LXX

Page 551. (1) *Mr. Gotobed*: see p. 251, note (1).

(2) *Ezekiel Sevenkings*: loosely based on Walt Whitman, perhaps, who was very well known in England since the selected edition of his poems published by William Rossetti in 1868, and whose *Centennial Edition* of *Leaves of Grass* in 1876 was much publicized and supported in Britain.

Page 556. *Anglican*: in the sense of Anglophile.

CHAPTER LXXI

Page 558. *Mr. Mildmay*: Whig Prime Minister between Lord Brock and Mr. Gresham, prominent in *Phineas Finn*, *Phineas Redux*, and *The Prime Minister*: bears some distinct resemblances to Lord John Russell.

Page 564. '*all the blood of all the Howards*': 'What can ennoble sots or slaves or cowards? Alas! Not all the blood of all the Howards' '(Pope, *Essay on Man*, Ep. iv, 1. 215).

CHAPTER LXXII

Page 567. *Islington*: then a rural north London suburb.

Page 569. *Darby and Joan*: the ideal elderly married couple of an eighteenth-century ballad. There is an echo of Glencora who is scathing of Palliser's desire for 'a Darby and Joan kind of thing' (*The Prime Minister*, Ch. XVIII).

CHAPTER LXXIII

Page 582. '*There is a tide . . . men*': 'There is a tide in the affairs of men/Which, taken at the flood, leads on to fortune' (*Julius Caesar*, IV. iii).

EXPLANATORY NOTES

CHAPTER LXXIV

Page 585. *caviare to the general*: *Hamlet*, II. ii. i.e., too good for popular taste.

CHAPTER LXXVI

Page 600. *buckram*: starch, false stiffening.

Page 601. *suasive*: persuasive.

Page 602. *the brewers were anxious about publican licences*: a Bill was introduced in 1874 which restricted the hours of licensing. In 1880, Brewer's licences were repealed and beer duty was imposed in lieu of the old malt tax.

CHAPTER LXXVII

Page 618. *leather or prunella*: a misapplication of Pope's *Essay on Man*, IV. 204: 'Worth makes the man, and want of it, the fellow/The rest is all but leather or prunella.' Pope uses it to distinguish between different classes of men: Trollope often uses it, in the sense of something to which one is entirely indifferent.

Page 621. *breaking up the Ministry*: the fall of this Conservative government bears no relation to real events in 1875 or '76. See note to p. 162.

CHAPTER LXXIV

Page 38: *centre* is *McCormack's*, *Donald, II, iii* i.e., too good for popular taste.

CHAPTER LXXVI

Page 601: *fustian suit*, takes silliness.

Page 601: *money* persuasive.

Page 602: the *brewer* their *nectar* about *problem*, i.e., a Bill was introduced in 1875, which matched the house of *Beresasi*. In 1880, *Brewers' licences* were repealed and *beer duty* was imposed during of the old *malt tax*.

CHAPTER LXXVII

Page 618: *Lay* of *sundaise* a *misapplication* of *Pope's letter to Miss M.W. 1717*: "North makes the *man*, and want of it, the *fellow*. The rest is all but leather or prunello." Pope uses it to distinguish between different classes of *men*; Trollope often uses it, in the sense of *something* to which one actually inclined of ...

Page 625: *Lord etc, this in the Moon, the Bill of this Conservative government bears no relation to any events in 1873 or '76. See note to p. 162.*

WHO'S WHO

IN

THE DUKE'S CHILDREN

(Characters whose names are in capital letters appear also in the other novels indicated.)

Amazon, Miss, a rowing girl, 245.

BEARGARDEN CLUB, 45.
See *The Way We Live Now*.

BEESWAX, Sir Timothy, Conservative M.P., 124; Leader of the House of Commons, 162; Lady B. and daughter, 551.
See *P.M.*

Boncassen, Ezekiel and Mrs., of the U.S.A.; their d. Isabel, 218, 251; in Brook Street (not Bruton Street), 539.

BRENTFORD, Earl of, former Liberal minister, father of Lord Chiltern and of Lady Laura Standish (Kennedy), 368.
See *Ph.F.* and *Ph.R.*

Bubbs, Mr. and Mrs., electors of Polpenno, 443.

Bullock, Marley, a racing man, now 'with nothing a year paid quarterly', 290.

Buttercup, Lord, a junior minister, 519.

CANTRIP, Earl and Countess of, of Custins in Dorset, 8, 38; two dd., 93 (see Nidderdale); 283.
See *Ph.F.*, *Ph.R.*, and *P.M.*

Capulet, Marchioness of, 252.

Carbottle, Liberal candidate for Polpenno, 437.

Casseway, Miss ('Miss Cass'), a distant cousin of Lord Grex, 72; her brother, 464.

CHILTERN, Lord, o.s. of the Earl of Brentford; of Harrington Hall; Master of the Brake Hounds, 488.
See *Ph.F.*, *E.D.*, *Ph.R.*, and *P.M.*

CHILTERN, Lady (Violet Effingham), 368.
See other Palliser novels.

Clanfiddle, Countess; her d. Lady Violet, 258, 269.

Comfort and Criball, of Crasham Court, Crutched Friars, money-lenders, 358.

Crummie-Toddie, a grouse-moor in Perthshire, 300.

663